Praise for *Romantic Comedy*

"Harvey at his best is as good a writer as the movies could ever hope to have, and his lengthy descriptions of scenes and stars are beautifully observed, sometimes astonishingly so."
—Neal Gabler, *The New York Times Book Review*

"This is the best book I've ever read—the most fun and the most thoughtful—about the movies I love most. Harvey raises plot summary to high critical art: as we live through each plot twist and camera angle, he lovingly reveals its farthest ranging implications."
—Lloyd Schwartz, *The Boston Phoenix Literary Supplement*

"You flow along easily through [Harvey's] conversational, jargon-free prose, always aware of its finesse but more aware of your own pleasure in reading, in seeing and hearing interesting things, in laughing a lot; the book wants to be like going to the movies and it succeeds. And then at the end you realize you've gained a full understanding of some of the freest art America has achieved. Romantic Comedy matches its subject so exactly that it's the best book about film I've read."
—Robert Garis, *Raritan*

"A fan's book in the best sense, *Romantic Comedy* catches the tone of real-life movie talk. . . . When Harvey writes of Myrna Loy, Joel McCrea, or Jean Arthur, it's with that twentieth-century brand of intimacy that turns film stars into family."
—Geoffrey O'Brien, *The New York Review of Books*

"To write well about comedy, give the facts and keep the reader entertained is a tricky task. Harvey succeeds on all fronts by conveying his love for the subject, by meticulous attention to detail, and by quoting liberally from the films themselves. A treasury of good reading and information."
—*Library Journal*

"Harvey succeeds in pressing these fleeting and ineffable moments he loves onto the printed page. His tribute to the screwball form seems richly deserved and terrifically realized."
—Tom Nolan, *The Los Angeles Times*

D1352617

Romantic Comedy

Irene Dunne,
Cary Grant,
and Asta in
Leo McCarey's
The Awful
Truth.

James Harvey

ROMANTIC COMEDY

in Hollywood,
from Lubitsch
to Sturges

DA CAPO PRESS • NEW YORK

Library of Congress Cataloging-in-Publication Data

Harvey, James, 1929–
Romantic comedy in Hollywood from Lubitsch to Sturges / James
Harvey.—1st Da Capo Press ed.
   p.   cm.
Originally published: New York: Knopf, 1987.
Includes index.
ISBN 0-306-80832-3 (alk. paper)
1. Comedy films—United States—History and criticism. 2. Lubitsch,
Ernst, 1892–1947—Criticism and interpretation. 3. Sturges, Preston—Criticism
and interpretation. I. Title.
PN1995.9.C55H37 1998
791.43′617—dc21   97-41564
CIP

Owing to limitations of space, all acknowledgments of permission to use
illustrations will be found following the index.

First Da Capo Press edition 1998

This Da Capo Press paperback edition of *Romantic Comedy* is an
unabridged republication of the edition first published in New York in 1987,
with minor textual emendations. It is reprinted by arrangement with the author.

Published by Da Capo Press, Inc.
A Member of Perseus Books Group

10 9 8 7 6 5 4 3

For Betty Ann Besch

For Mary Ann Youngren too,
and for all those who loved her

*Barbara Stan-
wyck and
Henry Fonda
in Preston
Sturges' film*
The Lady Eve.

Contents

Acknowledgments

IT WAS my editor, Bob Gottlieb, who first had the idea for this book, and also the idea that I should be the one to write it—and who gave me his unfailing support and encouragement through all the time of writing, as well as the benefit of his own knowledge and love for the screwball comedy. So that whatever this book is I owe in one way or another to him. And it was David Lindner, editor of the now sorely missed *Dance Life* magazine, who first invited me years ago to write about Astaire and Rogers—an assignment that started everything.

You need a lot of people to help you when you write a movie book. I'm specially grateful to all those at the film archives and film companies who enabled me to see movies (many of them rare and almost inaccessible) when I needed to—to none more than to Charles Silver at the Museum of Modern Art Film Study Center, but also to his colleagues, Ron Magliozzi and Ed Carter; to Stuart Lindner, who is at Films Inc., and to Don Rosen and Marcie Gollup and Rhonda Bloom, who used to be; to Herbert Nusbaum at MGM; to Barbara Humphreys at the Library of Congress; to Charles Hopkins and Robert Rosen at the UCLA Film Archive; to Ron Haver at the L.A. County Museum; to Ray Penn and Bonnie Berman of Swank Films; and to Rodney Recor at the Academy of Motion Picture Arts and Sciences. William K. Everson lent me many films and never declined a request I made. I also want to mention John Belton of Columbia University, who turned up a rare copy of Lubitsch's *Angel* just when I had despaired of finding it anywhere; and Howard Otway, who screened *Swing High, Swing Low* for me one night after hours at his Theatre 80 St. Mark's.

My friend Clyde Griffin at the New School guided me through my early days of running projectors and showing films, and would somehow always come up with a vacant room or space for me to show them in. Howard Mandelbaum and Carlos Clarens at Phototeque, and Mary Corliss and Terry Geesken at the Museum of Modern Art Film Stills Archive, helped me through the long and painstaking job of choosing the final illustrations. Lisa Rodensky of Wellesley College saved me months of labor by transcribing the dialogue of all the major Sturges films from videotape copies. And Bill Pass of UCLA did valuable research for me in the Sturges archive. I am also grateful to the staff of the UCLA Special Collections Library for their kindness—and above all to my cousins Grace and Glen Vining, who always made my visits to L.A. so special and happy.

Another sort of help—equally necessary—has come from friends I could always talk about movies with: Bob Garis above all, but also my friends Ann Noerdlinger, Richard Schwarz, Ron Overton, Nancy Goldner, Noll Brinckman, Howard Mandelbaum, and Peter Shaw. Andy Pawelczak and Nancy Cooper helped me through many small and larger crises over the writing days. And Charlotte Sky and Vic and Dylan Skolnick, by inviting me to hold classes at the Huntington Cinema, gave me the most satisfying experience of teaching movies that I've ever had. I also want to thank the Department of English at the State University of New York at Stony Brook—particularly my colleagues Joe Pequigney and Dick Levine—for all their understanding and support during the time I was working on this book. My thanks, too, to Lillian Silkworth and Joanna Kalinowski. And to Mary Maguire at Knopf, who guided the book through production, to Mel Rosenthal, who served as the book's production editor, and to Peter Andersen, who designed it.

There are *places* I'm indebted to, too: the Thalia and Regency theatres, the two movie houses that have done more over the years than any others to keep repertory cinema alive in New York. As I write, the Regency is still prospering while the Thalia (although it now has branches at the Thalia Soho and the Cinema Village) is endangered—by realtors and gentrification. What accounts for such places being around for us at all, it seems, is the commitment of the people who run them—of Frank Rowley at the Regency and Richard Schwarz at the Thalia. And everyone who cares about seeing the classical Hollywood movies as they were meant to be seen—on big screens, in real theatres, with responsive audiences—owes them a particular gratitude.

Some of the important people who figure in the history covered by this book—Irene Dunne, Claudette Colbert, Rex Harrison, Joel McCrea, Billy Wilder, Rouben Mamoulian, the late Walter Reisch—generously allowed me to interview them; and I want to thank each of them again. And for their recollections of Lubitsch and Lubitsch's Hollywood, I want to thank Mary Loos and Dorshka Raphaelson. My thanks, too, to Sandy Sturges—not only for permitting me to use the Sturges archive at UCLA, but for sharing with me so many extraordinary memories of her husband. Above all, I want to express my debt to the remarkable Samson Raphaelson—whom I came to know because of this book, who contributed so much to it, and who died before it was finished. I miss him still.

Finally I want to give my love and gratitude to Paula Fox and Sheila Gordon, to Bob Garis and Connie Harrier—who "lived" this book with me (so it seems to me) through the years, reading it in manuscript and sustaining both it and me by their responses and insights and friendship.   J.H.

Preface

. . . that sustained feat of careless magic we call "thirties comedy."
—PAULINE KAEL

THIS BOOK is about the screwball comedy, that extraordinary comic-romantic inspiration that invaded Hollywood in the thirties, that reached its climax, and end, in the forties, and that has left behind it an almost incredible number and variety of wonderful movie comedies—films that seem more astonishing to us now than they could have seemed to audiences of their own time, who took a certain level of wonder for granted, especially in romantic comedies. At the time, it was widely assumed that whatever else movies were, they were certainly ephemeral. It doesn't look that way now. Hollywood's so-called Golden Age seems against all odds to have left us some of our most enduring works of imagination. The movies in fact seem to have left us as many such works, as many permanent occasions of amazement and delight, as has any art form of our century. Especially the movies of the big studio era of the thirties and forties, the period of what André Bazin calls the classical American cinema. And at that period's height, probably the single most widely successful style—the mode that seemed to inspire the highest flights and tap the deepest energies, not only of individual filmmakers but of Hollywood and the spirit of Hollywood itself—was the romantic movie comedy.

It came to be widely known as "screwball"—originally a publicist's term—around 1936, when Gregory La Cava's *My Man Godfrey,* with Carole Lombard's dizzy rampaging heroine, seemed to compel the description. But screwball comedy was a wider category than the term itself suggests: it named a style associated less with scattiness or derangement than with a paradoxical kind of liberation, with romantic exaltation of a very down-to-earth kind. This paradox was the peculiar, energizing complication that made the style so congenial to Hollywood—so expressive of both the place and the fantasy—and so magical to audiences in general.

There was almost nothing in the screwball mode that wasn't familiar from long usage in theater, vaudeville, popular fiction, or earlier films. But watching Powell and Loy or Astaire and Rogers, audiences in the mid-thirties forgot they had ever seen any of it before. And in a way they hadn't. Nineteen thirty-four was the turning point, the year when it first began to seem as if the Hollywood movie had *invented* romantic comedy. Suddenly, in *The Thin Man* and *It Happened One Night* and *The Gay Divorcee*, in actors like Dunne and Lombard and Grant, Powell and Loy and Astaire—all the familiar, borrowed elements came together in combinations so new and fresh, so electric, and so intrinsically movielike that familiarity became revelation.

What follows is about that revelation: about the movies and the movie stars it generated, about the directors and writers who interpreted it to the world, and, above all, about the two filmmaking giants, Ernst Lubitsch and Preston Sturges, who gave almost the whole of their matchless careers to it. And just as Sturges can be said to end the great era of the romantic comedy movie—consolidating its triumphs with a remarkable series of films in the forties—Lubitsch begins it.

AUTHOR'S NOTE

The illustrations in this book (with the exception of a single chapter) are production stills—that is, photos taken on the set *between* filmings. Stills are meant for the most part to represent the action of the movie, but they don't exactly reproduce it. What they do convey, however, is the glamour and glow of the original film experience. That's why I've preferred them to frame enlargements—whose quality is always less glamorous than that of on-screen projection. The only place where I have used frame enlargements is in the Astaire-Rogers section, where I analyze a dance ("Let's Face the Music") in such detail that exactly faithful images seem crucial.

All the quotations from movie dialogue in the book are taken directly from the movie itself—never (unless otherwise specified) from a screenplay or shooting script, sources which nearly always differ markedly from what the actors on the screen finally say and do. And so also, all the directions and descriptions of action, intonation, or intention that occur in such dialogue passages, and which appear in parentheses and italics—such as the word "dryly," for example, below:

MAXFORD (*dryly*): That won't be necessary, Mr. MacDonald . . .

—are my insertions, my own interpretations of what's on the screen or in the performance, and not the director's or screenwriter's. The only exceptions are those instances where I quote from the written text of a play or screenplay; the parenthetical directions are then, of course, the original author's.

Jeanette MacDonald and Ernst Lubitsch on the set of Monte Carlo.

PART 1

The Lubitsch Era, 1929-1933

Jeanette MacDonald with her hairdresser, Jack Buchanan, in Lubitsch's Monte Carlo.

Lubitsch: 1
The Naughty Operetta

Lubitsch was a giant . . . his talent and originality were stupefying.
—ORSON WELLES, in a 1965 interview

"It's a silly story. Only possible with music."
—DUKE OTTO VON LIEBENHEIM, in *Monte Carlo*

COMEDY WAS Hollywood's essential genius. And probably no one, not even Chaplin, did so much as Ernst Lubitsch did to shape the spirit and style, even the substance, of Hollywood comedy. No one who made films did so without being aware of the latest Lubitsch triumph or ingenuity, the newest brilliant example of his famous "touch." And though his standing with critics and audiences fluctuated over the course of his career, the awe and respect he was held in by his filmmaking colleagues never varied. To many he was simply the best director in Hollywood—"the masters' master," as David Niven called him.

He was a small man with a cigar in his mouth at all times, a glinting eye, and a very downright manner. He had that most dependable of charms: the gift of being able to confer life and size and excitement on whatever took his interest, and to impart that excitement to others. If he didn't embody glamour by Hollywood standards, much better by Hollywood standards, he had it to give, impersonally and generously. Screenwriter Samson Raphaelson claimed that he never saw anyone in that "territory of egoists" who didn't light up in the company of Lubitsch.

He was a generally acknowledged "great" filmmaker who nonetheless worked comfortably, it seemed, inside the studio system instead of at odds with it. Unlike a Chaplin, or later a Welles, he never had to be ostracized or put in his place, never slapped down or disciplined. For the most part, he was a company man—so much so that he even became a mogul himself for a short time in 1935, when he was Paramount's production chief: the only time in Hollywood history that a first-rate film artist would be given so much actual power. The experiment failed, of course; but the wonder is that it was even tried.

It is hard to escape the suspicion that other filmmakers may have valued his films in a way for their *lack* of substance—that they admired Lubitsch for his ability to make much out of almost nothing. Such a talent could be only useful in the Hollywood of the great studios, and the filmmaker who had it (who more than Lubitsch?) was someone to be watched and learned from. Hollywood also admired—the exact word for it—his dirty jokes. A Lubitsch film was always famously risqué. And yet he was never hassled by censors, either before or after shooting. To people in the industry, that was no negligible accomplishment. Contests with the censor were not only a challenge but an industry-wide obsession. And the ability to get *really* dirty jokes into your script or picture, and to get away with them, was a universally approved one.

In this respect, as in others, writers and directors in the studio system often had the psychology of army noncoms. They felt powerless, but they knew where the power was, and there was no satisfaction or distinction in defying it and bringing it down on yourself. But to outwit it and mock it and then to be rewarded for your mockery (see Hecht and MacArthur's *The Front Page*) was almost the highest satisfaction—apart from the money—that labor in the studio ranks could offer. To this psychology Lubitsch was a model and an ideal. For it wasn't just mockery and dirty jokes that he got away with: it was intelligence itself, in a system that tended to empower stupidity. The spirit in those "wonderfully intelligent eyes" (in his associate Steffie Trondle's phrase) seemed to win over every obstacle—for a while.

Lubitsch films always had a certain highbrow following, even at a time when a fondness for movies was often something serious people either concealed or apologized for. Lubitsch, it's true, could be as "Hollywood" as anyone—as vulgar and philistine sometimes as any of his filmmaking peers. Still, a Lubitsch movie was something different. It was nearly impossible for an American intellectual of the thirties and forties to sit in front of a Lubitsch film and not feel—however much he might dissent from it otherwise—a certain kinship to the man and the mind that had produced it. No other major American filmmaker—not until Orson Welles, at least—produced this effect so strongly. You had to make allowances for a Capra or a Ford, even at times for a Chaplin. But not for Lubitsch. Movies, it was agreed generally, spoke a preliterate language. But not a Lubitsch film. A literate viewer might attack or dismiss his movies, but he didn't at least have to *translate* them. It was therefore not surprising that a cinemaphobe like George Jean Nathan should make an exception of Lubitsch (and *The Marriage Circle*) when deploring Hollywood, as he did frequently, or that Edmund Wilson could praise a Lubitsch film (as he did both *Kiss Me Again* and *Lady Windermere's Fan*) in exactly the same terms he might use for a serious new novel.

Ronald Colman with May McAvoy in Lady Windermere's Fan; *Bert Lytell (at right) looks on.*

But the Lubitsch career—which spans Germany and America, silents and talkies, and some thirty years—went through several phases, all of them remarkable. While still a minor actor in the Max Reinhardt Company, he began his movie career as a silent-screen comic, appearing as a stereotyped low-comedy Jew, usually a department store clerk struggling to make good, in a series of comedies he was soon directing as well as starring in, with titles like *Schuhpalast Pinkus* (1916) and *Der Blusenkönig* (1917). Even as late as 1919, when he had already become an important director of feature-length epics, he was still being seen on German screens as *Meyer aus Berlin*—though this was the last such film he would appear in.

The first serious feature-length film he directed was also his first film with Pola Negri and Emil Jannings—an Egyptian-curse melodrama called *Die Augen der Mumie Mâ* (1918). It was followed by *Carmen* (1918), also with Negri, and *Madame DuBarry* (1919), again with both Negri and Jannings. It was *DuBarry* that turned the minor Jewish clown into the most prestigious director on the international film scene. Lubitsch was twenty-seven. "The master of tragedy," he was called; "the Reinhardt of the cinema," "the Griffith of Europe." He had a gift (derived from his tenure with Reinhardt) for film spectacle, for the effective deployment of huge crowds and enormous budgets. And the worldwide success of *Madame DuBarry* virtually created the German film industry overnight, making it a force in world cinema. And even though Lubitsch continued to direct comedies, both short and feature length, it was his epics he was famed for— films like *Anna Boleyn* (1920) and *Das Weib des Pharao* (1922), which were marked by an ability to combine the large public event with the intimate personal detail. Like Griffith, Lubitsch was called a "humanizer of history." But unlike Griffith's, Lubitsch's personal detail was generally comic and ironic— rarely sentimental.

So he came to Hollywood at the end of 1922—but not, as it turned out, to make the bigger and better historical spectacles that "the Griffith of Europe" might be expected to do there. Lubitsch wanted, he said, to do "modern stories of American life."* This notion came to him, it seems, only after he had done *Rosita* (1923), his first American film, with Mary Pickford as a seventeenth-century Spanish street singer—and a box-office flop. (Pickford called him a "director of doors, not people.") Around this time he saw Chaplin's *A Woman of Paris* (1923), and it was a revelation to him. He signed with Warner Brothers and commenced a series of five films as small-scale as his earlier successes had been big. Sophisticated domestic comedies—*The Marriage Circle* in 1924 was the remarkable first one—with small casts of recurring performers (Monte Blue and Marie Prevost in three) and ingenious plots with recurring themes (sexual infidelity in all five). And with these films Lubitsch achieved once again— though on quite different terms than before—that combination of critical and commercial success which had distinguished his German career.

From one point of view, however, each phase in his early Hollywood career can be seen as a kind of retrenching, a deliberate act of scaling downwards. And there were always observers ready to note this reductive pattern and to deplore it. In 1926 writer-actor Jim Tully in *Vanity Fair* saw Lubitsch's decision to do films like *The Marriage Circle* as a refusal of "the greatest opportunity ever given to a director"—namely, the chance to become the "modern Moses" of Hollywood, someone who might lead the film industry out of its self-imposed wilderness; instead, Lubitsch had chosen to do "frothy films for sophisticated chambermaids and cinema critics." Later on, Dwight MacDonald, who differed with this view of the domestic comedies, nevertheless deplored Lubitsch's *next* phase, the operetta films of the early thirties. "Ernst Lubitsch enjoys the greatest reputation of any director now active in Hollywood," MacDonald wrote in 1933, and added: "but this is based largely on his silent films."

---

*Precisely what he never succeeded in doing—since nearly all Lubitsch's important American movies have European settings.

Films like *Lady Windermere's Fan* (1925), one of the silent cinema's most extraordinary achievements. Lubitsch boasted when filming was done that he hadn't used a single line of Oscar Wilde—no doubt because he knew just how good his own version was, even larger and richer than the original in some ways. Surprisingly, Lubitsch's approach emphasizes character and "emotional values" *over* wit. The movie's Lord Darlington (Ronald Colman) is genuinely ardent and troubled, a much more complex figure than Wilde's. And not again until Garbo in *Ninotchka* (1939) does a Lubitsch film offer such a complexly observed heroine as Irene Rich's Mrs. Erlynne. Lubitsch's general effect on the Wilde play is to move it closer to moral and psychological realism. Through most of his early sound films, however, he seems to move determinedly in the opposite direction—away from accepted modes of seriousness.

People are so used by now to talking about Lubitsch as a giant of film history, as a major artist and filmmaker, that it can be surprising to discover how paradoxical and even perverse in a way the larger part of his achievement was. As if he defied his own eminence: this most "important" of filmmakers chose for the most part to work on almost aggressively unimportant projects, in minor modes and on trifling materials. Partly, of course, like any Hollywood filmmaker, however important, he was maneuvering for survival. And more than many, he was a cautious and practical man. But in fact the kind of froth he was drawn to wasn't all that commercial. Nor was it even very prestigious. It wasn't "art" that he worked in the name of, but "sophistication." And a rather ersatz form of it at that: the Continental theatrical tradition of the boulevard comedy, a *haut bourgeois* kind of swank, having more to do with daydreams of elegance than with the real thing.

At his best, however, he could transform even this material. Clearly he took inspiration from it. His fondness for obscure Hungarian plays of the well-made school was a widespread Hollywood joke. ("It's not enough to be Hungarian," one saying went, "you've got to have a third act too"—Hungarian third acts being notoriously defective.) "I have a special weakness," he once told an interviewer, "for the Continental type of thing, works like Molnár's." And, he might have added, works like Lehár's. Lubitsch made five operetta films—all with Maurice Chevalier or Jeanette MacDonald or both—in the first five years of the sound era, beginning with *The Love Parade* in 1929.

ONCE UPON a time—in *The Love Parade*—there was a mythical kingdom called Sylvania, whose ruler, Queen Louise (Jeanette MacDonald), was not married. Nor has she ever been married (she is very young). This fact entirely preoccupies, it seems, all the people of her kingdom, from elderly cabinet ministers to children in school to the band in the palace courtyard, which plays

the wedding march under her bedroom window in spite of her express prohibition against such music. What can she do? The obsession is everywhere she turns. "Don't tell me you weren't talking about it," she says, opening a meeting with her cabinet. "You're always talking about it." Talking about what? the cabinet ministers inquire innocently—playing dumb. But she knows—we know—that they were talking about *it*. In Sylvania, they always are. . . . There is no escape. Even in dreams.

When we first meet this queen, she is being awakened in her cathedral-like bedchamber by a group of ladies-in-waiting, who are as interested in finding out about her dreams of the night before as they are in assisting at her morning toilet. Radiant against the bedclothes and clutching a pillow, the young queen gratifies their curiosity by singing to them. "Dream lover, fold your arms around me. / Dream lover, your romance has found me. . . ." She rises as she sings, descends from the dais, and stands at the foot of her bed in full-length undress. "Knowing too well," she sings in her lingerie, "dreams never tell. . . ." Now she idles before us in medium shot as her attendants take up the chorus. As they pipe away behind her, she lowers her head shyly, kicks her foot out, puts a hand on the back of her neck, stretches on tiptoe—then, with arm upraised before her, moves with sudden dramatic emphasis to the right, into a peignoir held out for her by one of the ladies. She seats herself, and the ladies, still singing, kneel around her and produce mirrors for her to see herself in; she fluffs her hair and joins the singing again. The music beedul-dee-umps to its close. The queen rises and sings the final prolonged note, her arm upraised again; and holding it aloft as before, she follows it out and off, sweeping through a curtained door with her retinue following. End of number, empty set—which the camera holds for a few frames, presumably allowing us to collect our wits. We'll need them: in the next scene she takes a bath. The "Lubitsch era" has begun.

It's all old stuff in a way. Lubitsch is frankly transferring the conventions of a stage number to the screen, retaining and even heightening the staginess. To movie audiences of 1929, the elements of the scene would have been familiar: the star in step-ins, the opening song about a dream romance, the proscenium arch framing: all occur, for example, in David Butler's *Sunny Side Up* (1929), released just before *The Love Parade*, and a great popular success. Janet Gaynor sings there about *her* dream lover ("He's ideal, but he's not real"); but she does so in close-up, gazing and dimpling right at us, sitting in a chair and fully dressed. She appears in lingerie later on. But she thinks she is alone—until she notices the bemused hero (Charles Farrell) sitting on the bed and watching her, causing her to pose prettily and then flee.*

What is new in *The Love Parade* is the way the familiar elements are combined, and the resulting Lubitschean tone: both dry and ardent, both dazzled and knowing. MacDonald is presented to us with a mixture of formality and leering, of operetta swank and strip-show prurience. The prurience has a benevolent quality. Those ladies-in-waiting are genuinely solicitous. The solicitude gets nuttier as it gets elaborated, however. "I'm held *in* your spell," the queen sings, and the ladies literally help her into the high note—lifting her from the bed to a standing position as she hits it. Once she is upright and on to

---

*The same movie includes a musical production number called "Turn On the Heat," in which undulating chorus girls not only melt igloos and glaciers but cause a forest of trees to come thrusting up through the ground around them: a sample of the kind of "risqué" effect Lubitsch was *not* interested in.

the next note, they bow and withdraw as discreetly as if curtains were parting around her, to leave her at the center of the frame. What's important to notice here is that the absurdity of all this, rather than destroying the affectionate tone the scene has set up earlier, really amplifies it. This effect is characteristic of Lubitsch, for whom pomp and ceremony tend to be functions of an essential good nature, especially when they are insanely elaborated.

Lubitsch, of course, is kidding the operetta style here, heightening its artifice and absurdity at every point. It would be a mistake to suppose that he is camping, however—or *seriously* making fun. He is not interested in subverting the style or in being superior to his audience's (presumed) enthusiasm for it. He shares that enthusiasm. In his way. The matter is complicated, to say the least, by MacDonald's lingerie. It's not just her figure that we're invited to admire but her dignity under the circumstances. This perilously maintained dignity is one of Lubitsch's great subjects. One of the strongest biases of his comic vision is to see us *all* as trilling in our underwear. And if he shows MacDonald this way here, it's not to undermine her song (that intention probably wouldn't even have occurred to him) but to remind us what it is she's singing about: the fact that all this operetta "prettiness," all the piping and trilling, all this gentility and civility and soprano rapture, are really about getting laid. Lubitsch isn't being sardonic when he makes this point—far from it. The contrast between these genteel theatrical forms and their final, very ungenteel meanings only makes those forms more treasurable to him—and to us, as he shows them to us. This wonderful joke—the identification of high aspiration with low cravings, of the most highfalutin forms with the most down-to-earth realities—is of course basic Hollywood. And though Lubitsch certainly didn't "teach" this joke to other moviemakers any more than he originated it, he did teach them more than anyone else did about how to shape and repeat and perfect it. And no one else, it is commonly agreed in Hollywood even today, ever told it quite as well or as elegantly as he did.

Q UEEN LOUISE's problems begin to be solved when Count Alfred (Maurice Chevalier), her military attaché in Paris, is recalled to Sylvania—in disgrace for his amorous activities. The queen reads the detailed official report on those activities in Count Alfred's presence. She smokes furiously on a cigarette as she turns the pages, more and more rapidly, pausing only to look up and glare at him. The ultimate outcome of this interview is a private supper in her quarters, while her aged cabinet ministers watch from the garden and note the count's progress. "If it goes on at this rate," one of them observes grandly, "then we are entitled to the highest hopes." The difficulty in all this, as these ministers have explained to the queen, is that a queen's prince consort really has nothing to do.

Nothing to do? cries the queen (can she have been misinformed?). Well, of course he has *something* to do; but such a marriage is not a situation that most self-respecting men would enter into. Count Alfred, on the other hand, seems to have been swept off his feet, and to be unsuspecting into the bargain. It isn't until the wedding ceremony that he gets a hint of what's in store for him—when the priest pronounces them "wife and man." The rest of the story details the predictable stresses of this arrangement, which climax when the prince consort decides to break loose from the palace and return to Paris, compelling his royal wife to submit at last to his husbandly authority. "My king!" she exclaims as they embrace, and reprise the title song, before fadeout.

In a way, the whole film is like that final duet: all the important scenes are between Alfred and Louise. And except for their low-comedy counterparts, his butler and her maid (Lupino Lane and Lillian Roth), who do their own duets from time to time, there are no other clearly personalized characters in the film. Still, there are several opportunities for spectacle, as might be expected in "the

Queen Louise (MacDonald) back in bed; Count Alfred (Maurice Chevalier) on his way back to Paris.

Griffith of Europe's" first talkie. The queen reviews her troops—and sings "The March of the Grenadiers" ("Ev'ry uniform / Taking a heart by storm . . ."). The palace sets emphasize vastness and grandeur, and when the queen goes to the opera, the halls and great staircases are lined with guards standing at attention—and singing. But mostly Lubitsch uses these spaces by emptying them out. Chevalier crosses a great hall to fetch his pajamas from another room. The queen runs up the grand staircase after him—in long shot, a tiny figure in the distance, with arm upraised futilely as she scuttles out of the frame's upper edge.

The royal wedding scene was described in the studio's publicity releases as "perhaps the most dazzlingly spectacular scene yet witnessed and heard in a talking motion picture." But Lubitsch's relation to spectacle and to big-budget effects has become by this time rather curious. Not only are his vast sets used mainly to diminish and isolate his characters: even when he fills those sets, he seems oddly remote from the effect that results. He shows us the great wedding procession with all the involvement of a tourist taking snapshots: now from this angle, now from that (including an aerial shot from above—why not?), with no kinetic relation to the spectacle itself. The sequence is a clear instance of something that was to become more and more a feature of Lubitsch's work in the sound period: a kind of alienation—a dry, chill distance—from his own biggest effects.

The joke he's building up to here is about the very different degrees of deference accorded to the queen and her new husband. In effect, we see two wedding processions: his and hers. First, hers. The guests are massed in the palace's great throne room. The lord chamberlain gives three great knocks on the floor with his massive staff. There is an answering fanfare of trumpets; a choir bursts into full-throated song; and two great doors swing wide to disclose the queen in her bridal gown, proceeding slowly forward, her great jeweled train supported by page boys, her ladies-in-waiting just behind them. She moves slowly and shyly down the great staircase under the arched swords of her grenadier guards—until she reaches the foot of the throne and the officiating priest. Next, the prince consort–to-be enters. Cut to what looks like the door to a small closet. *Bump-bump*, goes a page boy with a baton. An off-screen organ plays a jaunty little fanfare, and out comes the bridegroom, looking cheerful and vacant. The organ thumps and tootles and he walks quickly out of the shot. Appearing in the next shot at the queen's side. The humiliating (for him) ceremony ensues. "And you, Prince Alfred . . . do you promise to be an obedient and docile husband . . . ?"

Lubitsch turns Hollywood elephantiasis to almost delicate account. The massing of details in this sequence becomes a function of his wit and is characterized above all by its thoroughness. Nothing has been overlooked, for example, that might enhance or amplify the count's humiliation—from the size of his door to the look on his face. The sound of that off-screen organ is exactly, inspirationally right: a sort of vague cheerful tootling, encouraging but dim. In the same sequence, we watch a huge, beturbaned Turk—the ambassador "from Afghanistan"—expostulating in nonsense syllables against the marriage ceremony and its anti-male bias. But what is funny here is the way Lubitsch has framed this figure, in a long, static two-shot with an impassive Eugene Pallette, one of the queen's ministers. Pallette stares equably ahead, sunk in himself, while the bulging-eyed Turk at his side fulminates massively in a stream of plosives and popping sounds. It takes a particularly rude sound, however, to startle Pallette into attention, to make him give up that equable forward gaze. Pallette in this shot is a typical Lubitsch figure: we can tell from his face that his relation to the outside world is both fitful and reluctant. And he is contentedly remote from the furious figure at his side. It is also characteristic of Lubitsch to imprison two such figures in the same extended shot, and to end the "most dazzlingly spectacular" sequence in the film with this odd, slightly and slyly irrelevant "climax."

For it's clear that what he likes best about the spectacle in this film is the chance it gives him for waywardness, for anticlimax. And the effect isn't always a comic one. Later on, when the queen goes to the opera—she is dramatically alone, having been abandoned by her husband—she marches in formal progress and lonely splendor down the staircase and through the great hall of the palace, past the chanting ranks of her grenadier guards. Lubitsch ends this conventionally stirring sequence on an oddly rapt note, entranced and suspended, as his camera watches MacDonald in profile in a long, lateral tracking shot. As she walks forward, the line of her coat emphasizing the slouch of her body and the motion of her hips, she is as self-contained as Pallette was. But there is something else quite different: an impersonal, even unconscious pride of youth and beauty in the movement, underlined by the gaunt elderly cabinet minister who walks behind her. She walks to the beat of the grenadiers' song, raptly—and it's almost as if the movie is holding its breath as it watches her to the fadeout, sauntering into darkness.

But in *The Love Parade* it is less usual for the camera to follow movement than it is for a character to walk out of the frame, leaving the camera, and us, behind, where we stay for a few frames. An effect of cutting like a retard in music, it's also an editing technique of Lubitsch's silent films which persists in his talkies until well into the thirties. People don't just go out of a Lubitsch frame: they vacate it, leave it empty. We see them and then we see their absence, an empty chair or desk or space—a slight hesitation before we see where they have gone to, in the next shot. The signature step of this film is a quick exit, often in the wrong direction—or what looks like it to us. We are never quite sure where things are outside our immediate view. People enter Lubitsch's shots from unexpected points—how did they get there? The camera pans slightly and we see them where we didn't expect them to be. This evenly maintained, quiet, steady disorientation about physical spaces is crucial to Lubitsch's style.

The movie frame in this style becomes a sort of register of the world beyond it—a world nearly always dislocating, unexpected in some way. Alone in this frame, with its connections to the unseen, people tend to look uneasy (they haven't seen it yet) or discomfited (they have). Jeanette MacDonald has the ideal Lubitsch face: always slightly astonished. Even composed, she looks alarmed. And when she looks determined—as she often does, being a queen—that is a joke. Lubitsch conditions us to perceive almost any sign of determination or intention in his characters, any hint of autonomy, as primarily *funny* facts. Partly because the immediate world of the film is so unpredictable. But also because in a longer view it is just the reverse: Lubitsch's heroes and heroines are the puppets of a very conventional sexual fate. Whatever they *do* either to promote or to impede that fate, we learn to feel, is mostly beside the point.

Prince Alfred has declared his intention to leave wife and Sylvania at once—back to his carefree bachelor life in Paris—and he is packing his bags in his rooms. He doesn't even answer his phone when his wife calls him from *her* rooms. She sobs on the top of her bed, heartbroken. Next we see her crossing the great hall, her sobbing now very distant. She has decided to go to him, and she looks almost poignantly small and dim as she scurries up the great staircase and out of the frame. Outside his door, she gets no response. Until he comes out—in silence—and crosses the great hall in the direction of her chambers. She runs after him, then past him—excitedly—looking over her shoulder as she goes. She reaches her room again and jumps promptly into bed. He enters the shot, and she lifts the bedclothes: looking up at him, with a kind of witless jocosity. But he has only come to fetch his pajamas from a nearby chair; he does so and exits. And she is up again—and after him. Back across the great hall, for the third time.

Predictably, in this passage—extended, it seems, by almost nothing but its own confidence—those transits through the great hall culminate with the queen in bed "asking for it" again, lifting the bedclothes and then being rebuffed. Lubitsch never relents in his radical reductive Hollywood vision. The problem at the beginning of this movie was getting the queen laid, and it is still the problem here at the end. But the most Lubitschean joke of all is the fact that this particular "point" should be the payoff to such a nuanced and elegant passage of film, with its formal structure and repetitions. It's the structural equivalent to MacDonald trilling in her underwear.

And although the point is predictable (as always), the joke itself, its timing and form and inflections—that jocose look when MacDonald lifts the bedcovers—is (again as always) surprising. Just as we are never really uncertain about the ultimate intentions and fates of Lubitsch's characters, we are always uncertain about their *immediate* intentions—in crossing a room, or running to catch up, in entering a shot or leaving it. In *The Love Parade* we learn to expect that almost any pattern of movement will resolve itself in some unexpected way. And this moment-to-moment unexpectedness creates an important tension with the reductive, know-it-all meanings, the generic comic vision in which nothing is unexpected—in which either sex or money, or both, explain everything, or at least every human aspiration we can believe in. But as we see and experience a Lubitsch film, we are never made to *feel* as if we know it all, or that anyone could. The lubricity of *The Love Parade*, even with its implicit cynicism, is like MacDonald herself in the film: wondering and wide-eyed, full of happy energy and unquenchable surprise.

When MacDonald and Chevalier have crossed that great hall for the final time, we get to see Chevalier alone when he reaches his own room again: collapsing across his bed with a grin of triumph. Suddenly he hears a door. He looks frowningly out of the frame. Cut to a close-up of MacDonald in front of the door, which is now closed behind her. No longer wide-eyed and ardent and beseeching as before, she looks subdued, opaque, deliberately unreadable—and she is silent. The prince approaches her. They are in a two-shot: "The key, please," he says quietly. She looks away. No reply. "Trying to use force again, Madame?" She looks away still. At length it develops that she does have the key: she looks the way she does in this scene because she has hidden it in her sleeve. That overdetermined quality that André Bazin complains of in the basic Hollywood cutting style (shot/reverse-shot), in which the significance of each shot is all too readily fixed and declared, really seems not to be a feature of *The Love Parade*. There are too many images in it like MacDonald in front of that door—in which the point is precisely our uneasy *non*-recognition of the point, our uncertainty (even if only temporary) about just what this face *means*.

It's true that behind the surface is still another surface, and that the suggestions of privacy and mystery in Lubitsch people are always going to be resolved in a joke or a witticism or a double entendre. But the larger joke in these films is in a sense *about* complexity—about the fact that human beings are constantly and inconveniently surprising, self-deceived, contradictory. And in a way Lubitsch gives us the experience of complexity—the surprises, the perceptions of contradiction, the discovery of hidden meanings—without the content. *The Love Parade* is an exercise in style, rather purely. But it's a style that pays tribute to, even embodies, the unpredictable and incalculable. Lubitsch's style has a moral grace that undercuts the script's often complacent cynicism, the chortling naughtiness of some of the jokes. Lubitsch has put on the screen a world where people live in a more or less continuous state of mild astonishment: not the sort of place where the complacencies and attitudes implied by "cynicism" and "naughtiness" could seem very central. He is in full, happy command of a movie style that not only portrays but tends to induce the habit of wonder.

And Jeanette MacDonald is its chief interpreter. She is also the focus of the magical feeling in *The Love Parade*—as well as its chief comic agent. Lubitsch's own habit of wonder about *her* was something he would continue to explore in the even more accomplished comedies to come.

Jeanette MacDonald at the casino in Monte Carlo.

MacDONALD WAS an official Lubitsch discovery. She was a featured Broadway player when movie star Richard Dix saw her in a short-lived show called *Angela* (with Eric Blore) in 1928. Dix asked her to make a screen test for Paramount. Nothing came of this test, however, until a year later when Lubitsch saw it—and promptly entrained for Chicago, where she was appearing in a show called *Boom! Boom!* He decided that this was his Queen Louise and signed her up. Her early screen personality was largely a Lubitsch invention— a very different image from the one she is now mainly (and unhappily) known for: the genteel and often preposterous singing heroine of all those MGM operettas with Nelson Eddy. But this metamorphosis happened, of course, *after* her Lubitsch years. In 1930 it was different. The *Time* magazine reviewer then could refer to her as a player chiefly distinguished by "her aptitude for undressing before the camera quickly and almost completely, with becoming grace and without embarrassment." *Monte Carlo* (1930), her next film with Lubitsch, both confirmed this talent and revealed others. Lubitsch "the master," wrote the *Photoplay* reviewer, has turned "a conventional prima donna" into "one of the best comediennes on the American screen."

Their rapport from the beginning, it seems, was in their common sense of humor: in his movies she was always European, and she said of him after his death in 1947 that he had "the most American sense of humor" she had ever known. *Her* "Americanness" both challenged and baffled him. By several accounts, he was in love with her. And if the passion was unrequited, the friendship wasn't; it survived even Nelson Eddy and professional separation and lasted—close and funny and warm—until his death. It was just their mutual incongruity that Lubitsch valued, of course, and used for comic point. The contrast between them was like the one he put on the screen between her and Chevalier: European rake and nice American girl. He liked those lingerie shows better than she did, and there were some arguments—most of which he won. She had a singing coach in constant attendance, a woman with the richly evocative name of Grace Adele Newell. Lubitsch pretended never to know quite who this personage was—referring to her, when asked, as "Jeanette's morals teacher."

He knew what he had in her from the start. Under his direction she is more than a charming, elegantly self-mocking comedienne: she is the quintessential Lubitsch heroine, as exactly suited to his comedy of dry astonishment as anyone ever would be. She is not exactly a "natural" comedian. There is a faintly ceremonial air to even her lightest moments, a sense of decisions taken and lessons learned behind almost everything she does. But it was just this that endeared her to Lubitsch, who was never really attracted to "naturals" of any kind. It was just those tensions and contradictions in MacDonald's performing personality that made her "his type": her primness in undress; her essential reserve in gestures of abandon; her ability above all to retain a real and impressive dignity through the most adverse scenes and circumstances. His affection for her gallantry in such moments is something you can feel through his driest inflections.

She is always the slightest bit overemphatic. Even her beauty: the rather heavy-jawed plangency of her face; her big, lustrous, heavy-lidded eyes. She is not really a formidable woman; she is too indomitably good-tempered, too sunny and enchanted and enjoying herself for that. And it is one of Lubitsch's tenderest, most affectionate jokes about her to cast her, as he does over and over again, as a lady imperious, authoritative, domineering—a queen, a countess, the richest woman in Ruritania—a willful beauty, awesome in repose and awful in wrath.

Above everything, MacDonald has—as Lubitsch so clearly saw—a gift for ardent nonsense, a knack for playing absurdity with total, stunning conviction as well as comic edge. *Monte Carlo*, Lubitsch's second sound film, seems largely built around this facility of hers. In spite of the movie's title, we don't see much of the casino or the gaming tables or of any locale but the heroine's hotel suite—where she spends most of her time fighting an embarrassing yen she is getting for her hairdresser (Jack Buchanan). Grappling with a passion that she can't even afford to notice: she is, after all, a countess. (He in fact is a count, but she can't know that until the end of the film.) Soon, though, she yields to her desire quite fully and happily: it's the naming of it that she has to fight against. She *tries* to be affronted, even at the height of passion. "That's what you get," she cries brokenly after emerging from a disabling kiss with the hero, "for being nice to your servants."

Monte Carlo is an advance in many ways over *The Love Parade*—in lunacy and witty extravagance as well as its mastery of sound film techniques. It is also brisker, more streamlined, purged of all extraneous stagy elements (like the Lupino Lane–Lillian Roth interludes in *The Love Parade*). Everything is more intimate. There is less space around what it shows us: the cutting is faster and the framing is tighter.

It is also bawdier: the "ris-gaiety," as it was called, is even more relentless, more inventive than before. MacDonald makes her obligatory first entrance in underwear. But this time she is running to catch a train (when the middle-aged conductor looks startled at her state of undress, she explains coldly that she has "just come from a wedding")—escaping a marriage ceremony whose nutty logic is epitomized by the chinless and ineffectual bridegroom (Claud Allister) singing a song to the assembled guests about how he is going to get her back, "caveman style" ("She'll Love Me and Like It"). The songs in *Monte Carlo* are generally witty, and possibly even benefit from not having to be tailored to the requirements of a familiar screen personality like Chevalier's. English music-hall star Jack Buchanan makes his American film debut here as MacDonald's leading man. (His appearance wasn't regarded as a success, and his next American film wouldn't be until twenty-three years later, Vincente Minnelli's *The Band Wagon*.) The song lyrics are by Tin Pan Alley veteran Leo Robin and have the requisite Lubitschean flavor, especially "Trimmin' the Women," about how to get your kicks by being a hairdresser ("Satisfy the craving / Finger-waving!"). And some of the film's boldest jokes are set to strains of lilting melody, including an exchange about the heroine's calling the hero by different names (her imperiousness again) of her own devising, and his promising to "come" to all of them.

The bawdiness and the looniness are of course connected, mutually reinforcing. That connection is what MacDonald's look of alarm is about, and why the movie makes that look so central. The action begins with one of those classic movie images of successful flight and freedom: the runaway bride. Countess Helene Mara (MacDonald) has run out on her wedding to a silly-ass duke, Otto von Liebenheim (Allister)—a man who, she says, has "everything a woman wants . . . nothing but money." The countess, leaving her wedding gown behind and wearing nothing but her underthings and a coat, boards the first train out of town. When she finds out it's headed toward Monte Carlo, she resolves to gamble her future at the gaming tables and sings "Beyond the Blue Horizon" out the window, as the train rushes, chugging and whistling, toward the promise of a new day.

But promises of flight and freedom in Lubitsch films have a way of not paying off the way they should. Far from being the story of an adventurous and reckless heroine, coquetting her way through a glamorous and glittering capital, baffling and taunting a lovestruck hero, and so on—the movie is about a woman in her hotel room, the bills unpaid, falling in love with one servant while being coldly observed by another (her maid, played by ZaSu Pitts). The image of Countess Mara as breaking loose turns out to be mainly ironic. (Also, we learn that this is the third time she's escaped from the same marriage to the same man.) She is neither an adventuress nor a free spirit but a "woman of propriety," as she is described by the opera singers of the final sequence. And her creator wouldn't have it any other way: a lady's "propriety" is one of those elegant civilized arrangements he particularly values. For Lubitsch, it could almost be said, *all* constraints and formal manners are a dirty joke—a delightful one. But it's no wonder his favorite heroine looks steadily alarmed.

And Lubitsch's camera, like MacDonald herself in this film, tends to stare. It does fewer of the blinks, starts, and double takes that mark the style of *The Love Parade*. Those effects of dislocation and discontinuity that he gets by cutting in the earlier film, here tend to be contained in the same shot. Where the basic visual device of *The Love Parade* is the shot/reverse-shot, in *Monte Carlo* it's a two-shot—long, laconic, stationary—with two faces in the same frame, offering an image of violently opposed self-absorptions, registering simultaneous but radically different inner experiences. As when Buchanan, the disguised count, first "does" MacDonald's hair. He shampoos it by mistake, an error that calls for an immediate and strenuous rinse-and-dry. Followed by a shot of MacDonald sitting indignant under a billowing cloud of her own hair while Buchanan stands over her like some mad orchestra conductor and wields the hand dryer: the hair has a life of its own as she seethes below it and the ecstatic Buchanan "works" above.

But the movie's most memorable instance of fiercely missed signals between people trapped in the same movie frame is the opera box sequence between MacDonald and Allister. MacDonald has fallen in love with Buchanan, then quarreled with him and thrown him out—an event that has made her late for the opera. The compliant duke is waiting for her in their box, and the opera—*Monsieur Beaucaire*, about a hairdresser who is really a nobleman in disguise—is well underway when she arrives, distraught. "Have I missed very much?" she inquires. "Oh, no, no," replies her suitor, always anxious to make her happy. "Only the first and second acts." And when Allister—who has a monocle, an imbecile sunniness, a perpetually open mouth, and a tendency to lead with his teeth—asks her whether she found the hairdresser, MacDonald instructs him angrily never to mention hair or hairdressers to her again. She changes the subject; "What's the opera about?" she inquires. Allister looks forward, and struck to the heart. But he is obliged to tell her: it's about this hairdresser. She looks at him. "I can't help it," he says, reasonably. Once she has taken this information in, however—gravely and at length—she decides to hazard some questions about it.

COUNTESS (*looking away*): What's wrong with this hairdresser?
DUKE (*a toothy grin in reply*): It's a silly story. Only possible with music. . . . (*She looks at him.*) Imagine—a lady falling in love with a hairdresser.
(*Pause. She continues to gaze at him.*)
COUNTESS (*still staring at him*): That's possible . . . even without music. . . . (*She looks frontwards again.*) Things like that happen every day . . . I should say so . . . —Tell me—did she marry him?
DUKE: Oh, no. She had no idea he was a hairdresser. She's only just found it out.
COUNTESS: Then what did she do?
DUKE: What could she do? She threw him out, of course. . . .

The countess's astonishment at this last information is almost more than she can support. She turns and stares at the duke again, burningly. She draws back, still staring, her hand at her throat. At length, by virtue of scrutinizing the duke it seems, she appears to have taken this new and astounding fact in: she nods gravely. "She'll regret it," she says, in a tone so baleful and tragic that the duke looks suddenly terrified. He continues to look front.

The take here is nearly three minutes long: a steady, deadpan, unblinking contemplation of absolute impasse and mutual incomprehension, of burning-eyed blindness and choked passionate misunderstanding. It's the joke of human isolation, and the recurrence of such two-shot effects suggests just how fond of that joke Lubitsch is. It should also suggest why *Monte Carlo* features a heroine who is largely precluded from breaking loose, even when she sets out to do so. Lubitsch treats even space and motion in the film in a way that underscores the point: break loose to where? from where? Once again, as in *The Love Parade*, MacDonald walks in profile, with the camera tracking laterally beside her. She is walking—watched by the hero and his friend—through a garden on her way to the Casino: alone, in twilight, trailing a fan, moving purposefully and looking straight before her, with nothing on the soundtrack but the faint crunch of gravel under her feet. It is a deliberately odd, deliberately deadpan effect—like the shot of a Lubitsch door, oddly prolonged, oddly laconic (like the door too, it turns out to be the buildup to a joke). But also, like other such moments involving MacDonald, it is privileged and oddly beautiful. And the beauty has to do with something melancholy, with our sense that she is "going nowhere." The path seems improbably endless; her relation to the camera never varies; nor, seemingly, does the backdrop of shrubs and bushes she walks in front of. And Lubitsch cuts between her and the two men standing and watching her in a way that suggests she never gets any farther away from them.

It's appropriate, then, that the most stirring moment in the film should be a song number, by Buchanan and MacDonald, about going out—and that it should lead to their coming right back again. They are going to the Casino (but when they get there, the sight of the duke sends them hustling out again). Buchanan is meant to be "lucky," and this is the night when they expect to recoup MacDonald's losses. They are dressed in their evening clothes and ready to go. They sing:

Always
In all ways
Rely upon me . . .
Should any doubt come,
    Wait for the outcome
    Hopefully!

They walk on the second chorus—music-hall style—strolling and strutting into an outer room, where she dons her wrap, he knots his silk scarf and pops his hat on. MacDonald's stroll is a kind of sideways walk, leading with one shoulder and looking invitingly over the other. And they sing, of course, on and on, and out the door.

We'll find a happy ending—
If you will keep depending—
Always
In all ways
    On me. . . .

What's nice about this is the sense of a very qualified kind of elation—a music-hall number in a hotel room. But it's not like Astaire dancing over table tops and sofas: these singers don't transform or transcend their environment—indeed, they never lose sight of it. Nor do we. The constraint and limitation are there in the music, the movement, in the slight charming awkwardness, in the jaunty angle of MacDonald's elbow as she leads the way to the door, in the way the sexual and romantic excitement is modified by the slightly self-conscious, slightly self-mocking roguishness. Indeed, the whole music-hall strolling style—which Buchanan and MacDonald are both peerless at—is an image of excitement held back, of transport smiled over and shrugged at, of elation offered almost diffidently. What makes the number stirring is precisely this sense of constraints both accepted and surmounted. The Lubitschean festivity: gallantry and gaiety within limits that nobody dances beyond or away from—or even sings about very convincingly.

L UBITSCH MIGHT have been repeating himself dangerously with these operetta films—or so many people were beginning to feel. But another such film was just what Maurice Chevalier's screen career, faltering since *The Love Parade*, seemed to need by 1931. *The Smiling Lieutenant* (1931)—a Lubitsch-Chevalier film *without* MacDonald—was a hit both critically and commercially. It was made at Astoria, Long Island, while Lubitsch was also functioning as "supervising director" of the studios there. And it was co-written by Samson Raphaelson, the New York playwright who was quickly to become, and remain, Lubitsch's favorite screenwriter.

In the early days of talkies the movies seemed to take giant steps almost from month to month, and technically this is the most accomplished of the early Lubitsch sound films. In sets, camerawork, background music, alternations of sound and silence, the whole film achieves a fluency that makes *The Love Parade* and *Monte Carlo* look comparatively stilted. And yet nothing in *The Smiling Lieutenant* calls attention to these feats of smoothly functioning technique (no sequences as flashy as, for example, the "Blue Horizon" number in *Monte Carlo*): what's most impressive is the quiet confidence of it all. Although at times the sets seem constricted (this was Long Island, not Hollywood): the parade with Princess Anna in her carriage is very cramped and small-scale—even if we don't think of comparable moments in *Monte Carlo* and *The Love Parade*. And the various palace halls and chambers don't cover the daunting expanses that Lubitsch seems generally to have preferred in these films. But otherwise, the movie's locales are a triumph,* more articulated and interestingly detailed than ever (there are obvious painted backdrops in *Monte Carlo*, even in interiors), from the rococo and gingerbread of the palaces to the elaborate tracery of trees

---

* Hans Dreier is the credited art director—as he was on most Paramount films of the period, including all of Lubitsch's.

Maurice Chevalier sings about his bugle in The Smiling Lieutenant.

and street lamps in the beer gardens and street corners of the lieutenant's be-loved Vienna.

King Adolf of Flausenthurm (George Barbier) has a spinsterish daughter, Princess Anna (Miriam Hopkins), who takes both alarm and offense on a visit to Vienna when Niki, an Austrian lieutenant (Maurice Chevalier), smiles and winks at her as she is passing before him in official review. The fact, as we see, is that he is winking at his girlfriend, Franzi (Claudette Colbert), who is standing across the street from him making love signals just when the princess's carriage happens to pass between them. When he is called to account by the enraged King Adolf, Lieutenant Niki tries to save his neck by making an urgent personal appeal to Princess Anna. He is so successful that she insists—to his horror—upon having him for her husband. And soon, with the ensuing approval of Emperor Franz Joseph himself, Anna's infatuation has the power of the Austrian empire behind it. Niki has no choice. Neither does Franzi: she walks out of his life, passing under a street lamp and disappearing into the darkness to mournful theme music and a lingering fadeout.

But come the royal wedding night, Niki exercises in private what he has been denied in public: his chance to say no. Anna, who understands these things dimly at best (she even sucks her thumb at moments of stress), is left on her bridal night with nothing to do but play checkers with her father. And when, after a while, Franzi turns up in Flausenthurm—she is touring with her all-girl orchestra—she and Niki resume their affair clandestinely. But one night Franzi goes to the palace for their usual rendezvous and instead finds Anna waiting for her. When Franzi sees how unhappy the young princess is, she takes pity on her. She gives Anna some much-needed lessons in pleasing a man—and walks out of Niki's life for the second, and presumably final, time. The lessons do their job: Niki is so enchanted with his sexy new wife that he resolves to settle down with her.

It's all much like *The Love Parade,* of course—with elements of *Monte Carlo* thrown in. What's missing is the MacDonald heroine, and other things, too, that seem (for Lubitsch) to be related to her: those daringly extended privileged moments, like the opera box sequence in *Monte Carlo* or her back-and-forth pursuit of Chevalier through the marble halls of *The Love Parade. The Smiling Lieutenant* is a work of nearly total assurance. But that assurance seems cold, cautious, even lifeless. Having attained it, Lubitsch takes no chances with it, or so it seems: there are almost none of the risks or hesitations, none of the dislocations or daring suspensions-of-meaning before a joke, that mark the two earlier films. And that tone of dry astonishment that MacDonald in particular commands—that propensity to motions of surprise and wonder that transfigures the obsessive "naughtiness" of the other films—is mostly missing from this one.

We are left with the "naughtiness"—and a certain sourness, too, which surfaces in spite of the film's declared intentions. In a sense the MacDonald heroine *isn't* missing: she is divided between these two heroines. The prim, virginal side goes to Hopkins's Princess Anna; the dashing, ardent, yielding side to Colbert's Franzi. But clearly Lubitsch isn't easy with this split, or with the simplifications it entails. These latter, in fact, trigger something worse than unease. The jokes about Anna's sexual retardation—including the thumb-sucking—are crueler and cruder than they should be. And there is a tendency to punish the sexy heroine, too. The self-judgment of Franzi's "girls who start with breakfast" speech (the point being that they don't get invited to the *other* meals) is an example. So is the odd, cold way the film lingers over her suffering—with full violin threnody in the background—when she is shunted aside for the princess.

And Chevalier is alarming. Always animated, here he seems demented—particularly in his opening song (the score is by Oscar Straus and Clifford Grey), where he boasts about being a member of "the Boudoir Brigadiers." Chevalier sings this song right into the camera and makes a great play throughout of putting his thumb to his mouth and blowing a make-believe bugle:

We're famous near and far
For our *rat*-tuh-tuh-*tat*-tuh-tuh-*tah!*

What's unsettling is that each time he comes to this refrain—chortling and grimacing and rolling his eyes—he seems determined to outdo the last time. It's unnerving because, for all the leering, there is no suggestion of real carnality. Indeed, there hardly ever is in a Chevalier performance. (In some ways, ironically, he is the Nelson Eddy of the dirty joke.) And the more excited he gets, the less he suggests passion or erotic life of any kind—the more he suggests impotence and the effort to "get it up," joking and grimacing to the bitter, hopeless, soul-shattering end. Chevalier singing about his "bugle" could serve as an emblem for everything D. H. Lawrence meant by the modern audience's propensity for "sex in the head"—by our affliction with "the dirty little secret."

That affliction seems to trouble the whole film—at times like a madness. Lubitsch's method here is as unrelenting as his star's. Every reference to a musical instrument, for example (and there are many), carries the same charge of ribald meaning. Franzi, we are told, plays the violin. "You should see her fingers!" says one admirer. "She has the daintiest little fingers!" She plays it in public, too, Princess Anna informs her father, the king. He is not surprised. Do all women like that play the violin? the princess inquires. No, but they *play,* replies her father. "So you play the piano?" says Franzi to Niki, flirting with him. "Someday we may have"—she is *very* roguish here—"a duet." "I love chamber music," replies the eager Niki. And on and on and on. You begin to feel that the *real* Lubitsch touch is an elbow in the ribs—tirelessly, even maniacally reapplied.

But even when he's uninspired, Lubitsch can be funny. Just when we are beginning to give up on him, he does something comic and sanative. Niki and Franzi actually *do* play a piano and violin duet. And they do so in a perfect deadpan manner, as if to say: what did you *think* we were talking about? And the ribald music metaphor does in fact begin to take on some life near the end of the film, when the two women in Niki's life finally meet. This sequence is nearly the best in the movie: full of energy and wit and self-delighted outrageousness. It is also—and probably significantly—the scene in which the two "sides" of the Lubitsch heroine, sexy and proper, at last come together in this film.

Franzi, against her own best interests, decides to help the Princess Anna win her husband back. She asks first if Anna can play the piano. The answer is yes. But what can she play *on* it? "Etude for Five Fingers," "Cloister Bells," and "A Maiden's Prayer" turn out to be the unhappy Anna's specialties. Franzi is undiscouraged. "Let me see your underwear," she says. Anna lifts her skirts to reveal a pair of thigh-length panties secured at each knee with a ribbon. "Cloister Bells," remarks Franzi dryly. And she flashes her step-ins at us. This turns out to be a song cue. Franzi sits at the piano and sings:

Jazz up your lingerie!
Just like a melody
Be happy!
Choose snappy
Music to wear!

Viewers who associate Lubitsch with some idea of "good taste" have probably forgotten this moment, and the many, many others like it in his films. This song number works, if at all, precisely because of its bad taste, because of its sheer happy vulgarity. Especially when the two women start to jam it together at the piano, which is played throughout the sequence in a rollicking, ricky-tick style. "Get hot!" sings Colbert. "I'll try," answers Hopkins—and makes a sustained but off-key sound. "Not so hot," chants Colbert and thumps the piano keys. "It sounds like eighteen-fifty." Hopkins tries it again, better this time. "You've got it now, that's nifty!" cries Colbert, with a real high-rolling abandon at the piano and a slight squeak in her singing voice when she hits "nifty"—which is just the right word too for the break-loose jauntiness of the whole sequence.

A bit late, but the rest of the movie seems oddly freed by this new and lively tone, as if the romping, self-declaring vulgarity had set something off. At any rate, there follows a sequence with the dreamlike, hallucinatory edge that the best Lubitsch jokes often have: a series of swift tableaux designed to illustrate the effect of Anna's lessons on her husband. It's a passage both deranged and comic, far from the cautious leering tone of the movie's earlier parts. Hopkins is seen playing her own piano now, alone and unassisted, in a raffish barroom strut-and-slide style. Niki, on his way out as usual but attracted by these strange sounds in the palace, stares at her from the doorway, incredulously. She is smoking a cigarette—it dangles from the side of her mouth. She is dressed in a tatty-looking robe; she looks tough and experienced and a little bored. Niki stares. Now she is seated and is reading a book—in the same robe. A canary in a nearby cage starts to sing, piercingly. Anna rises, removes her robe, and throws it over the cage—silencing the canary and revealing herself in her new step-ins: she strikes a pose by the now shrouded cage, a waggish look over her shoulder as she does so. Niki is astonished—about time, too. The movie is nearly over.

AFTER *The Man I Killed* (see chapter 2) Lubitsch turned once again to the operetta film, once again to the teaming of Chevalier and MacDonald. Although he had originally meant only to produce *One Hour with You* (1932)—after he and Raphaelson had written the screenplay, George Cukor was assigned to direct—a close watch on the daily rushes left him dissatisfied with Cukor's work, and he took over the direction himself.

So there can be no question about it: it was Lubitsch himself who did this trashing, or at least trivializing, of his own most prestigious early work. *One Hour with You* is a remake of his first important American film, *The Marriage Circle* (1924), and is in every most obvious way a diminishment of it: the silent classic—sardonic, original, often grimly ironic—has been turned into this standard (by this time, *very* standard) Lubitsch musical.

One Hour with You at once follows *The Marriage Circle* closely and entirely transforms it. The plot, common to both films, revolves around two married couples, one happy, the other distinctly not so. The happy wife insists that her husband—in both versions he is a doctor, and wealthy—pay some personal attention to her best girlfriend, who is very *un*happily married. What the wife doesn't know is that the friend has already resolved to seduce the husband. And what all three of them don't know are the hopes of the friend's own husband—in both versions, a professor. With the help of a private detective, the professor has set a trap to catch his wife in an infidelity so that he can at last divorce her. And to round out this pattern, the doctor's wife is also being pursued by a would-be seducer. But he is an ineffectual Other Man type, a mostly comic figure, and therefore never really a serious possibility for the heroine, as Mitzi (Mizzie in the silent version), the sexy best friend, is for the hero.

The two versions of the Mitzi figure mark the differences between the two movies. In the silent film, Marie Prevost's mischief has a malevolent, even a pathological edge, whereas Genevieve Tobin, in the musicalized version, seems merely silly and reckless. And Adolphe Menjou, the professor of *The Marriage Circle*, has an acrid disdain and a weight of bitterness, both a weariness with his wife and an anger at her, that Roland Young in the sound film doesn't even hint at—in spite of the little chuckle he keeps giving ("I have no sense of humor at all," he insists ominously to the discomfited Chevalier) and the thin smile that accompanies it. The pain and hatred and discord that Menjou and Prevost convey so powerfully in the silent film are emotions entirely missing from *One Hour with You*—just as they are missing for the most part from Lubitsch's subsequent work.

For in trivializing (and, presumably, commercializing) the materials of the earlier film, Lubitsch is also, paradoxically, moving in the direction he was most

serious about. Not only does *One Hour with You* restore those elements of style and angles of view that *The Smiling Lieutenant* had scanted—the hesitations, the vacated frames, the daring long takes, the incongruous two-shots, the images of solipsist discord—but these defining Lubitschean traits are once again at the center of the movie experience, where they belong. *One Hour with You* not only consolidates past gains but makes new ones as well. The collaboration with Samson Raphaelson, with his special gifts for comic characterization, is clearly paying off here, in exciting ways. *One Hour with You* is the most richly *peopled* of all Lubitsch's early operetta films. And in this respect especially, it foreshadows the triumphs of *Trouble in Paradise* and *The Merry Widow* (which are also Raphaelson screenplays). It begins to define a Lubitsch specialty: his odd, funny mimicry of the inner life, intensely lived. The minor characters here— even the *very* minor characters—have a disconcertingly independent life.

There is a girl who licks envelopes in a government office (the film takes place in modern Paris). She appears fleetingly in one of those montages that detail the passage of a crucial document through various hands. This particular document is the legal announcement that names Doctor Berthier (Chevalier) as corespon-

dent in the professor's divorce suit against his wife, Mitzi. What we see when this particular girl licks this envelope, its contents so devastating to the film's hero, is that she rolls her eyes lasciviously—confirming our worst fears about all those unseen "girls" in all our lives.

The professor hires a detective (Richard Carle) to shadow the duplicitous Mitzi. We see this figure early in the movie, when he visits the professor, presumably one of their initial interviews. He is not what we expect from a movie detective, let alone a Parisian one: he looks more like a New England storekeeper or a rural county judge. What he looks most of all, however, is impassive: a shrewd, turkey-faced, white-haired, elderly man, keeping his own dignified counsel. He does so sitting next to Young, the professor, on a couch, in a two-shot. The off-screen object they are looking at (and musing over) is, it develops, a hanging portrait of Mitzi. Mitzi herself is on the premises in another room. She is, as usual, going out. She talks to her husband through the door. "Oh, sweetheart," she calls. "She's lying," says Young to the detective. "Lie back," the other advises. More melodious endearments through the door. The wife takes her leave. "I don't want to disturb you," she calls through the door. Young looks at the detective. The detective makes a face. More goodbyes are exchanged, and there is the sound of a door slamming. The two men, still in their two-shot on the couch, look blankly forward. The detective is gazing at a cigar in his hand—a gift from the professor. It is unlit, and he turns it slowly between his fingers. "In Switzerland," says the professor at length, slowly and thoughtfully, "we have a very peculiar law." The detective continues to look at the cigar. "If a husband shoots his wife," the professor continues, "they put him in jail . . ." Pause. The detective raises the cigar to his nose and smells it. End of scene.

No one else in Hollywood would have put *that* detective in such a scene, or given him the kind of emphasis that Lubitsch does. What's clear is that Lubitsch likes to surround his main characters—to "crowd" them in subtle ways—with minor figures of ominous reserve and opaqueness. Mitzi, for example, has a lady's maid (Barbara Leonard), a pretty blonde. This character has no name and practically no lines, but she is on the screen with Mitzi during all the latter's scenes at home. (Genevieve Tobin and Roland Young, on the other hand, are seen in the same shot only once—and even that occasion they share with a very nervous Chevalier, placed significantly between them.) Mitzi is a small, delicate, birdlike woman. Her maid is tall, big-framed, blank-looking. When she is seeing her mistress to the door, walking behind her deferentially, she is as faceless and withdrawing as a servant (slightly taller) could be. And, of course, we are intensely aware of her as a result. And whenever she is called upon (not often) actually to speak or to respond in some way, she and her mistress turn out to be at hopeless cross-purposes. Mitzi gives her the night off—to get rid of her—and she declines. Mitzi feigns an illness so that Doctor Chevalier might be called—and the maid rushes to her side instead of to the phone. It's Mitzi who loses her composure at these moments, berating and shouting at the uncomprehending girl. But when, near the end of the film, the professor finally watches his detested wife leaving for good—in a long parade of opulent baggage to a waiting car out front—he shares the window with the maid. They are side by side, leaning on their elbows, watching Mitzi go, and they are smiling—together—the same thin smile.

It's in a supporting character like Adolphe (Charles Ruggles) that we can most easily see what Lubitsch owed to the Raphaelson collaboration. Adolphe is the standard absurd Other Man figure—hopelessly pursuing MacDonald as the heroine, Colette—but with wonderful, surprising details within the familiar outlines. Adolphe is a dyspeptic-looking man, who dresses up as Romeo and then calls Colette on the phone: "What? *What?* . . . Not a costume party?" he gasps—and Lubitsch promptly shows him in a full-length shot, holding the telephone and looking distressed in tights and ruffles. Adolphe is always trying to make urgent love to Colette. Clearly he *thinks* of himself as out of control; but an odd prudential streak is always intruding itself, even at moments of extremest passion. "Let's run away!" he says desperately—then adds, fervently, "You're still a young woman." Though, of course, she *could* be younger, he keeps seeming to feel—and that notion keeps cropping up gracelessly: he seems helpless to resist it. Colette at one point tries to send him away by pleading her own sadness of heart, and he tells her that sorrow only makes her "more beautiful . . . more feminine . . ." He hesitates here, but he really can't stop himself: ". . . Younger," he concludes unhappily.

Colette, though, unlike us, never really hears any of this. She is always preoccupied when she is with Adolphe. And their relationship occasions some of Lubitsch's best solipsist joking. Colette and Adolphe are on the terrace overlooking the garden. She is out there looking worriedly for her husband André (she has good reason to be worried: he is in the garden with Mitzi). And Adolphe is by her side, making his usual ardent love to her—praising the moonlight in this case. "I tell you," he says, "if I didn't have such a splendid education I'd yield to the animal in me" and he makes a little face (he always does after an emotional outburst). At this last remark MacDonald turns, touches her throat, and gives him her best look of burning-eyed incomprehension—as if he had just made some hard-to-identify but possibly crucial sound. Presently she turns, lifts her skirt, and steps onto the gravel path below. The camera tracks slowly before them as they walk: MacDonald looking agitatedly about her, and Ruggles continuing in the same vein of thoughtful absurdity: "Colette, how does the moon affect you?" No answer. "It turns me inside out and upside down. . . . Yes, yes, I admit I come from a very refined family. But should a refined gentleman not have any luck? . . . Does one have to be a roughneck to get along in this world?" At this (the timing is very precise) they both stop, both looking in the same rightward direction—the first sign of union in the scene, and quite accidental. Pause—whereupon Colette utters her first words. "I wonder where André is," she says—and walks off, leaving Ruggles startled and alone on the screen.

The Lubitsch epiphany: alone on the screen, ditched and discomfited. In other movies, actors command the screen when they're alone on it; in Lubitsch, they are stranded there.

A STRANGE footnote to this period in the Lubitsch career is the fact that the Chevalier-MacDonald movie which probably most people think of as the pinnacle of the Lubitsch style, is not by Lubitsch but by Rouben Mamoulian, that most eclectic of gifted thirties directors: *Love Me Tonight* (1932). "The Lubitsch film that Lubitsch was always trying to pull off but never quite did," says critic Tom Milne. This time MacDonald is the Princess Jeanette, pining away in a countryside castle in France. Chevalier is Maurice, a tailor from Paris, who is trying to collect some overdue bills from the princess's spendthrift cousin, the vicomte (Charles Ruggles again). So that he can visit the castle without exposing the vicomte's impecuniousness, Maurice pretends to be a baron. Princess Jeanette suffers from fainting spells, and everyone in the castle is concerned about her, especially when she is brought to ground just after meeting Maurice in the woods. The doctor is called. He asks the princess to undress, and she does so. He learns during his examination that she is a widow. She had, she claims, been quite happy with her late husband. "It was the happiness of great peace," she says, looking sentimentally into the distance as she recalls it. The deceased husband, it emerges, was seventy-two on their wedding day. Once again, it's clear that MacDonald must be married—and quickly. "You're not wasted away, you're just wasted," cries the alarmed physician. But there are no eligible suitors among the old nobility, only the "Baron Maurice." A match with *him* seems ideal to everyone, and eventually even to the princess—until the "baron" blows his cover. Seeing the princess in her ill-fitting new riding habit, he gets carried away by a professional passion to remake it, is discovered in the act, and is exposed

Chevalier is exposed as a tailor when he takes MacDonald's measurements in Rouben Mamoulian's Love Me Tonight.

as both a commoner and a tailor. He leaves the castle in disgrace. Jeanette, at first shocked and angry, then bereft and lovelorn, mounts her horse and rides after his train. She brings it to a halt by standing astride the tracks: a Valkyrie with a riding crop. "I love him," she cries in explanation. "That's not a railroad problem," replies the engineer. But Maurice gets off the train, and they embrace in a cloud of steam.

Love Me Tonight really does deserve its reputation. The screenplay (by Samuel Hoffenstein, Waldemar Young, and George Marion, Jr.) sustains its wit and fantasy better than any of the Lubitsch-directed films do. And the Rodgers and Hart score is one of the glories of thirties musicals. Even the supporting cast— Ruggles, Charles Butterworth, C. Aubrey Smith, and, best of all, Myrna Loy, playing a sexually insatiable countess—comes close to outdoing Lubitsch. But similar to Lubitsch as the Mamoulian film seems (Mamoulian even reproduces some of Lubitsch's effects of delayed cutting and off-screen surprise), the comparison is still misleading. The spirit behind *Love Me Tonight* is very different from Lubitsch's. It is *not* the film "that Lubitsch was always trying to pull off." *That* film is *The Merry Widow,* still two years away. *Love Me Tonight,* in the meantime, doesn't even come close.

The Lubitsch films preceding it, even *The Love Parade,* are chamber films, essentially small-scale and intimate. *Love Me Tonight* is a kind of bravura effusion. That bravura element runs through all of Mamoulian's films, different as they may be in other respects: from *Applause* (1929) to *High, Wide and Handsome* (1937), from *Blood and Sand* (1941) to *Summer Holiday* (1948). Mamoulian is a spectacularist; Lubitsch, the erstwhile "Griffith of Europe," is not. The "symphony" of Parisian street sounds that opens *Love Me Tonight* is a fair sample of the Mamoulian "touch." (He had used the same device in his Broadway production of DuBose Heyward's *Porgy* in 1927, and then repeated it in his 1935 production of Gershwin's *Porgy and Bess.*) An even more dazzling instance is the way, near the film's end, he expands and orchestrates the castle's shock at finding out who the Baron Maurice really "is"—through a witty Lorenz Hart song lyric ("The Son of a Gun Is Nothing But a Tailor") and a montage in which each echelon of the serving staff absorbs the appalling revelation, from the valet ("To think I pressed his coat and vest / When he's the one who could press the best") to the chambermaid ("I used to flirt until it hurt / While he stood there in his undershirt") and on downwards.

This number—surely one of the great extended "reaction shots" of film history—has a largeness and sweep that characterize the whole film. And that use of a montage to open out a song and situation is a favorite Mamoulian device. When Maurice first comes to the castle, Mamoulian shows each of the principals waking the next day and singing an appropriate verse of "Mimi" (C. Aubrey Smith leads the sequence off), as a way to show Chevalier's enlivening effect on the place. Best of all, perhaps, is the early introduction of "Isn't It Romantic?": Chevalier sings it in the morning in his tailor shop, and it travels through various unlikely groups—Parisian cabbies, soldiers on maneuver, gypsies by a camp-fire—until it reaches the Princess Jeanette languishing in the moonlight on her castle balcony. Mamoulian's impulse toward this "integrated musical" style (as he calls it in interviews)—his impulse to expand his effects and then pull them together in showy and virtuosic ways—has almost no echo in Lubitsch's method and temperament. The distance between the two directors' styles is suggested by the different forms they give to the MacDonald heroine's "problem" in *Love Me Tonight* and in *Monte Carlo:* the distance, respectively, between the images of a fainting spell (a cry and a graceful arc to the floor) and a tension headache (a line in the forehead and a general irritability).

While *Love Me Tonight* is too much in the Lubitsch mode to be described as warmhearted, it does verge on a kind of fairy-tale sweetness, to a greater degree than Lubitsch with similar material was ever in danger of. It was just this aspect of the original story idea—"a kind of fairy-tale romantic magic"—that Mamoulian has said he was attracted by, when Adolph Zukor asked him to do the film as a way of keeping the two salaried stars working profitably (Lubitsch was occupied with *Trouble in Paradise* at the time). *Love Me Tonight* is a marvelously funny film, and nearly as enchanting as it is meant to be. And for all its dryness, it never risks being disagreeable or discordant—as Lubitsch, in spite of his resolve to be lighter than air, so often does. And yet it is partly this same risk that makes Lubitsch seem difficult and even mysterious and finally more considerable, where Mamoulian's film seems, by comparison at least, rather easily triumphant. Both at his best and at his worst, Lubitsch is closer to danger.

Lubitsch: A "Serious" Film | 2

The Man I Killed (1932) gives some idea of that danger. It's Lubitsch's only "serious" film of the sound period, and in relation to his work in general it is one of the most revelatory films he ever made. It was a commercial disaster, and thus became a turning point in his career. He never again risked the kind of ambition it showed: the moral centrality, the direct appeal to the conscience of his audience, the recognizable "importance" in both subject and style. When it opened, Robert E. Sherwood, speaking for middlebrow seriousness, called it "the best talking picture that has yet been seen and heard." While Dwight MacDonald predictably—writing for an arts journal called The Symposium—took an opposite line, dismissing it as "a Teutonic tearjerker." Samson Raphaelson recalled in 1978 that he worked on the screenplay with some feelings of aversion ("The whole thing gave me the creeps, in fact"), which apparently were not shared by Lubitsch. The Man I Killed is a monstrous, miscalculated, fascinating film. In fact it gives everyone the creeps—at least everyone who feels its power to any degree. And its relation to the comedies is deep and illuminating.

No doubt Lubitsch expected not only to extend his range with this film but to enhance his reputation. It's the first interruption in the cycle of operetta films (and the film he did right after it was another operetta, One Hour with You). At the time, probably no mode of seriousness was more generally available to audiences and artists of "good will" than the antiwar drama. The source play, by Maurice Rostand (son of Edmond, author of Cyrano), is in a debased Ibsenite tradition: the well-made play of social protest, with lots of carefully crafted reversals and ironies and an air of urgent self-consequence throughout. These qualities remain in the film: they even have something to do with its power.

Lubitsch begins with a montage: Armistice Day, 1919. Celebration: a parade framed between an amputee's stump and his crutch. Bells, and a long, slow tracking shot past beds full of wounded. A priest in his pulpit offers thanks for peace, and the camera tracks past rows of glittering sabers as the officers kneel

Phillips Holmes in Lubitsch's The Man I Killed.

in prayer. After the service a young man (Phillips Holmes) goes to confession and tells the appalled old priest (Frank Sheridan) that he has killed a man. In the war. We see the event in a flashback: the Frenchman Paul bayonets a young German who has leaped into his trench—then finds and reads an unfinished letter the German had written to his girl. The priest is relieved: Is that all? he says. "You are free from crime. You have done nothing but your duty." But this assurance only makes Paul more distraught and desperate: he no longer believes in duty. The priest has an inspiration. Perhaps Paul can find some help for his anguish by going to the dead man's home and family, by finding some way to make a personal reparation to them. Paul sees hope in this. "God is with you," says the priest.

And so Paul arrives in Walter Holderlin's home town, a small German village, where, being a Frenchman, he is met with suspicion and hostility. Not, however, from the family he has come to visit: Doctor Holderlin and his wife (Lionel Barrymore and Louise Carter) are happy with anyone who brings news of their dead only son, and Paul pretends to have known Walter in prewar Paris. But as time goes on, he is unable to tell the Holderlins or Walter's fiancée, Elsa (Nancy Carroll), who he really is. But Elsa and he fall in love, and she discovers the truth. She prevents him, however, from telling it to the Holderlins: he has begun to replace Walter in their hearts, and for their sake, she tells him, he must go on replacing him. The "family" gathers in the parlor. Doctor Holderlin produces Walter's violin, their dearest relic of him, and hands it to Paul—who draws back in horror. "Don't be afraid to make us happy," says the elder Holderlin. Paul takes it—and plays it. While Walter's fiancée accompanies him on the piano, and Walter's parents beam at him from the couch. A son has come home to them.

Samson Raphaelson in 1978 remembered the excitement of writing this last scene: he and Lubitsch together "riding high on the sheer corniness of the whole thing." But there was a problem, nonetheless, with the new "son's" final close-up, though the problem didn't emerge until shooting was completed. A viewing of the final film panicked the studio into flying Phillips Holmes back from New York just so they could reshoot that close-up: Paul playing the violin for his new family, no longer afraid to make them happy. What they couldn't do was get that appalled look off his face, even (as it turned out) with retakes. Phillips Holmes is the kind of actor who tends to look furtive under the best of circumstances, and in a scene like this one, the sense of entrapment he conveys almost help-lessly is stronger than the studio (thinking of the box office) or even Lubitsch (thinking of the happy Holderlins) wished it to be. But, finally, it is not really the actor's fault. There is a horrified spirit loose in this film that necessarily defeats such reasonable wishes—and it invades every scene.

The Man I Killed was in fact the first Lubitsch-Raphaelson collaboration. (*The Smiling Lieutenant* was written afterwards but filmed before.) Lubitsch wanted a specialist in "emotional drama" for the occasion, and so he turned to the author of *The Jazz Singer*, a play he admired and had once even hoped to film. But what he got in Raphaelson—it became clear once they started to write comedy together—was a reckless, off-the-wall comedian. Just like himself. "Lubitsch used a part of me that I never valued," Raphaelson said, "things I would have called too outrageous, too fanciful and preposterous. He'd snap them up. 'We can use it, Sam,' he'd say—and off we'd go." But temperamentally, it seems, and as a practicing playwright in a more or less realistic mode, Raphael-son was more interested in questions of consistency and plausibility and char-acterization than Lubitsch was. According to Raphaelson, this difference between them never created a problem—*except* on this first collaboration. "The nature of our quarrel, if you can call it that, was the hero [Paul]. I felt the last thing that person should do if he wanted to help was to go anywhere *near* that family. What could he do for them? I thought he was a self-important, self-pitying son-of-a-bitch. I wanted to change the situation, the character, all of it. But Lubitsch was sure. He'd say, 'No, Sam, *wait*—you'll see it on the screen, it'll be up there.' That was the only time he ever said that to me. On every film after that one, we had a tacit understanding that when one of us objected to something, we'd work on it until we *both* liked it—partly, I think, because he realized he had been wrong about *The Man I Killed*. The picture came out, and you *didn't* see it up there."

Raphaelson is probably right about Paul. What is surprising, though, is how little those well-founded objections matter to the final film. *The Man I Killed* is full of faults, many of them crippling: it never really transcends its air of fustian theatricality (the "Teutonic tearjerker" problem). But Lubitsch was also right in his instinct about it: he *has* gotten "it" up there on the screen. The film is charged with an apprehension that seems almost too much at times for the actors or for individual scenes to support.

It is, after all, a film about a monstrous fact: about the corruption of sons by their war-loving fathers, about the hatred of the old for the young. Yet in spite of its subject and its appalled tone, no one could mistake it for anything but a Lubitsch film: in its movement and editing, above all in its strange hesitations. As they do in the operetta films, reaction shots conventionally come before the shots that explain them. And the space within the frame is charged with the usual uneasiness about the space off-screen and beyond. Characters look off in surprise, walk off in haste. All the devices that Lubitsch had perfected to enforce in his viewer a kind of humorous discomfiture, a buoyant off-balance prickling attentiveness and readiness to be surprised, are here used to a generally ominous effect. There are doors, of course. When the obnoxious self-satisfied Herr Schultz* (Lucien Littlefield) points out to the grieving Dr. Holderlin that he himself and the dead Walter have the same first name, he is treated upon uttering this remark to a whole series of opening and closing doors—left by one person, joined by another—the Elsa he hopes to pay court to—only to be shown to the last door of all, to the street, and asked by her never to come again. But the Lubitsch door that figures most prominently here—the door that is most likely to cause people to hesitate, to look apprehensively off, to enter reluctantly—is the door to Walter's shrine, his locked and darkened room, where the violin is kept.

The film itself was a little like Walter's door in the effect it had on audiences: mostly they avoided it. Not even a change of title (to *Broken Lullaby*, just a few days after its New York opening) or a complete revamping of the publicity could make any difference. And yet in spite of the funereal tone, a good part of it is comic in the most bracing Lubitsch manner. A minor figure named Herr Bresslauer (George Bickel), proprietor of the local dress shop, sees Elsa looking at a dress in his window and steps out onto the street to talk to her.

---

*"Everything to do with Herr Schultz was supplied by Lubitsch," Raphaelson told me in 1978. "He knew this character. And I got to know him too—through Lubitsch. So that by *The Shop Around the Corner* I could write him too, in the character of Vadas."

Phillips Holmes, Nancy Carroll, and Lionel Barrymore— with Walter's violin—in The Man I Killed.

BRESSLAUER: You like dat dress?

ELSA: Yes, Herr Bresslauer, I like it very much.

BRESSLAUER: Well, you're wrong. Dat dress is for a brunette. *Here . . .* is a dress for you. (*She looks in the window.*) Listen, I'll tell you a secret. Remember, you must not repeat this to a soul. . . . It's a *French* model. (*She looks at him. He nods gravely.*)

ELSA: It's really very pretty.

BRESSLAUER: *Made* for you. . . . I haven't sold you a dress in a very long while, Fräulein Elsa. It's about time you got one. (*very confidential*) Let me tell you . . . a young girl should keep up mit d' styles. (*He leans back.*) It's bad to be left behind. . . . Dis dress is good for four years— because it's already two years ahead of d' style. . . . Come in and slip it on.

Herr Bresslauer's gently bullying intimacy—a mixture of con man and nice uncle—is wonderfully caught here. It also tells us a lot about the intimacies of such a town.

But the characteristic Lubitsch perceptions of people's inconsequence, illogic, irrationality have this time a savage, even a sinister force. Sometimes the point is pathetic—as when two mothers in a graveyard exchange recipes for their dead sons' favorite cinnamon cake. More often, it is sardonic—as when Herr Schultz lunches in a rathskeller with a group of elderly townsmen and they conclude that the new Frenchman in town is a spy, no doubt of it. For one thing, he carries a violin case. What does this case contain? asks Herr Schultz, with emphasis. "Maybe a violin," someone inappropriately suggests. "There you are," exclaims Herr Schultz, after fighting down his indignation and disbelief. "Always trusting. Believing anybody." There is general assent to this, and the food arrives. Herr Schultz continues: "A Frenchman comes along with a violin case—locked, mind you—and we take it for granted it contains a violin." Murmurs all round the table. He carves the sauerbraten. Sadly: "We never learn. . . ."

The cosseted, complacent, self-preening malignity of this is exactly right—and harrowingly familiar. An even nastier moment occurs earlier, in the scene that introduces Barrymore's Dr. Holderlin. He is in his office at his desk, interviewing a small boy with his father. The boy has just been fighting, and when he is reproved, he replies stoutly: "Nobody's going to call *me* a Frenchman!" His elders are undone by this explanation, and visibly moved. They collect themselves. "Great boy," says Barrymore, over the head of the child to his father. The proud father smiles. "He'll do," he says fatuously. And for one stunning moment, the foolish and the monstrous come together on the screen—dazzlingly. The observed silliness in this film is something familiar and willful and lethal. And it is not really comic.

PAUL AND Elsa are falling in love (that was the reason she was looking at that dress at Herr Bresslauer's) and they take a slow idling walk through the cobblestoned streets—and under the eyes—of the town, a walk that becomes one of the movie's great set pieces. It begins when the women in the butcher shop are alerted to what's going on by the Holderlins' maid (ZaSu Pitts): she orders five lamb chops for dinner instead of the customary four, and leaves them to draw their own conclusions. "Five lamb chops!" repeats the butcher exultantly, sharpening and flashing his knives. Outside, Paul and Elsa proceed gravely and silently side by side, down the winding cobbled street, watched by tradesmen from their shops and housewives from the windows above. Each time the couple passes a shop door, it opens and a bell rings. We follow them from a distance—watch their progress in a series of long shots intercut with a montage of quietly excited onlookers, of doors opening and windows flung wide, of women calling to their neighbors ("Frau Oglekinder!" "Frau Kugel!")—and close-ups of shop bells of various shapes and sounds shivering and going off as the couple passes by.

The walk through town, in a production shot from The Man I Killed. *(Lubitsch is the one in knickers in the center.)*

In spite of those exploding bells, the whole sequence has a hushed, dreamlike quality, forbidding and chill. The distance between us and the lovers (always seen in long shot) is an ominous one. And the scene is photographed in a cold early-morning sunlight (like the Armistice parade at the film's beginning), in bright whites and gleaming grays. Lubitsch's tact in this sequence is a marvel of balance and exactness: it's clear that the town's interest in Paul and Elsa is threatening but it is *not* malevolent. Empty, fussy, snoopy—even ominous—it's tangibly different in quality from the bigotry of Herr Schultz and the town elders.

After keeping its distance from Paul and Elsa, the camera suddenly joins them, tracking in front of them and framing them in medium shot as they walk slowly along, not saying much but clearly absorbed in each other, and oblivious. Paul, almost for the first time in the film, looks "well." He is gazing at Elsa: "I *like* this little town," he says fervently. And just as he does so, between this remark and Elsa's reply, two bells go off in the background, softly and discreetly—and ominously. The sound of the town. And subtle as this detail is, audiences invariably laugh in recognition. That sound effect exactly gauges— in the most poignant and gentle but absolutely precise and witty way—Paul's fatal isolation, even when he is falling in love. As always for Lubitsch, the two things are allied: being in love and being out of touch. For the first time in the movie, Paul's intensity is *not* misdirected or misconstrued—Elsa shares his feelings—but for Lubitsch it is still, in some important way, the intensity of *non*apprehension: "I *like* this little town."

The film's general performing style is portentous and theatrical. Each of the actors is obliged to show a characteristic, and isolating, intensity of his own (even the forthright, commonsensical Nancy Carroll), so that each appears sealed off, private, even misguided at times. Just as in the Lubitsch comedies, it's the intensity of people at cross-purposes, in complacent but complete missing of one another's points. But what is a joke in the operetta films—almost their basic joke—is here made an occasion for poignance, even anguish. The "joke" of the inappropriate response—sometimes transmuted into pathos, sometimes not—is nearly everywhere in *The Man I Killed*. In the way Elsa listens to Herr Bresslauer disclose that his dress is a "French model": with total and grave attention. In the way the two elder Holderlins listen to Paul's made-up account of having known Walter their son. Paul offers a Pinter-like recital of commonplaces, wrung from his own guilt and growing hysteria: "We went out together . . . two friends . . . we went out together. . . . We had a great time . . . oh a wonderful time. . . ." The Holderlins laugh when they hear this; they all but clap their hands; they are rapturous as children. Neither of them seems to notice the tortured condition of the speaker—or the fact that the words are almost meaningless.

Even when people *should* come together in some kind of mutual feeling and comprehension, they don't—quite—in a Lubitsch film. At the end of this one, the two old people have triumphed (so far as they know): Paul is to stay with them forever, just as they had hoped and dreamed he would. When they are seated together on the couch, holding onto each other, listening in rapture as Paul plays Walter's violin and Elsa plays the piano, Lubitsch directs these two almost uncomfortably histrionic faces, Barrymore's and Carter's, each showing its queasy version of bliss, to look at all times in *different* directions: toward the sound of Elsa's piano at one end of the room or toward Paul and his violin at the other. Whatever sound the one face turns toward, the other turns away from: it is very carefully done. So that even this final image of union, of life's-end happiness, is disturbingly qualified on the screen.

For to Lubitsch intensity *means* isolation—even, it seems, when he is trying to make it mean something else. Ardor can be funny, it can be tragic; it is always disproportionate. This fact helps to explain why Lubitsch, for all his fastidiousness, could apparently promote such a lack of proportion in performers like Barrymore, kvelling over the younger generation, or Chevalier, ogling the camera during one of his naughty songs.

But it also helps to explain something even more striking: the fact that even when Lubitsch is working within a romantic genre, operetta or romantic comedy, he makes films that almost no one would think to call romantic. Why in movies that are so convincingly about sexual attraction, there is no very convincing evocation of love. Cynicism is one explanation—the jaded sensibility of a "witty playboy," in Graham Greene's phrase for Lubitsch. But the movies themselves are too full of ardency, however it is ironized, for this to seem a plausible account of the temperament behind them, or of the intention. Lubitsch focuses on something allied to "love" but quite different from it. And it is that focus that makes his way of seeing things seem so distinctive, so unforgettable—a way of seeing that offers a quite unalienated and unmodish, a very direct, sensory, and particular sense of everyone's odd and disconcerting solitude. This intensely perceived solitude is at the heart of his comic vision. A central tragic fact for other artists is for Lubitsch the richest joke. In the world of his films, to feel strongly and passionately about anything, even in love, is to be alone.

It is no accident, then, that his one wholly serious sound film should be about a man who is isolated by his conscience from the world around him. *The Man I Killed* may be the only big commercial film ever made about conscientious objection—its not so thinly disguised underlying subject. Compare such box-office antiwar films as King Vidor's *The Big Parade* (1925) and Lewis Milestone's *All Quiet on the Western Front* (1930), which are about *victims* of authority, not apostates from it, and offer heroes that mass audiences could presumably identify with more easily.

But who could "identify" with Paul? Even his author Samson Raphaelson couldn't. Still, it seems clear that, in some complex way, Lubitsch could—and did. "No, Sam, *wait*—you'll see it on the screen, it'll be up there." And it *is* up there. Paul is only the most extreme and exaggerated instance of something that is always "up there" in a Lubitsch film. The British critic C. A. LeJeune saw it clearly in the German silents, when Lubitsch was making his name as a director of spectacles, like De Mille a specialist in crowd scenes:

Lubitsch had a way of manipulating his puppets that gave multitude, and in contrast, loneliness, a new force. No one before had so filled and drained his spaces with the wheeling mass, rushing in the figures from every corner to cover the screen, dispersing them again like a whirlwind, with the single figure staunch in the middle of an empty square.

The fact is that Lubitsch couldn't imagine *any* kind of crowd, even a crowd of two, without noting the detail that evokes that "single figure staunch in the middle of an empty square." Neither as an artist nor as a man did he function as a dissident. Like nearly all the working filmmakers in the Hollywood of the time, he played the game. And he made movies *about* playing the game. But more than most—more perhaps even than Preston Sturges did—he had the imagination of a dissident. It is the signs and motions and instincts of dissidence that always come to life in his work. He is instinctively averted and apart, fastidious and ironic, especially in those moments and situations where others experience common or even only mutual emotions. Experiences like love—and war.

His temperament is a main reason that intellectuals have always felt a kinship with him—even when he was falsifying and vulgarizing history, in *Madame DuBarry* or *Anna Boleyn*, as badly as De Mille ever did. In spite of such lapses of taste and judgment, and even the explicit philistinism of many of his comedies, he has usually been forgiven by literate audiences—because he *seemed* so smart. Indeed, he may even have seemed smarter than he was. He was neither an intellectual nor a specially cultured man. But he *was* ironic, and by his deepest instincts.

The Man I Killed is a pacifist but not a political film. Lubitsch is as remote from an ideology of pacifism as he is from the mentality of a booster or a joiner. It is notable that nowhere in the background or implications of the film's action is there a convincing appeal to anything like a brotherhood of man, as there are in other films of this period—no plea for a society of peace nor even apparently a hope for one. And when the Lubitsch hero does act on his conscience, he is more permanently alone than ever. Finally, he can only fulfill his debt to the bereaved Holderlins (as Elsa reminds him) by concealing his identity from them, forever.

What Lubitsch and his hero stand by is a kind of radicalism of common sense. It's a reductive stand, even a simplistic one. But it is the kind of stand that people usually have to take to be effective against very complicated evils and against socially entrenched lunacies. Paul stands by the single, simple fact of the movie's title, that he has killed someone. And in standing by that one clear irreducible fact, he stands, as it seems, against everyone else.

Just as Doctor Holderlin stands against the town when he tells his friends at the tavern off—old men like himself who have lost sons in the late war and who now speak darkly of "the next time" and proudly of their hatred for the French.

. . . Who sent that young man out to kill Germans? Huh? And who sent my boy? And your boy—and your boy? And your two boys? . . . Who gave them bullets and gas and bayonets? *We (tapping his chest)*—the fathers! Here and on the other side. We're too old to fight, but we're not too old to hate. . . . We're responsible. When thousands of other men's sons were killed, we called it victory and celebrated with beer. And when thousands of our sons were killed, they called it victory and celebrated with wine. *Fathers!* . . . drink to the death of *sons*. . . . (*He turns from them and walks away, then stops.*) Aah! my heart isn't with you any longer, old men. My heart's with the young, dead and living . . . everywhere . . . anywhere. . . .

He goes out—applauded by a young amputee who has been seated at another table throughout the scene. Supporting himself on his crutches, the crippled man follows Holderlin into the cloakroom and shakes his hand.

The most effective part of the sequence (beautifully and gravely played by Barrymore throughout) is what happens next, the quietest effect of all. After he has shaken the young veteran's hand: "I stood in front of this hotel," Holderlin confides to him, "when my son went by. He was going to his death. And I cheered. . . ."

For all its faults, its excess and sometimes hysteria, *The Man I Killed* never really loses its hold on the basic clarity and sanity of this scene and speech. Lubitsch isn't really on the side of morbidity or despair—though this odd movie and its odder hero sometimes make him seem to be. Quite the contrary. Being Lubitsch, a successful Hollywood artist, a practical, sensible man as well as a "genius," he is on the side of common sense. But being Lubitsch, he can't also help but notice—like Paul in *The Man I Killed*—that this sets him against the world.

Kay Francis and Herbert Marshall in Lubitsch's Trouble in Paradise.

Lubitsch: 3
Comedies Without Music

Dwight MacDonald, writing in 1933 about *The Man I Killed*, accused Lubitsch of having "a weakness for taking himself seriously." If so, it was a weakness the director would not soon again indulge. *The Man I Killed* was followed by the lighthearted fun of *One Hour with You*, and then by *Trouble in Paradise* (1932), one of his airiest and sublimest comedies. Of the latter film, MacDonald says, in the same article, that it "comes as close to perfection as anything I have ever seen in the movies." He goes on: "Its list of virtues is endless," even allowing for the "drastic limitations" of its genre and for the emptiness of its narrative ("which, by the way, is banal—and quite unimportant"); *Trouble in Paradise* is a film that "almost makes one believe in Hollywood again." And though it got mixed notices when it opened, MacDonald's view of the film is the one that has prevailed. *Trouble in Paradise* is not only widely believed to be Lubitsch's masterpiece—it even made money on its initial release, appearing on at least one list of box-office champions for November 1932.

After *One Hour with You*, Lubitsch's Paramount contract had run out. Columbia and United Artists made attempts to sign him. He seemed to be seized briefly by indecision and restlessness. He went to New York with an idea of directing for the stage but returned rather quickly to Hollywood. In the spring of 1932, he signed with Paramount again, a three-picture contract. It was under this contract that he made his first nonmusical romantic comedies, *Trouble in Paradise* and *Design for Living* (1933).

Trouble in Paradise is a cool and brilliant performance: as far as its director could possibly get, it seems, from the lugubrious tone of his antiwar film, or from its moral radicalism. Lubitsch himself seems always to have regarded it as his most supremely accomplished movie. "As for pure style," he wrote in 1947, in a backward look at his own career, "I think I have done nothing better or as good."

Herbert Marshall and Miriam Hopkins are Gaston and Lily, a pair of thieves

Miriam Hopkins is disguised by glasses; Kay Francis still doesn't like her (Trouble in Paradise).

who meet and fall in love in a Venetian hotel, where Gaston, pretending to b the hotel doctor, has just robbed a wealthy fellow guest. The two professiona thieves and now lovers move to Paris. At the opera, Gaston steals a handba from the immensely rich Mariette Colet (Kay Francis), owner of Colet and Com pany, the great parfumiers. Gaston discovers, however, that there is more profi in returning the handbag for a reward than in keeping it. He pretends to have found the bag at the theatre, and Madame Colet is so impressed by him that she hires him as her personal secretary. Whereupon Lily also joins the Colet house hold staff, and she and Gaston plot to rob their new employer. But Gaston fall in love with Mariette and begins to manage the Colet business empire as well— discovering as he does so that it is being systematically mismanaged by an ever bigger crook than himself, Monsieur Giron (C. Aubrey Smith). As events fal out, Lily discovers Gaston's affair with Mariette; Monsieur Filiba (Edward Ev erett Horton), a suitor of Mariette's, remembers Gaston as the hotel thief who robbed him in Venice; and Monsieur Giron threatens to expose Gaston as a criminal of international reputation. At one stroke Gaston counters them all: he confesses both his thievery and his love to Mariette, who seems ready to shield and forgive him. But being in the end both a practical man and a committed thief, he elects to go off with Lily and the loot.

The fecundity and cleverness and inventiveness with which all this is expounded in the Samson Raphaelson screenplay are astonishing. At almost every point Lubitsch and Raphaelson find some new and surprising way of narrating a scene or telling a joke or even just conveying information. It's as if they had set out to test the expressive limits of indirection—to make those closed Lubitsch doors achieve a kind of maximum eloquence. As a result, more than ever before in a Lubitsch film, our own responses become the subject of the film. It's less that the people on the screen illustrate comic and surprising ways of seeing things than that we ourselves do. Lubitsch makes us more conscious than ever of how we understand, of how we get the point of a joke, of the sort of things we know without having to be told.

Watching a garden party through glass doors which ostensibly screen out all the sound, we see Madame Colet take Gaston aside to remonstrate with him. We don't need to hear her in order to know what she is upset about, because we have just seen her seeing him making a group of young women laugh. Now—a lovely final twist—we see him make *her* laugh, and all is forgiven. And when *we* laugh too, it's partly because we are "seeing" so much without hearing—that we are in fact seeing just the things we don't hear.

And when we are not attending to our own patterns of recognition, we are watching those of the characters. One of the best gags in the movie is the running joke about Monsieur Filiba's efforts to remember just *where* he has seen Gaston before—not connecting him, of course, with the "hotel doctor" in Venice who entered his room and demanded to see his tonsils, then robbed him. When Filiba and Gaston first meet again at one of Mariette's garden parties, neither, it seems, remembers their previous encounter. Gaston, however, remembers *something*: he asks Filiba if they haven't met before. No? He shrugs and walks on. But Filiba is indignant—precisely because he is sure they have *not* met. "That man never met me before and he knows it!" he says angrily to his companion. From then on, Edward Everett Horton–like, he becomes more and more obsessed with Gaston. He fumes and dithers and glares, but no memory surfaces. He is *certain* they haven't met. Until finally, near the film's climax, Filiba is chatting pleasantly with his erstwhile rival in love, the Major (Charles Ruggles)—there is a rapprochement between the two gentlemen now that Mariette, the object of their contention, is preoccupied with Gaston. Filiba speaks of Gaston serenely now: he has passed beyond his obsession and is at peace. They speak of Mariette's unaccountable taste in men. "He's a secretary," says Filiba. "He always was a secretary, he always will be." "Funny . . ." says the Major, wonderingly, "the first time I saw him I thought he was a doctor." Filiba is on his feet and shouting: "Tonsils!" he cries, and goes off to denounce Gaston.

It's so carefully worked out that it amounts almost to a kind of epistemological joking. And it infuses the smallest details of the film. Instead of simply showing us the door and the sign, Lubitsch identifies the ladies' room at the opera by showing a young woman emerge from a door to get a coin from her top-hatted escort and then go in again. There is even one whole sequence where we see nothing but a series of clocks: we are meant to infer an important plot development from the time each one tells and from the offscreen voices. A round, very *moderne* table clock says 5:00, and we hear Lily saying goodbye to Gaston, leaving him with Madame Colet ("But if you behave like a gentleman, I'll break your neck"). At 5:12 by the same clock, we hear Mariette pretend to be looking for Lily and then inviting Gaston to dine out with her, with much knowing laughter between them. 9:05: a phone rings and is *not* answered. 10:50: laughter from the hallway. The voices of Gaston and Madame Colet, exchanging double entendres ("You dance like a dream." "The way you lead! . . ." "The way you follow . . ."). Now a second clock: a rectangular model on a table near plants. 11:00. The camera pans to champagne in a bucket. Dissolve to a church tower, chiming the hour. Dissolve to the moon in the trees. Dissolve to a third clock: the familiar and imposing hallway clock, with its sleek art deco lines, which stands between the bedroom doors of Gaston and Madame Colet. 2:00. The camera pans right to take in Mariette, standing outside her door and gazing up into the eyes of Gaston.

It is very ingenious, and still it comes perilously close to joking by the numbers—to a kind of *abstract* cleverness and comedy. But in fact this movement toward the abstract, toward the impersonal, is everywhere in the movies. The film itself has the lean, sleek "lines" of that hallway clock—aspires to the emotional equivalents of the art deco style it is always showing us in the wonderful Hans Dreier sets. There's hardly a frame of the film that doesn't emphasize the clean gleaming outline of an object, a stairway, a gown. Those clocks in the preceding sequence are not just ways to announce offscreen events. On the contrary, they are just the sort of thing Lubitsch wants to look at in this film: images of the *moderne*, the streamlined. And the offer to connect such images, as Lubitsch does, with images of traditional romance—the moon in the trees and the old clock tower—is a significant one. *Trouble in Paradise* is Lubitsch's first really contemporary sound film (all the others have been set either in the past or in a vague present). And it is full of the excitement of the contemporary. The "paradise" of the title is the here-and-now, where things suddenly really *do* look new (compare the look of this film to *The Man I Killed*, or even to *One Hour with You*). So do the people.

Gaston (Herbert Marshall) meets an even bigger crook than he is—M. Giron (C. Aubrey Smith). Mariette (Kay Francis), their employer, is between them.

MARIETTE COLET is going to the opera, attended by her two constant suitors, the Major and Monsieur Filiba. As usual, the men are fussing and quarreling at each other, and Mariette is trying to keep peace. As she enters her box with Ruggles, behind them Horton, in top hat and topcoat, opens the door, says an eloquent and wounded "goodbye," and withdraws. "Aren't you ashamed?" says Kay Francis, as she and Ruggles seat themselves in the box, faces front. "Two men of your standing, always quarreling."

MAJOR: He started it.

MARIETTE: But you're the more intelligent one.

MAJOR: That's true.

MARIETTE: Then why did you do it?

MAJOR (*impulsively, blurting it out*): Because-I-hate-him-because-I-love-you! . . . (*He blinks furiously, still facing front.*)

MARIETTE (*annoyed, sighs*): You should have more self-control. You were in the army. . . .

MAJOR: Well, he was in the navy.

Note the almost anonymous quality of the foolishness here: those successive appeals of Mariette's to "men of your standing," to intelligence, to the experience of army (or navy) life—all invoked as deterrents to quarreling. The whole thing has a kind of wonderful pompous lunacy, a free-floating preposterousness that brings it closer to the world of surrealist comics like Bob Elliott and Ray Goulding than to the "character" of Madame Colet, who actually says the words.

The glamour of *Trouble in Paradise* is the glamour of worldly style. But, like the joking, it is curiously impersonal, associated less with characters or with character types than with something detached from character, and yet something all the characters share in—both collective and complicated. Gaston runs up the staircase after Mariette—they are both glowing with the excitement of their first meeting, at which Gaston has returned the handbag—and says ardently: "Make that check out to cash." The moment is both funny and oddly romantic— in that ironic, almost perverse way that Lubitsch sometimes finds to *be* romantic: by surprise and with a heavy overlay of the "practical." It is part of Gaston's and Mariette's glamour, as well as part of the joke they embody, that they are able to incorporate this element of deliberation into their ardor, even when they are parting forever. "Do you know what you're missing?" says Gaston, as he hesitates in the doorway. "*Yes*," says Mariette, smiling and rueful. "No," he replies, "*this* is what you're missing." Producing a pearl necklace. "Your gift to her," says Gaston, "with the compliments of Colet and Company." Mariette assents, with a smile and a shrug. She and Gaston deploy a style that knows how to manage these things. Where Lily, less self-possessed, makes a fuss. *They*, on the other hand, make love as it should be made in this paradise.

"What are you going to do with my day tomorrow, Monsieur Laval?" asks Mariette, putting herself at the disposal of her handsome new secretary. But she also knows how to exert her power over him; even, best of all, how to exult in it. "You can't go," says Gaston, trying to detain her as she prepares for an evening out. "I'm crazy about you." She puts on a glove: "I know it," she says. "Then why do you want to go?" "Because," she says—with a smile both dazzling and confiding, her face lifted to his—"I want to make it *tough* for you"—and it is one of the film's most enchanting moments. A similar exchange:

MARIETTE: I've got a confession to make. . . . You like me. In fact, you're crazy about me. Otherwise you wouldn't worry about my reputation. Isn't that so? . . . But I don't like you. I don't like you at all! I wouldn't hesitate one instant to ruin *your* reputation—(*snapping her fingers*) like that!
GASTON: You would?
MARIETTE: Yes, I would!
GASTON (*snapping his fingers*): Like that?
MARIETTE (*snapping her fingers again*): Like that!

GASTON: I know all your tricks.

MARIETTE: And you're going to fall for them.

GASTON: So you think you can get me?

MARIETTE: Any minute I want.

GASTON: You're conceited.

MARIETTE: But attractive.

GASTON: Now let me tell you . . .

MARIETTE: Shut up—kiss me! (*They kiss.*) Wasting all this precious time with arguments . . .

Mariette combines languor with assertion, in the general style of glamour queens of the time. But Lubitsch underlines the assertion. This supreme, effortless, omnipotent authority and self-possession is the dream the movie is about, and it's incarnated everywhere: in Mariette's style and clothes, in the drooping lines and the sag of her posture, in Gaston's professional skill as a thief and in his general imperturbability, in the clocks and vases and mirrors. But Lubitsch, it seems, wants us to have the dream with a full and continuing ironic consciousness that it *is* a dream. The glamour is always slightly undercut (though more gently than usual in a Lubitsch film) by the comic exaggerations of glamour. So that the special quality of the film is both excited and dry. This is also the special quality of its best jokes ("No, *this* is what you're missing"), with their surprisingly emotional, almost melancholy resonances. "Your gift to her, with the compliments of Colet and Company." *Trouble in Paradise* offers a richer vein of feeling than the comedies preceding it do: a somewhat more wistful relation to his own tough worldliness than Lubitsch has so far conveyed.

At bottom, it's an idyll. And, perhaps most surprising of all in a Lubitsch movie, it even suggests a certain vision of community: that community of cleverness that exists not only between the leading characters in the film but between the film and its audience. (It should be remembered how much more intense this effect would be in the large theatres and large audiences movies of this time were calculated for.) If earlier Lubitsch comedies have been characterized by characters who don't know what's coming next, this one seems filled with people who know all too well—and with uncanny composure. That composure is one of the chief jokes: the complacency, the outrageous imperturbability with which Gaston and Lily not only rob other people but each other as well—simultaneously copping feels and property. "I hope you don't mind if I keep your garter." "Darling, tell me all about yourself! Who are you?" The general atmosphere of knowingness touches even servants and functionaries, who never in this film show that disconcerting, impenetrable quality that characterizes the usual Lubitsch menial. And this knowingness, like the glamour, is comically exaggerated. In *Trouble in Paradise* people understand each other to a degree that only reminds us how rarely, in fact and in reality, they ever do. Here is Gaston in Venice, ordering a seducer's supper for Lily on what is to be their first evening together, and talking to the waiter (George Humbert):

GASTON: It must be the most marvelous supper. We may not eat it—but it must be marvelous.
WAITER: Yes, baron.
GASTON: And waiter . . .
WAITER: Yes, baron?
GASTON: You see that moon?
WAITER: Yes, baron.
GASTON: I want to see that moon in the champagne.
WAITER: Yes, baron. (*He writes it down.*) Moon in champagne . . .
GASTON: As for you, waiter—
WAITER: Yes, baron?
GASTON: I don't want to see you at all.
WAITER: Yes, baron. (*He bows and withdraws.*)

Understandably, the idyllic strain of this film isn't something Lubitsch seems inclined to repeat. His next film, *Design for Living*, marks a turning away from it, a try at a tougher, more aggressive and up-to-date tone and style. Lubitsch loves the knowingness and the ultimate cool of the Gaston-Mariette style. But, as it turns out, there's a way in which the best side of him is opposed to it—is more at home with, more energized by, the bright, dazzled what-am-I-doing-here? mode of the operetta films, by the slightly rube-ish enthusiasm of Mac-Donald's heroines and Chevalier's heroes (compare Herbert Marshall's total savoir faire). The Lubitsch "type," if there is one, is not a leading man or woman but a character actor, either in fact (Edward Everett Horton and Charles Ruggles) or in spirit (as Chevalier and MacDonald are). The Lubitsch actor is an excessive personality. And Lubitsch's method with such types is nearly always to moderate them, to play them straight and constrained. The *look* of this constraint on the face of a Horton or a MacDonald is one of the surest signs of the Lubitsch touch. And it is one reason the slightest glimpse of a Lubitsch two-shot can set us smiling. The urbanity of *Trouble in Paradise* depends on different effects: among them, that universal knowingness. And the film's resulting tone—a marvel of poise and wit—still runs counter to Lubitsch's deepest and most persisting comic vision: of an ardent and universal human isolation, obsessed and irredeemable. *Trouble in Paradise* is both "perfection" or close to it ("As for pure style . . . I have done nothing better or as good") and a dead end.

Gary Cooper, Fredric March, and Miriam Hopkins in Design for Living.

Desesign for Living (1933), on the other hand, is a clear attempt to go forward—beyond Ruritania, even beyond the Venice and Paris of the last two films. It has the usual European setting, but for almost the first time in a Lubitsch film the leading characters and the performers who play them are unambiguously American. The heroine, Gilda Farrell (Miriam Hopkins), is an American in Paris (she is, we learn, from Fargo, North Dakota). What she is doing there, however, is working as an artist for an American advertising company, run by Max Plunkett (Edward Everett Horton). She draws pictures of Napoleon endorsing the Kaplan and McGuire Union Suit ("It was my unprotected rear that cost me Waterloo!").

Like the Noel Coward play on which it is based, the movie (screenplay by Ben Hecht) is a comedy about a woman who falls in love with two men at once and finally decides to live with them both. Gilda on the stage was played by Lynn Fontanne. Alfred Lunt and Coward himself were the competing, and finally cooperating, leading men. Indeed the whole exercise, in a distinctly more elegant style than the movie's (no talk of union suits in the play), had been conceived and written by Coward as a vehicle for the acting talents of himself and his friends the Lunts. On the screen, the two men, a painter and a playwright, are played by Gary Cooper and Fredric March. Lubitsch liked to boast that he had adapted Coward (as he had earlier adapted Wilde) without using any of his dialogue, apart from a single five-word phrase ("good for our immortal souls"— a drinking toast).

What Lubitsch *has* appropriated from the play, of course—along with its plot—is Coward's special line in contemporaneity. This Lubitsch movie strikes a note quite different from the rather impersonal glamour of *Trouble in Paradise*, with its fantasy about jewel thieves and sleeping-beauty millionairesses, staple and old-fashioned figures out of boulevard theater. *Design for Living* is, as the New York *Post* put it at the time, "Lubitsch's first film dealing with contemporary morals," a daring, up-to-date movie about daring, up-to-date people—about Noel Coward people, in other words. The sort of people who not only embody fashion but make it.

The difference between this movie and *Trouble in Paradise* can be measured by the two very similar final scenes. In both movies the reunited lovers are lined up in the back seat of a taxi, faces forward, in medium shot—except that in *Design* there are three people in the taxi. Gilda—after a fruitless attempt to be "a nice girl," a businessman's wife instead of "a mother of the arts"—is running off with her two rollicking lovers, bohemian adventurers who have come to rescue her and themselves from the death-in-life of the middle classes. The one she has run out on is Max the businessman—Horton—a standard version of the comic Other Man whom such heroines always marry or get engaged to for a time.

But Gaston in *Trouble in Paradise*, in the back of his taxi with Lily, has run out on Kay Francis. It's clear that he is returning to a challenging and rather dangerous career: he and Lily are both committed thieves, and they even show off their skills for us in this last scene by picking each other's pockets before the final clinch and fadeout. Still, in every respect but their thievery, Gaston and Lily are (one of the movie's basic jokes) a quintessential bourgeois couple, conscientious professional types with expensive tastes—yuppies before their time. Gaston and Mariette, on the other hand, are the really romantic pair, the adventurous and risk-taking lovers. In returning to Lily and lawlessness, Gaston is doing the sensible thing—returning to his "station," as it were, opting for the mundane life he knows. And he does so with full regret, apparent in his lingering final exchange with Mariette, full of rue and stylish ardor on both sides. Here, as elsewhere, Lubitsch and Raphaelson have chosen just those possibilities that ironize or undercut the elements of romance and adventure. But in *Design for Living*, on the other hand, the situation at the end is quite different: there is no way for Lubitsch to ironize the adventurousness of Gilda's final choice—of "marriage" to two men. Both the Coward play and the Lubitsch movie belong to that category of romantic fantasy in which adventure is precisely the point. And for Lubitsch, that creates a problem.

In the play, not only the adventure but the magnitude of it are insisted upon. Particularly in the final act, when Gilda and her two lovers rise to defy Ernest, her husband (the original of Horton's Max), by breaking into communal and uniting laughter, by asserting their own "wonderful" madness against the straight world and all the respectabilities and decencies that Ernest stands for. Unlike his movie counterpart, Ernest is no clown but an articulate and often persuasive spokesman for the values he represents. Coward even gives him some wit. But not enough. When Ernest tells Gilda she can't be "serious" in what she proposes, she replies that he's right, she's not: "That's what's so dreadful, I feel I ought to be but I'm not." But then: "Why shouldn't I be mad?" she cries, "I've been sane and still for two years!" And Leo, the playwright (Tom in the movie), sums up their common stand: "We have our own decencies. We have our own ethics. Our lives are a different style from yours. Wave us goodbye, little Ernest, we're together again."

This sort of moralizing, it goes without saying, is not something that Lubitsch could ever have found congenial. Or even possible. And there is no counterpart in the movie to the play's moments of high confrontation, to its over-the-top speeches and scenes. Lubitsch's Gilda has a big self-dramatizing moment and falls on a couch to underscore it: dust rises around her in a telltale little cloud. Her biggest moment of all in the film is a silent progress down a staircase, Horton running fussily ahead of her, into a room full of eager elderly couples, all waiting to play Twenty Questions: Hopkins takes her place and pauses, as Lubitsch's camera tracks solemnly towards her—"Is it animal, vegetable, or mineral?" she says, with a kind of wasted grandeur. End of scene.

These moments of towering absurdity in the film (there are several of them, mostly wonderful) are a long way from the spirit of Coward's play. There, the absurdity is nearly always within the control of the characters themselves, a function of their wit and mischief, a weapon against the Ernests of the world; it isn't the lurking, threatening, undoing thing that it is in the best of Lubitsch, where *everyone* is implicated in it.

From the start, Lubitsch felt uneasy in the world of Noel Coward. He hesitated over this project more than was usual for him, even discussing his reservations in pre-production interviews. And he finally committed himself to doing it only when he became convinced the whole thing could be redone completely. (If Coward could write his play for three particular actors, he reasoned to an interviewer, why couldn't it be rewritten for three others?) It was at this point, significantly enough (Raphaelson was busy*), that he turned to Ben Hecht,

*Before his death in 1983, Samson Raphaelson read the early parts of this book in manuscript, and wrote the following comment on *Design for Living:* "I may have been busy when he and Hecht worked on it, but I

co-author of *The Front Page* and *Twentieth Century,* even traveling to New York (where the Broadway production of *Twentieth Century* had just opened) to work with him on the screenplay. It was the first and only Lubitsch-Hecht collaboration.

Though Lubitsch must have been reassured by Hecht's taking the job. No writer in Hollywood had better credentials in the tough, slangy, specifically American style that Lubitsch wanted to impart to the Coward play. And together they transformed it. "Americanizing" the ménage à trois situation ("a decidedly continental" one, said Lubitsch to one of his interviewers) meant, at least in part, injecting a slight, saving note of hypocrisy: when Gilda goes off with her two friends in the final scene, she stipulates (ha ha) that there will be "no sex"— a "gentleman's agreement." But otherwise the play's celebrated amoralism is intact, and even more matter-of-fact in the movie version. "Conscience bothering you?" says Tom to Gilda the morning after (they have just made love, and he is thinking about the "betrayal" of George). "*No,*" she replies dismissively, as if the question were actually insulting. *Design for Living* is a pre-Code movie, of course, and if anything the movie's humor is more "audacious" than the play's (e.g., a long smirking exchange about Gilda's typewriter: she didn't keep it oiled, the shift is broken, but it still *rings,* and so on). It is also grimmer. "Now we'll have some fun," says Gilda at the end, but you don't really believe it. "Fun" is the problem: something that gets talked about but never really happens. And even in spite of its stars, *Design for Living* flopped at the box office. The reviews weren't that good, either.

For all its clevernesses and occasionally wonderful jokes, there is something dispirited about this comedy—a deadness at the center of things that nothing affects. Clearly, the Noel Coward original was no help to Lubitsch here—just the opposite. The self-congratulating bohemianism of the Coward characters, tentative and genteel as it may be, is beyond Lubitsch's range and powers of sympathy. (It is beyond Ben Hecht's too, though he tried harder over the course of his career to pretend that it wasn't.) While Lubitsch, as I've said, can well imagine being outside or opposed to "polite society," what he can't imagine, it seems, is *choosing* to be so—or being in love with the *idea* of such a choice, as Coward's lovers often seem to be. The Lubitsch "outsider" is either hapless like Paul, or disguised like Gaston. Lubitsch can't really believe in the *adventure* of nonconformity.

---

was free when he contemplated it. We were in Palm Springs on horseback, imagine. He asked me and I said, 'My God, another goddam sophisticated triangle. You need Coward like a hole in the head.' I turned it down, begging him to do a delightful and substantial novel (Russian, I think) that he was also considering, but he was afraid it might be too heavy. I can't remember the novel. (Don't ask me why I did *Angel* after that! There *was* a difference, although I had one or two misgivings about *Angel.*)"

But, finally, the problem that the failure of *Design for Living* reflects is a broader one than his differences from Noel Coward. In his relation to the great screwball comedies of the later thirties, Lubitsch is like the leader who brings people to the promised land but cannot enter it himself. Lubitsch's *Design for Living* is a comedy about freedom that never finds its own freedom—never even begins to suggest how such an experience might exist, or what it would be like if it did. The Lubitschean spirit is too dry, too detached. He gave a triumphant, delighted form to the movies' spirit of skepticism. But the freedom and exhilaration, the sense of possibility and triumph, that qualified and even transformed that skepticism in the later great comedies were qualities beyond him. Though once the style was defined and elaborated by others, he could make films that reflected it—as he did with *Ninotchka* in 1939. But the fact remains that the great progenitor of Hollywood's romantic comedy wasn't really a romantic. Obsession and solipsism were the great comic subjects of his early sound films. And love in these films was an obsession, not an adventure. To the sensibility that engendered them, the relations between men and women could never quite become what they became in the most brilliant American movies of the later thirties—a liberation.

Amanda and her unlucky new husband: Norma Shearer and Reginald Denny in Private Lives.

The Classy Comedy: 4
High Life and Smart Talk

The terrible habit of theater.
—ROBERT BRESSON, *Notes on Cinematography*

THERE WAS almost a glut of sophisticated comedies in the early days of talkies. They weren't very popular, they weren't very good, but they all came from the stage and there were a lot of them. And many of them offered something Lubitsch in much better films couldn't quite manage: a conception of the modern romantic couple.

Probably no romantic couple of the time made more impact than Elyot and Amanda in Noel Coward's *Private Lives*—especially when played by Coward himself and Gertrude Lawrence, as they were in London in the fall of 1930 and then on Broadway the following season. Audiences for the 1931 MGM film—produced by Irving Thalberg (uncredited as always) and directed by Sidney Franklin—must have sustained less of the impact, with Norma Shearer and Robert Montgomery in the same roles. But such was the power of Elyot and Amanda, as figures of wit, swank, and daring, of high spirits and high living and faintly scandalous romance, that the movie, entirely faithful to the play, repeated its success—and did so, of course, playing to vastly wider audiences.

It's not like Lubitsch: here the characters make the jokes, not the director. Elyot and Amanda have an autonomy and authority, a larger-than-life-size glamour, that makes them seem specially right for the movies. And at times they really do fill the screen, more than adequately. For example: they are alone in their Alpine hideaway (a Paris flat in the play). This is where they have fled to escape Victor and Sibyl, the people they are currently married to and whom they have deserted on their respective wedding nights. Now they are hiding, remembering and reliving their own earlier marriage—which failed, they agree, because they were "over in love"—"so ridiculously." They are making love now, and Elyot is recalling the trip around the world which he undertook to mend a

Elyot and Amanda: Robert Montgomery and Norma Shearer in Private Lives.

broken heart after their divorce. (Coward's heroes always go around the world for this purpose: so do the ones in *Design for Living*.) Elyot describes the wonders he saw. "Moonlight shining on old temples, strange barbaric dances in jungle villages, scarlet flamingos flying over deep, deep blue water." It was all, he says, "breathlessly lovely, and completely unexciting because you weren't there to see them with me." "Take me!" cries Amanda, "take me at once!" "Next week?" asks Elyot. "Tomorrow!" she replies. "Done!" he says—and they embrace passionately, and kiss. But not before Amanda has added one last remark: "I must see those *dear* flamingos," she says throatily, just before passion claims her, managing on the edge of that passion to condescend, in one remarkable breath, to Elyot, to "the flamingos," and to her own feeling, all at once. It's a wonderful and funny moment: real movie-star size. And yet it reminds us that the "charm" of Elyot and Amanda has as much to do with their awfulness—willful and boasting—as with anything else.

But in fact, as it turns out, they don't fit the movies as well as they should, despite their outsize life and glamour. We don't really want to be as close as the movie medium puts us to figures who "project" themselves so insistently, who talk and behave in such sustained and nervous raptures of self-awareness as Elyot and Amanda do. Even their poise seems a little shrill, their reserve a bit worked up. They are essentially theatrical conceptions. And only Lubitsch at this time among filmmakers seems to have felt that not only Coward's plays but the people in them had to be reimagined for the films. In one respect here, Elyot and Amanda *are* reimagined—inadvertently—in the casting strategy of having them embodied by two familiar and popular (and American) movie stars, neither of whom quite suits his role.

Robert Montgomery, in spite of his skill and intelligence, seems oddly not lightweight enough for the role of Elyot. Something similar is true of Shearer, who seems neither as skilled nor as intelligent as her co-star, but whose miscasting has an even more interesting effect on the play. Shearer works hard and daringly at times, is good in the fight scenes, where she achieves an appropriate comic hysteria. But most of her assets as a star—a kind of plangency in the face, the visual equivalent of a blues note, and an expressive high-pitched voice that breaks nicely at moments of stress and sorrow—are irrelevant to Amanda. And yet her basic lack of sympathy with the role, especially at the moments when Amanda is being most outrageous, gives her a coldness in it that a closer identification might have prevented. And there are moments when this detachment makes comic points one could at least imagine the more accomplished Gertrude Lawrence missing—whose Amanda may well have seemed less monstrous, less astonished at the heart than Shearer's does.

The screenplay makes some crude attempts at "opening up" the play. Instead of fleeing to Amanda's Paris flat, the lovers in the film go, for no clear or stated reason, to a remote Alpine chalet. This gives opportunities to show them sleeping and waking in a barn, riding a cable car, even scaling a cliffside. But in spite of some feeble interpolations about the cliffside (Amanda speaks of having "a high old time"), even in these new and improbable locations the movie sticks mostly to the Coward dialogue—which was, of course, the more or less proven element of success.

But in the end, Elyot and Amanda only illustrate the kind of problem a sophisticated couple is likely to make for the movies of this time, under the grave, steady, narrowing attention of a big-studio camera. The glamour the film is about seems to be more a matter of excited self-consciousness than of excited passion. This romantic couple are a bit too aware of their effects to be quite persuasively romantic. Even their effect on Victor and Sibyl (Reginald Owen and Una Merkel), those dependable, stolid, and not-too-bright spouses they are obliged to desert at the beginning of the film. It's significant that their third-act triumph over this pair—who seem less like betrayed mates than a visiting uncle and aunt—involves misbehaving at table, giggling and breaking up over jokes that both elude and mock the discomfited and disapproving "grown-ups."

Indeed, nearly all the moments of liberated feeling, even of romance, in Coward's play tend to be moments of triumphantly recovered childhood. "Let's blow trumpets and squeakers, and enjoy the party as much as we can," cries Elyot during one of the play's improbable love scenes, "like very small, quite idiotic schoolchildren." They are always referring to themselves like this—in diminutives: not just small but "very" small and "quite" idiotic. For all their daring and willingness to shock, Elyot and Amanda do tend, in the subtext, to make excuses. There is a steady little threnody of self-pity, a constant faint whine in the background of the entire play—and occasionally in the foreground:

> AMANDA (seriously): What happens if one of us dies? Does the one that's left still laugh?
> ELYOT: Yes, yes. Death's very laughable. Such a cunning little mystery. All done with mirrors.

"Let's be superficial," says Elyot. And we are clearly meant to feel that for Elyot and Amanda the superficial is a choice—and yet, gallant and brave as they are, that they pay somehow for making that choice. And for being in love. "How long will it last?" exclaims Amanda, "this ludicrous, overbearing love of ours?" There are frequent references, warranted by no circumstance in the play, to "philosophers" and "futile moralists" who "want to make life unbearable" and who pretend to have all "the answers." Though it would be hard to find any two people more insistent about raising the questions than Elyot and Amanda are—in their way:

> ELYOT: Don't you believe in . . . ? (He points upward.)
> AMANDA: No, do you?
> ELYOT (shaking his head): No. What about . . . ? (He points downwards.)
> AMANDA: Oh, dear no.
> ELYOT: Don't you believe in anything?
> AMANDA: Oh yes, I believe in being kind to everyone, and giving money to old beggar women, and being as gay as possible.

But it's only when *Private Lives* tries to be "serious" that it almost manages to be shocking: that reference to old beggar women in the mouth of an Amanda touches a level it's hard to imagine anything sinking below. "Sophistication," of course, nearly always runs the risk of offering this kind of horror, a species of the let-them-eat-cake sensibility. Lubitsch certainly wasn't exempt from it (the jokes about communism in *Trouble in Paradise* are an unpleasant sample), but in him it occurs without the self-pity at least, without the notation of gallantry.

But, interestingly, almost none of this—none of the passages just cited, for example—made it into the movie. So that the movie really improves on the play, as movies often did at this time, for reasons that almost certainly had nothing to do with anyone's taste or judgment, mostly to do with their caution and cowardice. Not only is Coward's more self-conscious sort of naughtiness missing from the film, but also most of his philosophizing and moralizing. Screen characters might talk at length in these early days of talkies, but *not*—if the front office could help it—about the meaning of life. As a result, some of the worst writing in the play is edited out (though Elyot still refers to mountain snow as "cleanness beyond belief," the Taj Mahal is still "a sort of dream," and so on).

But as a movie, and in spite of its popularity, MGM's *Private Lives* was too uneasy a hybrid of stage and screen, and of English and American styles, to have much impact on the development of movie comedy. Beyond that, Noel Coward's sophistication was too bloodless and chichi, too English, perhaps, and too dependent on an upper-U context, to be much more than a fleeting success in movies. His sentimentality too seems alien to Hollywood styles. Not, as we know, that the movies of this time didn't accommodate all kinds of sentimentality, much of it hair-raising—but not the subtler, more rarefied kind that *Private Lives* gives expression to. The narcissistic self-pity of Amanda and Elyot is a specifically theatrical "sophistication," a debasement of the Molnár style. Glittering people feeling rueful about their glitter: the it's-a-strain-to-be-wonderful blues. This kind of attitudinizing, so prevalent in the theater of the time, never really took root in the movies. This is at least one reason why, overall, the movies of this period wear better than the plays.

The real comic genius of the American movies is a tough, hardheaded, no-nonsense one. *Private Lives*—and the Noel Coward style generally—is too la-di-da. Not only the implicit self-pity but the wistful fake childishness are opposed to the Hollywood style of the thirties, which prides itself on being grown-up, with no apologies. In these respects too, Lubitsch is a significant contrast. He too was a bit swanky for the movie mainstream: *Trouble in Paradise*, for example, certainly puts on airs. But the dryness in Lubitsch—the detachment and toughness—is real. In Coward by comparison it's all a bit faked, worked up for company. Amanda's famous turndown to Elyot's second-act lovemaking—"It's so soon after dinner" (she says this, the stage direction tells us, "rather flauntingly")—though meant to be tough, is anything but. The flauntingness is too self-aware, too childishly self-infatuated. And everything is softened by the haze of adulation the author sees these figures through at all times.

W HAT *Private Lives* showed—both the play and the movie—was that a hugely successful entertainment could be built around nothing but a knockout couple. The Lunts showed this too, in their way, in a career stretching over four decades, appearing in plays that might have been nonexistent but for their presence—and their line readings. To theater audiences, they were the certified glamour couple of their time, the apogee of sophistication and comic style. To many people—to most, perhaps—they were a romantic couple as well. Still, they were generally considered too "grown-up," too classy, for the movies.

Irving Thalberg, predictably, saw matters differently. The movies, at least at MGM, should be *made* classy enough to suit the Lunts. And so in 1931 he brought them to Hollywood to film their 1924 hit, Ferenc Molnár's *The Guardsman*, again directed by Sidney Franklin. But unlike the Franklin-Thalberg movie of *Private Lives*, MGM's *The Guardsman* was not a hit.

Nevertheless, the Lunts and *The Guardsman* give the first important screen rendering of a joke that was to be central to the whole movie tradition of romantic comedy—a joke with almost no precedent in the sophistication either of Lubitsch or of Noel Coward: the male as the weaker sex—volatile and unsure, given to alarms and flutters and frequent losses of control, in almost constant need of reassurance and support. Thus the man becomes the more "feminine" partner, in the most unflattering sense of the stereotype—while the woman is the figure of strength and solidity, the one who is cool, knowing, and "potent." (Obviously, and as much as he owed to Molnár, this isn't a joke that would have appealed at this time to Lubitsch. In his films, both sexes are equally foolish, and equally humbled by sexual feeling. It's only later, when screwball becomes ubiquitous, that an imbalance sets in—in 1939's *Ninotchka*.)

The couple in *The Guardsman* are significantly unnamed: known merely as the Actor and the Actress. They are Vienna's leading theatrical stars, only recently married to one another. And "happily." But the wife, with a romantic past well known to both her public and her husband, is troubled by inchoate private longings that send her to the piano to play Chopin, even in the middle of the night. The Actor concludes, by a process of hysterical "logic," that she is longing for a soldier. So he becomes that soldier, disguising himself as a Russian guardsman, and begins to court her, hoping at each stage of the pursuit that she will reject him. But in fact she encourages him, without ever quite giving in. Until the final test—which she fails, summoning the guardsman, with a key thrown from her chamber window, to spend the night with her. The next morning, the husband "returns." He changes to his guardsman disguise in the next room and emerges to confront his wife with her "treachery." The Actress bursts out laughing at the sight of him and tells him that she has known it all along. But did she? as the plot synopses say. It is a mark of the film's sophistication that it ends (just as the play did) with this question pointedly unanswered—with the Actress looking slyly over the Actor's head, which is buried in her bosom. She exchanges this final significant look with a character called the Critic (Roland Young), whose principal function throughout the movie is to provoke and receive such looks: the amused observer to whom the two leading characters are constantly explaining themselves.

Both leading characters are somewhat absurd, of course: being theater

people, they are implicated in vanity of all kinds. But the suggestions of an ingrained emotional fakery are almost all reserved for the Actor. In his dressing room, for example, he utters a passionate threat to kill his rival—interrupting himself only long enough to check his hairline in the mirror. Whereas the Actress, in a parallel moment, thinks of her makeup (she is expecting the guardsman) while playing Chopin on the piano: once she has checked herself in a hand mirror, she resumes the musical phrase, with its delicate and controlled exultance, exactly where she left it off—triumphantly. Even her anxious little vanities take elegant form, partake of her composure and her control. The Actor's vanity is stupider; the jokes about it, broader. He is often foolish; she never is.

And it's amazing in a way how far, and in what directions, the Lunts and the movie extend this contrast. While Lunt looks as tall as she seems diminutive, in their close-ups together she is nearly always a head higher. In the love scenes he is either at her breast or, in one instance, at her feet. After a quarrel, she comforts and soothes him, fondling and cradling him in her arms. "You foolish

The Actor in disguise, testing the Actress's virtue: Alfred Lunt and Lynn Fontanne in The Guardsman.

boy," she says in her wine-rich tones as he lifts his suffering face to hers. "You silly child"—and the words as she speaks them are incredibly sensual, full of fierce rue and a strange bent ardor: it's no wonder he's undone by them—or by her. Once in the film—in the last sequence—he is allowed to loom over her, dramatically. But the inappropriateness of this effect (he doesn't belong *there*), even the unreason of it, is emphasized by the way it is shot: upside down, from her point of view, as she leans back from her book and sees him towering Othello-like over her chaise longue. She laughs. . . . By the final shot of the film, matters have righted themselves. His face has disappeared into her breast, while she directs that final ambiguous look of hers toward Roland Young—and toward us.

Where the Coward hero and heroine remind us of the triumphs of childhood, the Lunts here remind us of the defeats. Their boldest and funniest moments in *The Guardsman* say less about adult romance than about the persistence of undignified childish needs in all of us. It is, paradoxically, part of their sophistication (even, perhaps, of their glamour) that they take the joke so far. Quite possibly—for the movie audience of the time—*too* far. Thalberg wanted them to try again, in any case—to do another film. Instead, they returned to the stage for good, to the triumph of *Design for Living* and a succession of similar hits (they never varied their type of play much, though it was universally believed they *could* have) on into the sixties. They were dedicated artists and supreme technicians, and through most of their long career the most illustrious stars on the American stage. Everyone, it's been said, learned from them. Even the people who made the movies the Lunts weren't—it was generally agreed—suited to.

What "unsuited" them, then? It's not at all a matter of the obvious liabilities: his looks (nondescript) or her age (forty-five at the time of *The Guardsman* film). In some less obvious ways they don't really seem to be movie-star types. Theirs is a more interesting, more complicated disability than Elyot and Amanda's. But there are similarities: like the Coward characters, the Lunts too are a theatrical conception. With none of those specifically *anti*theatrical elements—even so simple as inattention or blandness—that most movie-star personalities seem to include.

They made their separate star debuts not as romantic leads but as character actors in what happened to be starring roles: he in Booth Tarkington's *Clarence* in 1919, she in Kaufman and Connelly's *Dulcy* in 1921. Their transformation into leading man and lady really began with the Theatre Guild production of *The Guardsman* in 1924. If Lunt had had a movie instead of a stage career, most likely he would have been a comic second lead, one of those presentable but almost professionally unimpressive actors who regularly appear as the Other Man (Victor in *Private Lives*—who was, ironically, played in the original production by Laurence Olivier). He is a big man, tall and broad-shouldered, and a comic type for the same reason that another big man, Ralph Bellamy, is a comic type in films: a certain lack of masculine authority, a thinness and lightness of presence that make it too easy for an audience to take him not quite seriously. Lunt's voice, for example, is remarkably expressive, but its richness seems actorish: even at its most orotund it never quite loses its thin, reedy base. We are always more conscious of an instrument when we hear it than of a human fact.

Fontanne, as the Molnár play emphasizes, makes quite a different effect. Her authority on the screen is unquestionable—though puzzling. She is often heavy with her own inwardness—as Lawrence describes Hermione in *Women in Love:* gripped and tranced in thought, walking with clenched hands held at her waist. Her gestures are characteristically those of clutching and gripping. She touches Lunt's face reassuringly—with the back of her hand. So that when, with the guardsman, she stretches her arms wide across the back of a couch, the gesture has a surprising, even disturbing, force. She is small, slope shouldered and broad hipped, with deep dark eyes. Their gaze is like her clogged, tranced manner: intense but unfocused. We may see what she is looking at but are rarely quite sure what she sees. But we are always interested. Her apprehension of the outside world is slow, reluctantly given. When she reclines on a chaise longue and reads a book, she moves her lips. But this peculiar detail is part of a seamlessly conceived performance. Only if you think about it later does it stand out or seem odd. Only later, in fact, does the whole performance seem odd: Fontanne creates the sort of character who might indeed have a difficulty with reading. But if she does, we unhesitatingly blame the book. If the outside world is difficult for her to attend to, we locate the failure *there*—certainly not in her. Her special triumph as an actress, as a star and as a comedian, is to maintain a steady suspense about whether that outside world, and most especially the part of it that Lunt occupies, will earn her attention. In short, it is Lubitsch's solipsist joke—but used here less as a joke than as an element of personal authority, a component of glamour.

Both the Lunts, in their different ways, command considerable presence in front of the camera. But that presence is a matter of style, temperament, formidably marshaled emotion: it is personal while at the same time giving no clue to a *person* behind it. Unlike most of the great movie stars, even exotics like Garbo or Boyer, or neurotics like Bette Davis, the Lunts have no moral presence. They give the effect of standing for nothing but themselves more or less as they appear before us—of embodying their own theatrical life rather purely. As a result, they are fascinating—but, in some crucial way, not interesting. Brilliant and funny as they are in *The Guardsman*, the effect on the screen is of an absence.

JUST THE opposite is true of Diana Wynyard, playing the Fontanne role in
the MGM movie of Robert E. Sherwood's *Reunion in Vienna* (1933), the last
of these Irving Thalberg–Sidney Franklin sophisticated comedies. A piece of
echt-Molnár tailored to the Lunts (who played it on the stage): once again the
heroine is visited by powerful romantic longings that the men in her life evoke
but are quite unable to gratify. Once again the men are rather bumbling and
foolish. Once again the heroine is authoritative. The wife of a Vienna psychiatrist (Frank Morgan), she is also the ex-mistress of the exiled Rudolf of Haps-
burg (John Barrymore), down on his luck and driving a cab in Paris, who returns
to Vienna to claim her, in a campaign of music, champagne, and ecstatic reminiscence.

John Barrymore, at this point in his career, is not a very romantic figure, but
he is a convincingly dispossessed one: posturing and bravado carrying a lack of
conviction at the center. With his twitching mustache and dancing eyebrows and

snake charmer's hand passes, he may be the only romantic hero on record who strides into a scene on buckled legs (and in short Alpine pants). The message we get is that he likes to swagger but that he doesn't believe in it; the result is that curious parody of the dashing male that he more and more specialized in. With the large and sweeping gesture always climaxing in something mincing or finicking: the sob in a whinny, the laugh in a grimace. He provides the whirlwind into which Wynyard's heroine—an impressively quiet, thoughtful, inward woman—is drawn.

Wynyard is the sort of dark, distant, beautiful woman that you see only across *very* crowded rooms—and very distinguished ones. Tall and regal, with black eyes set deep and far apart, she has a permanent vaguely quizzical expression. She twists a handkerchief and wears long earrings. She has something of the same witchlike quality Fontanne has, but she is altogether more prosaic: she is remote without being exotic, and her sense of humor seems more dependable. She has great natural dignity, and she does, certainly, even less in front of a camera than Fontanne. She controls her scenes, it seems, almost by pulling back from them, into a kind of stillness that informs her whole performance. One of the smartest things Franklin does—and this is the smartest and probably the best of these three Thalberg-Franklin comedies—is to let that stillness control so much of the film. Barrymore's competing tone seems like a flurry at the edges. What Franklin the director mainly does is to give Wynyard an unusual number of close-ups: reaction shots where the reaction is almost always masked and ambiguous to some degree. The effect is surprisingly powerful, and helps to fix Wynyard's quality of sharp, gracious, slightly mysterious intelligence.

Although she had a brief vogue, coinciding with the height of Hollywood's early Anglophilia when talkies came in, she never really made it as a star. Even in her native England—where her inescapably upper-class style would be both familiar and acceptable as it probably never could be in the United States—her films, including this one, rarely did well. She always seemed much older than she was; there was even something matronly about her. She was only twenty-seven when she filmed *Reunion in Vienna*, playing a woman much older. And in another MGM film of this period (*Men Must Fight*) she played Phillips Holmes's mother. (He was in fact only three years younger.)

She isn't so flexible and inventive, not nearly so brilliant, as Fontanne; not many actors are. But she seems a more sensitive human register. The interest of her close-ups is not in her blindness but in her watchfulness, her responsiveness. Wynyard suggests some of the human uses of the "sophisticated" presence—ways in which the coolness and reserve and poise may be more than flourishes or too-conscious effects. In Wynyard they seem like the functions of a serious intelligence, the inevitable declarations of complexity and tact. Her ability to convey, without any noticeable technique or "acting," all the ambivalence of her reactions to Barrymore in this film—the degree to which she is both responding to the past and recognizing that it *is* past, the fact that she is both swept up by him and not quite convinced at the same time—shows real movie-star magic. Even more than Shearer or Fontanne, Wynyard foreshadows the glamorously intelligent heroine of later romantic comedy—whose sophistication is less a style than a fate.

Ronald Colman—whose movie-star career was as long and dominant as Wynyard's was modest and brief—has some of this same serious force in the sophisticated mode. His first sound film, *Bulldog Drummond* (1929), was a civilized comedy spoofing the extravagant melodrama of detection and adventure, a James Bond predecessor. And it established Colman, already a major star of silent film, as "the pre-eminent talkie actor" (David Shipman). In the early thirties, Colman made a series of sophisticated romantic dramas and "dialogue comedies" for Samuel Goldwyn. Like Wynyard, Colman seemed to come from British aristocracy and was usually so cast, in movies notable for their Anglophilia, an enthusiasm for the British class system that Hollywood (or at least that aspiring, upward-climbing part of it that Goldwyn's "quality" filmmaking typified) often indulged. In *The Devil to Pay* (1930), one of the most skillful (a Frederick Lonsdale script) and popular of all these films, Colman is the scapegrace son of a peer who must choose between his showgirl-mistress, Myrna Loy, and a respectable Loretta Young.

There can't be much question: Colman is the most attractive "sophisticate" hero in early talkies. With his thoughtful presence, his gentle implacable melancholy, beginning with *Bulldog Drummond*, he succeeds with arch material more consistently than any other star of his time. His high spirits always seem real, although complicated—precisely because he distinguishes them so clearly from whatever it is that inspires the deep gravity of his presence. And that gravity is never theatrical or self-important: it's private, not really available to the outside world—except to an occasional heroine (his yearning toward May McAvoy in Lubitsch's *Lady Windermere's Fan* has a kind of embarrassed ardor that is unforgettable). Colman is almost a model of Norman Mailer's star with something else on his mind—one of the ways Mailer tries to identify a specifically *movie*-star quality. And James Cagney, Colman's opposite number in the roughhouse style, is really his counterpart in some ways. They are both playful, essentially *amused* presences in their films. If Colman is heavier than Cagney, less mercurial and audacious, it is partly because his private—his serious—world is a sadder, more disabused one. Where Cagney suggests the energy of intelligence, both its creative and its disruptive force, Colman suggests its melancholy.

Colman is a master of *light* conviction. He is lively and susceptible—ready (even suspiciously ready, given that sadness) to be delighted, engaged, moved.

But his approach to the constantly surprising environment he finds himself in is oblique and sidelong, always slightly abstracted. Like his gaze, which is bright and attentive but inevitably slides off people very quickly, as if he is afraid to intrude with it or to insist. He plays his entire role in *The Devil to Pay* as if it were an extended aside—and not to an audience but to himself, addressed to his own unfailing sense of how extraordinary it all is. He can transform an arch, Professor Higgins–like exchange: "Kiss me, Willie," demands ladylike heroine Loretta Young, tired at last of their quarrels. "Nothing could induce me to," replies the gruff manly hero. But Colman makes that reply surprising and funny, even oddly touching—mainly by pausing gravely just before he makes it—and then seeming surprised by it himself. He focuses *our* attention too in the same sidelong relation to the lines and material of a scene or of a moment. This way too he can make convincing to some degree the most preposterous encounters with the most unlikely co-actors—from George, the barking dog who figures so prominently in *The Devil to Pay*, to Sam Jaffe's prosing High Lama in *Lost Horizon* seven years later.

He commanded large U.S. audiences for a longer time—from the twenties to the fifties—than any other star of his eminence. It was the gravity, the wounded look at the center of his eyes, the solemnity behind the playfulness, that saved him from the world of Noel Coward. He is a presence on the screen as Alfred Lunt is not. And he has the kind of effortless dignity that Barrymore, for all his much greater talent, could only envy. He and Diana Wynyard are similarly instructive figures, different as they are otherwise. In an insubstantial mode, they give a striking impression of substance: "sophisticates" who also suggest seriousness—and "weight." Just the sort of weight that the Lunts—incomparably more brilliant and airborne—seem almost deliberately to have refused.

"POUR THE wine, there's a dear," says the queen to the commoner. They are ill-fated lovers, having their last supper together. Since this scene belongs to a Noel Coward play (an early one, *The Queen Was in the Parlour*), we can be sure that they care about the wine, and that the fantasy of royal swank is a particularly naked and infatuated one. Shortly after they enjoy this wine, and one last night of love, the hero gives his life to save the queen from a revolution—brought on, it seems, by her high living in Paris (those spoilsports are everywhere). But in the movie version, Paramount's *Tonight Is Ours* (1933), with Claudette Colbert and Fredric March, the hero survives, and the radicals are so delighted to find out that the queen is in love with someone just like themselves that they agree to call the revolution off—provided, of course, that she marries the guy. "You get what you want and we get what we want," says their leader with a grin. The queen is very much relieved.

Elissa Landi and Paul Lukas, registering dismay, in By Candlelight.

One of the curious things about the era of early talkies is how many films like this got made—how many of these tributes to British and European systems of rank and privilege the Hollywood studios turned out. None of these films set the box office on fire; most of them were flops. Still, the froufrou comedies came— not only from Thalberg's MGM and Lubitsch's Paramount but from RKO and even from Warner Brothers, which offered William Dieterle's *Jewel Robbery* (1932), a precursor of *Trouble in Paradise*, with William Powell as the dashing and well-spoken jewel thief and Kay Francis as his wealthy "victim," taking the bath with serving girls attendant that these films often feature (even Lynn Fontanne takes one in *The Guardsman*).

But under the pressure of finding ways to talk, the movies turned more and more compulsively to the stage, where the sophisticated comedy had a tradition of commercial success. Hollywood would try, and try again, anything that worked in the theatre. What's more, the film industry, as it grew from its early silent days, became increasingly Europeanized and cosmopolitanized, and more and more subject to the confused dim notions of culture and "class" that its uneducated European-born moguls could respond to. And in the perennial Hollywood hunger after "prestige," these movies—from plays by Coward,

Maugham, Molnár, Lonsdale, etc.—represented the kind of distinction that studio heads could recognize without difficulty: the distinctions of rank and power and money. The "classy" film is essentially an upper-class kind of film: a celebration of the elite and privileged.

Nowhere is this clearer than in Universal's *By Candlelight* (1934), directed by Englishman James Whale, a film very close in tone and style to Lubitsch. Except that the joke in the Whale film (from Siegfried Geyer's play, performed on the New York stage by Leslie Howard and Gertrude Lawrence) is less sex than class: it's about a butler (Paul Lukas) who pretends to be his master the prince (Nils Asther) in order to make love to a countess (Elissa Landi) who turns out to be a lady's maid. Lubitsch's version of this situation is of course in *Monte Carlo*, where a nobleman pretends to be a servant; but a servant pretending to be a nobleman is a joke closer to the painful nerve of such material than Lubitsch generally chose to get. And the element of panicked servility that Whale's film so much exploits in its leading man, Paul Lukas, was not something Lubitsch would have been likely (it seems on the evidence of his films) to enjoy. Not that Whale quite seems to be *enjoying* it. It seems instead like something painful gotten out of control—gotten into the center of Lukas's fearful eyes, into his nervous appeasing gestures, spreading from this performance through the whole movie, even to the orchestra on the soundtrack. There is not a joke or a nuance that the music track doesn't slug across with some suitable sound or comment.* A heavy jocosity afflicts every level of this film, all its hectic nervous motions.

But then there are good reasons for the nervousness. If *By Candlelight* makes explicit the dirty joke of class that underlies all or most of these comedies, it also shows—in salacious detail—just *how* dirty the joke is. "I'm very fond of foreign languages," says the disguised maidservant—and the orchestra gives her the raspberry. Just as it does when the prince (who knows the difference between a maid and a lady even if his butler does not) slaps her on the derrière. And the conception of a lower-class type that director Whale has encouraged Elissa Landi to perform is almost slaveringly grotesque. It's not just the stomping and slouching and flouncing and pouting—those moments when, presumably, the servant girl is being "herself"—but those moments when she's *not*—when she is dancing clumsily, draping herself across a pianoforte, suppressing a hiccup (the orchestra whistles), affecting to smell and caress a vase of lilies, even trying to read a book (the orchestra chuckles) and doing it upside down (it's in Greek)—that the movie particularly savors. Another detail about her that the director likes to show us (from behind) is the way she runs in her evening gown:

---

* W. Franke Harling, who composed the score, seems to have specialized in this sort of Mickey-Mousing: he also did it for *Trouble in Paradise.*

she lifts her skirts, sticks her butt out, and clomps off on high heels as if she were wearing lumberjack boots.

But *By Candlelight* is only an extreme sample of something quite general. The dead weight of the jocose—the awful, depressing *will* to lightness and jollity—afflicts all these classy movies, as it occasionally afflicts even Lubitsch. And in all of them there is the problem of tone. Only Lubitsch solves this problem more or less, and he does it by walking a high wire that almost no one less gifted could follow him on: the others only remind us of the abyss it was stretched over. The sophisticated theater tradition failed to suit the movies not because it was "stagebound" but because, finally, it seemed to have nothing to do with what Hollywood movies in general did best: evoking specifically American qualities of experience and consciousness. And that consciousness was programmed, whatever the actual and rampant injustices of American society, to a certain uneasiness on such subjects as class and wealth and privilege. Not that American movies didn't find a way to lie, and to lie consummately, about all these problems. What they never quite found was a way to treat them as facts (as the "continental" mode does) rather than problems. Such topics would nearly always be touchy, to some degree, in American films. This in turn creates a dilemma for the kind of comedy that we call "sophisticated," which is always a fantasy of upper-class freedom. Part of what separates Lubitsch and Noel Coward and the Lunts and others from the screwball comedy explosion of the mid-thirties is their indifference to, and even incomprehension of, this problem of tone.

DONALD OGDEN STEWART, appropriately, was one of the first people both to reflect this problem and to try to solve it—in a movie called *Laughter* (1930). "Appropriately" because Stewart is in so many ways a paradigmatic American figure: a writer whose life has turned out, at least from our point of view, to be exemplary. A man of genuine and lifelong amiability, he was visited early by Fitzgeraldian aspirations to worldly success and social status and by a taste for the company of the rich and famous. He was not only a famous wit—a best-selling humorist (*The Parody Outline of History*) and a member of the Algonquin Round Table—but a society pet, married to a rich and beautiful young socialite. He was a friend not only of Robert Benchley and Dorothy Parker but of Ernest Hemingway: Stewart was one of the little group that went to Pamplona on the excursion memorialized by *The Sun Also Rises*. He was a playwright: his most notable play was *Rebound*, staged in New York in 1929 and filmed by RKO in 1931. And he had a long, off-and-on career as a Hollywood screenwriter ("Most writers pretended to despise Hollywood," he wrote in 1975. "I found that I adored it."), notable in its later stages for his screen adaptations of plays by his friend Philip Barry, *Holiday* and *The Philadelphia Story*. (He also wrote, according to John Lee Mahin, the memorable last scene of *Red Dust*.)

Fredric March and Nancy Carroll—in search of Laughter.

In 1936, however, Stewart's life took a new direction: he met Ella Winter, ex-wife of Lincoln Steffens and an active political radical. They fell in love and married two years later. In midlife he underwent, as Katharine Hepburn says of him in a 1975 memoir, a conversion to "serious thinking," a perception that the society he had "laughed his way to the top of" was "not fair." The society wit became a man of passionate (and doctrinaire) left-wing conviction, "the pixy revolutionist" of Ben Hecht's sardonic phrase about him, and an exile from America from the red-baiting fifties onwards, until his death (in London) in 1980.

Stewart wrote the screenplay for *Laughter*—which the New York *Post* described in 1930 as "the nearest approach to sophisticated comedy which has yet been made in the talkies." It had the distinction for such a comedy of *not* being based on a play, which seemed almost audacious at the time. *Laughter* was conceived from the start as a *movie* comedy. And what is most interesting about the final film seems to have been due mostly to Stewart, although he was not the only notable talent involved in it. Herman Mankiewicz—to whose later work it bears some affinities—produced it. Harry D'Arrast—director of sophisticated, Lubitsch-like silent comedies like *Dry Martini* and *A Gentleman of Paris* (he was also an usher at Stewart's first wedding)—supplied the "original story" and directed. It was filmed at Astoria, Long Island, and cast with actors from the Broadway stage: Fredric March, Frank Morgan, Glenn Anders. The obligatory "name" in the cast belonged to Hollywood star Nancy Carroll. She plays a former chorus girl (which Carroll herself was), married to a super-rich daddums (Morgan) and coping with the return from Europe of an old boyfriend (March), a dashing but penniless young composer who becomes determined to unlock her gilded cage.

Laughter is regarded as a milestone film, but is really less "cinematic," less venturesome with the sound camera, than a lot of other 1930 releases—like George Cukor's (with Cyril Gardner) *The Royal Family of Broadway,* also produced by Paramount, also with March (as a thinly disguised John Barrymore), and also filmed at Astoria. This latter film features, for example, a bravura tracking shot that follows March from the parlor up a stairway through several rooms to his bath, and talking all the way. But if the Cukor-Gardner film is more "cinematic," *Laughter* is more like the movies. *The Royal Family of Broadway* is standard theatrical stuff: adapted from a play by George S. Kaufman and Edna Ferber (the screenplay was co-written by Herman Mankiewicz), one of the theater's frequent tributes to itself, about a weird but wonderful family of actors.

But in *Laughter* we can see the outlines of movie comedy to come. For one thing, the sophistication isn't brandished at us—used to put us in our places—as it tends to be in the sophisticated theater piece. The rich elegant world is treated matter-of-factly here, as just another backdrop. A backdrop with a difference, however: there is a pervasive unease on the whole subject of wealth that (as I've said) has no parallel in the films of Lubitsch or in the other "continental" movies of this time. Stewart's characters are mostly *depressed* about being rich. There is none of the chirruping animation of Kay Francis's rich young wife in *Jewel Robbery,* or the cheerful complacence of her rich young widow in *Trouble in Paradise.* The Nancy Carroll heroine lives with the daily dreary consciousness of having made a bad bargain in her mercenary marriage. As a wonderful moment near the beginning makes clear: Morgan has just given his wife a stunningly expensive bracelet, and as he bends to fasten it on her wrist, she looks appraisingly at *him.* What is unusual here is not the conventional moralism about marrying for money but the very real sense of money itself as a kind of oppression. And this sense in the film is very authoritative, often powerfully conveyed.

It wasn't a popular film, in spite of good reviews. Six years later, during the heyday of screwball comedy, Herman Mankiewicz recalled *Laughter* to an interviewer—ruefully. Reflecting on the success of such later films as *It Happened*

One Night and *My Man Godfrey*, Mankiewicz told the press: "we" did it first, *Laughter* was "the original of this madcap type of screen story." Why did it flop? Because, Mankiewicz said, "we" made "one mistake": "our heroine" had a husband who made "eighty-four million dollars every day," lived in "a sixty-room quadruplex" on Park Avenue, had a Rolls-Royce to take her from bedroom to bath when she was finally exhausted from trying on dresses and jewelry all day, and so on. "The elemental trouble with our plot was that we started off with the assumption that all this was no good because—she didn't have *laughter!*"

This description is interesting partly because it fits *Citizen Kane* (which Mankiewicz would write four years after these remarks) rather better than it does *Laughter*, an infinitely more modest film. And the "elemental trouble" with the latter film would seem to be something quite different from what Mankiewicz suggests. For a comedy it is uncommonly grave, even dispirited at times— named, it seems, after what most of its characters are missing. Including the maniacally embittered Greenwich Village painter (Glenn Anders) who finally kills himself for love of the heroine—and thus engineers (in one of the film's glummest and least convincing plot turns) the heroine's final decision to give her life to love and laughter. As she explains afterwards to her disbelieving husband, if a man can die for love, a woman like her can live for it. This confrontation with her husband is a very restrained one (the suicide, too, is discreetly managed)—a very quiet scene in a very civilized film. Where even the comic effects tend to be muted, vaguely troubled—like the sight of Morgan, a gentle, diffident man, dressed as Napoleon at his own masquerade party and looking *very* uneasy.

The hero and heroine are livelier, of course. And their escapades and jokes anticipate the screwball style of later romantic comedy: writing notes to each other on the butler's cuff (the butler seems happy); questioning tramps on an inland road about the way to the "ocean" (the tramp seems angry); breaking into an empty house, playing the piano and calling the operator on the phone to find out whose house they are in; spending the night (platonically) and wearing a bearskin rug at breakfast; and so on. But all these sports and pranks are like the briefest glints on the calm grave surface of the film itself.

And that gravity is more than surface. Laughter is a serious business, it seems. And it is just here that Stewart's script is most un-Lubitschean, and most interesting. Just *how* serious a business is evidenced by a strange scene between March and Carroll the morning after their night in the empty house. They have been arrested for trespassing, but when it is discovered "who she is," they are chauffeured back to New York with a police escort and sirens blaring. They sit grimly in the back of the limousine, and speak listlessly over the sound of the sirens (one of the film's few attempts at a complicated sound effect). When Carroll insists that she has "a good time," March tells her that she does not. A grave charge, gravely put. She is having "a ghastly time," he tells her—living a "dead," "false," "horrible" life. "Nothing you do is really you." He tells her that she is "dying." "God didn't mean you to live like this," he says—without "nourishment," without "laughter." "Laughter?" she repeats, incredulous. He goes on portentously:

> Yes, laughter. . . . You were born for laughter. Nothing in this life of yours now is as important as that. Laughter can take this whole life of yours—that home, those people, those jewels—and blow them to pieces. You're rich. You're dirty rich. And only laughter can make you clean. . . .

This is a long way from the world of the continental comedy and its sophistication. The implications of this amazing speech are not, however, quite borne out by the rest of the movie. We never see "laughter" doing any of these saving or destructive things: we barely "see" it at all. The heroine's longed-for release occurs not through the operations of laughter but because of an off-screen suicide. And the pallid constricted life that the movie dramatizes is never really exploded or transcended: that promised liberation into something exciting and exhilarating and fulfilling also takes place off screen—and so never convincingly takes place at all. In the end, *Laughter* is less a "madcap comedy" than a statement about the need for such a comedy. But as such, it now seems amazingly prescient.

Stewart has a powerfully romantic—and characteristically American—idea of a sense of humor, of the *uses* of irreverence and wit. Uses both social and spiritual, it would seem, as the Fredric March hero explains them to the heroine: humor as a revolutionary force, a weapon against wealth and worldly power, even against the kind of worldly calculation that would tell the heroine to stay with her rich husband. All this only seems extraordinary, however, when it is baldly stated: that it *should* be baldly stated, and should come so close to a prominent screenwriter's consciousness, is the extraordinary thing. The romanticism itself is an ordinary fact of American movies, an ordinary paradox of their American "sophistication." And when Herman Mankiewicz in that 1936 interview puts it down and dismisses it in conventional wiseacre fashion (a heroine who prefers laughter to *money*—are you kidding?), he is really forgetting how deep in the movies he knew—and some of them he even wrote—this romantic, idealist feeling about comedy is: the very *un*-"sophisticated" notion that we become somehow better, sharper and more dangerous, truer and even "cleaner," if we laugh more.

Love, on the other hand—which isn't so funny—can make us small, slavish, cowardly, stupid. In fact, Stewart suggests in his play *Rebound* that there are more important things than love—a strange idea to find at the climax of a romantic comedy. And the immediate result of it, of course (since this *is* a romantic comedy), is that the heroine finally does get the man she's been yearning after, so impressed is he by her new, *un*slavish character. But here again Stewart shows himself to be at a characteristic kind of variance with the continental mode. What is a joke to Lubitsch—not unkind, but a joke nevertheless, this tendency of love to reduce and even to humiliate people—is a *problem* to the characters of *Rebound*. And, indeed, it is one problem underlying the whole Hollywood attempt to appropriate the continental, neo-Molnár style to its movies. Once again, Stewart names the problem out loud.

Now it's easy to see how close to the mark he was. Hollywood was moving away from Lubitsch at the same time as it was learning from him. Something more important than love? It's a notion, after all, that would have left Elyot and Amanda feeling quite blank. That condition of "loving so desperately" that Coward so frequently and tinnily invokes is, after all, the "serious" side of his vision. But what Sara, the heroine of *Rebound*, comes to realize is the possibly greater seriousness of something she calls "grace"—dignity, self-respect, even self-possession. Like the most interesting suggestions of *Laughter*, this idea of "grace" never really gets worked out or convincingly dramatized, either in Stewart's play or in the RKO movie version that followed (with Ina Claire as Sara).

But subsequent movies do work it out. The comedies of the early thirties are moving (so we can see now, at any rate) toward a romantic-comic version of love that is neither sentimental on the one hand nor cynical and mocking on the other. Toward a notion of love as something that is not only *not* inconsistent with "grace," dignity, common sense, and self-respect—but that even somehow leads to higher, truer forms of all these qualities. This sort of romantic affirmation, of course—quite different from the Lubitsch spirit—is part of the genius of thirties romantic comedy. The comedy to come.

Doctor at work: Jean Harlow and Edmund Lowe in Dinner at Eight.

The Tough Comedy: 5
Low Life and Rough Talk

Contrary to what it seems, comedy was in reality the most serious genre in Hollywood—in the sense that it reflected through the comic mode the deepest moral and social beliefs of American life.
                    —ANDRÉ BAZIN, in a 1948 review

"LET'S GO Slumming" is a production number in Twentieth Century–Fox's *On the Avenue* (1936), and it is strikingly graceless. Alice Faye sings and dances it in front of a stage chorus of spiffy proles, all dressed in their flamboyant "Sunday best." They are setting out for Park Avenue, the Irving Berlin song tells us, to stare at the swells the way the latter come to stare at them: if the rich can "slum," why can't the poor? As Faye puts this question, she shakes her puffed shoulders and rolls her eyes and lifts heavy feet to dance, while the group ranged behind her shuffles and dips and clomps and raises their hands in front of one of those dark-gray backdrops with painted stoops and garbage cans that are meant to stand for the East Side tenement scene. The whole number is full of eye-rolling merriment and heavy raffishness throughout—it's dumb and clumsy, and it's a total success. As it would not be probably if it sounded and looked any better. Berlin's jingly song, with its crude lyrics and jokes ("Let's go smelling / Where they're dwelling"), above all with its dumb prancing jollity, taps something so deep and strong in our feelings about the tyrannies of class, that the clumping, moiling, tossing anarchy of the performance, even its being very close to ineptitude, seems a fact exactly right—even rousing. The whole number is about *wanting* to be dumb and heavy and cloddish. The people onstage triumph over sophistication by imitating it—and then compound their triumph by imitating it badly—and to hell with it.

This strain of defiant vulgarity runs deep in American movies—and in their audiences. It's one of the things that makes them seem American. Although British films, for example, traditionally get plenty of mileage out of lower-class

Alice Faye (center) sings about the rich people in On the Avenue.

vulgarity, they rarely recommend it (not, at least, until the fifties and the "angry young man" phenomenon). And if "class" is a nearly unmentionable word in early British talkies, it is heard often in American movies of the same period where people (especially at Warner Brothers) are always talking about having it or getting it. The kind of talk which is, of course, nearly always a joke *against* it—against elegance, sophistication, "culture," etc. The animus is always against the refined byproducts of class lines and economic privilege—never (or rarely) against the lines and the privileges themselves. For Hollywood films were no more likely than British ones to talk frankly about *class*—about those institutionalized arrangements of society that keep people in their places even in America. Hollywood sentimentalizes these arrangements, and only villains or madmen ever suggest in movies that any of them might be *re*arranged. But (and this is the odd and slightly heartening part) just as the movies characteristically exalt and endorse the status quo, they just as characteristically mock it. Hollywood encouraged just the kind of subversive mockery and institutional irreverence that would have been almost unthinkable in a British or European film of the period—but that was so much a feature of the smart-talking Hollywood comedy that by 1936, the time of "Let's Go Slumming" and *On the Avenue*, it was an established movie style. So much so that they could make a spirited but perfectly conventional song-and-dance of it. The sound of jeering . . . It was a mob sound—like a lot of the sounds the movies of the time made most convincingly. (It wasn't until the fifties that the movies began to lose this collective quality—their security in expressing *public* emotions.)

For just as much as Hollywood in one direction pursued sophistication, in another—and probably more authentic—spirit, it despised it. That hatred surfaced mostly in its comedies—even, occasionally, in the sophisticated ones: the acrid fumes in the general perfumed atmosphere of *By Candlelight* and *Tonight Is Ours*. It surfaces too in the on-screen complications of someone like John Barrymore—a baggy-pants clown in Alpine shorts "playing" Alfred Lunt (*Reunion in Vienna*). Barrymore was always thought of for the "Lunt roles," often played them, and gives the frequent impression of feeling trapped in them—trapped by his looks, his voice, his family, and his "culture" in a style he seems to detest. And although he could play beyond that style—Mercutio or Baron von Gaigern (*Grand Hotel*)—he couldn't play Hildy Johnson, or even a quite credible Walter Burns, whereas Adolphe Menjou—who also had a mustache, a profile, and an actorish (read "fraudulent") personality—could and did. A vastly more limited performer (Louise Brooks recalled to Kenneth Tynan how Menjou would "prepare": "Now I do Lubitsch number two," he'd say before a shot—and then, of course, Brooks adds, he'd be marvelous), still Menjou connected with images of a contemporary vitality in a way that Barrymore never could. And there's no mistake about it: the "heroes" of *The Front Page* were the heroes a movie actor of the time would want to play. Since it's hard to think of a major male star of the thirties, from Clark Gable to Cary Grant, who didn't in some sense derive from these figures or show a kinship with them.

THE FIRST film version of Ben Hecht and Charles MacArthur's *The Front Page* (there have been two since then*) was produced by Howard Hughes and directed by Lewis Milestone in 1931. It starred Menjou and Pat O'Brien. "This story," says an introductory title, "is laid in a mythical kingdom . . ." Hesitation. "—Chicago." And finally it is Hecht and MacArthur's Chicago, and not Lubitsch's Ruritania—his Marshovia, or Sylvania, or even his Paris or Vienna—that counts most deeply in the imagination of Hollywood. And their play, the first of the great newspaper comedies, did more to define the tone and style, the look and the sound of Hollywood comedy than any other work of its time.

His Girl Friday (see below), and then in 1974 Billy Wilder's *The Front Page*, with Walter Matthau as Walter and Jack Lemmon as Hildy.

Their mythical kingdom—as invented as any of Lubitsch's—was a place the movies could be at home in. Lively and unlettered, hustling, grungy, and noisy. But the first and foremost fact about "Chicago" is that it is a Terrible Place—categorically. Its principal charm is that you can relax and admit that—that you're even obliged to admit it. This consciousness, persistent and unrelenting, of how awful it all is, is a condition of being there. And what a relief it is: after Ruritania or even Paris, those mythical kingdoms where even Lubitsch has trouble keeping his (and our) spirits up. High spirits in Chicago are about as appropriate and useful there as good diction would be, or exquisite manners. You are *meant* to be depressed in Chicago, just as emphatically as you are meant to be elated and romantic in Paris. Whereas in Chicago, things like gaiety and romance are so antithetic to the spirit of the place that they happen there only by the sheerest and most improbable chance. Except that that chance is always—and always improbably—happening.

Hildy and Walter (Pat O'Brien and Adolphe Menjou) under arrest in The Front Page.

Physically, it is hardly a place at all. It has no look exactly—only a kind of gray anonymity. Tall, faceless buildings that the cabs and police cars speed past. Liquor stores, dry cleaners, florists, drugstores and lunch wagons where small-town types with a very citified sourness wait on you. It's less a city with characterizing details than an ambience, less a place than a spirit of place. An atmosphere of corruption, serene and endemic, where it's accepted that scoundrels will run things. The scoundrels who do are also gray—colorful only in the *scale* of their corruption, which compels a certain admiration. In spite of this, their exertions are joyless and automatic. They are addicted to pious rhetoric; but even that, gifted as they are at it, gives them no pleasure. They are crafty, but they are without imagination. What they have instead is a lovingly cultivated stupidity—a quality which they share, it seems, with all the people they exploit and oppress (at least all of them that we see). Everyone in Chicago mouths the slogans of rectitude, from the governor to the cops to the hoodlums and shoeshine boys—even the man in the jail cell, waiting to be "fried."

There are just a few people in this gray world who know better. They are select. And for them the pious rhetoric *is* fun. They are the "heroes" of this fantasy. And they may or may not be distinguishable from the others in Chicago by virtue of having a few qualms (Hildy does have them, Walter doesn't). But what does distinguish them, principally and always, is that they have fun. And the fun they have is what *The Front Page* is mainly about.

> HILDY: . . . Why, you ungrateful hound. Who wrote the Fitzgerald confession? Who wrote Ruth Randolph's diary? And how about the Dayton flood? Even the telegraph operator was crying!
>
> WALTER: All right, make me cry now! (*He crosses to* Examiner *phone.*) Duffy! Listen, Duffy. What's the name of that religious editor of ours? The fellow with the dirty collar? Sipper what? Well, where is he? . . . (*To Hildy*) Do you know what I'm gonna do? . . . (*Happily*) I'm going to get the Reverend Sipperly to make up a prayer for the city of Chicago—right across the top of the paper! (*He crosses center.*) "Our Father Who art in Heaven—there were four hundred and twenty-one murders in Chicago last year!" All in religious lingo, see? Eight columns Old English boldface! The God-damnedest prayer you ever heard! (*He crosses back to* Examiner *phone.*) God, what an idea! . . .

Unfortunately, not enough of this elation finds its way into Milestone's 1931 film version. Not until 1940 and Howard Hawks's wonderful *His Girl Friday* does the play's real energy and spirit get onto the screen. Milestone's actors—even Adolphe Menjou, who would seem to have been born to play Walter Burns (and who was to play many variants of him for the rest of his film career)—seem strangely distant presences in the film's basic medium shot. We are more aware of artfully arranged groups, photographed from multiple angles. And even more aware of a very mobile camera, within the one set—the press room of the Chicago criminal courts—the film is mostly confined to. Milestone seems determined (much like Rouben Mamoulian at this same period) to show that the sound film can *move* too. Some of the camera effects are simply bizarre: at one point Milestone swings his camera on a pendulum to the rhythm of a song the newsmen are humming in unison; each time the camera swings upward, it comes down and into focus again on the face of a different newsman, until it has covered them all. More damaging are those effects which are portentous: full-circle pans during a newsroom poker game (the camera is in the center of the table), a long melancholy track to the music of a banjo, and so on.

In spite of the inherent sleaziness of the material, Milestone seems conscious of filming an Important Play—placing as much of it as he can in a serious context of humane concern and enlightened outlook. The screenplay (by Bartlett Cormack and Charles Lederer) omits much from the play that won't fit this context—like Walter Burns's sentimental reminiscence of the Reverend J. B. Godolphin ("It seems we called him a fairy") who sued the *Examiner* and then "drowned in the river" on his way to the trial in a car with "all his lawyers and medical witnesses" ("Something seems to watch over the *Examiner*")—and adds things that do—an opening sequence of the hangmen rehearsing, with a shock cut to a sandbag falling through the gallows. Capital punishment seems an issue in the movie as it never does in the play. *The Front Page* is not, to put it mildly, a notably humane play. Though it sometimes pretends to be when it loses its nerve. And just those moments when it does are what Milestone seizes on. When "a Clark Street tart" named Molly Malloy (Mae Clarke) comes into the press room to denounce the newsmen assembled there to await Earl Williams' hanging ("Poor little crazy fellow, sitting there alone, with the Angel of Death beside him"), upbraiding them for their heartlessness and indifference to suffering, she speaks for all the humanity that these reporters (and the play itself) have outraged. In *His Girl Friday*, Howard Hawks turns this scene—stagy, poorly written, and out of key with the rest—into a set piece and thus isolates it from the rest of the film: it doesn't really work that way, but it doesn't do too much damage. Milestone, on the other hand, almost does make it work (Mae Clarke is very good)—and the damage is considerable. For the fact is that every time the Hecht and MacArthur play tries (and it often does) to moralize about the reporters' heartlessness or about Chicago itself, it goes back on its own boldest and truest impulses. Milestone puts Molly's denunciation ("It's a wonder a bolt of lightning don't come through the ceiling and strike you all *dead!*") at the emotional center of his film. And the result is dampening and obfuscating, substituting a dumb kind of "responsibility" for the real seriousness and achievement of the play.

That achievement is to get close—as almost no work before it had done so well—to a certain complexity, and even mystery, of the American consciousness and character: the combination of an absolute cynicism about public and social life with a kind of innocence and even hopefulness. It's a combination that almost invariably strikes Europeans, that often puzzles them in our films, where it seems particularly present and mysterious. The mystery is how you invent such a nightmare landscape as Chicago and then make precisely *that* the occasion for the sort of comic fantasy that seems not only buoyant but, in some subterranean way, optimistic.

But we shouldn't forget how powerful the opposite tendencies in American culture have always been (just as they are today): the positive-thinking side, pious, Pecksniffian, nobly attitudinizing. Against *this* strain, the bad news of Chicago—with its vision of a universal corruption—will almost sound good. What may *look* in these comedies like a kind of despairing cynicism was really—for their audiences as well as their authors—a liberating kind of truth-telling. And the worse the truth was, the more liberating it *felt*.

The heroes of *The Front Page* compel interest and admiration precisely because they know so supremely well how to *operate* in this landscape, how to maneuver and win the victories that Chicago has to offer—mainly the defeat and grudging admiration of other "operators" less skillful, less canny, less amused than themselves. When Walter Burns, who is trying to keep Hildy from quitting the newspaper game for marriage to a "respectable" girl (she wants him to go into advertising), tells Hildy they will be "naming streets after" him once the two of them have exposed the mayor of Chicago, Hildy is tempted—momentarily—to forget the girl. And though she takes Hildy off at the end, it is clearly conveyed by the play's famous curtain line ("The son of a bitch stole my watch!" says Walter into the phone, arranging to have Hildy arrested on his honeymoon for possession of his editor's wedding present) that Hildy will never be free of his boss or the newspaper racket. "Right in your class!" he says to Walter earlier on. "On my prat in a monkey cage!"

And yet all this confers an odd kind of integrity on the figures of Hildy and Walter. They are fundamentally disreputable, and though Walter is the boss of a big newspaper, they are both in some fundamental way outside the world of bosses. There is in fact no way to imagine them in anything but an adversary relation to any authority that human society could devise. Not that they are ideologically or even morally out of step with the society they inhabit; they are simply, permanently wised up. They are beyond the experience of belief—even the mingy, minimal sort of belief it takes to be hypocritical. But, finally, it is crucial to note that they are wildly successful—by the end of the play at least—and successful by the standards of the world they are wise to.

This is really the dream that *The Front Page* is all about: being cynical and clear-eyed and unappeasable in your bitterest knowledge—and being *rewarded* for it all. That reward, of course, is the special triumphant twist: confirming your cynicism beyond anything you could have hoped for. It's this element of success—the element of triumphantly getting away with your disbelief, of being acclaimed and cosseted in the camp of the smarmy enemy—that gives *The Front Page*'s cynicism its special force and élan, that turns its humor of defeat into something like a victory. And it is this victory and its excitement, above everything else, that the Hecht and MacArthur play gives to the movies—the many movies—that were shaped by it.*

It's a particularly American idea of community: a world of private skepticisms and public energies—where no one wants to be cut off from either the energy or the clarity of the skepticism. A community of wiseacres—in a larger society of fakes and fools (as we all at times believe all larger societies to be). The personal ideal in this arrangement is to be whole and sardonic and *still* to be connected, to have the kind of vision that *should* set you apart but only somehow binds you more deeply, more closely, to a group or family or job, even to a town or a Chicago, to the spirit of America itself. For America—in this vision—is the land of the privately wised up, of the quietly sardonic. A community of secret smilers. And their special movie incarnation is James Cagney.

C AGNEY PLAYED many fewer gangsters than he did operators like Hildy. It is only technically that he could be said *not* to have played in *The Front Page:* he was appearing in one or another version of it through most of his career. He plays Walter Burns, so to speak, in his penultimate film, Billy Wilder's *One, Two, Three* (1961): instead of the *Examiner*, it is the Coca-Cola company that he is scheming and double-crossing for, but the style and the ruthlessness are the same. In *Torrid Zone* (1940) he plays Hildy to the Walter of Pat O'Brien (the original movie Hildy): in this one a Central American banana company stands in for the newspaper, with surprisingly little effect on the essential Chicago tone. (The same movie, in Warner Brothers' cheerful tradition of interstudio plagiarism, borrows even more extensively from MGM's *Red Dust*.) Through the early and mid-thirties, when he was making up to five movies yearly, Cagney played several varieties of promoters, sharpies, con men. In *Jimmy the Gent* (1934) he specializes in fake inheritance claims. In *Hard to Handle* (1933), he is a press agent, promoting rigged contests and trick products ("The public is like a cow, bellowing—*bell*owing to be milked."). In *Blonde Crazy* (1931), he is a larcenous bellhop who keeps a scrapbook of swindles and confidence games culled from the newspapers.

---

*Samson Raphaelson wrote next to this: "It shaped Hecht and MacArthur too—they were among the victims—and in many ways befouled Hecht's career."

Loretta Young and James Cagney in Warner Brothers' Taxi.

And the scripts of these films are much like that scrapbook: anthologies of outrageous and funny con games, from the simple swindles of *Hard to Handle*— a treasure hunt with no treasure, a "reducing cream" that doesn't rub in ("so the yobs can *rub* the fat off")—to the elaborate legal maneuvers of *Jimmy the Gent*— where the hero has to manufacture fictitious heirs to unclaimed fortunes. He makes it big with a grapefruit diet in *Hard to Handle*. But in *Blonde Crazy* he never really makes it at all: *everyone* in that film, it seems, is a con artist. Even the moralizing heroine (Joan Blondell), who helps Cagney get back at an old enemy by setting the sucker up in a racetrack con of breathtaking complication. At the movie's beginning, Cagney sees this widespread sharpsterism as an opportunity. "This is the age of chiselry!" he tells the skeptical Blondell. "Everyone's got larceny in his heart." But by the end of the film that turns out to be just the problem—as he languishes in a jail cell, having been outsmarted by the heroine's respectable and "cultured" husband. As a chiseler his talents are only fair. And the competition is fierce.

But these movies are less interested in success than they are in a certain kind of audacity. They are just as likely to involve the Cagney hero in small degrading schemes as in big ambitious ones. The important thing is fooling people—and earning that secret smile, which is the real prize. And the most anonymous types often have the most ingenious plans for winning it. Like the dim, unsavory-looking party who wanders into Cagney's hotel room in the last reels of *Blonde Crazy*. He offers to cheer the disconsolate Cagney up (Blondell has just married someone else) by cutting him in on a mail-order con. First, he explains, they comb the obituaries ("I got two people reading them full time"), then they send a good-luck charm to "the stiff," COD $3.50 (the charms cost "two bucks a gross"). The family are so shaken to find that the deceased ordered a good-luck piece just before "kicking off" that they never fail to remit the charges: it's "the greatest thing in the world." Cagney listens to all this impassively, lying on top of his bed. "I been away so long," he says reflectively, "it all sounds strange to me."

But it all sounds very familiar to anyone who knows more than a few samples of this early-thirties Warner Brothers style.* The con artist movie: they are modest, often makeshift films, but they add up—with their endless, insatiable, utterly delighted interest in what people will do for a buck. The world they create is, of course, a lot like Hecht and MacArthur's Chicago, but different in shading and detail. There is less emphasis on political and official corruption. In fact, there hardly seems to be a government at all in the Cagney films, except for cops and judges and occasional prison wardens. Everyone seems to live in the same big hotel, and to check in and out as easily as they hail taxis. "Where's Helen?" asks someone in *Blonde Crazy* about a prominent (up to now) supporting player. "Aw, I sent her back to where I got her from" is the reply. And we never see *her* again.

There is always, however, a "high society"—people like dowager social leader Mrs. Weston Parks (Louise Mackintosh) in *Hard to Handle*, who reluctantly agrees under Cagney's pressure to "endorse" his new reducing cream. What, she inquires delicately, is "the honorarium"? (Her maid in the background rolls her eyes knowingly.) A thousand dollars. But her friend Mary Shortridge posed with a Simmons bed and got five thousand. "You can have me for two," she cries in outrage, "and nothing less!"

In the same film Cagney is seduced by a debutante (Claire Dodd) who turns out to be a slut, and then conned by her father (Robert McWade), who turns out to be a crook. Usually, however, it's Cagney's girlfriend who is most susceptible to the allurements of "class." Bette Davis in *Jimmy the Gent* is so impressed by Alan Dinehart's refined manners (he serves high tea in his posh office) that she assumes he is honest as well. Always a mistake: he is, of course, even crookeder

---

* Or even its later imitations—like Peter Bogdanovich's *Paper Moon* (1973), where a version of the same con game turns up (with Bibles instead of good luck pieces).

than Cagney. Joan Blondell in *Blonde Crazy* meets a well-tailored young man (Ray Milland) who takes a cinder out of her eye on the train, and then courts her by sending her volumes of Browning. Although she is not quite up to the Browning (she is a little too smart for *that*), she is impressed by the approach— and eventually marries him. He's from "a different kind of people," she tells Cagney, people who "like music and art and all that sort of thing." And this guy of course turns out to be a complete bum: not only embezzling from his firm but setting Cagney up to take the rap for it.

The function of these classy types is always the same: to make Cagney look better than he did in the first reel. To the audience, their treachery is never a surprise. It's only the heroine, hell-bent for culture and virtue, who fails to notice the signs of a hopeless creep: the nerves, the darting eyes, the self-satisfied little smirks of triumph, and so on. What these heroines are always out for, to their ultimate sorrow, is respectability. And one of the nicest things about these movies is their suggestion that there is no such thing—since the people most unquestionably in possession of it seem to be the worst types of all. As one result of this, there is no repining about the movie's fun—no hypocritical deploring of just what we have been enjoying all along. It's a less grim world than *The Front Page*—the corruption is more benign—but it is also less apologetic.

An instance of this light and unrepining tone is the way *Hard to Handle* offers its mother-in-law joke. The heroine (Mary Brian) has a mother (Ruth Donnelly) who is always and literally at her side. To underline the point, they both wear festive matching outfits—identical hats and gowns—throughout the movie. But except for their constant proximity and matching clothes, and a tendency to walk in step and move their heads in unison when they are walking down a hotel corridor looking for the hero, they don't, oddly, seem to have much connection. It's true that Mom thinks of daughter as an extension of herself ("We've got a good job and a real man interested in us," she tells Cagney, warning him off). But she does so in the most rigorously, most unsentimentally practical way: "We've reached a stage in life when we're *entitled* to relax," she says, as she prepares for "their" marriage to a "twenty-five-thousand-a-year man." Her interest in her daughter really seems quite impersonal. And while the daughter endures this interest equably, mostly she does as she wants in spite of it. She even rejects Cagney after he's become very rich—to her mother's horror, she goes back to that "twenty-five-thousand-a-year man." ("We're practically marrying a pauper," cries Mother to Cagney. "We're throwing ourselves away just for spite—we don't love that mug, we love *you!*") So that finally the joke of all this (and of those girlish matching outfits) is not so much that mother is awful (although she is) as that she is *there*—always. Less a joke about a daughter's victimization than about her fate. Mother is simply a condition of life; no one in the film thinks to wish her away or even to complain about her. Where an Alfred

Lunt or a John Barrymore might berate and threaten such a figure (as Lunt does his mother-in-law, Maud Eburne, in *The Guardsman*)—might even dream out loud about doing her in—Cagney knows better. He listens to the old bird—and smiles. In a way he enjoys her—why not?—this venal, outrageous, hard-as-nails old woman. In this world, triumph consists not in a grand speech or gesture but in that small smile—which Cagney smiles so especially well.

It's a function in part of that playfulness in performing which is always at the edge of his effects, and which suggests that any character he plays, whether a loser or a mug or both, could still surprise us. But the same Cagney smile—when he first showed it to effect on the screen, in fearsome close-up, in William Wellman's *The Public Enemy* (1931)—belonged to a killer on the prowl. This of course was the performance that made him a star, and that he was ever after identified with: it was scary, it still is, and reviews of the time talked accurately of the power of his presence and performance. But in fact it wasn't until seven years and some twenty-three films later, as Rocky Sullivan in *Angels with Dirty Faces* (1938), that he would show anything like this power again. And not until *White Heat* (1949), fourteen films beyond that, would he fully recall the menace and fearsomeness of his debut as a star by playing another psychopath gangster-killer.

But it probably wasn't, as it turns out, the cruelty or the scariness that audiences were mainly responding to in *Public Enemy*. The most famous single scene in it, the grapefruit scene, is a domestic one, and comic. And we register the cruelty of Cagney's gesture—its impact on the moll—much less than we do the boldness, the pure self-assertion. He is sitting at breakfast in striped pajamas, opposite girlfriend Mae Clarke. (Clarke, who gets it in the face here, is also the Molly Malloy who dampens everyone's fun in *The Front Page*.) She is complaining, wishing that he paid more attention to her. "I wish, I wish," he says murderously—"I wish I was a wishing well so I could tie you to a bucket and sink you!" He shoves the grapefruit in her face and walks off. This galvanizing gesture comprises both what we like most about his gangster—his wonderful, towering, unassuageable impatience—and what makes him most "dangerous": that blow against the moll is a gesture against romance as much as against domesticity, an almost iconic rendering of implacable, exultant contempt for and rejection of everything the girlfriend represents. And that reach across the breakfast table also propels him into an exit. Like all the jabbing, thrusting, punching he does—all those images of bursting, barely controlled energy we associate with him—it launches him into his own space.

Even here, where he is playing a thug and a psycho, that reach across the table, that launch into space, has a special grace. Cagney always liked to claim that he was primarily a song-and-dance man; and in fact that statement is a clue to his special quality, his distinctive effect. It accounts for the peculiarly lyrical edge that he gives even to his psychopaths. But he is not a "dancer" the way

Astaire is: that would imply an ability to partner that Cagney doesn't have. *He* works facing the audience—like all song-and-dance turns. It's a solo act. No regrets: it's simply the line he's in.

Still, it's mysterious. He is a conscious loner, but in a strange way he is also without self-consciousness: self-preening without narcissism, swaggering without vanity, "cocky," as he is always called, without eros. Cagney's egotism when he is "on" is both egregious and strangely pure, a public, not a private, event. Of course, nearly all the stars of Cagney's era have something of this public, almost pre-Freudian intensity: a quality that was largely to vanish with the stars of the fifties, with the Clifts and the Monroes and the Brandos. Cagney's energies are impressive and outsized but strangely impersonal.

It's that playfulness, that lightly disengaged quality—both his chief strength as a performer and his chief limitation—that most of his early movies exploit. And those qualities of his that the great gangster roles exploit—the doomed sweetness, the self-inflicted isolation, the prowling shrewdness, the insane high spirits—are really hyperbolic and tragic versions of the playfulness. Most of the time we don't feel his privacy or his essential aloneness as a tragic or even a regretable fact. It's a guarantee of his dignity, a function of his shrewdness: it goes with the smile.

And it makes him an *anti*-romantic. His self-assertion, his skepticism, his disengagement are all qualities that work against the romantic relation or effect. A famous still from *Taxi* (1932) shows him at Loretta Young's side, simultaneously leaning forward to kiss her hand and looking backwards to see how it's going over. This is the kind of love we can believe him making—shrewd and wised up. Playing it up for the lady and playing it down to himself: the con man's rapture. He can be lecherous of course, and lewdly inviting—as he is when he first meets Ann Sheridan in *Angels with Dirty Faces* or Joan Blondell in *Blonde Crazy*. In *The Public Enemy*, Jean Harlow calls him her "little boy" and presses his face down into her breast. The moment is affecting, even erotic, partly because it reminds us that the sexual necessity in the Cagney hero has a special and poignant force: it undoes him momentarily—it even calms him down.

COMPARE THE two great mug couples of early-thirties movie comedy: Cagney and Blondell seem in some respects like a "little people" version of their MGM counterparts, Gable and Harlow. The Warners couple is rounder, cuter, smaller—smarter, too—while Gable and Harlow seem to have the appropriate MGM size and authority, in longer, slower, more expensive-looking films. For example, no one could mistake the prison Harlow goes to in *Hold Your Man* (1933) for a Warners establishment: the MGM jail looks like an abandoned château, and has a distinct convent-school ambience.

But Gable and Harlow are also a good deal sexier than their Warners coun-

Clark Gable and Jean Harlow in MGM's Hold Your Man.

terparts. Gable relies on his female co-star more than Cagney ever could. An although he and Harlow are a bit too much alike to be a really romantic couple they *are* an erotic one. And so they bring the movie-tough tradition a bit close than anyone at Warner's could to the romantic mode.

In a way, Gable confronts the sophisticated tradition more squarely—an hostilely—than Cagney does. And precisely because Gable is a coarser, simple type, he seems a more authoritative representative of the tough style. Still, isn't until somewhat later on that he becomes the Gable who could reasonabl be called "the King" of the movies—a major comic figure and star. Somethin that happens most unmistakably when he is paired with a particularly "ladylike co-star: Jeanette MacDonald in *San Francisco* (1936) or Vivien Leigh in *Gor With the Wind* (1939), women whose gentility is aggressive in different ways an who offer him a certain incitement.

But the best tough comic of the early thirties—next to Cagney—is Jean Ha low. The moment when Harlow first leaps into full star life is neither as flamboy ant nor as famous as Cagney's grapefruit scene, but it is unmistakabl nonetheless. It happens some minutes into a movie called *Red-Headed Woman* (1932). The opening scenes have established her character—a scheming and sexy small-town girl—in a quick montage. (Trying on a dress: "Can you see through this?" Harlow asks the saleswoman. "I'm afraid you can, dear." "I'll wear it.") She meets her sidekick, Una Merkel, at a drugstore, and confides to her excitedly that she is going to deliver that day's office mail, which she has in her hand, to her handsome young boss's house, and in spite of the wife who lives there with him. Since she has failed to attract his notice in the office, she has decided to take this desperate measure. And she wants her friend to walk her to the boss's house. Her shocked friend, it seems, wouldn't miss this for the world. Off they go, Harlow striding ahead, with Merkel remonstrating breathlessly beside her: you can't do this, she tells her. But Harlow just strides purposefully, blissfully onward, with Merkel keeping up beside her. "Gee," says Harlow, striding toward the camera and in a tone of slight surprise, "I'm beginning to get a little *nervous*." She stops to make an adjustment, then turns to Merkel: "Here, hon, hold these." "I'd be nervous too, if I didn't have any more brains than you've got," says Merkel.

The sardonic friend gets the last word, of course, the topping line. Merkel is the "smart" one. And the joke, as is usual in Harlow films, is *on* Harlow. She is the "dumb" one, with her coarseness, her imperceptiveness, her lack of ordinary "nervousness." But she is "dumb" too because of spirit, energy, a strange kind of animal good humor. The point is complicated. Harlow striding toward the camera in this scene, clutching her steno pad and swinging her long arm, gazing happily and unseeingly ahead and talking about "nerves," is not just a comic sight but an inspiriting one too. She is in fact marvelous. And the joke about her dumbness is one way—partly defensive—of placing that marvelousness in the world of "smartness" and "nervousness" that the rest of us inhabit, with some regret.

But mostly Harlow's films have a hard time placing her at all: they alternate between celebrating her and putting her down. In *Red-Headed Woman*, her breakthrough film, she is made to be *very* simple and scheming—even a conventional "villainess" at times, as when, at the film's end, she whips out a gun and shoots the hero (Chester Morris) after he finally rejects her. But then the movie gives us *two* endings, as befits its warring tones: in the second and final one, Harlow is shown as the golddigger triumphant (the hero has survived his gunshot wound)—in the style of hardboiled comedy that at least part of the film belongs to—at a Paris racetrack with a very ancient rich husband and a sexy chauffeur (Charles Boyer in an early bit part). This uncertainty about how to take her, or at least how to show her, was something that would beset the rest of Harlow's career, brief as it was.

In her early, pre-MGM films, she looks almost dowagerish at times (she was nineteen when she appeared in Howard Hughes's *Hell's Angels*): the white hair, the heft of the bosom, the hard dark eyes. She is statuesque and inexpressive, sexy but formidable, even a little forbidding. Some of her early movies translate all this into "class"—i.e., upper-class-ness. In Hughes's *Hell's Angels* (1930) she is an English girl, and in Frank Capra's *Platinum Blonde* (1931) a Long Island debutante. *Platinum Blonde* is very much in the *Front Page* line, with a hardboiled reporter hero (Robert Williams) having to choose between a stuffy, ultraconventional marriage and the freebooting life of "the paper." Harlow is the stuffy, rich, insistently conventional fiancée—she is the blonde of the misleading title, but it is really the secondary role of the Other Woman, the Gail Patrick–Helen Vinson role, that she is playing here. It is Loretta Young who plays the tough, modern, breezy heroine that this sort of film requires: a woman reporter, one of the boys, and cute, too. Meanwhile, we get to see Harlow on a massage table, and to watch her from behind in a lengthy tracking shot as she takes a long, sauntering walk through palatial halls with the hero behind her. But she is not as improbable as you might expect as a society girl. She has natural dignity, and she translates her uneasiness in front of the camera into imperiousness. If her bearing isn't exactly regal, it's still impressive.

But it was MGM (not Capra, interestingly enough) that discovered she could be funny—first in *Red-Headed Woman* and then, even more triumphantly, in *Red Dust* (1932). Metro was the studio that built the remotest and grandest stars: they not only discovered her likableness but gave it the epic dimensions that star qualities got at that studio in the thirties. Today, her image in studio stills conjures up the whole era, or at least the era's daydream: the white marcelled hair, the penciled eyebrows, the clinging silk gown—a vision at once tacky and awesome. It was the tackiness that made the studio uneasy, especially as movies in general became more straitlaced and discreet. In the depressing *The Girl from Missouri* (1934)—with Harlow unwell during the shooting and looking more spookily unreal, more mannequinlike than ever—she spends the entire film trying to correct the impression, which everyone she comes across somehow gets, that she is the kind of girl who can be had without a wedding ring. By the time she has convinced them otherwise, the movie and its obsession have stirred up some very sour feelings in everyone.

A movie like *Bombshell* (1933) is less damaging because it's in the tough comedy style that suits her. And much of it—a film à clef concerning a Harlow-like movie star (Clara Bow, according to the screenwriter John Lee Mahin), her hangers-on and exploiters, and her various attempts (all comic) to live a "normal" life—is very funny and sharp. Lee Tracy (Broadway's original Hildy) is co-starred as the studio press agent who baffles not only her efforts to achieve ordinariness but all her attempts to find other boyfriends as well. The toughness is genuine and mostly uncompromised: jokes about motherhood and attendant sentimentalities, for example, centering on the movie star's project for adopting a baby. Nice . . . but still, there is something finally unpleasant in the film's making *such* a joke out of the idea of Harlow having a baby. The comedy at her expense—and it is almost all at her expense (the baby joke merely comes close to being the cruelest)—is saved from being unacceptably cruel only by the fact that Harlow performs it all with such enthusiasm and skill and intelligence, as if separating herself from the character in this paradoxical way, exorcising through the jokes all the possibilities in herself they stand for.

Her pictures veered between making fun of her and, later on, denying that there was anything at all unusual about her. In *Wife vs. Secretary* (1936) she is the nice, ordinary girl, destined for home and family, that in *Bombshell* she so ludicrously and hopelessly aspires to be, but this is more an act of studio willpower than a convincing piece of casting. On the whole, the roles that suited her best were the floozies—Gladys in the wonderful *Libeled Lady* (1936), and nearly all her early films with Gable.

There was, of course, a celebrated movie-star precedent for the comic-grotesque Harlow, and in *Hold Your Man* (1933), Harlow's costumes, her lines, even her style of delivering them, all seem quite clearly modeled on Mae West. Harlow decides it's warm enough in Clark Gable's apartment to take off her coat. "How 'boutcher hat?" he asks, grinning. "No thanks," she says, turning away with a slight inflection of hips and shoulders, "I'm pretty cool in the head." For a time there was even a plan to have West write Harlow's dialogue—fortunately abandoned. Mae West is a brilliant cartoon, a marvelous loony idea brought to full and complacent life in her screen persona. The Harlow persona is something else: fully human, staggeringly attractive, and moderately complicated. The funny thing about West is her absolute singlemindedness, both in greed and in lust. Sex, or indeed any other feeling, in Harlow isn't funny because it's single-minded but exactly because it isn't. In any situation, she is subject to distractions. In what is probably her best role, Vantine in *Red Dust* (1932), she finds herself having breakfast ("We haven't met yet, but don't let that stop you if you're hungry") with the straitlaced young wife played by Mary Astor—who discovers as they eat exactly "what" Vantine is. Astor rises coldly from the table and says good morning. "Arncha gonna drink your pineapple juice?" says Harlow, with a little frown. The question is both partly flip and utterly genuine: Harlow really cares about the answer. It's the sort of concern that sets her apart from almost everyone else in the movie—who all seem less human than she does—as well as from most other sex goddesses. She takes a direct unsentimental interest in the world around her, even in its irrelevancies. Unlike Marilyn Monroe and her imitators, Harlow seems not only sexually but humanly available and intact. She is the most intensely *likable* of all the "sex symbols."

Chester Morris and Jean Harlow in Red-Headed Woman *(above); Wallace Beery and Harlow in* Dinner at Eight.

"I'M POLLYANNA, the glad girl," she says by way of introducing herself, tartily, in *Red Dust*. Like almost every piece of dialogue she makes memorable, it's both a joke and not. In a way, she is a "glad girl." She has a smile like no one else in the movies—certainly no other glamour queen. It is not a "flattering" expression: it's broad, it always seems comically sudden, it scrunches up her features and all but closes her eyes—neither stirring nor languorous, even "radiant" seems an inadequate word to describe it when it happens. It invades her face. Like a feeling of relief—or an unmasking: a signal that we can all cut the crap—at last. Needless to say, in some of her movies (e.g., *The Girl from Missouri*) she doesn't smile much—she doesn't dare. This impulse to cut the crap, in spite of the makeup and the costumes and sometimes even the role—the necessity to be funny, friendly, and sensible whatever the odds against any of it being reciprocated or even noticed—this necessity seems nearly the deepest thing in Harlow's screen personality.

Vantine is a good-hearted but rather blatant whore, stranded on a rubber

plantation in Indochina, in love with Gable, the plantation boss, and having to endure his scorn while he pursues the respectable but rather hypocritical young woman (Astor) who is married to his foreman (Gene Raymond). The point of Harlow's role is its likableness. Slouching around in a wrapper ("I guess I'm not used to sleeping at night"), feeding the parrot, playing solitaire and cracking wise, reading "Little Molly Cottontail" to the ailing hero while his hand hippity-hops up her leg, she is the only one on the exotic premises who isn't either mealy-mouthed or dumb. She has the movie tough girl's wisdom and style. When Mary Astor is worrying out loud about her first yieldings to Gable—"It was just one of those excitement-of-the-moment things," Astor says (she has *her* style, too)—Harlow doesn't even look up from her solitaire: "Well, watch out for the next moment, honey," she says, playing a card. "It's longer than the first."

This is classical stuff, and she is very good at it. But she is more interesting when the joke is sexy. Harlow's relation to her own power to excite men is rarely simple. She is too shrewd and honest to be unaware of it, too friendly and nice to be preening about it. Entering a room in her wrapper: "Don't mind me, boys, I'm just restless," she says with her smile—she is neither vamping nor camping in the usual ways. The declared sexiness is funny because it is so opposite to practiced or whorish—because of her own sidelong relation to it. She is pleased, a little surprised, as amused as anybody at the stir she can create. Like her smile, like her "nerves" as she goes to confront her unresponsive boss in *Red-Headed Woman*, Harlow's feelings always seem to surprise her a little. She is comic partly because she seems constantly open to this surprise—in spite of the hard, almost calcified outer appearance.

Anger, however, is no surprise to her—not ever. She is always ready to scrap and yell, it seems. This combative streak was part of the studio's conception of her toughness. They decided she had a talent for denunciation and brawling, and in almost every Harlow movie from *Red-Headed Woman* on she gets a chance to blow up memorably at someone. In *Red-Headed Woman* she is even something of a virago—but never again. Like Cagney, she made her first impact as a star playing a role greatly less sympathetic than almost any she would play after that. When she gets angry in subsequent films, she is usually mightily provoked. Casual bitchiness, of course, was quite outside her range, and if she turned on another woman it was clearly jealousy or humiliation that prompted her. In *China Seas* (1935), an elegant Oriental woman, in the vicinity of one of Harlow's outbursts over Gable, makes a lofty (and unasked-for) observation: "The more violent the storm," she says to a companion, "the sooner it subsides." "When I want *you* to sound off, Golden Bells, I'll pull your rope!" Harlow rejoins exultantly.

It is this exultant quality that makes her so indelible in *Dinner at Eight* (1933) as Kitty, an ex–hat-check girl married to a thuggish and shifty entrepreneur played by Wallace Beery. Like most of Harlow's roles, Kitty is a character made up of conventions. This time, the signs spell dumb, venal, sluttish—the gold-digger who's hit the jackpot, sitting up in a luxurious satin bed, trying on pert little hats and eating chocolates (chocolate-eating while reclining was an unfailing sign of the type until well into the forties), screaming at her equally sluttish but very much slyer maid.

Why is Harlow so large and so definitive in this role? It is certainly not the role that accounts for it. Kitty is closer to the one-note venality of Lil in *Red-Headed Woman* than any other role of her starring career. In a way, Kitty doesn't even suit her: the part never calls on the energetic amiability of her other most indelible roles, notably the variants of Vantine. And Harlow's performance never challenges the simplicity, even the monotony, of the character's conception. She never even tries to make Kitty sympathetic. She just makes her loud—and richly funny.

The richness centers in her way with an epithet. Her insult style is eloquent, varied, inexhaustible, ranging from the way she speaks to her maid, addressing her alternately (and conversationally) as "yuh fool" and "yuh nitwit," to the vehemence with which she opens a discussion with her husband—"Listen, stupid," she begins—to the grimness with which in his absence she contemplates his taste in society. "That slug," she says, giving "slug" just the right kick-in-the-stomach heft, "never wants to meet any refined people." Later on, she reminds him of his first wife, the woman he "wore out" and buried in Wyoming when he was done with her. "That poor mealymouthed thing, with her flat chest, that never had the guts to talk up to yuh, yuh big windbag!"

It's only with this last information that we get any hint of an "explanation" (Kitty as an indirect avenger of another woman's martyrdom) for the unreasoning pleasure—the moral satisfaction, even—that audiences seem to get from Harlow's unleashed aggressions in this film. In fact, it's the same sort of satisfaction we feel when Cagney's stomach growls from drinking too much tea in polite company in *Jimmy the Gent*—or, even closer, when he wields the grapefruit in *The Public Enemy*. Watch Harlow winding herself up to insult Beery in *Dinner at Eight*. This is where her otherwise amiable energies go in this role—into the sheer, bursting force, the untrammeled delight and exultation, with which she lets him have it. . . . Not just "him"—it's the delight in coarseness, the defiance of gentility and "sophistication," of all polite constraints and graces—the whole let's-go-slumming pleasure and zest of the movies in general—that Harlow embodies in these scenes, and indeed in her whole career. She sounds this tough exultant note—the sound of the Hollywood genius, the movies' most authentic vein—more purely and sharply and triumphantly than any other star of her time.

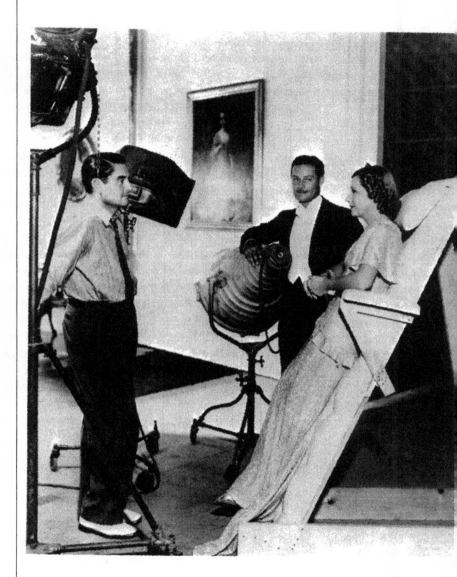

Leo McCarey and Irene Dunne on the set of The Awful Truth, *with Alexander D'Arcy.*

PART 2

The Romantic Comedy: Directors and Stars, 1934-1939

*Maurice
Chevalier,
Jeanette
MacDonald,
and Ernst
Lubitsch cele-
brate with the
crew of* The
Merry Widow.

1934: Turning Point | 6

Only the cinema is able in its most fantastic moments to give a sense of absurd unreasoning happiness, of a kind of poignant release: you can't catch it in prose . . . ——GRAHAM GREENE, in a 1935 film review

FOUR FILMS released in 1934 seem to mark the real beginning of screwball comedy. The first and most important of them was Frank Capra's *It Happened One Night*, which opened at New York's Radio City Music Hall on February 23 and played for one week ("Oscar Wilde's *Birthday of the Infanta*" was the spectacle attraction on the stage). The reviews were good but perfunctory, noting the usual Hollywood blend of the improbable (especially the newspaper sequences) with the familiar. Still, said the New York *Times* (Mordaunt Hall), there were "plenty of laughs" and some "bright dialogue."

It was, it seems, a film that no one had particularly enjoyed making—even Frank Capra, whose pet project it was from the beginning, when everyone told him that no one wanted to see another "bus picture" (the others having been flops). Clark Gable was fractious and disgruntled—he was being disciplined by Metro, sent to the Siberia of Columbia studio and Poverty Row picture-making. Claudette Colbert in 1981 remembered the filming as not especially pleasant, and she blamed this on Capra. Whatever the experience was, it wasn't long: the shooting was done in just four weeks, though the film itself, lasting an hour and three quarters, is almost dreamily overextended at times. For a comedy especially, its length was surprising. Capra would later claim that he was so tired of the whole thing that he couldn't bring himself to do the extra work of editing it down to a proper running time; he just wanted it off his hands and released. And so it was—with historic results.

The plot was familiar (runaway heiress), and the hero and heroine were standard types (tough reporter and crazy rich girl). What was new was something that went on between them at times, something harder to identify—something in the combination of love and toughness. Hero and heroine weren't condescended to (she wasn't really crazy, he wasn't really a mug), and they were more than equally matched. There was some new kind of energy in their style: slangy, combative, humorous, unsentimental—and powerfully romantic. Audiences everywhere were bowled over by it. So was the Motion Picture Academy later on, with an unheard-of sweep of all the major awards. There had never been a movie success like this before, so total and so utterly unexpected. Of course it was imitated—often by people who were not sure what exactly to imitate.

Not even Columbia knew. They really seemed to think that Howard Hawks's *Twentieth Century*, which they opened at the Music Hall just two months later (May 4), might have the same sort of success—another crazy comedy. But neither audiences nor reviewers took to it. Based on the Hecht-MacArthur Broadway hit, it was both raucous (its performing style) and sophisticated (its theatrical milieu) and had, as the *Variety* reviewer pointed out, no sympathetic characters at all. "General audience appeal" was "doubtful," said the same reviewer—accurately. But *Twentieth Century* was Carole Lombard's comic debut, and so it expanded the conception of what was possible to a movie's leading lady. If Lombard wasn't exactly (as has been often said of her) the first star to be both beautiful and funny at the same time, still, that's the feeling she gives you: that no beautiful woman has ever been quite so funny before in such an all-out way. Hawks's film was another sign that Hollywood was entering upon a new kind of comedy—comedy that was inspired by the styles and temperaments and skills of its most glamorous and romantic stars—and that a lot of those stars would have, as Lombard did, surprises in store.

Certainly William Powell and Myrna Loy did. His career had been flagging, hers going nowhere in particular—both of them at MGM—when director W. S. ("Woody") Van Dyke had the idea of putting them together in the film version of Dashiell Hammett's *The Thin Man*. Filming was completed in eighteen days—Van Dyke was famous for being fast ("One-Take Woody")—and the movie opened in the early summer (June 30 in New York). It was a success comparable even to *It Happened One Night* in the unexpected way it caught on with audiences. Early reviews remarked little beyond a certain pleasant conventionality: another lighthearted murder mystery, another sophisticated couple, another William Powell detective (he had been playing Philo Vance in a series at Warner Brothers). But "Nick and Nora" soon became a kind of national craze, and they made major stars out of Powell and Loy.

The Gay Divorcee—which opened at the Music Hall on October 12—was the first of the great Astaire-Rogers film cycle and their first starring vehicle. In the previous year's *Flying Down to Rio*, they were the comic second leads (Dolores Del Rio and Gene Raymond were the stars, and serious). Astaire was a cheerful Mr. Fixit sailor; Rogers was a chorus girl and band singer, performing risqué dipsy-doodle numbers like "Music Makes Me" ("My self control was something to brag about / Now it's a gag about / Town . . ."). They had small roles and

*"Lanky bru-
nettes with
wicked jaws"*:
*William Powell
and Myrna Loy
in* The Thin
Man.

almost no scenes together. But when they got up from their nightclub table to dance a brief section of an enormous production number called "The Carioca," the effect on audiences was to wipe everything else off the screen. This galvanizing, almost inadvertent debut meant that RKO would build their next picture around them. *The Gay Divorcee*—based on a show that Astaire had starred in on the London stage, *The Gay Divorce* (the Production Code required the title change on the grounds that there could be no such thing)—was tailored to their talents by the same production team (including producer Pandro S. Berman and director Mark Sandrich) that would turn out most of their subsequent films. It was a staggering success. Astaire and Rogers were a kind of apotheosis of the comic-romantic style—brash, breezy, and challenging—that seemed to be sweeping the movies by the end of 1934.

But Lubitsch that year—whose last Paramount film, *Design for Living*, had been a serious disappointment both commercially and critically—returned to scenes of early triumph, to Ruritania (or in this case "Marshovia") and another sound-stage version of Paris. The project brought together again his favorite screenwriter, Samson Raphaelson, and his favorite starring team, Chevalier and MacDonald. Lubitsch's Paramount contract allowed him one outside picture, and Thalberg at MGM had long been planning a sound film remake of *The Merry Widow*, filmed in 1925 by Erich von Stroheim and one of the studio's all-time hits. So Lubitsch came to Culver City, with much publicity and general fanfare. Thalberg scheduled the remake as an all-out spectacle, one of the most lavish, eye-popping extravaganzas in MGM history. It was in the event the studio's biggest-budgeted film* since *Ben-Hur* (though not as expensive as the same year's *Mutiny on the Bounty*). Filming took a near-record eighty-eight days (compare *The Thin Man*'s eighteen days, a record at the other end). The world premiere on October 12 at Loew's Astor in New York was accompanied by the sort of tumult that befits "the coronation of emperors," according to Andre Sennwald in the New York *Times*, including mounted policemen who "clattered up on the sidewalks and gallantly beat back the surging proletariat," and arc lights whose "weird blue mist was visible up and down Broadway." Sennwald was even more impressed by the film—by its wit, its performances, its spectacle. "All of the sets are consummately lovely," he wrote, "and a few of them are entrancing enough" to suggest "a paradise" beyond this world. "Everyone can now sit back and take a deep breath," he concluded. "The winter season has been royally crowned." But MGM presumably never took that breath. The winter season passed, and so did several more winters, and still Lubitsch's *The Merry Widow* hadn't recouped its enormous losses. It never did. The vast audiences that were responding to Astaire, and Powell and Loy, and Capra were staying away from Lubitsch's most ambitious and accomplished operetta film. He never made another.

"NO ONE has ever fully explained what gives this basically slight romantic comedy its particular—and enormous—charm," says Pauline Kael of *It Happened One Night*. "It's no more than the story of a runaway heiress (Claudette Colbert) and a fired newspaperman (Clark Gable) who meet on a long-distance night bus and fall in love." Ellie, the heiress, jumps her father's yacht in Florida and gets a bus to New York, where she plans to reunite with her aviator husband

* Over a million and a half. According to Aljean Harmetz, a budget of a million and a half was soon to become normal for a *big* MGM film, and eight weeks the normal shooting schedule.

("He's a fake, Ellie," says her father, and we know he's right). Reporter Peter Warne, who has just been fired for getting drunk and filing a story in "free verse," spots her as the escaped rich girl of all the headlines. Ellie thinks at first that he's just being helpful—she even thinks, though grudgingly, that he's kind of cute. She doesn't think he's on the make until a washed-out bridge forces the bus to stop at an auto camp and she finds out that he has registered them for the same cabin. She stands in the rain, holding a raincoat over her head—the manager, in passing, has just wished good night to her and her "husband"—and ponders this. Inside the cabin, Peter tells her that she needn't worry, that he's not interested in her that way, that he didn't have enough money to pay for separate cabins, and that if she tries to leave he'll notify her father. He offers her a deal: he'll keep her secret and even help her to get to her husband if she will give him the exclusive story, "all about your mad flight to happiness." She is standing by the door listening to all this and watching—incredulously—as he hangs a blanket from a clothesline he has strung between the two beds. She

Clark Gable and Claudette Colbert in Frank Capra's It Happened One Night.

stares. "That, I suppose," she says, "makes everything"—giving a feeble gesture toward the blanket, finding the right feeble phrase—"quite all right?" As
usual, disbelief is wasted on him. Since she refuses to move from her post by
the door, he proceeds to undress in front of her, giving a running commentary
as he does so ("I once knew a man who kept his hat on until he was completely
undressed. He wore a toupee."). She is soon on her side of the blanket. "Don't
be a sucker," he says gently. "The walls of Jericho'll protect you from the big
bad wolf." She prepares for bed, reluctantly and warily. She will, of course, wear
a pair of his pajamas.

She undresses in the dark. Gable, on his side of "the wall," lies with his hands
behind his head and stares at the ceiling. They are both just barely visible,
outlined and highlighted in the glow from their separate windows. Outside, the
rain pours incessantly (Capra thought it was sexy), streaking and beading the
windows, softening and diffusing the light. They lie in their beds in shadow, and
Capra cuts between them, conveying the intense mutual awareness, the gathering sexual tension. (Graham Greene wrote in a 1936 review of *Mr. Deeds Goes
to Town* that "Capra cuts as brilliantly as Eisenstein.") Each time in these alternating shots that the movie cuts away from Gable it cuts back to a slightly closer
shot of Colbert. The effect of this intensification (the device is almost invisible)
is breath-catching: a succession of mild, deftly registered little shocks, the
several-times-repeated jolt of a sudden unexpected nearness, making Colbert
look both powerfully glamorous and very vulnerable. The feeling of yearning in
this all-but-wordless passage is almost too much for the scene to sustain—until
Ellie has a thought. She sits up in bed: "Who are you?" she says. "Who me?"
he says with a slightly twisted smile (what's he going to pull now?). ". . . I'm
the whippoorwill that cries in the night. . . . I'm the soft morning breeze that
caresses your lovely face." Ellie smiles (not what she expected him to say)—
grudgingly. "You've got a *name*, haven't you?" She says. "Yeah, I got a name.
Peter Warne." "Peter Warne . . ." She repeats it ruminatively. Slight pause. "I
don't like it," she says decisively, nestling her butt into the bed and falling back
onto her pillow. Now they are *both* smiling—grudgingly. And there is one final
extreme close-up of Colbert as she sinks back onto her pillow and further into
darkness. Her face is only a shadowed outline now, until she moves her head
slightly and the camera catches a reflection of light in her eye—a gleam slight
but clear. Fadeout.

This is powerful filmmaking. Elegant too: the way it connects wit and yearning, going from the little smiles on each side of the curtain to the gleam in the
heroine's eye. And Gable's odd speech about the whippoorwill has a nicely precise and complicated tone: he is both alluding to a conventional romantic style
and establishing his own distance from it, a bit regretfully, but wry and humorous too. "I'm the soft morning breeze . . ." It's a legato version of his brashness.
The heroine understands him exactly, as her reluctant smile tells us. And when

he tells her his name, her surprising reply ("I don't like it") is her version of the brashness: a reversal, witty and unexpected. This exchange between them at the end of the scene is like a compact. It is also, given the extraordinary pressure of yearning the scene builds up, very sexy.

So much of the movie dwells, like this scene, on the mechanics and little suspenses of frustrated sex (Colbert flings her stockings over the "wall," Gable has to ask her to remove them, and so on) that it's remarkable that almost none of it seems prurient. But the atmosphere of yearning is too large and full a fact here ever to seem merely titillating or teasing. Joseph Walker's photography gives the world of the film a consistent refulgent, glowing-from-within quality— especially the night world, from the rain on the auto camp windows, to the rushing, glittering stream Gable carries Colbert across, to the overarching hay-stacks, moonstruck and sagging, that the couple find themselves sleeping under after they leave the bus.

There is a similar quality in Colbert's performance—of choked fullness and outer urgency, that mixture in her of primness and tactility which Capra seems to be the first of her directors to fully understand. Even when Ellie is insisting on the distance between herself and this upstart newsman, she is touching him. "I'll pay you," she says in the bus station when he first reveals his profession; "I'll make it worth your while"—her hand is on his chest and then on his arm. Colbert is one of those actresses who makes us feel her body, especially in the angle and set of her hips; she makes us aware in a special way of comfort and discomfort. She sits forward on her bus seat, with the roguish-looking Gable next to her, like a receptionist having a bad day. But when she falls asleep, she wakes up clutching his lapel, her head nestled against his chest. So that finally that gleam in her eye that Capra shows us at the end of the walls of Jericho scene—the smallest kind of detail, literally a glimmer—has the weight and momentum of the whole movie behind it.

The major social tragedy reflected by the film—the dislocation and uproot-edness enforced on Americans by the Depression—is treated with surprising matter-of-factness, even complacence. Everyone is on the move in this movie— even when they're off-screen (the aviator bridegroom, the millionaire father flying over the auto camp on his way home). What domesticity we see belongs to the auto camp, with people raking gravel in the morning and tending tiny plots of lawn. The blowsy, middle-aged women on line at the outdoor shower Colbert goes to all look emphatically at home: housewives whether they have houses or not. We don't get the feeling that people like this have left their homes so much as that they make them, or find them, on the road. The rootlessness is as much taken for granted here as its opposite might be asserted in another kind of movie (the kind Capra would go on to make, for example). It's not deplored, and yet it's certainly not glamorized.

There is, not surprisingly, a powerful undertone of melancholy through the

Peter Warne
(Gable) teaches
Ellie (Colbert)
how to dunk.

whole movie. It's not the whippoorwill that cries in the night here but the loco-
motive. Was there ever a movie, before or since, with so many unseen trains and
train whistles—haunting and mournful and always at night—on the soundtrack? Or a "gay comedy" with so many depressed sights in the background?
Those backgrounds are consistently, even conscientiously shabby. They are also
familiar and unremarkable, with that anonymous washed-out look that only very
familiar things acquire. Only at beginning and end does *It Happened One Night*
evoke conventional movie glamour: the Andrews yacht (at the start) and the
Andrews mansion and estate (at the end) "frame" the general drabness—the
buses and bus stations, the dusty country roads and dilapidated cabins. A world
of chintz curtains and traveling salesmen, of oilcloth and lunch wagons and
outdoor showers. Populated by thieves, mashers, and wise guys, sharpies looking for a fast buck, mean-faced housewives and their bratty children, truculent
landladies and their quashed, compliant husbands. It's such figures as these—
including the obligatory unlovely fat man—who sit on the bus, looking dispirited and isolate as they sway and creak along through the night and the unending
rain. Then suddenly these people start to sing a song—"The Man on the Flying

Trapeze"—and the bus becomes a scene of community. It's only for a moment, but the transformation is still amazing: one of those scenes that everyone who sees the film remembers, though it has no particular point and no function at all in the plot.

That transformation *is* the point, for Capra and for us. The world the movie shows us is a world waiting to be transformed. It's a peculiarly American landscape: what it shows us isn't exactly what it means—or values. Like the heart-stirring, oddly affecting plainness of certain midwestern Main Streets—broad, flat, unvarying—the drabness of *It Happened One Night* hides a kind of excitement: a deep belief in high spirits, in the ability of a joke or a song, a shared mood of elation or a witty inspiration, to transform and transfigure an unpromising environment. This landscape becomes something to triumph over—and its meanness becomes a measure of the triumph.

THEY ARE walking along a dirt road in the country: Ellie had been spotted on the bus and so they've been obliged to leave it. The camera follows them from behind in medium shot: Colbert is limping, clutching her purse and swaying on her heels; Gable carries a suitcase and his coat flung over his shoulder. She wants to know again, in a failing voice, what it is they are supposed to be doing. The answer is hitchhiking. But it's too early in the morning yet, he tells her, to expect any cars. "If it's just the same to you"—as she turns and walks out of the shot—"I'm going to sit right here and wait," she says, heading in the next shot toward a split-rail fence by the road. She climbs up and sits on it. Gable joins her, leans against the fence, and eats a carrot he has saved from the night before, cleaning it with his penknife, rather showily. Does she want some? "I hate the horrid things," she replies, though a bit regretfully (she is very hungry). Never mind: he chews and talks and cleans. He's going to write a book, he says. She doesn't doubt it. And he shows her—expansively, humorously, confident enough to mock his own confidence, and still dining on his carrot—the three important modes of flagging down a ride. "It's all in the thumb." There's the "short, jerky movement" (self-confidence), or "a little wider one" and a knowing smile (ribald comradeship), or "a long sweeping movement" and an even longer face (hard times). None of this—offered to a skeptical Colbert, perched on her fence, purse planted firmly in her lap, arms folded, face expressionless—ever really distracts him from his carrot, either the cleaning of it or the chewing: he is giving her a lesson *there*, too, in how to make do with little or nothing. Now a car approaches and he steps eagerly to the road. "Keep your eye on the thumb," he says over his shoulder, "and see what happens."

He presents both the thumb and an eager, open face—it's "movement number one"—but the car speeds noisily by. "I've still got my eye on the thumb," says

Colbert in the background, tonelessly—and somewhere a bird sings. "Something must have gone wrong," says Gable. "I guess I'll try number two." Colbert reclines on the fence now: "When you get up to a hundred, wake me up." He braces himself at the roadside, and not just one car but an explosion of cars goes suddenly by. Gable gestures futilely and frantically with his thumb, his hand, his arm, both arms—and finally just thumbs his nose as the last car shoots past him and off and away. Colbert is still reclining. He walks back to the fence. "I guess I won't write that book after all." She offers to try and he scoffs. "I'll stop a car," she says, "and I *won't* use my thumb." She gets down from the fence, pulls at her blouse in a businesslike way, and steps to the road—on her face a look of radiant vacancy. But something in her voice has gotten to him: "What're you going to do?" he says. "It's a little system all my own," she says as she looks down the road. And then, as a lone car approaches, she raises her skirt to well above her knee and pretends to be adjusting a garter, extending and displaying a very long and shapely leg. Close-up of leg. Close-up of car wheels grinding to a halt. Cut* to Gable and Colbert in the backseat of the open car, she looking happy, he looking depressed. She looks around at the passing scene, the very picture of motoring pleasure, occasionally casting a merry glance at him, the sore loser beside her.

A legendary sequence, of course—part of almost everyone's movie memory, of every TV tribute to the "golden age." In a way it's a pointless scene—like the song on the bus, it has no effect on the plot or its outcome. And it's so leisurely that we get to register things we haven't so clearly seen before in the styles of the two actors. Colbert's relation to objects, for example—the way she grasps them, settles into them. When she first perches on that fence, she clutches it with her hands and shifts her butt on it as if she were nestling into pillows—not so much a sensuous gesture as a practical one, an instinctive basic appropriation of an otherwise unwelcoming landscape. Gable's way with the same sort of landscape is to make hand passes at it, like a conjuror. And he has a conjuror's perilous balance, always working a trick of some kind: turning blankets into walls, carrots into meals, waves of the thumb into auto rides. While he stands and performs in the foreground, she sits behind him and lapses into herself, her shoulders slightly hunched, leaning forward and staring off. This image really crystallizes the difference between them, and it controls our expectation of the scene. That firm, literal hold on things is *her* way of managing them: sure, matter-of-fact, tactile. It's Gable who is dangerously off the ground—in orbit, even. We expect him to crash then, and he does.

But why does this outcome, when it comes—and Colbert's triumph—give such deep unreasoning pleasure? It always does. That's one reason everyone

---

*In fact it's a wipe, one of Capra's favorite cutting devices.

remembers the sequence. *Why* it does is a key to the way the film works at its richest moments, on levels below some of the apparent meanings in the script. Peter is cocksure of course—and has been through the film. But Ellie is arrogant and, being a rich girl, knows nothing about ordinary life. She thinks that a bus driver will wait for her if she just tells him to, or that a masher will leave her alone if she is just haughty enough in her manner to him. She has no idea about being broke, let alone being hungry and homeless. She's never seen poor people before, certainly not close up; but when she does, she gives the last of her money to them—to a needy mother and son on the bus. In short, she learns about reality (as we call it), and the Gable hero is her teacher.

Still, he is a very self-satisfied one. And his lessons have a sameness, a recurring point. He teaches not only about dining on raw carrots and hitching rides but also about how to dunk a doughnut ("Twenty million dollars," he exclaims, "and you don't know how to *dunk!*") and how to give a piggyback ride—as if to say that if you can't be rich, you can at least be fey. (Piggybacking, he tells her, is the mark of "a real human," and no rich person is ever good at it: the Capra version of class hatred.) But these lessons, beneath the surface chatter and the advertising package, are in a way dispiriting ones. This hero may have the manner and style of a conjuror, a man who works magic, but what he is in fact offering to work is the prosaic and commonplace. He is teaching the heroine how to be ordinary, how to fit in, how to look and act like everyone else. Both the plot and her character require this lesson, of course. But still . . .

But when Ellie stops that car with her leg display, all bets are off. Suddenly we are on another level of challenge and risk and funniness. It's not just the fact of her triumph but the nature of it. Where he had been proposing the plausible and ingratiating—all those mingy, wheedling faces and gestures with the thumb—she does something large and outrageous. Ellie, we recognize, goes farther than he ever could: she is unconventional and he is not, for all his air of risk and bravado. She could have stopped *forty* cars if she'd taken all her clothes off, he reminds her sullenly as they ride along. "I'll remember that when we need forty cars," she says, with that same look of radiant vacancy she had when she first stepped to the roadside. *She* is the magical one, then. And that fact has a lot to do—paradoxically—with the way she holds on to the fence when she sits it, the way she grasps and settles into things, while the hero chats and flies high. Ellie has—like the great screwball heroines who succeed her—the freedom and magic that belong to a sensible, down-to-earth, no-nonsense view of things. He may know a lot, but she knows what stops traffic.

This same pair, the spoiled rich girl and the hardboiled reporter, had been principal figures in an earlier collaboration between Capra and his favorite screenwriter, Robert Riskin: *Platinum Blonde* in 1931. In that film Robert Williams is the wisecracking newsman and Jean Harlow is the society girl he falls in love with, while Loretta Young, another reporter, loves him. Young is the film's real heroine (Harlow, as I said earlier, is really an Other-Woman figure), and she gets the hero at the end, once his eyes are opened to the humiliation of being a rich girl's husband. *Platinum Blonde* has almost all the elements of screwball comedy—the characters, the settings, the "madcap" stunts, as when a wonderfully raffish group of newspaper types invade Harlow's stately home, hell-bent on a party. It has almost everything but the élan. The spirit of *Platinum Blonde* belongs unmistakably to a movie era before *It Happened One Night*. The earlier film's central adventure, for instance—the romance between the reporter and the high-born beauty—turns out badly. It's like the way that party ends—when the stuffy types come home and throw everybody out. The movie is very aware of class lines, and even the lines created by differing temperaments and backgrounds: the hero doesn't belong in that sort of family or house or world, it tells us, and neither indeed do his friends. They are all better off going back where they came from, just as he himself is better off, as it develops, with a girl from the office. In this respect, *Platinum Blonde* is typical of early-thirties comedy: those Cagney and Harlow films, for example, which get a lot of their laughs from noting just such lines between people and such futile attempts to cross them as Cagney having high tea or Harlow meeting "the ritz."

The girl from the office, on the other hand, invites the hero to run just those risks that his society wife opposes—he is writing a play, as so many newspapermen seemed to be doing in those days, both in life and in fiction. So that when Williams finally walks out of Harlow's Long Island mansion, he is choosing adventure over security. But this climax isn't really effective: Williams' choice is framed too much in terms of things *not* working out. It's been clear from the start, in fact, that his marriage to Harlow is a mistake, that he should never have left his buddies or his job, that happiness is in his own backyard. But all these sentiments are, so to speak, pre-screwball—and dampening. On the surface, *Platinum Blonde* may endorse risk taking, but its feeling is the reverse of adventurous. The main sense it gives is of limits, problems, "realities." It's a very accomplished movie—with some accomplishments superior to *It Happened One Night*'s: brighter dialogue, a more interesting hero, especially in Robert Williams's wittily eccentric playing. But none of this counts for much next to the excitement of Capra and Riskin's "bus picture." Compare the climax of *It Happened One Night*, when Ellie breaks out of *her* mansion.

That climax takes a lot of setting up—one reason the movie gets overextended. Peter and Ellie are estranged over a misunderstanding (he's gone off to arrange his job so they can get married; she thinks he's deserted her), and Ellie is about to marry King Westley (Jameson Thomas) in a huge public ceremony on her father's estate. It's never entirely clear why she is doing this, since she is already married to him; but never mind—Capra knows what *he's* doing.

Westley plans to arrive at the ceremony by landing his autogyro on the great lawn. ("Personally, I think it's silly," says Ellie's father. "GROOM TO LAND ON BRIDE'S LAWN" says the headline.) He alights from the helicopter, in long shot, and is instantly surrounded by top-hatted well-wishers. They all cross the lawn to the house. And the society wedding—that occasion of ultimate conventionality—begins. It's an al fresco event, with the white-surpliced priest waiting at a very High Church sort of altar on the lawn. The organ plays the wedding march and the procession from the great house begins: ranks of men in black followed by solemn-faced flower girls in white, marching past banks of flowers and rows of guests. When at last we do see Ellie and her father (Walter Connolly) coming warily along, it's with some relief (Capra is a master of this sort of postponement), like a glimpse of friends in a room filled with strangers. Andrews is talking to his daughter out of the side of his mouth: telling her to blow this place, to marry Peter, who really loves her, to forget about Westley ("I can buy him off for a pot of gold"). "If you change your mind," he tells her finally, "your car's waiting at the back gate." They are at the altar. "Dearly beloved," intones the priest. But when he comes to the big question—"Ellie, wilt thou have this man to thy wedded husband so long as you both shall live?"—Ellie, who has been looking increasingly furtive and trapped, rolls her eyes madly, does a panicked little curtsy toward the priest and picks up her skirt, and runs: dashing in long shot, with cries going up and flashbulbs popping and news cameras turning, across the same lawn Westley had landed his autogyro on—her magnificent white veil streaming out behind her, as she makes for the waiting black limousine. She jumps in, shuts the door on her veil, and speeds off. Into the distance.

It's rousing, as everyone who's seen the movie knows. This final image of the heroine sprinting across the lawn, running out on her own wedding, taking off in full bridal sail, and even (since we never see her again, though the film has minutes to go) bursting out of the movie itself, seems when it happens not only something marvelous but a gesture of total conviction—the natural fulfillment of a film whose dominant motives are yearning and traveling. This ending became an emotional reference point not only for audiences but for the comedies to come. This new kind of comedy wasn't just funny: it was also exhilarating.

I T'S INSTRUCTIVE to watch Carole Lombard in *Twentieth Century* with her co-star, John Barrymore—whom she worshipped and reportedly learned from. The contrast between performances helps to define what's remarkable about Lombard at this point. When producer Oscar Jaffe (Barrymore) bursts into the apartment of his star and protégée, Lily Garland (Lombard), and discovers her attempting to go out for an evening without him, he is inconsolable. "What are you going to do?" she says. "Nothing," he replies grandly, "—while *you're* here." But as he stands at the window, hoping, it seems, to be deterred from jumping, Lombard starts to creep past him and out, with a look of fierce, crazed determination that becomes the funniest thing in the scene. They are both playing in the same familiar theatrical style: two roaring phonies in a comedy of hammy exaggeration and hysterical excess. But where Barrymore's hysteria is daunting, deranged, and wildly inventive, it's always a spectacle. Lombard's is an experience, something we don't just watch but get involved in too. There's a certain weariness, a deep disabling knowingness, at the bottom of Barrymore's effects. But when Lombard does that mad-eyed creep to the door, she seems really unsprung, desperate and recklessly exposed. We rarely feel that Barrymore's outrageousness puts him in any real danger on the screen. Not so with hers. Her excesses, although fully as calculated as his, seem to have a deeper, fresher source, a more dangerous life. In fact, she owed this all to him—or so she claimed. It was Barrymore, she said, "who taught me to 'let go,' to abandon myself to my part." And he in later years would call her the greatest actress he ever worked with.

Carole Lombard and John Barrymore in Howard Hawks's Twentieth Century—*"I'm going to start kicking him."*

Ben Hecht and Charles MacArthur adapted the screenplay from their own

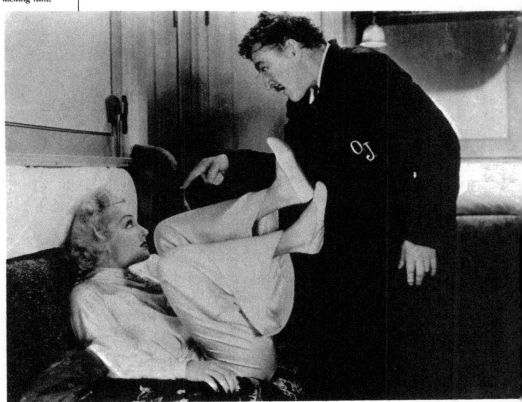

1932 Broadway hit, their biggest success since *The Front Page*. *Twentieth Century* is on the same model, in fact—in a theatrical instead of a newspaper setting. Just as in *The Front Page*, an unscrupulous and flamboyant boss is trying to reclaim an errant protégé(e). Oscar, the impresario, has been down on his luck since his star, Lily, left him (she is going to Hollywood). And so desperate measures are required, all of them more or less taken—including signing the Oberammergau Players for a Broadway engagement, passing a phony check from a demented millionaire who hands out "Repent!" stickers, and when all else fails (and it does), pretending to be dying—as everyone speeds cross-country on the Twentieth Century Limited train, Chicago to New York. The entire play takes place on the train, but the movie is almost half over before the characters even get to the station. In the movie we see the Oscar-Lily affair from its beginning—when she is Mildred Plotka, and he discovers her at an audition, casting her in the starring role over everyone's protests and making her an overnight star. We see them rehearsing, quarreling, making love, and breaking up when his possessiveness (he has had her phone tapped) becomes too much for her. The movie's Lily goes through several stages, then—from yearning young actress to sudden star to a very tough lady of the theater, looking sluttish in step-ins, striding in a fury past her swan-boat bed and stepping into the first dress "in three years that doesn't make me look like a Quaker."

It's a bravura performance, but it's also something more—something to do with Lombard's talent for *infectious* craziness. When she is quarreling with Oscar in her compartment on the train—she is sitting on the bed and he is in the doorway—she slumps down against the compartment wall (she has fallen there out of laughter over his Passion Play idea) and kicks out and up at him with her feet. He berates her. She listens fiercely—he accuses her of "traveling with a gigolo"—glaring up at him from her slumped position below. And as he talks—he calls her "vulgar little shop girl"—she revolves her feet in the air like dangerous pistons, "firing" them at him with little inchoate cries of rage as he bobs back and forth in the doorway flinging his insults. She is like a comic maenad in this film. That revolving of her feet in the air not only looks funny, as it's meant to, but *feels* inspired—a detail as natural and relieving as the choked cries of attack that accompany it. (Whenever Lombard began a new film after that, she would send Howard Hawks the message: "I'm going to start kicking him!") The heroine of *Twentieth Century* may have been drawn, as the movie reviews noted, without redeeming qualities, but Lombard gives her a redeeming recklessness. And this audacity came from an actress no one really expected it from—incredibly, *Twentieth Century* was her thirty-fifth film. More than that, Lombard showed ways to be funny that went farther toward abandon and transport than any leading lady before her had gone. Her zaniness in this performance is less like an aberration than a fulfillment. And she was really just beginning.

Nick and Nora (Powell and Loy) with their Christmas presents in The Thin Man.

THE MOVIE of *The Thin Man* was, as often happened, almost a cartoon ver-sion of its source, the distinguished Dashiell Hammett detective novel. The screenplay by Frances Goodrich and Albert Hackett makes the conventional murder-mystery plot even more conventional. "Suspects" (pronounced in the movie with the accent on the second syllable) multiply with almost every scene except the final one, in which they all assemble for a ritual showdown and un-masking. But any suggestion of the novel's mordancy—its ability to evoke a real corruption and to make us feel that it is pervasive, inescapable, built into the "civilized" arrangements its characters live under—is banished from the film. As a result, so also is some of Hammett's most vivid characterization—partic-ularly his Mimi Jorgenson, the scheming and avaricious widow of the missing man, the woman whose baroque duplicities are so funny and central in the book. In the movie she is a crude and boring grotesque, in both the playing (by Minna Gombell) and the writing. In fact, there is only one way in which the film is *not* a diminishing and coarsening of the book: Powell and Loy's Nick and Nora are even richer and more compelling figures than Hammett's. (He was arguably more interested in Mimi anyway.)

Someone has given Nick Charles an air rifle. He is lying in pajamas and robe on a couch in his hotel suite and shooting at the balls on the Christmas tree. Nora sits nearby in a fur coat—another Christmas present—and watches him dispassionately. This short, wordless scene is one of the high points of *The Thin Man* and one of the great moments of thirties movie comedy. In some ways it's a conventional scene. Its basic components are both banal and "cute": the grown-up hero behaves like a mischievous boy in front of his "mom" of a wife, who is disapproving but indulgent. What saves the scene from such archness? It *reminds* us of those banalities, but it doesn't convey them. For one thing, William Powell is so far from being or suggesting a boy that he can act like one and make such behavior seem like an essay in stylish (and rather cold) craziness rather than a move toward ingratiation. We can believe that this Nick Charles—who in general "plays" quite convincingly—might want to shoot the decorations off a Christmas tree. But we can never believe that he might think of such behavior as appealing or try to charm us with it, as another sort of actor might do in such a scene. Powell is at such an enormous distance from the thing he's mimicking here that he achieves a pure and controlled preposterousness.

After shooting out the hotel-window glass, he curls up on his couch, and then uncurls as if just waking up and says, "Where am I?"—all under Loy's unblinking and unamused gaze. And the close-ups of Loy looking at him are stunning ones: her beauty in this sequence seems almost hallucinatory. Yet her face is in some final way unreadable. The countenance she turns on her cut-up husband here is a deadpan one. It expresses nothing so clear as disapproval or sarcasm or even ruefulness. It suggests, rather, some kind of ultimate female resignation—so deep as to cast only the slightest shadow across her face—and it is very funny.

People said that Powell and Loy made even marriage seem like fun. But then it's a special sort of marriage they show us: rich, idle, childless—unless you count Asta, the dog. *The Thin Man* sets the pattern by which screwball couples always have an animal of some kind instead of a child. They drink, go to night-clubs, walk the dog, answer the door. They live in a hotel; at the end they leave town on a train. It's her money they are living on. There is no question of his being too proud for that: he is delighted—as he so often tells her. Nick is a "retired" private eye. No mug certainly, but he comes from the world of mugs, from the world of Cagney and Harlow movies. This is the world he introduces Nora to—at least when she insists, which she always does. He never wants to "take the case"; she always wants him to.

Certainly "the case" is peripheral to what interests us: those privileged moments between the two of them when they sound that same note of tough, chagrined tenderness that the couple in *It Happened One Night* evoke. But in *The Thin Man* that sound is a fully elaborated style between two people, in dialogue taken verbatim from the novel. Not my type, says Nick about another woman. "You got types?" says Nora, wide-eyed. "Only you, darling," he replies. "Lanky brunettes with wicked jaws." Later she tries to stop him from going off on a dangerous errand. "It's a dirty trick," she says, "to bring me all the way to New York just to make a widow out of me." "You wouldn't be a widow long." "You *bet* I wouldn't!" "Not with all your money." "Sugar" is his improbable way of addressing her—with a slight sardonic broadening of the final syllable: "Sug*ah*." The sarcasm is light but palpable—but directed at who or what? Just as with those amused sidelong glances she is always casting at him: we're not always sure why she's so amused, though we never doubt she has reason. Their humorous, slightly sardonic appreciation of one another is never sharper, it seems, than when the other's poise is being tested or severely shaken in some way—whether by gunsels or cops or importunate young women or even by Asta pulling too hard on his leash. This, in fact, is the way Nora makes her entrance into the movie: pulled off her feet by the dog and sprawling into the middle of a crowded bar where Nick is doing his usual drinking. She is somehow imperturbable. "Tommy, I don't usually look like this," she says to Nick's companion. "I've been Christmas shopping." And we get to see Nick's delighted recognition of both her embarrassment and her aplomb. ("The dog is well trained," he assures the head waiter.)

They embody a deep witty fastidiousness. The characteristic Nick-and-Nora joke is one, like the Christmas tree scene, where we're reminded of all the familiar possibilities in a familiar situation, only to find them all rejected for something lighter, richer, funnier. Take the way Nora discovers her husband in the arms of another woman—at their Christmas Eve party. Nick takes Dorothy Wynant (Maureen O'Sullivan) into the bedroom to talk. She is hysterical and waving a gun around, which he takes from her. "Oh, Nick!" she cries and collapses in his arms. The bedroom door opens, and there is a sudden dramatic pan of the camera to Nora in the doorway. She looks at this scene—ambiguously, widening her eyes. The camera pans back to Nick, holding Dorothy and looking back at Nora, with Dorothy's head buried in his chest. "Caught"—he makes a triumphant face at Nora and hugs Dorothy tighter. Back to Nora, who makes a face back at him and enters the room.

But that first swift pan of the camera to Nora in the door doesn't really evoke the *expected* suspense: uh-oh, the wife! Our suspense is about how Nora can possibly react to such a conventional "discovery," since we know that she can't or won't react conventionally (we don't suppose she'll misunderstand what she sees) or—and even more importantly—*un*conventionally (this isn't an "open" marriage). That's why the ambiguous look with the widened eyes is so funny and gratifying when it comes: it resolves the "suspense," underscored by the camera, in the right witty way. And the whole joke reminds us, very elegantly, of something else: our clear sense of how impossible it would be for Nick, even temporarily, to prefer a Dorothy to a Nora.

What *The Thin Man* evokes is not so much (as the conventional account of its magic has it) the compatibility of marriage and romantic love as the compatibility of romantic love with such supposedly unromantic qualities as humor and shrewdness and poise. This is what makes Nick and Nora unlike the couples in Lubitsch or Molnár who are made more or less ridiculous by love and its attendant emotions. Sophistication in the continental mode implies being absorbed by romance, being occupied by it even to the exclusion of everything else—but at the same time not taking it quite seriously, or at least taking it with a pinch of salt, with that leavening of worldly knowledge and cynicism that distinguishes a grown-up sensibility from an adolescent one. What felt new about Nick and Nora in 1934 was almost, it would seem, too apparent to be clearly said: they embodied a sophistication that was not a defiance of serious feeling but an expression of it.

T HE FIRST meeting of Fred Astaire and Ginger Rogers in *The Gay Divorcee*, their first co-starring film, is—like all their subsequent "first meetings"— ingeniously accidental and highly unpromising. *And* it makes her mad. Astaire is debarking from an ocean liner, and Rogers is on the dock meeting her aunt. She has caught her skirt in a steamer trunk, and he is trying both to assist her and to detain her. He manages only to tear part of her skirt off—making possible several amiable dumb jokes of the sort the script specially favors ("A man tore my skirt off." "Anyone we know?"). In any case, she disappears before he can learn her name (it's Mimi Glossop), and he resolves to search all London for her.

Now he is in his hotel room, where he has just explained to his comic sidekick, a dithering divorce lawyer named Egbert (Edward Everett Horton), how truly desperate his case is. Horton leaves—and Astaire sings. The song and dance that follow are, says Arlene Croce, "the number that first defined the Astaire character on the screen." The song, "A Needle in a Haystack" by Con Conrad and Herb Magidson, is the sort that Astaire characteristically transfigured: a plaintive, banal, faintly throbbing ballad, uptempo and full of odd mournful energy. "It's just like looking for a needle in a haystack . . . / Still I've got to find you." He sings it now in profile, in a high-angle shot, seated on the couch and clenching his fist for emphasis: "I've *got* to find *you*." Astaire doesn't just sing the song, he strains at it. Until its oddities become expressive, especially the melody's recurring and irrelevant emphasis on the word "It's"—a high, very extended note from which the rest of the phrase descends ("*It's*—just like looking for a needle in a haystack . . ."). This is the note that Astaire rises on, turning his back to the camera and walking to the balcony, still singing. The rise is dramatic, both light-elegant and powerful. He's not just straining now; he's floating too.

His valet (Charles Coleman) enters—the first of several such entrances in the number—holding a mirror in his hand and some ties on his extended forearm. Astaire whips off his dressing gown, throws it in a fancy hike from behind his back, and with a spillover of some of the growingly happy energy the song is about ("Still I've got to find *you*" has become less clenched, more buoyant), he selects a tie. He is going out: this number announces Astaire in one of his most characteristic relations to choice and action. Do we ever think of him as choosing to stay home? Or even of being glad to get there, as Powell's Nick Charles is, with his resistance to the world outside his hotel (he's been there too much), his picture-long resistance to taking the case? Astaire, on the other hand, is always on the edge of flight, poised to take off.

And soon he does—in a qualified way. The dance that follows the song draws us inside Astaire's own state of concentration, makes us feel all its pressures and countertensions as well as its purpose and force. He dances (just as he selects a tie) *because* he's got to find that girl. It's beyond logic and perfectly clear. He is now, his tie tied, at the fireplace. He taps the mantel with his fingers and the base with his toes—testing and in control. Then he walks, or, rather *is* "walked": in an odd turned-out traveling step, ending with a look behind himself, as he finds himself (surprise) away from the mantel and on the floor. But a happiness to get there, clearly. The dance—in its oddness—now begins. The music tootles jauntily, easy and perky. Astaire matches the perkiness, but not quite. As in his singing, there's a sense of straining against things. It's not a graceful lyric dance, nor is it a jaunty vaudeville turn; it's something in between. The concentration seems suspended *between* the two styles; the point is to preserve it. There are movements, hectic and fragmented, that seem to threaten it. Like the way Astaire now echoes that opening "walk"—with an odd, awkward kind of butt-switching step that seems to turn in on itself and "go nowhere," a churning rather than a traveling step. Again and again Astaire makes us feel the weight and heft and difficulty of movement—all the more to feel the takeoff when it comes, the lift and buoyancy.

This tension and alternation form the pattern of the whole dance as it develops. A baggy-pants flight. A kind of ecstatic clodhopping. A pirouette—followed by a shuffle. A leap—that ends in a buck-and-wing crouch and clatter. He takes off into the air—and flaps his elbows as he does so, storklike. Part of what this dance is about is an excitement that is almost too much to support. He seems at times almost to *sink* under the dance itself. The combination of buck-and-wing crouch and balletic flight becomes inexpressibly eloquent and beautiful. "Still I've got to find *you* . . ."

But it's also a dressing-to-go-out dance. The valet enters with a coat and

Astaire dances into it, puts a flower in his buttonhole, and vaults over the couch—all in the same miraculous motion. Back at the fireplace, then back onto the floor: the excitement of the music grows. And just as he falls again into one of those sinking, shuffling motions that seem almost to pull him into the floor, he is suddenly, heart-stoppingly in the air, in the number's single gesture from the vocabulary of classical ballet: in the air, on an angle, in a quick beating of feet. Then down again—the orchestra throbs and pounds as he lands—and just as he seems about to sink once more, he is in the air—again. These battements are always in counterpoint to the band's insistent, jazzy drumbeats—and

Astaire and Rogers at the end of the "Night and Day" dance i The Gay Divorcee.

although he repeats this leap with battement no less than three times, each time it seems startling—and wondrous. Astaire is not only dancing a feeling here but his relation to it as well—not only dancing "spontaneously" out of his own excitement (compare Gene Kelly's intentionality, for a different kind of effect) but beyond and around it, too, not only sinking under it at times but at times rising briefly, sublimely above it. He's done now: the valet brings him his hat and rolled umbrella, and he's out the door.

Of course he finds her, in one of those brushes in which he is all chipmunk eagerness, she is all bristling resistance—a resistance so marked and seemingly implacable that it presents a certain mystery, even in this initial film. She gives in, however, when they dance together. This happens much later: they meet accidentally for the third time at a seaside hotel. Rogers is there in the cause of her divorce, to rendezvous with a paid corespondent, and is doing her best not to be seen. But Astaire does see her: from a stairway high above the hotel café he spies her sitting below at a table with her aunt Mrs. Ditherwell (Alice Brady). Rogers flees in a panic. He follows her, just as the familiar Cole Porter strains begin on the soundtrack. He catches up with her at the esplanade, and in front of a back-projected ocean and moonlight he sings to her—"Night and Day."

And even at the height of the great romantic dance that follows, she manages to look suspicious of him. As the first orchestral drumbeat sounds ("the beat-beat-beat of the tom-toms"), he grasps her by the wrist when she tries to leave the dance floor and does a kind of supplicating step at her feet, crouching with his torso and flicking his legs out behind him in a quick now-you-see-it-now-you-don't shuffle and tap. The abasement is almost canine, adoring spaniel eyes and all, and we recognize that mixture of abashment and exultance she inspires in him. Later on in the dance, when Astaire repeats that same supplicating step but with a more confident manner and a more upright stance, and then Rogers responds with an answering version of the same step, the effect is stunning. Abasement overcome: exultance—or close to it—pure.

But never *quite* pure: she is always trying to leave him in this dance. As in every subsequent such dance, she is resistant and reluctant. But her reluctance in "Night and Day" has an extraordinary way of shading into backbends, into motions and gestures of consent. So that her resistance at times seems mysteriously continuous with her submission.

His problem in the dance is to hold her strange, dreamy attention, once he has caught it with that crouching, doglike shuffle. His attention—on her—never wavers, although the restless, changeable music is full of abruptnesses, sudden shifts of tempo and volume. His eyes never leave her. The step below may be quick and elated, flashy and high-spirited, but Astaire's gaze is grave, fixed, imploring. At one point they separate in order to do a jumping strutting step side by side. Rogers, rolling her hips and leading with her shoulders, looks at the floor, absorbed in her own movement. Astaire, doing the same step at her side, is absorbed in her. They are both in their different ways solemn, stepping out in this jaunty jazzy mode as if meeting a destiny.

Suddenly there is another shift in the music's volume and tempo, and now she looks, for a change, directly at him. He responds to the opportunity by doing a pirouette and a tap: she responds in kind—then turns suddenly to leave, like someone who has just remembered an appointment. He follows and grabs her by the wrist again. She looks startled at this, and her hand goes to his face: he staggers backward as if struck. She stares at this sight—this is a dream, after all, and she is a dreamwalker. But instead of going off the way she's headed, she runs back again to the balcony where he's just sung to her. Astaire then does a remarkable thing: a swift sidling step, one quick oblique movement, up the stairs to her side. He grasps her hand again, more gently this time. She looks back over her shoulder, but he leads her back down the steps and onto the floor—for the dance's climax.

The paradox is that he is dancing her not only into submission but into a kind of independence. All the gravest moments of the dance are those moments when he must leave her, must dance by her side, must watch for a step that answers his. In spite of his own ease and dexterity, he achieves actual nonchalance only when the dance is over (his famous gesture with the cigarette case); only then is he sure of her. Now the music heats up and they are on the dance floor. He twirls her around and supports her in a jump. Then he echoes that supplicating step by which he detained her at the beginning: she responds—it's that exultant effect I cited just above. The music swells: he has hold of her now. And suddenly that constant impulse toward flight of hers gets dramatically resolved by one swift, stunning, many-sided stroke: he swings her out, his hand over her head, until she is framed by her own arms—so that she is all at once going away, holding on to him, and enclosed by her own movement. There it is: in the midst of this stormy accelerating climax, Astaire has struck just the right fleeting image (it's gone almost before you can catch your breath again) to fulfill and resolve all the tensions of the dance. This sudden inspired "framing" is also the fulfillment of all that anxious, grave attention he has been showing her. He eases her onto a nearby couch and the dance ends.

After this, their next dance in the film, the overpowering "The Continental," seems remarkably appropriate. A big production near the movie's end was obligatory after *Flying Down to Rio*'s sensational "Carioca." These numbers (there's another one in *Top Hat*, "The Piccolino") conventionally enlist great masses of dancers, numerous singers, and seem to go on forever. "The Continental" is the longest (seventeen and a half minutes, a record) and spreads its dancing cast of anonymous hundreds over the movie's tallest, most splendid, most art deco–dreamlike set, the great esplanade of the Brightbourne Hotel. Astaire and Rogers, escaping the vigilance of Erik Rhodes, the corespondent, spin through the hotel's revolving glass doors and rush down its great staircase to join the fun.

They are only there for a few minutes, but it's enough. This number is a public event. And though their special genius would always seem most potent in their dances "alone"—numbers like "Night and Day," simply and even minimally staged and shot—it's still appropriate that the intensities of their greatest dance in this film should be succeeded by a public celebration like "The Continental." It's crucial to the kind of romance that this couple embodies that they should enter the world with it too—that they should find a public form for their ardor.

For the romantic couple represented by these new, dashing, specifically American "sophisticates"—by Powell and Loy, and Astaire and Rogers—implies a special relation to worldliness and public forms. They have neither the cynicism of the Lubitsch couple, nor the entrenchment in a specific world of privilege of the Noel Coward lovers: the Hollywood movie variants of these figures participate in a world they also somehow elude, and are finally untouched by. Astaire and Rogers dance among anonymous couples—but they would never think of refusing the dance. They rush to it eagerly: and they define themselves as clearly by their participation *there* as they do when they dance in a deserted ballroom.

They embody a romantic idea that welcomes the public world, but on curious, even paradoxical terms. *The Front Page* is in their background: and though Hildy and Walter Burns are certainly more than touched by the world they inhabit, the paradox and the result are similar—they have found a way to connect with that world which also sets them apart from it. "Oh, Nicky," cries Nora, embracing her husband at the end of their Christmas Eve party, as the hoods and molls they've invited raise their terrible voices in song, "I love you because you know such lovely people!"—although that hardly seems a plausible phrase for the floozies and plug-uglies they are surrounded by. But we believe her: she values him—and so do we—partly because he is surrounded in this way, by an alien world. These romantic couples are both alone together and surrounded, by their choice. At the end of *The Gay Divorcee*, when Astaire and Rogers have at last no more wonders to show us, they do a short reprise of "The Continental" in their hotel suite. It's also an echo of the "Needle in a Haystack" solo: now Astaire dances *her* over the furniture, too. They are packed, they are dressed in hats and coats, they bow off past a lineup of bellboys. The final point of *The Gay Divorcee* is the right one: they're in love—and they're going out.

WHAT A strangely beautiful film Lubitsch's *The Merry Widow* is. It's the same sort of experience as the earlier operetta films, and yet it's also very different. Some of the differences are easy to locate. It's an MGM, not a Paramount, film. And though Lubitsch has worked with big-studio largesse before, he hasn't done so on quite this scale. It gives a new eerie amplitude to the familiar effects: MacDonald isolated on the screen now, a small bonneted figure in black, against a creamy expanse of blindingly white floor and wall—the "hallway" of her Marshovian home, which seems, like her bedroom, to have been carved out of ivory. Oliver Marsh's black-and-white photography (he also photographed Stroheim's *The Merry Widow*) has the sort of glow and richness that make you almost regret the whole history of Technicolor. The long sequence at Maxim's, for example, has a ravishing footlit look that emphasizes the sag and weight of the players' flesh, the heaviness of MacDonald's glycerin-shadowed eyelids, the world-worn style of her glamour in this film. (*The Love Parade*, where she looks like a girl, was only five years before, but the change in movie styles, and in styles in general, make it seem much earlier: this was a period when even movies of *three* years before could look as if they belonged to a lost age.)

This is the first time Lubitsch has worked with a major score, and he fills the movie with it. There is hardly a detail of the intimate Chevalier-and-MacDonald scenes that isn't "played" to the Lehár music. (The score was arranged by Richard Rodgers, who also wrote new bridging melodies, while Lorenz Hart and Gus Kahn adapted the lyrics.) What particularly suits Lubitsch of course is the Lehár ruefulness—the way even a celebratory song like "I'm Going to Maxim's" seems both rollicking and hesitant, with an undertone of melancholy even. For if this Lubitsch operetta film has a new vividness and spaciousness, it also has a deeper gravity than the others have.* The odd and wonderful thing is that this gravity makes it funnier—makes it sillier and farther-gone in dementedness than the earlier films. And this particular cause-and-effect is not only central to the film but to all of Lubitsch.

Sonia (Jeanette MacDonald) strolls, veiled in her widow's weeds, under the stars. She is the richest woman in Marshovia, and she is listening to the servants—gypsy types, splendidly coarse and zestful at their balalaikas—playing and humming in her garden. Count Danilo (Maurice Chevalier), driven nearly desperate by a desire to unveil the widow's face, has climbed the garden wall. He accosts her in her solitude to deliver a confidential—and anonymous—letter. She takes it, lifts a corner of her veil to reveal a single blazing eye, and reads it aloud. "Madame Sonia," it says, "if you ever meet Count Danilo, let me tell you he is terrific." She is puzzled. She looks up from the letter—at him. "What is this?" she says with alarm. " 'Count Danilo'? 'Terrific'?" She looks at the paper again. Again she looks at him: he is falsely encouraged. "That's what people say," he replies, grinning fatuously. But she is still trying to puzzle the message out. "Danilo," she repeats—what can it mean? She repeats it again, fiercely—looks at him as he begins to look more and more foolish and uncom-

---

*One of the most cherished of Lubitsch's unrealized plans was to do a film of *Der Rosenkavalier*.

fortable. But it is beyond her. When it emerges, at length, that *he* is Danilo, she is not exactly reassured, and refuses to lift her veil. She leaves him and goes inside.

But she has been struck—forcibly struck. Her thoughtfulness has intensified. So has the film's, as it follows her traversing the gleaming white spaces of her palace, entering her chambers, where her maids prepare her for bed. She is in mourning, and a woman of unshakable conventionality: even her pug dog and her extra corsets are in black. She is in mourning, but she has been impressed. The maids throw the windows wide, and the gypsy music fills the room. She steps onto the balcony under the moon and sings "Vilia" from her tower: "The song of a shepherd who cried for the moon . . ." But in her bed she is unable to sleep and takes up her diary. She sighs over the long succession of empty pages (they all come after "Dear Diary: I am a widow . . ."). Repairing to her desk, she begins to write about all the feelings Danilo has reawakened in her. A full inkwell in close-up dissolves to an empty one. She is singing to herself now, a delicate, serpentine, inward-turning melody. Her pen scratches busily: "Men are not . . . not what they seem," she sings, with a hesitation in the middle of the line. So she resolves sensibly—singingly—to forget him. And she appears, as the music swells, now framed in the date panel ("1885") of her own diary, in various attitudes of forgetting Danilo: musing, sewing, not sleeping . . . "I have forgotten him, . . ." "I am still forgetting him," read the entries below, as the camera pans downward. It pans up again to show Sonia looking suddenly angry—with a sudden quickening fanfare in the music. She rises and walks out of the panel, and the camera pans downward to the page below as a pen enters from offscreen and writes: "I am fed up with Marshovia!"

We are back in her bedchamber. Sonia goes instantly to the door and calls to her maid. "Get everything ready," she says out the door. "We're going to Paris. Tomorrow. Tomorrow morning. As soon as possible!" "Yes, madame," replies an offscreen voice. Satisfied, MacDonald turns from the door and marches past the camera. "There's a limit to every widow," she observes to herself, as she walks past a flower vase and off, out of the frame.

This exit line cues a total switch of tone and style. In the next scene, MacDonald is trilling in her underwear, preparing briskly for Paris and a new life, while every article on the premises has been transformed to white, including the pug dog. "There's a limit to every widow": that sort of quiet, drawling, devastating afterthought is the Lubitsch version of the wisecrack sound—an elegant but abrupt descent to the incontestable. And all the elaborate legerdemain that precedes it is there, as it turns out, to remind us of the incontestable. There may be, in this fantasy, lovers and glamour and music, kings and queens and castles and balls; but there are limits, too. And everybody in *this* movie knows it.

It's one of the most generous and attractive things about the movie that they

do know it, that almost no one is excluded from the common perception—sardonic, resigned, more than a little depressed—of inevitable limits. And the *sound* of this knowledge is clearer than ever before in the Lubitsch-Raphaelson films: more drawling and sidelong, more unmistakably American.* Queen Dolores (Una Merkel) confides her worst fears about the political situation to King Achmed (George Barbier): "It looks like exile to me," she confesses, patting his hand and staring grimly ahead, like someone on a midwestern front porch contemplating the mortgage. This is the dominant voice of the film: wry and wayward and skeptical, reductive and puncturing and down-to-earth. And it's lovely—with the kind of authority and fluency that lets it range from nonsense and vulgarity to a blighted romantic lyricism. It has the same toughness as Gaston and Mariette give voice to in *Trouble in Paradise* ("That's the trouble with mothers," says Mariette when informed that Lily's mother is no longer alive. "You get to

At Maxim's: Jeanette MacDonald, Maurice Chevalier, and Minna Gombel in The Merry Widow.

---

*Lubitsch also shot a somewhat altered French version, *La Veuve joyeuse*, filmed simultaneously. Marcel Achard adapted the Raphaelson screenplay, and Chevalier and MacDonald (who was fluent in French) repeated their roles.

like them and then they die"), but not so prodigious, closer to common life. It's the comedy of lowered expectations—under the champagne and brio and enchantment, nobody kids himself.

Least of all, Baron Popoff (Edward Everett Horton), Marshovia's ambassador in Paris. With his dithering alarms, Horton is to Lubitsch pretty much what William Demarest was to be to Sturges later on: the nearly indispensable supporting player. But this Horton character is somewhat different. He looks distinguished, with graying temples and formal attire, a man of station and dignity. He dithers, it's true, but there is also a kind of equanimity. He has no delusions about himself in this film—unlike Filiba in *Trouble in Paradise* or Max in *Design for Living*, no aspirations toward the heroine nor romantic hopes otherwise. It's true that he enters the film enjoying what looks like a moment of glory, but that is quickly wiped out. He is leaving Maxim's with a blond cutie nestled in his arm. They pass through the outer lobby in silence: Horton's head bobbing on his shoulders with silent, smirking, all-but-bursting elation and pride, as he looks down at the prize on his arm and escorts her to the door. Unfortunately, no sooner have they disappeared behind that door than Danilo comes through it—and the blond cutie right after him. "Danilo!" she calls, the way every girl at Maxim's calls that name—with rapture. In the end, however, that universal female longing for Danilo suits Baron Popoff just fine: he has been assigned by King Achmed to arrange and promote Danilo's courtship of Sonia, "the richest widow in the world," so that her fortune won't get out of impoverished Marshovia. The baron knows this to be a commission requiring the highest tact and devotion to duty. He looks Danilo up and down: "Have you ever had diplomatic relations with a woman?" he inquires severely—then abruptly passes over the reply, which is embarrassed and halting. Above all, the baron is a realist. Part of his plan for beguiling the widow at the Embassy Ball involves his own dancing with her until Danilo arrives. At that point, the baron explains, "she gets the big thrill: I leave her."

King Achmed is also obsessed with the widow problem—a good thing, too, considering the propensities of Queen Dolores. He is preparing to go to a late-night cabinet meeting, summoned in response to the widow's departure for Paris, and Queen Dolores is watching him. She is sitting up in their enormous bed—an ebony extravaganza that rises at its apex to a giant overhanging ram's head—twisting the edge of the sheet between her fingers and inquiring in a hopeful, slightly kvetching voice whether or not he will be out all night. Achmed and Dolores are inspired creations, especially as embodied by George Barbier (a veteran of such roles) and Una Merkel. He is a foxy, chuffling, lodge-brother type. (Preparing to flee the revolution, he wraps the crown in newspaper.) She is a nasal-sardonic American "dish." Together, they evoke a whole world of traveling salesmen jokes and small-town bawdiness. (George Cukor would later claim—incredibly—that Lubitsch cast such actors as royalty because, being European, he never got the point of how American they were. Clearly, it's Cukor who never got the point.) The king is so preoccupied with the crisis that he is even able to discuss with his visibly restive wife (she still hasn't found out if he's going to be out all night) who among the men *she* knows might be up to the job of luring the widow back to Marshovia. His equanimity in this area is unshakable.

KING: Tell me. If you weren't married, if you weren't my wife, could you fall for Gabrilovitch?
QUEEN: If I weren't married—if I had it to do over again and had the choice between you and Gabrilovitch?—frankly I'd take you.
KING: Well, he's out.

The king is momentarily distracted from this problem when he returns for his sword belt and finds Danilo in the queen's bedroom. The queen protests that she was defending herself all the while: if he'd come back "an hour later," he'd have found Danilo "where he belongs—outside the door." King Achmed has a sudden thought:

KING: How does he compare with Gabrilovitch?
QUEEN: No comparison. Put Gabrilovitch and Sinkevitch together, and what have you? Gabrilovitch and Sinkevitch. But Danilo!—Oh, no! No comparison.
KING: Dolores . . .
QUEEN: Yes, Achmed?
KING: With my brains and your contacts, Marshovia can't miss!

No one in the film, it develops, is much more sentimental than these two—though some are more conflicted. But not even the romantic heroine has many illusions about romance.

Sonia belongs to that hallowed theatrical tradition of the ultrarespectable young woman who goes temporarily "loose" or "wild"—or, rather, pretends to do so—usually as a way of enticing and discomfiting the hero. The widow, despairing of encountering Danilo in Paris any other way, disguises herself as a cocotte—"a Fifi," to be precise—and appears in the anteroom of Maxim's with glinting eyes and a ribbon around her neck. "I'm just in the mood for a banker— you understand, don't you?" Danilo, taking her face in his hand and turning it from side to side, pronounces her "not bad." "Who is she?" he asks Marcelle, the madam (Minna Gombell). "She's new here," says Marcelle. But Fifi is not too encouraging: she has her mind set on that banker. "Who is he?" she asks Marcelle about Danilo. Marcelle and Danilo are equally incredulous: everyone knows *him*, they laugh. Sonia has her usual problem with the name ("Danilo?

Danilo?"—it doesn't ring a bell), then wonders brightly if he isn't the man who gave her "this bracelet." ("He doesn't give any bracelets," says Marcelle.) It's enough to make Danilo have the sulks. At that point she relents ("There's not much going on here tonight, no Americans") and agrees to go to a table with him—but not before taking his chin in her hand, turning his face from side to side, and pronouncing him "Not bad." "Come on," she adds, leading the way to the table.

The scene at the table has a familiar Lubitschean contour: what promises to be conventionally risqué turns into something unstrung and rather demented. They sit side by side without ever touching *above* the table, while we are cued to follow the invisible action below. He leans toward her: "Let go of my hand," she says. He looks soulful, then pained: "Stop kicking me," he sys. "Stop pinching me," she answers. She leans toward him, settling forward on her elbows and purring: "That's better. Now you're behaving like a gentleman." Suddenly she sits bolt upright, gasping. Then the words come, hoarse and urgent: "*Give* me back my shoe. . . ."

As usual, it's the MacDonald heroine who focuses the real interest of the film. And in *The Merry Widow* she has become something she hasn't quite been before: the film's intelligence, the sponsor of its consciousness and spirit. She has a new kind of control over the jokes, sponsoring the wit as well as the madness— as when she puzzles over Danilo's letter or announces the widow's "limit." Instead of an ardent virgin or a trusting wife, she is now a woman who knows a thing or two—and even the Chevalier hero is a bit chastened in her presence. Sonia embodies much of that rueful relation to his own knowingness that Lubitsch expressed more impersonally in *Trouble in Paradise*, his other masterpiece of this period.

And through her Lubitsch comes closer, in his oblique way, to a lyric-tragic account of sexual feeling than he has since his silent films. At the same time as he gives MacDonald a new degree of authority in this film, he emphasizes her vulnerability. There is a high angle shot, after Sonia and Danilo have left their table, that shows her climbing the stairway to the private dining rooms, frowning and lifting her skirts and limping slightly—Danilo has got her shoe now and is using it to lure her upstairs. The shot emphasizes both the plunge of her gown and her real disadvantage: it suggests several kinds of nakedness. The music from the dance floor chuckles away below as she ascends. Once she reaches the top and pauses before the open door to the private room—with a professionally complaisant waiter to one side and Danilo (and her slipper) within—the music changes, becoming plaintive and lyrical. Danilo is standing by a couch as she enters the room and goes to him, the door closing discreetly behind her. "May I put it on?" he says, indicating the slipper in his hand. And she sits.

The ensuing conflict—all the movements of troubled seduction, the backing and filling, the hovering and wavering—has a remarkable sort of force. Lubitsch stages it like a dance—and to music, of course. The lovers circle each other, and the camera, even more eloquently, circles them. But—unlike Astaire and Rogers' "Night and Day," for example—it's a romantic dance without turbulence or suspense. These circling motions are elegant and lovely, but they are also in some way inflexible. We're not meant to notice that so much as we are to feel it. And we do: this is a conflict strikingly without tension—with an air of deep fatality, a settled melancholy. The passion in this scene is more like a ceremony, sad and civilized. And it ends, of course, with a joke. (Sonia's Napoleon remark—see below.)

Sonia sits on the couch—very gingerly—as Danilo kneels in front of her to replace the slipper on her foot. Lubitsch shows Chevalier in close-up profile, leaning forward, looking upward. He smiles, very slightly—expectantly. There is an answering close-up of Sonia, who smiles down at him—uneasy, hopeful, beneficent. Danilo bends forward in his close-up to kiss her hand. Sonia reacts in her close-up—passionately, with her head back and her eyes closed. Now they are in the same shot together, Sonia seated on the couch and Danilo kneeling before her—as she draws her hand, very slowly, out of his. He rises, the camera following, to turn down the lamps, circling her as he does so. Another high angle shot of MacDonald: a ravishing one, again emphasizing her lushness and vulnerability. She sits forward as the camera looks down on her, her hands clutching the edge of the couch, her head back and her eyes lowered: a startlingly direct image of sexual longing and readiness. But Danilo, instead of bending toward her (as the camera has more or less just done), sits next to her. And speaks (it is a challenge): "And now, Fifi, if you feel in the mood for a banker, the door is not locked." She stirs at this, opens her eyes, and rises. Still under a spell, she moves to the door, the camera tracking behind her, and stops. She stands where she is with her back turned to us. Suddenly the lights go down and her shoulders rise—as does the music, swellingly. Danilo enters the shot now, takes her in his arms and kisses her. She moves away again, out of the frame. Danilo, quite confident, goes to the champagne. Abruptly the lights go on and the music stops. Sonia is standing thoughtfully in front of a large hanging portrait of Napoleon—who also, she remarks, "attacked too early." Danilo explodes ("I don't mind a little teasing . . . but this is absolutely demoralizing!") and storms out of the room.

He comes back, though, and they dance "The Merry Widow Waltz" together—just as big a moment as it's always supposed to be in this show—alone in the private dining room. And they part—and dance it again at the Embassy Ball, where their engagement is formally announced by Baron Popoff and almost instantly broken off by Sonia. The film's final sequence shows Danilo and Sonia trapped in a dungeon (he has been imprisoned there for his failure to keep her fortune in Marshovia, and she has come to visit him). They get married there too, before the final fadeout. The champagne, the ring, and even the priest (courtesy of King Achmed and Baron Popoff) materialize from behind a sliding panel in the wall. The final joke is certainly a Lubitschean one: love and marriage seen as a kind of delirious entrapment—even entombment, given the contours of that dungeon. Still, it's a tomb filled with the intensest kind of movie life Lubitsch could then probably imagine: a man in resplendent uniform and a beautiful woman in a pretty dress, circling each other, to the strains of a waltz—a moment at once mocking, sardonic, romantic, and ceremonial. But whatever chance—never, surely, a big one—this sort of fadeout had of seizing the popular imagination was almost certainly lost when Astaire danced Rogers over the furniture and out of the movie at the end of *The Gay Divorcee* (released, as if to underscore the point, on the same day as *The Merry Widow*). *That's* a finale in an Astaire movie—a world where there are neither traps nor tombs, only slammers and local police stations, laughable and vanquishable, like the furniture he dances over.

The Merry Widow was the last of the Lubitsch operetta films. It was also probably the best, with its wiseacre soul, its inspired and unrelenting nuttiness, its hints of troubling beauty and gallantly endured distress: a self-declaring trifle that never seems trifling—just the opposite, in fact. Under the lovingly elaborated nonsense and the sumptuous ritziness, the spirit of this film is deeply tough. The isolation Lubitsch likes to show us has ceased to be an astonishment and has become a settled condition. Yet the result is far from dispirited. Never before has the Lubitsch-Raphaelson collaboration seemed at the same time both so deranged and so grown-up: it's clear as it never has been before how much the looniness and inconsequence ("*Give* me back my shoe") have to do with a refusal of such things as complaint and repining, self-pity and self-importance. The elation of this movie comes from just such refusals: its artifice is a victory over softness and sentiment. *The Merry Widow* is in some ways perhaps the most brilliant of all their collaborations. But that brilliance has as much to do with coldness as it does with wit or inspiration. That's one of the things that makes it wonderful—it didn't help to make it popular.

Frank Capra | 7

No one else can balance the ups and downs of wistful sentiment and corny humor the way Capra can—but if anyone else should learn to, kill him.
— PAULINE KAEL, on *Mr. Smith Goes to Washington*

THE GIRL: *Is Capra nice, or don't you know him?*
SULLIVAN: *Very nice.*
— PRESTON STURGES' *Sullivan's Travels*, from the shooting script

This the land of the free! Why, if I say anything that displeases them, the free mob will lynch me, and that's my freedom. Free? Why, I have never been in any country where the individual has such an abject fear of his fellow countrymen. — D. H. LAWRENCE, *Studies in Classic American Literature*

FRANK CAPRA had no sooner inaugurated the screwball comedy cycle with *It Happened One Night* than he turned his back on it. Beginning with *Mr. Deeds Goes to Town* in 1936, Capra made the sort of film that looked like screwball comedy, even sometimes sounded like it, but whose intentions were inspirational. Nor were any of these films, it should be noted, very funny. It's *this* Capra, the Capra of *Mr. Deeds* and after, the artist of "Capracorn" and the laureate of "Capra humanity," who becomes the Capra of fame and legend, the Capra who is somehow in all our pasts.

In a way it's not hard to see how he got there. Apart from the enormous and unquestionable talent, the enthusiasm for filmmaking and film performers, he is exceptionally likable. Who can resist all that ambition and hope and risk-taking, that eager, open engagement with the largest and most pressing "issues" of his time, against the prevailing Hollywood landscape of cynics and time servers? Capra is bound to seem impressive, even now. So he seemed to Graham Greene in 1936, in a review of *Mr. Deeds:* "Capra has what Lubitsch, the witty

Frank Capra
directing Bar-
bara Stanwyck
and Adolphe
Menjou in For-
bidden (1931).

playboy, has not: a sense of responsibility," Greene wrote, and called *Mr. Deeds* "a comedy quite unmatched on the screen." It is, after all, a comedy about a rich man who gives his money away to the people who need it, and which more or less insists on the simple justice of such a course. The movies in general endorsed brotherhood and the golden rule, to be sure—but who besides Capra would go so dangerously and so logically far?

Except that it doesn't seem quite that way when you see the movie—neither far nor dangerous (nor even particularly logical). Not at all. The "sense of responsibility" that drives Capra to raise these issues doesn't prevent him from betraying them on the screen—from falsifying and condescending to the poor people he shows us and from sentimentalizing the impulse to help them. Deeds's conscience is first awakened when a maddened out-of-work farmer (John Wray) charges into his mansion, waving a gun and threatening to shoot him. But the man collapses in sobs, and Deeds (Gary Cooper) gives him supper. Deeds—and we—watch the man eat, and Capra underlines his abjectness and his desperate hunger. But the actor is a very stagy type ("I'm at the end of my [*sob*] rope!"), and so the discomfort that Capra induces in us here—by savoring every gulp and swallow and moist-eyed gaze of gratitude—has a lot to do with the feeling we're being leaned on. There is always a lot of talk in Capra's films about the dignity of people like this farmer, but what we get when we see them is wheedling and ingratiation and emotional blackmail. The poor man who comes on with a gun finally says "Excuse me" for pointing it and ends up just the way these movies like their poor people: weak and lovable and grateful. But the real focus of this sequence is Deeds himself, sitting across the table while the farmer eats—watching him in silence, chin in hand, making welling-eyed little grimaces and blinking his encouragement whenever the man looks up. Cooper's self-consciousness is so pronounced that Deeds seems moved by his own emotion as much as by anything else—just as he seems later on when he shares the simple sandwich of another poor man, batting his eyes at him as he lifts it to his mouth. Compassion in Capra is nearly always self-congratulatory.

And yet in spite of his intention of generosity, and his fondness for the feelings that go with it, Capra's attitudes toward the poor are depressingly and discouragingly familiar. Capra and his screenwriter Robert Riskin never portray an unlucky or hungry person without hastening to reassure us about them. The woman who faints on the bus in *It Happened One Night* is, we are told, on her way to a job. A man who goes through garbage cans in *Meet John Doe* does this, we are told with great satisfaction, because he has too much pride to take a relief check. And the nervousness about people who do take such checks never goes away. There are many knowing jokes in *You Can't Take It With You* (even more of them in the original Kaufman and Hart play) about the laziness of Eddie Anderson's black servant, Donald, while the idleness of his white employers is seen as a kind of higher wisdom. Capra seems nearly unable to imagine a poor person who isn't genteel, once you get to know him. Getting to know him is always the main problem—as it is with your neighbor, too. John Doe sees "the answer"—"the one thing capable of saving this cockeyed world"—in people's finally learning "that the guy next door isn't a bad egg." But what if you learn that he *is*—even worse than you imagined, or at the least more troublesome? Then what?—forget him? In a Capra film you don't even think of these questions. So that while you may feel there's a nice man trying to be helpful behind the film, you feel even more clearly that he's not trying hard enough. Just the opposite, in fact: the flow of rhetoric about goodness and kindness and caring about your neighbor seems so utterly remote from any real experience of doing good or attempting it that it becomes finally offensive. Even a little crazy. But that, I think, is finally its appeal.

There are times, though—notably in *Mr. Smith Goes to Washington* (the only one of these films *not* written by Riskin; it's by Sidney Buchman, who also wrote

Theodora Goes Wild)—when Capra's excitement about "goodness" gets beyond the self-congratulations of *Mr. Deeds*. All the glamour and excited sense of place in *Mr. Smith Goes to Washington* (1939) is an excitement about moral heroism. How many movies give us such a strong sense as this one does that we've experienced a place? We hardly notice that we don't really see much of that place, and we are less interested in the meticulous detailing of what we do see (that absolutely faithful replica of the U.S. Senate chamber) than Capra probably expects us to be. The movie keeps insisting, in any case, that what's *there*—nearly total venality and corruption—is less important than what *was* there once—the high idealism of the Founding Fathers. They, too, we are told (though it's a surprise), were surrounded by scoundrels and hypocrites. But "the odds" didn't stop men like Lincoln. "They were fools that way," Jean Arthur tells James Stewart at the Lincoln Memorial, "and all the good that ever came into the world came from fools with faith like that."

Capra, of course, wasn't the only popular moviemaker telling audiences how wonderful it was to be unpopular, to maintain your integrity and to go against the crowd. The crowd bought tickets for this sort of thing, as everyone in Hollywood knew, including Capra. But Capra also felt some of the unease and even contradiction of his own success: one of the greatest crowd-pleasers of them all ("The people are right, never wrong," he says in interviews) who is obsessed with the grandeur of heroes who defy the crowd. Fake heroism is one of his recurring subjects, and his version of the real thing is itself a bit fake: stagy and theatrical, without any of the irony that Preston Sturges brings to the same materials and moments; virtue seen uncritically from the outside, as in all those low angle shots of Jefferson Smith (James Stewart) suffering his agony in the Senate, slumping over baskets of hostile telegrams, looking up with such a stricken face that onlookers pale and cry out: "Stop, Jeff—stop!" cries the heroine from the gallery, sinking to the floor in sympathetic distress.

But if Capra isn't quite convincing about heroism itself, about the aspiration toward it he is sometimes close to eloquent—at least in *Mr. Smith*. He knows a lot, it seems, about the way people are drawn to heroism, yearn after it, are made unhappy and uncomfortable by it. The impact of Jefferson Smith's innocent idealism on sleek worldly Senator Paine is registered in detail—and with surprising pain and power in Claude Rains's performance. There is even more force in Jean Arthur's version of the same conflict: she is Saunders, Jefferson Smith's secretary in the Senate, a consummate Washington operator, who knows all the rules and all the angles, and whose knowledge and expertise finally save the guileless hero. "My favorite actress," Capra says of Arthur in his autobiography—and no wonder. Arthur's cynical heroines (*Mr. Deeds Goes to Town* is an earlier version of the same tough lady) are always able to suggest a deep susceptibility to higher feelings. It's in the famous cracked voice: a readiness to be

rapt, exalted, taken out of herself. And it's touching because it's controlled, like all Arthur's effects, by such brisk intelligence—by the crisp, dashing, almost mannish style.

She has been waiting for the new Senator Smith in his office, and when he finally turns up, it appears that he's been sightseeing. He's taken in all the spots—the Capitol, the Lincoln Memorial—and he's full of talk about all of them, all eager boyish patriotism. We can see from her face that she'd rather not listen to this, but if she has to, she has to. She looks at him pleasantly, a little blankly as he talks: her mouth tightens at the corners, her eyes slide off his face into some melancholy vacancy beyond, with just the slightest suggestion that he might touch something painful in her—*if* she looked at him, that is. Everything that seems rich and interesting in this scene comes from Arthur's way of listening to Stewart's enthusiasm, which exactly places the way this man is going to be hard on her.

Soon, after a painful conversion, she is on his side. And when he himself is disillusioned finally by the corruption and duplicity of official Washington, she turns up at the Lincoln Memorial to ask him what he's going to *do* about it: she is the believer now. One of the nicest things Capra does in this film—and one of the most improbable—is to associate Arthur's glamour with the Lincoln Memorial. Smith, betrayed and slandered by his friend Senator Paine, has gone there to say goodbye to Washington. Saunders comes out of the shadows and sits on his suitcase to talk to him. She is in ravishingly shadowed soft-focus close-up, with a rakish over-the-eye hat, leaning forward in profile and talking softly about the "fools" who go against "the odds"—about how Lincoln has been waiting for him, Jefferson Smith, to come along, to defy the scoundrels once again and to tell the truth. Or so she believes. It's very moving when such a sensible, fundamentally modest woman—and in such a hat—talks about greatness. You can believe in it happening, as Capra knows. And his intention to expand the moral and emotional limits of the romantic movie comedy really does fulfill itself in this sequence, where Jean Arthur's beauty and wit and style are like guarantees of the idealism the film is about.

SIX YEARS before this, Capra had made a quite different film about an idealist heroine: *The Bitter Tea of General Yen* (1933), with another favorite actress, Barbara Stanwyck. This was his fourth film with Stanwyck (the fifth and last was 1941's *Meet John Doe*) and the climax to an extraordinary partnership, crucial in both their careers. Stanwyck is Megan Davis, a New England girl who has come to China to marry a missionary and share his labors among the heathen. In the midst of civil wars and riots, however, she finds herself detained by a warlord named General Yen (Nils Asther) and held prisoner in his summer palace. The general hopes at length to wear down her resistance to him. She is ardent and beautiful, of a religious and enthusiastic temperament, young and inexperienced. She never seems younger than when she panics at the first sign of the general's amorousness and calls him "a yellow swine"—reacting just as a respectable white woman was expected to in such extremities, and then being instantly ashamed of it. After all, as she says with touching matter-of-factness, she came to China "to help people." She makes this last remark to an unreadable China doll named Ma Li (Toshia Mori), the general's concubine. Ma Li looks—and is, as it turns out—pettish, corrupt, duplicitous. She is also suspected of betraying the general to his enemies. And since she is friendless, as it seems, Megan befriends her.

And the parrying with the general goes on. Just as in *It Happened One Night*, Capra is eloquent about erotic tensions. General Yen is trying, as he puts it, to "convert a missionary." He talks about art and poetry, and she is drawn to him against her will. She has a dream about being saved from him by a hero who turns out to be Yen himself. He tells her that the loyalty of a selfish man can be bought, but her missionary fiancé "will betray [her] every time—for his God."

She pauses before replying to this, lowering her eyes and gathering her thought. "The subtlety of you Orientals," she says, achieving scorn as she speaks, "is very much overestimated." And she walks out.

But she is back again as soon as she finds out that Ma Li is under sentence for treason. To save the girl's life, Megan launches into a passionate plea to the general, a wonderful mixture of condescension and respect, of ardor and calculation. "Forgive her as God forgives," she says, "with no thought of return" and even "*because* she's betrayed you." She really does believe in the renunciation and self-transcendence she is talking about here. But the feelings she is tapping in herself are too tangled and volatile, and when she starts to talk about the "real happiness" his act of mercy will give him, she suddenly bursts into tears. Stanwyck makes us feel the complicated pain of this breakdown as well as its residue of triumph. But it's her ardor that impresses the general. He remarks that it's as if Ma Li were her own flesh and blood. "But she is!" cries Megan, realizing he's stumbled onto the point. "We're *all* of one flesh and blood." "Really?" says the general. "Do you mean that?"—and touches her

The Bitter Tea of General Yen: the riddle of Ma Li. Toshia Mori, Barbara Stanwyck, Nils Asther, and Walter Connolly (standing).

hand. "Of course I do," she replies, and withdraws her hand, placing it on her throat and looking at him. He stares at her, disgusted. "Words, nothing but words," he says. "You came here to preach!" Christ gave up His life for such words, she says. "What are *you* willing to give up for them?" wonders the general, now framed by his bedroom door. What does he mean? Is she willing to be hostage for Ma Li's future loyalty? In desperation and anger ("I'm not afraid of you!"), Megan agrees to "answer for" Ma Li.

When of course the girl does betray him, the disaster to his army and fortune is a total one. Megan goes to him, stricken and distraught; but the sight of her suffering offends his pride. Oh, did she think he meant *that?* Oh, no: "It was your *life* you put up as a forfeit for Ma Li's loyalty." "My life?" she repeats weakly. A sobering mistake. His anger turns to scorn: "You are afraid of death as you are afraid of life." He tells her he will send her back to the fiancé who "speaks the same meaningless words as you do"—and she staggers slightly as he says this. "He has everything you want," he says. She smiles to herself, then raises her eyes to look at him. Stanwyck's look registers all the pain and chagrin of Megan's sudden self-knowledge.

But it's interesting how close to comedy all this comes. Nearly all the big moments in this romantic drama are essential comic moments: scenes of sexual cross-purpose and misunderstanding, of sudden and disconcerting self-recognition. She says they're all of one flesh—and he makes a pass at her. She discovers she's staked her life, not her virtue. She discovers, too, where her preference lies: dishonor before death. The point is almost Buñuelian—but the style isn't. The *comic* meanings are unexplored. That's not surprising: so they would have been by almost anyone but a Buñuel in the Hollywood of this time. What's surprising is that Capra of all directors should have come so close to a Buñuelian possibility, to this kind of sardonic joking. But then *The Bitter Tea of General Yen* (screenplay by Edward Paramore, loosely based on a novel by Grace Zaring Stone) combines just those elements of moral aspiration and sexual conflict that Capra's filmmaking seems to have been most powerfully engaged by. And he must have been encouraged by Stanwyck's talents, too—her talent for chagrin and sardonic self-reflection. Probably his most remarkable achievement here is the balance of affection and irony he holds the heroine in throughout. But that balance, which seems so sure and impressive in the movie, might have seemed very perilous to Capra himself.

FOR CAPRA, as the rest of his career makes clear, didn't like irony—if he had, he might have been funnier. He liked conversions. And though he had a talent for bringing actors out on the screen, often in a way other directors hadn't (*It Happened One Night* was a turning point in the careers of both Gable

You Can't Take
It with You:
*Mischa Auer,
Jean Arthur,
James Stewart,
and Ann Miller
(standing);
Edward Arnold
and Mary
Forbes (seated).*

and Colbert), he moves away from the kind of subtleties implied by Stanwyck's Megan. What he promotes more and more in his work are the large vivifying effects that encapsulate a performer's essential quality or character. He had a talent for making actors "unforgettable," usually by simplifying them in some way. The personality he defined for Gary Cooper in *Mr. Deeds* became "Gary Cooper" ever after that. And his way with someone like Edward Arnold—an actor who specialized in powerful men and who was one of Capra's favorites— is to turn him on screen into something monolithic. Arnold is the ultimate villain in two Capra films: in *Mr. Smith Goes to Washington* and *Meet John Doe*, he is the Mr. Big behind everybody else, mysterious, remote, all-powerful. In *You Can't Take It With You* he is the ultimate Wall Street financier—also a villain. Arnold is wonderful at all this hyperbole. He is the embodiment of worldly authority very much as impressed children might see it—without any suggestion that it might be uncertain, might feel fake or foolish. Authority without irony. He radiates importance without ever suggesting self-importance. He is too grave, too powerfully preoccupied, too worried even. Even his own gestures strike him forcibly. His hand reaches out to switch on the intercom and his gaze follows, almost with surprise: So that's what I'm doing, talking on this now— then: Get me So-and-So! His looks never dart or glance; they travel, making contact with the intelligible other by painful, slow, often terrible degrees.

Capra liked to boast that he and Riskin really wrenched the play about to give Arnold this role in *You Can't Take It With You* (1938), rewriting one of Kaufman and Hart's best-known—not to mention surefire—Broadway successes. We made the villain the hero, Capra declares with satisfaction in his autobiography. In both play and movie, multimillionaire Anthony P. Kirby (Arnold) is finally converted from his joyless pursuit of wealth and power to the carefree ways of the happy loony Sycamore family, presided over by benign Grandpa Vanderhof (Lionel Barrymore). Capra was of course much more interested in this conversion experience than Kaufman and Hart ever were. (The Jean Arthur heroine, who usually undergoes it in his films, is among the faithful from the beginning in this one, being one of the Sycamores.) He makes it the central event of his movie, and Kirby becomes almost its main character, with many new scenes detailing his unhappy relations with his son (James Stewart) and his seizing of still more financial power. Capra even has him about to corner the world's munitions market. "Why, a war wouldn't be possible anywhere without us!" exclaims one of his henchmen, while Kirby, Jr., yawns. It's characteristic of Capra both to raise this issue and then to wipe it out: the main trouble with munitions making, it finally seems, is that it's gloomy and not fun. And it was generally felt at the time of the film's release that Capra had unbalanced the play by such changes, making it unduly solemn and pretentious.

But it's the movie, not the play, that seems authoritative now—with Capra at the peak of his filmmaking skill. His ability to stage scenes powerfully and then to edit them for maximum effect* is evident over and over again: in the happy, do-your-own-thing chaos of the Sycamore household; in the funny, meditative love scenes at the office between Stewart and Arthur; in the pandemonium of the nightclub, when Arthur exits on Stewart's arm with a "Nuts" sign pinned to the back of her cape, a classic "screwball" event; and above all, in any scene that has centrally to do with Arnold. Who plays some of his most galvanizing scenes with a harmonica—a characteristic Capra prop, winsome and childish and standing for vanished joys. Kirby was once a harmonica champion, he admits, though now, fatally, he's much too busy for such things. Grandpa Vanderhof, on the other hand, is never without *his* harmonica, always ready to break into a tune. When he and Kirby quarrel while sharing a jail cell (the Sycamores and their high-toned guests are all arrested when the "revolutionary" fireworks in

---

*Capra has said more than once that editing is his favorite part of the filmmaking process.

the basement go off), Vanderhof tries to make it up by slipping his own harmonica into Kirby's pocket. Kirby doesn't even find this gift until they are all being arraigned in front of the judge: he takes the harmonica from his pocket and turns it over in his hand, ruminatively, with all that machinery of fierce attention fixed on it now. His wife (Mary Forbes) at his side nudges him gently, a reminder where he is: pay attention to the judge—*I* am. He puts the harmonica back in his pocket and glares at her, then looks forward again.

But no one supposes that he is angry with his wife when he glares at her like that. It's simply, as we understand by this point in the movie, that she has intruded on a particularly intense motion of attention. The "anger," such as it is, is directed at his own abstraction. Just as when he first enters the movie, he scowls at the doorman who holds the car door for him and says good morning. Kirby's fierceness is reflexive: it's certainly not about the anonymous doorman. In fact, and curiously, it hardly matters what it's about. Whether it's empire building or indigestion (he is afflicted with both), it's the intensity that's impressive. Nothing is light to this man. And everything is impersonal. It's just that impersonal quality that makes the motion of his attention so interesting—and so momentous. It's never just *people* he's angry with; he's too busy a man. When he looks at someone—killingly—he is always seeing what looms behind him: some threat or challenge, some issue he'd rather not face or distraction he'd rather not suffer. He can do the same thing with a harmonica: he can look at it (as he often does in this movie) and almost make us believe in the very large meanings Capra invests it with—just as Jean Arthur can almost make us believe in that rhetoric at the Lincoln Memorial.

And the moment, so carefully built up to, when Arnold actually plays this harmonica is one of the great exhilarating events of thirties comedy. Does he know "Polly Wolly Doodle"? Grandpa Vanderhof wants to know (Kirby's missing son, Tony, is upstairs, and Vanderhof knows that if they play loud enough, he will come down and surprise his father). "'Polly Wolly Doodle'?" says Kirby, staring at the man. But in fact he does know it. "Yeah," he says: it escapes him like a sigh. "Of course you do," says Grandpa. "And swing it!" He himself starts to play. Kirby stares at him, more fiercely intent than ever. And as Grandpa plays, he takes his free hand and lifts Kirby's harmonica to *his* mouth—and before he knows it, and still staring fiercely at his companion, Kirby is playing, too—a duet, as Grandpa promised. Tony comes downstairs; so does Alice. Soon everybody, the Sycamores and all the neighborhood, is whooping and jumping and dancing in the living room: the unbending of A. P. Kirby is a public event (it means, among other things, that the bank won't take the house away). That seems perfectly appropriate to the man himself. His geniality seems as momentous as his fierceness, and almost as absorbing to watch: the way the intensity collapses into "Polly Wolly Doodle," whomping and reaming along, interspersed with hugs and chuckles and a turn at throwing Mischa Auer to the floor by a wrestling hold. The frightfully dignified Mrs. Kirby enters the happy bedlam just in time to see Auer hit the floor and is understandably baffled. "Oh, hello, Mother," says Kirby, sitting down again to his harmonica. "Come on, you do the Big Apple, too." She doesn't—she faints instead—but she's likely to be the only holdout to the fairy-tale pleasure, either on the screen or in the audience.

Still, it's all very calculated: it even feels that way while you're enjoying and giving in to it. The effects in this movie are *so* confident and surefire, and everyone on the screen seems locked into them most of the time. True, there are wonderful things here and there, and not just in Arnold's performance—inflections of behavior and detail that almost jump off the screen, like Essie (Ann Miller) pirouetting around the dining-room table while Donald sets it, or Rheba, the maid (Lillian Yarbo), going to answer the doorbell, shaking her shoulders to the Hungarian-Rhapsody-style music and giving a hand-pat to the pet crow as she passes it. Among the best things of all is Eddie Anderson's Donald, Rheba's boyfriend, twirling and trucking by himself in the background of the kitchen, then in the foreground of the big celebration at the end, leaping into the air and clicking his heels. *His* celebrations on the crowded screen are always a little apart from the others—his raptures separate but equal, and even a bit more so.

But mostly the "spontaneity" in this film is like the happiness of the Sycamore household: a noisy and skillful counterfeit, a hyped-up, efficiency expert's version of something Capra had done with more conviction earlier on. In all those moments in his films when the characters seemed to escape his or the film's control or intentions, to be suddenly and astonishingly "themselves." It was this talent for a surprising naturalness that first made people pay attention to Capra's work, and it had its culmination in *It Happened One Night*, where it connected with romance and took off into movie history. The movies in general, it should be remembered, were committed to a kind of fake, bland, dead-level "realism" (a situation that worsened considerably in the forties). Movies without surprises for people who mistrusted fantasy and invention, who wanted the same thing over and over again, who were made nervous by novelty or imagination. "Magic time"—for the dull and fearful. So that the run of movies offered a peculiar mixture of things: stories that were always a great deal *more* eventful than daily life—a surface texture that was always a great deal *less* so. One of the things movies could do for their audiences was to smooth those surfaces out, to offer a processed commodified reality, less baroque and troubling than the original— also very often a great deal duller. That was the catch, and the trouble with most movies.

Capra was one of those people in Hollywood who both challenged this situation and turned it to his own account. He said later that he liked to stop the story every once in a while and let us just "look at" the characters, as with the song on the bus in *It Happened One Night*. But he lets us "look" even *without* "stopping" in that film: the way he lets us notice that Gable and Colbert each smiles to himself at different moments after hostilities have been exchanged, building two separate sequences on the bus to the "punch line" of a smile out the window—or the way he shows us Colbert looking scared in close-up before she takes her defiant leap off her father's yacht. It's clear that Capra is in love with these small notations, these nervous looks before leaping, as confident of their power to move and hold his audience as he is of the big surefire moments, the leaps themselves.

Jean Harlow
and Robert
Williams in
Platinum
Blonde.

Among his first talkies at Columbia he made two formula "action" films, *Flight* in 1929 and *Dirigible* in 1931 (*Submarine*, their successful predecessor in 1928, was a silent), very impressive for their mastery of spectacle and large-scale suspense. But when the action lets up and the two male leads, Jack Holt and Ralph Graves, start to horse around and kid each other, you feel you're watching the real excitement: the sound and look of everyday human exchange, of odd details and random conversation, of behavior that *doesn't* fit a plot or pattern or make a wearyingly familiar point. It looks strange in such a movie. It also looks like fun—even for aging Jack Holt, comically square-jawed, implacably straightforward, heavily genial. Graves is the boyish one, physically thick and heavy like Holt, gangling too—a shit-kicker, glancing toward the floor while he mutters his lines, and often blowing them too, in a high-pitched adolescent voice, good-natured but with a hint of a whine. They are not a dazzling pair, but they are a pair. And they are touching and funny in those offhand moments Capra shows us, without a trace of sentiment or special indulgence, with a real and convincing amiability.

It was, and is, called "business"—giving actors shticks to do, bits and details of behavior. Capra had a talent for such details, things that expand in the mind afterwards when the rest of the film may be disappearing. Like the children's masks that Barbara Stanwyck and Adolphe Menjou use to talk to each other through in *Forbidden* (1931). Or even—a more melodramatic case—the ventriloquist's dummy David Manners uses to talk to Stanwyck with in *The Miracle Woman* (1931). But dummies and masks, with their high-flown expressionist aura, are less typical of Capra than the chin exercises Warren William and Guy Kibbee do together in *Lady for a Day* (1933), or the vibrating machine we see Marie Prevost in in *Ladies of Leisure* (1930). Prevost's character in the latter film—she is Barbara Stanwyck's roommate and fellow call girl—is almost entirely created by "touches" like that one. Her written character is that of sympathetic golddigger, a bit overage and a lot overweight. But she becomes someone vivid when we see Stanwyck massaging the back of her neck as they sit on a bed together, or when we see her trying to talk on a wall phone in her apartment while an unseen client is groping her off-screen: "One of those hysterical husbands," she explains, with a lopsided smile into the phone. She is a pillowlike woman, always being poked and pummeled in some amiable way, whether by a boyfriend, a girlfriend, or a machine, and smiling her rumpled, crooked smile of defeat through it all.

In *Platinum Blonde* (1931), when newlyweds Jean Harlow and Robert Williams have a disagreement in their bedroom—they are going out, and she wants him to wear garters on his socks, with all that that implies about shaping up generally—Harlow's wheedling and insisting suddenly turn into a playful little singing act. "Yes, you *will* wear garters," she sings, very baby doll–ish, burrowing with her finger into his chest. And Williams sings back, "No, I won't," while they are nose to nose and falling backwards onto the bed together. And it's as if we really are in someone's bedroom, in the middle of their intimacy and impasse. Partly because Capra has found in his characters' behavior that union of the bizarre or eccentric with the absolutely familiar and commonplace that marks the experience of naturalist art at least from Chekhov on. Just as he finds it in the way Walter Huston, the avuncular bank president of *American Madness*

(1932), greets Pat O'Brien, his favorite employee and surrogate son. Huston enters the bank and O'Brien is behind his cage, in place for the day. As Huston passes, exuding warmth and energy in every direction and making his good mornings to all, he fixes O'Brien with a special strenuous wink, which O'Brien returns with equal strenuousness. Huston's greeting is warm, paternal, genially patriarchal. O'Brien's response, though genial, is something else as well: distanced, slightly self-mocking, ultimately cool. This exchange tells us an extraordinary amount about the lines between these two people—not only where they connect but where they are drawn—reminding us what complicated relations such daily rituals of greeting are likely to express.

Such notations in Capra not only escape the film's more ambitious meanings and intentions, but they give those intentions a life and substance they wouldn't otherwise have. The *idea* of the bank in *American Madness*—as a genuinely benign and avuncular operation—is a preposterous one (it was too much for Depression audiences to swallow, in fact, and the film failed spectacularly). But the *life* in this bank is so rich and real and lovingly observed that the movie almost works anyway. A Capra film of the early thirties could be persuasive even when it wasn't especially coherent, mainly because it seemed to come from someone who was committed most of all, and in spite of distractions, to a connection with observable life—to a certain behavioral freedom and richness in front of the camera, to letting us "look" at people even if that meant "stopping" everything else. But beginning with *Mr. Deeds Goes to Town* ("my first all-out indictment of the inhumanities of our time") in 1936, Capra sets out on a quite different course than all this suggests, and the sort of freedom and spontaneity of effect that seems so prominent in earlier films begins to diminish. It's not freedom but constraint that marks the later Capra: the constriction of moralizing intentions and surefire effects. And *It Happened One Night*, oddly enough, seems to have been the turning point for him.

CAPRA TELLS about his conversion experience in his autobiography, *The Name Above the Title*. He was frightened by the great personal success he had earned with *It Happened One Night*—finally as bemused and puzzled by the film's impact as was nearly everyone else in Hollywood. What to do for an encore, then? He decided, as he tells it, to play sick, then discovered that he was really sick and couldn't get well—he couldn't even be diagnosed, but he *seemed* to be dying. It was at this point that he had a visitor, "a faceless little man" sent by friends (Capra claims he never learned the man's identity). The little man called him a coward, accused him of wasting his God-given talent and, above all, his opportunity as a maker of movies seen the world over. How many people can Hitler talk to in his radio broadcasts? asked the man. "Fifteen

Mr. Deeds
(Gary Cooper)
feeds a poor
man (John
Wray) in Mr.
Deeds Goes to
Town.

million—twenty million? And for how long—twenty minutes? You, sir, can talk to *hundreds* of millions, for two hours—and in the dark." Capra not only got well as a result of the faceless little man's visit but was from that moment, by his own account, a filmmaker totally committed "to the service of man . . . down to my dying day, down to my last feeble talent. . . . Beginning with *Mr. Deeds Goes to Town,* my films had to *say* something."

Although Peter Warne, the hero of *It Happened One Night,* is (as I said above) a prophet of the average and everyday, Capra never suggests in that film that there is a really serious conflict between the heroine's freedom and the hero's conventionality. But in *Mr. Deeds Goes to Town* he does—and there is. Claudette Colbert's Ellie turns into Jean Arthur's Babe Bennett, the first of several Capra heroines who must learn, through love of the hero, to repent her freedom and wit—much as Capra had learned, it seems, to repent his. The Capra hero from Mr. Deeds on is an embodiment of all the simple virtues, kind and sincere and boyish, full of patriotism and secular piety. "He's got goodness, Mabel," says the heroine of *Mr. Deeds,* talking to another tough type like herself (wisecracking

Ruth Donnelly). "Do you know what that means?" Then, not waiting for an answer: "No, of course you don't. We've forgotten. We're all too busy being smart alecks." It's a big laugh to the smart alecks at Tullio's restaurant (Capra's and Riskin's version of the Algonquin Round Table) that Longfellow Deeds (Gary Cooper) writes greeting-card verses, and they invite him to their table to mock him: "Can you recite one?" "Give us one that wrings the great American heart!" But as Deeds in his anger tells them, "A lotta people think they're good— anyway, it's the best I can do." These high-culture snobs are without tolerance or understanding or even ordinary kindness—the sort of civility you find in Mandrake Falls: "I must look funny to you, but maybe if you went to Mandrake Falls you'd look just as funny to us—only nobody'd laugh at you and make you feel ridiculous 'cause that wouldn't be good manners." Finally, he just knocks one of them down.

The only people who touch brilliance in these films are the villains (usually Edward Arnold) and the heroines (usually Jean Arthur). And if they learn anything at all, they learn to be sorry for it. Arthur makes the same radical mistake in two different films: she just can't bring herself to believe that someone as simple as Deeds or Smith seems to be isn't either a fake or an imbecile. In a screwball comedy, she would be right, of course. He would, in fact, very likely be *both*—anyone who wonders out loud, as Deeds does, why people can't "try *liking* each other once in a while"—and would be played by Ralph Bellamy.

Because Capra is not just departing from screwball comedy—he is making war on it, though the lines in that war were drawn independently of his efforts and long before *Mr. Deeds*. Almost from their beginnings, the movies had been polarized between naïve and sophisticated modes, between skepticism and innocence. The screwball comedy was a modern culmination of the skeptical mode. And it was the Capra version of the folksy comedy that now entered into a debate with that skepticism, speaking up for simplicity and ingenuousness and a pastoral-idyllic vision of America, and against the smart alecks. Partly because of Capra, the familiar polarities became a kind of dialectic, an argument that entered into individual movies, where one kind of movie was always reminding its audience of the other kind—and deliberately. Screwball comedies were largely meant for the city—meant to reconcile their audiences to living in one. Although Capra films idealized the small town (the hero always comes from one), they didn't seem to want to "live" there.* They took place in the cities they deplored, in newspaper offices and nightclubs and other such habitats of the screwball couple. Their heroines, too, were screwball comedy heroines— newspaperwomen, independent career types, very tough-talking—though at the

---

*When Capra finally reverses this pattern, he makes his most serious and most interesting film: *It's a Wonderful Life* (1946), where the hero feels really stuck in his small town and has to learn to appreciate its blessings.

end of the movie they are always headed for that small town and for that transformation into homebody which we never (happily) have to witness.

It was conventional in the screwball comedy, on the other hand, to make jokes
about small-town America that were fully intelligible only if you assumed, as
these movies did (the Tulsa joke in *The Awful Truth*, for example), that life in
that America was a terrible living death and that any reasonable person would
do anything he could to escape it. Whenever such a comedy actually shows us
one of those towns (e.g., *Theodora Goes Wild*), the place is characterized by
extraordinary meanness and ignorance. The sort of community (e.g., *Nothing
Sacred*) where a small boy may run out of his front yard just to bite you on the
leg, and where people charge you a fee even for talking to you, if you're a stranger and they can get away with it. The avarice of the down-home type is as
certain a characteristic as his hypocrisy is. In Mr. Deeds' home town of Mandrake Falls, however, they hardly seem to have *heard* of greed. The housekeeper's reaction to the news that Deeds has just inherited twenty million dollars is
to tell him to eat his lunch: "You haven't touched a thing!" she exclaims.

Gary Cooper in *Mr. Deeds Goes to Town* embodies both the intention and the
central problem of these Capra films. Cooper stands for naturalness, without
being quite wholly authentic—for "naturalness," in quotes. "The simple yet far
from simple face," as James Agee described him in 1944, "of the high-priced
male beauty." Capra is concerned more or less throughout his career (especially
in the screenplays with Riskin, and as early as *The Miracle Woman* in 1931)
with questions of honesty and public fakery. It concerns him that good ideas may
be used by bad people for their own bad ends—just as the deploring of worldly
success may be used to secure it, not only by evangelists and politicians but by
moviemakers, too. But the outcome of this concern in the plots of his movies is
always a comforting one: faking is not something you are drawn into by degrees,
but something you decide either to do or to stop doing, as in both *Meet John Doe*
and *The Miracle Woman*. Still, even here Capra is nervously aware of just how
good a good fake can be. "Look at that face—they'll believe him!" he has Stanwyck say about Cooper in *Meet John Doe* as she is setting him up to meet the
public. Capra knows (as he reminds us here) that he himself is involved in
exactly similar calculations about Cooper and others. So does Cooper. "When
they say I'm just being me," Cooper once said in an interview, "they don't know
how hard it is to be a guy like me."

Cooper was a man of extraordinary beauty: a *troubled* beauty, with expressive
wounded-animal eyes, with suggestions of cold mischief in them at some times,
of dumb suffering sensuality at others. Josef von Sternberg put a flower behind
his ear in *Morocco* (1930), made the sensuality proud and insolent (next to *this*
Cooper, Marlene Dietrich looks almost affable and outgoing). He tried to make
the Cooper beauty unapologetic. But it didn't work. How could it with a cowboy

type? Besides, audiences wanted that note of apology. It helped to make him seem what he more and more offered to be as his career wore on—a kind of transcendent ordinary man, a demigod bumbler, a man so legendarily inarticulate that the one-word sound "Yup" identified him everywhere in jokes and impersonations.

But he is a genuinely troubling figure. The eyes are *so* stricken, the face so lean and taut and clenched at the jaw when he is young, so collapsed when he is older. In repose, the beauty seems authentically tragic. And when a role or situation calls for stolidity and unwavering gravity—as most of his western roles did, beginning with *The Virginian* (1929), his first talkie—Cooper is unmatchably eloquent, seeming both vulnerable and monumental at the same time. And the sense of pain and defeat as he grows older—the rawness of some unuttered suffering or guilt—makes you almost want to turn away from his presence on the screen. Very few of his directors were willing to use this complicated pain: only Anthony Mann in *Man of the West* (1958), one of Cooper's last (and least popular) films, and quite possibly his best. They were more interested in monumentalizing him as the ultimate plain American, and using him in roles like Lou Gehrig in *The Pride of the Yankees* (1942), which connected the pain with a terminal illness, and everything else with decency and simplicity and wonderful ordinariness.

But this was a process that Capra initiated: he showed the way to all the others. Before *Mr. Deeds Goes to Town*, the Cooper image was still somewhat indeterminate, still hung up—even in less-than-ordinary films like *Now and Forever* (1934), where he plays a con man reformed by Shirley Temple—on some of Cooper's contradictions, like the suggestions of coldness and slyness. Capra both infantilizes Cooper and cloaks him in presexual, nondenominational piety: the ultimate good little boy, with shyness and stammerings and childish dreams intact into middle age and beyond. This was a triumph, no doubt of it. Specifically, it was a triumph for that persisting tendency in popular culture that tries to empty out our experiences for us—to deprive them of meaning or threat or seriousness. If the movies could banalize Cooper's face—if they could deny the defeat in *those* eyes—they could handle anything.

But it wasn't just the complications in Cooper that audiences and filmmakers refused to see. Since he was most effective when he did nothing in front of the camera, it was conventional to say that that was what he always did—nothing. And it has become even now nearly the universal testimony about Cooper— repeated in spite of the evidence of films like *Mr. Deeds*, or even *Pride of the Yankees*—that he is a uniquely *plain* sort of performer ("they say I'm just being me"). When in fact, he is an acutely mannered one, playing a plain man: arch and "cute" and almost painfully false at times, condescending to plainness in the same way that Capra does. When Deeds has to register his discovery of

Babe's betrayal (he has just learned she is the newspaper writer who has been making public fun of him all along), Capra very shrewdly has him play the scene in front of an onlooker, his press agent, Cobb (Lionel Stander), so that Deeds can also show the kind of self-consciousness an onlooker might reasonably provoke. This gives Cooper more things to *do* in the course of the moment—an important help for him. For although he doesn't grimace or make big dramatic faces, he is endlessly busy making small ones, almost as if running through a checklist of expressions: torn between crying and trying not to cry, between showing his grief and registering Cobb's presence; frowning, smiling, blinking, turning first this way, then that—undecided *where* to turn—until finally Capra has him step into a nearby shadow, leaving Cobb in the light, staring at him with concern.

"Look at that face—they'll believe him." Gary Cooper and Barbara Stanwyck in Meet Joe Doe.

The contrast to Jean Arthur's presence and performance in the same movie is enormous. Arthur has her mannerisms too, but she never has to mug to get through a scene. She *is* what Cooper often has to work at being: a natural. Watch the scene where they are first dining together at Tullio's. She has pretended to

be starving on his front sidewalk in order to meet him for her story, and he is being gallant to a lady in distress. When Deeds signals the restaurant's wandering violinist to play a schmaltzy romantic tune for her while they eat, and then watches her shyly across the table, with winks and blinks and mischievous eye widenings and boyish "oh, whoops" looks of alarm as she listens—and Arthur merely *looks*, first at the violin, then at him, then back at the violin again—the contrast in performers is like the difference between a powerful poetic utterance and a vigorous set of semaphore signals. Because as with all great screen actors (and it remains a kind of mystery), we can really *see* what Arthur is thinking. It's in her face and her eyes: the suppressed incredulity at the gypsy fiddler routine, the simple bafflement about Deeds himself, the determination to remain impassive and even seem pleased when she looks back at him.

But Cooper makes his discomfiture into a kind of purification rite in these films. And when audiences at *Mr. Deeds* took the impression of something powerfully "natural" in his performance, it was partly that they weren't used to seeing such discomfort in a star offered so sufferingly. For Cooper more than anyone incarnated the special Capra vision, enduring it in front of the cameras for the large numbers of people who wanted, like Capra himself, to believe in this sort of goodness. But it wasn't easy being the embodiment of simplicity: "They don't know how hard it is being a guy like me. . . ." And Cooper turns his problem with this situation into his signature as a star: he is self-conscious about being *un*selfconscious. And in this respect above all he represents Capra's dilemma, too.

CAPRA TRULY *wants* to be generous—but, finally, he is too unadventurous, too fearful and self-protecting, to be good at it. What happens to Deeds in the city, for example, would confirm the narrowest small-towner's darkest fears. Everyone *is* after his money: they talk about culture and so forth, but we know better. They want him to support the opera, and then they tell him it's losing money. Then it must be giving "the wrong kind of show," he retorts simply; that, as he says, is only "common sense." It's not bad business sense, either (Deeds runs a successful factory of some kind back home). And although the movie deplores the cruelty of the highbrows at Tullio's, it also gives the disturbing impression that it resents their "cleverness," which is very clumsily and unconvincingly mimicked in any case (the "poet" refers to a hat as a "headpiece," and so on). The whole episode—especially Deeds's improbable triumph at the end, making all the intellectuals feel ashamed and even knocking one of them in the jaw—has the feeling of scores being settled. If it works at all, it's likely to remind you of that joke that went over your head and that everyone else around you got—so loudly—and all that laughing you couldn't join and so you just had to sit there feeling like an idiot, maybe dreaming about a little revenge like Deeds's at Tullio's. So much of the emotional energy in this movie goes toward making people feel *ashamed* of laughing. "It's easy to make fun of someone," says Deeds to the highbrows, "if you don't care how much you hurt 'em." Capra spends so much time reminding us that laughter hurts—and it's not the villains or the moguls it hurts (who would laugh at Edward Arnold?), nor even the phonies (who are egregious but unfunny), but innocent people like Deeds. Here, it's the phonies who *do* the laughing. And the rest of us get to feel superior to it. Some fun. "I handed the gang a grand laugh," says the anguished heroine at Deeds's sanity hearing, contemplating the fact that *her* jokes have just about put the man she loves in the crazy house. "It's a fitting climax to my sense of humor." Indeed it is—in this movie. The pattern is so unrelenting that you begin to wonder if Capra has something against "humor" itself.

Of course, Capra wants people to be kind. But he also gives the impression that he wants them to be unthreatening, manageable, unimposing—a world of people like Jane Austen's Miss Bates, who had "no intellectual superiority to . . . frighten those who might hate her, into outward respect." That's one reason, perhaps, for his and Riskin's embarrassing rhetoric about the "little people," and the diminishing of all the so-called ordinary people in these films to a kind of Disney-like pathos and winsomeness, as with Deeds's starving farmer. Because if you just think about all those masses of people out there as "little" enough—cute and scruffy and starry-eyed enough—probably you don't have to think of them the *other* way these films show them: as ravening and demented, a mob clamoring for the hero's destruction. Capra's condescension is like Mr. Deeds's common sense—a protection from the world outside.

But that "little people" emphasis was widely objected to even at the height of Capra's popularity. And he himself parodies it when he has Cooper's John Doe pose for publicity photos with a midget man and woman. But in the same movie, Doe talks emotionally to D. B. Norton, the master villain of the piece (Arnold again), about the thousands of ordinary people who have come from "everywhere" to attend the John Doe Club convention which Norton now threatens to disrupt. Why have they come? asks Doe rhetorically, and answers: "So they could pass on to each other their own simple little experiences." And it's not worth asking, even rhetorically, whether Capra and Riskin could think of *their* experiences in this way—as "simple" and "little." The interesting question is whether they expect *us* to—their presumably ordinary audience. And it's just here that Capra's relation to his audience, the people he's trying to "say something" to, gets tricky indeed.

The Capra hero is, like his creators, always involved with an audience. And that audience, like Capra's real audience, is always a general one, representative and "ordinary." One of the most interesting features of Capra's work is the careful way he defines our relation to our surrogates on the screen, the audience in the movie. For example: John Doe is making a radio speech and he is in front of a radio studio audience. It's "the little punks" like them, he tells them, who make the difference in America, "because in the long run the character of the country is the sum total of the character of its little punks"! And the studio audience applauds wildly. We don't, however—and it's clear that we're not meant to, partly because that other audience's applause is so hard to believe in. What's cagey here, what's almost brilliant, is the way Capra and the movie itself have allowed for our disbelief—even solicited it. Doe tells his audience in the same radio speech that we all have a bit of larceny in us: he reminds them how they never pass a pay phone without feeling for a coin. And *his* audience laughs again. As if to say, "He's sure on to us!" But he's not on to *us*. Any real audience—anywhere, and even in 1941—is going to be farther gone in iniquity than that. Beyond that audience on the screen certainly—just as we are beyond most of the people in the movie, and invited to patronize them just as the movie itself does. If the outrageous condescension of *Meet John Doe* works at all, it's partly because we the audience are invited to bestow it rather than receive it—even to bestowing it on "ourselves." Those on-screen audiences—who both are and aren't us—are like the neighbor the movie keeps urging us to get to know: nicer than we could possibly imagine, or believe. Like the John Doe Club members from Millville who laugh merrily when a spokesman recalls how one neighbor's radio kept everyone awake at night. They seem as delighted by this recollection as the elderly neighbor himself is by the nickname ("Sourpuss") they now call him by to his face.

Because if that on-screen audience is always a lot nicer than the one we are sitting in, it is also, we recognize, a lot dumber—laughing at jokes that aren't funny and clapping for platitudes and speakers who call them "little punks." We can watch that audience on the screen, possibly even admire it, but we could never *be* it, any more than we could laugh at those jokes: the best we can do is think we might have laughed at that *once* perhaps—long ago. But this is precisely our relation to the "goodness" these films are always commending to us ("He's got goodness, Mabel—do you know what that means?"). We observe it from far off: it's nearly always a matter of being more innocent, more childish, stupider even, than we can ever be again. As when Longfellow Deeds is told that he has inherited twenty million dollars: he really seems not to have heard, or at least not to be that interested. The silence after he gets the news is lovingly, almost pornographically extended, as we and the lawyers wait for his response. He looks abstracted, more interested in the mouthpiece on his tuba, and when at last he does speak, it's to repeat his suggestion that they should stay and have lunch with him and to particularly recommend his housekeeper's "fresh orange layer cake"—"with the thick stuff on the top," he adds, smacking his lips. It's unbelievable, of course—just as it is in *Meet John Doe* when the "little people" of Millville (Ann Doran and Regis Toomey are their spokesmen) respond with passionate excitement to the "idea" that "the trouble with the world is nobody gives a hoot about his neighbor." Capra isn't at all saying that real people will respond this way: he knows that we won't and even reminds us of it. He's only asking us to imagine . . . well, how nice it would be if we *could*. And the impossibility of the virtue he shows us in these films is part of what makes it so pleasant, so seductive and entertaining. The goodness here is like the poor people: unreal and unthreatening; there is less of real kindness and real heroism than of a yearning nostalgic relation to such events. And finally what could be more hopeless?—below the affirmations, "the thick stuff on the top." It's no wonder that Capra, with all his energy and optimism, was also a depressive, that his movies have terrible undercurrents of discouragement and despair. Those who make serious claims for these movies usually point to the pessimism in the subtext (the power of fascism in *Meet John Doe*, the power of political corruption in *Mr. Smith:* the forces of evil are always inescapable and overwhelming) as redeeming and balancing the general optimism and uplift. But it's not the optimism in these films that needs to be redeemed (screwball comedy is an implacably optimistic mode); it's the condescension and falsity.

But this was the time of screwball comedy; and though the Capra films were massively popular, he had reason to feel, as a comic filmmaker at least, like an embattled minority. Probably he did—certainly he has a keen instinct for the enemy. He puts her, in fact, right into the middle of his own films. Can anyone believe, for example, that Barbara Stanwyck wouldn't see, in anyone else's movie, that the John Doe "idea" was a dumb one? Capra not only brings her into the fold—forcibly—he makes her confess her errors and behave as if that's where she always wanted to be. There could be no doubt about it at the time (and clearly Capra knew it somehow): the most dangerous enemy. the most beguiling antagonist to everything that the Capra films stood for, was the screwball heroine—that sexy and funny new "type" who was also tough, smart and independent, all the things the most brilliant of thirties women stars excelled at being. She is the Capra heroine, too—she is Arthur and Stanwyck, two of the women who did the most on the screen to make the condition of being skeptical, unillusioned, and even a little tough seem like a fully human, utterly attractive one. In the Capra films she is all these things, too—that, in fact, is her value for him. But precisely so she can learn to be ashamed of them—to repent what she is, a "smart aleck" and "wised up," and even be punished for it. "I wonder, Diz, if that Don Quixote hasn't got the jump on all of us," says Jean Arthur in *Mr. Smith* to a reporter buddy (Thomas Mitchell). "I wonder if it isn't a curse to go through life wised up like you and me." It is indeed—as she finds out very shortly.

This wise-guy heroine is always the instigator of the hero's public humiliation.

At the beginning of the film she is the one who gets the newspaper on his case. She acts out of ambition—and skepticism about him. But soon she learns better, and she falls in love as well. This reversal comes fairly early in the film, but her punishment and mortification generally go on to the end. Just as she herself achieves belief, she has to watch the hero—thanks to her—lose it, and then to confront the torment this causes in him. "Whatta yuh gonna *believe* in?" he says in *Mr. Smith*, and Jean Arthur tells him. In *Mr. Deeds* he doesn't even ask—he's been too hurt. As a result, Arthur falls into hysterical public contrition and must plead with him and weep even to get his attention (she fails). And Stanwyck in *Meet John Doe* must rise from a sickbed to plead with the hero in the snow not to throw himself off the edge of the building—to promise to go over with him if he does.

The Capra hero, like the movie star, is sustained by the interest of crowds. Friendship in these films always looks like fandom. When the judge (Harry Davenport) in *You Can't Take It With You* is told that the crowds filling his courtroom are *all* Grandpa Vanderhof's friends, he is astonished: "I didn't know anyone had that many friends anymore," he says. And when Longfellow Deeds departs Mandrake Falls for New York, there is a genuine mob scene at the railroad station. "Gosh," he says as the train pulls away and the throng cheers, "I got a lotta friends." And this isn't a joke, as it would be in Lubitsch ("It's great to be in love," says Danilo at Maxim's, clutching some dozen girls at once) or in a tougher kind of comedy. It's in deadly earnest: this hero requires the support of the crowd, and often his life depends on it.

Or, rather, he *makes* his life depend on it. Invariably in some form he makes this threat: believe or I'll die. And the heroine becomes Magdalene at the foot of his cross. (Christ, we are told by Stanwyck, was "the first John Doe.") But his agony is less like Calvary than it is like a failure at the box office: bad publicity and the loss of his audience. And the hero's response is always (like Capra's own self-induced illness) self-spiting, with mild variations allowing for the star: Cooper sulks and Stewart fumes (one prefers Stewart—and even as written, Mr. Smith is the least masochistic and self-pitying of these heroes). When Longfellow Deeds tries to give his fortune away to the dispossessed farmers, his competence is impugned and he is forced to submit to a sanity hearing. His response to this threat—along with his discovery of the heroine's treachery—is to stop talking. To anyone. When all the while it is perfectly clear that the absurd suspicion could be disposed of in an instant, and he could be saved from the loony bin if only he *did* talk, even just a little—no, never mind. Let his friends and supporters sweat and plead—they do, they do. He just sits there in the courtroom—*don't mind me*, he seems to be saying, as he turns his suffering beautiful face, mute and reproachful, to the heroine and the farmers, to the crowd, to the judge, to the camera, to us. . . . So who's laughing now?

Deeds, too hurt to talk—even to Jean Arthur. The judge (H. B. Warner) is in the background.

CAPRA BELIEVES in radical kindness and in American institutions. He never notices the contradiction. He is into denial, as we might say. But this propensity is exactly, I think, what gives him his famous power over audiences, even audiences of today: young people who get restive at the high romanticism of old movies, even laughing at Bogart's tough-guy style in *Casablanca*, sit rapt and unprotesting and apparently moved through the platitudes of *Meet John Doe* and *Mr. Deeds*. The Capra vision isn't dead.* We still have something invested in the *idea* of being American; certainly Capra's original audience did, at the depths of the Depression—the idea of Americanness itself as connecting somehow with a stronger plainness and decency, with a people's greater directness of manner and openness of feeling, a greater idealism even than other people's. And it's ideas like this, of course, which always seem to rationalize America's most dangerous (and most popular) national policies—like our fondness for weapons (what harm will *we* do?). It's as if being plain in manner might

* Unhappily. Reagan in the White House (a Capra event in itself, though certainly no joke) "explains" his economic policies to reporters by quoting "lengthy passages" from *Mr. Deeds Goes to Town*!

exempt us from being fake at heart. But the style of a national icon like Gary Cooper shows, if demonstration be necessary, just how fake even that plainness can be. As baroque in its way as the style of a Jack Barrymore or Noel Coward—and greatly more deceptive.

Capra was far from being the only filmmaker who dramatized such notions of the American character, but he was one of the most ersatz. In Capra, however, it's the ersatz that makes the difference. It isn't that he tells us more than other people do of what we wish were true about America: it's that he tells us, finally, that the truth doesn't matter compared to the wishing. This is exciting news—*if* you can get away with it. And Capra almost does. In his hands even those platitudes become magical counters. "There's something swell about the spirit of Christmas," says John Doe in his radio speech, "what it does to people, all kinds of people. Now why can't that spirit, that same warm Christmas spirit, last the whole year round?" Yes—why *not?* But . . . "we are already asleep," as Arkadina says in *The Seagull.* This conundrum is boring even to Capra, it would seem. He has the heroine, who presumably wrote this speech, apologize for it later on: "Look, John, what we give them is platitudes. . . ." We certainly don't believe those platitudes, any more than we believe in the rapture they inspire in the people on screen. But this is where the magic comes. Capra's secret is that he doesn't just stretch our credulity—he challenges it, openly. We are asked to take all this seriously precisely because it *does* defy belief, at least of an ordinary kind. A Capra film doesn't just tell us that small towns are wonderful places: it tells us that the people who live there are indifferent to money and not at all inclined (as those city people are) to make fun of strangers; it tells us small towns are wonderful in just the ways that no one can believe they are. This filmmaker, who once showed a special talent for evoking real behavior, gives us people who are almost programmatically unreal—no one more so than the "real" ones, the spokesmen for the common man, the representatives of grass-roots simplicity (the children in Capra, too, are always strikingly false, even for this period in Hollywood). But all this begins to seem less like a defect of talent or skill than a kind of choice. It is integral, in fact, to just what we respond to in Capra most strongly. His inspiration is always peculiarly energized by those situations and occasions where the evidence is all against him—like Jefferson Smith invoking the spirit of Lincoln against the fact of a corrupt Senate, filled to the bursting point with hacks and crooks.

During the Second World War Capra worked long and tirelessly, in an Army Special Services unit, at selling the war effort. The result was the monumental "Why We Fight" series. Long a propagandist for America in fact, Capra was now working at the job openly and happily, and often with marvelous effect. Could anyone else have brought quite the same conviction to a government film called *The Negro Soldier* (1944), praising the contribution of black troops to the war? This extraordinary movie begins and ends with what purports to be a Negro church service and proceeds to recount the history of American blacks from the Revolutionary War to the present. It does this, even comprehensively, without ever once naming or alluding to the event called slavery. An extreme case, perhaps, but in truth this wasn't so far from the customary way of dealing with such things at that time of national unity. Capra, however, brings a special flair and feeling to these accepted tactics—from the ringing falsity and theatricalism of his pious black congregation (worshipping the Flag, it seems)—to the excitement of the moment, in connection with the Civil War, when slavery is *almost* mentioned—then swept past and under by the narrator's rhetoric and the choir's exultancy. When Capra denies something, the moment isn't furtive or shameful: it's exalted.

Such deliberate implausibility—even fabrication—systematically applied to social issues that are real and painful and present to his audience, is, of course, exactly the method of Capra's "fiction" films—just as it has become the dominant mode of our American political life. And the message of this mode is an exciting one: telling us we can believe what we like really. It may seem unfair to compare him to Reagan: Capra, for all his faults, addresses our best instincts just as clearly and surely as Reagan addresses our worst. But in one respect, at least, they are fatally similar figures: each affirms our *will* to get good news, our inalienable right to have a good day. And Capra really believes in belief. That's why he didn't apparently feel, as others did at comparable moments in their Hollywood careers, that he was selling out (though, as we've seen, the subject was on his mind). Early on, he was a director with an affinity for experiences of yearning, longing, aspiration (*It Happened One Night*, or *The Bitter Tea of General Yen*). He turns that affinity into a statement about American life: the aptitude becomes a theme—and a calcification.

He knew where the enemy was, as we've seen—identifying it in the screwball comedy, with all its blithe, brilliant, coldhearted practitioners. And *they*, for the most part, identified him. Capra's success—his universally conceded ability to define and touch something deeply "American" in his audience's feelings—helped to define other comic filmmakers' subjects and choices, often indirectly, often not. Some, like Sturges, would take him on. Others, like McCarey, would finally decide to join him.

Powell and Loy | 8

IT WASN'T until two years after their triumph in *The Thin Man* that William Powell and Myrna Loy did another comedy together. MGM knew, of course, that they had a sensational romantic comedy team, but they also knew (as befitted the studio's eminence) how to make subject audiences wait. While lesser MGM stars like Rosalind Russell and Robert Montgomery were appearing in comedies about amusing detective couples—MGM's way of meeting the *Thin Man* demand without slaking it—Powell and Loy were teamed in *Evelyn Prentice* (1934) and *The Great Ziegfeld* (1936), heavy films and turgidly domestic. *Ziegfeld* at least was a hit, but it wasn't a comedy. *Libeled Lady* (1936) followed, however, and it was—the most delightful comedy of all the Powell-and-Loy films.

It's an MGM all-star special—Jean Harlow and Spencer Tracy are also in it— and it looks wonderful even before it begins. The starriness calls for a fanfare: between the MGM lion and the opening credits, there is a medium shot of the four stars walking forward arm in arm (left to right, Harlow, Powell, Loy, and Tracy), striding briskly toward us against a cyclorama sky and into a wind that blows the women's dresses backwards. They are smiling broadly, larger than life, on top of the world and loving it. Wanting to share it, too—coming toward us. But not getting any closer: stars, after all—both like and unlike the rest of us.

Not only do the cast trail clouds of familiar glory; so do the movie's various settings and plots. That familiarity is one of *Libeled Lady*'s special pleasures— that it evokes for us not only so many other movies of fond memory but so many *kinds* of other movies, and manages them all with so much authority. It begins as a newspaper comedy, full of shouted abuse and stylish double-dealing. Soon it becomes a rather high-toned comedy of manners involving Powell's pursuit of Loy on an ocean voyage. It finally hits its stride as one of those marital-mixup comedies ("She may be his wife but she's engaged to me!"), where Harlow, the

Two kinds of social dilemma: Loy on shipboard with bores (above); Powell on "honeymoon" with Harlow and her fiancé, Spencer Tracy. Libeled Lady.

bride, gives a prolonged kiss to Tracy, the best man ("An old friend of the family," explains Powell, the bridegroom, to the judge—and adds, as the kiss goes on, "A *very* old friend"), and where something called a "Yucatan divorce" magically changes everyone's life (or seems to for a reel or two). Myrna Loy is Connie Allenbury, the richest girl in the world, who is suing the *Evening Star* for libel. William Powell is Bill Chandler, the ace reporter and devil with women who is assigned by the *Star* to compromise her reputation and forestall the lawsuit. Spencer Tracy is the editor who gives him this assignment, and who is therefore too busy to marry Jean Harlow, who keeps showing up at the church anyway. The credit for this intricate screenplay is the usual gang of names: Maurine Watkins (the playwright-author of *Chicago*), Howard Emmett Rogers, and George Oppenheimer, "from a story by" Howard Sullivan. The director is Jack Conway.

The material here is, and was even by 1936, the stuff of tradition. It's important to the kind of experience the movie offers that we know where we are from

the very beginning, even from the opening scenes. Harlow, making her first entrance into the film, storms into the *Evening Star* newsroom in full bridal regalia and sweeps past rows of startled reporters at their desks to confront Tracy in his glass-walled office. He is dressed for a wedding, too, but he is pouring himself a drink and worrying about Connie Allenbury and about finding Bill Chandler, who has disappeared. "What are you doing here?" he says as she bursts into his office, as if forgetting momentarily that he's just stood her up at the church. "Well, what are *you* doing here?" she says, already losing her advantage. Of course he has a good excuse—he had all those other times, too. "First you said a trip to Bermuda—" "You went to Bermuda." "Yeah, but alone!" She puts the issue squarely: "If you don't want to marry me, just *say* so!" she screams. But he does, he really does. Get the preacher to wait, he tells her, and "I'll phone you just—just the minute I'm free." He is ushering her to the door now. "You look beautiful," he says tenderly as he passes her to the office boy, who has instructions to get her to a cab.

And we recognize it all: the waiting-at-the-church joke with all its nightmare exaggerations. But we recognize something else, too: that the people telling the joke to us this time know exactly what's funny about it, exactly what's *always* been funny about it. * Every choice they make here has a wonderful comic clarity and sharpness, an exhilarating rightness. From Harlow's march down the "aisle" of the newsroom, to her attempt to throw a bottle at Tracy's boss, who has spoken to her, she says, "like a house detective" (How do *you* know how a house detective talks? Tracy wants to know. "Don't you think I *read?*" she shouts without skipping a beat)—to her parting observation as she is hustled out the door that this is "supposed to be the happiest day in a girl's life."

Her name is Gladys Simpson, and she is indomitable. Almost the next time we see her she is reading *Real Love Stories,* sitting by the phone. It rings: Haggerty (Tracy) wants her to come to City Hall to get married. The catch, when she gets there, is that he wants her to marry Chandler, whom she hates. The plan is to frame Connie Allenbury for husband-stealing, and so they have to get Chandler married. "Oh, the things I do for that newspaper!" exclaims Gladys. The ceremony that follows is a rather tense one. "I'm taking *your* arm," she says to Haggerty as they all depart the bewildered judge's chambers: she may have married the wrong man, but she is determined to leave with the right one.

None of the jokes in *Libeled Lady* has a distinctive slant or flavor or bias. Unlike in a Lubitsch or a Capra film, the details and inflections here don't reflect any recognizable individual temperament behind them. What they do express is a commitment to what's most deeply, most irreducibly *funny* in our common experiences and common imaginings of experience. The brilliance of this movie is impersonal, almost anonymous—and accessible to absolutely everyone. The intelligence is not so much a director's or writer's or even a star's as it is— wonderfully—a common possession. This is one of the special, irreplaceable satisfactions of a movie like this one. Where a Capra film tries to blackmail us into a feeling of communality, movies like *Libeled Lady*—with their sense of an intelligence that is both heightened and publicly shared—suggest other possibilities: the communality of the ideal city, where we are all tough and funny and smart together, and connected because we're free instead of stuck with one another—different, of course, from the sustaining bonds and sheltering simplicities of the ideal small town. And a lot riskier.

Stars like Powell and Loy convey this riskiness, too. Loy is particularly glamorous here because she's so smart and (for part of the movie, anyway) so dan-

---

*It's often hard to distinguish between MGM's house directors: all of them were primarily servants of the studio style and look. But you can tell at least that Jack Conway—like W. S. Van Dyke and Richard Thorpe— knows what's funny in his scripts and materials, even when there isn't a lot that is. Robert Z. Leonard, on the other hand, seems never to know. Nearly all the Leonard-directed comedies—though the scripts and projects were no worse in general than those assigned to other MGM directors—are lifeless and misjudged.

gerous—the most dangerous of the four leading players. The four of them spend most of the movie demonstrating the various and refined styles of insult and putdown, from the prole-ish brawling of Tracy and Harlow to the lethal sparring of Loy and Powell. The controlling pattern is a series of personal contests. First Tracy puts Harlow down, as we've seen—and then is put down himself by the vastly subtler and more resourceful Powell—who finally meets *his* match in the superelegant Loy. And so on. Everyone in the quartet gets his turn at everyone else. Everyone wins, and everyone loses, at least one crucial encounter. And the effects are complex because we are rarely on the side of one or another of the combatants. We are involved in the *atmosphere* of insult—a very heady one—and in the ingenuity of the manipulations. The movie makes us want to see everybody put down—and eventually we do. With exact emotional logic: proceeding from the roughhouse of the newsroom to the civilized acrimony of the ocean liner, where we recognize that the most painful aggression of all is to be treated as Powell is by Loy—with infinite inattention.

The movie knows everything about this kind of embarrassment. All the great

William Powell, Myrna Loy, and Walter Connolly in Libeled Lady. *Loy is no longer suspicious—though she should be.*

screwball comedies participate in this painful social genius. And *Libeled Lady* takes us through Powell's discomfiture at Loy's hands twinge by comic twinge—not a nuance overlooked. Since it knows that this kind of humiliation is composed of nuances—and their accumulation. Bill Chandler is in the position both of trying everything he can to please the Allenburys (learning about trout-fishing, pretending to hate reporters) and of not being able to get their attention. It's in this sequence on the ocean liner that we see Loy's almost endless range in expressions of quiet distaste. They are all at a table together in the ship's lounge. In order to thank Chandler for an earlier bit of gallantry toward Connie (saving her from some insistent photographers on the dock—a set-up to get acquainted, of course), her father, J. B. Allenbury (Walter Connolly), has invited him for a drink before dinner; but neither of the Allenburys seems to be able to focus on him once he's there. There are so many interruptions: cables from New York, queries about the chartered plane, replies to the waiter, and so on. And neither father nor daughter can ever seem to get his name right—"Chalmers," they keep calling him, in spite of his gentle corrections. "Do you fly, Mr. Chalmers?" Connie asks graciously. "Uh, *Chandler*," he says softly, flashing a winning smile; but she looks at him as if he'd made a rude noise of some kind. Soon she turns to him again: "Are you having fun, Mr. . . . ah . . . ?" But this time he doesn't coach her: "Ah . . ." he repeats, like a playful schoolmaster, inviting her to find the word on her own. But already another thought has struck her—"Father, did you cable about my plane?"—she turns away again, leaving Chandler with his smile hanging. A little more of this treatment and this impeccable man of the world seems almost punch-drunk. At length the Allenburys rise to leave. "Good evening," they say. "Ah . . . huh?" he replies, as if stuck for the right answer.

But of course they are leaving too soon. He gets an instant second chance, however, when he sees that their departure from the lounge has been blocked by the two bores they have been complaining about and trying to avoid: the Burns-Norvells, a giddy mother-daughter pair ("We've been looking for you all over the boat!"), who insist that the Allenburys join them for dinner. Chandler darts forward—"Sorry if I'm late, J.B."—and saves the Allenburys by claiming his own dinner appointment. "We're dining with Mr. Chalmers," says Connie to the bores, and off the three of them go to the dining room. "That was fast thinking," says Connie to Chandler as they cross the lounge again: he takes her remark as a compliment.

They dance together after dinner; she is almost rigid with distaste and suspicion, while he is unflappably gallant.

BILL: I'm afraid that dancing isn't exactly my line.
CONNIE: I should say it was part of your line.

BILL: Hmm? Oh—may I be frank, too?
CONNIE: Why not?
BILL: You dance superbly.

It's hopeless. He stumbles slightly and apologizes: "I wasn't concentrating," he says, then adds, more gingerly than ardent: "It was your eyes." "Beautiful, aren't they?" she replies. And so it goes—until the Burns-Norvells intrude again, from their table by the dance floor, enabling him to "save" her again: the two women want her to lunch with them tomorrow, but Bill tells them that Connie is dining with him again tomorrow. Connie is more rigid than ever as they dance away from this encounter: clearly it's not the Burns-Norvells she's thinking about. "You know," says Bill, jocular, "it's just dawned on me that I seem to have made myself a permanent member of your party." "Yes," says Connie, "it's dawned on me, too"; her look is dazed, her voice is eerily distant. But he has at least convinced her father of his credentials as a fisherman. "So you fished Gluckman's Point," says Allenbury excitedly, when the couple returns to the table. "Well, you're an angler all right!" "I should say Mr. Chandler is quite an angler," says Connie, and says good night. She plans, she says, to spend the rest of the voyage in her cabin with a book. At last she has gotten his name right.

It's love, of course—or at least its inevitable prelude. Powell's Bill Chandler is the consummate man-about-town, the ultimate smoothie—guaranteed, according to Haggerty, to "meet anybody in the world, from Gandhi to Garbo." He can handle the Harlow and Tracy characters with almost no hitch at all; but confronted with Loy, he is suddenly reduced to snubs on the dance floor, pratfalls in a trout stream (one of the great slapstick routines of the decade), and the humiliating necessity of having to manipulate and deceive three separate people at once. And to every challenge and abasement, to every new threat of exposure, this hero responds not only with aplomb and good temper but with a new lie, a new strategy, another willingness to risk his dignity. He is *not*, as Connie, falling in love with him and still unaware that he is a reporter from the hated *Star*, says of him later on, "impetuous" and "guileless." Far from guileless, he is something more important in the moral scale of these comedies: he is endlessly inventive and ingenious. And he is in love.

It's a measure of the movie's tact and intelligence that once Connie *does* find out who he is—not only a hireling of the *Star* but her would-be blackmailer—it gives her no problem: they are both in love by that time, and they are both of them too smart and too serious to waste time in recriminations or more misunderstandings. They're a wonderfully nice couple, in fact. It's true that the movie loses some of its excitement and sharper energies once they give up their hostilities. What's surprising is that we don't really mind the quieting down: the feeling between Powell and Loy in the straightforward light romantic moments is so attractive and full. It's really what we want to see, after the sparring of the early scenes. But the way in which that aggression, satisfying as it is, and the romance, satisfying as that is, remain more or less separate experiences, marks *Libeled Lady* as a somewhat transitional film. Like all the great screwball romances, it seems to come out of both the tough and the sophisticated modes of earlier film comedy. But in *Libeled Lady* the two modes are less blended than juxtaposed. Even the two couples divide this way: the classy couple and the mug couple. And the movie's richness comes from such juxtapositions: the feeling it gives of an almost breathtaking comic range, the number and variety of tones and styles and jokes it manages over its length, from repartee to pratfalls and back again, from bitching to brawling to a convincing romantic poignance. What it doesn't manage—oddly, in a way—is to owe anything at all to *The Thin Man.* Powell and Loy's hero and heroine here have almost none of the complication and resonance of Nick and Nora. It turns out that the loveliest and most satisfying comedy they appeared in is not the movie in which *they* are most interesting.

P OWELL —who is meant to be a dashing, romantic type—demonstrates the successful masculine manner to a very dim and unsuccessful young man named Waldo (John Beal), in a movie called *Double Wedding* (1937). Waldo, it develops, can't even smile with conviction. That's not a smile, Powell tells him. "*This,*" he says, "is a smile," presenting it with a little gesture of the hand, widening his eyes and exposing his teeth. Women want forceful men, he tells Waldo—"like me," pointing at himself, then going quickly, nervously on. Later on, he is talking to an unsympathetic Myrna Loy, who disapproves of his character: "blackguard" is her word for it. Still, he tells her, "we blackguards can be rather sentimental"; and he describes men in his Foreign Legion regiment who rode into battle and certain death "carrying a rose in their teeth." But his face falls when he gets to the part about the rose, losing conviction even as he hears it. Powell has so many different ways in nearly all his performances to suggest the slight, slowly creeping suspicion of one's own terrible foolishness: it's possibly his greatest single comic gift. He is a virtuoso of the vocalized pause, making stammers and hesitations as precisely informative as words. In one extended "ah" in *Libeled Lady,* a reply to the Allenburys ("Yes—ah . . . ah-*huh?*"), he manages to convey assent, then dismay, then final puzzlement. It's because of this gift for comic unease that Powell almost never seems for all his worldliness either supercilious or complacent, even in encounters with dim young men named Waldo, or even dimmer police sergeants on a case.

Double Wedding—a modest MGM farce, intelligently directed by Richard Thorpe—allows both Powell and Loy to indulge their considerable talents for

Marriage in a trailer: Powell is trying to marry Loy's sister (Florence Rice, center), even though he doesn't really want to, and Loy is trying to rise above it, though unsuccessfully. In a moment the big fight will start. Double Wedding.

light self-mockery. Loy, a prim and unmarried businesswoman, has to fight her unadmitted love for Powell throughout the film. It's an agonizing plight, since he is everything she despises: a "bohemian" who lives in a trailer, wears a beret and a raccoon coat, and writes plays about desert sheiks and their captive love slaves. At first she thinks he's come to do the wallpapering ("They sometimes get to look like that"). But once she knows him for what he is and her appalling passion begins to grow, she is lost. She manages to keep her composure and civility at least in front of Powell himself; but the sight of his thuggish sidekick, Edgar Kennedy, invariably snaps something in her. "That ape!" she cries, her voice rising out of control, every time she sees the unfortunate Kennedy. As a result, he's not eager to see her, either. But at Powell's wedding in the trailer (he is marrying Loy's sister), Kennedy arrives late and with the mistaken impression that Loy is the bride. So he conquers his revulsion and kisses her. She has to gather her wits before hitting him with her purse. "What's wrong?!" cries Kennedy. "Ain't I supposed to kiss the bride?" "I'm not the bride, you ape!" she screams, and starts to pound his chest in terrible anger. In the skillfully staged melee in the trailer that follows this, Kennedy pulls the chin strap on her perky little hat until it snaps back under her nose. And in general, Loy's portrait of an excessively civil lady gone bonkers is wonderful farce. It is also, like Powell's version of the "bohemian" lover, an elegant, amused comment on the stereotype she is playing.

They made thirteen films together (fourteen if one counts Loy's unbilled "guest appearance" in Nunnally Johnson's *The Senator Was Indiscreet* in 1947), all of them comedies after *The Great Ziegfeld* in 1936. Of the ten Powell and Loy comedies, three of them were miscellaneous farces, ranging from good (*Double Wedding*) to passable (*I Love You Again* in 1940) to almost unwatchable (*Love Crazy* in 1941). Six of these comedies, however, were *Thin Man* films, spanning some thirteen years (the last of the series, *Song of the Thin Man*, was released in 1947), making it the longest-running major film series of studio days. For the most part the sequels follow the pattern of the first film. Nick always declines to take the case at first, and Nora always wants him to. There is usually an ingenue spin-off of the original Dorothy to spur him on—though after this figure turns out to be the killer in the third film, this pattern lapses. There is always a nightclub sequence, and there is always a tough, ambiguous blonde more or less derived from the original Mimi—Muriel Hutchinson in the third film, Stella Adler (best of all) in the fourth, even Gloria Grahame in the last. And even in that final film, as in all the others before it, the suspects are gathered in a room at the end for the identification of the killer: the *Thin Man* films were observing this convention long after it had disappeared everywhere else.

MGM wasn't the only studio making *Thin Man*–like comedies in the two-and-a-half-year interim between the original and its first sequel (Powell himself made two of them at RKO: *Star of Midnight* with Ginger Rogers in 1935 and *The Ex-Mrs. Bradford* with Jean Arthur in 1936). But when *After the Thin Man*—by the same director (Van Dyke) and writers (Goodrich and Hackett) who did the original—finally appeared in 1937, almost everyone was happy with it. It was longer and more expensive than the original and generally felt to be more "surprising" at the end (Jimmy Stewart did it). It begins and ends just as the first film does, on a coast-to-coast train (Nick and Nora are returning from the New York trip of the first movie as the second one begins). But there is a depressing little surprise in the sequel's final moment: Nora is pregnant. Even the manner of the revelation is ominous: she is knitting a bootie, giving Nick his first "clue" ("And you call yourself a detective"). Thus begins a process that continues by degrees through each of the subsequent films in the series: the taming and safe domesticating of Nick and Nora.

Nick's liquor consumption, for example, is gradually scaled down. So are Nora's wit and sharpness. At first the process is almost painless: barely noticeable in *Another Thin Man* (1939), the only film in the series with a Dashiell Hammett screenplay. There are some itchy-koo baby jokes, but there is also the wonderful "baby party" thrown by all the plug-uglies Nick knows to show off their babies, even the borrowed ones. But by the next film, *Shadow of the Thin Man* (1941), the "baby" is able to read lines and participate in cute domestic scenes with Mom and Dad. Still, there are compensations: this is also the film in which Nick encounters Stella Adler as the ambiguous blonde, meeting her plummy outrageousness with his complicated gallantry and irony. Even *The Thin Man Goes Home* (1944) has its moments (a comic routine with a lawn chair, and Nora's jitterbug encounter with a sailor), but they no longer make up for the rest of it. Robert Riskin, appropriately, was called in to do the script, which shows Nick and Nora keeping up with the times, as well as with the creeping sanctimony that was overtaking most of Hollywood (especially MGM). It looks like an Andy Hardy film: the art deco sleekness of the series' furnishings is now replaced by the chintz and polka-dot look, done with the usual MGM amplitude. Most significant of all, however, is the way Nora's character has tilted toward the dizzy, lovable helpmate of domestic comedy tradition—cute but dim-witted. (When she demands the sheriff arrest someone, he tells her the man has to do something first. "He does?" she replies. "Why?") This seems right for a film that tries to turn Nick into a small-town type at heart: he has come back to his home town, and he doesn't drink at all, it seems, in spite of his reputation. And the kid, Nicky, Jr., who was "away at school" for this one, is back in the next one—*Song of the Thin Man* (1947)—lecturing his guilty parents about not spending more time at home with him ("*Look* what time it is," he says to them when they finally get in one night) and played by the kind of child actor who seems born for just such a moment. This final film is also the series' nadir. Its concluding image—and the final image of the series itself, once known for its risqué fadeouts—shows the child actor in bed with Asta.

B UT POWELL and Loy were always so much better than even the best of the *Thin Man* movies. They escaped their own vehicles somehow (as stars often did in those days), just as they were always extrinsic to the murders and intrigues that provided the plots. They were the quintessential thirties couple. Other romantic comedy pairs—Astaire and Rogers, Dunne and Grant, Grant and Hepburn—might seem more dazzling, even perhaps more obviously talented. But Powell and Loy were definitive: they embodied the romantic couple itself with an authority—and implied monogamy—that belonged only to them.

They are both rather oblique performers. Loy's glamour on the screen seems always related to meanings held back, diffused, refracted. Her expressiveness, which is considerable, is indirect, light, oddly angled—as Carole Lombard's, for example, never is. Lombard's expressive power is overt, almost overforceful: she can listen to Oscar Jaffe's description of his Passion Play production in *Twen-*

Nick gets stopped for speeding in Shadow of the Thin Man; *Nora looks on.*

tieth Century and then devastate the whole thing with a simple satirical smile. But that sort of effect is almost beyond Loy's powers. She can't, at her best and most characteristic, *look* anything "simple." Both she and Powell are masters of the ambiguous glance or gaze. Nick Charles, as a rule, offers the same pleasant, polite face to all. The mustache and the poise of the mouth suggest a certain alertness; but the eyes, big and wide, are often flat—gleaming but dead. He turns them on others, all eager inattention. Marjorie Main, a crusty but still susceptible landlady in *Another Thin Man*, mistakes this eagerness for "interest." But I'm married, he tells her. "That don't matter and you know it," she says roguishly and tries to clap him on the shoulder—and he darts back playfully, with that mock archness he specializes in: the smile is fixed, but the wide bright eyes are deader than ever. In all these films he walks and stands just as he listens: full of complaisance, with a slight narrow-shouldered forward stoop. He is everybody's servant in a way—and totally beyond their reach. All this changes when he turns to *her*. She has his real attention, unmixed and delighted—whether she is sprawling in Asta's wake on a nightclub floor, lecturing him about not getting killed, soothing a gorgonish old aunt (Jessie Ralph), or returning from an unintended visit to Grant's Tomb (where he sent her to get rid of her).

Nick and Nora, unlike other movie couples, never have to court or to break up and then come together again. All those plot things needed at the very least to keep a movie going are taken care of in the *Thin Man* series by the "case." And the low level of energy and inspiration of these mystery plots allows the two stars to be as comfortably, even happily uninvolved with them as they are with the murders themselves. Nick and Nora are untouched by action; they're involved in a state of being. So are we. We never see their relation tested or challenged in these films, nor do we want to. We only want to look at it, to be around it. And that's the real point of the films themselves, as oblique in its way as the style of the stars.

There is, for example, the way Nora looks at Nick—or, rather, doesn't look at him—when they are driving in an open car over the Golden Gate Bridge in *Shadow of the Thin Man*, the fourth film in the series. They are going to the racetrack, and Nick at the wheel is singing tunelessly to himself. She smiles to herself beside him, looking sidelong at him every once in a while. A motorcycle cop stops them on the bridge for speeding—very hostile and wisecracking. Nora looks straight ahead, still with a slight smile but firmly turned away from the colloquy between Nick and the cop. "Nick Charles!" exclaims the cop over the driver's license—not *the* Nick Charles? Nick is pleased, and the cop is overjoyed. Nora is still looking straight ahead, still smiling, but more firmly than ever turned away from the two of them—as if the encounter were all somehow arranged for her, and she is not going to be taken in by it even if it *was* arranged for her pleasure. Since it's her delight that dominates the scene, simply by existing in the corner of it. By now the cop is even praising Nick's car: you can do eighty in a car like this and hardly feel it, he says, smiling broadly—and making out the speeding ticket. "You're feeling it now, aren't you, dear?" says Nora, breaking her silence. And the remark, instead of being a little triumph, is like a spontaneous outbreaking of her pleasure: irresistible.

What *is* that space they create between them? It's there as richly and palpably in the fourth film, and even in parts of the fifth, ten years after the beginning of the series, as it is in the first. It's not in the scripted lines, nor even in the situations. Why, in *After the Thin Man*, does she look at him like that—and why is it so funny when she does? They've returned from New York to their posh San Francisco home only to find a noisy and inexplicable party going on, the place full of strangers. In order to get to their kitchen and find their servants, they decide to dance their way through the throng of merrymakers. Nick takes Nora in his arms and off they go—a rather dainty two-step in the middle of a jamboree (get some of the Napoleon brandy before it's gone, someone advises them chummily). As they go, Nick surveys the action, but Nora simply looks at *him*, steadily, levelly, gravely, as they mince and pump along through the pandemonium. Explain *this* to me, her look says—as a way of suggesting the hopelessness of anybody's ever doing so. It's one of their odd, unstated, pervasive jokes with each other to react to the most impersonal event as if it were somehow the other's idea—like a last-minute gift, well intended but misjudged.

At the Ly-Chee Club, the obligatory hot spot in the same film, we follow Nick and Nora as they enter the place, going from door to checkroom to their table near the crowded dance floor. This time she is surveying the action (it's her kind of place: sleazy and full of low life) and he is looking at her as they move through the crowd. He is less attentive to what people say to him as they pass (some of them seem to be threatening him) than he is to the way Nora hears what they say, watching her with settled amusement: so how do you like the Ly-Chee Club? It's not her discomfiture he's savoring, however, but her refusal to show it, her refusal to give anything away in these situations. At such moments, of course, they always touch banality (she knows the speed limits, he knows the dives, etc.)—and they always elude it (or at least most of the time). This, in fact, is their special vocation as stars: to inhabit the hackneyed and transform it—for all of us. It goes with their gift for the oblique response, for the unexpected nuance. They enact something in their dazzling oblique way that most of us feel about our own lives: this may *look* like the cliché but it really isn't, not at the center of things where it matters. That's why that puzzling, elusive quality in their most ordinary exchanges seems so right and funny, so repeatedly satisfying.

At the end of *Shadow of the Thin Man*, after the big showdown and unmasking of the killer, the guilty man whips out a gun and aims it at Nick. On an impulse Nora rushes the killer and he is disarmed. A moment later, when it dawns on her what she's just done, she collapses onto the couch, in something close to a faint, with Nick sitting next to her. We are inhabiting *pure* banality here, needless to say—and it goes on. It's disclosed now that the gun Nora rushed at wasn't loaded at all; Nick had known this at the time of course. Nora, taking this in, sits up and looks at him. "So I'm *not* a heroine?" she says to him—reproachfully. As their eyes meet, hers are wary, the glance sidelong again, and her tone is accusing. But why accusing? And why accusing *him?* Of course she *is* a heroine. Those large possibilities are never quite excluded in their world. What's been taken from her—with the news about the gun being unloaded—is something else: it's the *idea* of herself as a heroine, the possible self-congratulation. He's done it to me again, that sidelong look seems to say. Another potential piety—vanished. Loy always lets us see that part of Nora that might possibly be attracted by sentiment and conventional pieties and images of heroism—the conventionally soft, conventionally "feminine" Nora. And indeed he *does* do it to her: it's her bond with Nick—and even her connection with the tough world he mediates for her, the world of mugs and dames and crooks—that keeps her from yielding to that possibility in herself, though it doesn't keep her from looking at it regretfully from time to time.

For that matter, even Asta does it to her (she directs some sidelong looks at him, too). No matter that Nick and Nora soon have a "real" child (or even that Nora does finally become conventionally "feminine")—no matter even that he should be as repellently typical a Hollywood child, combining rectitude and winsome appeal in every glance, as the casting offices of the time could provide.* By that time the point had been made. Who remembers or cares about Nicky, Jr.? And who forgets Asta? Other screwball comedies even borrowed him (he is Mr. Smith in *The Awful Truth*, George in *Bringing Up Baby*): he became an emblem of the screwball spirit and style. He is not even a "doggy" dog: shaggy, drooping, melting-eyed, and lovable. But a trim little terrier, crisp-haired and beady-eyed, elegant and snappish. Standing where he does in these films—in place of the child—he confronts Hollywood (and American) piety very squarely. From one point of view, the bond between Nick and Nora is a deep refusal of cant. And Asta is its issue.

---

*The child actor grew up to be Dean Stockwell—who gives such an extraordinary performance in *Blue Velvet* (1986).

Astaire meets Rogers in Shall We Dance, *the usual unpromising start— she thinks he's a "toe dancer." Jerome Cowan is between them.*

Astaire and Rogers | 9

[Balanchine] has called Astaire the best male dancer of the day . . .
— BERNARD TAPER, *Balanchine, A Biography*

How can one render the inside? Precisely by staying prudently outside.
— JEAN-LUC GODARD, in an interview (1962)

WHAT MAKES Astaire and Rogers so wonderful together? The legendary movie team have been an occasion for wonder of all kinds, from awe to speculation, almost from their first screen dance together—"The Carioca" in *Flying Down to Rio* (1933). Arlene Croce, especially, has written with great perception, in *The Fred Astaire and Ginger Rogers Book*, about the Astaire-Rogers magic. So has Stephen Harvey in *Fred Astaire,* and John Mueller in the indispensable *Astaire Dancing.* But about Astaire and Rogers—as about any complicated fact or any triumphant work of art—there is always more to say, always more to see and more to discover, especially by taking a close and detailed look at the major dances.

One such dance is the climactic number from their fifth movie together, *Follow the Fleet* (1936)—"Let's Face the Music and Dance," music and lyrics by Irving Berlin. The sequence has only the most tenuous relation to the story of the movie (Astaire and Rogers are putting on a show to save Harriet Hilliard's ship so that she can marry Randolph Scott, who likes ships) and in fact comes with its own story. And the figures of high sophistication the two stars appear as in this "story dance" exactly reverse the proletarian types they play in the film itself: a gob and a dance-hall girl.

We see Astaire, in evening clothes, first; and in a brief opening tableau we see him losing all his money at roulette and being promptly deserted by the four elegant young women at his elbow (picture 1). Then, in a quick dissolve, the curtains close and open on the main set, a terrace outside the casino windows.

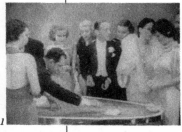

And the music, which has been vamping restlessly, relaxes into the melody of the Berlin song as Astaire appears, leaving the casino, in a very low-angled shot of the entire looming set (picture 2).

Usually, Astaire sings the song, and then he and Rogers dance to it. But there is a lead-in to the song here, and to Rogers' appearance: a two-minute-or-so mime sequence to the music, in which Astaire not only develops the "story" (nobody knows you when you're down and out) but fixes certain basic patterns of movement and meaning. The sequence itself is almost nothing but a series of attitudes, of poses struck and held—postures of turning away, of leaning forward, of drooping inward. Like the meanings of the "story," these attitudes are in a very conventional theatrical style. But from the beginning Astaire makes something stirring out of them—partly because he never strikes an unearned pose, never implies a meaning or a feeling except through a continuous mimetic development of meanings, even in this simple prologue sequence, where the movement into dance, always present, is always checked and pulled back on itself.

The sequence shows four strolling encounters, in each of which Astaire is snubbed. First it's a top-hatted man—Astaire salutes him and the man walks by (picture 3). Then three women, chatting and smiling. Just as they reach him he bows, and they turn on their heels and sweep out (4). What's notable here is the timing. The movements of these walk-on players are always received and completed in the inflections of Astaire's own body. As here: the slight caving-in of his stance seems to complete the sweeping, turning movement with which the three haughty women start to leave the frame. And it's clear that these gestures of rejection are confident and beautiful—whereas Astaire looks for this instant almost *too* exposed. A suggestion which he confirms in a startling way when he suddenly takes two steps and turns his back to us. And just as the last of the women is leaving the frame, he leans toward them—in a kind of arrested stagger, and a sudden startling image of pure longing (5).

From the opposite direction, the right of the frame, comes the third group: a man with two women on his arms. Almost as soon as Astaire—and we—see them (in a cut to a long shot), they are upon him, and step around him, without skipping a beat (6). He turns his head and watches them go. Their departure from the frame prompts the first violent movement of the sequence: Astaire spins suddenly around in their wake, with palms down, fingers splayed, and coattails flying (7). An outburst of feeling that ends gently in that same leaning posture of loss and longing that is clearly the basic image of the sequence (8).

The fourth and final group is the most imposing of all: two women, a sleek brunette and a statuesque blonde (Maxine Jennings and Lucille Ball). The camera, in medium shot, pans just slightly enough to the right to show them coming backwards into the frame, twirling slowly as they do so (9). And just as Astaire bows to them— everything in the shot is tightly framed—they complete their turn away from him and go elegantly off, looking along their shoulders as they do so. This time, as Astaire takes two, three steps after them and makes that yearning movement into a lean, he seems for the first time as if he might fall—a slight but telling emphasis (10). Then he straightens, puts his heels together military-style, drops his cigarette and steps on it.

He has kept that burning cigarette in his hand through the whole sequence. For it's hard, once the music starts, to "believe" in Astaire as a down-and-outer of *any* sort. Not just his supremacy as a dancer makes it hard—but something in his temperament, too, a deep unflappability somewhere beneath the startled eyes and despairing motions. The tableau shows him being rejected. But even in this light stylized mode, it takes four examples to convince us that he *is* being rejected. Whereas with Gene Kelly one example would surely do—and be almost too much as well. For where Kelly seems willfully good-natured, Astaire seems really so. And Astaire is both too reserved as a performer and too inexpressive in the ordinary actor's way, to lay direct claim to the big moments and effects. It is partly his

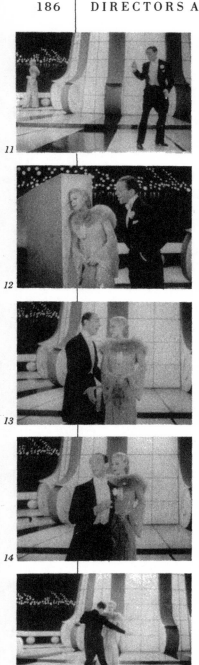

native incapacity for overt poignance, for any kind of overt emotionalism, that makes his turned back in this sequence such an eloquent statement.

And even the set, in this marvelously realized number, suggests a kind of restraint, dramatizes an appropriate paradox and tension. It is not one of the "Big White Sets" for which thirties movie musicals (e.g., *The Merry Widow*), and Astaire-Rogers movies in particular, were noted. Rather than big and outflung, it seems rather cramped and shallow; rather than bright and white, it is dark and gray. Yet it successfully suggests distance and height. It represents the casino terrace. There is a low terrace wall and stylized city lights in the flat black "distance." Dominating the foreground dancing area, the opaque casino windows form a broad, massive, glowing white pillar, both rising out of sight and slanting downward at the set's center. It all looks like a stage set, however—deliberately insubstantial and even papier-mâché. At the same time, it conveys the "idea" of mass and weight and heaviness. All its main lines, both the vertical of the terrace wall and the horizontal of the white pillar, end in massive, squat outward curves. Everything in this visual effect—like the lugubrious, insistent melody of the song—seems to pull inexorably downward. And, equally, everything is theatrically unreal.

Rogers appears—in one of those slight panning motions of the camera—in the left background of this set. Just as Astaire is about to shoot himself in the temple with an elegantly produced revolver (picture 11), he sees Rogers enter and poise herself with equal elegance to jump from the terrace wall. He saves her. He sings to her . . . (12) "There may be trouble ahead, but while there's moonlight and music and love and romance . . . let's face the music and dance. . . ." Rogers's hair is pulled tightly back in a chignon—it's the sort of severe hairdo that heightens her characteristic air of hauteur and singleness, and that brings out something ineradicably melancholy in her looks. Her sheer clinging gown, with its big fur collar, is sewn with metallic threads in the billowing sleeves and long skirt. Its

weighted downward fall gives a breathtaking line to the
curve of her body, of her back and hips. Astaire takes
her arm, still singing, and they walk forward into the
center of the set . . . The camera tracks backward in
front of them. As Astaire sings the last notes of the song,
she raises her eyes and looks at him (13)—and the wonderful dance begins.

She starts to walk. He leans with his back into her
path (14), then whirls around in front of her and faces
her. Blocking her way with his back to the camera, he
simultaneously leans to the left and makes a hand pass
to the right (15). But it's exactly this leaning motion that
was the basic movement of the earlier tableau, an image
of lyrical despondency. Suddenly—thrillingly—Astaire
transforms the whole movement. Here, he is almost literally leaning into her rather than leaning futilely after
her. And the accompanying hand pass gives the basic
image of longing a sudden dynamic intention, and a new
shape. This is just the beginning, of course: this long-
ing-leaning image recurs throughout the dance in different shapes and meanings, many of them astonishing.

Rogers moves forward again, rather uncertainly, and
he "surrounds" her—by a renewed pattern of hand
passes (16), then by an encircling run. A bit dazed
and still uncertain, Rogers leans into a hand pass of her
own—her forearms stiff and upraised (17)—and they
come together. With one arm he clasps her waist (18).
She leans back on his arm, and as she does so, he propels her forward (19). This combining of forward pro-
pulsion and backward pull characterizes the whole
dance. It's also in the Berlin melody, and in the visual
components of the set. The whole number is a kind of
extended, relentless retard.

Now, in this same movement, as they fall away from
each other and as he catches her by the right hand (with
the other, she flings her handkerchief away), Astaire—
remarkably—falls into a kind of buckle-kneed stance
(20), a sudden and dramatic sag at the knees, as he sets
himself for Rogers' return on the reflex of their fallaway.
She comes back to him, does three finger turns under
his hand, and comes to rest at last with her upraised

21

22

23

24

25

hands against his chest. They hold the pose, a conventional but extraordinarily beautiful image, which is astonishingly inflected when suddenly they both seem to buckle, to sag together (21). Rogers' right leg is bent forward at the knee (the slight inflections of Rogers' knee are important through this whole section); her head droops and lolls backwards, all but disappearing into the fur collar; and as Astaire leans forward, the line of her body (that incredible back) sags even more dramatically. In the following passage this coming-to-rest pose is repeated and varied. In addition, each time Astaire swings her out now, there is a suggestion of drooping in her fallaway, of the head lolling backwards again; but each time the suggestion is more muted than before.

The pose reminds us of other great moments in their dances—when Astaire's attention to her seems as much an aesthetic impulse as a romantic one: that amazing moment, already described, in "Night and Day" (*The Gay Divorcee*) when at the height of a very rapid and stormy climax he frames her with an overhead port de bras—a sudden consciousness in the midst of passion that is breathtaking. And the held poses that punctuate the last bars of "Cheek to Cheek" (*Top Hat*)—when she comes to rest in a backbend across his arm and nearly to the floor, rising more and more slowly each time. But none of these moments have the special quality of the held poses here: the inward-turning line, the huddling and shrinking and buckling, indeed all the variations on "sagging" that Astaire has devised for this dance. There is, of course, a deliberate tension between this huddling and cringing impulse and the tendency to the large outward-flung gesture of the Big Romantic Dance. But here it's a tension and not an opposition. It's a tension that informs the whole dance and gives it its special complexity. For what Astaire gets us to see here is not how the two kinds of movement oppose each other but, rather, how they mold and blend and even turn into one another. He gets us to see the continuity between caving in, so to speak, and bursting outward. At least that is *one* of the things he gets us to see. The whole remarkable number is built around different ways of seeing the expressive and troubling line of a body bent inward.

Now there is a very tentative outward flourish: Astaire promenades her, and she raises one knee as he does so (picture 22). He swings her out—they pause on the fallaway and she raises her knee slightly (23). He promenades her again. The music quickens and they break apart. The movement is faster now and the scale larger, no longer so cautious and inward. Now, separately but in unison, they do a grander version of the hand passes, but without the leaning inflection (24). They turn and move toward the back, still doing the hand passes. Astaire is behind her and a step-level above her and gives the impression of watching over her as they dance (25). They come forward. He circles her again in a run. They come together and twirl around the floor. They join hands again—and again he swings her out. But this time on the fallaway we see that Rogers' body (26) is perfectly straight, and for the first time: not even a slightly uplifted knee interrupts the line. But Astaire's body—on the other end of the same movement—is almost ludicrously staggered at the knees. It's a mysteriously affecting detail, with its suggestions of a sudden powerful intimacy, of a deep human exchange. And it is characteristic of Astaire's art. That buckle-kneed stance is something he uses at big climactic moments in nearly all his romantic dances with Rogers. (Its most notable earlier use is in "Cheek to Cheek.") It is his way of qualifying what another dancer might turn into a moment of triumph—and of triumph over Rogers in particular. Astaire takes such a moment and makes something almost quizzical out of it. That he does—and does so characteristically—helps to explain why, even in dances more overtly and directly about sexual seduction than this one is ("Night and Day" being the great example), we never feel uneasy about Astaire's demonstrated power over her. (In *Carefree* in 1938, however, that power is total. He literally hypnotizes her into doing the main romantic number, "Change Partners," and the result is an Astaire-Rogers duet with almost none of the force or nuance of the great dances.)

26

27

28

29

30

31

32

33

34

35

As the dance goes on, the movement continues to expand and open out into larger and larger gestures and patterns. But also there are strange modulations of this largeness, patterns of movement that interrupt the gathering power. These movements both limit and comment on the expansiveness, and are similar in their effect to Astaire's staggered stance. At one point, Astaire and Rogers face away from each other and in a swift aborted little jump (a movement along the floor rather than up and off it) they change feet (27). The step is both finicking and decisive. And the emphatic delicacy of it—in the midst of so many urgent, fateful sweepings and circlings—is both moving and troubling.

Another example: Astaire holds his arms out, encircling her waist, while within the circle Rogers does a series of chaîné turns across the floor (28). She holds her own forearms upraised, and she moves her uplifted hands in a kind of fluttering motion as she turns—a curiously fussy motion for such a composed and formidable woman, and it stands out oddly. But in a moment Astaire will make us see the point of it. As they come to the front of the stage and begin to dip and sway side by side, Astaire accents the dip by a strange little strut-and-shuffle step, his elbow pointing jauntily upward as he dips and rises (29). This is the strutting masculine equivalent to Rogers' vaguely fluttering hands. These curiously "personal" details, flourishes of bravado almost, seem a kind of reply to the larger, more impersonal dance movement and design. Also a way to counter the resistless pull of the music.

Now a quickening in the music ("Let's Face the Music and Dance"), a step up in the excitement of the rapt, insidious melody. Astaire and Rogers begin leaping and circling in wider and wider arcs around the floor (30). He seems almost to be leaping and driving into her (31). Then a chain of shoulder movements (32), which emphasize the implacable melody. Another heightening in the music, and they are front stage again, dipping and swaying, making enormous sweeping hand passes (33), directed now at nothing but their own absorption and transformation in movement. Then Astaire to one side

does a quick cabriole (34)—then passes in front of her
and does another, even quicker and higher (35). A sudden, stunning effect, since everything in the number
(the set, the music, the dance movement itself) has contrived to make us feel the impossibility of such a jump,
of *any* unencumbered upward movement. But as Astaire
does it, it seems something casual—a spontaneous
overflow of that sweeping and passing movement. And
as he leaps, Rogers, to his left, makes a lovely pass with
her hands across her chest, reminiscent of that earlier
chaîné flutter. And as a "response" to Astaire's leap (she
is *not* looking at him—it's as if she is registering his
movement on some other, deeper level of herself), this
hand gesture is very moving: a formalized image of almost maidenly wonder, limp hands rising to the face.
But as the face here is Rogers' glamorous (and severe)
deadpan mask, the effect is both surprising and surprisingly eloquent (like the admiring equivalent of a silent
scream).

He lands, crouches into a run, and circles her in the
manner of the dance's opening. But now the run is low
and swooping and the momentum seems in some mysterious way to come really from her. He passes her and
turns. She reaches out with her arms. And just as he
seems about to leave the frame (at left), he reaches out
and takes her by the hand (picture 36)—and as he is
pushing back, he simultaneously pulls her toward
him—and past him—and they come together and turn.
His arms go around her waist, she raises her arms (with
those ballooning sleeves) into the air (37), then brings
her right arm to rest on his shoulders, as they face left
and sink into a kneeling posture near the wings (38).
They touch the floor with their knees and look at each
other. (Since their eye contact at the start of the dance,
Rogers has seemed to register him by almost every way
except looking at him.) They rise and rear backwards—
one, two, three, four steps. And pause . . .

This pause (39)—as they draw back before gathering
to their exit—is nearly the most heart-stopping moment
in the dance so far. They are entwined and in profile,
facing left. Rogers is on the camera side, her face and

41

body to the right of Astaire's. Her left arm hangs at her side, her right arm is around his shoulders. Her back is arched, her profile is at a level slightly higher than his, and her downward gaze rests on him, with that combination of imperiousness (the downward look) and submission (the relaxed left arm) that she alone seems to have the secret of. Astaire, in a crouching position, has one arm around her waist and the other extended leftward. He dominates the frame: in this moment and in this stance he seems to gather everything including Rogers into himself, into the ease and force of his own body, and to aim it all outward along that extended arm. This is the final powerful statement of the huddling, turning-inward motif—they are both gathered in and aiming sublimely out. They hold the pose; then they rise slowly, looking at each other—as they take four gliding steps toward the wings (40). Then just as they reach the curtain, they throw their heads back, pull their knees up (41) and—in this final astonishing attitude—they look at us . . . And leap off.

That afternoon [London, 1933] . . . [Lincoln] Kirstein poured out his admiration for Balanchine's creations, his grand dreams for ballet in America, his lofty ideals for the future of the art, his fervent hope that Balanchine would join him in the endeavor. Balanchine said that he would like to try it. As far as he was concerned, Europe had become a museum. . . . He added that, furthermore, he would dearly love to go to a country that produced girls as wonderful as the movie star Ginger Rogers. It can only be guessed what Kirstein thought of that remark. . . .
— BERNARD TAPER, *Balanchine, A Biography*

T HE GENIUS in all this, of course, is Astaire's, as both choreographer and performer. But just how much Rogers' temperament and gifts meant to that genius became more and more apparent in his long career without her. Their later reunion in MGM's *The Barkleys of Broadway* (1949) was unhappy for a number of reasons. Among them the fact that Rogers, at a desperate phase in her tenacious career by that point, had become almost unwatchably mannered and arch—strangely, almost eerily subject to just those painful airs and pretensions that she had seemed to be the instinctive enemy of in their thirties films. Astaire's post-Rogers career was still a distinguished one. At times it was even glorious. In the big romantic dances of *Ziegfeld Follies* (1944), "This Heart of Mine" and "Limehouse Blues." In *Easter Parade* (1948) with Judy Garland and in *The Band Wagon* (1953) with Jack Buchanan and Cyd Charisse. There was even in *Ziegfeld Follies* a partner named Lucille Bremer who seemed to suit him in some of the intangible personal ways Rogers had. But none of these later women sparked the fun and transcendent high spirits that he managed with Rogers. And never again were the big romantic dances to seem so dense and rich, so authentic or so deeply realized. Those Astaire-Rogers RKO films may in fact be the greatest movie musicals ever made. And if that is so, it is because of Astaire. But it is also because of the relationship he found with Rogers—a screen miracle that was never to be repeated, not even in his extraordinary career.

They made six of these films—an average of two a year between 1934 and 1937—before they got restless with the pattern and the glory began to depart. What made them so special together? There are plenty of clues to the answer in "Let's Face the Music and Dance." The central imagery of that dance—the drooping and huddling—is moving partly because it is such a marvelously gentle expression of, and such a generous comment upon, Rogers' characteristic tension of resistance. And there is that climactic moment of turning inward, of turning away *together*—which develops by the internal logic of Astaire's choreography into the showy defiant bursting forth and turning out of their exit. A moment that might be preposterous if it were any *less* audacious: it is convincing partly because it is so astonishing. All this is all the *more* astonishing—and moving—because it engages Rogers: her physical authority, her skeptical temper, her native imperiousness. Her submission in these dances is an interesting and complex event that magnifies both of them.

There is, after all, something almost bodiless, something lighter than air about Astaire. And under that unshakable good temper, under that personal unflappability, there is a deeper, almost impersonal unease. His solos in the RKO films show something we never see in his dances with a partner: a readiness to be distracted, even disconcerted, by his background—a faint harried sense of things getting out of his control. Even the fact of a background (Rogers is always in the foreground of his attention) seems to be a slight strain. His relation with us, the audience, is easy—not so his relation with *them*: the marching sailors in "I'd Rather Lead a Band" (*Follow the Fleet*, 1936), the shadows in "Bojangles of Harlem" (*Swing Time*, 1936), even the machinery in "Slap That Bass" (*Shall We Dance*, 1937). Astaire rarely appears before a chorus (or an animated background) to *lead* it—at least not simply or confidently. The sailors march the wrong way, the shadows go out of sync, the machinery proves resistant to imitation, and so on. He must constantly look over his shoulder at whatever he finds himself in front of, it seems. As if he hadn't that much "weight" to throw around, so to speak—that much authority to dispose of. But behind this suggestion is something much deeper and more significant: a deliberate refusal to dominate his environment that is similar to his refusal to simply "triumph" over Rogers.

In "Top Hat, White Tie and Tails" (*Top Hat*, 1935), the top-hatted male chorus is a constant mild irritant to him. They come too close and he turns. They do a tap step and he blinks. He walks in front of them and grins and shakes his head at us. Yet when they disappear, the lights go down and the music goes low and ominous. His infectious swaying motion ("*I'm* . . . puttin' on my top hat") becomes a stagger. He takes his hat off in greeting—is it? or in defense? Every movement suddenly implies its opposite; his cane becomes a "rifle," he confronts phantoms. He whirls, jumps, crouches—but recovers his jauntiness every time—then loses it again. Until the lights go up again and the top-hatted chorus reappears. Whereupon he shoots them all down . . . and exits to wild applause on the soundtrack. This is Astaire's own reported favorite among his solos, and it is his most complicated reflection on the condition of being "weightless."

It's nice in *Swing Time* when he assumes (quite without mockery) a Jolson stance while singing "Never Gonna Dance" to Rogers—appealing to her as she stands above him on a glittering staircase. It's nice partly because Astaire is so far from having the Jolson kind of all-purpose authority, or anything like that kind of theatrical and personal intensity. Astaire's intensity is marked by the kind of indirection and reserve that can make the gesture of a turned back into a powerful effect (as in "Let's Face the Music and Dance").

Rogers, on the other hand, is not at all "weightless." And this fact about her reflects not so much her different style nor her inferior skill as a dancer as it does something about her temperament. She has "both feet on the ground," as they used to say of common-sensible people. And where it's easy to think of Astaire as leaping and flying, we most easily think of Rogers as strolling. (As Arlene Croce observes: "Rogers never walks, she always strolls.") And that stroll is one of the glories of film history. The line of her back and the mold and movement of her hips are surely among the most extraordinary natural gifts that a dancer—or a beautiful woman—could have. Gifts that Astaire knows how to display, of course (her melting backbends are made the point of dances as different in mood and tempo as "Cheek to Cheek" and "Shall We Dance")—as does Rogers herself. Notice the way she often highlights the marvelous hips by the set of her shoulders—squared, slightly raised, in a kind of counterpoint to the fluid line and motion of her lower body. Sometimes a forward-leaning set of those shoulders seems almost to propel and carry her along—notably when she is escaping Astaire, either in alarm (as in the midst of "Night and Day") or in a huff (as in the dog-walking number in *Shall We Dance*).

But though she resists him in all their big dances together, "Night and Day" is the only one in which she actually tries to leave the floor in the middle of the

After the dance: Rogers has just asked him to marry her—but warily. He accepts. Follow the Fleet.

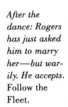

dance. Just as it is the only one in which the issue of seduction is to be so clear-cut and relatively uncomplicated. When that dance rises to its stormy conclusion and Astaire lets go of her by easing her onto a nearby couch, she sits there looking up at him in dumb amazement—which seems, in fact, after what we have just seen, just about the only possible response. For it's true: this first of their major dances (in their first starring film) *is* wondrous—with the special excitement of something beginning, as well. And Astaire caps it all by a feigned casualness that only confirms our wonder. No sooner has she come to rest on the couch than, almost with the same gesture by which he has let her down, he reaches into his jacket and produces a cigarette case. "Cigarette?" he inquires. . . . She shakes her head.

It's a marvelous moment, but it can never again be repeated, given what Astaire and Rogers are still to become. Astaire can never again afford to overpower her so completely—as he well knows. Compare the ending of "Cheek to Cheek," two films later. In this dance, too, Astaire is storming her resistance to him, dancing her into compliance and tenderness. But instead of rising to a climax at the end, the dance winds down slowly in a long diminuendo passage. As the music starts to subside, Astaire holds Rogers over his arm in the last (and longest) of a series of backbends. She rises after a dramatic while into a slow finger turn. They two-step to a terrace wall. He lets her out, and pirouettes gently into a leaning position against the wall, relaxing on the same elegant movement into crossed legs, folded hands, and a social smile (the equivalent of that cigarette case). Rogers, on the other hand, is not so composed: we notice her bracing herself slightly with one hand against the wall, and as she leans on it and looks at him, we can see her breathing quickly underneath her feathered dress. She starts to move toward him. Then suddenly chagrin—her constant temptation—overcomes her again. Instead she turns, pushes off from the wall, and strolls composedly away. . . . This is the real end to the dance, and it is breathtaking, an even more marvelous period than Astaire's cigarette case. But its special significance, in the development of this magical partnership, is the fact that Rogers is allowed to walk off, even from such a marvel of a dance, with many of her reservations intact—with her resistance in some degree reaffirmed.

What exactly is this resistance—so central an element in nearly all their great dances—about? The nonsense plots of the movies themselves sometimes suggest an answer, sometimes don't. In *The Gay Divorcee* and in *Top Hat*, the problem is mistaken identity. She thinks he's a gigolo in the former, her best friend's husband in the latter. That timeworn device may "motivate" the dances (and successfully extend the movie itself), but it hardly throws any light on them. But in the plot of *Swing Time*, it's worth noting that he almost costs her her job as a dancing teacher in the first reel. And in *Follow the Fleet*, he both threatens her job in a dance hall and spoils her audition for a big producer. This sort of issue, on the other hand, does fit our sense of what is going on in the relation between the two of them. He, after all, is the mercurial one—just as she seems the one more likely to know and care about the importance of a job. We can see *that* in the carriage of her shoulders.

It's only in *Swing Time*—of the major films—that Rogers' temperament is importantly denied. For a good part of the film she is placed by the plot in the position of yearning openly after Astaire (who is "committed" to marrying Betty Furness instead). This is the Astaire-Rogers film that many people like best of all—for the excellent reason that it probably contains more consistently won-

Rogers among the "Ginger Rogers" masks in Shall We Dance.

derful dance numbers than any of them ("Pick Yourself Up," "Bojangles," "Romance in Swing Time," "Never Gonna Dance"). But in some ways it seems to me their most unfortunate major film. It was directed by George Stevens (all the others, except William Seiter's *Roberta* in 1935, were done by Mark Sandrich), a gifted but rather fancy (for the time) filmmaker, with a very heavy light touch and a taste for endlessly extended "cute" moments. It is only in *Swing Time*, for example, that the famous pair have to submit to such indignities as kissing coyly behind a door, and then going all giggly and pant-y (these sounds are actually on the soundtrack) when they are discovered. This sort of thing suits Astaire no better than it does Rogers—and he clearly has less heart for it. In all the films we wait for the dances and songs, but only in *Swing Time* do we feel embarrassed by what sometimes precedes them.

Shall We Dance (1937), their last major film (the two RKO films that followed it, *Carefree* in 1938 and *The Story of Vernon and Irene Castle* in 1939, were both untypical in different ways and both disappointing), is opposite to *Swing*

Time in ways both good and bad. *Shall We Dance* has wonderful enough dances but barely enough of them, and the wonderful opportunities of the Gershwin score are often wasted. "Let's Call the Whole Thing Off" is "danced" on roller skates, for example. And the thrilling dance to the title song seems over almost as soon as it begins. And footage that might presumably have been given to Rogers goes instead to a "balletic" contortionist named Harriet Hoctor.

Still, *Shall We Dance* is a high point. It has the George and Ira Gershwin songs. It has Edward Everett Horton and Eric Blore at the peak of their odd forms. And it has the best script of the entire series, with genuinely funny scenes and situations and often witty lines (credited to Allan Scott and Ernest Pagano) in the best tradition of thirties movie comedy. But above all, *Shall We Dance* is the most moving and satisfying of all the Astaire-Rogers films precisely because—at what turned out to be the climax of their career together—it is the only one of their films in which plot and screenplay consistently amplify and enrich the great dance numbers. And *all* the great dance numbers of the series, not just the ones in this last climactic film.

For this film makes clear that if we ask the "meaning" of Rogers' formulaic resistance to Astaire, we are bound to see that it is not primarily a sexual reluctance that is being dramatized and danced. When Rogers yields to Astaire, it is not so much maidenliness (so to speak) yielding to passion—but rather common sense yielding to something that looks suspiciously like its opposite. Astaire plays a ballet dancer named Petrov here, while Rogers is a musical-comedy hoofer, with a pronounced suspicion of "toe dancers"—which Astaire at first does nothing to allay.

This conflict is carefully drawn. Because, like so many of the great women movie stars of this period, Rogers is a figure of overwhelming, almost awesome common sense. Her glamour and her personal authority are connected not only to intelligence but to a tough, astringent and skeptical view of the world. Even in her toniest and most elegant guises, she carries (to her credit) an air of chorus-girl knowingness, a powerful suggestion of street smarts. (This was a side of herself that she would do her best to obliterate later on, unfortunately.) And this reductive knowingness is exactly Astaire's problem with her. The wall around *this* sleeping-beauty heroine is a kind of no-nonsense radar, an invisible shit-detector—which gives her an almost pathological sensitivity to any suggestion of phoniness or pretense. To Astaire, therefore, with his enthusiasm and his romanticism, she is a special challenge. All that might be said against him—and even his romantic obsession about her might be a count in the indictment—is summed up in Rogers' perfection of the deadpan comment, in her unforgettable sidelong glance from time to time at his slightly skittering presence (as when she learns in *Shall We Dance* that his real name is Peter P. Peters).

For the Rogers sidelong glance, and her sardonic deadpan, express just the kind of honesty that not only the Astaire-Rogers films but all the great thirties comedies celebrated: the virtues of skepticism, wariness and tough-mindedness. The liberation of having no illusions. But in these romantic comedies, this liberation is also sometimes a trap. As it seems to be for Rogers in *Shall We Dance*. She is determined, like so many heroines of the screwball genre, to marry for no given or coherent reason a comically impossible suitor (the wonderful William Brisbane), a man with a dementedly fatuous grin and below it, it seems, no chin at all—who, when complimented on his healthy appearance, replies delightedly, "Oh, nothing shows on *my* face." And as Rogers contemplates her future with this nightmare exaggeration of Ralph Bellamy, she announces that she is facing "real happiness for the first time in my life." And just because her resistance to Astaire is not otherwise "motivated," we are encouraged to see one of the final meanings of her intimidating common sense: a fear of the freedom of feeling, of the risk and ambition, that Astaire's dances with her so transcendently express.

One of the inspirations of *Shall We Dance*'s final big number is to reproduce the Rogers deadpan some thirty or so times. The chorus of girls that Astaire dances with in the title number are all wearing—literally—Ginger Rogers masks. "He said if he couldn't dance with you, he'd dance with images of you," Jerome Cowan explains to the astonished Rogers. And for us, too, the sight of these masks is astonishing—and resonant to an amazing degree. For the masks underline a central fact: Astaire, happily, is sui generis; Rogers, happily, is not. And understanding her effectiveness with him calls for registering (as audiences of the thirties did with no effort) her likeness to other women performers of the time—Joan Blondell, Barbara Stanwyck, Ann Sothern, Glenda Farrell, Eve Arden, and so on. Women who represented both a real and familiar American type and a wonderfully effective style and ideal. Within this type, of course, there was only one Ginger Rogers—there was certainly no danger of confusing her with any of the others, in memory or otherwise. But part of her glory as a star was her participation in the common type that they collectively embodied. (It's hard to imagine a Katharine Hepburn mask, for example, being used any way but cruelly. Witness *Stage Door*, her movie with Rogers and other "dames.") So that when Rogers, in the last number of *Shall We Dance,* decides to join the chorus of dancers who are wearing her "mask"—and when Astaire discovers her in their midst and *without* a mask—that exciting moment celebrates both her uniqueness and her representative quality. And the exultation of reunion in the dance that follows is one of the most thrilling passages in all their films. And it is an expressive high point that casts a retrospective light over all their great moments.

For when Astaire persuades Rogers to dance—as he must do over and over again—what he is transforming and transcending, in her and in us as we watch, is the quality of ordinary intelligence, carried by Rogers in these films to comically extraordinary extremes. Astaire never affronts this intelligence. The appreciation and the autonomy that he gives it are palpable facts. But next to *his* human qualities, such "sense" is bound to seem rather a burden. And the *strain* of being tough and clear-eyed and relentlessly reasonable was something that all these women performers were adept at conveying. (Think of Eve Arden's exaggeration of the weariness.) Astaire with Rogers transforms this burden into a source of energy and freedom. That is one reason at least why those moments of Rogers' capitulation to him are so permanently resonant and moving. For it is only with Rogers in this period that Astaire's sunny, almost Mozartean art fully reveals one of its final and most urgent meanings: the conviction that romance between men and women is not so much a matter of sustaining illusions as of penetrating and even "dancing" over them. That warmth and tenderness and love may also mean humor and intelligence and style.

Carole Lombard | 10

C AROLE LOMBARD probably more than any other leading lady of her time, was identified with the lunatic comedy: the "queen of screwball," as she was called by press agents. Lombard was one reason the public indulged and tolerated some of the wilder excesses of that comedy: she was so lovely, so sexy, so widely beloved. She was like an ambassadress to the sane prosaic world; she mediated the craziness even while she exacerbated it. She was—and is—brilliant, peerless, unique.

And she knew about Getting Out of Town—one of those defining gestures of the screwball heroine—even before screwball began. In 1932, in Wesley Ruggles' *No Man of Her Own*, she gives one of her best early performances as a girl who will do anything—almost—to get out of a place called Glendale. As it is, her mother (Elizabeth Patterson) won't even let her go away for the weekend— not to Inspiration Lake, anyway, a notoriously romantic local spot. The notoriety is totally undeserved, Lombard tells her mother as she readies herself for work, standing in the front hallway and planting a trim little hat on her head, tucking the hair in all around the brim with darting clawlike motions of her hand—and she wishes it weren't. Sometimes, she says, she goes out in the woods by herself and just screams "to keep from bursting." "Just like her Aunt Hattie," her mother gasps, recognizing the family strain. "Aw, Hattie's all right," drawls Father from off-screen. He and younger brother are at their breakfast in the dining room. And the contrast between these two unconscious men, affable and eating, and the tense women in the hallway, fretful and driven and painfully connected to each other, tells us a lot about why Lombard screams in the woods—and why she threatens now: "Oh, if I disappear someday, you'll know I ran off with the first traveling salesman who didn't have gold teeth!" Having hurled this at her mother, she barges forward out of the frame, her toilet complete, her purse held up in front of her, an image of the matron she threatens to be: despair with a clutched purse. In the dining room she gives her big teddy-bear father (George

William Powell as the "forgotten man" with Carole Lombard as the dizzy heiress in Gregory La Cava's My Man Godfrey.

Barbier) a kiss, and her brother, over Mother's protest, money for the movies. Another exit—and she is out the front door. At the front gate a seedy-looking salesman with a traveling case approaches and launches into his pitch. "Madam, you wanta make your little home here in Glendale attractive, don't you?" "Sorry, it can't be done," she says briskly, and exits left.

And through Glendale: with its Civil War monument in the center of the town square, its evergreens and gabled storefronts and graceful multi-bulbed street lamps. Lombard strides down Main Street at that eager, furious, faintly purse-clutching angle she left the salesman with—coming toward the camera with a frown and burning eyes, looking like a combination of madwoman and thrift shopper, stopping only to play a quick and winning game of Lotto at the corner newsstand and to notice Clark Gable, who has been trailing her. (This was their only film together.) He is a gambler and con artist from New York. He follows her to the library where she works; he even takes out a book. He goes to church with her and the family the next morning, and joins them for ice cream in the parlor. "Not the skim milk you get in the city," observes the father. There are other comparisons favorable to Glendale: "I bet," says Mother, "Mr. Stewart doesn't hear any better preaching in New York than he heard today." "I'm afraid you're right, Mrs. Randall," Gable replies mildly. "Ma," says younger brother Willie, injecting a lighter note, "I just can't make my ice cream and cake come out even." Lombard looks despairing ("He's just a boy," says Mother, simpering).

She does go to Inspiration Lake, however. So does Gable. They are alone in a cabin, but she is still hesitant. Just as he is about to take no for an answer, she calls him back to offer him a bet. "I'll gamble on anything," he says. On her virtue? Tails, he wins and she loses it; heads, they get married—and go to New York. She wins. (But the movie loses: she spends the rest of it as his wife reforming him.)

She is even more desperate in William Wellman's *Nothing Sacred* (1937)—to get out of a town called Warsaw in Vermont. And no wonder: if Glendale stands for boredom and complacency, Warsaw has gone beyond boring into a kind of transcendent meanness. The children bite you. The natives don't, in their own grudging words for it, "shoot their mouths off"—and even expect a tip for saying so. "I wouldn'ta talked atall if I knew I was gonna do it for nothin'." "Pardon me," says the hero as he reaches for his money, "I forgot I was in Vermont." The watch company that owns this town gives its employees a two-hundred-dollar bonus if they die there. And Hazel Flagg (Lombard), diagnosed as incurably ill with radium poisoning, would seem to qualify ahead of time. She is planning to spend the money on a trip to New York. But now her doctor, an elderly alcoholic named Enoch Donner (Charles Winninger), tells her that the diagnosis was an error. ("I got so I was seeing radium poisoning everywhere," he explains.) She is of course glad to hear this—but it does sort of kill the trip to New York. As she says, explaining her sudden burst of tears to the doctor, "It's kind of startling to be brought to life twice—and each time in Warsaw." He understands. She rushes from his office, sobbing. And stuck in Warsaw again.

This time it's Wally Cook (Fredric March) who's waiting at the front gate for her, as she comes out of Dr. Donner's house, weeping. He is a reporter from the *Morning Star*, he tells her. "I have nothing to say now," she says through her tears. Then adds: "It's sort of too late," and walks away. He follows. She tries to explain about the reprieve she's just gotten but is first prevented by her own tears, then by his words. He wants her to come to New York with him, he says, as a guest of the *Morning Star*. "Now don't say anything till I tell you," he says. "Oh, I'm not saying anything," she replies, looking at him with eyes shining and jaw dropped. She looks almost preternaturally beautiful and glowing as they walk and talk and she listens to him. "If you were my sister or somebody close to me, I'd take you outa Warsaw, dead or alive, Miss Flagg!" She lifts her face to these words as if turning to the sun. "You've lived here all your life?" he asks. "Twice that long," she says briskly, frowning a little at the interruption of her own voice. "Poor kid," he says—and as his words sound, again her face is serene. "You've never been to New York?" Well, yes, she has—with her grandmother when she was three. "But I didn't appreciate it," she assures him eagerly, with the same radiant smile. Lombard has a way of *embracing* banality when she utters it—like someone who has just learned to talk in this stupid way and is offering it proudly, knowing it will please. "Oh, I've always wanted to see the world outside," she tells Wally, "before I—" and she leaves the phrase uncompleted, making the little face of grief such an elision calls for.

Still, she hesitates over his offer—just a little. She tries to talk about it. Wouldn't she be, well, *imposing* on everybody? "Imposing? In what way?" says Wally. Wouldn't she be "kind of a killjoy"—with her wasting terminal illness? Not at all, says Wally. "Listen," he says, "I'll be frank with you—even if I sound like a ghoul. You'll be a sensation. The whole town will take you to its heart." They have stopped by a tree, and a thick branch conceals their faces for a moment.* "You mean they'll like me," says Hazel, as she stoops under the branch and reappears from behind the tree, "just because I'm dying?" Wally follows her, and his voice goes nicely dead—the way it always does when he has something particularly smarmy to say—as he replies: "Oh, that's a cruel way to put it. No. They'll like you because you'd be a symbol of courage and heroism."

She is always coming up against language like this. Everyone in New York, it turns out, is implicated in this sort of smarminess. Even she isn't immune to it—crying at her own memorials, especially when she is drunk, starting to break up even at the sound of her own name. Though she also feels nervous: "Oh, I hope it's going to be a *little* funeral," she tells Wally (the hope is vain: half a million is the projected attendance). This Ben Hecht screenplay is less the *Front Page* view of the city, as a center of hopeless political and social corruption, than the Holden Caulfield one: the place is full of phonies. All of them weeping over Hazel—jaded sophisticates, working-class slobs at wrestling arenas, and self-important public figures in private delegations to her hotel suite. The reporter-hero—who has himself made good, as he tells her, "over your poor pain-wracked little body" (Hazel smiles weakly)—draws the moral: the "daffy public" likes to cry so they can feel themselves crying. They try to confuse feeling generous with *being* it. Hazel's slow public passing (some would say *too* slow, but that's another matter) gives them a long, leisurely chance to kid themselves about their own good-heartedness.

But could anyone involved in *Nothing Sacred*—either David Selznick (the producer) or William Wellman (the director) or Ben Hecht (the writer)—have known quite how much the particular situation and character of Hazel Flagg would be transfigured by Lombard? Where the heroine of her earlier triumph, the previous year's *My Man Godfrey*, had seemed to be an odd if finally shrewd

---

* A tree or a pole momentarily between the actors and the camera is a recurring Wellman touch.

piece of miscasting (a woman of such intelligence playing a dimwit), Hazel Flagg seems to focus the Lombard character and temperament in a kind of permanent, intoxicating radiance. It's Lombard who makes something inspiriting and moving out of Hazel's big lie—who redeems the situation and Hecht's script from its jokiness and its knee-jerk cynicism. By being so full of troubled life on the screen that she makes the jokes about death (the hero describes the gamble of marrying her: "like honeymooning with the hearse at the front door") seem not just funny but oddly stirring.

Hazel is possessed with a vision. We can see it on her face in that walk through Warsaw when Wally first talks to her about the trip to New York. He is embarrassed—he worries about sounding "ghoulish," and he promises to be frank, he reminds her that they'd better fly to New York—since "we haven't much time." "Oh, I'm sorry," he adds hastily. "I mean, the sooner you get there, the more time you'll have to enjoy yourself." She doesn't mind—oh, no. Her

"It's sort of too late": Fredric March and Carole Lombard in Nothing Sacred.

reaction to the sanctimony she inspires in others, whether in the hero or in everybody else, is exultation. She is like someone in a state of irrepressible maniac elation who's compelled to attend a wake. She would never stay home. And she understands the others' feelings—she even enters into them up to a point. Though some of the nuances are lost on her. "Stop looking so happy and gallant," says Wally, apropos of nothing but a glance in her direction. "You're breaking my heart." "Cry? Why should they cry?" she says of her public—but then she remembers why, and stops looking happy for a moment. And there are times when she is clearly uneasy about the swindle she is pulling on everyone, a consciousness that causes strange discordances in her tone, as when she and Wally and Doc Donner (he wanted out of Warsaw, too) are flying into New York in a private plane. She is slumped down in her seat, watching the skyline go by and almost passing out from mingled excitement and nerves. Since it's hopeless anyway, they mustn't try to put her to bed, she tells them, or take her to doctors. "You know," she says merrily, her head lolling and her eyes glinting, "I'm not going to bed until I have convulsions and my teeth start falling out"—and she taps her teeth in ghastly illustration. "*That's* when I begin worrying," she adds, grinning at them.

This panicky kind of elation is a Lombard specialty—her particular contribution to the screwball heroine. She is not one of those heroines, like Garbo's Ninotchka or Dunne's Theodora, who transform themselves. She may, however, attempt to transform her circumstances—usually by taking some desperate chance, attempting some monstrous deception or imposture. But she remains herself through it all, cursed with consciousness, mired in the intractable.

In Wesley Ruggles' *True Confession* (1937), for example: the way she sits next to her husband (Fred MacMurray), leaning into his back, looking at him anxiously as he struggles with himself, his face turned away from her. Like two shipwrecked people, in their own living room. Their physical attraction—so evident in this and other scenes in the film, none of them technically love scenes—is something she accepts better than he does. He is still fighting her: talking about going to China or some comparable distance, when everything in the image suggests he can hardly get off the couch they are sharing. A scrupulously honest (and consequently poor) young lawyer, unimaginative, humorless, and likable, married to a compulsive liar—"I'm living a nightmare," he says, as she watches him tensely from behind. No matter what he does or threatens to do, no matter what she herself promises, he is always catching her in another lie. Mostly, as she says, she lies to please him (telling the butcher they owed money to that he was dead)—and *would* please him if he didn't keep catching her. She invents someone and then forgets the name—"McCarthy," she says. He supplies it—"McDougal"—balefully. Every time he catches her, he is forced again to threaten to leave her; and against everything he really feels, all the impulses that keep him anchored to that couch, he has to assert all those troublesome things he *ought* to feel.

She is as glowing here as she is in *Nothing Sacred*; but her radiance in *True Confession* is more like nerves. The world of the film is more like a mine field. She clutches at even the objects in it—the telephone, the typewriter, even the sandwich she is eating—the way she leans against her husband's back: as if she had to keep it all from turning on her. Helen Bartlett is a visionary, too, but a harrowed one: sitting at her typewriter and composing stories that no one will publish or believe, lifting the phone to take the job her husband has forbidden her even to think about. (Another of his principles: that a husband should be able to support his wife without help from her.) But Helen figures she can get away with *this* job without ever having to tell him about it, since it's only three hours a day of being a private secretary to a wealthy broker, an "old friend" of her family, who has hired her after a single interview. She has no secretarial skills, but she expects she'll learn. "That isn't all you're gonna learn," observes her friend Daisy (Una Merkel again).

It turns out that Mr. Krayler (John T. Murray) works at home, and that home is a Park Avenue mansion. "Shall I show you to your room?" asks the butler when she reports for her first day of work. "What room?" she says, alarmed. "Say, what kind of place is this, anyway?" But she is reassured when he shows her to the library and she sees some mail on the desk that she can open—or something. But then the "boss" enters, and the secretary role really begins to claim her. "Good morning, Mr. Krayler. I'm late." "Aren't we all," the indulgent boss replies, beaming at her and fixing a flower to his lapel. First of all, he wants her to call him Otto. "Yes, sir . . . Otto," she replies, businesslike. "You're going to work out all right," he assures her. "Thank you, sir," she says eagerly. "If I only knew—" He holds a finger up: "Otto," he corrects her. "Otto," she goes on, "if I only knew how to get *started*. . . ." But he is evasive about this. He asks her about her husband, then asks her to sit closer. Finally, all other conversational avenues having been explored, he asks her to take a letter. It's a faux pas. She looks at him, appalled: "Oh, I *can't*," she exclaims. Then, leaning forward shyly: "Remember?" she says hopefully. "Oh, that's right," says the affable Otto, his hands flat on the desk in front of him. "D'you know any word games or anything?" No, she doesn't, but she *is* going to learn shorthand: she's going to get "one of those little booklets." In the meantime, perhaps if he talks *very* slowly . . . "I think you should be getting something for your money, don't you?" He agrees—and soon he is trying to. He pursues her around the desk until she socks him in the stomach—"Let go of me, I quit!"—and leaves.

Helen isn't really as dumb as this makes her sound—she is simply desperate, as are nearly all the great Lombard heroines. It's her unconquerable hopefulness that makes this conventional sequence wonderful: her eagerness to open mail

and her dreams of a future shorthand, her troubled but not *too* troubled responses to Otto's questions about her husband and her weekends, her way of
saying "Yes, sir . . . Otto," both appalled and businesslike at the same time.
She is in the grip of her determination that this job *should* work out, just as
Hazel Flagg is in the grip of her dream of New York. If only the unfortunate Otto
didn't keep disturbing things, throwing her hopes into question. But he can't
affect the intensity—nothing can.

That intensity is Lombard's special comic vehicle, putting her in touch with
her audiences as few other leading women on the screen would ever be. When
she is angry, for example, she doesn't just convey the rage but the ecstasy, too—
kicking at Barrymore in *Twentieth Century* or staggering forward, blazing eyed
and heavy lidded, to aim a woozy uppercut at the jaw of Fredric March in *Nothing Sacred* ("Yeah, yeah, lemme hitcha just once—just once on the jaw—and I
don't care *what* happens . . ."). What might be routines for another performer
are epiphanies for her. The recklessness that makes her scream in the woods or
toss a coin for her virtue, pretend to be dying or confess to a murder she didn't
commit (in *True Confession*), always has the same source: in her deep impatience
with everydayness and with the ordinary limits of ordinary life. She is consumed
by this recklessness—isolated by it and cut off from almost everyone else on the
screen. But it's the recklessness and impatience that connect her to *us*—even
powerfully. So that Lombard's solipsism—and this is the special screwball
twist—is not just a joke, as the Lubitsch heroine's is more or less, but a kind of
triumph.

IT WAS a long time and some thirty-five movies before they identified Lombard's talent with screwball comedy itself. But off the screen her image
wasn't so indeterminate. She was, in fact, just the sort of "heroine" those later
comedies would be about: straightforward, high-spirited, intelligent and delightful—a no-nonsense girl. She was a distinctive figure among Paramount's young
contract players and, the story goes, attracted the notice of both Sturges and
Lubitsch in her, and their, early days at Paramount. Her biographer Larry Swindell calls Lubitsch her closest male friend in Hollywood; Sturges, he says, was
both a brief love affair and a friend. (Robert Riskin was a longer, more serious
romance.) Donald Ogden Stewart is also said to have fallen under her spell at
this time. When he was working on *Laughter*, he tried out an early draft of the
script on her, and many of her reactions are said to be incorporated in the cuts
and revisions of the final screenplay. Though its leading role was meant from the
beginning for Nancy Carroll, Lombard wanted to play the second lead, the role
of Carroll's stepdaughter. Apparently she would have done so (director Harry
D'Arrast was also a friend and admirer) if Preston Sturges hadn't written a role

for her that she wanted to play even more: a showgirl in love with a rich playboy in *Fast and Loose* (1930), Sturges' second screenplay, produced and filmed at Paramount's Astoria studios (Miriam Hopkins starred, in her screen debut). Sturges wrote the part for her, even modeled it on her, he later said, because he liked her: "Everybody did."

Unlike most of the women who came to prominence in the early talkies, who had begun their careers on the stage, Lombard really felt at home in Hollywood. The place *was* home to her: she went to school there, appeared in her first movie at the age of thirteen, had her first dates with the sons of Hollywood royalty and her first dances at the Cocoanut Grove, grew up to marry William Powell (very briefly) and Clark Gable. She was ambitious, but she also seemed really to enjoy herself. She was a big party-thrower, a practical joker, and the most famous dirty talker in Los Angeles County. A regular girl, as they all said—immensely popular on her sets and furtively generous to people less famous and lucky than herself. "Marvelous girl," said Howard Hawks of the offscreen Lombard—then added: "Crazy as a bedbug."

She was perceived as a beauty early on. She enjoyed that job too, it seems—submitting to more stills than any other star on the lot except Dietrich. Like most of the screen beauties of that period, she is in the Garbo style: gaunt, hollow cheeked, languorous. (She is made to look like Garbo's Queen Christina in the jail scenes of *True Confession*. And in *The Princess Comes Across* she plays an aspiring "Garbo" named Princess Olga, Swedish accent and all.) She tries for hauteur at times, but that is never as convincing in her as the suggestion of something more down-to-earth, something anxious that calls attention to the set of the excessively square jaw, something careworn and mind-driven at the center of the improbable glamour. The Lombard look was in fact paradigmatic—a familiar kind of American woman's beauty given a special authority by the challenge of the Depression: a worrier with a sense of humor. (Compare the sleek, self-armored, playmate-of-the-month look favored later on.) At her most serene she looks harrowed, with a gauntness that suggests not the ideal but the grimly palpable—a fineness and delicacy that have nothing to do with "breeding" or "background," everything to do with chagrin.

Before *Twentieth Century*, Lombard was a leading lady at Paramount (with occasional loan-outs to Columbia) for some twenty films over four years, a dependable, attractive performer available for musicals (*Bolero*), melodramas (*White Woman*), or spook shows (*Supernatural*)—the ordinary gamut that a secondary, not very distinctive star might be expected to run. Lombard plugged along at stardom instead of shooting to it or falling from it. What's unusual is that she somehow never lost ground over this span of time and films; she kept both audience and studio interested and hoping, it seemed. But a strain begins to show: a hectic, inchoate quality in her performances that gets worse rather

Ken and Helen Bartlett (Fred MacMurray and Carole Lombard) on the couch (above) and in the courtroom. True Confession.

than better as the movies roll by, one after the other. More and more her emotions seem discontinuous, disproportionate. She tries posturing but never seems to get away with it. Her face is almost haplessly expressive, sending messages she can't control. She talks about hope, and the eyebrows rise hopelessly. She smiles, and the eyes look angry. Her variableness is so marked that *We're Not Dressing* (1934) tries building one of its song routines around it: as Bing Crosby croons a love song, she looks fierce each time his gaze is on her, melting and love-struck each time he looks away.

In such a dilemma it seems appropriate that she should end up berating her leading men, as she does in scene after scene and movie after movie—making dumb, empty dazzlers like George Raft and Gary Cooper and Gene Raymond feel foolish and ashamed. If there is a single kind of big moment that characterizes the early (and even somewhat later) Lombard film, it's that time when she rains on the hero's parade—when he learns to see himself as *she* sees him. "I'm ashamed of you!" she tells Charles Wadsworth in *Fast and Loose*—and then makes him apologize to the judge. She makes Gable get an honest job in *No*

Man of Her Own—then does the same for Gene Raymond in *Brief Moment* (1933). She also has to deal with the latter's drinking, just as she must rebuke Gable for being nothing but a crook—and Gary Cooper, too, in *Now and Forever* (1934). But I didn't *know*, pleads sharpie George Raft, thoroughly ashamed of himself at last, in *Bolero* (1934). Of course you didn't, replies Lombard: "How would you know about anything but yourself?" It had to happen sooner or later, she tells Gable in *No Man of Her Own*, "my finding out you're a cheat." She already knows that Gary Cooper is a cheat in *Now and Forever*, but when she finds out that he is also a liar, it's too much. "You've lost your size, Jerry," she tells him sadly, "and I could never chase trains with a little man."

This censorious mode clearly fits *something* about her—the line in her forehead, the blaze in her eye. But it doesn't move her toward major stardom. There are complaints from the fans about her looking "hard." The studio knows what they mean but are still not really sure how they want her to look—or be. She doesn't have a "tragic" quality, like Sylvia Sidney or Kay Francis. She isn't even good at pathos, as Nancy Carroll is: she isn't lightsome enough, and she was never girlish. She is a woman of mystery in *The Eagle and the Hawk* (her glamour), a woman of evil in *Supernatural* (her fierceness), but is unconvincing in both, clearly unconvinced herself. She is certainly intense on the screen—but about what? Since no one seems to know the answer, least of all Lombard herself, she becomes faintly ludicrous as she goes from one conventional heroine to another. She doesn't so much play these roles as stalk through them like some restless ghost.

She'll be a sensation, Howard Hawks reportedly told John Barrymore on the set of *Twentieth Century*, if we can just keep her from acting. "The worst actress in the world" is how he later remembered her at this time. But it depends. She always seems to work well with Wesley Ruggles (she made three movies with him, one more than with any other director); and *No Man of Her Own*, two years *before* Hawks and Barrymore, shows her giving a beautifully controlled and judged performance throughout: a performance much like the later Lombard, in fact. Ruggles spoke about the film to Larry Swindell in 1974:

> When we ran it off for the first time I was damned impressed, though nobody else seemed to be. I loved the first part of the picture—it had a lot of realistic comedy crammed in, and this was what we had decided to work for. Carole and Clark both knew exactly what they were doing. . . . Yet I thought Carole was the revelation. . . . Look at the picture today. It's dated, but her work hasn't. She's very fresh. She's playing straight but using comedy technique too. Those idiots who'd taken over the studio— they couldn't even see that. Well, the critics didn't see it either. She was wonderful, but it just passed by. . . .

So almost did *Twentieth Century*. Since the film did poorly, Lombard's breakthrough into frantic comedy ("I hardly recognize myself," she said in a contemporary interview; "I am certainly not the Carole Lombard of the past four years") wasn't as widely noted an event as it should have been—or as it has since become. Paramount still persisted in casting her conventionally. Her next two assignments there were *Now and Forever*, in support of Shirley Temple and Gary Cooper, and *Rumba* (1935), with George Raft, a not-so-disguised sequel to their 1934 hit, *Bolero*. She did two loan-outs between these films. In *Lady by Choice* (1934), back at Columbia, she had the sole top billing, but the movie was built around character actress May Robson and a hoped-for confusion with *Lady for a Day*, Robson's hugely popular Capra film of the year before. *The Gay Bride* (1934), Lombard's sole MGM film—a kind of unofficial tryout for a contract there—was a flop. Though it got some good notices (notably from Andre Sennwald in the New York *Times*), the studio lost faith in it even before it played widely, booking it on the lower half of double bills and forgoing ads. Directed by Jack Conway and written by Sam and Bella Spewack, *The Gay Bride* is about a chorus girl who marries a series of racketeers for their money and their short life spans (one of them is called Shoots Magizz, enabling her to be known later as "the Widow Magizz"). It's a tough rather than a screwball comedy—a *very* tough comedy, with a consequent nervousness of tone and uncertainty of outline, in a mode that already by 1934 seemed a bit dated. But Lombard's venality as the bride is very funny—in a role at least as unsympathetic as her Lily Garland was, though a good deal less coherent. (She herself hated the role, referring to the film later as her worst ever.)

At this point Lubitsch stepped in. He had influenced her tryout at MGM, praising her pointedly to the studio bosses when he was there doing *The Merry Widow.* Now (though briefly) he was production head at their own studio, in one of the shifts of power frequent to the erratic fortunes of Paramount in the thirties, and so in a position to affect her career directly. It was through Lubitsch that Lombard made the first film intentionally designed as a showcase for her. Lubitsch (uncredited) supervised the production and Mitchell Leisen directed, with Fred MacMurray co-starring (the first of his four films with Lombard). *Hands Across the Table* (1935) is about Regi, a fortune-hunting manicurist who sets out to marry a rich playboy (MacMurray) only to find out that he is poor and hunting a fortune himself. He is engaged to the daughter of "the Pineapple King" but moves in with Lombard; they become buddies and partners in their separate pursuits of the big money, falling in love with each other but fighting it.

It was a big success for Lombard, a popular film and a vindication of Lubitsch's confidence in her. It was not only the first Lombard vehicle but her first real screwball comedy. But it's also, unfortunately, a misguided one. Regi and Ted, the romantic couple, are almost programmatically madcap—their "giddy fun" gets to seem very deliberate very quickly. They go to a posh nightclub and get the hiccups and try to cure them by drinking water upside down. You can't come in here in those clothes, says the stuffy maître d' at the entrance—and they proceed to take their clothes off. Ted calls Regi at work, imitating (if that's the word) her Japanese houseboy, to tell her that he has "boiled" the lamb chops. He pretends to be her outraged husband when an unwanted date calls on her, while she collapses with stifled laughter in the other room. And when he phones his fiancee and pretends to be in Hawaii, Regi pinches her nose to make a nasal voice and pretends to be an operator who keeps interrupting the call. This makes them laugh so much that they fall on the floor together ("Oh, my jaws hurt," says Regi). At the very end of the film, riding on top of a doubledeck bus, they decide to settle an argument about whether to have lunch or get married that day by tossing a coin. But the coin rolls under a car. They leap off the bus, stop all the traffic on Fifth Avenue, and crawl under the car to see how the coin has landed (on end, as it happens).

But this is screwball comedy *without* the joke—or the risk. Regi and Ted are wonderfulness on a rampage, without threat, mockery, or doubts. This is exactly how a lot of filmmakers understood screwball comedy (which they now began turning out in great numbers): as another kind of Capra film. But without that cutting competitive edge between the couple—without the recklessness of the hitchhiking scene in *It Happened One Night,* the hints of danger and chagrin that glint beneath the surface of Nick and Nora's banter, the skepticism that finally resolves itself when Astaire and Rogers dance—the screwball couple, with all their public high jinks, seem offensively complacent rather than daring or adventurous.

It's never a surprise, then, when they also turn out to be mealymouthed: Fred MacMurray assures us solemnly near the end of this film that he is no longer "the enemy of the ordinary." And he's going to get a job, too, in case we're worried about that. In spite of its Lubitschean ambience and high Paramount gloss, *Hands Across the Table* illustrates most of the ways that the standard and uninspired screwball comedies of the time went wrong—and sentimental. And it even adds a few kinks of its own. The Other Man figure this time is neither a phony nor a fool (though he is still Ralph Bellamy) but a cripple, radiating benevolence from what looks like an art deco wheelchair. "You're so right," exclaims Regi as she kisses him off at the end, "it *is* love that counts!"—and leaves him with his butler. A certain sadism even creeps into the comic routines—as in a painfully prolonged scene where Regi gives Ted a manicure and the file keeps slipping, leaving his fingers and cuticles bleeding. She is supposed to be nervous because she thinks he's rich, but since she seems so supremely competent otherwise we never really believe the scene, which thus adds the discomfort of seeming gratuitous.

And at times Lombard's performance shows those undertones of depression and irritability that mark her earlier assembly-line films. Here, too, she seems unfocused and overinflected—looking martyred when she's supposed to look discontented, bad-tempered when she's supposed to look blue, and so on. The surprising fact is that the first "real Lombard film" doesn't really seem to suit her very well.

Her next film, a Universal comedy called *Love Before Breakfast* (1936) is also in the screwball vein. (This is the movie in the famous Walker Evans photograph: the billboard showing Lombard with a black eye.) But it's a shambling, disconnected film.* Here she is a crazy, willful rich girl. Although she looks beautiful and does some skillful slapstick, the empty and effortful script prompts her to another frantic and strained performance. She is wonderful, however, in her next film, Paramount's *The Princess Comes Across* (1936)—again with MacMurray—

---

*Preston Sturges worked briefly on the screenplay, though none of his work appears to have survived into the film.

though the movie itself disappears from under her, collapsing before its midpoint into the kind of narrative chaos MGM would never have permitted in a released film. She is an American girl aspiring to a movie contract who masquerades as "Princess Olga," a Garbo clone. Who is her favorite movie star? the reporters on board the ship ask her. "Mickey Moosey," she replies, and does a snuffling little laugh of satisfaction into her scarf. ("I think I smell a moosey," she says dryly later on, fingering the hero's calling card.) Lombard's popularity with audiences was high, and both these films, despite their flaws, were box-office successes.

But it was Gregory La Cava's *My Man Godfrey* (1936) that made her a major star—and a specifically screwball star at that. As a dingbat heiress who picks up a tramp in a scavenger hunt and brings him home to be the butler, and ultimately the savior, to her addled and improvident family. Her ex-husband, William Powell, had wanted her to do this role opposite him, even made it a condition of his own signing for the film. And yet it doesn't seem a very probable kind of casting: Lombard, with her air of fierce intelligence, as a giddy halfwit. The character of Irene Bullock in this film derives from the Dizzy Little Woman of comic strips and popular radio shows and even other movies (where she is usually a supporting part, not the heroine): Gracie Allen or Jane Ace of radio's *Easy Aces* serial, with their complacent straight-man husbands. She is less a character than a comic routine, featuring general incomprehension and muddle, lightning changes of subject, and a relentless propensity to talk nonsense, however much her patient male companion may try to talk her out of it.

This abstraction of dumbness, it should be pointed out, is an abstraction of dumb femaleness, quite specifically; no leading man could ever have been conceived in these terms. The heroine of *My Man Godfrey* really reverses the joke that lies at the center of most screwball comedies: the woman is smarter, stronger, and finally more independent than the hero. Irene, however, is dumber than everyone, except possibly her mother (Alice Brady), who is a shriller variant of the same comic routine. One of the problems with this routine is that it forces almost everyone around it into a kind of straight-man smugness. And the joke in *My Man Godfrey* verges even more than usually on ugliness: Irene is the romantic heroine, and yet she is clearly not someone anyone could want to be around for very long—as her mother's marriage shows. ("Take a look at the dizzy old girl with the goat," says a man at the scavenger hunt to Eugene Pallette's Bullock, Sr. "I've *had* to look at her for twenty years—that's Mrs. Bullock," says Pallette.) Most damaging of all, perhaps, the character simply isn't very funny. Her inconsequence is too predictable and mechanical—too dumb, in fact. As when Irene tells Godfrey that he is different from her late, lamented Pomeranian: the Pomeranian had fleas, she explains, and didn't use big words. The nonsense is reflexive and tired, in just this style, throughout.

It isn't only that Lombard rescues this role from its own impossibility or that she saves it from tedium and offensiveness: she does much more. She makes it into a triumph—mainly by that sense of careless, rapturous going-too-far that also infused (though to different effect) her performance in *Twentieth Century*. "See you in church," she says to Godfrey, her butler and "protégé," as he leaves her room after unsuccessfully trying to serve her breakfast. It's the same exit line she throws at Gable in *No Man of Her Own* after he kisses her in the library stacks; but there it is comically tormented, a cry of distraction. Here it is serene—Irene is leaning forward on the edge of her bed, wreathed by the collar of her feathered negligee, her fierce broad brow covered with blond curls, her face ravishingly lit from above—a vision, in short, of movie-star glamour. And at the center of it all, firmly in place, is a grin of derangement. The whole performance is like this: ecstatic, with an air of radiant fulfillment. It's that that makes it funny finally—and compelling in its odd way. And though it doesn't quite make it romantic, it helps to suggest how a man like Powell's Godfrey might be in some way drawn to this figure. (Their wedding at the final fadeout is appropriately dreamlike: "It'll all be over in a minute," she tells him.)

But most important of all, perhaps, Irene Bullock seems to give Lombard a central clue to the wonderful performances that follow—in 1937, her *annus mirabilis*—in *Nothing Sacred* and *True Confession*, the decade's two best Lombard films.* Though Hazel Flagg and Helen Bartlett are remote indeed from the antic stupidity of *Godfrey*'s heiress, they have in common with her their self-fulfillment in states of desperation and extremity that cross over into relief, abandon, self-forgetfulness. It's in *My Man Godfrey*—in the discordances and incoherencies and near-impossibilities of the leading role—that Lombard first hits upon the screwball idea that she all but made her own: craziness as a kind of transcendence.

THE LOMBARD heroine is both a visionary and a realist. If her imagination is sufficiently stirred, she can be very disinterested: sitting at her own trial for murder and listening to the prosecution, "I want to see *myself* electrocuted," she admits in *True Confession*. Earlier on, she likes nearly all the hypothetical confessions that policeman Edgar Kennedy proposes to her when he is grilling her for the murder of Otto Krayler (the police found the millionaire shot to death

---

* Mitchell Leisen's *Swing High Swing Low* was the first of that year's three Lombard films, and it too was a big success: the highest-grossing Paramount film of 1937. A melodrama, based on Arthur Hopkins' and George Manker Walters' play *Burlesque*, about a trumpet player and his long-suffering wife, updated with some screwball romantic scenes. But Lombard's performance is uneven—often arch and hectic. Leisen seems not to be a director who brought out the best in her, either here or in *Hands Across the Table*. He thought she was wonderful, and it looks from the films as if he may have spent time telling her so: in any case her effects in both their films together are very conscious.

Hazel Flagg (Lombard), on the brink of public exposure—with a swollen jaw: she's just had a fist fight with Wally (Fredric March, in background—note his swollen jaw).

in his mansion a few hours after Helen's departure). You killed him because you loved him and he threw you over, Kennedy suggests to her, in rich and lurid detail: "So you stand lookin' at this man, lookin' and hatin' as only a dame can hate!" She's not so crazy about this scenario—besides, she points out, it doesn't explain the missing money. "*Now* I know what happened," cries Kennedy, undiscouraged. "You *don't* love him, see? You never did love him—you don't love nobody. You're that type of a dame!" She likes it. But finally she prefers her own version: a straying wife who kills her lover to save her husband from knowing about her infidelity. But she is puzzled when Kennedy thinks she means it. Helen doesn't actually decide to confess to this murder until she is persuaded later on that it's the only practical thing to do. Her decision pays off. Her final acquittal on grounds of self-defense leads to fame and wealth, a lecture tour, and a serialized autobiography (*My Life, My Struggle*).

It's clear early on, of course, that her lying is as much a response to her husband's needs as it is a defiance of them. And when he visits her in jail and gets the first hint that she might plead not guilty at her trial, he is appalled: "[Don't] even *think* of trying to convince a jury that you didn't fire those shots," he tells her. "Do you know what'll happen to you?" He is scared just to think about it. Suddenly so is she. Part of his problem is that he'd assumed beforehand that they were going to plead self-defense: he's been building his plans for her defense around that ("A woman has the right to protect herself from a brute")— and he is not, to say the least, very flexible. She, on the other hand, is—endlessly so. She sees what he's getting at right away: a defense attorney fighting for the life of his own wife. "In defending me," she says excitedly, "you'll be pleading the cause of all womanhood!" It's her kind of scenario. The difference between her and all the others, including her husband, is that she doesn't really believe in it—the same crucial element that isolates Hazel Flagg from the people in her movie.

It's this outsider status that Lombard plays so particularly beautifully in *True Confession*. Sitting beside Ken, her husband, in jail—the same tableau as in their apartment—he is turned away from her and facing forward, she is leaning into his back and regarding him gravely, with wide, wondering eyes. Every time he turns to look at her, however, she assumes a slight frown, as if quickly remembering how she is *supposed* to look: solemn, disturbed, etc. He turns away and the frown goes away, he turns back and it reappears (a wonderfully rich and subtle counterpart of that earlier routine in *We're Not Dressing* where she looks alternately frowning and loving while Crosby sings to her). It's not that she *isn't* disturbed (she is scared to death); it's just that she knows she hasn't found the right *look* for being disturbed, the one her husband will like. Lombard puts on a conventional face the way she finds the conventional words about death in *Nothing Sacred*: with relief that she hasn't forgotten the trick. "How's the food?" Ken asks her. "All right, I guess," she says absently. Then, quickly, frowningly: "I haven't eaten any." *Now* she has his serious attention. "Oh, you should eat," he says concernedly. And she looks at him imploringly.

Lombard is not a nonconformist figure, like Hepburn in *Bringing Up Baby* or Dunne in *The Awful Truth*. Just the opposite: she is *trying* to conform, desperately, if only because she has so much to hide. Trying to get that face or remark or attitude *right*—it's never easy. What makes it even harder is that she's likely to be the only undeceived person in the movie—besides her girlfriend, if she has one. It's instructive in *True Confession* to see the way she and Una Merkel enter a space full of somber, threatening men (the cops at the scene of the crime) chattering and clutching at each other like a pair of daft forest creatures. It's mostly the men in her films who talk about truth—and mostly to invoke it against her. She lies to them, of course; but *they* lie to themselves. And if her deceptions do pay off in the end (as they do, richly), it's mainly because of the contradictions and deceptions of the world around her. Hypocrisy doesn't come naturally to her; she always has to learn it, and so she is always in danger of lousing it up, of giving the whole game away. And she is always troubled—as others are not— by knowing better. We'll win because we're honest, says Ken about her trial, or else we don't want to win at all—and Helen bursts into tears. Much later on, when he finally finds out that she lied about shooting Krayler, he accuses her of making "a farce of our lives," making a mockery of justice and the legal profession and him, too. And he isn't far wrong. She is a subversive in spite of herself—an involuntary outlaw.

Nothing Sacred and *True Confession* were the peak of her screwball career. Both films were hits, and both were released nationally on the same day, Thanksgiving, 1937. *True Confession* reunited her with the two men who had, according to her, done the most to form her as an actress: director Wesley Ruggles and John Barrymore, who plays the featured supporting role of a mandarin drunk who holds the key to the murder. A modest film, shot in half the time *Nothing Sacred* took (Lombard had only a weekend off between the two films), it was almost inevitably overshadowed, and still is, by the Selznick film.

Nothing Sacred is probably the most famous of all the Lombard films next to *My Man Godfrey.* And it impressed people at the time with its evident ambition. It wasn't to begin with the sort of project David O. Selznick was normally drawn to (i.e., it was a comedy); but once convinced (mainly by his principal backer, Jock Whitney, who had been carried away by seeing *Godfrey*), Selznick determined to make the classiest of all screwball comedies. Lombard, after *Godfrey*, was a necessity. And so, Selznick felt, was Ben Hecht, nearly the hottest screenwriter in Hollywood at the time, especially for comedy. People were impressed not only by the cast and the credits and the Technicolor (the first movie of its sort to be filmed in that process); *Nothing Sacred* was also the first screwball comedy to lay apparent claim to larger satiric meanings, to make scathing observations about American life and society. It sets out to demonstrate what a more modest comedy like *True Confession* simply assumes: that the corruption and phoniness are nearly total.

This is a newspaper comedy, but it opens (after some travelogue shots of Times Square and Rockefeller Center) not in a press room but in a magnificent banquet hall, where Walter Connolly, the owner and editor of the *Morning Star* (a character later described as "sort of a cross between a Ferris wheel and a werewolf"), is introducing his newspaper's latest public-spirited project. This is New York, not the grungy early Chicago of Hecht's *The Front Page.* Everything is plusher and posher in this version of the city; even the scams are on a grand scale. Connolly announces the building of a monumental new arts center and introduces the donor—"with a heart as big as his pocketbook"—"the sultan of Mah-zoo-pan" (Tory Brown), an enormous black man in a pink turban seated complacently beside him. Then the editor unveils a massive, gasp-inducing mural of the project. "Twenty-seven halls of learning and culture," he intones. "Twenty-seven arenas of art!" The sultan, however, has no sooner risen to give the invocation ("Peace be to you my friends," he prays over the bowed heads below him, "peace and the blessings of cul-chuh") than an indignant Hattie

McDaniel barges in (her only scene in the film), trailing four children and two policemen. "That's my husband!" she cries—and so the sultan is unmasked as a shoeshine boy. POTENTATE SHINES NIFTY SHOE, reads a rival paper's headline. ACE REPORTER'S EXCLUSIVE PROVES HOAX OF CENTURY.

Hecht's racial slurs, in jokes like this one, were not casual—unlike most other people's in the Hollywood of this time. The ugly and incessant racial joking of *The Front Page* is part of the meanness of spirit the play is about. It's also part of the disreputable comic energy that Hecht likes to plug into. He was simply more knowing about the meanness—and more ready to get a laugh out of it—than other writers working the same territory.

But this strain of Hechtian ugliness, very much present in *Nothing Sacred*, has an odd visual counterpart there. Hazel Flagg's New York is heartless, hypocritical, corrupt. But it looks—in the delicate and ravishing pastels of early Technicolor—like Oz, unreal, rainbow-hued, magical. From the sky as Hazel's plane flies in from Vermont, from the Hudson River as she and Wally go sailboating there, it's an enchanted place. Even its interiors, the arenas and nightclubs and banquet halls, suggest space and freedom, flight and elation.

Just as they should. *The Front Page*, after all, had no Lombard. But it's just that bleak Chicago landscape which Hecht and MacArthur made legendary that the screwball heroine inherits—and transforms. And *Nothing Sacred*'s overproduction (as it might be called) makes that transformation palpable, a visual as well as an emotional fact. Hazel's relation to the city is crucial. The Lombard heroine is not a city type, either in the tough comedy sense (Harlow or Blondell) or the sophisticated one (Shearer or Colbert). She isn't a small-town type, either—though she was *once* (just as a good part of her audience was)—a city girl with a small town in her past. What makes New York so wonderful? Mainly that it's not Warsaw. The alternatives are grim, to be sure, but they are real. And the screwball heroine turns grim realism into magic, the grim city into Oz. And yet Lombard never makes the magic look easy. She reminds us always of just how perilous and hard to master the trick is.

This finally becomes the expressive use of that variable, oddly intense temperament—paraded so fruitlessly through so many uncertain movies and unsuitable roles—focused at last in these embattled, obsessed, uneasy, and ultimately rapturous heroines. *Nothing Sacred* jokes obsessively about Hazel's "gallantry" in facing death, but the most powerful effect Lombard conveys is the gallantry of someone facing life. The movie tells us that everyone is implicated in hypocrisy and self-deception, but Lombard tells us that some people are mysteriously, triumphantly untouched by this general atmosphere: they are simply too daring, too funny, too full of sense and life. The Lombard heroine stands for that extraordinary promise American life once seemed to hold out: that *anyone* might grow up to be a crook.

Irene Dunne | 11

About It Happened One Night *I said that its appreciation depended on a certain acceptance of Claudette Colbert; but my sense of* The Awful Truth *is that if one is not willing to yield to Irene Dunne's temperament, her talents, her reactions, following their detail almost to the loss of one's own identity, one will not know, and will not care, what the film is about.*
— STANLEY CAVELL, *Pursuits of Happiness*

THE GRANT family never expected her to crash the Governor's Ball—in *Theodora Goes Wild* (1936). And then they look across the floor and see her dancing with the Governor himself—the man who had just a moment ago been asking them about this "notorious woman" the papers have been linking their name with. "Caroline Adams," as she is called, (Irene Dunne) is the scandalous author of a sexy best-selling novel. Bad enough that she has moved into the penthouse apartment of Michael Grant (Melvyn Douglas)—a married man and the son of the Lieutenant Governor—just about the same time as she has made headlines for breaking up her publisher's marriage. Now she is here—and her only purpose is to create a scandal for them, to embarrass Michael and to ruin his father's political career. If the Governor should find out . . .

The Governor (Frederick Burton)—a tall, distinguished, elderly man— seems almost too important to have really heard about all this. But he has heard *some*thing about it—or why else his "notorious woman" question? He prides himself especially, as he has just pointed out to Michael and his parents, on having never been touched by scandal. Now there he is: pumping magisterially across the dance floor with the notorious woman herself. *He* may not know who she is, but everyone else surely does. Especially the excited reporters with their cameras.

From the Governor's point of view, he is being quite lucky. This woman is charming. And if the Governor has a weak spot, as we have seen, it's for com-

The Awful
Truth. *"Lola"
at the Vances'.*
*Irene Dunne
with Claude
Allister (whose
role got lost in
the cutting).*

pliments on his dancing. We see this earlier on when his wife reminds him, as she dances away on the Lieutenant Governor's arm, that "there are a hundred women just palpitating to dance with you." The Governor almost seems to believe her: the stern face suddenly collapses into helpless chuckles. Of course he knows it's a joke. But still . . . he is ready to dance. And chuckling. "You dance divinely, Governor," says this pretty young woman as they dance. "Thank you, Miss—ah—?" "*Ad*ams," she says, with emphasis. "You're a splendid dancer too, Miss Adams," he says, and chuckles over his own remark. He even chuckles when the flashbulbs go off in their faces, "Miss Adams" making sure that they are both turned forward into the cameras.

The dance ends and the Governor introduces her to the Grants—to the Lieutenant Governor and his wife, to Michael and his wife. Although they of course *know* who she is they aren't giving it away—except that they look at her murderously. "Allow me to present—uh—Miss—uh . . ." "*Ad*ams," she says, again with emphasis: a little lurch and jump as she says it at him. "It's a delightful party, isn't it?" she says to the Grants, and the Governor smiles and nods. "I don't know when I've enjoyed myself so much," she goes on. The Governor is chuckling insensately now: he knows what she's going to say next (don't they all say it?). "And the Governor dances *divinely*," Miss Adams says. There is much laughter at this, most of it the Governor's. The Grants are smiling, but they look glaceéd as they do so. "Thank you, thank you," says the Governor. "But give me a charming lady to dance with and"—he pauses for effect—"we-ell, I'm young again." The object of this compliment looks astonished at the Governor (oh, yes?), then delighted at the others: as if to say, it's true and isn't it wonderful? The music resumes and the Governor dances her away again.

When the by now quite desperate Michael tries to cut in, the Governor is playful: "Young blood trying to force an old boy on the sidelines, eh?" Not a chance. "Miss Adams is *my* discovery"—while Miss Adams looks shy in his arms—"and I'm going to keep her." Michael then gets his wife (Leona Maricle) to *demand* that the Governor dance with her ("I'm simply expiring to dance with you and you've no use for me whatever")—on the grounds that she "can't wait." "Of course I know just how you feel," says Dunne, as Michael dances her away from the Governor at last. But not in time to prevent the explosion that's coming.

It's one of the triumphs of the screwball style that it's occasionally able to "throw off," almost in passing, a figure like the Governor—a character so lightly and fleetingly sketched that he might even escape notice, but nearly unforgettable once he attracts your attention. The Governor is a delight because he captures a certain kind of fatuousness so perfectly and purely. He is a happy man—even to knowing ahead of time that his jokes will be laughed at, his compliments blushed over, his words hung on. What makes the Governor delightful is that he really doesn't seem to know *why* all this is happening—doesn't seem to have the least clue that it's anything but himself that people around him are responding to with such enthusiasm. Now for instance, not only is he dancing, a pleasure in itself, but people keep telling him how wonderfully he is doing it—in a series of compliments that mount crazily out of control, from "charming" to "fascinating" to "I'm afraid I can't wait." Can complacency be ecstatic? The Governor is almost fuddled with satisfaction by the time this sequence is over.

But it's Dunne who controls the scene—and its comic meanings. Just as Caroline Adams is controlling the situation. She is the bombshell in his arms. Looking spacey and adorable as they move across the crowded floor and knowing exactly what havoc she is wreaking. Savoring the banality of the Governor's remarks—even offering to share her pleasure with the Grants. She creates the context that makes the Governor (who is played quite straight by the actor) as funny as he is. When Dunne turns him gently around on the dance floor so that they are both facing into the photographers, you might never notice the telltale little eagerness with which the Governor leans forward into the cameras if Dunne, below him, weren't showing a corresponding eagerness, leaning forward a bit more even than he is, with an inflection of mad avidity in her eyes. Her light parody of celebrity exposes the Governor's heavy and earnest pursuit of it. Her style is highly elaborated (after the avidity before the flashbulbs, for example, she does a kind of was-that-me? take and recovers) but never seems overdone or excessive precisely because it seems so consistently inspired. Dunne is like someone possessed by their own delight.

So they go across the crowded dance floor, Miss Adams in what looks like the lead (the Governor's dancing, from behind at least, looks remarkably like doddering in place), hanging on her partner's condescending smile, echoing his satisfied chuckle with a slightly unmoored ascending laugh of her own, letting him turn her around in front of the appalled Michael. She's beautiful: a good little girl (she even wears a high-fashion version of a hair bow in this scene) who has learned all her lessons—and who is now gleefully, systematically, lethally misapplying them. She fulfills, in her genteel feminine way, *The Front Page*'s ideal of social success: to be both destructive and esteemed, subversive and fawned over at the same time. Not only to have the goods on all of them—but to have them take you in their arms—and to music, too . . .

Dunne is the kind of comic performer who *feels* the joke, in her bones and blood. In a way, she has nothing to do to *play* a scene like this but to be *on* it— and then try to hold herself back. It's that wonderful funny *brimming* look she has whenever she looks at the Governor. And those little lurches and jumps she gives are like breakouts of elation and triumph. It's the triumph of wit and intelligence that this movie is mainly about. And it's the final reason that it and the hero are in love with her. Irene Dunne is the most dazzling screwball comedienne of them all.

IT'S TRUE that by 1936 a lot of leading female stars with careers as tearjerker heroines much like Dunne's had been, had gone screwball (even Joan Crawford had tried it). But none of them made the sensation that Dunne did: *Theodora Goes Wild* was another sleeper for Columbia, a huge and unexpected hit. It became the precursor and paradigm of almost every important romantic comedy to follow it, from *The Awful Truth* to *Ninotchka* to *The Lady Eve*. Like all those later films, it deals in impersonations and magical transformations. And the screenplay, by Sidney Buchman (who also wrote the best Capra film of this period, *Mr. Smith Goes to Washington*), is one of the most brilliantly constructed in the screwball cycle.

The small town that Theodora (Dunne) lives in is a particularly nightmarish one: entirely populated, as it almost seems, by fussy old aunts. It's in Connecticut and it's called Lynnfield, after Theodora's family, now entirely represented by herself and her two formidable maiden aunts, Mary and Elsie (Elizabeth

Theodora (Dunne) dancing with the governor (Frederick Burton) and sharing her pleasure with Melvyn Douglas and Leona Maricle; Henry Kolker in background. Theodora Goes Wild.

Risdon and Margaret McWade). When the local newspaper starts to serialize a sexy new novel called *The Sinner*, the aunts go into battle, with Theodora delegated to lead the charge. She phones the editor (Thomas Mitchell)—the aunts, as always, at her elbow—to announce the family's displeasure. "Aunt Mary and Aunt Elsie simply can't approve, Jed." Nor can any of the other ladies in town, who deplore the serial almost as avidly as they read and discuss it. But Jed is unmovable. Rebecca Perry (Spring Byington), the town's worst busybody and the president of its Literary Circle, fires off a telegram to the publisher: "brazen filth" and so on.

The New York publisher, Arthur Stevenson (Thurston Hall), is reading this telegram—with great pleasure—just as Theodora herself slinks into his office in a state of guilty nerves. Stevenson is the only one who knows the scandalous author's real identity—so far. At this point Mrs. Stevenson (Nana Bryant) happens into the office—"Don't tell me *you're* Caroline Adams!"—and so does the painter who did the book jacket, Michael Grant (Douglas). Theodora, feeling cornered, agrees to go to dinner with them all. The probings continue, however.

Theodora (Dunne) dancing with the governor (Frederick Burton) and sharing her pleasure with Melvyn Douglas and Leona Maricle; Henry Kolker in background. Theodora Goes Wild.

"Your modesty, my dear, your girlish *sweetness!*" exclaims the poisonous Mrs. Stevenson. "I'm baffled." Does she drink? Michael wants to know. She *looks* as if she doesn't drink, he says. Oh, yes? She puts her order in to the waiter: "Straight whiskey." A few of these and she is dancing, too—and going to Michael's apartment: a woman of the world, just as Caroline Adams should be. "Some soft music would be nice, don't you think?" she says—displaying her bravado. Yes, in fact it's been playing all the time, he replies.* Recovering from this mistake, she is still not quite equal to his attempt to make love to her, and she bolts the apartment in a panic. In the next shot, she is singing "Rock of Ages" back home in the choir: Sunday-morning services.

But Michael has tracked her to Lynnfield—with a stray dog he's picked up on the way. Threatened with exposure, Theodora installs him and the dog in her toolshed. He can do the gardening, she says over her aunts' protests—and there is much "talk" around the town, eagerly led by Rebecca Perry. In the meantime, Theodora and Michael go fishing and berry-picking, and Theodora falls quietly

*A nice joke, because we're surprised, too—we've assumed that it's just soundtrack music before this.

in love. "I'm gonna break you outa this jail," Michael promises her when she asks him to leave town. He is on the familiar movie mission—for a movie hero—of liberating the prim and repressed heroine. He makes all the familiar appeals: seize the day, do your own thing, live! Everything she writes about she is afraid to do, he tells her. What if I'm happy? she says. Nonsense, he tells her; "no quaking rabbit was ever happy." "Break loose, be yourself"—and so on. What all this is building toward, however, is that rich and magical moment near the middle of the movie when Theodora finally does take his advice—and we realize just on the instant that Michael himself does, that he wants to take it all back.

It all starts when the Literary Circle meets at the Lynn house. The assembled ladies are shocked to see Theodora in the toolshed with "the gardener," laughing—he is in his undershirt and they are both sitting on his bed. Her mortified aunt summons her to the house to serve tea. But when Theodora enters the parlor with the tea tray and sees all those mean, censorious faces set and waiting for her, something snaps in her. She tells the Literary Circle off. They want to know why she went out to the toolshed: it was to tell the gardener he had to leave, "to tell him that he's got to go because *you* want him to!" But they've been telling her what to do since she was three years old. "Now I'll tell *you* something—I'll tell you something you'll never forget! There's no law that can put that gardener off these premises and he's going to stay *right here!*"—with her teeth flashing and her eyes blazing. Dissolve: to a framed photo of the Literary Circle sitting in rows and looking thunderstruck—as Theodora's voice goes on without interruption, and the camera tracks back from the photo to reveal that it—and we—are in the toolshed now, where Theodora is repeating her speech for Michael's appreciation. "This is a free country, I said—I'm over twenty-one, and what I choose to do is none of Lynnfield's business. I invite the whole town to take a jump in the lake"—we hear her say. But when the camera finally takes her in—panning across Michael, looking delighted, on his cot with the dog—we see that Theodora is quite impressively wild-eyed, standing at the top of the stairs and reliving her big moment. "That gardener's going to stay here as long as I want him to—forever—because I love him!" Michael's grin collapses. Theodora in her transport looks demented: "What's Lynnfield going to do about *that?* I love him!"—making a fist—"I always *will*"—the fist again—"and there's nobody in this town who's going to *stop* me!" "Swell," says Michael, and rises from the cot.

The mood of what follows—the comedown from this lovely turnabout—is reflective, wistful, a bit enigmatic. Theodora looks "delivered" and glowing; Michael looks trapped and miserable. She puts her head on his shoulder. "When you finally did let go, you certainly rocked the world, didn't you?" he says gravely. "Are you proud of me, Michael?" His reply is a considered one: "I'll tell the world, baby." She laughs: "And Uncle John said nobody in Lynnfield would ever call me 'baby.'" But the next morning Michael runs out on her, leaving a note. It turns out that this traveling apostle of life and love and freedom has his own reasons for playing that role—and that it *is* a role more than something he entirely means.

But it's just at this moment of sardonic revelation that this up-to-now rather mild movie takes off—on a flight of inspiration and incident that hardly lets up till the ending. The joke on Michael here is not a sour or dispirited one; it's not even cynical or knowing in the usual way. But it *is* immensely sophisticated—though, again, not in the usual way. This is a joke on a character's "idealism" that works like an expansion, an opening up of feeling and possibility, instead of a closing down or a simple undercutting of what the figure stands for. First of all, there's the adroit way Michael has been set up for this moment. He is rather tiresomely sure of himself from the beginning (shades of Gable's Peter Warne). He let *his* family know he wanted to paint, and that was that. "It was the battle of the century, but I won," he tells Theodora in the woods. "I knew you would," she says, laughing and dropping berries in his mouth. If he is a bit hard to take—well, these humorously dashing heroes nearly always are. They are also nearly always *right*—especially when they are commending love and freedom to a prim heroine. But Michael up to now has been the sort of character who makes us wish he weren't right—who makes us feel the oppressiveness of the movie patterns he belongs to.

All that changes, however, when Theodora "lets go"—and he pulls back. The revelation that this hero has his own comic problems about freedom is like a deliverance from the blacks and whites the film has been threatening us with, the usual movie spectrum in these matters. It isn't that Michael's ideals of freedom are destroyed or even importantly discounted: how could they be? Still, it's helpful to be reminded that one person's "freedom" may be another person's cue to look for the exit. Michael *does* liberate Theodora. But the joke on *him* liberates the movie itself—into just the kind of complexity and comic shrewdness that Dunne's heroine turns out to be most at home in. Her "Caroline Adams" in the next part of the film both parodies Michael's freedom and makes it seem like fun. She even makes it seem serious—as his glib advocacy never does.

Theodora takes the stray dog and follows Michael to New York. He tells her that he loves her, but it seems he has this wife, whom he neither loves nor lives with, and a domineering father (Henry Kolker) who is lieutenant governor of the state. Michael feels bound to the promise he's made: no divorce while his father holds public office. Theodora resolves to set him free. She "goes wild"—becoming a celebrity of the scandalous sort. She moves into his apartment: he moves out, but she is still able to give his address to the papers, even to hold interviews there. She dresses in feathers, ties a ribbon around the dog, and visits her publisher to demand—to his consternation—more publicity. She counsels "the modern girl" to be free and to express herself; gets quite flustered when reporters ask her about Michael Grant; hints at revelations to come in her next book; and is named corespondent in a headlined divorce action filed by her publisher's wife. It's with this recent history that she attends the Governor's Ball. And when Michael finally wrests her from the Governor's embrace on the dance floor and drags her onto a terrace to bawl her out, all the photographers (at her signal) follow. As a consequence, the papers get a photo of the Lieutenant Governor's married son in the arms of the week's most infamous homewrecker. And Theodora explodes the scandal that "frees" them both.

But there is a coda, enabling Theodora to return in triumph to Lynnfield. Since she is now a certified national celebrity, the town has all but forgotten her supposed transgressions. But she tests this new civic tolerance by getting off the train and confronting the mob at the station with what appears to be an illegitimate baby in her arms (not hers, of course, and not even illegitimate, but Rebecca Perry's daughter's: the plot machinery needed to set this valuable moment up is very intricate). And on this final note—with this final towering affront to Lynnfield propriety—the lovers come together and the movie ends—ecstatically.

Theodora's going wild works as well as it does chiefly because the people she affronts have such fullness and life in this film. And there are a lot of them, both in Lynnfield and New York—supporting actors doing their usual thing with more than usual conviction: members of the Literary Circle, Thurston Hall's publisher, Elizabeth Risdon's tough old aunt, Leona Maricle's and Nana Bryant's two styles of bitchy city wife. There are even some interesting castings *against* type: Spring Byington's malicious Rebecca Perry and Robert Greig's warm-hearted Uncle John, rich and scapegrace. (Greig was one of the great movie butlers and rarely played anything else: he later became part of the Preston Sturges "stock company.") There are occasional oddities of tone—forays into expressionist-style lighting and montage in the Lynnfield sequences, for instance—but the direction by Richard Boleslawski is secure and intelligent throughout, even at times (as at the Governor's Ball) inspired.*

At the center of everything of course is Dunne's calculated outrageousness. Blowing at the feathers of her outlandish and stylish new frock and looking at it when it moves ("A thing like this is darned expensive!"). Going all timorous when Michael scolds her at the ball, and twirling her handkerchief at a bunch of waiting reporters, gunslinger style. Playing the grand piano Rachmaninoff-style and discoursing madly to Michael about the joys of breaking loose and expressing yourself ("You'll be so happy!"). Describing her next book at a press conference—about a small-town girl who longed to be called "baby" and the man from out of town who obliged her ("I guarantee it for interest, if you know what I mean")—while brandishing a feather boa and a cigarette holder. Dunne is funny exactly because she's *not* the type. She's not actressy in the way these effects might lead you to expect: whiskey-voiced and shoulder slinging, vamping and camping it up for the fans. What she is—what she was for audiences at the time—is an embodiment of the genteel feminine, the nice (but not *too* nice) young woman. But as Theodora, she shows suddenly how such a personality could extend itself—daringly—without at the same time disappearing. What possibilities of wit and imagination, of recklessness and risk such a temperament—such a plain sort of woman—might be capable of.

For the first half of the movie, Theodora Lynn is a Lombard heroine, involved in a nervous imposture, hectic and out of her depth, her reactions to the world around her startled, wary, defensive: drinking "straight whiskey" and dancing on her partner's toes; doing a little dance of panic (to indicate casualness) when she stumbles into a man's bedroom; fending off the Literary Circle and her aunts and her blackmailer from the city all at once; fighting for the man she loves and scaring him away in the same outburst. Theodora's novel sets forces in motion she can't control or even fully comprehend—just as Hazel Flagg's X-ray does.

---

*Boleslawski, who had once worked and studied with Stanislavsky at the Moscow Art Theater, didn't have a very distinguished Hollywood career. Dunne remembers him as being unwell during the shooting of *Theodora*. He died the following year, at age forty-eight, while making *The Last of Mrs. Cheyney* at MGM.

But in the second half of the movie, the more distinctive Dunne heroine begins to emerge, and the screwball heroine herself takes an important evolutionary step. Where Lombard is almost helplessly outrageous, Theodora is deliberately so, choosing her craziness with full intention—the first important screwball heroine to do this. (*The Merry Widow*, of course, is an important antecedent.) Dunne enacts that crucial connection between lunacy and sense ("A Lynn may go wild but never silly," her uncle observes)—between abandon and the acutest kind of self-awareness—that underlies all the great screwball comedies. Lombard is "nutty"; Dunne is "wild." It's a difference in temperament as well as performing styles. Where Lombard seems driven and distrait, Dunne seems intoxicated, magical, high-flying. Both women had to do, for example, a lot of on-screen laughing; the collapse into "spontaneous" merriment became almost a screwball heroine's signature after a while—an obligatory moment. Lombard, if anything, did even more of these moments than Dunne (she got started on them earlier)—collapsing on the floor with Fred MacMurray in *Hands Across the Table*, on a terrace in front of an unamused Preston Foster in *Love Before Breakfast* (she has just played a practical joke on another woman). And yet Lombard on screen almost never laughs happily or freely, it seems, never without some edge of will, of anxiety, of abrasiveness even. But one of the most striking and most characterizing things about the Dunne heroine is how easily and naturally she *does* laugh—so naturally that we are never invited to think how hard *that* must be (Lombard almost makes you squirm with the thought).

The "wild" Theodora is that ultimate glamorous figure: the one who sees the joke—better than anyone else around. More than that: Dunne doesn't just see the joke—she is radiant with it, possessed by it and glowing with it. Nobody else does this so completely or to quite the same degree: Dunne takes us *inside* her own amusement—rich, energizing, seemingly inexhaustible.

INCREDIBLE as it seems now, Dunne actually fought against doing *Theodora Goes Wild*. It was to be the first film in her new Columbia contract (for one picture a year). *They* insisted—it's one of those stories that makes the studio system look good. She even went to Europe to get out of the assignment, staying two months. When she got back, though, they still insisted—and put her on suspension until she gave in. She was always, she later recalled, a reluctant comic. She liked the "serious" roles. Comedy felt "too easy."

She began on the stage, as a singing ingenue. Florenz Ziegfeld was struck by her beauty when he saw her in an elevator and cast her as Magnolia in the Chicago company of *Show Boat*. From there she went to Hollywood with an RKO contract, arriving just at the time (1930) when musicals had become box-office poison. Studios were filming the musical shows they had bought and cutting out

Irene Dunne and John Boles in John Stahl's Back Street.

all the songs. Her first film, *Leathernecking* (1930), was like that, with a missing score by Rodgers and Hart (*Present Arms*). It was her second movie that she made an impression with: as the heroine of Wesley Ruggles' *Cimarron* (1931) she "aged" from a young girl to an old woman and was nominated for an Academy Award.* After Edna Ferber, she proceeded through Fannie Hurst—in *Back Street* (1932) as a kept woman, and in *Symphony of Six Million* (1932) as a crippled slum girl (the hero operates on her)—on to Lloyd C. Douglas—in *Magnificent Obsession* (1935) as a blind woman (the hero operates on her again). She became identified with tearjerkers—as were other talented stars, like Barbara Stanwyck and Ruth Chatterton. And like them, too, she managed to give these occasions dignity and interest, and often a great deal more than that. If there was occasionally something too invincibly ladyish in a performance—a suggestion of matronly rectitude, even—that was a trap that went with the territory (and did several careers in, too, such as Ann Harding's, another RKO star's).

Dunne's soap-opera heroines are richly detailed, intensely imagined crea-

---

*The movie itself won Best Picture Award.

tions. Her performance in *Back Street*—under John Stahl's direction—is remarkable from the first close-up: she is sitting at a table in a raucous turn-of-the-century beer garden, drinking with eyes lowered from a brimming mug. The look is rapt, inward, almost devotional—a disturbing, strangely beautiful effect. Dunne compels the camera (this is only her sixth film) by her privacy, by a sense of powerful ambiguity, of mysterious reserves of meaning and intention. She is Ray Schmidt, "the toniest girl in Cincinnatuh," as the drummers call her. And when she rises to dance with eyes gleaming, fluffing her bustle into place and setting her jaw, you suddenly see it all: she is after a good time, and she is even having it, and she doesn't believe any of it, not for two seconds. Later on, when she is forced to face another kind of disbelief, compelled finally to see her lover for what he is (she asks to have a baby by him, and he reminds her, stunningly, of "the morality": "After all, Ray, you're *not* my wife . . ."), the moment is silent, endless, harrowing. Stahl's camera stays at an unmoving middle distance: Dunne seated on a couch, her eyes lowered this time in numb pain, in some simple final insight of hopelessness.

Although she was less noted for it, she also played feminist types—strong, independent women, almost fatally sensible: the M.D. daughter-in-law who faces down the devouring mother of *The Silver Cord* (1933), the social worker who crusades for prison reform in *Ann Vickers* (1933). And when musicals returned to box-office favor, she did the sort of heroines she had originally been signed to do (all of them in Jerome Kern shows): the Helen Morgan role in *Sweet Adeline* (1935) (she sings "Why Was I Born?"); the heroine of *Roberta* (1935), with Astaire and Rogers in supporting roles; and Magnolia in *Show Boat* (1936), with Paul Robeson and Helen Morgan. It's in these last films that you can see something that's there in some form in all her performances but most noticeable here when she sings: a note of restlessness, even impatience. She has a habit of rising on her toes with the highest notes, shifting and bobbing slightly as the voice sings away, almost as if she were tapping her foot or drumming with her fingers until it was done. And in *Show Boat*, when Helen Morgan sings "Can't Help Lovin' Dat Man," followed by an uptempo reprise of the same song by Hattie McDaniel, the most exciting moment of all in the sequence is when Dunne as the sheltered young heroine breaks out into a grotesque, mad minstrel-show shuffle, trucking and weaving and sashaying, hips melting and collapsing as she goes, leading a parade of excited children and deckhands into dementedness. A revelation: there is something really crazy about this ladylike woman with her gentle beauty, something reckless and infectiously insane—an attraction to absurdity that could get out of hand. And so it did eventually. After *Theodora Goes Wild* came *The Awful Truth* (1937), *Joy of Living* (1938), *Love Affair* (1939), *My Favorite Wife* (1940). Mostly triumph: this was her screwball period, and the height of her popularity.

No one could have been more different from Lombard in her relation to her own career or to Hollywood itself than Dunne was: withdrawn, remote, private to a fault. She struck a different kind of bargain with her fame, in what seems at times a rigorous detachment. Joel McCrea (*The Silver Cord*) remembers her as "a lady." Rouben Mamoulian (*High, Wide and Handsome*, 1937) remembers her as remarkably unworldly, susceptible to all the tall stories he told her as they passed the time traveling to location. The ladylike image was her public one, certainly; and to many it could be off-putting.* But people who worked with her or even just watched her work tend to focus on the same point about her: her capacity to be both deliberate and spontaneous at the same time. "A craftswoman," Douglas Fairbanks, Jr. (*Joy of Living*), called her: "nothing is instinctive" or "left to chance," but "instead of being dull and perfect" she's "enchanting and perfect." Lucille Ball told an American Film Institute seminar in 1974 about how she used to watch the stars at work during her days as an obscure contract player at RKO. Hepburn "telegraphed," she said—"Well, I'm going to be funny"—whereas Dunne always surprised, even in repeated takes of the same scene. "But I watched her do takes—literally, one day there were thirty-two takes—and twenty-five must have been different. She really worked on how to do that scene. Where Kate would do it the same way every time and telegraph it every time." Cary Grant told Garson Kanin that Dunne was his favorite leading lady partly because she was always so inventive and delightful on the set: doing a movie with her was less like work than like a long and always surprising "flirtation."

D UNNE'S NEXT film after *Theodora* was the peak not just of her career but of the screwball style itself: Leo McCarey's *The Awful Truth* (1937) is the definitive screwball comedy—and the purest of all such films. Probably only McCarey, with his zest for comic routines and improvisatory style, would have had the nerve to do what this movie does: to bank almost everything on the screwball couple themselves. There is no murder mystery, no social satire, no music or dancing, no gallery of supporting comic stooges, no sentiment or gestures toward populism—almost, in fact, no plot. There is "only" Irene Dunne and Cary Grant, the wittiest couple of them all. And Asta—borrowed from MGM—as Mr. Smith, their dog.

Jerry and Lucy Warriner (Grant and Dunne) break up their marriage over an issue of jealousy, then spend the rest of the movie trying to break up one another's subsequent romances, until they finally agree to get together again. The

*When I was a child in parochial school, Dunne's was always the first name on any list by anyone of Hollywood's "good Catholics," though the two or three other names (Pat O'Brien, Loretta Young, Bing Crosby, etc.) would always vary.

structure of this marvelous film is no more than a series of routines in which
each tries to embarrass, outwit, or radically impress the other. It's like a full-
length movie extrapolated from the hitchhiking scene in *It Happened One Night*:
the same witty antagonism in a romantic situation, in the same tough, disabused
style—a competition of risk and imagination. (And in both Capra and McCarey
it's the woman who comes out clearly if narrowly ahead.)

"Darling!" cries Dunne, running to embrace her husband and burying his face
in the foot-high sleeve of her white fur jacket—while he pulls the fur down and
peers over it with one eye at the handsome music teacher (Alexander D'Arcy)
she has just come home with. It's a definitive screwball image: one Cary Grant
eye rising in skepticism from a bank of white fur. The romantic couple are in
each other's arms but not disarmed. He has been away on "a trip," but she has
just been out all night. They are surrounded by visiting "friends," catty types in
tweeds—the country-club set—who depart, though reluctantly, when they
sense a domestic crisis impending. The music teacher is harder to get rid of: he
is gallant (he compliments Lucy on her "development"—she looks at her nails)

Listening to Ralph Bellamy: Cecil Cunningham (left), Irene Dunne, and Asta. The Awful Truth.

but a bit thick-witted. Never mind: Jerry resolves to be jealous. Lucy is at first incredulous—even amused by some of this. But when Jerry flings the challenge down—a marriage without mutual trust isn't worth going on with, he says—she takes it up. "Do you *mean* that?" she says, and in a moment they are phoning the lawyer. Who tells them that "marriage is a beautiful thing"—or tries to: his wife keeps telling him to come to dinner before it's cold and he keeps telling her to shut her mouth—between peacemaking efforts on the phone.

This breakup scene is conventional, the obligatory beginning; but it's also odd in some ways. We know where Lucy was last night—she told us (a car breakdown) and we believe it even if Jerry doesn't. But where was Jerry the last two weeks? That we are never told. All we know is that he's lying to her about having been in Florida—even to the extent of bringing her a basket of "Florida oranges." Except that she notices the "California" stamp on them while they're quarreling—and tosses the incriminating orange across the room to him. "You never mentioned the rainy spell they had in Florida," she says. "The papers were full of it." She seems more amused than anything else. But he accuses her of trying to change the subject. It's curious: we don't really believe in the issue between them, and yet we do. And it is curiously defined: Lucy has cause to be jealous, and yet she isn't, it appears; Jerry has no cause and yet he is. Still, it seems oddly momentous—and suddenly so—when Lucy flicks a beaded sleeve and tells him to call the lawyer. The actors seem determined but alarmed: as if something were getting out of control.

The divorce, in the next scene, is just as swift. The only issue the judge (Paul Stanton) has to address, it seems, is the custody of Mr. Smith—who has been ordered from the courtroom for "contempt." He is brought back so the issue can be settled: Jerry and Lucy are both to call him at the same time, and whichever one he goes to, gets him. It's a dilemma for the dog, resulting in paralysis— until Lucy cheats (she has concealed his favorite toy in her fur muff) and breaks the impasse. "I win, don't I?" she says to the judge—with the slightly dizzy public manner, so different from her private one, that she seems to reserve for authority figures like judges and cops. She takes the dog, and a *real* basket of fruit (congratulations from friends), and sails out of the courtroom.

But in the next scene, she and her Aunt Patty (Cecil Cunningham) are glooming around the penthouse in their evening gowns. Aunt Patty, a tough old bird, is frank about the problem: no man to take them out. She finds Daniel Leeson (Ralph Bellamy) in the hallway and brings him back to Lucy. He is rich, single (lives with his mother), in oil and from Oklahoma, and laughs hard at one of Patty's feebler jokes (Mr. Smith growls at him). Jerry comes along to see Mr. Smith—his legal "visitation right"—and tries to distract them all by doing a routine at the piano: he plays and Mr. Smith barks. "Tell me some more about Arizona," says Lucy, with a sudden new interest in her guest. "Oklahoma," replies Leeson—but who can hear him?—Mr. Smith is taking the "melody" now.

Jerry is laughing and banging the keys—and making such a racket that he soon drives them all to go out, just as Patty wanted to do from the beginning.

What she hadn't wanted is that Lucy should take a jerk like Leeson seriously. But Lucy is determined to do so: she describes him as "sane and considerate"— so different from her soon-to-be-ex-husband (the decree will be final in fifty days)—and "the finest man I ever met" (what could be more ominous?). We see the fateful outcome of these sentiments when she enters a nightclub with him in the next sequence. She looks depressed. "Just think of it, Lucy," says Leeson. "You're gonna be my wife." "Yes, I am thinking of it," she says in a small voice, fingering her glove and looking off into the distance. Jerry—at the same club (one of those Big White Sets that stood for the movies' idea of a New York night-club)—looks even more depressed at his table. But he brightens perceptibly when he sees Lucy and Leeson come in. He takes his girlfriend and joins them. "Now, you're sure we're not intruding?" "Uh, what do you mean?" says Leeson. "Wouldn't you like us to have a drink?" They sit down. Lucy and the girlfriend chat amiably. She (Joyce Compton) is from the South, and her name is Dixiebelle Lee—she changed it, she explains, because her family objected to her going into show business. In fact, she is the entertainer at this club; she excuses herself and promises they will soon see her number. "A nice girl," says Lucy. And they turn to other matters: Jerry likes to ask questions about Oklahoma, to imagine Lucy living there, and so on.

The very funny sequence that follows is both audacious and unique—very close to McCarey's deepest springs of feeling, and bold even for him. Now, instead of watching Jerry and Lucy's "show," as we've been doing, we watch *them* watching a show: Dixiebelle's terrible song number. The whole sequence (*except the song number itself*) has a quality of appalled understatement. Grant arches an eyebrow slightly. Dunne looks numbly toward the camera. And we know exactly what they mean. It's exactly what *we* mean—so to speak. It's a sudden and powerful experience of identity.

And McCarey's comic timing here is as exquisite as his two stars': the cutting in this scene—between Dixiebelle's performance and Jerry and Lucy's table— has an unmatched deadpan brilliance. Dixiebelle begins her song ("I used to dream about a cottage small, /A cottage small by a waterfall") in a gown of bouffant tulle, on a great white bandstand with a basket of hovering white balloons high above the orchestra. There is a dead-on medium shot of the people back at the table, turned to the show and each in his or her own way expectant: Leeson grinning (he's going to be entertained), Jerry with his hands folded in front of him, Lucy sitting forward, impassive but attentive. "But I wound up with no dreams at all," sings Dixiebelle, a bit plaintive now. "My dreams have gone with the wind!"—as an air vent in the bandstand blows her skirts up over her head and the orchestra makes a whooshing sound behind her.

WHAT'S FUNNY back at the table is how slight, almost imperceptible, the first reactions are—in another deadpan medium shot of the three people. Bellamy looks at the floor, embarrassed. Grant is immobile, looking straight ahead and stunned; then suddenly his eyes go up into his head. Dunne, trying not to look *anything*, touches her forehead with her fingers, raises her head and touches her chin. But Dixiebelle and the song go on from there. Not knowing where to look, Dunne looks at Grant. He puts his hand over his mouth. There is another blast from the air vent; he puts a hand over his eye. Dunne looks forward stoically, with slightly parted lips. She steals a glance at Grant— then decides, as she turns away, to smile, weakly. Grant looks at her miserably—then looks forward again. "There's bound to be stormy weather," sings Dixiebelle—the band is swinging it now—and this time when the air vent goes off, she sidesteps it, cute as a button. Grant is now slumped down in his chair. Dunne is sitting straighter than ever, pleasantly attentive. But Leeson—who is the only prudish one and the most *simply* embarrassed of them all—is now becoming furtively responsive: McCarey underscores the point with a close-up of Bellamy looking lustful (the only close-up in the sequence). "I just met her," says Grant to Dunne, who gives him a pleasant impersonal smile in reply.

Dixiebelle ends her song, stands over the air vent for a last stunning exposure—a glimpse of garter and panties—and runs off to big applause. Dunne makes the obligatory remark at last, looking down and pulling on her glove: "I guess it was easier for her to change her name," she says softly, "than for her whole family to change theirs." "That'd go great out west," says Leeson, as the orchestra launches into a dance (the theme from *Theodora*). "It seemed to go very well with the cowboy here," says Lucy. Jerry concedes defeat: "Why don't you two get up and dance?"

At the same time as we laugh during this sequence, we're aware of the most precise kinds of judgment and evaluation. Leeson has the conventional reactions to Dixiebelle's song—shocked and then leering—both of which the sequence disowns. It's not the "naughtiness" or the daring quality of Dixiebelle's act that we laugh at or see so comically mirrored in Jerry and Lucy's responses: it's the amazing dumb vulgarity, funny in itself. But the discrimination about that vulgarity, which we find ourselves seeing just as Jerry and Lucy do, is a very careful one. And we laugh partly because we feel it so clearly. None of this would be quite so funny in the same satisfying way if Dixiebelle had been a floozie or an idiot—as the "stripper" figure usually tends to be in these films. And as a 1937 audience might well know, this was just the sort of "sophisticated" number, full of witless roguishness and aspirations to carnality, that you might find in such a high-class club. What's more important to note, though, is that Jerry and Lucy's involuntary judgment against such "sophistication" sets them more or less apart from the world we see in the film: everyone else in the nightclub seems to enjoy it. Just as their marriage seems different from all the other marriages, prospective and real, that we see and hear about—all of them bad jokes of one kind or another.

This difference really defines Jerry and Lucy. Who are they, anyway? Everything about the way they live—the nightclubs and penthouses and evening clothes—tells us that they are "café society," forerunners of the jet set and the Beautiful People. But does anybody believe it? The Dunne and Grant characters really seem to transcend this identity, just as much as the people around them seem trapped by it. Lucy's aversion to the idea of Oklahoma, her future home with Leeson, which we can see on her face every time Jerry sounds the word (it's the way he amuses himself while they are waiting for Dixiebelle's act to begin), has none of the affectation or reflexive snobbery that we could attribute to an Aunt Patty, with her predictable Tallulah-voiced sarcasms (is it possible to believe that Lucy could ever become *that* woman at any age?). Lucy's Oklahoma reaction is funny just because it seems so helpless. "Oklahoma!" says Jerry, watching her wince, as they sit at the nightclub table together with Leeson.

"Ever since I was a small boy, that name has been filled with magic for me." He likes to *roll* the name across his tongue: *Ok*-la-*ho*-ma. . . . And each time he does Lucy registers the impact, with a thin, toothachy look and a slight vertical line between her brows: the distress is acute but controlled. "We're gonna live right in Oklahoma City," says Leeson. Jerry is delighted. "Not Oklahoma City it*self?*" he says. He turns, shoulders and all, to Lucy—staring at her: "Lucy, you lucky girl." "I know I'll enjoy Oklahoma City," she says numbly. "Well, of course," he replies merrily. "And if it should get dull, you can always run over to Tulsa for the weekend"—giving a funny spastic twist to the first syllable of "Tulsa."

It's significant that the screwball style, which sets so much store in "letting go," should also be clear about the kinds of letting go—such as Dixiebelle's act—that won't do at all. It's like the distinction Theodora's Uncle John draws between going wild and going silly. The screwball couple are committed above everything to common-sense standards. It's this that primarily distinguishes them from their counterparts in the theater of the time. The screwball hero may be fancy and elegant and even aristocratic (who could be more elegant than Grant?), but he is never affected or preening or pretentious (he is never an actor, for example). Nor does he ever throw amusing tantrums or indulge in any of the flamboyancies that heroes of sophisticated comedy traditionally allow themselves. Cary Grant is, God knows, a man of complicated vanities and ambiguous temper—but he is still in some sense a plain man, self-declared. Otis Ferguson, writing in 1939, argues that the great distinction of the Hollywood comedy (the implied comparison is the stage) is its sense of ordinary life. At first this insight could hardly seem to apply to movies about heroes and heroines who live in penthouses and have dogs for children. Except that the screwball couple *are* plain people, figures of ordinary life in all but their fantasy trappings: in their common sense and downrightness, in their aversion to anything high-flown or disproportionate (by comparison with them, Dixiebelle is "pretentious"). They are temperamentally conservative in this respect, with as acute a sense of how things will look to the neighbors as any small-town matchmaker might have. With this absolute difference: they concern themselves with appearances finally so that they can defy and rise above them. They immolate themselves like other great lovers—but for laughs. The skeptical and reductive comic vision—the wonderful wised-up voice of the movies themselves—becomes in them something overtly romantic: an element liberating and transcendent as passion is. And connected with passion: the life that stirs in this comic world is a passional one.

This, then, is exactly why Jerry and Lucy *can't* laugh through most of their movie—and why the effort to keep from laughing, their struggles with suppressed amusement, form most of their activity on the screen. Laughing is like love: both dangerous and impossible to resist. Just as Rogers mustn't dance, Dunne mustn't laugh. And for the same reason. Even when the situation is as grotesque as the one where Leeson insists on reading a love poem he's written to her ("To you my little prairie flower, / I'm thinking of you every hour . . .") while Jerry is hidden behind a door and tickling her in the ribs. "That's really beautiful, Dan," she cries—giving a manic uncontrolled laugh right in his face, right in the middle of "beautiful." So she repeats it: "It's *really* beautiful," she says solemnly. Lucy's laughter here is anguished and reluctant. But the laugh she gives when she decides to give in to Jerry at last is free and full and straight out—a total capitulation. It happens when Jerry breaks in on her song recital (he thought he would catch her in an assignation with Armand, her music teacher) and then has a complicated accident with a chair in the back of the room. This time she laughs in the middle of a sung word—exultantly and on the song's final note. An extraordinary image—of both lapsing and control—for what she is doing here, giving in to the best part of herself.

In the next scene she tells Aunt Patty that she is breaking off with Leeson. "I'm still in love with that crazy lunatic and there's nothing I can do about it." But now it's the "lunatic's" turn to lose his sense of humor—with a chic tight-faced socialite named Barbara Vance (Molly Lamont). And it becomes Lucy's turn to break the place up—with a foray into the middle of a Vance family gathering (*very* stuffy) so witty and outrageous that it leaves Jerry no choice but to laugh and give up. And get out—fast.

The screwball couple are always getting out like this—leaving an aghast lot of people behind them. From *It Happened One Night* on, this is the usual way for their movies to end: with a gasp and a breakout. Wally and Hazel sail away on a ship at the end of *Nothing Sacred*, and Jerry and Lucy head for Aunt Patty's place in the country, where they finally get together again. In a way, these movies told their audiences something the crowd in the movie house would seem to deny: that to be clever is to be alone. That the wit and humor of the romantic couple finally set them apart, leading quite logically to that place in the country. But who could imagine they would stay there? All these comedies are about being in love and being in the world and both at the same time. They are almost as romantic about being in the public world as they are about being in love. About being in the world *without* in some sense belonging there. The screwball couple are not really in flight from that public world, nor are they in a masochistic subjection to it. But they are deeply involved in it, in a kind of continuing productive conflict with it. That conflict is part of their romance. And the friction that sets them apart also sustains them. That's why it seems so right, though it really makes no other kind of sense (it takes a lot of awkward plot maneuvering to get that baby in her arms when she steps off the train), that Theodora should go back home at the end of her film to offer one final topping insult to the community—and that the community should welcome her anyway, more or less. Even when the screwball comedy refuses "social criticism"—is as devoid of it even as *The Awful Truth* is—it endorses the sort of feelings, both dissident and attached, that give rise to it. And the most romantic possible version of those feelings.

The screwball couple always try to deny this dissidence—to simplify their relation to the world and to escape their own intelligence and honesty. Mainly they do this by trying to join the enemy—and almost always by getting engaged to him, to a yokel like Leeson or a snob like Barbara Vance. They always fail of course. And always because of the humor problem. The Other Men and Other Women figures may vary a lot in their *kinds* of unattractiveness, but one thing they all have in common: they don't get the joke. Not the one we get, anyway. It's true they often *like* jokes—quite a lot. Leeson laughs so long and loud at one of Aunt Patty's remarks that Asta has to growl him into silence. But the jokes they like are always dumb or, even more importantly, safe. Jerry warms up to tell the Vances "a funny story" all about his father at Princeton (class of '92) playing football against Yale. Football against Yale? The Vances stir with anticipatory pleasure and amusement, Barbara smiling on the couch next to him as he begins. "And with the ball on Princeton's two-yard line, Yale fumbled." This, they recognize, will be just the sort of joke they like, full of innocent fun and reminders of status—a *good* joke. But Lucy, who is now pretending before the Vances to be Jerry's "sister," knows a better kind of joke. She interrupts Jerry's story: he was telling them about Dad at Princeton before she came, he explains to her patiently—if she *remembers* "Dad at Princeton." Of course she remembers—how could she forget? Dad loved Princeton, she says. "He was there nearly twenty years. If ever a man loved a place, he did—he just adored it." Slight pause here. "And he certainly kept it looking beautiful. . . . You've seen the grounds, of course?" The Vances are *not* amused.

This is a fulfillment of the screwball promise. The Lubitschean joke is nearer to something else: a kind of weary sardonic assent to worldly power. The screwball joke is a confrontation, an explosion. The sort of comic moment Donald Ogden Stewart more or less prescribed in his screenplay for *Laughter* when he has Fredric March lecture Nancy Carroll in the back of her limousine: jokes that destroy and save, that subvert worldly arrangements, that "blow them to pieces" and that "make you clean." And worldly arrangements are what the other-man and other-woman figures stand for in these comedies: some sort of permanent practical accommodation to the way things are, to practicality and realism. Leeson and Barbara stand for everything that matters—if nothing matters. For money, security, position, reputation and worldly power—they stand for the *wrong* kind of worldliness, the kind that ritualizes its own emptiness, for the hegemony of stupidity that runs the world. And by being so emphatically *unat-*

tractive as they always are, the Other Man and the Other Woman make a point that's intrinsic to the spirit of these comedies: the suggestion that emptiness and stupidity are not just things that happen to us, but often things we seek, even become "engaged to" if we can—certainly warmer and safer than the alternatives often are. The temptation of cleverness, like the temptation of goodness, can be—to paraphrase Brecht—a "terrible" one.

So the screwball couple try to escape their cleverness. This is the wonderful liberating absurdity at the heart of these comedies, with all their terrific people trying *not* to be terrific or smart, engaging in the hopeless and fruitless pursuit of everyday awfulness. Love in this comic world is not a blindness, something that impairs and muddles, but an illumination so bright you might even want to get away from it for a while—and understandably. It's also a lot like laughing. These fantasies don't suggest, as Capra's do, that people are soft and warm and harmless, but that they are sharp and bright and dangerous—that cleverness is a fate, intelligence a temptation we're all bound to succumb to. You can run from it, as Jerry and Lucy do, but you can't escape it.

O F T H E great glamorous comediennes of her time, Irene Dunne may be the one least well remembered. Lombard and Hepburn, Colbert and Loy are probably all more widely known today, more readily recognized. Even middle-aged TV watchers seeing *The Awful Truth* for the first time are likely to ask who she is—to be enchanted by her and even then have trouble remembering her name. (Who has trouble remembering Hepburn?) She has been off the screen for three decades, but even when she is on it, in a curious way she lies low—always, in even her flashiest performances. Her flamboyance is less the real thing than a witty self-delighted imitation of it. More interesting and more complicated than the real thing—perhaps even more finally sympathetic. Because Dunne shows us what such human qualities as complication and essential reserve, native tact and intelligence are capable of—what flights and surprises and even transformations.

It's these more impersonal qualities—of tact, taste, wittiness—that mark her screen presence. More than a striking personality—like Lombard—or an indelible individual style—like Hepburn. If Dunne weren't so irreducibly American, she would have been an ideal Elizabeth Bennett in *Pride and Prejudice*. She *is* Elizabeth in essential ways: in her combination of charm and shrewdness, of recklessness and seriousness. And like Jane Austen, Dunne is a comic artist who seems to put some final value on experiences of wit and playfulness. She generates antipathy too, it seems, for some of the same reasons Austen sometimes does: the ladylikeness, the commitment to propriety. In any case, Dunne's bad press over the years is a notable phenomenon particularly because it comes—and with such violence—from some of the best and smartest critics. Pauline Kael, the smartest of them all—a Dyan Cannon fan, we should probably remember—says that she finds herself wanting to "slap her" (it's "a trick with her teeth," Kael says). James Agee says (in 1946) that "as a rule" she "makes [his] skin crawl." Agee—a Teresa Wright fan—objects to Dunne's irony and playfulness. She is "painfully miscast" as Mother in *Life with Father* (1947), he says, being the sort of actress who "would probably keep her tongue in her cheek uttering the Seven Last Words."

You know what he means, anyway. Theodora suggests the kind of temperament that might see the joke in *anything*—and be dangerous for that reason. But of course Agee wouldn't have noticed or felt the glint of madness behind this activity—the *passion* for absurdity. It's partly this that gives Dunne her protean quality in these comedies—the first of the screwball heroines to specialize in transforming herself: not just getting out of town but getting out of and beyond her own apparent limits, especially the limits of female gentility. And Leo McCarey understood the power of this effect even better than the makers of *Theodora* did.

The Awful Truth may seem random in its structure—a series of routines, as I said—but it is still moving purposefully toward that union between rapture and skepticism that all these comedies move toward or at least aspire to. It happens here decisively when Dunne's Lucy has her big moment, in the comic climax of the film, impersonating Jerry's stripper "sister," "Lola" from the Virginia Club (the nightclub we saw Dixiebelle in), before an appalled assemblage of all the Vances. It's a miraculous sequence: at once funny and wondrous, excited and dry, disturbing and inspiriting—and Dunne offers one of the most astonishing flights of comic performance the movies have ever recorded.

It all starts when Jerry gets caught—as people in the movie are always getting caught—with the wrong person in his apartment. Lucy, who has come (ostensibly) to have a farewell drink with him on the eve of their final decree, answers his phone when it rings—and it's Barbara Vance. "Have you made up your mind who the woman is?" says Barbara, when Jerry, after a flustered conference with Lucy, finally comes to the telephone. "My sister," he says. Barbara invites his "sister" over to meet the Vance family that evening. She can't make it, says Jerry flatly.

But just as Jerry has settled in with the Vances for a "cozy" evening—in their palatial marble-floored library—and is entertaining Mr. and Mrs. Vance (Robert Warwick and Mary Forbes) and Barbara with the beginning of his Princeton football story, his sister *does* make it. "Miss Lola Warriner," announces the butler, as Dunne comes up behind him. And even though you've been expecting her, it's a bracing entrance: her hair in frizzy curls, a jacket with puffed sleeves and a dress with a hula-skirt fringe, trailing a long silk handkerchief and offering a face radiant with vacancy and expectation. She *is* happy to be there: Jerry's sister. Jerry of course is trapped.

It develops in the shambles that follows that "Lola" once worked at the Virginia Club. She even shows them—at the climax of her disastrous visit—what she does there. "The number has some wind effects in it but you'll just have to use your imagination about them." But not *much* imagination: she sings "My Dreams Have Gone With the Wind" to a record, trucking and shuffling jazzily, and when the orchestra makes those wind sounds she goes "Woo-woo-woo!" and buckles her legs—she wants to be *sure* they get the point. When the song ends, and she does a last shuffling step backwards, Jerry is already in the doorway behind her, holding both their coats. He takes her by the arm and they both bow off—out of the world of the Vances. He really thought she was funny—as we could see. He looks rather like her manager, in fact, escorting her offstage.

"Lola's" act—significantly—is even vulgarer than Dixiebelle's was. And it seems especially right that Lucy should appropriate and amplify *that* particular vulgarity. It gives those earlier reactions in the nightclub an even larger and

An evening at the Vances': Jerry (Grant) joined by his "sister" (Dunne). The Awful Truth.

richer context—a payoff we never expected. It even amplifies Lucy's characteristic generosity toward Dixiebelle ("She seems like a nice girl"). This imitation, such as it is, is another act of generosity. We're reminded that the real Dixiebelle isn't at all like "Lola"—she is, as we have seen, a straightforward sort of working girl, without airs or complications. Dunne's Lola is, however, what the Vances would expect her to be—even worse. She is in fact so richly worse that we are left almost gasping. It is Lucy's (and McCarey's) ability to know exactly what will strike the Vances as *worse*—to know exactly what will pain them the most—that controls the whole sequence. It's not just that Lola is lower-class (Jerry has just told them that she went to school "in Switzerland")—with her references to the ham she had for dinner or the phonograph they have to wind up at home, from her pride in her Princeton father's caretaking to her glee about her brother's sneaky drinking habit ("We call him Jerry the Nipper"). But this coarseness is also overlaid with "manners" and with painful little affectations. Like that skirt: when Jerry introduces her to the lordly Mr. Vance, she turns abruptly, all happy eagerness, so that the fringe whips out around her: she obviously wants them to notice the skirt. Worst of all, though, is her awful chumminess, her presumption and familiarity. "I think my brother's pretty swell, don't you?" she says sentimentally to the glacial Barbara. Then, not waiting for an answer: "He's always been pretty swell to me." She doesn't mean to be rude, but can she have a drink? "I had three or four before I got here, but they're beginning to wear off, and you know how that is," she says to Mrs. Vance, as they sit together.

This last arrangement is a particular disaster: Mrs. Vance, chilly but gracious, invites her to share a lounge seat with her. No sooner are they seated than Lola notices something. It's her long kerchief: Mrs. Vance is sitting on it. Lola pulls on it gently, apologetically. "Excuse me, Mrs. Vance," she says. The imperious Mrs. Vance looks startled—then rises, Lola rising with her. But *she's* the one sitting on it. She shrieks with delight. "It's me!" she cries, laughing wildly. "—Isn't it?" Mrs. Vance casts her eyes up, and they resume their seat together. But again Lola pulls on the kerchief. "It's you this time, Mrs. Vance," she laughs—as Mrs. Vance shoots like an arrow to her feet. She hesitates before sitting down again too. "Listen," says Lola, "I'll just put it over here"—shifting the kerchief to her other hand—"and get it outa the *way!*" Mrs. Vance resumes her seat—then shrieks and leaps up again. She has sat on Lola's hand this time, it turns out. Even Lola is getting disaffected with this. "That could go on and on and on," she says dryly. "I *hope* not!" says Mrs. Vance weakly, collapsing into place again.

Lola is just the sort of in-law you might wish on a group like the Vances: a constant embarrassment. But if she affronts their gentility by being low-class, she affronts ours by being awful. That awfulness has an independent life—and a complicated value in the relation between Lucy and Jerry, and between Lucy and "Lola"—that leaves the Vances far behind. (McCarey uses almost no reaction shots in the whole sequence: the times we see the Vances are mostly when they are in the same frame with Jerry or Lucy.) It's like the joke about Dixiebelle's song number: the Lola joke depends on some very shrewd and dead-on discriminations about personal vulgarity. And Lola's deepest and most hilarious vulgarity, it soon becomes clear, is her profound lack of interest in whoever it is she seems to be talking to. This problem is slightly disguised—as it is in most people who have it to any degree. Lola is deferential, polite, attentive—as she is with Mrs. Vance when they are coping with the kerchief crisis—attentive but obtuse. It grows gradually quite apparent that this woman, for all her shrinking and nervousness, really *needs* to have the floor—that she gets restive and even a bit testy if not hearing the sound of her own voice. Happy if she is, though—and blissfully out of touch: as when she confides in Barbara that her brother Jerry made her quit her job at the Virginia Club "the minute he started doing *better*—you know what I mean?"—while Barbara, the source of the good luck referred to, stares murderously at her.

Moments like this are funny, it should be remembered, precisely and primarily because it's *Lucy* who is in control of them. Because what is most brilliant of all about the Lola impersonation is all the ways in which it exactly and deliberately inverts Lucy's—and Dunne's—most essential qualities. Her tact and taste and humor; her generosity and imagination and essential reserve. Her ability to pay *attention* to the other performer in a scene, with a special sort of clarity and power. This last quality is one reason she's so good with Grant: she really seems to give him his due. And one reason her *Back Street* performance is unforgettable: she transfigures John Boles just by looking at him with interest. But when her co-star is someone like Grant or Boyer, and Dunne gives him that same intentness of response, the effect is powerfully romantic. "We never won any cups," she says at the Virginia Club, after Leeson has boasted of his dancing prizes—and with that one slightly bitten-off phrase, and one uneasy glance in Grant's direction, she summons up a whole ardent love affair.

This reversal of her essential character is apparent from "Lola's" first entrance—coming up behind the butler with her dreamy dumb look of eagerness. The initial impact is one reason it's breathtaking. And goes on being breathtaking—as Dunne shows her total simultaneous command of both the broadest effect and the smallest comic nuance within it, from the kerchief routine to the raucous song with "wind effects" that she bows out on. The song isn't Lola's apotheosis, I think—but rather a moment that occurs just before it. She rises from the couch where she's been sitting between Barbara and Jerry, and stops in her tracks—it's clear that something's wrong. She looks narrow-eyed around the room. "Sa-ay, what is this?" she says, understanding dawning. Blankness from the others. She comes out with it: "Don't anybody leave this room, I've lost my purse!" Fortunately, they find it—between the cushions of the couch. "Oh, well, am I *relieved!*" she says, on one of those deep delighted laughs of hers. But before going off to do her song number, she slips the purse to Jerry—very confidential. "Kinda keep an eye on this for me?" she says to him from the side of her mouth.

Dunne makes us feel all the satisfaction of this extraordinary moment: bad taste on a level that seems almost exalted. Certainly it's exultant. And it's a familiar kind of movie feeling and satisfaction—full of that animus against gentility that's been central to movie comedy from its beginnings. So central that a genteel woman star may even be carried away by it—may even become its most passionate interpreter. Dunne's Lola is a kind of ultimate moment in the experience of freedom that all these comedies mean to evoke in the end. And partly because of that lying-low quality in Dunne herself, that something elusive, almost anonymous, in her still-vivid screen presence. Her Lola impersonation never permits any distraction or raises any of the wrong questions—like, why is that woman going to such elaborate and improbable trouble? We *know* why she is, from the moment Dunne enters the Vances' library. She's there because the joke is so good—borne not by plot or design but by terrible inspiration. Dunne is a vessel of the funniness, even a victim of it—the instrument of an impersonal force. Not primarily, as other screwball actresses tend to be, its instigator. For a Dunne heroine, funniness is something like romantic passion: awesome and consuming, a force that can take you over and remake you.

When Lombard breaks loose, wonderful as it is, it's more or less what she's led you to expect. When Dunne does so, it's always unexpected in some way—and tantalizing. In fact, Dunne on the screen is mysterious in the way that only the greatest movie stars are. Like Garbo, she both submits herself to the camera and retains her privacy before it. Of the great women stars who dominated the movie comedies of the thirties (and forties)—movies which finally come to be *about* these women as much as or more than about any of their ostensible subjects or plots—Irene Dunne is probably the greatest, the loveliest and funniest and most skilled, the most complex and affecting. She is one of those transcendent comic players who reminds us that there is a comic equivalent—even a laughing-out-loud one—to the tragic experience of being deeply moved: at her best, as in *Theodora* or *The Awful Truth*, she is *deeply* funny. More than anyone else, she is the paradigm of the screwball heroine: a powerfully sensible woman with a passionate, even dangerous susceptibility for being amused, for "going wild." No one conveys a certain mystery at the heart of this heroine as strongly as she does. No one else gets the odd sober lunacy, the combination of common sense and uncommon passion, so exactly, so exhilaratingly right. Dunne is to playfulness on the screen what Garbo is to weariness: the keeper of mysteries.

Leo McCarey understands people better than anyone in Hollywood.
— JEAN RENOIR

That boy McCarey is one of the best . . . brilliant.
— ERNST LUBITSCH, in a 1936 interview

[Mailer] came at last to the saddest conclusion of them all, for it went beyond the war in Vietnam. He had come to decide that the center of America might be insane. The country had been living with a controlled, even fiercely controlled schizophrenia which had been deepening with the years. Perhaps the point had now been passed. . . .
— NORMAN MAILER, *The Armies of the Night*

NINETEEN THIRTY-SEVEN was Leo McCarey's year of triumph—and as baffling in its contrasts and extremes as the rest of his career was. He made two extraordinary movies that year—probably his two greatest films. As different from each other as their box-office fates turned out to be. *The Awful Truth* was a huge hit. *Make Way for Tomorrow*—which he had made at Paramount just before that—was a disaster.

Still, the two films have deep and surprising similarities. Like *The Awful Truth*, *Make Way for Tomorrow* is a movie about a smashing romantic couple next to whom everyone else on the screen looks dismal and gray and diminished. And it culminates in a final, exhilarating breakout, just as most screwball comedies do, with the hero and heroine going defiantly out on the town, leaving the dull followers of "sense" and "sanity" behind and gasping. But this is no screwball comedy: the couple in this film have their breakout triumph on the eve of going to a nursing home—to die. They are aged and helpless and victimized—and their climactic triumph over the dull ones can't really affect their plight.

Leo McCarey with Harpo Marx on the set of Duck Soup.

This is a movie that dwells almost obsessively on just the kind of event the romantic comedy is obliged to omit: aging and dying and children who grow up to be awful. Leo McCarey was screwball's classical master, the style's purest, most instinctive practitioner. He was also the author and sole begetter of one of the most delicately and unremittingly painful narratives a major Hollywood studio ever made the mistake of releasing. But the pain of one film can tell us a lot about the buoyancy of the other—and about McCarey's odd, astonishing talent in general.

Make Way for Tomorrow opens on a family conference. Barkley and Lucy Cooper (Victor Moore and Beulah Bondi) are losing their home of fifty years to the bank, and so they have called their four middle-aged children together to tell them the bad news. These "children" are disconcerting from their first appearance. One daughter, Cora (Elizabeth Risdon), is tight-faced and quiet, given to looks of private satisfaction. The other one, Nellie (Minna Gombell), is clamorous and silly and abrasive. Both in their different ways seem bad-tempered. A contrast to their brother Robert (Ray Meyer), a genial type, round-faced and merry-eyed (he is referred to in the family as "the good-looking one," which seems at once both accurate and cruel). Robert is a drinker and joker, and no one, including himself, takes him seriously. It's his brother, George (Thomas Mitchell), who functions as head of the family—a solid-looking man, thoughtful and quietly authoritative. But there's also something pettish about him, even a slightly furtive quality. His first action when he enters the movie— greeting his mother in the hallway of her endangered home—is to look at himself in a nearby mirror and announce that he has a cold. He kisses Nellie, though, before he "thinks"—then turns away, smiling to himself. "I shouldn't have kissed *you*," he says, while Nellie looks indignant behind him—and he proceeds to the family business.

It's soon determined that Mother and Dad must be separated, at least temporarily. Nobody at the moment has house room for the two of them. Bark will go to Cora's home in New England—and Lucy to George's and his family in their New York apartment.

Bark and Lucy are mostly withdrawn and watchful during this family scene. The children are ranged in front of the piano in the small, rather cramped parlor space, and the parents face them, Bark seated comfortably by the fireplace, Lucy standing beside him in front of it. McCarey keeps each group in its separate shot, cutting between them (only George, the administrator, "crosses over" occasionally). And though on the surface all is pleasant, we don't suppose these parents have any illusions. They sit in their shot and listen—and occasionally look at each other. Mother's style is hopeful and mollifying: "It'll be very nice— living with the children for a while. . . ." Father is skeptical and dry. He even makes stinging little jokes from time to time, but no one seems disturbed by this: it's his way, clearly, and they're used to it.

But for us it's the children who are disquieting—George and Nellie and Cora and Robert. More than any problem they announce—their marriages or straitened incomes or lack of house room—they seem so *dreary*. And we're not really quite allowed by anything in the scene to distance ourselves from that dreariness. We feel their edginess and tension and discouragement. We're even compelled to understand their selfishness—and in a very uncomfortable way. You begin to feel it's bad enough to grow up to be Cora or Robert or Nellie—but then to have to take your mother in *too*, really does seem insupportable in some way. This understanding—which the whole movie enforces—is nearly its most painful feature. There's no way to escape it, and no way to feel good about it, either. "Are you going to be nice to your mother when you grow up?" says elderly Mr. Rubin (Maurice Moscovich) to the little boy in his store. "What do I say?" asks the boy, with reasonable bewilderment, turning to his mother for the answer. And what can any of us "say"?—to this movie? Which becomes more and more complexly painful as it goes on.

As Bark says to his friend Mr. Rubin: "The world is filled with what-you-call-'em—*schlemiels*—and I guess somebody has to raise 'em." Bark is in the country, at Cora's house. While Lucy lives on Manhattan's Park Avenue with George and his wife, Anita (Fay Bainter). Neither arrangement is working. But there is a contrast in styles of failure. At Cora's there are none of the reticences or gentilities that Anita insists upon. Cora lives in a state of settled discouragement, in a shabby old-fashioned bungalow. She wears aprons, has an out-of-work husband in an armchair, and a couch in the living room for her father to sleep on—except when the doctor comes to see him; then she moves the old man to the bedroom. She cares about these appearances. But she has none of Anita's aspirations to civility and a lowered voice: just bad temper, barely controlled. It's Cora who gets the idea at last of sending her father to California to their sister Addie (never seen in the film) for "his health." And once this idea gets going through the family, no one ever really questions it: it simply gets settled that he will go. After all, Addie hasn't "done anything" up to now. So that at the end of the film, Bark is going to one coast, and Lucy to a nursing home on the other—a final separation.

Lucy tells George that he is her "favorite": Beulah Bondi and Thomas Mitchell in Make Way for Tomorrow.

Fay Bainter's daughter-in-law is especially interesting—more interesting than either of the daughters, and McCarey spends more time on her. Next to Lucy, she is the film's principal woman character. And given movie tradition, Anita would seem to be a setup for a heavy. She is—in Bainter's wonderful performance—a hoity-toity, cello-voiced, rather frosty woman, given to nerves and teaching bridge and ordering "fancy" sandwiches from the delicatessen when she entertains ("How 'fancy' can a sandwich be?" asks Mother-in-law). She is just the sort of affected semi-dowager that the movies generally go hard on. But she is also the sort of character—fastidious and wincing, impassive on the pleasant surface but suffering beneath it—that McCarey as a rule most identifies with. George and Anita are going out for the evening, and Lucy, seeing them off, urges them to enjoy themselves. And they mustn't worry about her: as she points out, "it isn't the first time you've left me alone." Though in fact she does have "a little dyspepsia tonight." "I know how you feel," says Bainter, at the receiving end of this treatment, looking wide-eyed and resting a splayed gloved hand on her diaphragm.

Earlier on, George and Anita are discussing the problem of what "to do with" Mother in the small apartment once Anita's bridge class arrives. But Lucy, it seems, has overheard them. Anita tries to smooth the resulting awkwardness over. "George was only trying to be kind to you, dear," she says. "My bridge pupils drive him *mad*." And the camera stays on Bainter while we listen to Lucy's off-screen reply: "I guess you won't ever have to explain George to his *mother*," she says firmly—while Bainter's look of effortful pleasantness widens into a ghastly smile.

Anita *tries*. But there is something about the trying—as that smile tells us— that carries the seeds of its own doom. The situation in the apartment is difficult, as George knows. "Mother just won't fit in at all, will she?" he says hopelessly about the bridge class. And Anita understands that her mother-in-law likes to "look after" George, even now (Lucy has just—disastrously—sent all his shirts to the laundry at once). But as the daughter-in-law gently explains: "So do I— and though I don't do *much* talking about it, I like to run my home, too." "I only wanted to help," says Lucy. Then adds: "You're so busy playing bridge." "I don't *play* bridge," says Anita, still smiling but rather biting off the words, "I *teach* bridge. There's a difference you'd notice if you had to meet the bills of this apartment." Pleasant—but firm. These things have to be understood, that's all.

But there is altogether too much smiling and hand patting and reasonable discussion. Anita knows, even as she tries—just as they all know—that this isn't going to work. The apartment is just too small. Their daughter, Rhoda (Barbara Read), has to share her room with her grandmother, and she can't really bring her friends home the way she used to. Even the maid (Louise Beavers) is complaining about losing her nights off. And one night when Rhoda doesn't come home at all, it seems easy to lay the blame for the new disruption in their lives on Lucy. Especially when Anita learns that Lucy had known all along about Rhoda's clandestine romance and had promised not to "tell on her" in exchange for Rhoda's promise to break it off. Anita blows up: "You had no right!" she cries. "You raised five children of your own—you might at least let me raise one!" And her hand is up in an arrested gesture of anger—her eyes wide as she realizes how clearly and unforgivably she's named the trouble between them. But Lucy tells her now that she fully understands how upset Anita is: "So there won't be any hard feelings," she says. But the declaration has a piteous sound—not even Lucy believes it.

Eventually, then, George must speak to his mother about going to the nursing home. And the complexity of feeling in this scene—probably the most harrowing one in the film—is almost passionate. George and Anita come home and see Lucy in the parlor, sitting as usual in her rocker. They exchange a look and Anita goes into the bedroom. George goes manfully into the parlor—to break the news to his mother. Lucy has already gathered what he's up to, though. She's seen a letter from the nursing home among the day's mail. She interrupts him before he even gets started. "There's something else I've got to tell you," he says, his head hanging and his voice trembling. "Well, there's something I'd like to say to you first," Lucy says. He raises terrible eyes to look at her: "Let me do it while I can," he says. But she goes on as if she hasn't heard this: she hates to hurt his feelings but she hasn't been happy here, alone all day in the apartment. "Would you mind terribly if I decided to leave you and go to the Idylwild Home?" He looks at her—with a little smile. She goes on. "Well, it's a fine place . . . I'd meet friends my own age—" He interrupts: "But, Mother, I didn't—" "Let me finish, dear," she says. She'd hoped that she and his father would be together again soon, but now that she realizes that won't happen, she really wants to go to the Home. Really . . . He looks at her speechlessly, from under his brows—he is leaning against the back of a chair, his arm hanging limp at his side like a stroke victim's. He knows what she's done—just as she knew what he was about to do. She's saved him from his own shame—as much as she was able to do under the hopeless circumstances. They both "understand."

McCarey makes us see this understanding from the very beginning of the scene. Lucy and her son have been communicating with half-averted looks from the moment he entered the parlor. They even make the same gesture of preparing to speak: touching the tips of their fingers together as they begin. But George's version of this gesture, like his gaze, is troubled, constricted, tentative, in contrast to his mother's assurance, her self-containment even in distress. They both understand, and so the exchange between them is essentially a matter of form. They are both saying things they know better than—and each knows that the other knows. But McCarey makes us feel that they *must* say them, that these formal matters are important indeed. It's through this sort of tact, taste, discretion that affection somehow survives—even scenes like this one. Lucy is being noble about it—as they both know. But she's a mother and that's what she's meant to be, in the common idea of a *good* mother. Only once in the scene does her deep resentment at this role break out: when she insists that Bark must never know where she is once she has gone to the Home, that he must still believe she's with George and his family. "And you tell Cora and Nellie and the others that he must *never* know. This is one thing that has to be handled *my* way!" she says, tapping her knee with an emphatic finger, her voice breaking.

Well, it's over anyway, this difficult conversation. And Lucy rises with a sigh. Up to now McCarey has kept mother and son each in their separate spheres of distress, cutting between shots, George standing, Lucy sitting in her rocker. So that when Lucy rises and stands now—the camera rising with her—it's a slight shock to find George directly at the right of her in the same frame: we hadn't known he'd been standing so close. Or, rather, almost standing—the whole sequence has been building to this collision between Bondi's straight unassertive back on the left and Mitchell's slumped profile on the right. That turned unburdened back of hers—in her plain black dress—lands on the screen like a blow. And we actually feel it connect in the collapsed outline of Mitchell's body as she moves by him—and he lists slightly after her.

But she doesn't pass—she stops and turns to him, in the same tightly framed shot. His head is hanging but he raises his eyes to her, and for a moment the intimacy between them seems almost unwatchable. She lowers her eyes and touches him with her hand, first on the coat, then the tie. His body is curled toward her, in a kind of infantile receptiveness. He is at least a head taller but he looks now like an abashed boy, buttoned into his tightly fitting suit and high round-tipped shirt collar. "Here's another little secret," she says, looking into his chest, "just between us two." She touches his cheek. "You were always my favorite child. . . ." He embraces her, she holds him and pats his shoulder comfortingly. A less pious filmmaker than McCarey was might not get us through these moments without at least some suggestion of martyrdom or repining in the mother's generosity, but there is no such ambiguity about Bondi here. She is a clear-sighted woman, doing the things she *can* do under the circumstances. And this final "secret"—undoing to her son as it is—is one of the last gifts she has to give him.

In the next scene he is himself again. He walks into the bedroom where Anita sits at her dressing table, waiting for him. "Well, that's that," he says. He goes up behind his wife, clasps her by the shoulders, and looks into the mirror. "As the years go by," he says, "you can always look back on this day and be mighty proud of me." She raises her eyes and they look at each other in the mirror, as the shot fades. But he touches her with real tenderness in this guilty exchange—just as Lucy had touched *him* in the scene before. No ambiguity here either. But this is a movie in which touching kills—in which tenderness only heightens the misery. A vision of devastation.

And the whole film is imbued with it. McCarey captures an aspect of thirties America—a certain grayness of feeling in all the arrangements of middle-class life—that no other film comes close to. And he captures it powerfully. Anita's bridge class, for example, is really unforgettable. The formally dressed middle-aged couples, grouped at their tables in the parlor and studying their cards, listening to Anita's dulcet-voiced instructions from the blackboard. But why are they all wearing evening clothes? you wonder. It *looks* right, but why? To come here and learn bridge? And suddenly you're reminded that *everyone* in these apartments—parents, children, maids, even guests—is going out or trying to. Just like the people they go out to the movies to see. These small controlled rooms with their small controlled families—like genteel holding areas—both deny life and promise it: somewhere else. Outside, in the city beyond—the theatres, the hotels, the parks and streets and stores full of people. The magical city world that Bark and Lucy—who might seem in many ways disqualified for it—finally enter near the end of the film, leaving both the tense apartment (Anita's) and the shabby small town (Cora's) behind them.

It's their last day together before the final separation. Bark's train is leaving that night. And the children are expecting them for supper at Nellie's place. But now they stroll the streets of Manhattan, they sit in the park, and they have a series of chance and happy encounters. A limousine salesman (Dell Henderson, a McCarey regular) takes them for a demonstration ride, deluding himself that they might be potential customers. They let him believe it—a bit guiltily, laughing and making faces in the backseat while he drives and makes his pitch from the front. But when the salesman discovers his mistake, he isn't angry or irritated—he's amused and even charmed. He had nothing else to do anyway, he tells them, plausibly enough. He even lets them off at the hotel they spent their honeymoon at long ago. When they tell the girl in the checkroom about this, she is delighted. She even calls the manager to meet them. He (Paul Stanton) is *very* distinguished, with a rich baritone speaking voice and an FDR pince-nez, and he invites them to be the guests of the hotel for the evening, dining and dancing. But the children are expecting them, Lucy reminds Bark. He offers to take care of that. He pushes Lucy out of the phone booth ("Excuse me, young lady, this is private"), gets Nellie on the wire, and tells her to *shove* her dinner. "Was it all right?" asks Lucy as he emerges from the booth. "She took it very nicely," he says. "Shall we join the others?" He extends his arm; she takes it and smiles—and with a lift of the camera and a swell of music, they go into the ballroom. It's the only exultant camera movement in the film (it's really a cut to a long shot, but it has the effect of a crane shot), and it conveys real exhilaration.

And just as it should do, we feel. The whole sequence is a kind of daydream reversal—including the phone call to Nellie—and yet none of it is unbelievable. Bark and Lucy are a terrific couple—funny and shrewd and charming—as we've known all along. Now, at last, they are getting their due. No one in this big city world is irritated with them—or bored or cruel or condescending. The manager joins them at their table. He laughs with them and listens to their reminiscences. They drink, and dance—and there are large helpings of sentiment now: tears and memories, a shy kiss and a sentimental verse, the strains of "Let Me Call You Sweetheart," and so on.

But then it's gradually borne in on us—as the sequence goes on—that we've seen all this *before*—different as it is. We begin to feel not so much a contrast with the rest of the film, or a reversal of it, as a certain recurrence. For the fact is all the signs in this sequence that Bark and Lucy are at last being appreciated and sympathized with—the moist eyes, the understanding smiles, the grave attention to their words, the warm laughter at their stories—are things we've been seeing throughout the movie: in Bark's and Lucy's tormentors. Because in fact, there's no one who mistreats this wonderful couple who doesn't feel that indeed they *are* wonderful in some way, who doesn't understand their plight and feel sorry for them. Even Cora has her moments of piercing recognition. Even Rhoda, who wants her room back. Even Mamie, the maid, who wants her nights off again. Even the bridge club, who are interrupted in the middle of their lesson by Lucy's over-loud phone conversation with Bark. All are moved—all are struck—all are finally sympathetic. The most stricken and sympathetic of all, of course, is the favorite son who consigns Lucy to a nursing home.

What's genuinely new—and relieving—in this hotel sequence is the *freedom* of people's responses. There is no constraint or conflict in their appreciation of the old people, as there nearly always is in the family's. But then the nice people in the hotel are getting to do something no one in the family gets to do: they're saying goodbye to Bark and Lucy. For good. Like the bandleader in the ballroom, who plays "Good Night Sweetheart" for them, smiling and nodding at them as they leave the dance floor. He is moved—as everyone in the place has been, and as we all can be so easily—by the nearly unfailing charm of Other People's Parents. The point, as always in this movie, is double-edged—and finally grim.

No Capra movie—in spite of the sentiment. Why can't people "try *liking* each other once in a while?" asks Mr. Deeds, with the full force of his movie behind the puzzlement. But McCarey knows something that neither Deeds nor his creator, it seems, could ever admit to consciousness: the fact that we can like each other quite a lot, really and even deeply—and *still* do each other in.

Shopping for clothes in Paris with Charles Ruggles: Charles Laughton and Mary Boland show their alarm. Ruggles of Red Gap.

I T'S BECAUSE he did know such things that McCarey is a deeper—and a funnier—artist than Capra is. He was compared with Capra even at the time. He was also compared to Lubitsch. ("The McCarey stamp on a picture has been described as being 'somewhere between the Capra and the Lubitsch touch,'" said the *Saturday Evening Post* in 1946.) The comparisons were inevitable: these were the two dominant figures in contemporary movie comedy, and Mc-Carey was a contender. Yet in some ways, in his muddled and fitful career, he went beyond them both.

It was to put Capra in his place that Harry Cohn brought McCarey to Columbia to make *The Awful Truth*—right after the fiasco of *Make Way for Tomorrow* and the end of McCarey's Paramount contract. And the heroine of *The Awful Truth* is *also* named Lucy. There are several signs, in fact, that for McCarey the two movies were connected by more than chronology. He told an interviewer in 1946 that he had made the Columbia comedy while "feeling like a guy slugging with tears running down his face," he was so angry and frustrated over the reception of *Make Way for Tomorrow*—his favorite of *all* his pictures, as he would say to the end of his life. And you can hear an echo of that anger in his last interview, with Peter Bogdanovich in 1972, where he is still incredulous over getting an Academy Award (best director, 1937) for "one of those My-God-my-husband jobs," as he calls *The Awful Truth*. The "anger"—as well as his rebound from the harrowing, highly personal earlier film—may have surfaced in the film itself as a kind of recklessness. There is something daring, something even defiant, in the way McCarey centers *The Awful Truth* in his own sensibility—in his own native fastidiousness, his instinct for complication and nuance, his responsiveness to matters of taste and form. *The Awful Truth* is not a populist work—by any means.

But it is Lubitschean in many of these ways. Though neither Lubitsch nor anyone else, it seems, would go as far as McCarey does—building scene after scene on the dismay induced by aesthetic infractions: Lucy's "Lola" act, Leeson's terrible poem, Dixiebelle's song. Or Leeson's dancing—a kind of enthusiastic clodhopping step. And Lucy is forced to do it with him—in full view of the ecstatic Jerry, sitting at ringside. In full view of *everyone*. In a McCarey film, any embarrassing display in a nightclub always commands a large and riveted audience—and lots of space. (In his 1925 two-reel comedy *His Wooden Wedding*, with Charley Chase, the people on the dance floor watch Chase bounce his partner around trying to dislodge some money from her dress, and they make the same grave attentive circle around this spectacle that they do around Dunne and Bellamy.) And only McCarey could prolong the embarrassment—and Jerry's delight—over so many details, over so many awful and plausible "steps" devised by the elated Leeson (he won a cup back in Oklahoma) for Lucy's mortification. He pushes her out—he pulls her in. He crouches in front of her—and turns her around. He spreads her arms out (to fly?)—and then they hop in little traveling jumps all across the floor. The whole thing touches another level of awfulness when Lucy sees Jerry watching—and decides to defy him, to carry it off, setting her jaw and lifting her chin, even glancing coolly over her shoulder with attempted hauteur, as the maniac Leeson push-pulls her around, pitching and rolling and hopping. At another point she tries to treat the whole humiliation as a wonderful joke, even to look as if she's really had fun with it, sort of—now that it's winding down. Except that then it starts up again: Jerry has bribed the bandleader to play an encore of the same piece. Leeson pulls her back onto the floor, hops into the air, and kicks her in the shin. Fadeout.

McCarey began his directing career at the Hal Roach studios doing silent two-reelers, notably with the new comedy team of Laurel and Hardy. With McCarey at this time the comedians developed their basic characters and routines. And their basic style: they don't just do a gag; they unpeel it—revealing *layers* of feeling and response. Laurel, reacting to something like a statue with its posterior misplaced, offers a whole chain of reactions: incredulity, dismay, acceptance, terror, and so forth. They were "slower" than other comics—more elaborate and nuanced and likelier to be surprising.

In McCarey's *We Faw Down* (1928), Stan and Ollie are obliged because of an accident to change their clothes in the apartment of a pair of good-time girls, the blowsier one of whom is now "playing" with Stan as they all sit around a table, waiting for the boys' pants to dry. Laurel is just sitting there in his bathrobe, but the woman keeps tousling his hair, tweaking his Adam's apple, twisting his nose—generally "making whoopee," as Hardy calls it, while looking on approvingly. He urges Stan to get into the spirit more. Laurel tries, manfully, but the fact is he really *hates* having his throat tweaked, he even starts to cry, and finally just knocks the lady over. Having done so, he rocks from side to side on his chair, looking replete and bleary-eyed. He even says "Whoopee!" after he's pushed her down for the third or fourth time—although she comes up grinning each time, ready for more. Can she really be enjoying this? Laurel is not sure, but he is certainly doing his part. And she's coming at him again. This time he tears the shoulder off her dress—goes "Whoopee" at Hardy—and rocks again, smiling that complacent chin-lengthening smile of his. Until he notices with a little frown of alarm that his flannel bathrobe has fallen away from the calf of his leg—he replaces it hastily, then resumes his smiling and rocking. Not that he ever really sees what's so funny—while Hardy and the women are laughing harder than ever.

Hardy believes in the surface of things—especially events like this one. If people are smiling and laughing, they are having fun, even if it gets a bit rough. He even has a name for the particular *sort* of fun they are having. It's called "whoopee"—as he tells Stan. And that really takes care of the difficulties—supposing there are any. As usual, Laurel doesn't understand. And as always, he is right. It's always the same in these wonderful routines: Laurel's confusion and bewilderment are always nearer to the real truth of things than Hardy's misguided assurance, his often disastrous complacency. Laurel can *see* that this woman is smiling and laughing—that's the confusing part. But he also knows that he is being mauled and attacked, even violated (the detail about the bathrobe), in some way that is not at all friendly. He is upset—and angry. "Whoopee," he says—and rocks, after hitting her again. To Hardy's approving eye, this is all as it should be. In general, he takes more or less the Capra view: people singing on a bus, for example, or hugging over a harmonica mean just what they offer to mean—they are having fun, what else? Laurel is the McCarey figure: the one who knows that fun doesn't always feel that great, that touching can leave marks.

Hardy, then, is the spokesman of the pair—the one who elects to address the outer world, to deal with other people, and generally show off his manners. The social adept. But Stan is the register of social truth—in troubling anxious contact with his own inner currents, always a beat or two behind his own intimations. He looks—and is—unfocused in some way: things come at him obliquely, through a condition of fog. He is always fuddled—and "out of touch." But he is never blinded by the kind of clarity that Hardy insists upon. They go home to their wives now, and they have some explaining to do. Since they can hardly admit they've spent the afternoon with a couple of party girls, Hardy takes on the burden of making up a story, while the two wives listen patiently. For this event McCarey puts Hardy in the foreground of a close shot, with Laurel behind him. So that Laurel is *literally* unfocused, his outline in the background of the shot a rather blurred one. Hardy starts to talk (it's a silent film), and we watch the succession of strained expressions on his face as his story increasingly and disastrously fails to convince the wives. But we also see Laurel's reactions—if they can be called that. He is in profile, looking dreamily off as is his custom. He doesn't even seem to be listening. But as Ollie goes on, Stan begins to feel the trouble in the room—registering it more and more in the way he shifts and rocks, and frowns and blinks, ascending gradually to a panic. He is like a dismayed seismograph, registering the degrees of unease in the air by precise and delicate calibrations. While Hardy in the foreground—the slave of reason—sweats and smiles through the social moment.

McCarey worked out nearly all the basic jokes of his career with Laurel and Hardy. It's at this time that he makes his crucial discovery: of fastidiousness as both a style and a subject. He was getting discontented, he told Peter Bogdanovich, with the things they were doing on the first Laurel and Hardy comedies. The silent comedy style was too "jerky," too hyperkinetic. They were killing the laughs—partly because, like most comics of the time, they were doing "too much." He determined from then on to do just the opposite:

> I came in one morning and I said, "We're all working too fast. We've got to get away from these jerky movements and work at a normal speed." I said, "I'll give you an example of what I mean. There's a royal dinner. All the royalty is seated around a table and somebody lets out a fart.—Now everybody exchanges a *glance*. That's all."

That glance around the table leads directly to *The Awful Truth*, of course. In some sense McCarey characters are always reacting to "farts" of some kind—by nonreacting. The wince (Dunne's reaction to "*Ok*-la-*ho*-ma," for example, as Grant rolls it on his tongue) is nearly the basic expression of a McCarey performer. Controlled dismay in the face of some unspeakable noise or sight, some vulgarity or gaucherie, is the basic McCarey joke. It's in the way Fay Bainter in *Make Way for Tomorrow* listens to her mother-in-law's homilies, or in the way Victor Moore listens to the pleasantries of his unappetizing, not-too-bright children. It's in the way Irene Dunne responds to Charles Boyer's practiced but rather tacky come-on in *Love Affair* (1939), or in the way Barry Fitzgerald's old pastor takes in his curate Bing Crosby's golf clubs and sports clothes ("You do meditate?") or overhears him at the rectory piano giving a crooning lesson in *Going My Way* (1944). "We three can talk more freely when you two are married," says Cary Grant to Irene Dunne and Ralph Bellamy. Who just look numbly at him: *this* idea hadn't really occurred to them yet. Some idea of good taste— of what you *don't* talk about or mention—underlies most McCarey routines. There is even a minor character in *Make Way for Tomorrow* who is offensive in ways that can't even be named, it seems. We never learn what it is about Harvey, Nellie's husband (Porter Hall)—but we see the toll that it takes on the others. Thomas Mitchell picks up the phone and dials. "I hope," he says fervently to his wife as he listens to the ring, "I don't get Harvey." The hope is instantly dashed. "Oh, hello, Harvey," says Mitchell—wincing. We never get to hear what Harvey is saying—we only watch Mitchell hearing it, watch his look of distress turn to one of positive alarm. Then, "Put Nellie on, will you?" he says weakly—but we can tell from his look that it is already too late. This look—of the struggle with invincible repugnance—is valet Charles Laughton's central action through the first half of *Ruggles of Red Gap* (1935), whether he is confronting his first master's betrayal or his second master's taste in clothes. Both he and Mary Boland spend one whole sequence on the train watching in suspense to see if Charlie Ruggles will or will not blow his nose on his elegantly arranged pocket handkerchief. (He does.)

In *Love Affair*, the two elegant lovers, Dunne and Boyer, are always wincing at themselves. They have just met—on shipboard—and they tend to hear themselves as they imagine the other hears them. Very uncomfortably: they stop, turn away, look askance, rephrase. They are always catching the false ring, or noticing the cliché, in the words they've just uttered. Boyer is an international playboy, engaged to an heiress; Dunne is a rich man's mistress. They exchange life stories by the ship's rail. Her protector first came upon her when she was singing in a joint, Dunne relates—uneasily. "He told me," she says, her voice breaking slightly on the too predictable words, "I didn't *belong* in a place like that. . . . What did you say?" "Nothing," replies Boyer, who is giving nothing away at this point. Later he tells her moonily how he has just spent a sleepless night, "wishing. . . ." She knows what he means. "My father," she says, "used to say that wishes are the dreams we dream when we're awake. . . ." But then she *hears* what she's said—and looks suddenly at the impassive Boyer as if daring him to make a crack. "He drank a lot," she adds, making the crack herself with a sudden liberating laugh.

Just as he values reticence between people, McCarey likes indirection—as between George and his mother, or between Dunne and Boyer at the end of *Love Affair*, where they discuss her not keeping their crucial appointment to meet months ago by pretending it was he who stood *her* up. I waited two hours, she says. No, he says; you waited four—in the rain. Oh, she says—and so on. Like Lubitsch, McCarey loves this sort of obliquity, especially between lovers. But McCarey's elegant indirections are always closer to breakdown and danger than Lubitsch's. Closer to *in*elegance and the temptation to say the hell with it. That tension is always part of the effect.

Boyer has the style of a makeout artist. He tries it out on Dunne. He had been thinking, he tells her, that there were no attractive women on the boat. "I got scared. I said to myself, don't beautiful women travel anymore? Evidently not. Then I saw you—and everything was all right. And I was saved. I *hope*. . . . Cigarette?" She declines, walks past him, and turns—thoughtfully. "Have you been getting *results* with a line like that?" she says, with real interest, sitting on the arm of a chair. "—Or would I be surprised?" It's a marvelous deflating line, a sure laugh. But with McCarey at his best, these little triumphs are never simple, nor entirely clear. There's the suggestion that Dunne's downrightness is as much a conscious style as Boyer's charm, that she is a wise-ass and her victories are too easy. "If you were surprised," replies Boyer with deceptive mildness, "that would surprise me." She bristles: "That sounds like a nasty crack." He doesn't deny it. And there is the following rapid exchange, with the overlapping bickering sound very funny and light:

DUNNE: I could make a few too if I felt like it.
BOYER: Sure you could.
DUNNE: I know I can. (*drums her fingers*)
BOYER: That's what I say.
DUNNE: I think I will. —How's your fiancée?

It turns out well, of course: they really do like each other. The crackle of bad feeling here is really a kind of excitement. It *feels* almost daring. Because with all the classiness it's so close to life in a way, so close to *real* irritability. McCarey likes to be close to the edge.

That's one of his differences from Capra. Because where Capra more or less mimics spontaneity, McCarey really risks it. Capra may show us casual sorts of everyday behavior, people kidding and horsing around and breaking into song— Jean Arthur and Gary Cooper playing "Swanee River" on garbage can lids and so on. But McCarey at equivalent moments shows us something much richer and more finally impressive: the involuntary motions of temperament, of people's deepest natures, those instinctive signals of sympathy or recoil that can't be taken back once they've been given away, and that nearly always tell more about ourselves than anything we choose to tell.

From Laurel and Hardy on, he relies on couples. A McCarey film is a succession of two-person routines. Unlike Capra or Sturges or Hawks, McCarey isn't interested in groups. Even the family dynamics portrayed in *Make Way for To-morrow* are largely the occasion for two-man scenes: between husband and wife, mother and son, father and daughter, and so on. He kept it simple—that way he could "improvise." McCarey "played" these scenes the same way he played his on-set piano: he knew where the life was, where to touch it, how to summon it up. And it's only by citing some deep instinct for getting life on the screen, I think, that you can begin to explain the miracle of a scene like the one in *Ruggles of Red Gap*—a piano scene—where Roland Young and Leila Hyams render an old standard called "Pretty Baby," she at the parlor upright, he at an adjoining set of snare drums. Nell Kenner is her name, a Red Gap hostess and party girl (her status in town is never very clear). He is Lord Burnstead, just over from England—and quite bowled over by this girl, whom he has just met. At his request she has just tied his tie for him. And when she tells him no, she does *not* believe in love at first sight, he tells her neither does he—"that's why I'd like to stay a little while if I may," he says. She grins at him, head back and hands on her hips. "Come on in," she says, taking him by the arm to the piano (where else?).

They are in a medium close shot: Lord Burnstead has a little go at the drums while Nell sits on the piano bench and watches. "Fascinating, your American rhythm," he says. But we've just heard him and we know he hasn't got any. So, of course, does she—the reason for that thin expression on her face. Never mind: she begins to play and sing the song, in her pleasant light soprano. "Ev'rybody loves a baby / That's why I'm in love with you / Pretty baby. . . ." She stops. *"Boum!"* she says, indicating his drum, looking at him inquiringly. Well? He looks at her—he is happy just to be near her. But now he senses a difficulty. "Why do you say 'Boum'?" he asks, still looking at her in that sweet dazzled way he does. She turns slowly on her bench and explains that there is one "Boum!" after *every* "Pretty baby." She demonstrates this to him and they proceed. Once again she sings: "Ev'rybody loves a baby / That's why I'm in love with you / Pretty baby. . . ." She stops and waits. "Boum," he says, leaning toward her and smiling, as if paying her the prettiest of compliments. "You do it on the *drum*," she says, controlling her impatience. "Of course, how stupid of me," he says, looking down at the drum now. But there is a *second* "Pretty baby" in the song's refrain, and just as they seem to be rolling along now, he misses that "Boum" too. And so it goes.

She knows as well as he does, of course, what is really going on between them. But she is the one who has to carry and manage the social thing—this music lesson that neither of them is all that interested in. Except that the familiar little song really *is* sort of nice—cheerful and fun and finally infectious, especially the way it rides into those "Boums" he never gets right till the end. So that Nell's mild impatience with him, partly fooling, is also genuine, something we get to feel, too, when he *never* gets it right. But she's also amused, and excited—delighted by the man in spite of the dimwit. It's a love scene, with a funny, disarming complexity to its tone: irritability and elation all at once, and a final wonderful triumph of good feeling. There is a second "Boum" now, she tells him. "Oh, a *ditto* 'Boum,'" he says, hazarding a little joke. She looks hopelessly at him: what is he saying now? "So we'll ditto-boum," he persists, nearly beside himself with happiness. "All right," she says, laughing and giving in, "we'll ditto-boum!"

And so they play and sing the rest of the song (at last), getting it all together now—and the effect when they do really is like some sort of intoxication: a delight so intense and so contained that Nell has to turn her head away to smile—the kind of excitement that has to attach itself to something neutral and dumb and delirious or else explode inside you (you think). You smile and you laugh and you chat—while you *think* you should be holding the top of your head on: so you sing—and you take off, together. It's all here—in this marvelous mild scene, with its offhanded elation. McCarey captures romantic intoxication so extraordinarily well exactly because he includes it all: all the elements of satire and prickliness and even irritation that other filmmakers might leave out or not even know about, that become part of the laughter and release in a McCarey scene, even part of the affection. It's this free powerful susceptibility— he doesn't censor anything in these elated moments—that makes McCarey a great screwball artist, maybe even the definitive one.

MCCAREY WAS twenty-two when he gave up a just-beginning law career to go into the movies. He was Tod Browning's assistant on *The Virgin of Stamboul* (1920), his main job being, as he later recalled, to keep the director's gin sufficiently watered so that he could finish the day's shooting. At the Hal Roach studios, McCarey went rapidly from prop boy to gag man to director of one- and two-reel comedies with Charley Chase and then Laurel and Hardy. By the time of the early talkies, he was directing feature comedies, free-lancing until 1933 when he signed with Paramount. He was widely described as "brilliant," and actors liked to work with him, and yet mostly during this time he worked with comic stars whose characters and routines were already set, unalterably: Eddie Cantor in *The Kid from Spain* (1932), the Marx Brothers in *Duck Soup* (1933), W. C. Fields and Burns and Allen in *Six of a Kind* (1934), Mae West in *Belle of the Nineties* (1934). It was *Ruggles of Red Gap* (1935) that made McCarey himself a comic "star." About an English manservant (Charles Laughton) out west among the cowboys, it seemed as distinctive in its way as a Lubitsch or a Capra film, even though it had been filmed twice before. It was a ramshackle affair, like most Paramount comedies; but for once it all came to-

Charles Boyer and Irene Dunne in Love Affair *(above);* Ingrid Bergman and Bing Crosby in The Bells of St. Mary's *(right).*

gether—like the layers of a Laurel and Hardy routine—with delightful perform-ances (by Laughton, Young, Hyams, Mary Boland, and Charlie Ruggles), a real feeling for its people, a real small-town, barroom conviviality. And it was an enormous hit. Laughton, who was well known for being hard on directors, was full of nothing but praise for this one, calling McCarey in interviews "the great-est comedy mind now living." No one seemed at the time to notice how Stan Laurel–like Laughton's performance was—in his drunk scenes at least, he has the same look of complacent blissed-out imbecility, the same chin-lengthening closed-mouth smile, the same troubling contact with his own inner currents.

McCarey had trouble enough with his own inner currents. Elsa Lanchester in her autobiography remembers his "weakness for pretty women"—and his guilt. He couldn't help it, he told Laughton. He'd see someone in the commissary; "You eat your lettuce so pretty," he'd say, and he'd be in love. He was always in love, and always guilty—since he was both a married man and a most serious Irish Catholic. He was a dashing, darkly handsome man—interviewers would often compare his looks to Cary Grant's. Though his photos don't really sustain

the comparison: McCarey is too sporty and amiable-looking, too eager to please. Lanchester remembers him as "full of charm" and "extremely shy," with "an apologetic smile that would melt an agent's heart."

People also remember him as brash—even famously so. No doubt he worked at that. Just as he worked, in his early days as a director, at being colorful. News stories about the Hal Roach studio describe McCarey's puttees and checkered cap turned backwards and the special tiny megaphone he carried for use, as he explained it, in "death scenes." He was known then as "the Beau Brummell of directors." He was living up to Hollywood, of course—and to his father, a turn-of-the-century fight promoter and supremely colorful himself.

To Hollywood sophisticates like Billy Wilder and Herman Mankiewicz, McCarey was a primitive—as were nearly all the directors of his generation.*

---

*Wilder even suspected him of being an anti-Semite. This seems unlikely; at any rate, McCarey's films seem even to go out of their way both to include minor Jewish figures and to depict them as lovable. And Wilder also remembered, in a 1978 conversation, how he once heard loud uncontrolled sobbing at a memorial service for a Jewish friend and turned to find that it was McCarey, in a yarmulke.

Still, he had one talent in personal life that people like Mankiewicz were more than obliged to admire: at the Hollywood game of outwitting the bosses, Mc-Carey had few equals. He was a gifted con artist and a spellbinding talker once he got going. Probably his most famous success in this line was the "original story" he simply improvised "on his feet" one day in Sam Goldwyn's office. It was called *The Cowboy and the Lady,* McCarey said—and Goldwyn was delighted by both story and title. Whereupon McCarey sold him all rights to the property—and went his way. But when Goldwyn assigned his writers to do a screen adaptation as a vehicle for Gary Cooper and Merle Oberon, it turned out no one could make out what he'd bought. And McCarey by that time had forgotten. (Even the title, it was learned, was owned by another studio.) Would McCarey like to work on the picture himself? Goldwyn hopefully inquired—perhaps even direct it? "What makes you think," answered McCarey—and the exchange became an instant Hollywood legend—"I would want to spend my valuable time on a piece of crap like *The Cowboy and the Lady?*"

He must have talked his way into *Make Way for Tomorrow:* it remains something of a mystery how such a project ever got started at a major studio, even as liberal a one as Paramount. Maybe they banked on the reviews—and the "prestige." After all, you'd have to be asleep in the screening room not to see that *this* one was "sensitive" and "courageous"—about as gloomy a story as anyone had ever heard, with no stars, no love interest at all, not even in the supporting cast. (In those days it hardly qualified as a *movie* if it didn't have two young lovers somewhere in its cast, preferably the leads.) The nearest precedent—and it couldn't have been a comforting one—was Lubitsch's *The Man I Killed,* another downbeat "emotional drama" about parents and children, by another comic director, and one of the direst flops in studio history. But even *The Man I Killed* had some compensating features: Nancy Carroll, a love story, and a slightly exotic setting at least—not the consistent dreariness of the McCarey project.

Victor Moore said in a 1947 interview that studio president Adolph Zukor "was on the set most of the time," for much of it trying—in vain—to persuade McCarey "to make the ending a happier one." But McCarey's commitment to the rigors of his subject had been strengthened by an event in his own life: the death of his father shortly before filming began. Still, the set, as was usual on a McCarey film, was a happy one. Everyone involved felt passionately about this picture. "We neither knew or cared when quitting time came," said Moore. Even the grips and light men were coming up to tell the actors how moved they had been. And perhaps reports from the sound stage were helping to reassure Zukor and others in the front office. Sure enough: the film opened and the reviewers were rapturous. They even praised it for its political implications, calling it an "eloquent plea for Social Security." But of course nobody really wanted to *see* such a movie, eloquent or not. It died a quick death at the box office, to its director's everlasting bitterness.

This failure may have damaged his stock at Paramount, but it didn't do any harm at all to his reputation for "brilliance." That—and the success of *Ruggles*—was what McCarey took to Columbia with him. Where he was given more freedom than he had ever had at Paramount. He took advantage of it. There was never a completed script for *The Awful Truth* (Vina Delmar, the screenwriter of *Make Way for Tomorrow*, was credited with the final result; Dwight Taylor, who had worked on it, asked that his name be removed; Sidney Buchman seems also to have contributed to it). There was only McCarey, waiting on the set, genial and impenetrable. Ralph Bellamy arrived for his first day's work without even knowing what his part was—and went in front of the camera in the clothes he came to work in: "Just the thing!" exclaimed McCarey when he saw him. *Nobody* knew what they were doing, according to Bellamy—nobody but McCarey. But they all learned to trust him—all except Grant, who spent his first days on the picture trying to escape it. He begged Harry Cohn to let him out of his contract. He asked his friend Joel McCrea to replace him. He even tried to get Bellamy to switch roles with him. He was sure he'd make a fool of himself, it seemed. Something McCarey never quite forgave him for, in spite of their later friendship.

Many mornings McCarey would arrive on the set and just go to his piano. He was an amateur songwriter, and he liked to doodle around at the keyboard while he thought—and while cast and crew waited. When inspiration struck—often not until the afternoon—he would take the newly conceived scene or business and run it through with the actors, then write it all down with the script girl, give the performers their lines, and film it. By this method, more or less, he shot the whole thing in six weeks. After that, he got on a boat and went to Europe for an extended trip with his wife. And *The Awful Truth* became Columbia's biggest hit since *Mr. Deeds Goes to Town*.

He could make his own terms now. But it took him almost two years—typically—to get the next project together. It started with Charles Boyer—who owned his own prints of *Ruggles* and *The Awful Truth* and who reran the latter film endlessly (he also admired *Make Way for Tomorrow*). Boyer—according to his biographer Larry Swindell—had come to regard McCarey as "an unappreciated major artist." And so the two men resolved to do a picture together, with Irene Dunne as co-star. But the first idea for a story—something about a French diplomat's clandestine American romance—foundered when the French government protested it. McCarey then appealed to screenwriter Delmer Daves for help, rousing him from his bed one morning at six a.m. (the situation was desperate). Daves remembered a shipboard love affair he'd had and wrote a scenario from that. And they were on their way. McCarey had signed Dunne to a personal contract. He now made a deal with RKO for her services and his own. Donald Ogden Stewart was also signed to write "additional dialogue"—the classy kind.

But Boyer, like Grant before him, was unhinged by his first days on a Mc-

Carey set. A methodical and reflective sort of actor, he now had to learn *not* to learn his lines beforehand (they were always rewritten on the set), and to deal with a director who seemed to have no interest in motivation or character analysis. But then the character was always changing: Boyer himself was invited to contribute to this enjoyable process—as McCarey actors usually were. And soon, in fact—to the surprise of many—Boyer was enjoying himself more than he ever had on a film. They were all enjoying themselves, it seems, as long as they were "on" the ocean liner (the setting of the film's first part), with Dunne and Boyer parrying and flirting over champagne. And the rushes had all the élan that McCarey banked on. But once the ship "docked," as Dunne later recalled, it was like the letdown after a real trip. Whatever was planned for the rest of the film now seemed inadequate. Writers were called in, and there was a general atmosphere of panic. It was almost like beginning the film over again.

In a way, that seems to have been what McCarey intended. He had meant from the beginning to make a movie in two halves, with contrasting tones and materials—light and heavy, screwball and tearjerker. He succeeded. *Love Affair* (1939) in its final form embodies the split in McCarey's temperament—between Lubitsch and Capra, so to speak—with startling literalness. Except that even Capra might have balked at the hokiness of *Love Affair*'s second half, where Terry (Dunne), on her way to meet Michel (Boyer) at the top of the Empire State Building after their six-month separation, is run over by a car and crippled. In her wheelchair then, she gets a job teaching singing to orphans. While Michel, who has become a successful New York artist, thinks he has been jilted. Until they meet by accident (she has bought one of his paintings—of her in his grandmother's shawl) and he discovers the tragic truth.

It was a big hit—McCarey's second in a row. And now he decided he would function solely as a producer for his next film at RKO. He did the screenplay with Sam and Bella Spewack and assigned the direction to Garson Kanin: *My Favorite Wife* (1940), an Enoch Arden farce about inadvertent bigamy, starred Grant and Dunne again—and it was another hit. Though it's a forced and feeble comedy, it's unmistakably a McCarey one, especially since it repeats (over Kanin's objections at the time) whole jokes and routines from *The Awful Truth*.*

It was around the time of this production that McCarey had the car accident that nearly ended his life, laying him up for many months—the most spectacular misfortune yet in a spectacularly accident-prone life. One Hollywood reporter noted that by 1940, and the age of forty-two, McCarey had spent more than six years of his productive life either in a hospital or convalescing at home. The

---

*Dunne does another "Lola" routine, impersonating a dumb Southern "cousin" to embarrass Grant in front of Gail Patrick. And McCarey ends the film with the same shtick that ended *The Awful Truth*: with Dunne in bed under the covers and Grant in a nightshirt in the doorway trying to find a strategy for getting in with her.

drinking, too, was getting steadily worse (though he never apparently drank on the job—as his old boss Tod Browning had). And the intervals between films as his career went on got longer and longer. It was two years before he returned to RKO to produce and direct *Once Upon a Honeymoon* (1942), from his own "original story." It's another film with a complicated tone: a romantic adventure among the Nazis. Cary Grant is an American reporter in Europe on the trail of one of Hitler's top operators, a German baron (Walter Slezak), to whom chorus girl Ginger Rogers, another kind of operator, is married—at least until she falls in love with Grant and reawakens to her American heritage. The movie is full of weird lapses and misjudgments: a scene in which Rogers is supposed to look like the Statue of Liberty; a concentration camp scene with the inmates singing their Jewish hymns in the background like darkies on the old plantation. In spite of its stars, it was neither well reviewed nor profitable.

But then everything turned around again with a Paramount project that couldn't have been anyone's idea of a blockbuster but that became one of the most successful movies in Hollywood history: McCarey's *Going My Way* (1944), with Bing Crosby and Barry Fitzgerald as a pair of priests. It was familiar McCarey ground—he even got Frank Butler, who'd worked with him on the Laurel and Hardy films, to do the screenplay with him. A comic couple in a movie-length routine that rambled along genially from shtick to shtick and left audiences feeling expansive and gratified. True, it was a new and somewhat unlikely movie subject: life in a priests' rectory. But treated with so many clichés that it was made to seem familiar. It was a way of telling audiences, even the non-Catholic ones (it was popular everywhere), that they were at home in this world even if they thought they wouldn't be—a way of making the world Irish Catholic. McCarey's next film followed quickly (for him), and it was a sequel: *The Bells of St. Mary's* (1945), with Crosby reprising his Father O'Malley role opposite Ingrid Bergman, the hottest new star in Hollywood, as a nun. It was nearly as successful as the earlier film. No surprise to McCarey: "God had his arm around me," he said, about the experience of making the film.

It's important to note that this was the *stratosphere* of success. McCarey was now not only the hottest filmmaker in Hollywood; he was listed as the highest-paid man in all of America. No screwball comedy, not even a Capra comedy, had come close to making the fortune these two films did, with their mixtures of sentiment and "religion" and gentle laughs. *The Bells of St. Mary's* was the biggest hit in RKO history. In a recent adjusted-for-inflation list of the all-time top-grossing comedies (in David Pirie's *Anatomy of the Movies*, 1981), *Going My Way* is fourth, coming between *Animal House* and *American Graffiti* in third and fifth places. And *The Bells of St. Mary's* is seventh.

And not everyone thought they were shlock by any means. James Agee joined the chorus of reviewers' praise for *Going My Way*, with the usual reservations about its "sugarcoating"—praising the acting, the "loving attention to character," to atmosphere and detail, the "leisure and spaciousness" of McCarey's style. But then he disliked *The Bells of St. Mary's*. Though it had many of the same virtues, he thought it too calculating—as did most of the reviewers who had praised the earlier film for freshness and naturalness. If it was shlock though, it was shlock with a complication: namely, the McCarey touch. The mixture of rich behavioral observation with an essential falsity was often hard for people to disentangle. At the least, these McCarey movies really did seem to show an interest in character. (*Going My Way*, wrote Agee in *Time* magazine, "points the way to the great films which will be possible when Hollywood becomes aware of the richness and delight of human character for its own sake.") What else could it be? So much attention given to the details of human types, so little attention to "plot"—it hardly seemed credible (at first glance anyway) that this "loving attention" was being lavished on stereotypes of behavior and personality as rigid and hollow, as consolingly counterfeit, as any the movies could offer. But then, of course, that was also the point, and one reason for both films' astonishing popularity. In effect, McCarey is extending something he first tried out with those singing orphans that Dunne coaches in *Love Affair*. The kids' faces (freckled, gat-toothed, "homely," etc.) make it clear at a glance that McCarey has gone out of his way to get "unaffected" and "natural-looking" types. But when they open their mouths to sing ("Wishing Will Make It So," the movie's hit song), the sounds that come out—courtesy of the Mitchell Boys Choir—are so souped up, so practiced and corrupt, that the effect is almost like something out of *The Exorcist*.

There are singing delinquents (led by tough guy Stanley Clements) in *Going My Way*, making the same sort of unsettling sound. But the children in *The Bells of St. Mary's* are first-graders putting on their own version of the Nativity story, under the delighted eyes of Father O'Malley and Sister Benedict. This sequence—one of the most famous in the film—was *really* improvised by the children themselves, with McCarey's camera running—and, unlike the rest of the film, is unquestionably "natural." It's charming—Agee calls it "almost magically deft and pretty"—but it's troubling too. It represents such a familiar sort of exchange between children and grownups: asking them to tell us one of "our" stories, even such a harrowing and majestic one as the Nativity (you have a feeling McCarey might even ask them to do the Crucifixion)—so that we can glow and chuckle, with Father and Sister, at their sincerity, their sweetness, their "little" mistakes. A moment like this one almost *defines* "cuteness." And it's typical, as McCarey knows, of the uses we often put children to: to blunt our own grown-up-ness, to make something "deft and pretty" out of even our harshest knowledge. But to McCarey it's even more—an epiphany, the most transcendent moment in his film. This is the kind of reality he touches now—the kind of relation he wants not only with children but with his own material. It's what his audiences wanted, too, perhaps: for movies in general—not just Mc-Carey's—were becoming more infantilized.

There is a child doing a grown-up piece in *Good Sam* (1948), McCarey's next movie, but she simply recites in a mechanical voice, sitting in her mother Ann Sheridan's lap, several verses of "The Night Before Christmas." But the scene is so lifeless it's inexplicable: it goes on as if McCarey were determined to make it go on, the child seeming as bored as any audience could be. It had been three years since *The Bells of St. Mary's*—but this new McCarey film didn't seem to touch *any* kind of reality. Though it wasn't for lack of trying in its picture of a struggling middle-class family headed by a good-hearted man who is always being taken advantage of by the people he tries to help. (McCarey himself was legendarily softhearted and generous.) But *Good Sam*, with Gary Cooper and Ann Sheridan, was a calamitous flop. Curiously, McCarey seemed almost to be imitating another box-office disappointment of the postwar period: Capra's *It's a Wonderful Life* (1946). Both movies concern themselves with the problems of benevolence and with a retrospective self-questioning hero; they even have similar details of plot. But where Capra shows a new growth, even a new level of seriousness, McCarey only shows a loss of old powers. The obsessive patterns recur—the wincing, the concern with parents and children, the delayed-fuck routine, etc.—but without conviction, often without making any sense. What's most remarkable about the film is the behavioral unreality of almost every moment in it—as if McCarey had been visited by some weird affliction reversing and blighting his strongest talent.*

It was some four years before the next McCarey film appeared. And not even *Good Sam* could have prepared people for this one—the bizarre *My Son John* (1952), with Helen Hayes and Robert Walker. John (Walker), a Washington official of unspecified eminence, has returned home to visit his parents (Helen Hayes and Dean Jagger) just at the time his two brothers in the Army have gone off to Korea. But the reunion isn't a happy one. John, a very prissy and snotty type, is behaving even more suspiciously than usual. And he is even followed by a mysterious man (Van Heflin) asking questions about him—who is soon revealed to be an FBI investigator. John of course—wincing away from his parents, who are bumptious and noisy, like a *pair* of Leesons—is the figure who carries the McCarey-like fastidiousness in this film. But for the first time in a McCarey film that fastidiousness is given a name. It turns out to be communism. And not just fooling-around communism, pamphlets and speeches and nutty ideas: Helen Hayes's favorite son is, in his own remorseful words, "a native

---

* All the scenes are slack and overextended. One of them goes on so long and so pointlessly that McCarey (like the audience) seems to forget what's gone on in it: Ann Sheridan hears the same information about another character's asthma at two different points in the same scene—and is surprised each time.

American communist spy." Eventually he repents, but too late. He is killed by the other commies once he realizes the enormity of what he's done—betrayed not only his country and his church but his parents, almost the worst thing a son can do. Though his parents, it's clear, have a duty to betray *him*, once he's gone wrong. It's not easy for Helen Hayes to cooperate with the FBI. She resists and suffers, as mothers do in these situations. She has never wanted to face the truth about her son. Father, on the other hand, has suspected it from the beginning.

And it all began with that wincing of his—as Mother soon comes to realize. She even thinks back on his reactions to football. "You never played, did you?" she says speculatively, after she has learned the worst about him. "I sometimes think it hurt you when your father and I jumped up and down cheering for . . . Ben and Chuck" (the football-playing brothers). The problem was he thought he was brainy. John admits that himself in the posthumous speech he has recorded for the graduating class of his alma mater. It was at college that he was first "recognized as an intellect," flattered by "liberal professors" and "invited to homes where only superior minds communed." It was in these circles that "the serpent lying in wait" for him struck, recruiting him to treason. "Even now," he tells the students, as the camera tracks past their impassive faces, "the eyes of Soviet agents are on some of you—they've observed your abilities, seen qualities that I once possessed." Seen—as they once did in him—the telltale signs of the potential traitor. A curl of the lip at a football game, perhaps, or a lift of the eyebrow at a mother's song. "When it gets to the stage where you're making fun of a mother's love!" cries Hayes, after singing, noticing the look on her son's face. "Making fun of my lullaby! Spoiling my memories!" She's just like "all the other mothers," she says—she "can't take it."

The whole film has a raving, disconnected quality—even down to its conversations, its most casual exchanges. Mother asks John if he has a girl now, and he replies—with a little smile—that "sentimentalizing over the biological urge isn't exactly a guarantee of human happiness, dear." John reminds Mother to take her prescription tablets. "What about Moses and the tablets *he* left," she ripostes, "with the prescription written right on them?" John has just finished a conversation with his father—who has spoken excitedly about taking John out in the backyard and shooting him ("*Both* barrels!"). "I can't understand Father's attitude toward me," says John to his mother. "That," says Hayes, "is because you're not a father." It doesn't help when the FBI agent comes along, either. Since he can't talk about his work any more than John can about his. "I know," Heflin says darkly to Hayes, "that our methods are very often criticized—by certain sources." But, he tells her, he can explain that: it's "because we're after them day and night."

But whenever this fogginess is dispelled by a reference to something exactly named, the result can be even more bewildering. They are talking—or so it seems—about John giving himself up for arrest, when suddenly Mother starts to play an imaginary football game: "Take the ball, John!" she cries. And when he declines: "That was a tough one to lose," she says and collapses on the couch. "Your conscience must be nauseating," says the FBI man to John. Much earlier, during an impassioned late-night conversation about John's idealistic beliefs, his mother, encouraged by all their points of agreement ("Love thy neighbor . . . I go along with you so far"), asks him if he'd be willing to swear—though it's not at all clear to what. "How does it go?" she asks, pressing the Bible on him, whereupon John raises his right hand and promptly recites, "I swear that I am not now and never have been a member of the Communist Party," while Mother kneels at his side, holding the book and looking up at him with shining eyes. "Feel better?" he asks. Does she ever. "I can't wait for your father to come home," she says.

It really seemed loony, even at the time. And it was another sign of Hollywood's disarray: no major studio would have allowed such a certifiable case to escape into theaters in the old days. But this was 1952, and it was also a time in Hollywood when no one would attack a filmmaker for his anticommunism.* That's not to say people couldn't be embarrassed by it—especially if the film was a box-office embarrassment, as *My Son John* emphatically was. In this situation McCarey himself became the fart at the royal table: people in Hollywood exchanged uneasy glances over this film, that's all—even though it had sent them reeling. Eventually—slowly—they deplored it publicly. Helen Hayes, it was said, had "no idea"; it had been another script altogether when she accepted the role. Certainly not *his* script, said John Lee Mahin, who gets the writing credit on the screen, with McCarey as co-writer. According to Mahin, he left the project and then the whole thing was rewritten, by McCarey and Myles Connolly. Mahin himself, like Connolly, was one of Hollywood's most active red-baiters and a champion of the blacklist. But he wasn't crazy. McCarey *was*, however, as Mahin told an interviewer in 1980: "Leo McCarey was a brilliant man who let communism absolutely drive him crazy. He actually went crazy. . . . I was aghast when I saw the picture. So was Helen."

EVERYONE WAS aghast. But not just—if they were honest—because of the craziness. People were used—in 1952—to the movies being dumb. Everyone knew and said that movies were dumb. But their dumbness was their own, so to speak—a function of their solipsism, their clichés and systems of self-reference. But what was coming off the screen from this movie was *our* dumbness—registered by McCarey with embarrassing fidelity and obvious approval. This movie's sound was less like "the movies" than like what we'd just heard in the lobby or the street or the local bar. The sort of remark people make

---

*McCarey's "original story" was even nominated for an academy award.

and believe mainly because they've just heard themselves making it—with belief. "That's a communist specialty, breaking up homes," says Father. "I may not be bright, but I know *that*." "Every life has some purpose," observes the FBI man. "Even Judas'." "*There's* a mother's instinct for you," he remarks to a colleague when Hayes looks over her shoulder to see if he is following her—as, of course, he is. And so on. It's this sound—of familiar conversational fatuity—that is the film's *real* craziness.

Especially where it touches the subject of communism. "How are things down in Washington, son?" asks Father in a characteristic early exchange. "Everybody's beginning to see things as they are, aren't they?" "Well," replies John with his little smile (he has understood the question perfectly, of course), "some of us, Father, are not so much interested in seeing things as they are as they are [sic] in seeing things the way they'd *like* them to be." In fact, we never learn anything about John's life as a communist. And for good reason: it's clear the moviemakers themselves know nothing about it. Or, rather . . . they know what they know, and that's good enough for them: how communists break up homes, encourage young people to sneer at their parents, use "liberal" ideals to spread "despair . . . disguised as hope," and so on. They know communism threatens everything that we believe in. What else do they need to know? There are, of course, those who know more—but *they* can't tell. As the FBI man says, rebuking a questioner, "We *gather* information, we don't give it out." The obfuscation is a necessity, then. Is that why we always get the feeling in this movie that when people are talking about communism they are really talking about something else (intellectualism, homosexuality, youth, "liberal" idealism—or just ordinary critical intelligence), and that when they talk about something else, they are really talking about *It*? It's a funny feeling—but a familiar one. The movie is obsessed by communism but utterly unable to focus on it, to know about it or look at it or even to talk about it directly. And in this respect McCarey exactly reflected American political life, American anxieties, and even our American conversations.

One of the most inexplicable things about the movie, it was commonly felt—one of its most perverse and McCarey-like features—was the portrayal of John's father. The most ardent and unwavering exponent of Americanism in the film is also a clown. A schoolteacher and a Legionnaire, he teaches "basics" to the children and lectures the men at the post about the need to be "alert." But it's really a Ralph Bellamy role: noisy, humorless, thick-witted. When Father takes the Bible out, he ends up hitting John over the head with it (Walker crosses his eyes on the impact). He gets drunk, storms noisily up the stairs, and falls down them. He sings (sober) a ghastly parody of a patriotic song, loudly and tunelessly (even Mother winces at this one): "If you don't like your Uncle Sammy," he sings and marches in place, "Then go back . . . to the land from whence you came!"

Making Mother Happy: Robert Walker and Helen Hayes in My Son John.

His "discussions" with John are really old vaudeville routines, with Father playing the stooge. When John accuses him of "copying" a line in his speech from someone else, "What difference does that make?" he says. "Copying doesn't make it right," says John. "I copied it right!" replies Dad indignantly.

All this may have been meant as an oblique reference to Senator Joe McCarthy—who was also a clown, but "fighting on God's side," as Hayes says about Ben and Chuck, her sons in Korea. McCarey even has Dean Jagger mimic one of McCarthy's most notorious public gambits: his habit of both dangling and withholding what he claimed were "lists" of communist names. "I've got it!" cries Father to John, brandishing his Legion speech at him. "It's all here! It's packed with dynamite!" ("I'm sure it's loud," says John.)

It's no surprise, then, with all this flailing around, that Father also has a violent side. He collects guns, and he thinks in terms not only of singing to the communists ("go back . . . from whence you came!") but of killing them too, a consideration which naturally and eventually extends itself to his son. "We're alert," he assures John about the Legion. "And *you* sound to me like one of those guys we should be alert about. . . . 'Cuz if I thought you *were* . . . I'd take you out in the backyard and I'd *give* it to you, both barrels!" A reminder that in nearly all their scenes together Father has been looking at John with something like detestation.

But then John *is* one of those guys we have to be alert about—after all. Father is right—and has been right all along—about this little creep. Not blinded by love the way Mother has been—the way mothers *should* be. This simple man is able to see things more clearly than anyone, as Mother tells him after she too has faced the truth about their son, because he listens to his "heart." "You're not blinded by it," she says, "but you think with it too—clear and honest and clean!" The astonishing conclusion, then, is the one that she draws: never mind intelligence, or even sobriety: Father has "wisdom"—"more . . . than any of us." And this is the judgment of him that the movie, in its peculiar way, clearly supports.

Why, then, has McCarey made this normative figure so brutal and appalling? Partly, it seems, because it's just this appalling brutality—this embodied violence against his own sensitivity and sophistication and better judgment—that McCarey needs to affirm. But then this is the sort of transaction within ourselves that most of us learn to keep quiet about—unless we're "crazy." In which case we become an embarrassment. With a friend like McCarey, do Legionnaires need enemies? No wonder John Lee Mahin and the other Hollywood red-baiters were "aghast" at this movie. McCarey, out of his own necessities, has more or less given the game away—all but endorsing stupidity, it seemed. The point about Dean Jagger's Father is not that he has "wisdom" in spite of his crudity and ignorance and belligerence but that he has it *because* of these attributes, which in him are quite unspoiled and untroubled, "clear and honest and clean." John's original crime, it seems, was in trying to escape this paternal heritage—in wincing, and in turning away from it.

But then, of course, there is no way that John *can't* wince away from this father. As McCarey knows very well, this son's position is a hopeless one. That doesn't, for McCarey, lessen the guilt, or mitigate the villainy of his betrayal. McCarey is describing a universal villainy—which implicates us all. Since we are all helpless not to betray *these* parents—the ones who give us a make-believe America (significantly, John's father teaches at "the little red schoolhouse"), which we may never get over yearning for but which we betray repeatedly and necessarily with every act of grown-up perception. So that McCarey, like Capra—whom he so much admired ("the cleverest director in the business")—offers finally a kind of willed simplicity. But it is more desperately willed and much less simple than Capra's, who for all his talents never seems to have had quite the option of grown-up perception that McCarey did—the vision behind *The Awful Truth* or *Make Way for Tomorrow.* What *My Son John,* with all its "craziness," shows is McCarey's dim but persisting consciousness of that option. He was too smart to be dumb without knowing there was a choice involved. That knowledge is somewhere behind all the hysteria and disconnection of *My Son John*. Though the choice, it seems, has been made some time before.

The two priest pictures, in the mid-forties, would seem to be the turning point. It's not hard to imagine what their extraordinary success must have meant to McCarey—in the midst of growing personal and working difficulties, to have the greatest triumph of his career in films that at once consolidate his talents and falsify them. Old men and young men alike in these films are cute and elfin—rascally, perhaps, but harmless. McCarey has learned to tell just the kind of joke that the Vances like and require in *The Awful Truth*: the kind that makes his audience feel more secure and safe, more pleased with themselves than ever. Jerry and Lucy's air of challenge and risk are replaced by the twinkling complacency of Bing Crosby's Father O'Malley, with his air of bovine mischief. Women appear only in rigidly defined—and sexless—roles: mother or housekeeper or nun. In both priest films, there are fractious and rebellious younger women, but they are minor figures—and cautionary, since they are no match for Father Crosby's certainties. Nor for his singing, with its relentlessly upbeat philosophizing ("Aren't You Glad You're You?").

It's not surprising, then, that McCarey should find his own security, and a worldly triumph as well, in films about "fathers." In this respect as in so many others, he reflects Hollywood itself. Because what he does in turning away from the screwball mode and its heroines is to opt, just as the movies in general did, for exactly those patriarchal values and visions that the great screwball comedies—with their emphasis on the peculiar foolishness of the masculine mode, the superiority of the feminine—implicitly rejected and subverted. But it seems those screwball subversions ran very deep in McCarey even to the end. They resurface in a distorted, nightmare fashion in *My Son John*, in the conflict between womanish son and mannish father. The masculine mode here is *still* foolish—more than ever, perhaps. But it's asserted like a kind of madness against the "feminine" virtues of the son, whose shrewdness, humor, and fastidiousness become in this odd vision the incitements to treason and evil.

In *The Bells of St. Mary's*, Ingrid Bergman's Sister Superior clashes with Crosby's Father O'Malley over a typical issue: whether one of her students, a favorite boy, should be encouraged to fight. She seems to get the better of the priest, verbally at least—

> FR. O'MALLEY: I like to see a lad who can take care of himself. On the outside, it's a man's world.
> SR. BENEDICT (*with a smile*): How are they doing, Father?
> FR. O'MALLEY (*embarrassed, with a laugh*): Well, they're not doing too good, but you know what I mean. . . .

But in the end, of course, she gives the boy boxing lessons herself—in secret (that mischievous tone). It's a familiar joke, the sit-com stuff of its time. (Boxing *lessons* were always automatically funny in movies like this, and always involved someone's taking an archaic John L. Sullivan stance. But then to have a *nun* doing all this—what could be better? But it's a long, sad way from Laurel and Hardy.) In a "man's world" the women make trouble sometimes, but then that's what they're meant to do (it's one of the film's principal jokes: how "hard" these nuns are on the priests and businessmen who run things)—anyway, what would we do without them? The movie's tone directly evokes the familiar tones of our own world—as when a Secretary of State Haig, for example, refers smirkingly to "the good sisters" of his boyhood while discussing the murdered nuns in El Salvador. So that it's no surprise to us—then or now—when "the good sister" in this fantasy ends up teaching about left jabs and right hooks. That outcome is predictable not only because of the cliché but because in the world this film evokes the "fathers" always win—however much you may counter them with your charm, your natural tenderness and concern, your gentle irony. You expect such things from women (or they wouldn't be women)—but you don't expect them to make any difference.

The Screwball Years: 13
The Leading Men

I N A 1937 poll of movie fans he was voted "the King" (Myrna Loy, his frequent co-star, was voted Queen), and the title stuck. No other star since then—not even the few like Wayne or Eastwood who have surpassed his box-office record—has succeeded to it. During the screwball years, 1936 to 1940, he was the top box-office star, just as he was *the* MGM star—associated with the studio in the public mind, and with its dependable glamour. He was leonine, too, like the famous studio logo. He was well barbered, even impeccable, with his trim little mustache—but still there was always something shaggy about him. Reminding us, too, that we don't always associate the animals we call "kings" with the greatest energy or skill or even interest. If you're Clark Gable, you don't *have* to be special.

Nor was he the sort of man who left a lot of anecdotes behind. But Donald Ogden Stewart, in his autobiography, does tell one that's memorable. Stewart, in 1939, was married to Ella Winter, a dedicated left-wing journalist and author (*Red Virtue*, a study of the Soviet Five-Year Plan, and *I Saw the Russian People*, about her experiences as a foreign correspondent). She was a fierce, lively, handsome woman, but not welcome in every Hollywood home. The marriage was a controversial one to Stewart's friends. Though not to Gable and Carole Lombard, themselves just married (Lombard, of course, was an old friend of Stewart's) and eager to meet and welcome Don's new wife. It was "a hilarious evening" at the Gables', according to Stewart—just the four of them, drinking and laughing and talking inevitably about the war in Europe. When they were leaving, Gable kissed Ella good night, clasping the author of *Red Virtue* in his big arms and patting her encouragingly: "Don't worry, little girl," he said, "we'll protect you from Hitler."

Even on screen Gable specializes in awkward moments, and in misjudged effects. "Gee, I like to look into those big lamps of yours," he says to Jeanette MacDonald in *San Francisco* (1936), leaning over her, overwhelming her with his size and avidity while she is backed against a wall. In *Strange Cargo* (1940) he has to creep among some oilcans on the dock to reach Joan Crawford (he is a convict laborer on Devil's Island, and she is a local whore) and then hold her by the ankle to keep her from running away, while he makes his pitch: "You're from Paris, aincha?" he says, while Crawford looks down at him with fierce, haunted eyes. He is even jauntier in *Idiot's Delight* (1939), where he sings and dances "Puttin' on the Ritz" with straw hat and cane and a backup of six "Les Blondes." And in an ambience calculated to remind us of Astaire, Gable is deliberately and compellingly awful. It's one of the oddest star turns in movies. There is something like it in *The Gilded Lily* (1935), when Colbert is maneuvered into doing a nightclub act even though she can't sing and dance. But her incompetence is really a caricature: while we watch her failing at her act, we can admire her skill as an actress and a comedienne, so that finally the joke feels like a safe one.

But with Gable it's just the opposite: he really *can't* sing and dance. We're not watching a parody of that deficiency but the real thing in painful action. He sings in a loud, dead voice, overbearing the girls. He hops and pivots, he picks his foot up, comes down on his heel and grinds. He kicks his feet and claps his hands. He points at his shoe with his cane—and looks very pleased with himself. Then, as if to prove it, he shakes his shoulders at us and comes forward— a slight loss of confidence here, dispelled by a triumphant bump of the butt directed at Norma Shearer's table (she reacts in a close shot). For a finale the girls carry him out: he reclines across their arms, wagging his finger and rolling his eyes at us. It's really dreadful—but there is some applause, and he comes back and does it all over again, even more enthusiastically, strutting and prancing and grinning, jumping a little higher, grinding a little heavier, trucking and shuffling with one hand in the air and the other on his stomach, and so on.

And why should it all seem so wonderful (just as in another way his goodnight remark to Ella Winter seems wonderful)? There's a real daring behind it. Gable offers his gracelessness straight in this film. There are none of the exaggerations that might get him off the hook. With other stars we're mostly not supposed to notice when they're inept at such things (as they often are). With Gable we *can* notice; we're even invited to. It's the ultimate kingly gesture, in a way—showing us what he *can't* do, too. His famous cocksureness is nearly always slightly misguided, his self-assurance slightly misplaced. It's part of his authority that he may even *know* this and still be undiscouraged. Even if he has to hold onto her ankle ("You're from Paris, aincha?").

Most of all he is a tough-comedy hero, embodying at his most characteristic that strain of defiant vulgarity central to the movies in general. Even *Gone With the Wind* (1939), with his apotheosis as Rhett Butler, is a kind of ultimate tough comedy, its vitality more a development of thirties movie comedy than of any historical romance tradition. It's a "romantic epic" that is neither especially

romantic nor notably epic—but does have these two terrific, hard-as-nails lovers at its center. And what other romantic epic ends the way this one does—with the romantic hero thoroughly fed up with the heroine's illusions and stupidity, out of love with her at last, and telling her that he doesn't "give a damn" what she does—a Gable moment that never fails to rouse an audience to cheers and applause?

Even so, Rhett Butler is smarter, more polished, more conventionally glam-

Even with her boyfriend and her priest in the room, he keeps coming on to her: Gable, Jack Holt, Spencer Tracy, and Jeanette MacDonald in San Francisco.

orous than most Gable heroes—a gentrified Gable with none of the rough edges of Blackie Norton (*San Francisco*) or Harry Van (*Idiot's Delight*) or Chris Hunter (*Too Hot to Handle*). For all his glamour and authority, he is still the sort of star who seems less to be transcending his limits than reminding us of them. It's what he has instead of amiability: a certain clumsiness, which he accepts, of body and spirit. He embodies all the limitations of the masculine mode: he can be incurious, self-satisfied, even cloddish. And yet, though he is often complacent, he has none of the weird laid-back composure of an archetypal star like Bing Crosby—at least the Crosby of the forties. Gable could never play a movie priest, not only because of his roguishness and his carnality but also because he could never be *that* pleased with himself.* Characteristically, he played the kind of hero who "knew all the answers"—but the audience always knew that

---

San Francisco, interestingly, pits him against one of these priestly figures of omniscient rectitude: Spencer Tracy's Father Tim, with his glow of angry piety, bleeding accusingly from the side of his mouth after Gable has slugged him. You're all on Gable's side in such clashes—though the movie, of course, with its official line against him (his "godlessness"), invites you to pretend you're not.

he didn't. And he knew it, too. That's why he nearly always looks a little un-happy.

He was one of the great leading men, but often a reluctant one. He worried a lot about being upstaged—by "actor" co-stars like Spencer Tracy and Charles Laughton, but particularly by the women. That was one reason he didn't want to do *Gone With the Wind*—because it was Scarlett's picture—or *San Francisco*—because he didn't want to sit around listening to MacDonald sing, he said. But then of course that's exactly the sort of thing he does almost better than anyone. MacDonald is Mary Blake, an out-of-work singer, and Gable is Blackie Norton, the owner of a Barbary Coast saloon named the Paradise Club. When she first auditions for him, she sings "Love Me and the World Is Mine"—and he looks at her angrily as she begins. But she goes on. As her voice goes up ("I care *not* . . . for the stars that shine . . ."), his eyes travel down. She gets the job: "You've got a pretty fair set of pipes, kid." But then in rehearsals for the big show she turns out to be a stiff: she sings *everything* as if it were "Love Me and the World Is Mine." Until Blackie intervenes: she sings it "the Paradise way" or else. And when she finally does—she is onstage, and he is watching from his customary box—singing "San Francisco" *his* way, jazzy and syncopated and Jolson-like, the reaction shot of Gable smiling as he watches, his head slightly turned away from the camera, overtaken by reluctant delight, is a bigger event than the song itself.

This is the Gable specialty with these ladies: being dazzled, disbelieving—head turned away as the dimpled grin gains across his face—and deep down delighted. Even when he's watching a roaring phony like Norma Shearer's Irene in *Idiot's Delight*. He plays a tinhorn vaudevillian in this film (from the Robert Sherwood play, which starred the Lunts on Broadway), a song-and-dance man named Harry Van, traveling across Europe with a troupe of six chorus girls. He is *not* high-class. Shearer, on the other hand, is nothing *but* class. He is on the dance floor, doing a brusque fox-trot, when he spots her doing her grand-lady number at a nearby table. He grins and starts to dance Bowery-style: cheek to cheek with his partner, bending down and sticking his butt way out—hefting it toward Shearer's startled face at one point as he executes a swift shuffle to the orchestra's drumbeat. Shearer is an American masquerading as a Russian countess and traveling with a munitions magnate (Edward Arnold). She regales the people in the hotel with tales of her Russian girlhood. Chaliapin gave her singing lessons. "Your father," remarks Harry, "spared no expense." "That," she says, "was in the *old* Russia." But Harry keeps thinking she's this girl he knew in Omaha—as, of course, she is. But when she starts to talk again, he is lost in grudging admiration. She tells of her "escape from the Bolsheviki" ("For four days I was alone with his body, sailing through the storms of the Black Sea . . ."). He points out that this escape is different each time she talks about it.

She shrugs and gestures: "I made several escapes," she explains airily. Another "singer," in full, rhapsodic flight—and technically the moment belongs to Shearer as clearly as the "San Francisco" number belongs to MacDonald. And yet, just as before, it's Gable's reaction of wry but undisguised appreciation that makes the scene memorable.

Most of the scenes with Vivien Leigh's Scarlett O'Hara are like this. They are focused on her but they are focused *by* him—by his bemusement, his disbelief, his final enchantment: "Sir, you are no gentleman!" "And you, miss, are no lady." Once again he is the heroine's impresario—complimenting her on her "passion for living," making fun both of Ashley Wilkes' language and of Scarlett's romantic delusion. The running joke about Scarlett throughout the film, which Rhett invites us to share and enjoy, is how tough she is in spite of her ladylike airs, how utterly remote her real nature is from any kind of ladylike or "finer" feeling. The movie invites us to a complicity with Gable's vision of her— to that wised-up understanding common to all tough comedies.

By the time of *San Francisco* he was almost monolithically roguish, coming securely into his special looks and style in middle age as many stars do. And it's partly—paradoxically—that he's such a cheerless man, with something inconsolable at the center of his eyes and his performances, that his delight in these flamboyant women seems so momentous when it occurs. And his most popular movie—the most popular movie *ever*—reflects this same paradox. *Gone With the Wind*, too, has a somewhat uneasy relation to its own surfaces.

That movie offers a highly romanticized portrait of middle-class greed and ruthlessness ("I'll never be hungry again!" vows Scarlett, with a breathtaking camera pullback and angelic voices on the soundtrack), and yet consistently manages to imply possibilities *beyond* that view of things. There is, of course, the implied ideal of married love that makes Scarlett and Rhett's failure with each other all the sadder—that was conventional. But beyond that, there is the strong suggestion (as there is in the novel, too, of course) that Rhett's and our view of Scarlett—the wised-up one, without illusions—may be finally somehow wrong, that Melanie with her forgiveness and charity may in some mysterious way be closer to the truth about Scarlett than Rhett or any of us. This redemptive view of human nature is, we are aware, very different from the view of the movie we are watching and yet at the same time is always somehow implied by it. This is one of the things that make people think of the film as "epic." The movie teases seriousness in this way. It's a reductive epic, both hyped up and scaled down at the same moments. It achieves largeness in part by insisting on its own limits—like Gable himself.

So that in spite of all that's wrong with *Gone with the Wind*—its soap opera and stereotyping and racism, the letdown and sometimes leaden filmmaking of its lengthy second half—the movie has a genuine mythic feeling. After Scarlett

leaves the library at Twelve Oaks, where she has just been rebuffed by her beloved Ashley and then "insulted" by the maddening Rhett, she stops under the
stairway to hide and dry her tears—just as we hear, from voices offscreen, that
war has been declared. Scarlett hears only that people are coming. She composes herself and starts up the stairway, just as crowds of excited young people
come bursting through the doors behind her and down the stairs around her,
whooping and shouting and calling, and the bright strains of "Dixie" sound
stirringly over it all. The camera draws back to show Scarlett lifting her skirts
before her and moving steadily up and against the tide of movement and excitement. It's a powerful image of self-absorption in the midst of "history," sad and
oddly touching. And it's characteristic of the film that one of its grandest effects
and moments should be an image of the heroine missing the point.

THAT'S ANOTHER way in which Scarlett belongs to the tough-comedy style:
screwball heroines rarely miss the point. Screwball heroes, on the other
hand, often do. But screwball was a special kind of women's game, nearly always
favoring the heroine to win. It began more or less as a response to these heroines—that sort of woman star who was funny and glamorous at the same time
and numerous enough in the thirties to seem almost like a new type. And once
these comedies caught on in mid-decade, they dominated thirties movies the
same way film noir dominated movies of the late forties and early fifties: attract-
ing and inspiring the brightest talents in the business, so that, for a while at
least, it seemed to filmmakers that this style was where all the life was, that no
other kind of film was quite so contemporary, so up to date and exciting.

They turned these comedies out in such numbers that after the mid-thirties
"screwball" came to be a word people might use for *any* romantic comedy—
certainly if it had any trace of "craziness" to it. And yet everyone knew in a
general way what a screwball comedy was: both swanky and slapstick, slangy,
irreverent, and skeptical—and powerfully, glamorously "in love with love." As
in all such cycles, characters and situations tended to recur. The vogue proceeded by imitation, especially of those first resounding hits, *It Happened One
Night, The Thin Man, My Man Godfrey, Theodora Goes Wild*—with permutations
such as ghosts (*Topper*), the "sick joke" (*Nothing Sacred*), a pet leopard (*Bringing Up Baby*), and so on, which were imitated in their turn. (Not the leopard,
though: his film was a flop.) Most of these comedies were run-of-the-mill, and
many of them were much worse than that. There are no points for falling short
of intoxication, after all—only embarrassment and sour memories. And the
cycle, though bright, was short-lived; it began to die out in the early forties. But
even in the late forties and the fifties, as if refusing to believe the magic had
vanished, Hollywood still turned out occasional pictures about runaway heir-

esses, playful detective couples, crazy rich families, or small-town girls cutting loose in the city. Jane Wyman played the Dunne role in a 1953 remake of *The Awful Truth* (*Let's Do It Again*). June Allyson did the remakes of both *It Happened One Night* (*You Can't Run Away from It*, 1956) and *My Man Godfrey* (same title, 1957). And Leo McCarey himself remade *Love Affair* in 1957, at times reproducing the original line for line and shot for shot: *An Affair to Remember*, with Cary Grant and Deborah Kerr, in color and CinemaScope.

Nineteen thirty-four—the year of screwball's beginnings—was also the year that the studios, mainly in response to pressures from the Catholic Church and its Legion of Decency, began to enforce the Production Code. With the result that as comedies got "crazier," they also got cleaner. Some people see a connection: "Screwball" antics in this view were a kind of reaction to the growing repression. Screen lovers couldn't be sexy anymore, so they had to be funny— they had to do *something*, after all. But the fact is that sexy couples on the screen weren't up to that much even before 1934, since the explicitness of our own time was always out of the question. The main effect of the new prudery, at least at first, was to make filmmakers work harder at something most of them were al-

Life in Greenwich Village: Robert Montgomery, Robert Benchley, and Rosalind Russell in Live, Love and Learn.

ready practiced in: finding an acceptable code for their bawdier sexual messages. It's true that innuendoes got less blatant—there could be no more gags
like the one in *Lawyer Man* (1932) where William Powell looks down a girl's
dress while the cigar in his mouth rises slowly upward—but they certainly persisted, even proliferated. And audiences were as adept at reading meaningful
ellipses—like the fadeout on a kiss—as filmmakers were skilled at devising
them—the many ways of signaling a whore or a whorehouse, for example. In a
way, this indirection was just the sort of thing that Lubitsch had taught them
about. Though the new restrictions were especially hard on *him*, perhaps of all
the major filmmakers—if only because sex rather than "love" was so central to
his material. Both *The Merry Widow* (1934) and *Desire* (1936) had to be toned
down during their productions. And both of them still contained scenes and
lines (e.g., Dietrich placidly announcing to a very horny Gary Cooper that she
may put her hand in his pocket, when he doesn't know that she has hidden a
stolen necklace there) that would be unthinkable in a movie two years later—
about the time of *Bluebeard's Eighth Wife* (1938), in fact, a Lubitsch comedy
that almost certainly would have been better, less hectic and abrasive, if it could
have been bawdier.

In any case, if comedies got "crazier" as they got less raunchy, they also got
more persuasively romantic. Certainly the romantic comics were less inconve-
nienced by the burgeoning censorship than the proponents of the tough comedy
were. It was teams like Gable and Harlow and stars like Mae West who *really*
had to clean up their acts. And the tough comedy itself survived mainly by being
absorbed into the screwball mode, just as the classy comedy was more or less,
with its high-toned people and settings. The newspaper scene, that staple background of the tough comedy, became a standard locale for screwball. So did the
upper-class drawing room—and often in the same screwball movie, as when
heiress meets reporter.

Warner Brothers in the early thirties was the home of the tough comedy—
making more and better movies about mugs and dames, con men and golddig-
gers than anyone else. Warner films had a working-class look, with grainy, over-
exposed photography and conscientiously shabby interiors. And whether they
were comedies or melodramas or tearjerkers, they were short and fast-paced and
crammed with incident, with abrupt turns of plot and character, and surreal
juxtapositions of event.* As a studio style it worked best of all: Warners produced more good and interesting *ordinary* films than almost any other studio in

---

* Warner Brothers also had a line in sumptuous historical films, with George Arliss as Voltaire and Richelieu
or Dolores Del Rio as DuBarry. But even these films clipped along briskly—at least at first. They got
ponderous later on in the thirties, with *Anthony Adverse* in 1936 and Paul Muni playing Pasteur and Zola.
(One producer is supposed to have complained that "every time Muni parts his beard and looks down a
telescope we lose a million bucks.") It's ironic, but by the mid-forties, Warners was making the longest,
slowest pictures of anybody, and the fewest per year. For Jack Warner, it would seem, the alternative to being
brisk and hard-hitting was to be heavy and long-winded—and so he was.

the first half of the decade. But it wasn't a style that suited the screwball comedy. Nor were the Warner stars—Cagney and Davis, Robinson and Flynn and Bogart—exactly romantic-comedy types. As a result, Warners was the one major studio to be more or less untouched by the screwball craze. They turned out a few such comedies (you were hardly a movie studio if you didn't)—Bette Davis in *It's Love I'm After* (1937), a wacky spinoff of *The Guardsman* with Leslie Howard in the Alfred Lunt role; Errol Flynn and Olivia de Havilland in *Four's a Crowd* (1938), about the dizzy rich—but Warner screwball never quite worked, seeming both halfhearted and ham-fisted.

If Paramount was a studio where people of cultivation could feel somewhat at home, that was because it was so disorganized and poorly run. Warners was just the opposite—efficient, tyrannical, a kind of police state among studios.* The Warner operation didn't at all encourage the kind of relaxed filmmaking that screwball really thrived on. Nor would it ever have put up with directors like McCarey or La Cava—or even a Capra, with his notions and demands.

Screwball *did* thrive, however, at an almost equally regimented lot—at MGM. But then MGM had Powell and Loy and the *Thin Man* series, it had directors like Woody Van Dyke and producers like Hunt Stromberg and contract players like Robert Montgomery and Rosalind Russell and Melvyn Douglas (shared with Columbia)—and the Thalberg tradition of quality and class. It also had a studio history of sleek, glamorous comedy production dating from at least the beginning of talkies. And the MGM look—of gleaming amplitude, with its glossy high-key lighting and dreamlike art deco sets—might have been invented for the screwball comedy alone.

Columbia, of course, had just the wrong look for it: cramped and underlit and B-picturish most of the time. But that didn't really matter: it was also the studio that had Capra and Jean Arthur under exclusive contracts—and, when it could get them, McCarey and La Cava, Grant and Dunne and Colbert. Columbia and RKO were the poor branches of the major-studio family (Columbia isn't even listed as a major studio in some histories). But they were also more receptive to experiment, more tolerant of chaos on the set. It was at these two lesser "majors"—often moving back and forth between the two of them (both were less likely than the bigger studios to require exclusive contracts, with either stars or directors)—that nearly all the preeminent screwball directors did their important films: Hawks and La Cava and McCarey and Stevens. Paramount, the Lubitsch studio, was widely regarded as the most sophisticated, and certainly the

---

*It was also the place—judging from latterday reminiscences—where the "workers" seemed to have most fun, and to feel the greatest camaraderie. The writers, especially, remembered it fondly. "It was a great place for a writer," said Casey Robinson in 1974—partly because Jack Warner was too cheap to pay for rewrites and retakes. If you wrote something at Warners, it was likelier than at other studios to get onto the screen intact.

one with the heaviest investment in all kinds of comedy: the Marx Brothers and Mae West and W. C. Fields as well as Lombard and Colbert. But the Paramount comic directors of the mid- and late thirties—Lubitsch and Mitchell Leisen excepted—were a generally undistinguished group, and much less efficient than their counterparts at MGM.

Twentieth Century–Fox, like Warner Brothers, didn't seem to have much knack for the screwball comedy. But unlike Warner's, Fox kept trying, turning out great numbers of such films all through the time of their vogue. But Fox screwball always seemed imitative and pale, never first-rate or even quite convincing, except for the occasional performance (William Powell in *The Baroness and the Butler*, 1938) or screenplay (Nunnally Johnson's *Wife, Husband and Friend*, 1939). Fox comedies had a built-in handicap most of the time: instead of stars like Powell and Loy or Gable and Colbert, these films nearly always featured Tyrone Power or Loretta Young, either one or the other or both together. It's one of the oddities of Darryl Zanuck's tenure as studio production head that the contract stars—Loretta Young and Alice Faye, Tyrone Power and Don Ameche and Sonja Henie (the first ice-skating star)—were consistently so much less interesting than the stars at other studios. This problem may not have impaired John Ford's work as a director very much, but it was mortal to Gregory Ratoff's.

BUT WHETHER you did screwball well or not, you did it, it seems—especially if you were a woman star or even just a leading woman. So many women, like Dunne and Lombard and Arthur, had pulled off such transformations by "going screwball" that who was to say the magic wouldn't work for others? Almost everyone gave it a whirl: Margaret Sullavan as a madcap actress (*The Moon's Our Home*, 1936), Janet Gaynor as a con woman (*Young in Heart*, 1938), Joan Bennett as a kidnapped heiress (*She Couldn't Take It*, 1935), Virginia Bruce as a runaway one (*There Goes My Heart*, 1938), just like Madeleine Carroll and Merle Oberon and Wendy Barrie and dozens of others. Joan Crawford made *her* grim attempt on the escaped-heiress role in 1936 in *Love on the Run*; Bette Davis in 1941, in *The Bride Came C.O.D.*, opposite Cagney as the Gable-type hero, both of them looking too old and too short for their roles (she is trying to marry Jack Carson, and he is a pilot hired by her millionaire father, Eugene Pallette, to stop her). In fact, the willful, dizzy rich girl became such a familiar figure that audiences lost any sense of her being a type: it was a heroine role, and a billing above the title seemed nearly the only requirement for playing it. How else to explain Barbara Stanwyck as *The Mad Miss Manton* (1938), a madcap debutante trailing six chattering girlfriends in her giddy wake as she tries to solve a murder and outwit newspaperman Henry Fonda? (Stanwyck could of course act nearly anything, and she's not too bad even in this bizarre miscasting.)

On the whole, the biggest male stars in the screwball style were the "monogamous" ones—William Powell and Fred Astaire—who were identified with a single co-star. The roving types, who went from co-star to co-star, somehow made less impression, seemed more lightweight. Melvyn Douglas was in some ways the definitive leading man of these comedies. He was an established star, well liked by audiences, who worked steadily and often wonderfully (it's hard to imagine his performances in either *Theodora Goes Wild* or *Ninotchka* being improved on). He had charm and versatility, and yet he was somehow finally colorless. At MGM he often filled in for Powell (*Ninotchka*, for one instance, when Powell was ill), but he had none of the latter's irony or dry elegance. Still, it was just this odd neutrality that became a kind of advantage to Douglas's career. He was greatly in demand during the comedy craze—MGM and Columbia shared his contract, and in between times Paramount borrowed him. Talented as he was, it was almost always his woman co-star who made the occasion. Indeed, his name on a film was practically a *promise* of such an occasion. It was his women co-stars who made his whole career. He was the romantic comedy's prince consort.

Robert Montgomery was the other leading man at MGM, a farceur even more skilled than Douglas, more urbane, less stolid (he could never convincingly play the philistine types Douglas sometimes did), infinitely knowing and amused. With his bright-eyed, closed-mouth smile, his cat-with-the-canary expression, he was boyish and mischievous in a way that struck even him as slightly absurd—with his infantile profile and snub nose. But he could be ardent where Douglas could only be insinuating: open unguarded passion for the heroine was one of the young Montgomery's eagerest specialties. As the rake surprised by love in *But the Flesh Is Weak* (1932), making urgent unmercenary declarations to wrenlike Nora Gregor looking uncertain in her clinging silk gowns, he really seems radiant with the feelings he talks to her about—a mixture of passion and prankishness, both funny and touching at once.

He is even better in the screwball *Live, Love and Learn* (1938), sharing a Greenwich Village bohemianism with Rosalind Russell and Robert Benchley. For at least half the movie (the other half is more "serious") the three of them keep up a running exchange of low-key loony wisecracks that achieve a kind of gathering risibility: it's an in-group sound, a body of shared jokes and responses that the audience gets tuned into, too, and all having very much the sound of Benchley's *New Yorker* pieces. Though he doesn't get a screen credit, Benchley was said to have written (or rewritten, more likely) some parts of the film. And Montgomery is the perfect Benchley hero, so to speak—wry and offbeat, with an air of complacent derangement in his look and manner.

James Stewart in one of his rare early tough-guy roles—as the private eye of It's a Wonderful World, wit Claudette Colbert.

But, unlike Douglas, Montgomery never had a great screwball comedy. The vogue largely passed him by. Mostly, he didn't get the choice roles at MGM—and the ones he wanted and did get were the tour-de-force parts, like the killer with the hatbox in *Night Must Fall* (1937) or the gangster peer in *The Earl of Chicago* (1940). He got bored with the conventional romantic leads—he'd been partnering MGM ladies like Garbo and Shearer and Crawford since the beginning of talkies—and his comic playing begins to reflect a certain smugness. That was always his temptation: he was so clever and so conscious. The charm and buoyancy he showed in the early thirties are replaced in many of his later films by a kind of glum impassivity.

But then the men in screwball comedy were nearly always a greater casting problem than the women. Paramount, for example, may have had two of the greatest comic women, Colbert and Lombard—but it hadn't the men to go with them. Lombard and Fred MacMurray were a team at Paramount, but they were almost no one's idea (least of all Lombard's) of a good match-up. With Colbert the tactic was different: instead of one dim leading man, she was generally given two—MacMurray and Ray Milland (*The Gilded Lily*), or MacMurray and Robert Young (*The Bride Comes Home*), or Robert Young and Melvyn Douglas (*I Met Him in Paris*)—and even at that they had to borrow Young and Douglas.

But the dimness, as I've said, almost went with the job. The leading man of romantic comedy rarely had any limiting sort of background or identity. He could play a square or a playboy, a salesman or a jazz musician—none of them memorably but all without apparent strain. But he was on the whole an urban type. He didn't, or couldn't, play a hick or a rube. There was another line of player—less important to the screwball style—who could, of course: the Gary Cooper line. More homespun and boyish types like Henry Fonda and James Stewart. These actors, however, did play the city types from time to time: Fonda is a smart-talking newsman in *The Mad Miss Manton*, for example, and Stewart is a terrific hard-bitten private eye in *It's a Wonderful World* (1939). But on the whole they were the Capra hero sort—small-town boys at heart, if not always in fact.

Probably Joel McCrea belongs to this line. He was known in Hollywood as "the other Gary Cooper"—the first one they thought of for any role that Cooper turned down. But McCrea really *isn't* a Capra type, at least in the sense that it's very hard to imagine him in a Capra role. He is too direct, too gruff even—and too lacking in self-consciousness. He is utterly incapable of pathos or winsomeness. A cowboy hero like Cooper—he was so immensely tall and good-looking that Anita Loos once claimed to have fainted when she saw him striding out of the sun on a beach one day. But the startling handsomeness has a slightly pinched, slightly gimlet-eyed quality, too—Apollo crossed with a small-town storekeeper—and the reverse of Cooper's lambency. That paradox, however, is a clue to McCrea's complication. He is unflappably good-natured, for example, but always with the threat of something irascible as well. In repose, he has an odd serene grumpiness.

He is so self-contained and withdrawn at times that whatever feelings surface on his face tend to surprise us, though they're always convincing. He keeps us guessing in a lot of his films. In the intensely screwball *Woman Chases Man* (1937) with Miriam Hopkins, he is either cautious with his millions or wildly spendthrift, depending on how many drinks he's had. In both *Chance at Heaven* (1933) and *The Richest Girl in the World* (1934) he is poor, with a real uncertainty—hard on the heroine—as to whether he'll be mercenary in his love life or romantic. Probably his best pre-Sturges role is Huntley Haverstock, the hero of Alfred Hitchcock's *Foreign Correspondent* (1940). McCrea evokes Hitchcock's comic-absurdist world with uncanny pitch and accuracy, establishing just the right bemused tone at the center of the film. "Well . . . we meet again," he says to a startled dowager after crawling through a bathroom window in his underwear and robe (killers on his trail). Then adds helpfully: "Quite a lot has happened since I last saw you." He hasn't the irony of the great urbane heroes like Grant and Powell, but he has his own kind of comic aplomb. He was one of the most ubiquitous leading men of the thirties, appearing in every kind of film and playing nearly every kind of hero; but it wasn't until the forties, in his films with Preston Sturges, that audiences would see how interesting and original a figure he was.

Cary Grant in
Bringing Up
Baby: *he's lost
his glasses but
acquired a
negligee—as
May Robson
and the maid
have clearly
noticed.*

Cary Grant | 14

*Willing but not forward, Cary Grant must be the most publicly seduced male
the world has known, yet has never become a public joke. . . . Cary Grant is
the male love object. Men want to be as lucky and enviable as he is—they
want to be like him. And women imagine landing him. . . . Cary Grant has
said that even he wanted to be Cary Grant. . . . [He] has had the longest
romantic reign in the short history of movies.*
     —PAULINE KAEL, "The Man from Dream City"

*Everyone tells me I've had such an interesting life, but sometimes I think it's
been nothing but stomach disturbances and self-concern.*
     —CARY GRANT

GRANT, a cockney, began his career in London music halls as an acrobat-comic named Archie Leach. He came to America and appeared in musicals in New York: he was in *Boom Boom* with Jeanette MacDonald in 1929. From Broadway he went to Hollywood in 1931. At Paramount, in his early days as a leading man, he appeared with the sort of women who necessarily took center screen: Dietrich in her von Sternberg phase, and Mae West. A strong handsome presence, he was also discreet, complaisant, infinitely obliging in the way he occupied the background of a scene, the foreground of his co-star's attention. He partnered all the big Paramount women: Nancy Carroll on her way down (*Hot Saturday* in 1932 and *A Woman Accused* in 1933) and Sylvia Sidney on her way up (*Madame Butterfly* in 1932 and *Thirty Day Princess* in 1934). By the time he "appeared" in the multistar cast of *Alice in Wonderland* in 1933, audiences knew who he was even behind impenetrable makeup—as the Mock Turtle, singing "Beautiful Soup." Like W. C. Fields as Humpty Dumpty in the same film, or Gary Cooper as the White Knight, he was a recognizable star if only by the sound of his voice.

Mae West took one look at him on the Paramount lot—so the story goes—and demanded him for her leading man, first in *She Done Him Wrong* and then in *I'm No Angel* (both 1933), her two best films. And Grant, as always, makes the star look good, looming over her nicely, his romantic style leavening her brashness. But West was tough on leading men—their discomfort was part of her joke. The joke works better, though, with Warren William or Randolph Scott: in those cases where the man seems a little fat-headed. With Grant, it just seems wrong, and discomfiting. At one point in *I'm No Angel* he has to sit clasping her on a piano bench while she and her constantly chortling "colored maid" exchange appreciative and bawdy comments about him. This—like Dixiebelle without *any* restraints—really isn't his style, even back then. The best he could do was be a good sport about it. But the smile he wears through most of the film—offered to West as she tosses off her one-liners and *meant* to be amused and admiring—is the sort usually described as "shit-eating." "I could be your slave," he says. "Well," she says, "I guess that could be arranged." And so on.

He can't be aggressive like Gable, but he can't exactly be passive, either, as

the West films show. He has none of Gary Cooper's ingrown, sensuous, dreamy quality, as von Sternberg captured it in *Morocco* (1930). In fact, von Sternberg tries a similar enterprise with Grant in *Blonde Venus* (1932), but it misfires. The director's gleams and highlights and soft-focus lenses bring out something essential and vital in the personalities of Cooper and Dietrich, but they just make Grant look out of focus, baffled, and hidden.

If nothing quite worked, he was still a workhorse in his early Paramount days. In 1934, the screwball year, he appeared in five movies (his yearly average at the time), all of them routine, and three of them built around women players who were much less prominent than he was: Frances Drake in *Ladies Should Listen* and Elissa Landi in *Enter Madame* and Helen Mack and Genevieve Tobin in *Kiss and Make Up*. Audiences might go to see Cary Grant partnering a woman even when they didn't care about the woman that much. It wasn't until George Cukor's *Sylvia Scarlett* (1936), on a loan-out to RKO, that something besides the prototypical leading man emerged, with Grant playing the supporting role of a lively but rather sleazy cockney entertainer. Audiences shunned the movie,

though—one of the biggest disasters in RKO's disaster-strewn history. And yet, while it certainly hurt Katharine Hepburn (who did a male impersonation in it), the word about Grant's performance was very good indeed. By the end of 1936, Grant had quit Paramount and signed a joint contract, including script approval, with both Columbia and RKO. He'd hated the work he'd been doing at his home studio, and in the next fifteen years he managed to work at every major studio *but* Paramount.

At first it looked as though he'd taken his chains with him. Since the first script he "approved" at Columbia was a leading-man job of particular dimness, a wheezing Grace Moore vehicle called *When You're in Love* (1937). (The attraction for Grant must have been Robert Riskin, who both wrote the screenplay and directed—the only film he ever did direct.) And at RKO the same year, Grant played second lead to Edward Arnold in *The Toast of New York*, a fictionalized account of the career of Jim Fisk. *Both* these films were notable, and expensive, failures. Like Carole Lombard, another Paramount workhorse, Grant was a well-liked, even popular star who had never had a very good picture, let alone a hit. And like Lombard, too—though a bit later than she—Grant was saved by the screwball comedy. His *other* two movies in 1937 were *Topper* and *The Awful Truth*.

Topper—produced for MGM by Hal Roach and directed by Norman Z. McLeod—came first and was a terrific hit. It had novelty (all those special effects with the ghosts) and glamour and modishness: its central idea was that the sort of witty couple who'd taken over the movies should now take over life and death, in a witty, offhand way, of course, materializing as sportive ghosts. The script derived from a 1926 novel by Thorne Smith, a prolific and popular writer who specialized in mildly risqué fantasies of the supernatural: the ancient gods coming to earth for a party, or a husband and wife magically changing sexes, and so on. George and Marion Kerby (Grant and Constance Bennett) are a rich, high-living couple who die suddenly when George runs their sports car into a tree. They resolve before leaving earth to do one good deed—to save the timorous and henpecked Topper (Roland Young) from a life of dull servitude to his bank and his wife (Billie Burke). As ghosts, the Kerbys are as high-living as ever, but subject to invisibility. The main action of the film is the redemption of Topper to playfulness and freedom—teaching him to drink and brawl and generally disgrace himself, with spiritual aid.

It's really Roland Young's movie, as the reviews praising his performance duly noted. But Grant and Bennett are a memorable couple. Although Bennett had lost her dominance as a star by this time (Hal Roach was one of the last big filmmakers to gamble on her), she never had more authority or stylishness. She is small and gleaming and sinuous: her body, draped in glittering bias-cut gowns, droops in a dramatic art-deco curve from shoulders to slightly out-thrust hips. She leans back, against a piano or a husband, with her long elegant fingers splayed and upraised, like someone who is always drying her nail polish. The effect is both voguish and feline. Grant, the one she leans into, is as big and dark as she is slight and fair. And there is something feline about him, too—a hint of danger, a look of sheathed-claw contentment. They look so smashing together that the production stills are almost better—certainly more elegant and suggestive—than the movie is. Grant's role, practically a supporting one, doesn't give him much to do, but with it he becomes an icon of thirties glamour and fun.

And with *The Awful Truth* he becomes a major star. And just the performance he was afraid of giving—afraid it would make him look foolish—turns him into the Cary Grant we all know. It's not hard, in retrospect, to understand his nervousness: only the screwball women were giving this kind of performance, being sexy and funny in the same roles, with the kind of abandon McCarey was asking *him* for now—risky indeed for a romantic leading man to attempt. But Grant pulls it off: a virtuoso screwball performance, full of slapstick, loony antics, impeccable timing, and breathtaking wit. No leading man had done anything quite like this before. And never before, oddly enough, had *this* leading man seemed so powerfully romantic as he did now in this all-out screwball style. It was this kind of performing that was Cary Grant's breakthrough, just as it had been for the great women stars before him—a fulfillment and a liberation.

THE ONLY male star to spring full-blown and solo (without an identifying co-star, that is) from the screwball mode. A slapstick farceur, a clown really, whose name became and remains the synonym for masculine glamour. Grant was not only the greatest leading man of his time—he was different from all the others.

Norman Mailer in 1960 described the male movie star ideal as the sort who "could fight well, kill well (if always with honor), love well and love many, be cool, be daring, be dashing, be wild, be wily, be resourceful, be a brave gun." It's a nearly unarguable list in its way. It certainly fits Mailer's examples—stars like Cagney, Flynn, and Bogart. But not much of it fits Grant, who is nobody's "brave gun," who is not even "dashing" in the way that Mailer evokes. One of the oddest and most interesting things about Grant is how he manages at once to be a paradigm of masculinity and yet at the same time to elude and even to defy most of the categories of the masculine romance.

The defiance wouldn't be open, of course—that wouldn't be his style. But what audiences felt about him very strongly was his elusiveness. And some of his most interesting films seem to be about just that—especially Alfred Hitchcock's *Suspicion* (1941). The movie-long question about the Grant hero in this

*Cary Grant
with Ethel
Barrymore in
Clifford Odets'
None but the
Lonely Heart.*

one is whether he's a killer or not, whether he's about to kill the heroine just as he may have killed others before her. In the novel (*Before the Fact* by Francis Iles) he *was* a killer; but in Hitchcock's original plan for the film, it was all to be in the wife's neurotic imagination. And the movie went into production without anyone having a clear idea how it would end (the exact reverse of Hitchcock's usual procedure, and a situation he detested) or who exactly the hero was. There was general agreement that Cary Grant couldn't be a murderer, just as there seemed equally no question he could be a man you could take for one. In the film's final scene he is revealed to be innocent, and the heroine's fears about him to be quite groundless—all a misunderstanding. Almost everyone involved in the movie felt they had a disaster on their hands; Hitchcock was sure of it.

That wasn't how it turned out, though—and mostly because of Grant. This virtually unplayable role—with no definition or center, where everything is ambiguous and teasing and ultimately misleading, all foreshadowing with no payoff—turns out to suit him beautifully. *Suspicion* succeeds partly as a movie about Cary Grant's equivocal quality. The melodramatic possibility of his being a murderer becomes almost a metaphoric way of exploring his complication. There is, after all, something dangerous, menacing even, in the charm, and quite different from the equivalent qualities in Cagney or Gable. But we also know that the danger isn't criminality. It's only *like* it.

What it is is anger—at least in part. If Gable seems disconsolate at his heart, Grant seems fierce. It's that note of deep-settled anger that arms and energizes him, that separates him so markedly from the other farceurs and sophisticates— from the world of elegant chat and drawing-room bitchery, from Noel Coward, even from Lubitsch. Grant's ironies seem challenging, his intelligence danger- ous, never light and spinning, never fooling or trivial. Of course, he never—or rarely—*expresses* anger: he only glows with it. And he pays close attention to whoever is speaking, giving the clear impression that he'd *like* them to make sense. He illustrates "throwing your weight around" better almost than anyone else on the screen: putting his hands in his pockets and tucking his chin in and bearing down on a fluttering Hepburn in *The Philadelphia Story* (1940). He likes to move in on people this way; and, like Hepburn, they usually panic and give way. Only once—in his most untypical film—is he matched to an actor with an equivalent angry force, even a similar sort of gleam in the eye: Ethel Barrymore in *None But the Lonely Heart* (1944). They are mother and son in a cockney slum—like two hooded giants, at odds with themselves and each other, mis- trustful and sardonic and grudgingly attached. They are especially eloquent when they are dissembling their feelings for each other: Barrymore's pleasure at his appearance in a new suit of clothes, his pleasure at her reaction, both turning aside from the other. And in the early scenes between them, when the dominant note is a kind of challenge and bitterness over the past, the pain is almost over- whelming. "Mean to do my best for you, Ma love," says Grant, moving in on her with chest out and shoulders squared. He grins down at her and she strikes him across the face—to our relief.

Grant's fierceness makes even his mildest, most uninflected remarks echo troublingly at times. "You wouldn't actually want to live on your wife's allow- ance, would you?" says Joan Fontaine in *Suspicion*. "Of course not, darling," he replies flatly and without hesitation, his gaze on her unwavering. But neither she nor we are at all sure what he *has* said: the reply is almost *too* uninflected. "You always give me the feeling that you're laughing at me," says Fontaine. And we know what she means. But we also know that he's not exactly laughing at *her*, though we're less sure who or what he is laughing at. And he makes this uncer- tainty seem like a weapon—even, at times, one directed at himself. "I'm told that the sight of an eligible male is a rare treat in this part of the country," he says to Fontaine again, upon first meeting her, stepping from a group of women and "presenting" himself to her. But he inflects the flippancy with something not only mocking but faintly chilling, and an effect that might have been just playful or even a bit arch—the practiced charmer coming on both strong and "cute"—is instead disquieting. Even in less ambiguous roles than this one, he promotes uneasiness, both on the screen and in his audience. Where other stars—if only by their familiarity—may make us feel calmed and reassured, Grant may make us feel edgy, watchful, challenged.

He is dangerous. But it's not violence he threatens us or the other characters with, but a certain knowledge. He is often cast as a figure of conscience, or at least of consciousness. If he isn't a bounder making comfortable people nervous, as in *Suspicion*, he is an idealist of some sort making them guilty: Ingrid Bergman in *Notorious* (1946), or Ronald Colman in *The Talk of the Town* (1942), or Hepburn's snobbish family in *Holiday* (1938), or Hepburn herself in *The Philadelphia Story* (1940). But whenever his movies make an attempt to specify that idealism, to give him a nameable commitment or ideology, something goes wrong. He is simply unbelievable as a radical agitator in George Stevens' *The Talk of the Town*. And as a Leo McCarey patriot in *Once Upon a Honeymoon* (1942), reproving the Nazis for their birth-control policies and encouraging Ginger Rogers' dormant Americanism, he is mostly just embarrassing. The Cary Grant "conscience," like the anger, seems nondenominational.

He's a kind of intelligence on the loose—threatening to all, even to himself. A kind of uncontrolled alertness—like a moral insomniac, he pays attention even when he doesn't want to. The fierceness is a function of the alertness. He moves among dissemblers and sleepwalkers. He is sardonic but *never* waspish: the playfulness is always a serious matter, even at times a grave one. He uses line readings the way other heroes use fists or guns: to bust the place up. "You hardly know him," says Hepburn about the twit she's going to marry in *The Philadelphia Story*. "Well, to hardly know him is to know him well," says Grant. The one they're talking about is Kittredge (John Howard), a self-made man, as we call them, and a fake. Kittredge is also fatally prim. He thinks, mistakenly, that Tracy (Hepburn) has spent the night before their wedding with another man. Dexter (Grant)—who is in love with Tracy himself, of course, and so rather happy with the way things are working out—advises Kittredge not to "be too hard on her." "I'll make up my own mind what I'll do!" snaps Kittredge. Grant gives him a sidelong look, both pleased and disbelieving: this guy is even worse than he supposed. "Well," he says—and the smile promises a lot—"we're all only *human*, you know." As Grant says it, it's a line that explodes in several directions at once—against Kittredge, against Tracy and himself, even against the sort of person who might say such a line and *mean* it—as if being "human" could be an excuse for anything.

Not in *his* view, certainly—not with the look he gives Kittredge, or turns on the world in general. A look that penetrates excuses and shams—and signals in a way his own isolation. There's a clue to that isolation in George Stevens' *Penny*

Serenade (1941). Grant is showing his wife (Irene Dunne) their new home. As they enter the bedroom, she walks into the foreground of the shot, while Grant in the background removes a kitten from a lounge chair and sits down in it yoga-style, with crossed ankles. As he does so, he raises the kitten to his mouth and kisses it on the top of its head—*smack*, quite audibly—before settling back into the chair. It's only one detail in a flow of details and given no particular emphasis. What's most interesting about it in a way is that it is almost unnoticeable—as it certainly would not have been if a Gable or a Cooper had kissed that kitten. Nor does the gesture seem, with Grant doing it, the slightest bit winsome or ingratiating. Any more than it does when he gets down on his hands and knees to play with Asta in *The Awful Truth*. Or when he steps back with the baby in his arms in *Penny Serenade* in order to say a few urgent unsounded words into its ear while Dunne is going to the door to let the social worker in. We're reminded at such moments of just how guarded and defended this supremely confident man is—guarded, that is, with other humans and other grown-ups: kissing the kitten before addressing himself to his wife, whispering to the baby before facing the social worker.

There's something disconnected about him, detached from ordinary life. His power on the screen—his exceptional forcefulness—seems to come from something besides the usual and conventional springs of human feeling and motive: sex or greed, love or ambition, et cetera. It even seems remote from ordinary egotism. He is the only major romantic star to play both a ghost (*Topper*) and an angel (*The Bishop's Wife*, 1947), and both convincingly. In direct contacts he is oblique and evasive, but in oblique ones he is devastating. One of his most distinctive talents is for being a sardonic bystander. In *The Philadelphia Story*, among his best performances, he doesn't so much act or do things on screen as send out a field of force, grounding Hepburn and the others with his piercing common-sense presence, with his gleaming eye and sort of smile.

George Stevens' *Gunga Din* (1939), a rousing comic adventure film "based" on Kipling, makes Grant's human disconnection more emphatic than ever. In the movie's trio of swashbuckling heroes—Douglas Fairbanks, Jr., and Victor McLaglen are the others—he is the only one without "ties." Fairbanks has his girl, Joan Fontaine, and McLaglen has his pet elephant. Grant, however, is the one with the greatest and zaniest energies—the most acrobatic and demented, with his cockney bravado and rolling sailor's walk, his straight-backed crouch and high whinny of excitement. It's an unrestrained comic performance and the closest he ever comes to playing an authentic crazy man, full of life and fun and a weird lunar isolation at the center of it all. Fairbanks, torn between his loyalty to his buddies and his engagement to Fontaine, is the movie's romantic hero. Grant is really a version of the comic (and sexless) sidekick. A triumph of inhumanity.

That's one reason—paradoxically—that we come to trust him on the screen. We know he'll never cop a plea the way more sentimental performers do: "We're all only *human*, you know." That he won't be arch or smarmy or ingratiating. We're even surprised when he turns out to be macho, as he does in Howard Hawks's *Only Angels Have Wings* (1939). He's a barnstorming pilot, running an airline of flying "crates" in the Andes, the sort of flyer who goes up himself "only when he thinks it's too tough for anyone else." He wears a sombrero, white flaring trousers, and a pistol belt, spends most of the movie giving men orders or quelling their resistance or fending off the heroine's romantic advances.

And there's no overlay of lunacy here, as there is in *Gunga Din*. It's all deadly serious in its boys'-adventure way. But because it's a Howard Hawks film, it's infused by the actors'—and particularly the stars'—personalities and systems of behavior. The role of Jeff Carter, the hero, is as much tailored to fit Cary Grant as he exerts himself to fit it: the final result, odd as it is, is hard to take your eyes off of. Making us aware, for one thing, of how much simultaneous abandon and reserve Grant gets into a typical gesture. He crouches in front of a woman he hasn't seen for a long time, as if to catch her—though we know he's *not* going to catch her, that thanks to the crouch, in fact, he's not even touching her. His most expansive movements are inflected with constraint. Waving a doomed pilot off from the doorway of the flight shack, he makes a huge sweeping arc with his arm; but the gesture is puppetlike, the arm stiff and straight: a subtext of disbelief. The entire performance has this double-take quality: is this *me?* Then again, why not? He conveys the feeling that he'll give anything a try—that he has his doubts but, more important than that, he's having fun. And he makes the feeling infectious.

But even playing this familiar hero—perhaps most of all *this* hero—he makes us edgy. One of the most attractive things about Grant's career—especially at his peak, in the late thirties and early forties, long before he started walking through most of his roles—is the way he makes us look at these heroes. The stardom of Cary Grant is a visible demonstration—one of the most heartening the movies have to offer—of just how savingly subversive a sense of humor can be. He looks and seems like a macho ideal; he's forceful, manly and athletic, authoritative and aggressive. And yet he's never right in such roles, never really convincing. Or convinced. He can't quite manage the faith required—a faith that other stars of the time possessed without effort, as did their audiences. But that fiercely humorous sort of masculine intelligence that Grant embodies above everyone, with its angry helpless clarity, is very hard on the "brave gun" ideal. Grant's version of this figure, in *Gunga Din*, is a clown and a madman. And in *Only Angels Have Wings*, his "cool," "daring," "resourceful" type—to use Mailer's categories again—is infused with mockery and playfulness and fundamental skepticism. Just the "values," in fact, of the screwball comedy.

Howard hawks' *Bringing Up Baby* (1938), with Grant and Katharine Hepburn, was one of the greatest of these comedies. It was also a box office disaster. It cost Hawks his contract with RKO (he had let the picture go way over budget) and ultimately his chance to do *Gunga Din*, also with Grant. It finished Hepburn's career at the same studio—the one flop too many that did it for her.

It didn't, however, seem to hurt Grant—but then, nothing did in those days. He had just done *The Awful Truth*. *Bringing Up Baby* even contains a spoken reference to the earlier film, at a time when such cross-references, especially to a rival studio's picture, were rare and even frowned upon: Hepburn tells the sheriff that Grant's real "moniker" is "Jerry the Nipper," the same name Dunne had given him in her scene with the Vances. (Hepburn's name in the film is also Vance.) And Asta is in this screwball movie too—playing a dog named George.

Marvelous as *Bringing Up Baby* seems to audiences now, it was more than they could take, apparently, in 1938. Reviewers said it was screwball gone *too* far—it was too silly and crazy. For one thing, there was the plot. . . . David

Huxley (Grant) is a paleontologist who is reconstructing a dinosaur skeleton. He is also going to get married the next day—to a Miss Swallow (Virginia Walker)—though he tends to forget this. Just as he nearly forgets, until stern Miss Swallow reminds him, that he has a golf date with a lawyer named Peabody, who may give him the money he needs to finish his brontosaurus. But on the golf course David is distracted from both his game and Mr. Peabody (George Irving) by a young woman (Hepburn) who insists on sinking his ball (she thinks it's hers) and then driving off in his car (she thinks that's hers too). That night at the country club he runs into her again—she drops an olive and he slips on it—and she tears his coat.

What's maddening about her is her unconsciousness. "Oh you've torn your coat," she says with dismay, holding onto it by one of the tails she has just ripped in two. Without meaning to, of course. She is the dizzy rich girl—just as he is the absent-minded professor, complete with horn-rimmed spectacles (Hawks had told him to model the character on Harold Lloyd). But there is one ominous difference, from the moment this dizzy rich girl enters the movie—striding across the golf course in full beautiful sail, with hair streaming and golf club swinging. She is almost awesomely self-assured. And unreachable. For one thing, she never really understands what he's going on about—when he is trying to get his golf ball back. And after all, as she points out to him, "it's only a game." He seems to take it *very* seriously. So it seems to *her*, at any rate. And now he is standing on the running board of the car, even refusing to get down, just as she is preparing to drive off. He keeps saying it's *his* car. "*Your* ball, *your* car," she says incredulously, "is there anything in the world that doesn't belong to you?" And she drives off, with the madman on the running board gesticulating and shouting as they go.

Her name is Susan Vance. She is disoriented, of course. In the wrong—even "dumb." But it should be noted that she does win that golf game—and also that she is the one who drives off with the car. Her complacency is crazy, but it's not, it would seem, unwarranted. It even suggests a certain mastery of reality. The movie never condescends to this heroine the way *My Man Godfrey* condescends to Lombard, or even the way *It Happened One Night* does to Colbert. Hepburn's slaphappy rich girl will never have to learn about dunking or piggybacking or common life—or, apparently, much of anything else. She not only won't be condescended to—in some infuriating way, she *can't* be.

David is angry about his tailcoat. She gets angry in turn—they are in a foyer of the country club—and starts to walk away from him in a huff. But just at that moment he is standing on the train of her evening gown—inadvertently tearing it off. "Get behind me, get behind me!" she cries—when she discovers, after some moments of bickering and misunderstanding, that her entire backside is now exposed to public view. Instantly, he claps himself into place behind her, they hold onto each other desperately, front to back, and march out: one of the most famously funny scenes of the movie decade—moving forward in a kind of spastic lockstep, Grant wearing his crushed top hat and Hepburn her glassiest public smile, as they shuttle through the buzzing and startled patrons of the country club to the revolving door and out. This movement is so sudden and demented it leaves you gasping—like one of your worst dreams of embarrassment coming to sudden demonic life. The effect is like something out of the Marx Brothers' sublimest moments: Harpo's mad lurching tiptoe when he is being Groucho's mirror image in *Duck Soup*, or "Doctor" Groucho's little dance of embarrassment when he discovers he's been taking his own pulse ("Either this man is dead or my watch has stopped") in *A Day at the Races*.

But there's more than a mad comic inspiration in this slapstick moment; there's also an important transaction between the hero and heroine. David— who has been telling Susan that he only wants her to go away and leave him alone, who really doesn't even *know* this woman apart from unhappy accidents (if that's what they are) like this one—is still suspiciously prompt in responding to her call for help. "Get behind me!" she cries, and he is already in place and ready to go, on their mad spastic progress to the door, through an aghast public assemblage. It's true that he accidentally tore her dress—but it's more than that, almost as if he felt implicated in some way in her embarrassment, as if he were even drawn to it—he is so ready to join her public predicament. In any case, it turns out that she knows Mr. Peabody. The man is her aunt's lawyer, in fact. To Susan, however, he is known as "Boopie"—and she insists on making amends to David by taking him directly to Boopie's house for a talk. Never mind the hour: Boopie won't mind—and, anyway, she knows exactly which room he sleeps in. As she tells David when neither Boopie nor anyone else responds to the doorbell. A simple matter to go round to the back of the enormous and stately home and throw pebbles at the bedroom window. David stands beside her, transfixed and looking upward, as she picks up a rock and prepares to throw it at the bedroom window. "I know I should run," he says dreamily—just before Boopie gets creamed with the rock—"but somehow I can't."

Of course he can't. They have been tied together by that mad Marxian lockstep out of the country club as surely as they could be by anything. The screwball equivalent of music and moonlight and a fadeout kiss: a moment of transcendent—and shared—social embarrassment. He hardly understands it himself, and he tries to put it into words when they are saying good night; after the country club and the stoning of Boopie, she is letting him off at his place— seeing him to the door, as it were. Once again he asks her to leave him alone. She is stricken, and he tries to explain. "In moments of quiet," he concedes, "I'm strangely drawn to you, but—well . . . there haven't *been* any quiet moments."

This way of seeing his dilemma is certainly confirmed by what happens next. Susan has a leopard named Baby in her New York apartment, sent from Brazil by her explorer brother. Still, there's no use in getting *excited* about it, as David is doing. She is rigorously logical, as usual: "The *point* is I have a leopard, the *question* is what am I going to do with it?" But there are no easy answers to this question. "I don't like leopards!" cries David, rather weakly, as Baby flings his powerful body against his legs. "David, I think you've found a real friend," says Susan, with one of her most radiant smiles—though she does suggest that he stand still. "Let *him* stand still!" cries David. "Don't be silly, David"—it's her patient manner—"you can't make a leopard stand still."

You can't, as it turns out, make a leopard do anything. Unless you sing to it. The particular song that mollifies Baby when he's excited or upset is "I Can't Give You Anything but Love, Baby." "This is probably the silliest thing that ever happened to me," says David; but he sings, loud and often. And whenever Baby is placated in this way, his purring thrums on the soundtrack like an ominous and fearful alarm. "Just think of him as being a housecat," advises Susan, unflappable as always. "Well, I—I don't like cats, either," says David, in his terror. Too bad. "Baby" *is* a baby—and they are stuck with him. All Susan can think to do with him now is to take him to Connecticut. All David wants to do is to be left alone—he is getting married, after all. "I will not be involved in any more of your harebrained schemes," he says firmly. And certainly *he* would never have gone to Connecticut too, if Baby hadn't gotten out of the apartment and followed him down Park Avenue.

The auto trip to Connecticut is also eventful. Among other things, Susan runs into a poultry truck and Baby gets loose and devours most of its contents. You'd never have had to pay for those swans, she tells David as they drive on at last, "if you'd run as I told you to." "Susan," he replies patiently, "when a man is wrestling a leopard in the middle of a pond, he's in no position to run." He's acquiring, we notice, her sort of reasonableness—at least in conversation. But his ordeals have just begun. At her aunt's country house, she steals his clothes while he is in the shower (she's trying to prevent him from returning to Miss Swallow). So that David is obliged to answer the door—it is the aunt returning home—in a negligee he found. This aunt (May Robson), it turns out, is the same woman who was supposed to give a million dollars to David's museum. "Oh, David!" exclaims Susan. "Well, I'm afraid that you've made a rather unfavorable impression. . . ." She is thinking of the negligee. While he was making that impression, and the commotion that went with it, George (Asta)—it is soon discovered—had slipped into the room and stolen the irreplaceable dinosaur bone David had brought with him. "My intercostal clavicle!" This means that they have to start following George around, encouraging him to dig the bone up again. Even, at times, helping him to dig. An activity which inspires the aunt to ask once again just who this young man *is*. He's a big-game hunter, says Susan. "You call that big-game hunting?" demands the aunt, as David is glimpsed on all fours, pursuing George around a tree in the garden.

"Now, George, we're not angry," coaxes Susan, as they kneel before the impassive little dog. "That's David's bone. Now Susan'll get you a nice fresh bone if you'll just show us where it is." But David is hopeless. "He's not paying a *bit* of attention!" he says, in a rage just to think about it. But just then George runs to a tree and starts to dig. They fall to the ground beside him. He has something, it seems. "Oh, look, David—a boot!" exclaims Susan. "A *boot!*" echoes David, in a rage of disgust—and he raises the thing threateningly over her head. "Don't hit George, David," she says. He is ready to kill: "I wasn't gonna hit *George!*" he snarls. But he throws the boot down.

He has—understandably—these outbursts quite often. Just contemplating the imperturbable George can do it to him: "Oh *look* at the nasty little cur!" he cries—from the heart. It is too much. Just as *she* is. But all this rage is making a change in him nonetheless. Before he had reason to feel it—before Susan and Baby and George came along, before he slipped on that olive or got his coat torn or got leaned on by a leopard or had his intercostal clavicle stolen by a dog— David was a wimp, feeble and dithering and henpecked. But this murderousness does something for him. It snaps him into focus until he almost leaps off the screen at us. It even turns him into Cary Grant—with eyeglasses.

But that night Baby gets away. And so they must go into the forest to look for him. This is the most overtly dreamlike of all the film's episodes. They come upon Baby and George playing together in a clearing in the moonlight, for example. And Baby himself is dangerously replicated when Susan releases another leopard who looks exactly like him but who is a killer. But this nighttime forest sequence is also in some ways the movie's most *prosaic* section. As Susan and David prowl and crawl through bushes and brambles, fall into ditches and get drenched in streams, the movie gives a sense of difficulty and impediment, of physical intractability, that we haven't gotten before. For the first time—and even though she carries a butterfly net trailing lyrically behind her—Susan is involved in the physical awkwardness. When she loses one of her high-heeled shoes, she limps ecstatically and chants: "I was born on the side of a hill." When she and David actually tumble down the side of a hill, they land in sitting positions at the bottom of it, with her butterfly net fallen over his head. She looks at him and laughs—a little cascade of mirth, with her head up and her mouth open. David glares at her through the net. By this time he has been through too much to attempt to remove this impediment: he understands why it's there, he even understands why it may be hopeless to try to remove it. He is thinking, as it turns out, about choking her to death.

But the clue to the way the whole movie works is in this image, this shot of

Grant and Hepburn sitting at the bottom of the hill. His face—through the butterfly net—is sharp, intent, menacing. Hers is all diffuse radiance and airy incomprehension—like her laughter. And they nearly always look this way when they're together: with Hepburn as dreamily free-floating as Grant is locked in a terrible fixity.

But then it's precisely Grant's fixed steady rage that holds the slapdash structure of the movie together, that even makes most of the jokes work as well as they do (particularly the ones about the leopard). If *Bringing Up Baby* finally seems more than an inventive and occasionally inspired funny movie, seems a lucid and coherent and oddly inevitable experience, it's primarily because the movie, too, is locked into Cary Grant's fixity. We are inside his rage and confusion and frustration at all times, inside his "sanity"—but also inside his helpless complicity with the craziness that oppresses him. David may be a nebbish and a clown, but he has Cary Grant's solidity and gravity, his strange seriousness of spirit. So that even the silliest situation seems somehow, and mysteriously, to matter.

Grant's partnership with Hepburn here is different from those with the leading women in his other great comedies—with Dunne in *The Awful Truth* or Rosalind Russell in *His Girl Friday* (1940)—where he is in competition with a heroine whose wit and skills match or even outdistance his own. In *Bringing Up Baby* the hero presumes from the beginning a superiority to the ditzy heroine—of sanity and reasonableness—which turns out not to exist, or at least not to matter if it does. With Hepburn's Susan he is not in competition but simply out of his depth. So are we. She makes us, like him, dazzled and bemused spectators. Although *Bringing Up Baby* was Hepburn's debut in screwball comedy, it didn't give new impetus to her career, as it did for other women stars. In the end, it compounded Hepburn's problem with audiences: Susan Vance seemed as remote from those audiences in her way as the star's serious heroines were felt to be.

Eventually everybody, even the two leopards, gets thrown into jail by a comic sheriff (Walter Catlett)—one of the profusion of comic types, including a twitching psychiatrist (Fritz Feld) and a timid-soul big-game hunter (Charles Ruggles), that populate the film's supporting cast. The upset is too much for Miss Swallow, who promptly breaks the engagement and tells David, back at the museum by the brontosaurus, that he is "just a butterfly." Then Susan turns up again, excited: to announce that she and George, after an intensive three-day search, have found the brontosaurus's missing bone. But David seems more disturbed than pleased by her visit. He has climbed his ladder again, to the platform high atop the enormous dinosaur skeleton. "Why did you run up that ladder when I came in here?" asks Susan. "Well, if you must know," he replies, "I'm afraid of you." But as she insists on climbing the ladder anyway, something comes over him. He's discovered, he tells her now, that he had a good time when they were together—"I never had a better time!"

But this is exactly what Grant's performance—in its intensity, in the glow of its anger, in the murderous glare through the butterfly net—has been telling us all along. "The best day I've had in my whole life!" as he says now. Cary Grant's relation to pleasure, as to everything else, must always be oblique—a bystander even at his own satisfaction. "But . . . but *I* was there," Susan reminds him, hardly daring to hope. "That's what made it so good!" he says. By now she is so excited that she starts to sway on the ladder from side to side. They are both excited—and shouting. "That means—that means that you must like me?" "Susan, it's more than that." "Is it?" She is swaying in such wide arcs now that he has to dash back and forth on his platform above her just to keep up with her. He shouts even louder now: "I love you I think!" And there is no pause, no implied comma or shifting of gears, between those two clauses: "I love" flows into "I think" in one firm, full and continuous declaration as Grant reads the line. In the end, then, the hero's ambivalence toward the heroine, far from being dispelled, has simply become exultant, and triumphant. Inseparable from his romantic excitement, a mingling of fear and transport.

This scene—which finally ends just as we've been expecting it to, with Susan swaying out of control on the ladder and demolishing the brontosaurus skeleton ("Oh dear, all right" are David's final words as they embrace above the dust and wreckage)—is more than a conventional windup bringing hero and heroine together. Just as *Bringing Up Baby* is more than a conventional series of farcical routines. This final slapstick love scene is utterly convincing in its way—and powerfully, convincingly romantic. Because laughter in all these great movie comedies *is* intimacy. A deep involuntary motion of the spirit, often at levels in ourselves we can neither touch nor predict otherwise. Best of all when we can't. And fun at the pitch and intensity Susan has brought to David in this movie can be a very serious matter. You can be joined to someone forever once you've been funny together—provided you've been really deeply, *helplessly* funny.

*Ginger Rogers
at the Foot-
lights Club
in Gregory
La Cava's
Stage Door:
Eve Arden
(with cat)
at left, Lucille
Ball standing
at center, Ann
Miller behind
her.*

Stage Door (1937) is like going to wisecrack heaven. The beautiful tough-talking heroine of thirties Hollywood—drawling and shrewd and street-smart—has an amazing apotheosis in this movie. She is multiplied, with anywhere from five to a dozen of her in the same shot, until she literally fills the screen: every variety of her, from cute kid (Ann Miller) to sleek bitch (Gail Patrick), from chorus cutie to southern belle to European artiste, from major star (Ginger Rogers) to minor star (Lucille Ball) to permanent supporting player (Eve Arden). It's a great idea—with a great idea's simplicity—to put them all in the same film, even to put Rogers and Ball and Arden in the same shot.

Gregory La Cava, the director, was the sort of filmmaker who took inspiration from his own players; and he is clearly entranced by this tough, independent woman. The movie seems all but designed to show his excitement. Its last twenty minutes, it's true, are conventional melodrama—a suicide, a first night, the show must go on. But before that it's all wisecracks and banter and lounging around. It takes place at a theatrical boarding house named the Footlights Club—one of those Terrible Places that the tough comedy always thrives in—where twenty or so young out-of-work actresses sit and stroll and saunter and talk, where they are nearly always either waiting for their dinner or digesting it. In either case they are complaining about the food. The lamb stew tastes so much like iodine they ought to serve it with bandages. If the soup were a little thicker it could pass for hot water: if they try to serve it again, says Rogers, "I'm gonna bring a bar of soap to the table and wash out a few stockings." "It's so beautiful I hate to cut it," says Andrea Leeds about her birthday cake. "That's one of Hattie's cakes, maybe you can't cut it," says Lucille Ball. "If it's not food, it's men—can't you talk about *any*thing else?" complains Olga, the pianist (Norma Drury).

But in fact they *don't* talk about men—only about "dates" who will take them to dinner somewhere, *anywhere*, else. One of the oddities of the movie's version of feminine glamour is its independence of men: there are no romantic male figures anywhere in the film, only Adolphe Menjou's lecherous producer.* They don't talk much about the theater, either, except as something that consistently shuts them out. What they do talk and joke about—obsessively—is failure. Eve Arden watches Rogers go whooping out the door to a nightclub audition and observes that "she hasn't worked in so long, if she does get the job it'll practically amount to a comeback." The joking is communal. You hear the wisecrack, you're not always sure which girl it came from—and it rarely matters. The joke floats above them, and they all take turns giving it a spin. There are *levels* of noise—bells ring and the piano plays and everyone talks at once. And a remark often seems funny because we just catch it, over so much aural chaos that our hearing it at all makes us feel ready to laugh. Two blind dates from Seattle come to call—they are big and dumb and chortling, embarrassingly rube-ish—and one of them knew Judy (Lucille Ball), he says, from her home town when she was "that high—in pigtails." "Well, let's skip that," says Ball quickly, putting on her coat, eager to get them out and away from the show they are providing for the gang in the parlor. "In those days," says the laughing yokel, "nobody ever thought Pete Jones' daughter would ever be an actress." And the men laugh again. "Well, the odds are still the same," mutters Ball under the noise, looking at them merrily. "Don't say anything here or I'll wrench your back," she says to Rogers through her teeth.

But then right into the middle of all this—breathtakingly—comes Katharine Hepburn, with her air of intensity and burning conviction: not the Hepburn of *Bringing Up Baby* but the Hepburn of *Morning Glory* and *A Woman Rebels* and even *Mary of Scotland,* the Hepburn that audiences, it was reported, were finding increasingly hard to take, just as the girls at the Footlights Club are. She is looking for a room, she says—she calls it "finding accommodations," though. And as soon as she walks into the place, she encounters Rogers, who takes one look, bristles, and cracks wise—to the audible delight of the gang in the parlor. "Evidently," says Hepburn, taking note of the laughter, "you're a very amusing person." And passes on. She settles in, too. And in a place where people joke grimly and incessantly about bad luck and worse food, Terry Randall (Hepburn) talks about a vocation to the Theater and about Shakespeare. (Hamlet? Never heard of him, says one. "Certainly you must have heard of *Hamlet!*" says the southern girl. "Well," replies Arden, "I meet so *many* people.") Terry, we soon find out, is an heiress, concealing her millions and trying to make it "on her

*There is a conventional love story in the original play by Edna Ferber and George S. Kaufman, and a conventional boy-gets-girl romantic ending. In the movie's ending, Hepburn and Rogers are explicitly *without* men, and explicitly resigned to being so. It's interesting that the movie should not only be much better than the play (even Kaufman admitted it was) but bolder and more unconventional, too. Since the play was partly an attack on the movies, a celebration of the theater, in which the heroine (Margaret Sullavan) demonstrated her character and integrity by refusing to give up Broadway for Hollywood.

Lucille Ball has arranged this date for them with a couple of out-of-towners: that's why Rogers is looking at her—while the boys (Jack Carson on left) chuckle. Stage Door.

own." She is also trying to be one of the girls. But she is finally too much of an inspirationalist, and she dissents vigorously from their collective tone, all those despairing wisecracks. She exhorts them to think positively, to talk about success, not disappointment, to do something about their failure and not just sit around lamenting it. "My grandfather sat around till he was eighty," says Lucille Ball. "Well, *my* grandfather didn't," says Hepburn, "and if he and a lot of others hadn't crossed the country in a covered wagon, there'd still be Indians living in Wichita!" Eve Arden in a close-up widens her eyes: "Who do you think's living there now?" she inquires.

But that's just what Terry means. "The trouble is you're all trying to be comics," she says. "Don't you ever take anything seriously?" This appeal makes no impression. "It'd be a terrific innovation," says Terry, taking her leave for bed (she's an early riser, too), "if you could let your minds stretch a little beyond the next wisecrack." But beyond the next wisecrack, so far as we can tell, there is *always* another wisecrack. That's the beauty of the style: it never lets you down. And its apogee in this film—its boldest, brightest exponent—is Ginger Rogers.

It's like the Ginger Rogers masks in the finale of *Shall We Dance* all over again. But when we first see her at the beginning of *Stage Door,* she emerges from the crowd of Rogers doubles not to dance but to quarrel over a pair of new stockings. Her hated roommate Linda (Gail Patrick) has taken them, and they are now on their way out the front door—until Jean (Rogers) stops her. "I didn't go without lunch to buy *you* stockings," she tells Linda, a haughty type, but one who gives as good as she gets in these encounters—which are a regular feature at the Footlights Club, and always diverting to the audience in the parlor. Rogers shows her special sort of authority in this scene, her unqualified poise in the mundane—peeling the stockings from Linda's legs, inspecting them for damage ("I knew it, I knew it!"), and managing a barrage of dry, round-voiced wisecracks through it all; her versatility is as offhand as her wryness.

There are some odd types at the Footlights Club (Eve Arden wears a somnolent white cat named Henry draped around her neck through the whole film). But they've never seen anyone quite like Randall. Is she a social worker? someone wonders. "I'm quite sure you'll get on together," says Mrs. Orcutt, the landlady (Elizabeth Dunne), as she shows Terry the room she's to share with Jean (Linda has moved out). And at that moment Rogers prowls into the frame, entering a close shot from the left with lowered head, looking fatally from under her brows at this new provocation. But why don't they like me? Terry wonders out loud in a later scene. "You're just different, that's all," says Kay (Andrea Leeds). But Kay is pretty different herself—sensitive and stricken and spaniel-eyed. More Sylvia Sidney than Ginger Rogers. And the only one in the house who doesn't wisecrack. (She is also the only sentimental figure—there, presumably, to balance the others, and also to precipitate the melodrama at the end by killing herself.) Kay, however, is the house pet, beloved by all, and valued for her misery.

Terry, on the other hand, seems impregnable—and she is the house antipathy. The scenes with her and Jean as "roomies" are nearly the richest in the film, with all the contrasting details of the ways the two women move and dress and look at each other. When she goes to bed, Rogers slaps a limp little doll into place beside her, as briskly as she would plump the pillow: so much for *that* necessity. Otherwise, Rogers' absorption in her clothes and belongings is almost sensual: examining her recovered stockings, patting the fur coat she's just borrowed—as different as anything could be from Hepburn's quick glances and darting gestures as she unpacks her commodious trunks. Hepburn doesn't unbutton her stylish coat; she plucks it open, like someone undoing a parcel.

Terry wonders, once she has gotten into bed, what to do about that electric sign that goes blinking on and off outside their window. "I usually leave it there," says Jean. She climbs into her bed and hands Terry a sleeping mask from the bedside table. Terry holds it up and looks at it. "What do you do with this, put it over your eyes?" "No," drawls Rogers, "you take it with a glass of water." But

Hepburn is delighted by this solution: "That's a *very* ingenious idea—thanks." "Don't get sentimental," says Rogers, trying to turn her off. But it's no use. With sleeping mask in place and settled into her bed, Hepburn makes just the sort of confession Rogers might have been afraid she'd make at this point. "I've always longed," she says, "to live in a place like this."

No wonder they all hate her. It's almost as if a character had walked into *The Front Page* and started talking about what a wonderful place Chicago *really* was, if people only learned to appreciate it. Terry Randall is a threat to the house style. Though, of course, by the end of the film she accedes to it. Or does she? Hepburn's real secret is that she may be tougher and smarter than any of these tough girls (imagine *her* taking a doll to bed). The tragic Kay tells us why they all joke so much and so relentlessly: to hide their fears, she says, and to keep up their courage.

But then Kay is the sort who supposes that people must always have some reason for joking—or why else would they do it? In La Cava's *Stage Door*, on the contrary, being a wise-ass is its own reward. Kay may see it as hiding a breaking heart or a faltering will, but the girls themselves don't finally convey that message. They are too bright and too lively and too funny, their collective style is too fully and humanly attractive. They give no quarter—to Kay or to Terry, to themselves or to us. They are hard cases and they never let up, it seems. They are not what we call "supportive." They testify to a different possibility: the power of negative thinking—as Terry, it seems, never quite understands about them. The loyalties in this group are unconditional. But there is never, nor could there be, any attitudinizing about loyalty. Compare any *male* camaraderie film of the time. La Cava has caught something almost bedrock-tough, without illusion or self-consciousness, that lies in the special camaraderie of women.

Two things happen to Terry at the end of the movie. The first: she becomes an overnight Broadway sensation. Which is much less important than the second: she becomes at last Jean's friend. They embrace each other and cry over Kay's death together. After that, they are tougher than ever—in the final scene and back at the Footlights Club. Hepburn, of course, is the film's heroine—and its most complex figure. But it's Rogers who has the authority of that collective style. And it made her a major star—even without Fred Astaire.

I T'S NOT just that she played a chorus girl so often and so well, from *42nd Street* (1933) to *Stage Door* (1937) to *Roxie Hart* (1942), but that the role somehow defined her even when she wasn't playing it. There's a fleeting but memorable image of her in *Stage Door*, when Adolphe Menjou first spots her in a chorus line at the rehearsal studio. She is in the middle of a line of girls, all

A late night for Rogers: Hepburn—who is always in early—helps her to bed. Notice the doll. Stage Door.

in rehearsal clothes, arms linked behind their backs, heads turned to the left, eyes lowered, as they kick their legs out to the tinny piano sound. It's the basic chorus-girl stance, legs out and heads turned away; but for Rogers it's almost epiphanic, capturing something so essential about her that it brings a shock of recognition when you see it: it's that mixture of displayed flesh and averted eye, both presenting and withholding herself at the same time. Just as when Menjou goes backstage at the nightclub to ask her for a date, she seems both agreeable and hostile at the same time, wisecracking herself into a yes. It's that paradoxical guardedness that gives Ginger Rogers *her* kind of radiance—and no one had it more.

She is the movies' emblematic wise girl—with her glamorous, sardonic deadpan style. (It's no accident that once she starts to animate her face in a purposeful way, mainly by lifting her eyebrows, the decline sets in—beginning with *Tom, Dick and Harry,* the first of her films to feature those eyebrows.) In *Kitty Foyle* (1940), she tells the young man who's come to pick her up for their date that she shares the small apartment with two other girls. "In times like these," he says fatuously (he's the positive-thinker type), "what could be better?" Rogers' response is toneless, but it opens vistas of disaffection and knowingness: "Sharing it with one," she replies—hardly looking at him or inflecting the line as she says it. Rogers doesn't *need* to inflect these common-sense replies. After all, this knowingness isn't something she asked for. She is afflicted by wryness the way other people are overcome by yawns, or vertigo. It's the offhandedness of her astringency that makes it seem special, even definitive.

But there's a catch. Can there be any other major star who was so variable, even from film to film, as she was—alternating performances of plain, unaffected dignity and charm, like the heroines of *Carefree* (1938) and *Kitty Foyle*, with mannered and painfully misjudged ones, like *Vivacious Lady* (1938), the film before *Carefree*, or *Tom, Dick and Harry* (1940), the film after *Kitty Foyle*? The denaturing of the wise girl was, of course, partly inevitable. Just as studio strategists thought Harlow had to be a nice girl at last—or audiences, it was felt, would turn against her—so Rogers had to turn into a sweet one, without astringency or sarcasm. *Vivacious Lady* is the first of her major films to insist on this idea of her—largely due to director George Stevens. There are no tough girls in any of Stevens' films (a remarkable achievement, considering the prevalence of the type). He had already gone some ways toward softening Rogers in *Swing Time* (1936); now he goes much farther. Although the heroine of *Vivacious Lady* is a nightclub singer, she is unimpeachably ladylike—except when (as quite often) she is girlish. She even does baby talk: "I'll be home as soon as Papa learns me all about the flowers," she says, batting her eyes. The Rogers persona is "opened up" in this film—no guardedness at all. She is revealed to be without suspicion or rancor or wit, all wide-eyed and glowing, all compliant warm femininity. It's a style, including the baby talk, that she would favor more and more as her career went on. And it's hopeless. Whenever she tries to be "starry" or radiant in any conventional way, all that really registers is the falsity and the effort.

Stage Door had been her first major film without Astaire. *Vivacious Lady* was her next, and it was a hit. The next Astaire-Rogers film, however, was not. *Carefree*, with its Irving Berlin score and crazy comedy plot (involving psychiatrists and hypnotism and Rogers running around with a rifle), lost money and reinforced the team's determination to split up. Their final RKO film, the very untypical *The Story of Vernon and Irene Castle* (1939)—a biographical drama with a score of old standards and no big Astaire-Rogers numbers at all—was also a money loser. It was Rogers' next film that really confirmed her stardom, almost beyond expectations. *Bachelor Mother* (1939) was a huge hit, and Rogers was its only star. (Her leading man was David Niven, up to then a supporting player, whereas *Vivacious Lady* had co-starred James Stewart.) A modest film, directed by Garson Kanin with a screenplay by Norman Krasna, it turned out to be RKO's biggest sleeper of the decade. It wasn't a film that Rogers wanted to do (the old story); producer Pan Berman had to force her.

She has never looked lovelier—or more imperious or more hopelessly sardonic—than she does here, achieving an almost transcendent version of herself as she stands behind a toy counter surrounded by Donald Duck windup dolls that quack and walk. She is a salesgirl in a big department store called Merlin's, and these ducks are what she sells. It's interesting: Jean Arthur in *The Devil and Miss Jones* (1941), another RKO comedy about a department store written by Norman Krasna, plays a salesgirl on an exactly similar set (most likely the same one) and looks uneasy and rather out of place there. Rogers, on the other hand, looks grimly—and deeply—at home standing behind that counter. Especially when we hear her floorwalker boss: "Keep those ducks in motion, Miss Parish," he enjoins her cheerily from behind his pince-nez, over the din of mechanical quacking that is an incessant feature of her day at work. It all seems deeply right, with the rightness of a dream: that if Rogers had to sell a toy it would be an officious and noisy and clamorous one that walked and waggled its tail while it quacked; that it would surround her, and be constantly in motion. A kind of ultimate test of her ability to register lunacy without letting it throw her, of her deep capacity for *not* being surprised.

Like Colbert and Arthur, she was identified with working-girl heroines. But she seemed much closer than they ever did to the real thing. It was this identification—heavily promoted in the ads—that helped to make *Kitty Foyle* ("America's White Collar Girl") a runaway hit, winning Rogers an Academy Award. She has a kind of supreme matter-of-factness that always seems to fit and even to dignify these matter-of-fact environments—typewriters and time clocks and steno pads, department stores and dress shops and offices—where there is really nothing much to be expected one way or the other. She is a noncom type— almost never a boss—with a noncom's lowliness and sense of fellowship. Her wiseacre style and her striking self-possession are ways of affirming that fellowship (we're all in the same boat, aren't we?) with the girls at the Footlights Club or the salesgirls at Merlin's. And we all know what's going on: that the exchange department doesn't exchange anything, or that big producers don't see anyone. She has a department store job in *Kitty Foyle*, too—faking a faint to cover the fact that she's just set off the store alarm. A young intern (James Craig) starts to attend to her while she's stretched out on the floor of the dress department. "Lay off," she says to him out of the side of her mouth, "be a good guy and go away." Nothing winsome about this appeal; it's just that good guys in trouble cover for each other—what else? We may expect to see other stars with the Una Merkel kind of sidekick or girlfriend, but for Rogers such a companion would be superfluous. She is her own sidekick. In some sense she *can't* be alone. She carries the prosaic workaday world with her. It's both her grace and her burden.

The "burden" may help to account for something else about her: her dreaminess. The impression she often gives—standing behind the toy counter or walking the streets looking for a job—of being slightly suspended outside her own predicament. It's when she is in this state that she sees a woman leaving a baby on a doorstep in *Bachelor Mother*. She frowns as if she's just had a troubling thought: but you *can't* leave that baby there, she tells the woman—who is gone. The doorstep, however, belongs to a foundling home; and the people inside assume, when they find her with it, that the baby is Polly's (Rogers'). They are even more convinced when she denies it, and they report her to the store. She denies it to them, too. "Those are experienced people," cries David Merlin (David Niven), the store owner's son. "They know a real mother when they see one!" So many people think they know the "real mother" that at length Polly "admits" it. She keeps both the baby and her job at Merlin's, settling into the imposture with the same air of sardonic acceptance she faces those ducks with. And she begins to spend sleepless nights with the baby. "How long," she wonders numbly, at the counter winding her ducks, "can a person go without sleep?" But the conniving stock boy Freddie (Frank Albertson) misunderstands the question: he thinks Merlin's son has been keeping her awake.

He hasn't, but he does take her out on New Year's Eve when his regular girlfriend (Louise King) turns him down, wondering rather bitchily over the phone whether it isn't too late for him "to get anyone presentable." He gets Polly—while her landlady baby-sits. And with "nothing to wear," Polly is outfitted from the store, Cinderella-like. They go to a nightclub, where all his awful friends are gathered for their party. But what will I say to them? wonders Polly as they enter the place. "Just say no to the men, and the girls probably won't speak to you anyway," replies David. And they go forward to the table. In a sudden access of inspiration David introduces Polly as the daughter of a Swedish manufacturer, "just come over," and "she doesn't speak one word of English." Polly dances with all the men, exchanges nasty-sweet smiles with David's now quite put-out girlfriend, and speaks "Swedish" for the table in general, which David obligingly "translates" (the English usually turns out to be insulting in some way). But just as they are leaving, the "Swede" hazards, with David's encouragement, some fractured English: "Oppy . . . Noo . . . Cheer," she says—very proud of herself when she's done. "How do you like her?" says David to his girlfriend, as he helps Polly into her coat at the checkroom. "She's not bad for a fill-in," says the angry girl. Then adds: "Personally, I'd just as soon go stag." "You could, too, with those shoulders," says Rogers in her lowest voice. And out the door they go, leaving the flabbergasted girl behind.

Out the door to the New Year's Eve crowds on the street. The bickering and bitchery of the nightclub give way to this sudden expansive feeling of celebration: people are laughing and dancing and tooting their horns, they are singing

"Happy Days Are Here Again." David and Polly, laughing too, are quickly separated; and when midnight strikes, they have to jump up and down just to see each other over the heads of the others. Horns blow and honk, streamers drift and fall, and people join hands and dance in long snaking lines. They sing "Auld Lang Syne," and as the gay-mournful chorus rises, so does the camera— to a stirring crane shot, high above the crowd (there's a discreet plug for *Love Affair* on a theater marquee in the background), with spotlights playing over the heads of the twisting lines of dancers. It's a powerfully romantic version of an essential screwball moment—the screwball couple's almost inevitable rite of passage. They've just told the swells and phonies off—now they're free, exultant, and delivered to the welcoming city.

LIKE OTHER notable 1939 comedies (*Midnight, Love Affair, Fifth Avenue Girl*), *Bachelor Mother* seems almost remarkably soft-spoken: screwball comedy without any of the frenetic tone. It's almost as if the style itself had gained a kind of assurance by the end of the decade, a confidence in its audiences and its own effects. Everything in this film is underplayed. Nothing is hurried or slugged across. Jokes are both lingered over and "thrown away" at the same time. And yet there is nothing self-conscious about this understatement, nothing italicized—as there might be in Lubitsch, who often likes to make a joke of his own reticencies. This was young Garson Kanin's (he was twenty-seven) fourth RKO film, and it's almost certainly his most graceful and interesting one. (Compare the heavyhandedness of his two subsequent comedies, *My Favorite Wife* in 1940 and *Tom, Dick and Harry* in 1941.) There is a running joke, for example—if "joke" isn't too strong a word for it—during a breakfast-table argument between Merlin Senior (Charles Coburn) and his son. Every time Merlin gets angry, he throws his spoon down at such an angle that it bounces off the tablecloth, sails out of the frame, and disappears—to the confusion of the infinitely discreet butler (E. E. Clive), who replaces the thing silently each time it disappears, each time with growing unease. This is just the sort of detail—so securely sketched into the background (the quarrel itself is the main joke, and a good one), given just the right delicate stress and no more than that—that gives density to the comic texture of these films, that can make even a modest comedy like this one seem finally memorable. In a way, the whole film is like an extension of Ginger Rogers' deadpan laid-back style. The jokes and the absurdities are allowed to speak for themselves. The way Rogers looks at those ducks—or at the little man who tells her cryptically that she now has "the greatest gift that any woman could possibly have"—is just the way the movie itself "looks" at its own materials: sidelong and deadpan.

One of the effects of this style is that the risible effects accumulate as the

His name is
John—and
Charles
Coburn is
moved. But
Ginger Rogers
and David
Niven
are puzzled.
Garson Kanin'.
Bachelor
Mother.

movie goes along. Merlin's Department Store, for example, is one of its most successful jokes. It's not a Terrible Place, as it would be in a tough comedy— just a discouraging one, alternating tedium and hysteria, full of officious little bosses and underpaid workers. And the Exchange Department *never* exchanges anything. As anyone who's ever *tried* to exchange something knows. This may seem hard to believe, but it's enforced by countless details in the film: by the way the salespeople look and sound when someone says he's going to exchange something (they all make the same high-pitched sound of incredulity); by the worn, rather defeated look of the two or so people on line at the exchange window when David Merlin goes there (in disguise) to prove that you *can* exchange something; by the ring of hopelessness in the voice of the woman who has just been told to "have it signed by the section manager and then bring it back here." "Oh, all right," she says, on a sigh. Now it is David's turn at the window. He has, he announces, "a defective duck." (He has broken it at Polly's place the night before, trying to wind it up.) How did it break? asks the exchange man. What? After all, "we have to know where to place the responsibility." "Place it on the duck and give me a new one!" shouts David. "Do you have a sales slip?"—and so on. Until it all ends in a slapstick melee, with David sending ducks flying.

The movie is complicated, and immensely enriched, when Charles Coburn enters it as John P. Merlin—drawn into the plot by his conviction (he has a letter from "A Friend") that his son David is the father of Polly's baby. He tracks the young people to the park, where they have taken the baby. But when he actually sees the baby, he is undone.

> MERLIN: I'd know that chin anywhere. . . . What's his name?
> POLLY: John.
> MERLIN: *John* . . . (*moved—then turning to David, reproachfully*) Thanks for *that*, anyway.
> POLLY: (*concerned about him*): . . . Is there something *I* can do?
> MERLIN: You've done it.

Neither Polly nor David, of course, knows what he is talking about—at first. When it dawns on them—in an extended two-shot, with both of them facing front, after Merlin has left them ("We'll discuss this matter at home!")—David is distressed but Polly is amused. Later on she realizes that Merlin's delusion— and passion for a grandson—have created a problem. Afraid that the rich man will try to take the baby away from her, she gets her landlady's bookish son to pose as the "real" father, a ruse which fails either to deceive or to deter Merlin. The whole thing sorts itself out, of course—and the film ends—when David tells her he loves her.

This interfering but beneficent old rich man is another standard screwball element. And he gave steady work to a whole roster of avuncular overweight character actors: Walter Connolly more than anyone, perhaps. But also Eugene Pallette—in *My Man Godfrey* and *The Lady Eve*. Even Robert Greig—who was usually a butler—as Theodora's scapegrace Uncle John. He is always a millionaire, always imposing and powerfully authoritative, always both fat and irascible—sharp in temper, but in actual contour soft and reassuring. It is always important in these romances to placate this figure, and the lovers must always come to terms with him somehow. "Merlin" is a lovely name for him, because he is in fact magical—a fairy godfather in many ways. And not only because he is rich and potentially bounteous: he is always, in some fundamental way, smarter than anyone else. He's a touchstone of sanity and wholeness for the lovers, and though they are always in temporary opposition to him, none of these films could end with that opposition unhealed, any more than they could end with the lovers separated. It's interesting that although screwball romance tends to omit or deny such facts as children or motherhood (*Bachelor Mother* is an exception to this pattern, though not entirely: since Polly's motherhood is a fiction, exploited more for its scandalous and sexual implications than for domestic or sentimental ones), it makes this father—or grandfather—figure a central one. There are deep emotional issues here—that will be explored later on by Preston Sturges in particular.

Charles Coburn, it's clear, however, is some kind of great actor. He thought of himself as a man of the theater and a Shakespearean (he and his wife, Ivah Wills, formed the touring Coburn Shakespeare Company in 1906). He resisted the lure of the movies until the mid-thirties, when he himself was almost sixty. And he became one of those familiar supporting players—like Edward Arnold, a related type—whose name appeared frequently above the title. He transforms *Bachelor Mother* when he appears in the movie's final third, and just when the farcical complications would seem to be running down, it moves onto a whole new level of richness and interest. Coburn isn't just a performer with almost breathtaking comic timing and intelligence: he's the sort of figure who ends a quarrel with his son in a moment of self-recognition. "What you need is—" he begins one peroration, and as David goes out the door, ends it: "—more sleep." Feeling foolish. And the conjunction of sanity and madness as he pursues his elusive "grandson" is both funny and troubling to behold. He is possessed—the *exalted* screwball style—and he achieves a comic grandeur that no one else in the movie approximates. When Polly's ruse in introducing the baby's "real" father is unmasked, there is a sudden chorus of confessions from the men in the room. "Your son put me up to this," cries the conniving Freddie. "*He's* the father!" Says Niven: "Dad, this is the truth," and he points to the landlady's son— "*He's* the father!" "Wait a minute!" cries the latter, "I'm not the father!" "I don't care *who* the father is," says Coburn, surveying them all, cigar in his mouth exultantly aloft, "*I'm* the grandfather!" And at that moment he *is* Shakespearean.

G REGORY LA CAVA's *Fifth Avenue Girl* (1939) was Rogers' next film (her second with La Cava) and like *Bachelor Mother* it was a surprise hit. La Cava hadn't worked on a film since *Stage Door* two years before (in the same period Rogers had appeared in five films), but his stock was still high: he'd been on a roll before that two-year interruption. His mid-thirties comedies—including *She Married Her Boss* (1935) at Columbia—had all been successful; and one of them was *My Man Godfrey*. In fact, *Fifth Avenue Girl* (screenplay by Allan Scott) is a distaff version of *Godfrey*, with Rogers in the William Powell role, as the down-on-her-luck outsider who sets to rights the rich silly family that takes her in. This time it's the father (Walter Connolly) who picks her up—in the park, not the dump—and brings her home, and the son (Tim Holt) who falls for her. Though his first reaction is to try to buy her off. They all think she's a golddigger—a misimpression the father has deliberately fostered. He even keeps her in the house just to upset them. His wife (Verree Teasdale) gets jealous and ditches her gigolo. The playboy son gets so nervous about the family business that he takes it over—just as his father had wished him to. And the debutante daughter (Kathryn Adams) gets married. Mary (Rogers) is both a catalyst to action and their adviser on common sense and reality, just as Godfrey was to *his* family.

But just as *My Man Godfrey* was hectic and noisy, this La Cava film is muted and almost somnolent. Can there be another movie comedy where the pressure is as low as it is here? *Fifth Avenue Girl* is a comedy that never seems to ask for an outright laugh anywhere. It has neither jokes nor wisecracks. It "has" slapstick—a nightclub brawl, and the cops bringing people home in their paddy wagon—but it's all off-screen. We learn about it all the next morning, through distant-sounding reminiscent accounts, as if the memory were already fading. A more typical sort of "action" in this movie is three characters lined up and facing front like a Moscow Art Theater tableau, exchanging abstracted remarks about the "problem" they now find themselves with. For movement La Cava sets many of his scenes on the mansion's broad and magnificent main stairway:

At the foot of the grand stairway: Walter Connolly and Ginger Rogers in La Cava's Fifth Avenue Girl.

people go up and down a lot, very slowly, talking as they go, and mostly not looking at each other.

What's most surprising of all is that the movie was so popular—one of RKO's biggest moneymakers that year. But the general movie context made the film look less eccentric then than it now does. Audiences at these comedies were accustomed to certain kinds of restraint. One of the impulses of later screwball, as *Bachelor Mother* exemplifies, was to get quieter. Though it's true La Cava turned the volume down lower than anyone had before. Why? His two most successful comedies, *My Man Godfrey* and *Stage Door*, had both been, in their different ways, quite noisy. But in spite of their many contrasts, *Stage Door* and *Fifth Avenue Girl* are remarkably and interestingly alike. In both movies La Cava cultivates our response to a dominant sound. The actual wisecracks in *Stage Door* are always less important, from scene to scene or in the movie as a whole, than the overall wisecrack *sound*. And instead of the Footlights Club kind of rat-a-tat-tat, the sound of *Fifth Avenue Girl* is a steady low hum of chat, murmurous rather than staccato.

And it *is* chat—not at all the "chatter" of sophisticated comedy tradition, with its aspirations to brilliance and style. The dialogue here has a consistent soap-opera banality: it never even tries to be apt or notably expressive. But in the end—in a limited way—La Cava's gamble pays off. Because the overall sound *is* expressive, just as it was in *Stage Door*. We really do *hear* a way of behaving, of being a group—reserved, reflective, sidelong. People talk in this film as if thinking out loud. If they seem on the whole almost eerily restrained and "civilized," that was partly what audiences expected from such movies. And the success of *Fifth Avenue Girl* suggested that they could enjoy the civility even when it came without the jokes.

This was La Cava's calculation, of course. And it couldn't have been made around anyone else but Ginger Rogers. No other star of the time could have given or submitted to such an impassive central performance. Mary Grey (and the name is a tipoff) is the deadest-panned of all Rogers' deadpan heroines. And the film itself is, even more than *Bachelor Mother* was, an extension of the Rogers temperament and performing style. This was characteristic of the way La Cava worked: designing his films *on* his performers, like a choreographer. "More than anybody else I ever met in this business," said Pan Berman in a recent interview, "La Cava was capable of exploiting the personality of an actor." Before starting to shoot *Stage Door*, La Cava assigned the supporting actresses—practically the complete roster of RKO "starlets"—to live together at the studio for two weeks in just the conditions of boardinghouse intimacy the movie would depict. A script girl transcribed their actual talk, and a lot of it turned up in the film. Not surprisingly, as they started shooting "with no script," Hepburn recently recalled.

In working style he was like Leo McCarey. People tend to remember the same sort of stories about both directors: tales of confusion on the set and panic in the front office and last-minute inspirations to the rescue. And pianos. "Between scenes," wrote a Hollywood reporter on the set of *Unfinished Business* (1941), "a little man climbs onto a rubber-tired truck upon which rests a grand piano and plays soft music. The gray-haired La Cava goes into a corner and figures out what he's going to shoot next." People on a McCarey film or a La Cava film had fun—if they weren't having a breakdown. And actors in general adored them. Joel McCrea said in 1978 that La Cava "talking about a character" was "a magic thing" ("he would take you aside and talk very quietly"). La Cava was one of McCrea's three favorite directors (Sturges and Stevens were the others)— someone he "loved," someone he "always learned from," who "could get you to do things you couldn't do for anyone else." La Cava beginning a film, he said, "never had but half a script, and then he just read it to us."* He would often, said Hepburn, "let the scene sort of shape itself," rehearsing and rewriting on the set. Though apparently in his more "serious" films he was less likely to wing it in this way (in contrast to McCarey, who "improvised" parts of even *Make Way for Tomorrow* and *My Son John*). According to Claudette Colbert, there was no improvising during *Private Worlds* (1935), a melodrama about a mental hospital, though there was during the very next film she did with La Cava, *She Married Her Boss* (1935), a screwball comedy.

Fifth Avenue Girl may be tailored to its star, but it also makes a serious—and immensely interesting—miscalculation about her. In heightening the Rogers deadpan to the degree he does, La Cava has also deadened its expressiveness— or, rather, he's made it express (inadvertently, it would seem) the wrong sort of meaning. Rogers' wariness has always made her a problematic sort of screwball, or romantic, heroine. But it's also, as in the Astaire films, what's made her interesting and complex, what's given her her special style and attractiveness. But this time La Cava gives us the wariness straight, so to speak, without the other things that make the Ginger Rogers heroine—the wonderful dryness, the humor and incredulity, the energy and physical authority, and so on—giving us the Rogers disaffection without the wit or the dreaminess. "It's my birthday," confides the unhappy millionaire to this girl he's just met in the park. "It's not mine," she replies, looking straight ahead. We never understand in this scene why he feels encouraged. He invites her to a birthday celebration and names a posh restaurant: would she like to go there? "I'd rather go to the Automat," she

---

*Screenwriter Allan Scott (*Primrose Path* and *Fifth Avenue Girl*) denied this in a recent interview with Pat McGilligan. According to Scott, La Cava would conceal the degree to which he prepared a film ahead of time: "We had many conferences, and I would write sometimes as many as four or five versions of each scene." But Scott also describes La Cava as spending all morning on the set deciding what to use from these versions each day before he began shooting.

replies, "and keep the change." And as it turns out, keeping the change is one of her favorite things. She refers complacently later on to her "Scotch blood." And when someone asks her if she had a good time at the posh club, she says, "I must have, I spent a dollar of my own money." And though she is praised throughout the movie for her unaffectedness and common sense, she seems to *us* mostly glum and irritable and unimaginative. She is meant to be direct and plainspoken, but instead we get this ill-natured killjoy sound. "People annoy me," she announces while having her "good time" at the nightclub. But she hardly needs to tell us: she *looks* annoyed, as she does for most of the movie. The leading man (Holt) looks and sounds the same way, and their scenes together are like contests in petty irritation. Almost the worst thing that La Cava imposes on his star here is her lack of energy, so that the bad feeling seems grudging in *every* sense. Just as she says, people make her tired. . . .

Clearly, La Cava—to his credit—is taking conscious risks in this movie: trying for a kind of bristling, cranky amiability, for example, in the exchanges between the heroine and the millionaire, a mock irritability concealing interest and affection. But neither his director's touch nor his writing skill is sure and delicate enough to pull the trick off (as Preston Sturges would do later on, over and over again). In the Rogers character only the bristle and the irritability seem real. La Cava made three films in a row with Rogers—*Primrose Path* (1940) was the third—and each of them offers a different, interesting version of her, each of them authentic, as increasingly her films and her roles were not. There seems to be no evidence that he specially liked or got on with her: the only way you could get her to cry, he told an interviewer during the filming of *Stage Door,* "was to tell her that her house was on fire." But La Cava never does to her what George Stevens, for example, tries to do in *Vivacious Lady*—to turn her into June Allyson, into a more acceptable, less troubling sort of heroine. La Cava likes to bring out his performers, not disguise them. When he makes what seems a major mistake about them—as he does with Rogers in *Fifth Avenue Girl* or with Lombard in *My Man Godfrey*—it's generally because he's emphasized one aspect of their temperaments too heavily and exclusively. But the mistakes derive from a real interest in them, in their temperaments and gifts, rather than in some stereotype they can be made to fit.

Like McCarey, too, La Cava had a drinking problem. But if McCarey was a nice drunk, La Cava was a mean one, a quality that finds its devious way into his work—the sourness that comes from bad nights and worse mornings. His friend W. C. Fields (who once called La Cava "the second funniest man in Hollywood") found a way to turn the bad feeling into brilliant comic shtick. La Cava never did. Or, rather, he never put his mind to it: he aspired to *all* sorts of comedy, as well as to sentiment and social significance, going from J. M. Barrie (*What Every Woman Knows,* 1934) to the "problem" of mental illness (*Private*

Worlds, 1935). A former cartoonist and animator, he began his career as a director with two-reel comedies, just as McCarey and Capra and Stevens did. He and McCarey were friends, but they ran in different crowds. McCarey's was the Irish set, with a penchant for gathering around the piano. La Cava's drinking buddies were John Barrymore and Bill Fields, probably his closest friend of all (one of the dates who comes to pick up Lucille Ball in *Stage Door* is introduced as Mr. Dukenfield, Fields's real name). They called themselves the Doxology Club. La Cava even drank on the job (McCarey apparently didn't). There are stories of his nodding off while shooting *Stage Door*, even falling into the orchestra pit while filming the theater scenes.

And he made trouble for himself in other ways. He was never very good at the Hollywood game of conning the bosses: he held them in contempt, all right, but he never really learned how to outwit them. He was too truculent, for one thing. And if it weren't for Pan Berman—his shield and defender at RKO and even thereafter (Berman produced La Cava's last, sad movie at MGM in 1947, *Living in a Big Way*)—his career might have been even more fitful and foreshortened than it was. Joel McCrea thinks that what "did La Cava in" was that "he got to hating the establishment too much." In any case, it seems to have become reciprocal.

But in some ways, it seems, he identified with an "establishment." A La Cava film is no likelier than any other Hollywood movie of the time to attack the basic inequity of American society. But a La Cava film is likelier than most to bring the subject up, and to reveal a more than usually tortured ambivalence about it. *My Man Godfrey* offers images of this inequity—the scavenger hunt, William Powell's "forgotten man," the men on the dump and the people in the mansion— as eloquent as any of the movie decade. But then it turns out as the story unfolds that this poor man who shows all the rich people up is really a rich man himself, in cunning disguise, and recovering from an unhappy love affair. And so in the end he shows all the *real* poor men he's been living among, all those tramps, how to turn their degradation into a good thing: by opening a "hobo nightclub" for the rich. La Cava was characteristically drawn to these subjects, but he was never able to bring anything more to them than a balky temperamental conservatism—mixing a vague populist tone with a stubborn and cantankerous snobbery, a kind of Beverly Hills egalitarianism.

Fifth Avenue Girl offers Hollywood's favorite indictment of the rich: they don't have any fun. But *this* time the indictment seems angry. The La Cava touch. And the anger is clearly registered, mostly through the Rogers heroine: through her even sullenness, her snappish comebacks, her denunciations of the upper class—complainers and "cadavers" and "wax dummies," as she calls them. "I know you don't like the rich," Walter Connolly says to her, "but I'm not a capitalist. I'm a victim of the capitalist system. . . . All I wanted was a family and some fun." But if you're rich, you can't have either—as this movie seems to show. The lucky ones in this setup, as it turns out, are those servants. (How much do we pay them, anyway?) After all, *they* have nothing to worry about. "We servants," butler Franklin Pangborn shyly confesses (not his finest moment) to his boss, "enjoy the luxuries of the rich with none of the responsibilities." As Rogers says in one of her more tolerant moods: "I guess rich people are just poor people with money." But even poorer in a way, since their money brings them so much grief. Yet certainly no one (except maybe a communist) would ask them to part with it. They're *supposed* to enjoy it—but then they *can't*—and so it goes. It's no wonder this heroine seems irritable.

More than irritable. There are outbreaks of bad feeling in the film, so at odds with the general civility that it's almost as if something were out of control. "You talk too much," says Rogers to the communist chauffeur (James Ellison)—and then picks up a kitchen knife: "I think I'll cut you a new mouth," she says, while the debutante daughter screams in terror. At first you wonder if you can have *heard* that rightly. Apparently you did. And she is kidding, of course.

But this handsome young chauffeur, who is mostly a kind of clown, also has a way of sounding surprisingly plausible at times (something else out of control?). In the kitchen he remarks on the cases of champagne that are being laid in for a party: "There are forty million people in these United States—this land of opportunity—whose annual income is less than twelve cases of that." But then we realize that the precision and the statistics are meant to make him sound pedantic ("Seventy-eight percent of the population have less than twenty-five cases"), even when he goes on to cite the overwhelming numbers who can't even afford medicine "without depriving themselves of the basic necessities of life."* But Rogers has the answer to all this talk, and she lays it on the line: "You haven't the courage to be a capitalist yourself," she tells him, "so you try to drag everybody down to where you are." And of course she is right. All he needed was a little capital of his own—enough to open a repair shop—to forget this nonsense. But "I shall never forget my proletarian beginnings," he announces at the end of the film, before departing with his new bride. "Come on, babe," he says to her—and we know he really will be all right.

Mary speaks, of course, for good old American horse sense, of the kind that the movies were usually promoting (the idea that political radicals were really frustrated conservatives was a particular favorite). And as it becomes clear what she stands for as the movie goes on, we realize that the Jeane Kirkpatrick style of this heroine is no accident. La Cava has connected to something he perceived in the Rogers temperament, and it's *not* generosity. *Fifth Avenue Girl* betrays the real meanness of feeling behind the received American attitudes it endorses,

---

*There were 9.5 million unemployed the year this film was released, over 17 percent of the work force.

coming as it does from a filmmaker who pursues truth of feeling. The movie reflects a deep disgruntlement: the feeling of being unhappy with your life and yet knowing you're not going to change it, and unhappiest of all with those who suggest you change. Bad enough to be stuck with your life; but then to have to defend it, too, against jerks like that chauffeur—and what do *they* know about it, anyway? It's the kind of impasse that can make you *feel* mean, or at the least a little bit sullen.

Similar as the two filmmakers' methods were, La Cava never really matched McCarey's talent for snatching coherence from chaos. He never approximates the controlling vision or force of McCarey's best work, McCarey's genius for making a brilliant whole out of a succession of loosely related scenes. Even the tough, ribald *The Half Naked Truth* (1932), with Lee Tracy and Lupe Velez— certainly one of La Cava's funniest films, full of marvelous gags and scenes throughout—seems structurally inert. There are other kinds of inertness, too, even in *Stage Door:* characters made of fustian, sentimental contrivances, embarrassing conventionality. La Cava liked stock-company mad scenes, it seems: Joan Bennett in *Private Worlds* and Andrea Leeds in *Stage Door* both play one on a stairway. His best films seem erratic. And, finally, so was his output. After *Fifth Avenue Girl*—and in the last decade of his life—he made only four films. He died in 1949 at the age of fifty-seven.

Claudette Colbert | 16

MGM's *It's a Wonderful World* (1939) was more or less dismissed when it came out—*another* madcap comedy, said the reviews—and did practically no business in spite of its two stars, Claudette Colbert and James Stewart. And yet now it seems an example of how almost *casually* terrific the screwball mode could be. It's a modest film in every way, one of four Colbert films that year—sandwiched between *Midnight* at Paramount, her home studio, and *Drums Along the Mohawk* at 20th Century–Fox—and one of the fastest the star ever made. Director W. S. Van Dyke outdid himself in the speed he shot this one with: a record twelve days, six fewer than he took on *The Thin Man*. But just as with *The Thin Man*, the speed shows up on the screen in mostly good ways—in crackle and verve and spontaneity. In some respects *It's a Wonderful World* is an even more accomplished film—the comedy counterpart to the supremely assured and high-spirited work Van Dyke had done on *San Francisco* (1936). Ben Hecht, another speed specialist, wrote the screenplay (from a story by Hecht and Herman Mankiewicz); it's in his *Front Page* vein, with admixtures of *It Happened One Night* and *Bringing Up Baby*, as well as surprising adumbrations of the forties private-eye film.

Guy Johnson (Stewart) is a private detective in New York. He has a sardonic older partner named Cap Streeter (Guy Kibbee) and a taciturn, mysterious boss named Major Willoughby (Richard Carle). This odd trio is right out of Hammett, except that they're not at all sinister or disquieting. In fact, they're not even offered as picturesque: they are simply there, at the beginning of the movie. Guy has one lucrative client—a little shnook of a millionaire playboy (Ernest Truex). This character barely comes up to Guy's hipbone, but he still manages to get into momentous troubles with fortune-hunting women. As a result of one such liaison, he is framed for murder and sentenced to the chair. Guy is arrested for harboring a fugitive when he tries to hide his client, but on his way to jail he jumps off the train and escapes. He then embarks on a hunt for the real murderer—there's a hundred grand in it for him if he succeeds. Unfortunately, he is spotted almost right away by Edwina Corday (Colbert) and so is obliged to take the woman along with him—against her will. Soon, however, she becomes his ally—against his will. With cops and newspapers on their trail, they make their way to a Connecticut summer theater, where—during a noisy production of *What Price Glory*—they trap the murderers.

It's an involved plot that never really pays off, in spite of the time it takes. And in spite of its eccentricities and byways (Major Willoughby, *What Price Glory*, etc.), the detective story never really becomes interesting. But the screwball couple in this film are. Stewart's irascible private eye is right out of *The Front Page*. He's in a lower key than either Hildy or Walter, but he could be one of the reporters in the press room playing poker and mouthing off. He is grumbling and hard-bitten and irredeemably cynical. "I never knew they took *detectives* to jail," says the skeptical Edwina. "Just the good ones they do," he replies. When he learns that his dumb hapless client has made a suicide attempt in jail (if the little playboy dies, Guy loses the hundred grand), his reaction is swift and anguished: "That's the kind of breaks I always get!" he cries. "He'll start swallowing *spoons* next!" Like Cary Grant in *Bringing Up Baby*, Stewart is a man on a quest, and saddled with a companion whose blitheness and inconsequence fill him with mounting and helpless fury. Like Hepburn in the same film, Colbert is "trying to help," with approximately the same results.

But the Colbert heroine is neither rich nor dizzy. And though she, too, has great self-assurance, it's more like a suburban matron's than a blueblood's. From her first appearance (she's just seen Stewart climb out of the water handcuffed to an unconscious cop)—peering out from behind a tree with wide, startled eyes, in a mannish suit and an absurd little flowered pillbox hat—she evokes the clubwoman world of Helen Hokinson cartoons. We even learn that she is on her way to lecture to a woman's group. Or was, before the hero kidnapped her.

And it's not wackiness or irresponsibility that she oppresses him with but a kind of aggressive gentility. She "believes," as she tells him, in "love and high adventure." As if this weren't bad enough, it takes a while even before he learns the *full* horror of what he's stuck with. He discovers it from the newspaper accounts of their flight. EDWINA CORDAY, FAMED POETESS, says the headline over her photo, "MISSING." His despair this time is almost more than he can give words to. He looks up from the newspaper and stares at her in disbelief. "Oh, well, don't look so *impressed*," she says, misinterpreting the look. "I'll think you're just a celebrity hunter." He really *can't* believe this. "You're a poetess?" he says weakly. Yes, she is. "Well, *I* don't know," he says, "I guess some people are just *born* unlucky." Finally—and reluctantly—she gets the point. "Too manly for poetry, huh?" she says, dropping her voice in that distinctive Colbertian way. Though she is not above trying to win him over: she has written

*James
Stewart—in
scout leader
disguise—and
Claudette
Colbert: she
has to tell him
what they're
looking at.
It's a Won-
derful World.*

a poem—about them—just the night before, she tells him. And recites it: "The night will be here when we are gone. . . ." He is not interested.

Gable on the road with Colbert in *It Happened One Night* was full of scorn for the rich; Stewart in this film is full of rage at almost everything. His pessimism is so vehement it seems almost buoyant. But occasionally he shows a "softer" side—and if there is one thing he knows, he tells Colbert, "it's kids." As they contemplate the toadlike child in front of them now. She, on the other hand, is not so inclined to trust this kid. She and Guy are the objects of a statewide manhunt. And so now there's this Boy Scout on their trail in the woods. What's he doing there, anyway? "Looking for—uh—mushrooms," he says. He has a compressed mouth and wears spectacles so thick that we can hardly see the glint and shift of his eyes behind them. Guy persists, however: he swears the Scout to secrecy before telling him their story. "Now my name," he begins, "is Armand Applegate—and this is Miss Hortense Doolittle." The eyes shift behind the glasses. "I am," says the boy, with the slightest of hesitations, "Stanley Cavendish." Well, continues "Armand," he and "Hortense" are eloping ("You know what that means?") and need a place to hide from her angry father. Stanley agrees to show them to "the old mill" ("You'll like it—it's haunted"), and off they go, with Stanley leading the way through the woods, looking inscrutable and malevolent. "That's a kid for you," says Guy to Edwina. "They live in a world all their own. Much better world than ours any day." But Stanley, in front of them, is flashing covert signals with a small mirror. Edwina spots this and tackles him: "He was signalling for help!" They tie him up. His real name, Edwina reveals, finding it in his hat, is Herman Plotka. (Lombard's real name in *Twentieth Century* was also Plotka: one of Hecht's favorite funny names.)

She is of course no dumbbell—the poetry notwithstanding. She may chatter and moon and say things like "I swear by my eyes" (her version of a solemn oath), but she doesn't really miss anything. If she makes mistakes, it's her over-eagerness. That, however, is a problem: backstage at the summer theater she hits the wrong man over the head—Cap Streeter, Guy's partner, in fact—and disables him. But she is finally the one who breaks the case, leading the cops to the killers' motel by pretending to have the goods on Guy: "He's the murderer!" She prefers to be honest, but when she is lying successfully she gets very excited—even elated. As she does in the back of the police car, urging them on to the motel, with Guy in handcuffs and the police in triumph because they think they've nailed him at last. Edwina, in the middle of them all, is on some kind of mad high of inspiration and duplicity, using the same words both to denounce Guy as the murderer and to share her exhilaration with him. "And keep him covered," she cries, "he's a *desperate* man!"—with a roguish, rolling-eyed look at Guy, who is smiling, incredulously. She is pulling it *all* off: not only breaking the case and saving his neck but being funny about it too. And she is as dazzled by what she's doing as Guy is. Colbert makes us feel it all, not just a funny moment but an intoxicating one.

Colbert is irresistible whenever she's sharing a joke with us—when she's in full, conscious control of the point. After they get out of the woods, Guy ditches her—but then finds her at the summer theater when he arrives there himself. Edwina is already quite cozy with the Madam Impresario (Cecil Cunningham), who is looking for an actor who can do a southern accent. Edwina introduces Guy as Mr. Hemingway, a native-born southerner, from Virginia. "Alabama!" he snaps, furious at her but still not declining the gambit (he is looking for the murderer among the cast of the play). Edwina makes a little face of concern at his violence and turns back to the Madam. They are in a dressing room, Edwina wearing a head scarf and tinted glasses, standing between Guy and the Madam, looking up at them both. Guy now offers a demonstration of his "southern" sound: "Madam, I'd be delighted to read for you all," he says with great and visible effort, torturing both his voice and his face into what he imagines is a southern drawl. And below him, as this painful demonstration goes forward,

Colbert looks up at the Madam with a kind of shy-mad Woody Allen smile behind her tinted glasses—a moment of deranged complicity with the performance
taking place above her: So what did I tell you? Southern . . .

The movie is filled with wonderful sight gags—not something Van Dyke usually seems to care about. But here he clearly does, even to routines for the minor
actors. Edgar Kennedy is one of the dumb cops on Stewart's trail; but it is the
other two cops, Nat Pendleton and Cliff Clark, who do all the familiar Kennedy
shtick in this movie, clapping the tops of their heads in elaborate slow burns.
Pendleton even does the hand sliding down over the face while the eye peers out
between the fingers—practically a Kennedy trademark—with Kennedy himself
sharing the shot and looking on impassively.

But the most sustained and elaborate of such comic routines involves Stewart.
To disguise himself, after they have bound and gagged both the Boy Scout and
his scoutmaster in the woods, Guy dons the scoutmaster's uniform, short pants
and round broad-brimmed hat, and puts on the boy's disfiguring eyeglasses; he
looks like an enormous wallaby—and a startled one. His eyes behind the
ultrathick spectacles are huge and swimming. Every time someone comes toward him, he loses his balance. At first Edwina has to prop him up and aim
him—when talking to the highway police, for example. Later on, he just sits—
and looks out at things. As he is doing at the boathouse, waiting for the ferry,
when the announcer on the radio starts to read the latest bulletin on "missing
poetess Edwina Corday, the vanished authoress who leaped into fame with her
memorable lyric 'This night will be here when we are gone. . . .'" Edwina looks
sheepish: this is the poem she told Guy she had just composed. And as the
announcer reads the rest of it—"Other throats will sing in the dawn / It's a
wonderful world, my dear!"—Van Dyke shows us Stewart's monstrous eyes shifting and rolling hopelessly in the depth of those glasses, like something at the
bottom of a fish tank.

The film is brightly lit throughout, even the exteriors in the forest. *It Happened
One Night* without shadows or rain. The sexual charge of that rain is missing,
too. This comedy's intensities have an almost prepubescent feeling: the howl of
outrage Edwina gives—"That's no fair!"—when Guy, changing his mind about
letting her go, kidnaps her a second time: "No, no! You let me go *once!*" Or the
disgust Guy registers when he learns that this pest he can't get rid of no matter
what he does, has told people they're married. "Of all the lunkhead tricks!" he
cries. "Well, I had to say something quick," she says. "Well, why didn't you say
I was your brother or something—*normal?*" Finally we get to believe in the
romance between these two funny people partly because their resistances to it
are so childish. *It's a Wonderful World* takes a sunny view, literally and figura-
tively, of the hostility between men and women.

And Colbert is wonderful. It's an all-stops-out kind of performance that never seems frantic or excessive. She does everything full out: the giddiness and alarm and panic, the hysteria and gullibility and mooniness. She didn't normally play heroines so naive as this—a woman who writes sappy poetry and who says "How thrilling" when the hero tells her his phone is tapped. When Colbert reads a line like this, she gets a laugh out of the naiveté—as almost any competent performer would. But she does something else, too, more her own: she makes us feel the logic of such a response, reminding us that it really *is* thrilling in some way to have the cops after you. She wouldn't say it if it weren't so, would she? Everything in *her* Edwina is modified by that irreducible sensible core at the heart of every Colbert performance.

JUST AS Ellie in *It Happened One Night* did, Colbert herself gives an impression of supreme competence—through her whole career. Though she played working-girl roles—was even, like Jean Arthur and Ginger Rogers, identified with them—she had the kind of range and versatility that the thirties careers of Arthur and Rogers never aspired to. She was a mousy spinster in De Mille's *Four Frightened People*, the title character in his *Cleopatra*, the mother and businesswoman of John Stahl's *Imitation of Life*—and all these films were made in 1934, the year of *It Happened One Night*. So it went thereafter: she is a psychiatrist in a mental hospital in La Cava's *Private Worlds* (1935), where she has some nice scenes of camaraderie with Joel McCrea, as another doctor. In *Under Two Flags* (1936) she is Cigarette, a Foreign Legion canteen girl who gives her life to save Ronald Colman. She is a Puritan woman accused of witchcraft in *Maid of Salem* (1937), a White Russian refugee working as a maid in *Tovarich* (1937), a music-hall cocotte in *Zaza* (1939), a frontierswoman fighting Indians in *Drums Along the Mohawk* (1939). Like Hepburn, she was an actress-star, though with a greater range, and a clearer acceptance by audiences.

But she always seemed so sensible. In some way, almost too sensible for an actress. That candid quality might be a threat to *any* kind of pretense. That was one reason she was mainly known, and had her greatest successes, as a comedian. Her clarity is both her strength and her limitation. She has no recesses. Whenever a role lays claim to them, she goes the slightest bit fake, though remaining always skilled and intelligent. Her glamour comes from her forthrightness. She has none of the spiritualizing or aspirational quality of Arthur or Hepburn. Just the opposite: she is hopelessly, helplessly down to earth. That's what her audiences loved her for—that tactility that threatened even the Gable hero in *It Happened One Night*. The same quality could also make her seem powerfully sexy. It's probably the one thing De Mille got right about her. And he got it into every one of their films: the shower under the waterfall in *Four Frightened People* and the bath in asses' milk in *The Sign of the Cross* for example.

Her half-ironic impersonations of Cleopatra and the Empress Poppaea (in *The Sign of the Cross*) have also the quality of real carnal inspiration.

She knows what's going on: that's the clearest message of the famous tilted head and glittering smile. For that reason she is almost funniest of all when she does her imitations of obliviousness, of baby-doll incomprehension. When those wide appraising eyes go adorably blank—listening to *him*, usually—the effect in its violence is like another comic's pratfall. Gary Cooper is being masterful in Lubitsch's *Bluebeard's Eighth Wife* (1938): the sly fellow has gotten her drunk on martinis. There she is in his arms—daddy's girl in excelsis, unresisting at last. But she has just—unknown to him—taken a huge bite out of a nearby bunch of onions, a vegetable he's violently allergic to. "Kiss me," she says, giving an adorable little doo-wop sound to the words. "Kiss me, Michael." He holds her and exults: "What does a nice girl say?" Chin on his shoulder: "Please," says the nice girl—even more adorably: she seems almost to *squeeze* the word out. "*Please*," she says again, even more urgently, all but expiring from desire and itchy-koo preciousness. He turns to collect—and she lays him low with one breath.

If she never seems to miss anything, we have the same feeling about ourselves when we watch her. She astonishes us often enough, but she never leaves us behind. Of all the screwball heroines, she's the closest to us, because she remains the most reasonable. In all her triumphs of wit and imagination, she remains stubbornly—happily—untransfigured. She always levels with us. It isn't that she isn't magical, but rather that she always shows us what she has up her sleeve—and she's *still* dazzling. That openness *is* her magic. When she first appears in *Bluebeard's Eighth Wife*, for example, we know that she knows the scene is a preposterous one. She also lets us know that she's going to pull it off: just watch. Gary Cooper is trying to buy just the tops of a pair of pajamas, and the store management is balking, when Colbert comes along and offers to buy the bottoms. "Yes, I may buy the trousers," she says, entering—and she plays the whole scene that follows with a kind of high, elated artifice: looking Cooper over before she lets go with a line, giving him her what-a-chump glance before she turns away to smile, full of pleasure at her own power, her own sound, at the general absurdity. He is definitely "the stripey type," she tells him—neither checks nor solid colors. "If there was a stripey type, it's you"—and she turns away. This is almost too easy, but it's certainly fun.

They decided early on that her line was candor. And being down-to-earth. This idea of her is at the center of the three Colbert vehicles tailored for her at Paramount in the mid-thirties, all directed by Wesley Ruggles and written by Claude Binyon. She's a working girl on a hard-earned vacation in *I Met Him in Paris* (1937). In *The Bride Comes Home* (1935), she's a dispossessed heiress who puts ketchup on her french fries: "I like 'em that way," she tells a disgusted

Englishman Ray Milland has an experience of the New York subways in The Gilded Lily. *Claudette Colbert is his guide.*

escort. In *The Gilded Lily* (1935) she is a stenographer who likes to eat peanuts, sitting on a park bench with Fred MacMurray. What she really wants to be, as he tells her, is Lizzie Glutz, "the ideal existence." "You'll do your own cooking and washing and you'll lose your figure," he says. "And I'll love it!" she replies. He goes on: she yearns for this ideal, but she won't achieve it. Because, he explains, she is not dumb enough: "Lizzie Glutz is Lizzie Glutz simply because she's too darn dumb to be anything else—and that's not you." Although she is smart enough to know, he says, that there is nothing better than *being* Lizzie Glutz.*

What this heroine becomes instead is an overnight celebrity—"the 'No' Girl"—when she publicly rejects the proposal of a rich and titled Englishman (Ray Milland). Because of the publicity she is signed to do a nightclub act; but it turns out she really can't sing or dance. (In fact, Colbert *could* sing—as audiences knew from *Torch Singer* just the year before, where she sings in her own voice a terrific bluesy number called "Give Me Liberty or Give Me Love.") So

---

*Such whimsical Hollywood populism is parodied later on in *The Lady Eve*, when Barbara Stanwyck tells Henry Fonda about her romantic ideal: short and fat and with lots of money! "Mine is a *practical* ideal: You can find four or five of them in [any] barber shop . . ."

she confesses this to her opening-night audience. This honesty—along with a klutzy, halfhearted dance in her feathered gown—turns out to be her "act." And it's a hit. She even takes it to London, where they also love it.

It really is an odd idea, even for the movies: an act that features the performer's inability to *do* an act, winningly confessed at each show. But it certainly demonstrates what idea of Colbert had gained in the studio mind. As if *all* she had to do was level with us. Provided she turns out to be Lizzie Glutz of course, who can't sing and dance either.

But we don't really believe it—just as we know that a movie that tells us how wonderful it is not to be wonderful is being disingenuous at the least. But the same condescension to their audience poisons all these Ruggles-Binyon comedies, which aren't very funny in any case, though they were very successful at the box office. What these misguided vehicles call attention to, mainly by denying it so strenuously as they do, is a certain complication, even contradiction, in Colbert's disarming candor. She is, after all, capable of working the room with it. If the poorest Colbert comedies exploit this candor, the best ones are those, like *Midnight* and *The Palm Beach Story*, where she herself exploits it. It's then that she's most interesting—and funniest, too.

She arrives in Paris at the beginning of *Midnight* (1939)—having staked everything she owned on the roulette wheel at Monte Carlo—in a third-class train compartment, with nothing but the gold lamé evening gown on her back. Outside the train station in the rain, she has to wave away all the cabbies who take her for the rich lady she looks like. One in particular (Don Ameche), standing by his cab and eating an apple, can't resist a remark as she passes: "Madam enjoys the rain, huh?" he says between emphatic bites on the apple (shades of Gable's Peter Warne). Something in his voice, it seems—the sound of a come-on, a certain complacency, or stupidity (the chump sound), or something else—makes her stop and turn, with a speculative look as she does so. She sizes him up: it just takes an instant. She comes forward, putting her thumb to her mouth and her head to one side. Quizzical—but radiant. *Very* big smile. "Here's how things stand," she begins. "I could have you drive me around town"—gesturing toward his cab—"and then tell you I left my purse at home on the grand piano." She pauses and shakes her head, a very Colbertian inflection: overcome by her own frankness even before she puts it into words. "But there's no grand piano," she says, unable to keep the delight at this news from breaking into her voice, "no home—and the *purse* . . ." She holds it up and produces a coin. "Twenty-five centimes with a hole in it—what's left of the Peabody estate." She needs taxi service to find a job, she tells him—and if she lands one, she'll give him double what the meter says. "Double or nothing," she says roguishly (what fun this is), appealing to his sporting side. "Oh, and a great big dandy *tip*." Then a big smile: "Whatayou say?" But he says no—and the smile vanishes.

Of course, he finally does take her up on it. She has decided—being in Paris at night and in an evening gown—to try for a job as a singer. And being hopelessly attracted to imposture, she tries to pass herself off as "the famous American blues singer." It doesn't work. "Is that your last cigarette?" she asks him, before settling back to enjoy the ride she's just bummed—it is, but she takes it anyway. He pulls up in front of a café and offers to buy her dinner, but she demurs: "Listen," she says in her throatiest voice, "you *lost* a gamble, you don't have to *feed* it." Once inside the café, though, she orders the special. "I wouldn't have taken oysters only I thought they were on the regular dinner—honestly," she explains happily, as they dance after dinner. She even *looks* full in this scene.

It's curious: there is something really retrograde about the Colbert heroine. Her performance notes it all, with the usual Colbert clarity—the conjunction of the openness, frank and free ("you don't have to *feed* it"), with the petty chiseling. You know that she can't help ordering those oysters. You also know that

Claudette Colbert in Midnight: *arriving in Paris (below) and settling in (right). But John Barrymore (beside her) and Hedda Hopper (behind) suspect a party crasher.*

she's glad she has. The amorality is pervasive and triumphant: that glittering attention can be as easily taken by oysters or people's last cigarettes as by bank-rolls. The hero, hearing her hard-luck story in the café, accuses her of "wanting something for nothing." Of course she does. Who doesn't?—except for people like him. "If you want peace of mind," he tells her (and you knew he'd be inter-ested in *that*), "get yourself a taxicab." She almost landed herself a lord, she tells him, but the family objected. "His mother came to my hotel and offered me a bribe," she says. "You threw her out, I hope," says Ameche. Colbert looks for a moment as if this question had interrupted some other train of thought, before replying: "How could I with my hands full of money?" As she says, "I've got a few ideas about peace of mind myself."

"Say, are you interested in finance?" asks millionaire playboy Gary Cooper in *Bluebeard's Eighth Wife.* "You bet I am," she says with a deep-throated laugh. A bit later on they are in a nightclub, staring dreamily across the table at each

other. "Ninety-five to ninety-seven and a half," she murmurs in luminous close-up. Cooper is puzzled. "Oil," she says huskily, showing him she can talk his language. "It went up two and a half points." But later, when he's about to marry her, there is a hitch. Her Aunt Edwige, the head of the family (Elizabeth Patterson), spurns the millionaire's offer of a marriage settlement for her niece Nicole (Colbert). But fifty thousand dollars! protests Nicole's father (Edward Everett Horton), who wants to accept it. "We're discussing a matter of the human heart!" cries the old lady, "what's fifty thousand dollars!" But in fact it sounds like even *more* (a very Lubitschean joke) when you balance it against the hollow sound of "a matter of the human heart." This is the sort of thing Colbert is always reminding us of. She is the most amoral of all the great screwball heroines. It's a function of her clarity: devastating to the matters-of-the-human-heart style, and very hard, too, on the people who talk about peace of mind or who disapprove of getting something for nothing. Colbert never has to make a flourish of this hardness, or indulge a tough-girl manner of any kind. But in some happy ways she's the toughest of them all—as you know when she turns those wide, attentive eyes on the one who's just said something like "You threw her out, I hope?"

As a result, probably her best roles of all are in her three love-and-money comedies: Leisen's *Midnight,* Lubitsch's *Bluebeard's Eighth Wife,* and Sturges' *The Palm Beach Story* (1942). (She is the only great comedienne of her time to work with both Lubitsch and Sturges.) Her sexiness isn't the only corollary to that tactility of hers; another is her materialism. Colbert does for golddigging what Lombard does for craziness: she makes it seem like something liberating.

ONE OF the peculiarities of *Midnight* is the way Ameche's wet-blanket hero—he's a Hungarian named Tibor Czerny—virtually disappears once he's established his claim to the heroine in those first scenes. He turns up again in the climactic scenes, where he becomes the focus of some wonderful new farcical inventions; but he is missing from the movie's center. As he almost has to be if the heroine is to have any fun or adventure. Eve ditches him (she must leave him, it says here, precisely because she is so attracted to him) by jumping out of his cab and into the rain again. She ends up under an awning and being inadvertently ushered into a party with a lot of other posh-looking types (it's her evening gown). And with this lovely, quite reasonable mistake the movie really begins—or at least the magical part of it does.

And it *is* like a magic act, piling surprise on surprise almost effortlessly. The Colbert heroine may have nothing up her sleeve, but the movie she's in does—inexhaustibly, it seems. The original story is by Edwin Justus Mayer and Franz Schulz and the witty screenplay by Charles Brackett and Billy Wilder. Directed by Mitchell Leisen, the whole film has that look of discriminating opulence

The card game
in Midnight:
Francis
Lederer, Mary
Astor, Rex
O'Malley,
Claudette
Colbert, John
Barrymore.

which Paramount movies especially (and most especially Leisen's Paramount movies) so often did have. There are two knockout parties in this movie, and they both *look* terrific, in sets combining a kind of Old World elegance with art deco spaciousness and vistas of glittering white. The second big party—at the Flammarions'—takes place on multiple levels and curving stairways, with dazzling long shots from above of everyone in the ballroom doing the conga while they discuss the latest turns of the constantly self-renewing plot.

But when Colbert's Eve Peabody steps into the first of these parties, she is like Alice down the rabbit hole or through the looking glass—entering a place where predictability takes on a different meaning. It is, of course, a boring party—that's agreed upon. "It always rains when Stephanie gives one of her dull parties—even Nature weeps," says one of the entering guests (Elaine Barrie), having fun even before she gets inside. But at the door, as Eve approaches, people are showing their invitations. Eve takes the Monte Carlo pawn ticket out of her purse, and with a wonderful smile-at-no-one-in-particular, the partygoer's official pleasantness, she hands it to the doorman and goes in. Inside, people are gathered in a vast room listening to an overweight soprano accompanied by a fuming long-haired pianist. Eve eventually finds an unoccupied chair (the one she just tried a minute ago had an angry Pomeranian in it) and settles down with relief. Safe at last: her round-eyed catbird seat expression, back straight, elbows at her side, face blankly blissful, as she sinks purposefully, concentratedly down into the cushions. But she is being observed, even studied, by a strange-looking man standing against the wall—she gives him a frosty smile. And then it turns out that the pawn ticket, with her name on it, has been discovered among the invitations. The hostess (Hedda Hopper) makes a public announcement: a Miss Eve Peabody? The strange man looks. "No?" continues the hostess. "Well, does anybody here *know* a Miss Eve Peabody?" Colbert looks pleasantly around. No response, and the musicale resumes. But now another man is watching her— and he approaches.

She thinks she is done for now, but instead she is being invited to make a fourth at bridge in a private room away from the concert. "Why did you pick on me?" she asks at the door. "You looked charming," says Marcel (Rex O'Malley), "you looked bored, and you looked as though you wouldn't trump your partner's ace." But the bridge game itself is a rather tense one, mainly because Eve's partner, Jacques Picot (Francis Lederer)—one of the most dangerous men in Paris, as Marcel describes him—is flirting with her, notwithstanding his liaison with the *other* player, the seething Madame Flammarion (Mary Astor). What's more, Eve finds herself playing a high-stakes game and calling herself (she had to supply a name) "Madame Czerny." These tensions intersect alarmingly when Jacques, distracted by his partner's charms and not really paying attention, passes right after Eve has bid two spades. "Now," says Colbert in a small dry voice, "I know why you called him dangerous." When it comes time for her to pay up, she starts muttering something about IOU's, only to open her purse and find a thick wad of bills inside it. The strange man from the musicale—who has turned out to be Madame Flammarion's husband, Georges (John Barrymore)— is still observing her. And then, when she pretends to go to "my hotel" (the Ritz, where else?) with Jacques escorting her, dogging her into the lobby and even to the door of the room, she finds she really *does* have a booking there—or at least that "Madame Czerny" does. And when she wakes up the next morning, she finds a closet full of clothes and a chauffeur and car waiting for her downstairs.

It all gets explained when Flammarion arrives at the hotel. He spotted her as a phony right away, he tells her. He also spotted Jacques' interest in her. And since Flammarion wants his wife back, he wants Eve to go about winning Jacques away from her—by continuing her masquerade as the "Baroness" Czerny while being a house guest at the Flammarions'. And so it goes—dazzlingly, for the most part, with jokes and inventions and surprises nearly to the end. "Get what you can out of this deal," Flammarion encourages her when she reports to him that Jacques has been trying to give her an emerald. "That's what

I'm doing," she assures him; Jacques, she says, may even be on the point of asking her to marry him. Flammarion is skeptical. "You don't know Jacques Picot," he says. "*You* don't know Eve Peabody," Colbert replies, walking off. And when her "husband," the real Czerny, turns up, determined to expose her, she outwits him too.

If it doesn't quite work to the end (the last sequence, a comic courtroom scene with Monty Woolley as the judge, is both flat and sour), that's because once Eve has finished outwitting Czerny, she has to be reclaimed by him. As if Cinderella should go back home to the stepsisters instead of off with Prince Charming. It's true Jacques is a little too equivocal a figure—handsome and aristocratic, but also a bit sleazy somehow—to be a convincing Prince Charming. Marry him, says Flammarion. "Nice kind of marriage," says Eve. "As we turn from the altar I start explaining, I suppose." But does the alternative to this figure—nonrich, nonaristocratic, nonsleazy—have to be quite so dismal as Czerny, the moralizing cab driver?

Well, if it's a Brackett-Wilder script he does, it seems. The cynicism of their films (and this becomes even truer in Wilder's later films as writer-director) is always the kind that has to be renounced by movie's end—and always *is* renounced, but in ways that only make us feel uneasy about both it *and* the renouncing. Brackett and Wilder don't quite have the courage of their cynicism, and in fact you're just as glad they don't; but then you feel them taking a kind of revenge for *not* having it, in the slightly smarmy quality of their romantic affirmations.* Even when the tone remains as light as it does in *Midnight*, the effect is queasy. As when Colbert gives a comic speech in the courtroom scene in defense of wife-beating (it shows he cares).

It's only when the whole movie begins to collapse that the heroine does too. Otherwise, she is the center of its strength. *Midnight* is a sophisticated comedy with one crucial difference: it has this tough slangy heroine, who ultimately outclasses everyone else on the very classy premises. And we really don't want or expect her to marry Jacques, precisely because we don't expect her to affirm the empty "sophistication" that he and the others represent. One reason that Eve can be so bitchy, even in an unprovoked way, to Madame Flammarion (that hat looks good on you, she says: "It gives you a chin") is that Madame Flammarion—at least by the standards the movie evokes—seems to ask for it. And she does so mostly by being what she is: "Oh, Marcel," she cries, examining a newspaper photo showing the "Baroness" as a chorus girl, "this is *heaven!*" The sound of that is so opposite to Eve's that it seems almost to define another order of humanity. And it defines by contrast almost everything we like best about the chiseling, golddigging Colbert heroine.

---

*Wilder's best films, I think, are the ones where the misanthropy and disgust are frank and unapologetic—the "unpleasant" (and unsuccessful) ones like *Kiss Me Stupid* (1964) and *Ace in the Hole* (1951).

She is a party crasher, first by accident, then by design. It's not only her central action in the movie; it's her nature. To be classy without ever quite believing in it. She is swanking around (Flammarion's instructions) at a shop called Simone's Chapeaux, mainly because Jacques and Madame Flammarion are there. She asks to see some hats "for the weekend," and the saleswoman complies eagerly. "I'll show you some amusing models," she says, as she goes off to get them. Colbert looks suddenly alarmed: "Not *too* convulsing, please!" she calls after her. Later on, when Jacques is proposing to her as she predicted, under the moonlight, he envisions the moment when he will bring her to his family home to meet his mother. He waxes lyrical over the scene: "'Mother,' I'll say, 'here she is' . . . and the dawn will be pale behind the oak." Colbert has her doubts, though: "It won't be as pale as Mother," she says. Earlier, when she first turns up at the Flammarion estate posing as the Baroness, she and Barrymore walk ahead of the others. "Nice little bungalow you've got here," she says under her breath—as if they were *both* freeloaders. (Barrymore acts as though he were too: it's one of the things that ties them together in the film, more closely than she ever seems tied to Ameche.) This tone is almost a Colbert signature: it's like her line when she first enters the movie on the train from Monte Carlo, leaning out of her third-class compartment and looking at the rain: "Well, so this, as they say, is Paris, huh?" She's come for the enchantment, all right—but on her own terms. Just as she enjoys the swank of the Flammarions' world without ever being taken in by it. "I thought the big idea was to get away from this party, not into it," she says in response to the search for the Eve Peabody of the pawn ticket.

The Colbert heroine may dream of and pursue the world of wealth and luxury—but in *our* dream of her, and in her final vision of herself, she is outside that world, happily and irredeemably. It's that dream of essential detachment that infuses all these comedies—and American culture itself. The dream of triumphant outsidership. The fun of the party is crashing it—*not* belonging at it.

Jean Arthur | 17

No one was more closely identified with the screwball comedy than Jean Arthur. So much was she part of it, so much was her star personality defined by it, that the screwball style itself seems almost unimaginable without her. And yet, at the same time—surprisingly—she does without most of the screwball heroine's standard effects. She neither goes "crazy" in her films nor "wild." If she is involved in a disruption, she is as confused and surprised by it as anyone. She hasn't Lombard's temperament or Dunne's brilliance. She doesn't have Rogers' sardonicism or Hepburn's radiance or Colbert's assurance. She is more querulous than sardonic, and she's almost never entirely sure of herself. She spends a whole movie (*Only Angels Have Wings*) hanging out with the boys in a dive in Baranca, and she doesn't even wisecrack with them. But then she almost never does wisecrack.

Though she *is* distinctive, even idiosyncratic. For one thing, there's her famous voice—a phenomenon people have trouble describing adequately. "Low, husky—at times it breaks pleasingly into the higher octaves like a thousand tinkling bells," writes Frank Capra in his autobiography. Another writer, Andrew Bergman, simply calls it "the most wonderful speaking voice anyone had ever heard." And it is a speaking voice: it never sings or flutes or declines into pathos. It's candid and direct, just as she is. And it had none of the classy overtones— *either* upper-class or lower—or actressy ones that other distinctive stars' voices had, like Hepburn's or Margaret Sullavan's. It was both remarkable and ordinary—a paradox that Arthur herself embodied.

In some ways she is the most original of all the screwball women—if only because she did away with so much of the equipment, the ingenuity and the subversion and the gags. She offered what she was, so to speak: smart and resilient and generous, with a killing smile, at once reluctant and adventurous, candid and quizzical at the same time. In a way she completes the cycle of screwball heroines, confirming the tendency to move their glamour closer to ordinary life. Possibly the most distinctive thing about Arthur is that she's always so nice: that's the only word for it. And that quality is central in her as it could never be in the Colbert or the Rogers heroine. It's also helpless: she could never have played the opposite qualities, as Hepburn and Stanwyck and Lombard occasionally did. Arthur has this special talent for making ordinary niceness on the screen seem somehow remarkable—and interesting. And with her this plainness often has the same mysterious effect, even the same exotic force at times, as more conventional glamour.

Easy Living (1937)—directed by Mitchell Leisen—is the clearest instance of this effect: where Arthur's Mary Smith (again, the name is a tip-off) is even less characterized than most such heroines, without a history or a sidekick or any striking personal qualities. But in this case the transparency of the character fits the transparency of the performer. Arthur shows her mysterious faculty for compelling the camera, for inviting the audience's absorption. There is a long wordless sequence in her rented room that might have been played for pathos and winsomeness: it calls for her to blindfold her piggy bank with a handkerchief

Jean Arthur— in the hands- on style of Capra (below: Mr. Smith Goes to Washington, with James Stewart) and the hands-off style of Hawks (right: Only Angels Have Wings, with Cary Grant).

before smashing it open to get her last coin out. But Arthur plays it for pensive-
ness—smelling some nearby cooking at the window, hearing the vague jaunty
strains of someone's radio playing, reading her landlord's notice about the rent,
then smashing the piggy bank and looking for the coin on the floor, finding a
telegram instead, and *then* the coin—the whole sequence is suspended in a kind
of meditative calm, the effect of Leisen's direction and Arthur's concentration.
Outrageousness makes her quiet. When Louis Louis (Luis Alberni) shows her
"her" hotel suite, a place of Versailles-like size and splendor (it occupied the
entirety of Paramount's biggest sound stage), she sits down when he's gone and
lets out a sigh: "Golly," she says softly, her only remark. ("When Jean's being
shown her hotel suite," Leisen told David Chierichetti in 1969, "the obvious
thing would be to have her react to every little thing. So I did just the opposite.")

When the same film puts her between two enormous sheepdogs, like panting
laundry bags, in the back of a speeding taxicab, with police sirens screaming in
the background, the effect is like a revelation—to see her sharp lively presence
framed by these two eyeless, faceless ones, like otherworldly companions. Her

hair, too, has fallen over one eye; she is looking distracted and clutching the dogs. She may not be conventionally characterized, but in a way it tells us almost everything we might hope to know about this heroine that when she makes it big on the market—as she just has—the first thing she would want would be this big, impractical, unmanageable sort of dog, that she would get two of them and hold onto them in the midst of traffic. She is both accommodating and intransigent, both hopeless and hopeful. Just the sort of extraordinary "ordinary" type—capricious and contradictory and embattled—that Preston Sturges often writes about.

He wrote the screenplay for *Easy Living*, and it has his characteristic interest in the insane arbitrariness of American experience. Everyone remembers it as the movie where the fur coat falls on the heroine's head. Even at the time (though the film was a flop) this image was a famous one. Arthur is riding on the open top of a Fifth Avenue double decker bus when the coat lands on her. For J. B. Ball (Edward Arnold) it was simply the one-too-many sable coat his improvident wife (Mary Nash) had tried to get away with: he had snatched it from her in a rage and thrown it from their penthouse roof. So it becomes Mary's, though she never quite understands why, and causes her to lose her job at a magazine called *The Boy's Constant Companion* and then to be installed in "the Imperial Suite" at the near-bankrupt Hotel Louis. Everyone thinks she is J. B. Ball's mistress—though the movie is nearly over, and a financial empire in ruins, before anyone really explains this to her.

Most of the time, she is just bemused. And Arthur registers and conveys every nuance of that condition—one of her specialties. She knew more about it than Howard Hawks did—at least that seems to be the real and quite unintended point of an anecdote Hawks told (in 1974) about directing her. A breakfast scene in *Only Angels Have Wings* (1939): Cary Grant, who sent her away the night before, comes down and finds her still there. Hawks wanted her to show her nervousness and confusion at this awkward moment by buttering her bread with a spoon and stirring her coffee with a fork. Arthur refused, categorically. (She was well known for being "difficult.") "I can't do that," she told Hawks. Wouldn't she even like to *try* it? he inquired. "No," she replied, giving as her reason that "it would just upset me." And that was that: Hawks reported that he "gave up." But this story, meant to illustrate her contrariness (the only person he ever worked with, Hawks told her after filming was done, "that I don't think I helped a bit"), really shows her good judgment: as a performer, Arthur knew too much about real unease to want to attempt the crude cartoon of it Hawks was proposing to her. She plays the scene her way: with no gimmicks, bright and chatty and glassy-eyed, somehow carrying the difficult moment off, mainly by talking. "And you know, she was *good*," Hawks conceded in the same reminiscence—about the only time in these late interviews he does make such a concession.

On the set of
The Whole
Town's Talk-
ing: *Edward G.
Robinson and
Jean Arthur.*

Where Colbert's authority comes from her security about the real world, Arthur's comes from her persistent unease about it. But she is never fussy or silly or distraught. That unease always seems justified, a function of intelligence rather than a failure of nerve. The Arthur heroine is bold and dashing —ready for anything in one way, not up to any of it in another. She is simply not *sure*, not really, about anything. What makes her so specially attractive is that she never is really disabled by this uncertainty. So that we are never really surprised, for all her doubts about things, to find her, at once intrepid and dubious, in Baranca or Washington or way out west, being a star reporter or in the arms of a public enemy or surrounded by hostile Indians.

Her most characteristic reactions are the appraising look, the double take, and the sidelong glance. Just as when she walks off—decisively—she almost always looks back: did she really see that, or hear it? Even the famous crack in the Arthur voice is a kind of aural double take—a way of changing directions, of registering a new perception in mid-utterance. She is a virtuoso of the delayed reaction—that wonderful *"Hey!"* when she discovers the double-headed coin Grant has given her at the end of *Only Angels Have Wings,* for example. Or in *Easy Living,* the way she sits bolt upright some moments after Ray Milland has kissed her, while they are both falling asleep. "Say—" she says, face half turned away—then the smile growing. She has a way of taking a second look at someone she's just been pleased by—by some piece of wit, or courage, or just niceness—throwing her head back, looking down along her nose, and smiling. You're out of work, too, Milland reminds her, having just lost his own job at the Automat trying to smuggle her a free meal. But there's a difference, she reminds *him,* in that rather severe tone that she's been taking with him as they walk along side by side: "When you're hungry, no one's going to lose his job trying to feed *you*"—but then she pulls back, unseen by him, and gives him that sidelong smile.

She plays a dual role in *Diamond Jim* (1935), the first of the two Preston Sturges screenplays she appeared in; and the doubling seems curiously appropriate, like another version of her double take. In an early part of the film she is the idealized first—and finally lost—love of Jim Brady (Edward Arnold again): a delicate southern belle, girlish and pretty and somehow melancholy, appearing when she enters the film on a surge of nostalgic music, like a John Ford heroine, and always referred to by Brady, once she's vanished from his life, as "an angel." In the second role, she is a high-class party girl, a New York demimondaine, appearing at a banquet Brady is giving for his raffish cronies on the arm of a distinguished gray-haired type. The escort takes her cape and she stands in the doorway of the banquet room, looking around with a composed little smile. It's that incredible movie-star expressiveness again: Arthur does nothing but stand and look, it seems, but we know instantly what "sort" of woman she is, even how she feels about it; there's a kind of consciousness in the stance and eyes, a kind of resignation in the cheerfulness. Brady, of course, takes her for "an angel"—and she lets him, more or less, accepting the situation as she accepts so much in her movies, with a kind of rueful heartiness. The escort has introduced her as his niece. Are you his brother's daughter or his sister's? inquires the bedazzled Brady. "Oh," she says, sucking her cheek in, "—sort of a stepbrother." In their scenes together Arnold tucks his chin in and looks up at her, sheepish and adoring, just as she lifts her chin and looks down at him along her nose, but uneasily—sympathetic, but from a precarious height.

Any kind of eminence makes her uneasy—even the relation with servants. She rarely has them at all in her movies, and when she does it doesn't work out well. Like that greasy, smirking chauffeur (Ivan Lebedeff) her sadistic husband sics on her in *History Is Made at Night* (1937). The man locks the door of her hotel room and then tries to kiss her. "Michael!" she cries, "give me that key"; but she doesn't even *sound* as if she expects to get it. (Charles Boyer saves her.) Even in an extremity like this one she has trouble giving a convincing order. But that is a significant incapacity, one of the things that marks her uniqueness. After all, even the gamines could turn imperious—Luise Rainer or Margaret Sullavan or (later on) Audrey Hepburn; it was one of the things they did.

Arthur, on the other hand, seems to have no grand-lady possibilities of any kind—alone among the leading actresses of her time, maybe of any time. No more could she be bitchy. Not even with Rita Hayworth in *Only Angels Have Wings*, where the situation is clearly set up for that—at least for a few good cracks (like the ones Lauren Bacall levels at Dolores Moran in *To Have and Have Not*, Hawks's later version of the same characters). Colbert's "It gives you a chin" or Rogers' "You could, too, with those shoulders": such ripostes are part of the standard repertoire. And yet from Arthur they are simply and flatly unimaginable. And she was never given such lines, it seems—or else she refused them, as uncongenial to her performing style, like stirring her coffee with a fork. And it's not that she's too "sweet"—not at all. She is uncommonly aggressive at times, prickly and challenging almost always.

But even at her boldest and most dashing, she is never quite impervious. Her panache always has this paradoxical quality: it seems to offer something exposed to the outside world. When she swashbuckles into the office at the beginning of *The Whole Town's Talking* (1935), the effect is stunning especially because she seems to register the *risk* of what she's doing, the risk of what she *is* in this world of impossible jobs and even more impossible men. If Harlow is the tough girl who doesn't know what it is to be nervous, Arthur is the tough girl who does. Still, she's so splendid that the only time Jonesie, the fainthearted hero (Edward G. Robinson), has the nerve to kiss her is after he's had a couple of whiskeys in the boss's office. Later on, when they are just married and sailing for Shanghai (Jonesie has become a hero after capturing and killing his public-enemy double), the reporters covering their embarkation want a picture of them kissing. "How about it, Jonesie," Arthur says, "do you need a slug of whiskey?" Of course he doesn't. And a line like this—with its suggestion of bullying and reproach—makes her seem all the more irresistible. It's the way Arthur always triumphs over the hints of bad feeling, in both her lines and her roles. She has a freedom that comes from her own vulnerability. She can tell Jonesie not to be scared, call him "a rabbit," challenge him to kiss her in public, and make it all somehow sound perfectly sensible and friendly—and why not? And when she tells the apparently unemployable Johnny (Ray Milland) in *Easy Living* that he's just—well, "underdeveloped" (choosing the word carefully), she makes it sound like a love message. Which is just how he takes it. One of her most delighted moments in that same film is when she gets to make fun of the way he talks. "Go over to the hot dish window," he mutters to her in the Automat as he pretends to be cleaning her table, and she gives him her say-what-is-this? look: "*Hotchkiss* window?" she says. "What's a matter, you got something wrong with your teeth?"—enjoying herself a lot.

Easy Living is her most "violent" role: she actually hits people in this one—always wimpish little men, not unlike Jonesie. Mr. Gurney (Barlowe Borland), her treble-voiced boss at *The Boy's Constant Companion*, makes an insulting innuendo, and she crowns him with an enormous framed picture. Later when Louis Louis, the frenetic, fractured-English–speaking hotel owner, makes a similar sort of remark (it's that coat), she hauls off and slaps him twice, very smartly, before running off with her two sheepdogs. "Such humiliation!" says Louis, clutching his stinging face. ("Put dat back in de icebox!" he screams at a man who's just walked in with two big birdcages.) But then the "humiliation" happens again—at the end of the film, with everyone talking at once and Mary (Arthur) trying to explain herself to the hero and his family over the hubbub. "Isn't that right, Mr. Louis?" she says at one point, turning to the flustered little man for corroboration of her story. He draws back, shaking his finger at her: "I don't want to be complicated," he says (he means "implicated"). "*Oh,*" she says, like someone who's just been struck by a twinge of pain—and instantly slaps him again, almost at the same instant as her attention is claimed by someone else. What makes this moment so funny and startling (it's in no way emphasized either by the camera or the staging) is its inexorableness. It isn't, we know, that she really *wants* to hit him—it's that he's done it again, and so gets hit again. In a way it has nothing to do with her. Even her anger is oddly—obliquely—generous-spirited. She strikes, but she never wounds. The blows may hurt (we can hear them land); but like her challenge and her mockery, they don't really seem to be meant personally.

IN MANY ways her career paralleled Lombard's. Screwball comedy made them both big stars in the mid-thirties, whereas both of them had been more or less routine leading ladies up to then, and both veterans of the silents (unlike the women who came from the stage, like Dunne and Colbert). They both had identity problems on the screen that were solved only by the screwball heroine. Jean Arthur had made over twenty-five films, most of them low-budget westerns, even before she made her first talkie, *The Saturday Night Kid* (1929) with Clara Bow. And in these early sound films—she had a brief ingenue career at Paramount—she seems unpromising. Like a distracted bird, with an odd flickering presence and a piping voice. She decided after a while to learn how to act on the stage. She left Hollywood and went east in 1931.

After two years of theater experience she went back to the movies, to leading roles in B films. But the third of these assignments—*Whirlpool* (1934), starring Jack Holt as her escaped-con father—got her a long-term contract at Columbia. It wasn't a first-rate studio, of course; nor did they give her first-rate pictures. A sample of what they did give her is *The Most Precious Thing in Life* (1934). She is a scrubwoman at college, cleaning the room of a rich, spoiled freshman (Richard Cromwell) who doesn't know that she is really his mother. Not surprising that he doesn't: though Arthur was a girl when she gave birth to him in the film's early scenes, now—eighteen years later—she is well into her sixties, wearing long skirts and a granny wig and dispensing an old person's wisdom and mellowness. (She's worried about her boy: now that he's been raised by rich people, will he have the character to get through freshman hazing? Money, it seems, has spoiled him for fraternity life.) Clearly, the studio thought she was an Actress. But *what* actress? Beulah Bondi at this time conventionally played women in their sixties and seventies when she herself was forty (forty-five when she played Lucy in *Make Way for Tomorrow*). Arthur was only twenty-nine when she put on her first granny wig. The portents could hardly have been more ominous. There were, after all, any number of *Most Precious Thing* opportunities for a screen heroine like Arthur, with a break in her voice and a suggestion of vulnerability.

But then with her next Columbia movie everything turned around. *The Whole Town's Talking*, written by Robert Riskin and directed (oddly enough) by John Ford, is a comedy with Edward G. Robinson playing both a milquetoast office clerk and the dangerous public enemy he is mistaken for. Arthur is the girl in the office. And with this role she becomes at one stroke a thirties comedy heroine, brash and funny and enchanting. She loses her job in this film, too—in her very first scene, entering the office with her head down and cigarette puffing. "You're late!" says the dithering little office manager (Etienne Girardot). She turns pleasantly from the time clock: "For what?" she inquires—and gets cheerfully fired. Jonesie (Robinson) watches her from his desk, hardly daring to breathe in the presence of such courage and glamour. "Hiya, Jonesie," she says on her way to clean out her desk, like some visiting celebrity being friendly. Her real dream, as she tells him later over coffee, is "to hop a freighter to Shanghai." Nobody seems to notice—least of all the bedazzled Robinson—that this was the sort of thing *men* in movies said. Anyway until heroines like Arthur came along.

She made an impression. And after this film, Columbia gave her script and director approval. Her next few films weren't horrendous (no more *Most Precious Things*), but they were mostly run-of-the-mill. Then Frank Capra saw one of them in a screening room and insisted on using her—over Harry Cohn's objections—in *Mr. Deeds Goes to Town* (1936). It was Capra who singlehandedly

Arthur with Richard Cromwell in The Most Precious Thing in Life *(above); with Gary Cooper in* The Plainsman *(right).*

turned Columbia into a major studio: with *Mr. Deeds* he also turned a studio contract player into one of the decade's biggest women stars. And Cecil B. De Mille's *The Plainsman* (1936)—a loan-out to Paramount—more than confirmed Arthur's new status. She was Calamity Jane, dressed in buckskins ("Don't you *ever* wear a dress?" "I might if I had one.") but much blonder-haired and more glamorously made up than ever before, cracking a bullwhip and yearning hopelessly after Gary Cooper's no-time-for-love Wild Bill Hickok. It wasn't a very plausible film, but it caught the public's imagination. And she and Cooper seemed to apotheosize themselves in it, both movie-star-beautiful and androgynous, tied by their wrists to a pole inside a tepee, straining toward each other while hostile redskins whoop it up outside. The De Mille touch.

She was *the* Capra heroine: his favorite actress, he says in his autobiography, "probably because she was unique." But Capra used the same qualities in her that had been exploited by *The Whole Town's Talking*—the independence and toughness and rakishness. He saw clearly that she was no sentimental heroine, in spite of her superficial resemblances to one. (It's the Capra *hero* who is the sentimental figure.) And once she became a major star, Arthur—uniquely—

never again made an out-and-out tearjerker.* She made, in fact, almost nothing but comedies. It was a career with no parallel among the women stars of her time.

But she was also a Hawks heroine—for at least one film, *Only Angels Have Wings*, opposite Cary Grant. Arthur was thought to have a special appeal for male audiences (another reason she did no tearjerkers, whose audiences were principally women), affecting them in some of the same ways heartthrob stars like Boyer affected the women. It was Arthur's total lack of coyness—the direct disabling way she looks into Boyer's eyes between the taxicab kisses of *History Is Made at Night*, for example. She is, in fact, a Hawks ideal—companionable and feminine and desirable but like a man, too. Though perhaps not *quite* enough like: her problem with the Grant hero is that she has to learn to be more so, to take Grant more or less as his buddies do, not to be hysterical and possessive like a woman, before she can win him. "Did you ever know a woman

---

*History Is Made at Night, directed by Frank Borzage, is a borderline case—almost too weird a film to be categorized. Most people seem to remember it as a romantic comedy, but in fact it's mostly soap opera, and more lugubrious than high-spirited.

who didn't want to make plans?" he asks her. They are sitting at the bar late at night. "What," says Arthur, "if she were the type who didn't scare so easily?" He thinks this over, then asks her if she'd like to see his room. Lots of pictures of himself there, he continues facetiously. Any baby pictures? she wonders. Yeah, those too. "Sure," she says, lowering her eyes and turning to get down from her bar stool—and she is on her way to his room. Just the slightest—characteristic—hesitation before she takes the decision ("Sure"): no fuss, no drama, but no kidding herself either. (Just as when she walks into the office of *The Whole Town's Talking:* we know she's measured the risk—she always does.) But it's Grant who backs down (one of them has to, of course, given the Production Code), and we're invited to infer that he doesn't want her to "get hurt." He takes her to the doorway and points her in the direction of that boat she keeps missing.

She is the first Hawks heroine to say to the man, "I'm hard to get—all you have to do is ask me" (Bacall says the same line to Bogart in *To Have and Have Not* in 1944, and Angie Dickinson says it again to John Wayne in 1959's *Rio Bravo*). The Hawks heroine of whatever period not only never says no; she does all the pursuing. She moves in on the hero, who keeps telling her to get on that boat or that stagecoach, and lays siege to him. It's the Hawks hero who is coy, who plays games—who often talks in codes and riddles, part of the way he fends her off without quite losing her. Geoff (Grant) never does ask Bonnie (Arthur) to stay with him. He flips a coin, over her loud objections: heads, she stays. It is heads—and he goes out the door to the plane they've been warming up for him. But since he's left the coin behind, she discovers that it's heads on *both* sides—in one of her funniest and most radiant double takes. *"Hey!"* she calls after him, holding the coin out in front of her and rushing to the door to wave him off jubilantly for the movie's fadeout.

Through most of the film Arthur wears the same kind of mannish tailored suit, with the same checks and wide lapels, as Bacall does through *To Have and Have Not.* Like the hero of Hitchcock's *Vertigo*, Hawks tends to repeat even the smallest details of his favorite heroine. Though Arthur often resisted him, he complained in latter-day interviews.* But then it's clear even by his own account that he was trying to impose on her something out of his own head, something he successfully imposed on—and triumphantly embodied in—Lauren Bacall some five years later. And yet much of the interest of the Arthur heroine in *Only Angels Have Wings* is the offbeat casting, just as it is with the Grant hero. And both stars as a result give performances tinged with incredulity. This situation only seems to embolden Grant, to enliven and delight him. But to Arthur it gives

---

*Capra, too, found her troublesome—and pathologically shy. He claims, in *The Name Above the Title*, that she vomited before and after every scene!

an edge of poignance. Bonnie seems a long way from home in *every* sense: Arthur makes that dislocation part of our sense of the character's gallantry.

W HEN THE coat falls on her in *Easy Living,* she is sitting on the top deck of the bus, hands crossed in her lap, looking off into space—then suddenly it envelops her. She gives a muffled scream and pulls it down off her head, breaking the feather on her drab but perky little hat. She turns and looks at the man behind her: he wears a turban and is reading a book. "Say, what's the big idea, anyway?" she demands. "Kismet," he replies, and goes back to his book. She sits there, fighting tears and breathing through her nose—rising to resentment, as it were, but at what? at whom? They've done it to her again—but *who* has? She pushes the buzzer to stop the bus and gets off, giving the turbaned man another look as she passes him: after *all.* . . . On the street now, she crosses, looking both ways for traffic as she goes, with a kind of bustling intentness, emphasized by our watching her from behind. She is going to try to return the coat—unsuccessfully.

J. B. Ball (Arnold), otherwise known as "the Bull of Broad Street," is America's third-biggest banker, and he is used to dealing with people peremptorily. He is leaving his house for work when he sees this young lady carrying the coat he has just snatched away from his wife. So far he is having a good day—he's successfully thwarted his wife and he's just won an argument with his servants— even though it started off badly. He's in a hearty mood and chuckling a lot. He sees this girl with the coat and he goes charging up to her. "Where did you find it?" he asks. She flinches away from him, suspicious. Is the coat his? But now he starts firing questions at her. Does she work for a living? Well, of course she does, what does he think—and what business is that of his? "Say, look what you did to my *hat!*" she says, remembering the broken feather. "You own a fur coat?" he asks. "No," she says, holding on to the feather, "I don't—but I still don't see—" "That's where you're wrong," he says, waving his finger at her, then tapping the coat. "You own *that* one. Happy birthday!"—and he goes off laughing. "Now just a minute, Santa Claus," she says, and goes after him.

He is about to get into his chauffeured car. What does she want? (He is a busy man.) She's not exactly sure. "Is it hot?" she asks—meaning stolen. "I don't know," he says, "I've never worn one." "What kind of fur is it, anyway?" He looks at it with distaste; he fingers it. "Zebra," he replies. "Anything else you wanta know?" He is getting irritated with her now, and she is getting more confused. When she hesitates, he wags his finger at her. "Let me give you a piece of advice, young lady." He wags it laterally. "Don't be too wise." A passerby stops and stares at them. "Don't think you know all the answers. Things have been *done* for people"—finger up and down—"many nice things. Remember

Easy Living:
*Arthur,
Edward
Arnold,
Esther Forbes,
Mary Nash—
and the
heroine's two
sheepdogs.*

that!" He is shouting now. She is looking, if no less confused, somewhat abashed. A crowd has collected. "Well, whatta you want!" he barks at them, and they disperse. His car is waiting by the curb.

But she needs a dime—she forgot when she got off the bus that that was her last dime. "What's a matter with *this* bus?" he says, indicating the car. She protests, but he overbears her again and she gets in. "The boy's *who?*" he says, as he leans over her to direct the chauffeur. *"The Boy's Constant Companion,"* she repeats, then explains: "It's a magazine for boys." "Never heard of it," he says, settling back in the cushions. They have over a million readers, she tells him. "Well, they haven't got me," he replies, with satisfaction. There is a pause after this exchange. They both look forward and ride: Arnold with his settled bilious expression (the chuckling mood has passed), Arthur with hair over one eye, her head moving slightly on her neck, and the coat she has just been given held in her lap—looking like I-*think*-I'm-enjoying-this, and achieving a kind of nervous complacence as she rides. It's soon interrupted: Arnold turns and looks at her fiercely. She looks back, questioningly. "Stop at a hat shop," he leans over and says to the chauffeur—that broken feather. She protests again: she is late to work already. He overbears her again: "Well, if I can keep waiting what's waiting for me, I guess *The Boy's Constant Reminder* can wait a few minutes also." "*Companion*," she says softly, looking at the feather.

It's like a Lubitsch two-shot—Jeanette MacDonald and Charlie Ruggles, or Jeanette MacDonald and nearly anybody—two self-absorbed people in the same frame but in different worlds, and looking straight ahead. The comic point in Lubitsch is always the isolation and cross-purposes of the people in the frame. It is here, too. But there is something else very different from Lubitsch in this extended shot: Arnold and Arthur in the back of his car, riding along, in their separate worlds, also seem powerfully connected as they sit and look out at us— connected in a way we can recognize even if we can't name it.

"You know," she remarks—they are now on their way to the hat store—"I was going to buy a fur coat. You can get it for two dollars a week and one percent on the balance." Unlike *The Boy's Constant Whatsis*, this does catch his interest. "That's one percent a month," he says, incredulous. She thinks it's wonderful they can do it for so little. But that's twenty-five percent a year, he exclaims. Twelve percent, she points out, since it's well known there are twelve months in a year. He shifts in his seat, patiently. "You, of course, don't know who I am," he says, "but I'm very good at computing interest." "I'm sure you are," she says, beginning to sniff through her nose again, "but having passed through high school myself, I think I can safely say that one percent a month is twelve." She can't *believe* this argument. And he can't penetrate the misunderstanding. "You don't have to get mad just because you're so stupid," she says—but now he is furious. "You don't seem to understand," she says, almost crying with anger and vexation. "Twelve times one can't possibly be six hundred—" But even as she says it she is overcome with disbelief: "A small *child* would be able to—" He throws a hand up: "All right, all right, let's forget all about it." She sits back, breathing and looking at him. He sits back and looks forward again. There is a pause.

He narrows his eyes, however, after a moment—and starts to compute with his fingers. She sees this, with disgust. He turns, raises a finger to speak—but she draws back, looking at him warningly. He thinks better of it, and subsides again.

She asks if the coat is mink. It's Levinsky, he says, approximating what his wife had called it. "You mean Kolinsky?" she says. "You shouldn't be giving away a real Kolinsky." "I'll tell you," he says, "we'll look at it another way now"—his brow furrowed in thought. "A farmer borrows a hundred cows . . ." She lets out a little cry and falls backward. "Y'understand?" he persists. Though he hardly seems to be talking to *her* in a way, she looks at him with repugnance, her teeth showing. Still, he goes on, with unseeing eyes, repeating now: "He borrows a hundred cows . . ." And she draws back from him as if he had something loathsome and catching. But when they get out of the car to go into the hat shop, he is still at it. "Now how much does a farmer pay?" he demands. "Twelve cows," she says hopelessly—and they go in to buy her a hat.

He selects it, of course—not the one Franklin Pangborn wants to show her, either. "It looks like a salt shaker," says Arnold. "We," counters Pangborn, "think it's very recherché." "That's the trouble with it," says Arnold. He finds the right hat and she tries it on, overborne again. She wears it out of the store with the coat, and he drops her off at her job. "Keep the moths out of Levinsky," he says with a hearty grin as his car pulls away. She tries to thank him, but she didn't get his name.

Exactly. She runs into him again at the Hotel Louis, and she still doesn't get it. Nor he hers. They are the liveliest, most interesting couple in the film—and very much a couple—and yet in some way they hardly seem to notice each other. And yet all their encounters are full of this life and energy and detail. Intimate strangers: they make us feel as if they know each other very well—at some place prior to names or identities or even personalities—bringing out energies in each other that no one else does. From one point of view they are perfectly, even oppressively, ordinary figures: a businessman preoccupied with his business, a working girl preoccupied with her living. What makes them seem special and vivid is their freedom of response, their passionate impersonal engagement with each other, making them seem stirring and funny and generous. They are "above personalities"—even their own. Beyond invidiousness or acrimony or suspicion—they are shouting too loud. They encounter each other several times in the film, but they never really "meet" until the end—when Ball becomes Mary's father-in-law, "blessing" by his delighted approval the young people's union. And yet that familial, personal connection seems a lot less deep and interesting than the one enjoyed before they "knew" each other.

They enact that remarkable impersonal energy and aggression that characterize Preston Sturges' work in general—many of his early screenplays and all of his films. Just as the same sort of energy characterizes the screen personality of Jean Arthur. She was a Capra and a Hawks heroine, but she was also, finally and most deeply, a Sturges heroine.

Lubitsch in the Late Thirties | 18

Lubitsch was and still is a great talent. . . . Specializing, however, in the so-phistication and realism of promiscuous sex relationships, a theme in keeping with the old post-war days, his most recent films do not show that he is keep-ing abreast with the swiftly changing times. The leadership he enjoyed dur-ing the pre-talkie era has been lost; his influence today is of minor proportions. —LEWIS JACOBS, *The Rise of the American Film* (1939)

THE YEARS of the screwball enchantment, when this new native strain of movie comedy really flourished, were not years when Lubitsch flourished. Not at first, anyway. For him the period was difficult and transitional. It culmi-nated for him in the successive triumphs of *Ninotchka* (1939) and *The Shop Around the Corner* (1940). But in the meantime, during the peak of the screwball craze, he did a lot of casting around and made fewer movies than ever. The new style of romantic comedy, which owed so much to his example, was in many ways uncongenial to him.

It was improvisatory, for one thing—if not always in its method, at least in its effect. Frank Capra didn't actually improvise on his sets—a Capra-Riskin script was nearly as inviolate as a Lubitsch-Raphaelson one was—but Capra made his movies *look* as if he did. Almost any screwball comedy couple gives an impres-sion of spontaneity that makes the sparrings of a Lubitsch couple seem almost ceremonial (as they often were). And the best screwball directors—McCarey, La Cava, Hawks—were notoriously off-the-cuff on their sets. Even George Ste-vens, famous for his brooding silences and endless retakes, made these same retakes in search of an elusive spontaneous life that he might discover only in the editing room. And Howard Hawks, according to John Wayne, *never* shot a scene as written. A Hawks comedy was always subject to the temperaments of its players and to last-minute revisions. For McCarey and La Cava, it seemed to be nearly *all* revisions, and the later the better—filming on the brink, as Kath-

Leon (Melvyn Douglas) helps Ninotchka (Greta Garbo) with the map of Paris in Lubitsch's Ninotchka.

arine Hepburn recently described the La Cava technique. Directing in this style was like being an action painter or a jazz musician; it was part of what people meant (whether they knew about it or not) by "screwball."

There's a story about Lubitsch (recounted by Maurice Zolotow) that when B. P. Schulberg visited his set and asked him why he was filming something or other a certain way, Lubitsch replied that he could no longer remember. What did it matter, anyway? "It is in the script," he said, "which is good enough for me. If I didn't have a good reason, it would not have been in there when Sam Raphaelson was writing it in the first place." Like Hitchcock, Lubitsch was committed to working out his movies, even to details, *before* he began filming them. Rarely was anything changed on a set, and whenever it was, the *writer* was called in to change it. "Lubitsch believed in a script that carried every possible detail," says Samson Raphaelson. "We both distrusted inspired after-moments—our own or from actors. We courted spontaneity and were ready at the drop of a hat to improvise, but only during writing time, when we always made creative elbow-room."

And writing time could be wild. Ben Hecht threatened to turn "pansy" if

Lubitsch grabbed him one more time to show him how a love scene should be played. Charles Brackett and Billy Wilder, in their published eulogy of Lubitsch, recalled how he acted out every gag for them—even the gags that were literally impossible, doing them so brilliantly that you began to think they might be possible after all. This "cigar-puffing magician" was so funny he could make you believe anything, even make you forget the "flesh-and-blood actor," no magician, who would have to do the gag in front of the camera. Never mind: one simply, they said, "rolled on the floor," crying, "That's it! That's it!" "He directs all the time," Ben Hecht told the New York *Sun* in 1933:

> He never stops. Every word you say he photographs. You try to write some dialogue and he stops you to say, "But where are they standing?" He gets up and walks across the room. "Now he's standing here, and she is there. And the camera should be so. And the table. And the chair?" He photographs it all. Yes and he lights it too. Then he comes back and asks, "Now what are they saying?"

The *Sun* reporter noted that Lubitsch, also present for the interview, responded to this description with "a tired smile."

And on the set he acted for the actors too, showing them how to do it. "He gave you every move you were to make—when to put your hands in your pockets, when to light a cigarette," recalled Fredric March in 1973, adding that Lubitsch "was too meticulous in his direction of actors." He was, said March, comparing him to Wellman and Wyler, "a different kind of director." He held extensive rehearsals—the only director she ever had who did, according to Claudette Colbert. "I was mad about him," she told the New York *Times* in 1984. "First of all, he was an actor himself, and he was the only director I know of who wanted to entertain his actors." And he acted every role for them, male and female, leading and supporting. One reason a Lubitsch film, unlike most, seems so consistent in its tone and style and voice is that the actors are imitating *him*— the way he did it or said it for them. Colbert claims that he got her to do outrageous things on the screen—like the onion scene with Gary Cooper in *Bluebeard's Eighth Wife*—by making her laugh so hard when *he* did them ("That's it! That's it!"). "He was a little man," she told the *Times*, "and he sat down right in Gary Cooper's lap and played that scene. He said to me, 'She's drunk and she's eating onions,' and acted out grabbing a bunch of scallions and shoving them in his mouth and turning to wait for Gary's kiss. I laughed until I cried." And all his favorite actresses had this same susceptibility—Colbert and MacDonald and Lombard, and even Garbo when they were alone together: they all laughed a lot. And in interviews it was always their "sense of humor" that he singled out for praise.

Nineteen thirty-four was a watershed year for Lubitsch. After the peak—and the failure—of *The Merry Widow*, the final flowering of his naughty-operetta style, the question was, What next? There were no easy or obvious answers, but the one he finally supplied astonished everyone. After six months or so of relative inactivity, Lubitsch became a mogul. On February 4, 1935, he was appointed Paramount's production chief, assuming "full creative control" of *all* Paramount films. It was an extraordinary appointment, one not easy to explain even now. As *Variety* pointed out—but only after Lubitsch had flopped at the job and was leaving the studio altogether—he never had been a moneymaker for them. (Only two of his Paramount films, it said, had been "real" hits. It doesn't name the films, but presumably they were *The Love Parade* and *The Smiling Lieutenant*.) So why offer him control of the studio? He was qualified for that position, it seems, by his prestige, his taste and intelligence, and his knowledge of filmmaking. But this *wasn't* a job description for a mogul—not so far as anyone knew. Irving Thalberg was supposed (not everyone agreed about this) to have some of those qualities, but even Thalberg wasn't a world-renowned filmmaker. Nor was any other magnate or near-magnate in Hollywood. The New York *Times* called the Lubitsch appointment "the most interesting experiment in Hollywood history." Was that what drew Lubitsch to it—that view of it? "It had always seemed odd," said the New York *Sun* in 1936, "that one of the world's most celebrated directors should take over an executive position." At that point, after having been fired, Lubitsch agreed. "I just wanted to see what it was all about," he said. "Just curiosity—you know, like Alice in Wonderland."

Surely Paramount was the only major studio that would have appointed him. Just as MGM (under Thalberg) had come to be known as a producers' studio, so Paramount was a directors' studio—a place where directors like Lubitsch and von Sternberg and De Mille were more or less given their head, at least for a time. But then so were (also for a time) directors like Norman Taurog and Alexander Hall and Stuart Walker and Marion Gering (B. P. Schulberg's special favorite). Paramount's house directors—the "script shooters" as Lubitsch called them, as opposed to the "creative directors"—lacked both the efficiency and the skill of many of their counterparts at other studios. And there was a general lack of production control. It was the major studio most often in financial crisis, most often in the throes of reorganization. "Paramount was always hit-or-miss," recalled W. R. Burnett, the novelist and screenwriter, in 1981. "They had people coming in and out. It wasn't a well-run place at all, ever." The disarray showed up on the screen, particularly in the narrative line of films. Paramount films of the early thirties, even those with major stars, seemed to lose their coherency and point as they went along—a contingency that Warners and MGM in their different ways had mostly learned to prevent (Warners in particular had perfected a kind of terse, fluent, suggestive style in the short feature film). Fortunately, a number of the biggest Paramount stars—Mae West and W. C. Fields and the Marx Brothers—didn't at all depend on narrative coherence. Those who did, however, often had to prove themselves first at other studios, as both Colbert and Lombard did at Columbia in 1934.

What did Lubitsch do in this Wonderland? For a start, he really ran things—or tried to. No property could be purchased, no director or writer or actor could be either hired or renewed, without his approval. Directors were no longer permitted, as they had been before, to withdraw from a picture in mid-production. Lubitsch gave contracts to Lewis Milestone and King Vidor and Frank Borzage. He renewed Wesley Ruggles, and he "liquidated" (von Sternberg's word) Josef von Sternberg—whom no one could have saved at that point. (Von Sternberg later claimed that Lubitsch both disliked his films and knew how much von Sternberg disliked his.) He instituted the Thalberg system of doing retakes of finished movies if they were judged to be in trouble at previews. He quarreled with Mae West—so roundly (even to making ungallant public references to her weight and age) that all business concerning her had to be turned over to William

Lubitsch with Margaret Sullavan and James Stewart on the set of The Shop Around the Corner.

Le Baron (who shortly afterward got Lubitsch's job as well). He gave Carole Lombard her first major Paramount vehicle, *Hands Across the Table*. And he attempted, by producing a film called *Desire*, to salvage the sagging career of Marlene Dietrich.

Jewel thief Marlene Dietrich is trying to look chastened here, so that she and John Halliday can get rid of moralist Gary Cooper in Desire.

D esire (1936), in fact, was almost the only thing from his year as a mogul that he could cite later on as a solid accomplishment. "I really produced it," he insisted to an interviewer, as if it was important to insist. "I worked on the story, the script, casting, everything like that." Starring Dietrich and Gary Cooper, and directed by Frank Borzage (Lubitsch himself directed retakes of several scenes), *Desire* was Dietrich's first film after the breakup with von Sternberg and, more important perhaps, her first real comedy.

She is a jewel thief, pulling one of the most elegant cons in movie history. A Lubitschean con, with lots of manner and ceremony, lots of strolling and eye-batting and intricate. lovingly detailed misunderstanding. Dietrich saunters into Duvalle's, the jeweler's, to look at a necklace. She stands, waiting to be attended to, hand on hip, the slightest of smiles on her face, both imperious and amused. When it develops that she is ready to spend three million francs if the necklace is "really rare"—and she manages to give the phrase a full libidinous charge as she says it (turning the *r*'s into *w*'s)—M. Duvalle (Ernest Cossart) promptly shows her their most valuable pearls. She decides to take them. Her name, she tells him, is Mme Pauquet; her husband is the renowned psychiatrist. M. Duvalle knows of him, of course—as he observes, who in Paris doesn't? Would you like to meet him? asks Dietrich, looking *really* amused now. And it is quickly arranged: M. Duvalle is to deliver the pearls to Dr. Pauquet's office. She will meet him there.

But when she gets there herself, it seems that she has an appointment—and she gives her name now as Mme Duvalle. She has come, she tells the doctor (Alan Mowbray), not for herself but for her husband, the well-known jeweler. But she has difficulty when it comes to the point in explaining the problem: she is embarrassed. "Oh, Doctor," she breathes in lambent close-up, "it's too terrible to speak of. . . ." But it has to be told. "When we were married," she says, and something in the memory lights up her eyes, "he was such a strong, *vir*-wile man. . . ." She lowers her eyes. "And now—" she says, darting a look at him. But she doesn't finish; she only sighs. "Oh, Doctor," she breathes, and turns away. There are other things, too—like the nighties he wears, and his obsession with money. He likes to present people with fictitious bills, it seems. The doctor agrees to see him, and she feels better already. "I wouldn't be a bit surprised," she says purringly, drawing her gloves on at the door and looking roguishly at the doctor from under her hat, "if he comes in here and presents *you* with a bill." The doctor assures her that he will know how to handle the bill, and she departs. When Duvalle arrives at the office with the necklace and the bill, Dietrich is waiting for him in the reception room. She takes him inside and introduces him to the doctor—each man is now under the impression that he is meeting her husband. By the time they straighten it all out, she—and the necklace—have disappeared.

It's in her getaway that she runs into Gary Cooper, an amorous car salesman from Detroit. She plants the necklace on him to get it through Spanish customs and then has trouble getting it back again. He pursues her to her hotel, then to a Spanish villa where she is hiding out with her confederate (John Halliday). He persists until love triumphs over the excitements of successful crookedness. All in all, it's clearly a Lubitsch film: the centrality of luxurious objects, the coldly controlled lunacy of the big moments, the visual double entendres (there is hand play under the dinner table as well as in Cooper's pockets), the long languorous buildups to shaggy-dog payoffs ("Oh, Carlos, he thinks you're a wonderful man," is Dietrich's report from Cooper's bedroom as she emerges to reassure an anxious colleague outside), and above all the excitement about thievery. "Now let's be calm, all we can get is five years," says Carlos, with the police at their door. "No, seven," says Dietrich, fluffing her hair. "I looked it up"—as she turns her face to receive the inspector.

It was the first time Lubitsch had worked with screenwriters Edwin Justus Mayer and Samuel Hoffenstein, two renowned New York wits who would help him to write two of his most important later films, *To Be or Not To Be* and *Cluny Brown*, respectively. (The third credited writer on *Desire* is Waldemar Young.) Frank Borzage's direction is an effective but softened version of the Lubitsch style: the pacing is slower and the rhythm less disorienting; shock cuts are less jarring, comic discontinuities less emphatic. When people walk abruptly "out of the frame" in the Lubitsch way in this movie, Borzage's camera tends to follow them, to see where they're going. The moralizing that takes over the end of the film—as well as the encomiums to the respectable life in Detroit the heroine is finally headed toward—is probably due much more to Production Code requirements (the cheerful amoralism of *Trouble in Paradise* was now out of the question in a Hollywood movie) than to those of Borzage's temperament, which was romantic and sentimental (films like *Seventh Heaven* and *Little Man, What Now?*).

But the real triumph of *Desire* is Dietrich herself. She is sublimely funny, in a forthright comic way no one had seen in her movies before this. It's an inspired solution to "the Dietrich problem." Audiences who had begun to resent the exoticism were now being invited to enjoy it in just the way Dietrich herself does—from the inside, watching and calculating its effect on those others. Now, just like the screwball heroines who had seemingly displaced her, Dietrich was offering a collusion with her own wit and intelligence and playfulness.

But *Desire* was only a modest box office success; and the change in the Dietrich image was too subtle to arrest her decline—or Lubitsch's. In February 1936, one year after he took on the job, Lubitsch was replaced as production head by the aforementioned William Le Baron. During Lubitsch's tenure, it was now reported, Paramount's costs had gone up, its production and profits had gone down. A lot of this misfortune, of course, was simply out of his control and had been from the beginning. But the *quality* of Paramount's production, he felt, was not; and the sad fact was that he seemed to have made very little difference to that quality, if any at all. The sixty or so Paramount films produced and released during the Lubitsch year are generally indistinguishable from those of the year before or the year after. In an interview after the fact, Lubitsch cited, rather wistfully, three he had "liked" (*Hands Across the Table, Anything Goes,* and *Collegiate*) and was even more enthusiastic about a picture not yet released, the very funny *The Milky Way,* starring Harold Lloyd and directed by Leo McCarey. "That boy McCarey," he said, is "brilliant," "one of the best." There wasn't, however, much else to boast about. He had made, it now seemed, a kind of devil's bargain. Toward the end of his year of power he had even begun to *sound* like a mogul, denouncing the "genius" sort of director who can't produce "honest entertainment" (von Sternberg?) and defending the same studio practices that he had once attacked (assigning teams of writers to a single picture, giving the producer control over the director, and so on). In the end, all he had achieved, it appeared, was an evasion, or postponement, of his own creative problems.

He took off for a three-month tour of Europe. A belated honeymoon: he had married for the second time the summer before (Vivian Gaye, a former lady-in-waiting, it was said, to the queen of Denmark—just the sort of ritziness he always loved). He even made a visit, by invitation of the Soviet government, to Russia. When he returned to Hollywood and to Paramount, it was announced that he would now head his own production unit at the studio, and would henceforth be in charge of all Colbert and Dietrich films. But he only made two films under this arrangement, *Angel* with Dietrich and *Bluebeard's Eighth Wife* with Colbert. These two movies, however, took up the next two years of his life. They also ended his career at Paramount.

Angel (1937) is the ritziest of all the Lubitsch comedies: the most discreet, the most soft-spoken, the one with the most impeccable manners. It was a curious response, if that's what it was, to the explosion of crazy comedy—to make a comedy so well behaved as to seem almost stuffy. It's as if Lubitsch had decided to out-"class" the competition. It was almost three years since he'd functioned as a director. And like his last film, *The Merry Widow, Angel* seems more a leave-taking film than a new beginning. Once again, his screenwriter was Samson Raphaelson.

Marlene Dietrich is Maria, Lady Barker, the bored and neglected wife of Sir Frederick Barker (Herbert Marshall), a League of Nations diplomat. She has a secret fling in Paris with an American, Melvyn Douglas, who then, to her consternation, turns up in London as a friend of her husband's. Tony Halton (Douglas) is looking for a woman he knows only as "Angel"; and the heroine, it develops, must "choose" between the men. This conventional sort of plotting gives no clue to the oddity of the film itself—even its daring. If Lubitsch was indeed, as it now appears, closing out one aspect of his career, he was also going to "new" extremes in a familiar style before doing so.

It's the Lubitsch passion for indirection, taken farther than ever before, that gives *Angel* its quiet but distinct excitement. He exerts himself more than ever, it seems, to keep climactic moments off the screen, and to call our attention to his ingenuity in doing so. Tony loses Angel in a Paris park at nighttime—forever, he thinks—and we watch the whole event reflected in the changes on the face of an old flower woman (Louise Carter). (There is a scene in the screenplay where an impasse between Maria and Sir Frederick is entirely visualized on the face of their Great Dane, listening: it was apparently never filmed.) Later on, just as we know that Tony has gone off-screen to look at a photograph of Lady Barker—and so to discover that *she* is Angel—we watch Sir Frederick on-screen placidly mixing a drink until the fadeout.

Above all, *Angel* has doors—in even greater range and variety than usual. From the flat, plain, concealing doors of the grand duchess's modish, brightly lit and rather sinister "salon" to the massive, baroque, baronial doors of Sir Frederick's vaulting Tudor-style mansion. And if the doors seem more prominent than ever, that's partly in the nature of the film. *Angel* is almost the movie equivalent of one of those doors—as close as Lubitsch ever came to making a whole film that expressed itself through a closed and impassive surface.

The Grand Duchess Olga, for example—a very doorlike type. She is the mistress of an elegant and thinly disguised house of assignation in Paris. Maria comes there at the beginning of the movie, in flight from her unhappy marriage. Lubitsch has cast the grand duchess brilliantly against type: Laura Hope Crews is a round, rumpled, pillowlike little woman with glinting eyes and a pie-shaped face. She had been a leading lady on the stage in her youth, but in the movies she specialized in comic-hysteric roles—Aunt Pittypat in *Gone With the Wind*, Prudence in *Camille*. In this role she is meant, improbably, to be stylish and imposing. And it is just that improbability that makes her convincing—a *real* grand duchess—and in some way threatening. She is a disturbing figure, and Lubitsch observes her discontinuities almost lovingly. Her salon is a maze of low-ceilinged hallways and connecting rooms. The camera watches her going silently down a corridor—observing her from the front, never from the back, the way it watches the other characters when they walk (the grand duchess's front *is* a back). And as she walks, we see the way her face collapses the moment she doesn't have to show it to someone. Just as she turns a corner to another meeting and she is smiling again. She gives nothing away, though—not ever. Not even, when Maria comes to the salon to seek her "advice," exactly what their previous connection has been. Clearly there has been one, in some former life of Maria's; but we never find out what it was. And when Tony, who has just met the mysterious Maria in the same sitting room, inquires who that lady was who just left the room, the grand duchess looks at him fixedly. "Lady?" she says—and it's an extraordinary moment—"I don't know. *Was* there a lady here?" "You know there was," Tony replies. "Really I don't know," she says, so absolutely equably that *we* almost believe her. "I swear," she adds, in the same even tone. Lubitsch stages this exchange in a single take, with the two actors in profile, facing each other and talking quietly and locked into each other's look. It's like a Kubrick conversation, without the suggestion of violence but unsettling nonetheless.

That lock into the other's gaze is a basic feature of the movie. A lot of the

Dietrich wants to know what Herbert Marshall is thinking about in Lubitsch's Angel. *The answer is surprising.*

jokes (a long exchange of double entendres between Tony and Frederick about a French girl they both "knew" during the war, for example) are told in this way—with one character gazing at the other, a smile playing on the lips, a pause between each phrase, then again before each reply. Above all, jokes are made *quietly*—until (characteristically for Lubitsch) the style itself becomes a joke. "What's worrying you?" asks Dietrich, dazzling in her negligee, leaning invitingly against the doorway and looking up concernedly at her husband, who is in his pajamas and looking off into the distance. No answer. "France?" she prompts. "No," he says, still looking off. Then, after a pause: "Yugoslavia . . ."

People tend to talk in code in this film, especially at moments of tension or emotion. Tony and Maria are obliged to talk that way, of course, when they first meet in the presence of her husband, who has no idea they've even met before. But even when Sir Frederick leaves the room, Maria maintains this cryptic style of discourse, denying to Tony's face that she is Angel, the woman he met and loved in Paris. She says this so equably—like the grand duchess—that for a moment he is a bit thrown. "Look at me here in the light," she says to him. "Look at me carefully—and I am sure you will realize—as clearly as I do—

that I'm *Lady Barker* . . . and nobody else." He understands her now, and replies in kind. "The resemblance," he says, "is amazing. But when I listen to you, I begin to see the difference. . . . You are *not* Angel." She is, she says, "greatly relieved" to hear it.

The indirection of the movie's final showdown is even more elaborate. Sir Frederick, with his suspicions about his wife at last aroused, has gone to the grand duchess's, hoping to dispel them. Is Maria "Angel"? He has learned that Tony is meeting Angel there and that the two of them are going away together. Sir Frederick's worst fears seem to be confirmed when, after a typically oblique and unsatisfactory interview with the grand duchess, he is joined by Maria, who enters from the next room. She tells him that she, too, is here to see Angel. To find out if the resemblance between them is as remarkable as she has been told. In fact, she has just now seen her, she says—at this moment she is in the adjoining room. "And does she look like you?" says the miserable Sir Frederick. "Exactly," she replies. She invites him: why doesn't he see for himself? All he has to do is to step into the next room. He declines the gambit—and momentarily threatens the whole game by blurting out, "*You* are Angel!" But she has an answer to this:

> MARIA: Why should I be Angel? Why should I be so foolish? Why should I do such a thing? Don't I have a lovely home—a celebrated husband—the best servants—every comfort—social position? (*Bitterly*) Is there anything more a woman can ask? Why should I be Angel? What reason could I have? . . . Perhaps *you* can think of one.
> (*Frederick looks back at her in complete despair. Then he looks in the direction of the door. He is just ready to go to it as Maria speaks, stopping him.*)
> Now, Fred—if you go into that room, I'm afraid our marriage is over. If you find Angel in there, you will be happy that I'm not Angel—and you'll want to continue our old life. That would not be satisfactory to me.
> FREDERICK: And if I don't find Angel. . . ?
> MARIA: In that case, I think you'll want to see your lawyer as soon as possible. (*Slight pause*) On the other hand, if you don't go in at all—you will be a little uncertain—you won't be so sure of yourself—or of me. And that might be wonderful.

But he can't resist: after a hesitation, he opens the door and goes in, closing it behind himself. The room, of course, is empty. But in the room he has just left, Tony now enters. He has come to claim Maria. Her marriage is over, she tells him, and prepares to leave with him. "It's silly how upsetting a little thing like saying goodbye to one's husband can be."

But just as they turn to go, Sir Frederick re-emerges from the empty room. He has seen Angel, he tells her. "And she looks exactly like you." He asks

Maria to go to Vienna with him that night: he has two tickets on the night train and will be at the station waiting for her if she decides to go. He turns without another word and leaves them. The camera follows him out the door and down the hall, tracking behind him. Just as he reaches the front door, Maria walks silently into the frame beside him. He takes her arm and they go out the door together. The last shot of the film—appropriately—is of retreating backs.

And it's curiously affecting. The real emotion in this movie is invested just there—in those turned backs. Lubitsch has never seemed more in love with obliquity itself than he does here. And the moments of real tension and interest occur not so much when the marriage is threatened as when the obliquity is. This final sequence, for example, is less about a man who regains his wife than it is about someone who temporarily loses his elegance, then rallies and recaptures it—triumphantly.

And yet, interesting (and accomplished) as it is, it all seems deeply wrong. A movie that feels both portentous and trifling. *Angel*, much more than most Lubitsch comedies, offers to be about serious emotional dilemmas—and what it delivers is novelettish talk, full of women's-magazine sentiment and psychology. The absence of felt life or experience in the film makes the elegance seem very oppressive indeed, and deeply vulgar—less elegant than chichi. And Lubitsch's absorption in that elegance begins to seem like self-exposure: evidence of a strong and unpleasant infatuation with swank. That impression is more than confirmed by the movie's comic subplot: about the Barkers' servants (Edward Everett Horton, Ernest Cossart, and others), who delude themselves, through identification with their masters, into thinking that they too are important and glamorous figures. This is meant to be quite a rich joke, and it is lovingly elaborated through several scenes below stairs. (There are precedents for it in Lubitsch as far back as *The Love Parade*, but it never seems quite as smug as it does here.)

Strangely enough, it's Dietrich who saves the film's central situation from seeming wholly preposterous—with that odd flair she has for grounding even her most outrageous effects in something hausfrauish and sensible. At the same time, she does seem to walk through the part, as reviewers (and Lubitsch) complained—as if she'd lost some vital spark. The role doesn't serve her well. If Maria had wit at least, like the heroine of *Desire*; but all her most telling effects are rhetorical-grandiloquent: "Why should I be Angel?" etc. The wit, such as it is, tends to be sibylline, as when Tony, begging her to stay with him, tells her that her refusal doesn't make sense. "I am a woman," she replies, "and it is the privilege of a woman not to make sense. Men who expect women to be logical are likely to be failures in love." Dietrich speaks this mouthful in one steady, excited flow—so breathlessly we can hardly believe we've heard it when she's done. But then how would *anyone* say that? Especially Dietrich: there's too much irreverence in her nature for this sort of self-important Ann Landers sound, offered without irony or satire, and without the ambiguity that von Sternberg customarily gave her.

Angel was a notable failure at the box office. It finished Dietrich's Paramount contract—and almost her career as well. It was two years before she appeared on screen again: as the brawling saloon floozy in *Destry Rides Again* (1939), one of the most famous—and successful—"image reversals" in Hollywood history. Lubitsch, it seems, never really got along with her. There were stories of friction on the set of *Angel* ("The director and Miss Dietrich," reported *Variety*, "were frequently at odds")—a nearly unheard-of thing on a Lubitsch production. And the *Angel* production stills (mostly photos of director and star together) are probably the only ones in existence showing Lubitsch looking unhappy on a film set. Mary Loos, the screenwriter and Lubitsch's close friend and confidante, says he never liked Dietrich too well, notwithstanding their common background as Berliners: he was put off, Loos believes, by her swashbuckling private life, in spite of his own vaunted sophistication. To his friend Walter Reisch he complained that Dietrich seemed more interested before the filming in her wardrobe than in her role. And he was no happier with her performance once filming began. But once it had, as it now seems, they were both trapped—in a misconceived project. Still, it may have been a necessary sort of project for Lubitsch. Once he'd gone as far in techniques of indirection as he does in *Angel*, he seems to lose interest in them. At any rate, he never made another film like it. And the direction he took in the next decade was an altogether different one.

H IS NEXT film was different enough. A contrast to the languors of *Angel*, *Bluebeard's Eighth Wife* (1938) was a bona fide wacky comedy. Although Lubitsch insisted—significantly—that it wasn't exactly a screwball comedy: "No, not the *My Man Godfrey* type of comedy," he said in an interview, but rather "a kind of mental slapstick." But for audiences surely the distinction was moot: *Bluebeard's Eighth Wife* was close enough to screwball to pass. It was calculated for a big success (Lubitsch badly needed one): it had Paramount's two biggest and most popular stars—Gary Cooper and Claudette Colbert—instead of, as in *Angel*, one problematic one. And it was the first collaborative effort of a screenwriting team who would soon become famous for their own skill and wit: Charles Brackett and Billy Wilder.

It's hard to know what Lubitsch may have meant by "mental slapstick," but in any case *Bluebeard's Eighth Wife* is fairly prodigal with the real kind—like the scene where Colbert eats onions and breathes the fumes in Cooper's face. She also hires a prizefighter (Warren Hymer) to knock Cooper out (he slugs David Niven instead). There is a lot of falling around and smashing things—

even a comic crazy house at the end where the inmates think they are animals. (When the authorities refuse entrance to Colbert, her father, Edward Everett Horton, knocks on the door and barks at them—and they show him right in.) It's closer to knockabout farce than anything Lubitsch had done since his early silent days. Clearly he is trying to "Americanize" his work in some way, short of actually setting a film here.

This one begins on the Riviera, where American playboy Gary Cooper pursues French girl Claudette Colbert, of an aristocratic but indigent family. It's a comedy of "the delayed fuck"—a very popular line (*It Happened One Night* belongs to it). In this case she marries him (the Production Code) but then refuses to come across. In view of his marital record (seven previous wives, all collecting alimony). And it's the agony of his situation that causes much of the falling around. By the end he is in a straitjacket and love triumphs (she loosens the strings a bit so that he can kiss her). But as it turned out, all this "fun" seemed a little rough—not to mention bizarre—to the general audience it was aimed at. And Lubitsch had another box-office failure.

Claudette Colbert has a premarital disagreement with millionaire Gary Cooper— with Edward Everett Horton, Cooper's anxious prospective father-in-law, looking on. Bluebeard's Eighth Wife.

It might have been different if he'd been Leo McCarey, for example. McCarey knew how to tell this joke (and did so repeatedly) in a way that audiences liked—by turning it into a cock tease, just as the Doris Day movies of the sixties did. But Lubitsch is as incapable of McCarey's crowd-pleasing kind of prurience as he is of Capra's sentimentalism. His approach to the same routine of the endlessly postponed wedding night is to give it a kind of off-the-wall grotesquerie, to redeem it by refusing to "humanize" it.

But the coldness of the resulting film, though preferable to the "warm" alternative, is genuinely disturbing. The toughness—unlike the equivalent quality in *The Merry Widow* or *Trouble in Paradise*—seems without a point somehow, without resonance or affect. The problem with *Bluebeard's Eighth Wife* is not its cruelty or tastelessness (it alienated audiences, according to one version, because they didn't want to see Gary Cooper as a roué) but its inadvertence. In a way, it's not tasteless enough. The "cruelty" is off-putting only because, finally, it doesn't seem really or fully *intended*. So that in the end the movie seems almost *idly* mean.

Though it's a frequently very funny, very stylish comedy. It's Lubitsch, after all, and it shows him at the peak of his powers, assured and masterly. And Colbert's performance is certainly a Lubitschean triumph, as are Herman Bing's as the loopy private detective and Edward Everett Horton's as the avaricious father-in-law. Finally what it has in common with *Angel*, different as the two films are, is a kind of emptiness. There is no urgency of feeling in either of these movies. If the result in *Angel* is a kind of high-class diddling, in *Bluebeard's Eighth Wife* it's a string of gags, many of them funny, but no real joke—anywhere in the film.

It was not just the lack of *any* joke but of a particular one—of a certain adversary force, that hostility to authority, that American movie comedy, whether tough or screwball, had always thrived on. One way of seeing the failure of these two Lubitsch films is to notice how strikingly they lack that energy of opposition that infused the screwball genius as much as romantic love did. But then Lubitsch, in spite of his sympathies with dissidence, had always had less of this subversive impulse toward power, this up-the-boss mentality, than his American followers did. He began to see the problem, when he publicly reassessed his career at this time, as one of materials: the mistake of trying to make contemporary films about rich idle wives and amorous playboys. From now on, he told reporters, one had to make movies closer to common life, about people who *worked* for a living.

In any case, he left Paramount, after eleven years, in March 1938—the same month *Bluebeard's Eighth Wife* was nationally released. With the agent Myron Selznick, Lubitsch formed an independent production company. He and Samson Raphaelson were preparing the screenplay of *The Shop Around the Corner*, a film about ordinary working people that was to be the new company's first release. But this Lubitsch-Selznick company never worked out. It was at this point that MGM, at the request of its star Greta Garbo, made him an offer. They would take over the *Shop Around the Corner* project if he would first direct a Garbo film for them—a story about a lady communist who falls in love in Paris, from an original story by Melchior Lengyel (who had written the play *Angel* was drawn from). Lubitsch agreed eagerly and signed a two-picture contract with the studio in November 1938.

Nineteen thirty-nine, as it turned out, was even more a turning point for Lubitsch than 1934 had been. He was now beginning the period of what are arguably his greatest films of all. And the first of them was *Ninotchka*.

"**G**ARBO LAUGHS!" said the ads for *Ninotchka* (1939), and everyone understood the message—not only the reference to the star's fabled glumness (she had in fact laughed a lot in *Camille*, but that was a tragic film) but exactly the kind of transformation that was being promised: an event on a par with "Garbo talks!," the 1930 slogan that heralded her talkie debut in *Anna Christie*. Garbo—the paradigm for all stars in her beauty and mystery and final inaccessibility—was now a screwball heroine, too. And the mystery compounded: she was funny.

And she certainly does laugh—with the same alarming wholeheartedness she once made love to John Gilbert with. Count Leon D'Algout (Melvyn Douglas) has pursued her to a restaurant in a working quarter where she is having a solitary lunch. She had found out the night before, after a romantic interlude in his apartment, that he is both the adviser and the lover of the Grand Duchess Swana (Ina Claire) and so the enemy of her mission in Paris. In Russia, she tells him—as she eats her soup and her bread in her grim way, while he sits at her elbow—his "business methods . . . would be punished by death." "Oh, death, death!" he exclaims. "Always so glum! What about *life?*" And what about smiling? he wants to know. At what? she wants to know. At anything—"if you can't think of anything else to laugh at, you can laugh at you and me." "Why?" "Because we're an odd couple." "Then you should go back to your table." He decides to tell her a joke. But this works no better, mainly because the joke is so dumb. "Maybe the trouble isn't with the joke," he says angrily, "maybe it's with *you.*" "I don't think so," she says. He tries again, with another joke—no better—then again, getting angrier and angrier and sputtering with each try. Until he leans back in his chair and falls sprawling onto the floor.

She laughs. In fact, she howls, she collapses, she chokes—falling across the table, throwing her head back to let the sound out, collapsing across the table again. Everyone in the restaurant is laughing now—while he looks up from the floor. What's so funny? he wants to know. *Now* she is pounding the table with her hand. He gets up from the floor, recovering his dignity. He sits next to her and she composes herself. Until they both break down, collapsing together as the scene ends. Garbo "laughs!"—as it turns out—as wonderfully as she "talks!"*

MGM knew she had to do something different. European markets for her films were being threatened by the war, and her appeal to American audiences alone was an uncertain thing at best. And by this time it was clear that if anything could transform a woman star's career, it was a screwball comedy. (It didn't do that for her, of course: *Ninotchka* was her next-to-last film.) According to some accounts, the whole project *began* with "Garbo laughs!": once they had the slogan, they looked for a movie to go with it. It was Melchior Lengyel, a Hungarian playwright now on the MGM payroll, who came up with the idea of a Soviet girl in Paris succumbing to capitalist delights. Gottfried Reinhardt (Max's son) was originally scheduled to direct, and there were repeated attempts at a screenplay by such different hands as Lengyel, Salka Viertel, Jacques Deval, and, finally, S. N. Behrman. Several years before this, Garbo and Lubitsch had talked wishfully of one day doing a picture together, and now Garbo asked for him. But Lubitsch, arriving on the project, was unhappy with the Behrman script. He had his friend Walter Reisch assigned to the film, and Charles Brackett and Billy Wilder followed. *Ninotchka* is one of the few Lubitsch films that weren't his idea to begin with. More importantly, it's his first film in the authentic screwball mode: a true comedy of romantic liberation. Though this was much less noticed at the time, *Ninotchka* was as truly a transformation for Lubitsch as it was for Garbo.

Garbo later called him the only great director she ever had. And Samson Raphaelson has recorded his recollection that Garbo was the only star that Lubitsch ever seemed even faintly in awe of. "The only star I ever worked with I did not have to drag away from the mirror," Lubitsch told the New York *Post* in 1939. "Most stars spend more time in front of the mirror than in playing their parts. But she won't look in the mirror unless you tell her to. . . . A wonderful girl!" That same year he contributed a piece to the New York *Times* about her ("Garbo as Seen by Her Director"): "Probably the most inhibited person I have ever worked with . . . but finally when you break through this and she really feels a scene she's wonderful. But if you don't succeed in making her feel it, she can't do it cold-bloodedly on technique." Garson Kanin has recalled Lubitsch talking about how funny Garbo was *off* the screen, talking about moguls and producers they both knew, or describing her travels with Leopold Stokowski.

---

* Melvyn Douglas says in his autobiography that she managed all this without making a sound that he could hear—on the set. The sounds were dubbed in later.

Even her tragic playing, said Lubitsch, had humor: "Most of them are so heavy. . . . But she was light, light always, and for comedy nothing matters more . . . and it doesn't hurt if they're beautiful."

In many ways *Ninotchka* is the plainest Lubitsch film yet—a particularly striking development after the mannerist extreme of *Angel*. Samson Raphaelson has noted that it was around this time (of their collaboration on the *Shop Around the Corner* script) that Lubitsch seemed to lose interest in specifically filmic effects and ways of telling the story, the epistemological joking of scripts like *Trouble in Paradise*. In *Ninotchka* we are hardly aware at all of the director's controlling presence, of his ironies or ingenuities or jokes. There is barely a single indisputable "Lubitsch touch" anywhere in the movie—hardly even any doors.

But then—as he must have felt—he hardly needed doors when he had Garbo. Who is a Lubitsch touch all by herself. That ardent isolation, that intensely perceived solitude which is the essential Lubitsch joke, at the heart of his greatest movies and comic moments, is precisely the Garbo specialty—though offered solemnly in most of her films, now for the first time at the center of a comedy. And this is the first Lubitsch comedy to be clearly centered by the necessities of its star. This new directness of technique is partly a reflection of *her* directness: "if you don't succeed in making her feel it . . ."

She is a typical Lubitsch butt: stranded on the screen from the beginning by her own private intensity, ardent not about love but about duty and socialism and the welfare of the Russian people. She arrives at a Paris train station where she is met by her nervous Russian colleagues, Buljanoff, Iranoff, and Kopalski (Felix Bressart, Sig Rumann, and Alexander Granach)—an envoy extraordinary from Moscow sent to check up on them, to find out why the sale of the crown jewels they were sent to Paris to accomplish hasn't gone forward as planned. She is humorless: "Don't make an issue of my womanhood," she says in response to a conventional gallantry. And when a porter at the station tries to take her bags, she asks why he wants them. "Well, that's my business, madame," the porter explains. "That's no business," she says balefully, "that's social injustice." "That," says the porter, "depends on the tip." She is frequently set up for ripostes like this one, but she never seems to notice. Her three guilty comrades—who have been living it up in Paris—are sweating. And they aren't encouraged by her tone—as when she observes a rather foolish hat on display in one of the hotel shop windows. "How can such a civilization survive, which permits their women to put things like that on their heads?" She shakes her head and turns away. "It won't be long now, comrades," she says, as they stare at her in horror.

This is familiar Lubitsch territory: the grim ones are always scaring the frivolous ones somehow, and then walking off and leaving them in the frame. It all feels even more familiar when Garbo comes to inhabit the Lubitschean two-shot, that relationship of intense cross-purposes, shortly afterwards. She is on a traffic island with Leon (Douglas); both are waiting for the light to change. How long does it take? she inquires of the stranger, out of her insatiable statistical curiosity. He doesn't know, of course, but he is intrigued by *her*. Can he help in any other way? "You might hold this for me," she says, spreading a map. "Correct me if I am wrong," she says, raising solemn eyes from the map (he holds one end and she holds the other). "We are facing north, aren't we?" "Pardon me, are you an explorer?" "No," she says, still intent on the map, "I am looking for the Eiffel Tower." He offers to point it out on the map for her, but he needs her finger. "Why do you need my finger?" "It's bad manners to point with your own," he replies. She looks at him. He looks right back. He has her finger now and is pointing it at the Eiffel Tower, in a close shot of the map. "And where are we?" says Ninotchka. "Where are we?—now let me see, where are we?" says Leon musingly. Again, the two-shot of their faces above the unfolded map—except that now *he* is looking at it intently, and she is looking up, one sardonic eyebrow lifted. "There you are," he says, "and here am I. Feel it?" The eyebrow stays lifted. "Must you flirt?" "Well, I don't have to," he says chucklingly, "but I find it natural." "Suppress it," she says.

She folds the map. She has heard of men like him, "the arrogant male in capitalistic society. It is having a superior earning power that makes you that way." At last he understands—and is delighted. "A Russian!" he exclaims. "I love Russians!" She looks at him. He leans forward on his gloves and cane. "Comrade," he says, "I've been fascinated by your Five-Year Plan for the last fifteen years." He smirks at her. "Your type will soon be extinct," she says, in her low, sad voice, and leaves the frame.

He follows her to the Eiffel Tower. She proceeds implacably to walk to the top: "There's an elevator included in the price of admission!" he calls out as she disappears up the winding stairs. At the top—it's the first time he's ever been there, and they are both impressed—he decides to show her something through the telescope: "the most unique spot in all Paris."

LEON: What do you see?

NINOTCHKA (*looking through the telescope*): I see a house. Looks like any other house. What's remarkable about it?

LEON: Oh, it's not the structure. It's the spirit that dwells within it. It has three rooms and a kitchenette dedicated to hospitality.

NINOTCHKA: So it's your house?

LEON: Um—well, let's say I live in it.

NINOTCHKA: Hm.

LEON: It's such a pleasant little place. It has all the comforts. Easy to reach—near the subway, bus, and streetcar.

NINOTCHKA: Does it mean you want me to go there?

LEON: Oh, now please, please, don't misunderstand me.

NINOTCHKA: Then you don't want me to go there?

LEON: No, no, no, no! No, no, I didn't say that either. Naturally, nothing would please me more.

NINOTCHKA: Then why don't we go there? You might be an interesting subject of study.

They go there. There is a butler (Richard Carle), and the place is in a posh art deco style (Douglas's apartments in these films always are). He wonders if he could be falling in love with her. "Why must you bring in wrong values?" she says. "Love is a romantic designation for a most ordinary biological, or shall we say chemical, process." And "chemically," she acknowledges, "we are already quite sympathetic." She sits on the floor, straight-backed, leaning with her elbow against the cushion of a big leather chair. He sits in front of her, like a petitioner. "My father and mother," she says, "wanted me to stay on the farm. But I preferred the bayonet." "The bayonet," he repeats, in his dazzled way. "Did you really?" "I was wounded before Warsaw," she tells him, in a lovely open-faced close-up, both childish and proud. She was a sergeant in the Third Cavalry Brigade. "Would you like to see my wound?" "I'd love to," he says. And she bows her head and throws her hair forward, exposing the back of her neck to him. She sits up again. Leon is speechless. "A Polish lancer," she says softly, "I was sixteen." "Poor Ninotchka," he says, genuinely distressed for her. "Poor, poor Ninotchka." "Don't pity me," she says gently. "Pity the Polish lancer. After all, I'm still alive."

They are more tightly framed now, in a medium close-up, and Leon proceeds (it's about that time) to make the obligatory love talk. (Unnecessarily, as it turns out.) "Ninotchka, it's midnight," he says. "One half of Paris is making love to the other half." "You merely feel you must put yourself in a romantic mood to add to your exhilaration," she replies.

LEON (*in a rush*): Oh, you analyze everything out of existence. You'd analyze me out of existence, but I won't let you. Love isn't so simple, Ninotchka. Ninotchka, why do doves bill and coo? Why do snails, the coldest of all creatures, circle interminably around each other? Why do moths fly hundreds of miles to find their mates? Why do flowers slowly open their petals? Oh, Ninotchka—Ninotchka, surely you feel some slight symptom of the divine passion. A general warmth in the palms of your hands—a strange heaviness in your limbs—a burning of the lips that isn't thirst but something a thousand times more tantalizing, more exalting than thirst? . . .

NINOTCHKA (*giving him a sidelong look*): . . . You are very talkative. (*They kiss.*)

This is close to being screwball's primal scene: the hero flying high and making a fool of himself while the heroine looks sardonically on—before bringing him down to earth. With this difference: it isn't so much the screwball heroine's common sense that Ninotchka opposes to Leon, in those killing glances she gives him as he talks, as her own literal-mindedness. In the Lubitsch variant of this scene, *both* the man and the woman are a bit foolish, both a bit missing the point.

But Garbo's way of missing a point, or of looking for it, is devastating indeed. Typically in these two-shots, Douglas is in profile, turned toward her and talking. And Garbo is looking inexorably forward, into space, as if he were coming to her over a short-wave radio full of static. As they stand by the telescope and he describes his apartment, "a pleasant little place" with "all the comforts" and so on, she frowns into the distance. It's like talking to a sibyl. But an attentive one. It's clear that she looks away to *listen* better, to take it all in somehow. All that stuff about the circling snails ("coldest of all creatures") and moths finding their mates makes her look especially intent and faraway and pondering. She is humorless, and you could say that she is missing the point; but it is hard to think of an audience (or an image) that could make *his* point look more foolish, or the sophisticated hero himself more fatuous.

Certainly Ninotchka in these early scenes seems odd and distant to us, too, just as she does to Leon ("What kind of girl are you, anyway?"). But then, just when she seems *most* unreadable and remote, she says exactly the right deflating thing: "You are very talkative." Almost as good as "Suppress it" was. She is complicated—and surprising. Though there is inescapably something foolish about her, about anyone who says things like "Your type will soon be extinct." Except that when Garbo says it—with her characteristic note of melancholy, of impersonal sadness—we're not at all sure she isn't right. Nor is Leon. "You are something we do not have in Russia," she tells him later. "That's why I believe in the future of my country." "I'm beginning to believe in it myself," he says, unprotesting. But then she finds out who he is—the grand duchess's kept man—and starts to leave. He stops her in the doorway. He holds her by the elbows and she slumps slightly forward; he reminds her that they've just been in each other's arms, after all, that she just kissed him. She lowers her eyes. "I kissed the Polish lancer, too—before he died," she says. She looks at him and goes out.

The cleverness of that is Lubitschean—pulling a switch on something we had almost forgotten in a way he often does. But the somberness is new. Not quite, though: it's an echo—not just the tone of it but the shape and dying-fall rhythm too—of Lionel Barrymore in *The Man I Killed*, talking about his dead son to the crippled veteran outside the hotel: "He was going to his death—and I cheered." The ironies of Ninotchka's remark, however, are even richer and subtler. It's a curious effect: in a movie where "reality" is sacrificed to gags over and over again, where the surface texture of certain scenes (Leon at the Russian In-Tourist Bureau, for example) has no more density and depth than a vaudeville sketch, this "Polish lancer" seems very real indeed. At least he does when we hear about his death, and about Ninotchka's kiss. It's an effect—and an echo—that reminds us of at least one reason why Lubitsch was never quite fully at home in the screwball comedy: he wasn't hopeful enough.

Though once Ninotchka laughs, it's not easy to remember that. The movie becomes romantic in an eager, full-hearted way that almost nothing else in the Lubitsch canon comes close to. Ninotchka reappears at Leon's apartment wearing the silly hat she had once deplored. She puts lipstick on for him and confesses her love to him. They go dancing, in a delirium of love and champagne. And of course they act up in public, as screwball lovers do. But this time the shocking element in the heroine's behavior is not some impropriety or scandal but socialism: addressing the swells on the dance floor as "comrades." And they are finally thrown out of the place because she is preaching communism in the powder room, inciting the attendants to strike.

One of the most remarkable things about *Ninotchka*—in spite of the gags and the tone of radio-show satire ("Who am *I* to cost the Russian people seven cows!" protests Ninotchka about the price of her hotel room)—is how judiciously and even at times sympathetically it treats the subject of communism. And it really seems to know—unlike almost every other Hollywood film of the time—what a believing communist might be like, what such a person might believe in and why. (It's ironic in view of this that it should have been the movie always cited for its anticommunism in the late forties and early fifties, when the movies were being probed for "subversion.") Ninotchka's commitment is made fun of, but it's also seen as a reasonable, even admirable, if frequently discouraging, choice. The character may talk flippantly about mass trials ("There are going to be fewer but better Russians") and solemnly about the price of things in cows—but she also speaks with moving eloquence about things like hunger and injustice, especially in her clashes with the thoroughly unsympathetic grand duchess. And although Ninotchka is "made human" by love and by Paris, she isn't made anticommunist or even procapitalist—a remarkable sort of tact for a Hollywood film, where such idealistic figures are usually required to "sell out" vehemently in the end (like the chauffeur in *Fifth Avenue Girl*), just as the sexy ones have to get married or die.

Above all, however, she is touched with Garbo's profundity. "I can't say it," Ninotchka says, trying to tell Leon that she loves him. But she turns her face to him—and to the camera—with an expression of longing and panic that makes her seem almost unbearably exposed: she offers *that* instead of the words. Lubitsch was right when he spoke to Garson Kanin about her "lightness." It's not the usual point about Garbo, but it's true. Mostly, she indicates Ninotchka's

deepest feelings by what she *doesn't* show us (the Lubitsch door again): lowering her eyes rather than exposing them; smiling at a memory of the Eiffel Tower— "Hmmm"—then looking down, turning masklike as she recites the words that Leon had shouted up the steps at her . . . "But there is an elevator included in the price of admission." Back in Moscow, alone and unhappy, she turns her radio on; she gets a stentorian official voice declaiming government propaganda. She turns the dial and gets another version of the same voice. Once more—with the same result. Then, with a little twist of her mouth, pulling her chin in with a

kind of smile, she switches off. The smile is important. She is trying to be indulgent to Moscow, to the voices—to her own unhappiness. But once she's
switched off, she stands a moment, lost in thought and slightly frowning. It
escapes her involuntarily, like a little moan: "No music," she says softly. That's
it, of course—not the voices themselves (what do they matter?) but what they
get in the way of. Garbo makes the point poignantly exact.

Just as she transforms all the rather tacky, coarse-grained jokes about lipstick
and lingerie and so on. She gives them the sort of attractive gravity that she gives
to carrying her own suitcases. "I don't look too foolish?" she says to Leon, as
she appears at his door in her new hat and Paris outfit. But Garbo doesn't belie
the words at all: she *does* look foolish, just as she feels, pained and clumsy and
really wanting a compliment more than anything. From Leon, of course, she gets
a very professional one. But it suits her fine—making her look even more sheepish than before, grinning and hanging her head as she enters the apartment.

The trouble with the earlier Ninotchka—the Ninotchka before the laughing
fit in the restaurant—is that she never feels foolish. Now she does—and she is
transformed, in the accustomed screwball equation between love and humor and
regeneration. "Oh, Leon, don't ever ask me for a picture of myself!" says the
new Ninotchka in the new dress and hat, in an overwhelming close-up. "I
couldn't bear the thought of being shut up in a drawer—I couldn't breathe, I
couldn't stand it!" she says, eyes tearful and bright, her head back in something
like a laugh, conscious of the "silliness" but exultant with it, too—as Leon
moves into the shot to embrace her. "You know the jokes you told me a few days
ago?" she asks just before this, while they are sitting on the couch together. "I
wake up in the middle of the night and I laugh at them. You know that's wrong."
She looks both hopeless and unreasoningly happy. "They aren't funny, they're
silly." Now looking at him: "They're stupid—and still I laugh at them." This
new relationship to foolishness makes her both more resigned later on (there is
always another radio station to turn to) and more painfully vulnerable (there
really is *no* music).

It's an extraordinary collaboration between director and star. Lubitsch is no
longer merely evoking or mimicking complexity, as he does so wittily in early
films like *The Love Parade*. With Garbo he is filming and exploring the real
thing. And it affects the Lubitsch style: the "touch" in *Ninotchka* is most dis-
cernible in a rich kind of anti-joke, a scene winding down and then ending
unexpectedly in a complex and quiet irony rather than building to a more conventional kind of witty payoff. As when Ninotchka first tries on the foolish hat
she has bought. She sees her comrades eagerly out after a business meeting.
She closes and locks the door behind them, then nearly runs to the place where
she has hidden the hat, in a lower drawer. She kneels and takes it out. It's cone-
shaped; she holds it up and looks at it and walks to the mirror, a full-length one.
She stands in front of it and stares—and then puts the hat on, settling it firmly

on her head with both hands. She stands and looks—hopelessly. Then she sits, leaning forward rather tensely with her hands on her knees. Then, still gazing at herself, she puts her chin in her hand—and the scene ends in a dissolve. It's an unmistakable Lubitsch moment. To watch Garbo's grave and gradual acceptance of the "silliness" of the hat, of its subtle but absolute wrongness over such a face as she sees in the mirror, is to experience something like revelation. A rich, funny reminder—a re-experience in a comic mode—of that unrescindable social contract we've all entered into.

There is a story about Garbo that she once seriously expressed a wish to play St. Francis of Assisi.* In some ways she comes as near to that unconventional aim as she could do in *Ninotchka*. Whose heroine—puritan and visionary, humanitarian and ideologic—has some of the qualities we associate with the Christian saint. The St. Francis story is usually offered as evidence of Garbo's eccentricity. But in fact it makes sense. One of the elements of the Garbo mystique was always the degree to which she could make idealism seem as much a felt human need as love or food. So that in *Ninotchka* she can speak of getting "foreign currency to buy tractors" (Lubitsch gives her a full glowing close-up) and be powerfully moving as she does so. Garbo, Lubitsch, and the screwball comedy itself come together in this film in a most astonishing result: the closest thing to a convincing socialist heroine the English-speaking cinema has yet produced. It's a nice payoff to the screwball tradition: that it had the freedom to offer even this surprise.

T HREE MONTHS after winding up *Ninotchka* at MGM, Lubitsch began shooting *The Shop Around the Corner* with Margaret Sullavan and James Stewart at the same studio. Once he'd begun, he worked quickly, finishing in twenty-eight days (*Ninotchka* took twice as long). And he seemed at pains once he was done to emphasize the modesty of the whole enterprise. "It's not a big picture," he told the New York *Sun* three days before the New York premiere (January 25, 1940), "just a quiet little story. . . . It didn't cost very much, for such a cast, under $500,000. . . . I hope it has some charm." "Its chief distinction," he told the New York *Post* in the same vein, was that it gave Frank Morgan "his first chance to play straight" in over a decade. The tribute to Morgan was undoubtedly heartfelt; his performance as Matuschek is one of the greatest in the Lubitsch canon. But the modesty of these comments might also have been a case of nerves: this was a picture that Lubitsch had been promising both to his inter-

---

* Kenneth Tynan had an even better idea for her. If anything, Garbo is a Chekhov heroine, and it's one of the tragedies of her career, as Tynan pointed out, that she never played Masha in *The Three Sisters*. Garson Kanin was "surprised"—as he has written—during his first meetings with Garbo in Hollywood, by "her wide knowledge of Chekhov and his works."

viewers and to himself—the comedy about ordinary life and ordinary people that he'd been saying he should make. A new move.

The Shop Around the Corner is about a prosperous gift and leather goods store in contemporary Budapest. "This is the story of Matuschek and Company," says the opening title, "—of Mr. Matuschek and the people who work for him. . . ." They are a family, in fact—in a self-contained world. The movie rarely ventures outside the store itself. And it has more than "some charm," though it has plenty of that: it has that combination of exaggerated delicacy and unexpected power that Lubitsch at times seems almost uniquely to command. And it holds a unique place in his work. It's the Lubitsch film which is most overtly about experiences of love and affection. Less about romantic love—though it's certainly about that—than about the achievement of benevolence. It was indeed a new sort of Lubitsch comedy.

Of course, there are many familiar components: the obscure Hungarian source (a play called *Illatszertar* by Nikolaus Laszlo), the Samson Raphaelson screenplay, and above all the central situation—a romantic couple at intense cross-purposes with each other, involved in an ardent, elaborate, and feature-length misunderstanding. Kralik (James Stewart) and Klara Novak (Margaret Sullavan) are both clerks in the store, and they have come to detest each other there. But in private correspondence, begun through an ad in the personals, they are lovers, known to each other only by their post-office box numbers and a ritual salutation: "Dear Friend. . . ." When at last they make an appointment to meet, Kralik looks in the café window beforehand and discovers that it is Miss Novak who is waiting for him. He goes in anyway—after first going away, then coming back again. He joins her at her table. She explains, patiently at first, that she is waiting for someone. But as usual he seems bent on tormenting her. When he is really trying to make friends with her now, difficult as that is for him, and goes on being. Since she not only dislikes him but also feels obliged to compare him out loud with her letter-writing ideal, with all his grace and learning and feeling for beauty, his love of art and literature. A man who writes poems to her and who knows her value. Not a "little insignificant clerk"—as she calls Kralik when he pushes her too far—with a handbag for a heart and a cigarette lighter for a brain. But then he's just called *her* "cold and snippy like an old maid." From her point of view, she only gives as good as she gets.

But she makes us nervous all the same. For what she's said and for what she *might* say. It's not only that she's out on a limb, not knowing what we know and what Kralik knows. It's that disturbing sense she gives of living a life in her head that nothing or no one can quite get at. With all her spunk and wit, her looks and charm, there is something hopeless about her. She seems both vulnerable and aimed like a weapon, both self-possessed and hysterical. So that we're certainly not surprised when she faints at the news of Kralik's promotion to manager, or takes to her bed out of nervous exhaustion the next day. She is under a strain always—with her aspirations to love and learning and beauty, and those wide eyes that never quite meet the other person's. Sullavan is remarkable, getting the exactly right balance of nerves and yearning, making Klara both upsetting and irresistible, funny and painful at once.

Klara is like the movie itself—under the sleek, impeccably functioning comic surface, there is the threat of something disruptive and undoing. For one thing, there is so much touchiness in the air, so many hurt feelings: people feeling slighted or dumped on or simply unappreciated, impugned for their rumored bow legs (Kralik's) or their chronic red hands (Klara's), their necktie or their blouse or the way they wrap packages, put down by their boss just when they think they least deserve to be. In Kralik's case, the sense of the injustice done him by Mr. Matuschek mounts to a kind of agony. "I'm not going to stand for this much longer!" he says, his voice breaking, after Matuschek has humiliated him in front of the others. "What does that man want of me, anyway? Why does he always have to pick on me?" "Well," says Pirovitch (Felix Bressart), "you are his oldest employee." "That's a fine reason," says Kralik.

But of course it is. The boss, as usual in Lubitsch, is the touchiest one of all. And Matuschek is in a state of exacerbated egoism even before he finds out that his petted and adored wife is cheating on him with one of his own employees (he thinks that it's Kralik, his favorite—it turns out to be Vadas, the snitch and the flatterer). Kralik is not only his oldest employee but his most trusted and valued one. That's just the problem, however. Matuschek trusts Kralik's judgment, but he doesn't really welcome it. The young man is not only likely to be right when he makes a business judgment; he is usually *sure* that he is right. Unlike Matuschek, who is rarely sure, and rarely right. And Kralik (we soon learn) is the only one in the store who will give the owner the "honest opinion" he is always asking for. About the cigarette boxes, for example, that Matuschek likes so much (because they play "Orchi Tchornya") that he proposes to buy them in quantity. He asks the salespeople what they think. Ilona (Inez Courtney) equivocates. Vadas (Joseph Schildkraut) lies eagerly: he says they're "sensational." Pirovitch simply hides in the stockroom ("The other day he called me an idiot. . . . I said, 'Yes, Mr. Matuschek, I'm an idiot.' I'm no fool."). In the face of all this "support," Matuschek demands that Kralik give him just "one reason" for his feeling against the boxes. Kralik, of course, gives him several, all of them very convincing. Which makes Matuschek angrier than ever. So much so that he ends up shouting at the man he's buying them from—and not buying them. (At least until Klara appears and intervenes: she gets a job by selling one of the boxes.)

Worst of all, after one of these episodes Matuschek feels like a fool. Why does Kralik do this to him? When it happens once again—and on the same day—he calls him into his office.

MATUSCHEK: Kralik, why did you put me in that situation in front of the whole shop?
KRALIK: Well, I'm very sorry, sir, but it was not my fault.
MATUSCHEK: Well, whose fault was it? Mine?
KRALIK: Well, yes . . .

He knew it was, of course. But he's a little startled at this reply all the same. But not angered: instead, he seems suddenly overcome by hopelessness, and when he speaks next, it's gently:

MATUSCHEK: What's the matter with you, Kralik? You're my oldest employee. I do everything I can to show my appreciation. I . . . I . . . I ask you to my house . . .
KRALIK: Well, I'm very grateful, sir.
MATUSCHEK: Well, you have a funny way of showing it. You know how much I value your judgment, and on every occasion you contradict me. Whatever I say, you say no.

Kralik, with exasperated sarcasm, offers to say yes from now on if that's what Mr. Matuschek wants. But the older man, who doesn't want that at all, now tries to make it up with him—asking Kralik, almost shyly, if he had a good time last night at the Matuscheks' party: "I . . . I had a lot of fun. Didn't you?" Almost like a suitor. And Kralik, who is now the offended one, relents.

The ironies and jokes in this film are not about people's sexiness (remarkably for a Lubitsch film, there are no double entendres, not a single risqué line or gag) but about their touchiness, their petty anxieties, their vanities and uneasy egoisms. Like Matuschek, we may cherish the sons—like Kralik—who can take our place; but on the other hand they *are* taking our place. A serious matter. And Frank Morgan's Matuschek is the ground of all the movie's pain. No other Lubitsch film is so directly in touch with the *anguish* of feeling. This is—for the first time—a Lubitschean comedy in which the adultery really hurts. And there are *no* jokes about it. Matuschek is, to be sure, a man of experience as well as years, and he can understand (once the detective has disclosed it to him) his wife's infidelity. He can even comment on it with insight: "She just didn't want to grow old with me," he says. And then he tries to kill himself (off-screen, of course) and is saved only by the intervention of Pepi, his delivery boy (William Tracy), who hasn't left work yet.

But people are never quite left alone in this film: it's one of the meanings of the Matuschek "family." And it affects the Lubitsch two-shot very directly: characters are given, as always in Lubitsch, to ludicrous intensities, but the other person in the frame is likely to be more sympathetic than alarmed. Even the reticencies and turnings away are not sly but tactful—signs of support and concern. And the background figures—far from being opaque and ominous, the way they are in *Monte Carlo*, for example—are likely to be compassionately involved in the foreground figure's plight: the discreet way Flora (Sara Haden), the soft-spoken cashier, stands to one side while Kralik, who's just been fired, says his goodbyes to all the others. Or the way Ilona, the pretty bookkeeper, supports him with anxious eyes when Mr. Matuschek is putting him on the spot. Even the camera seems sympathetic. Far from being a challenging presence, as it often is in Lubitsch—stranding a character on the screen, emphasizing his isolation and exposure—here it's almost a confiding one, discreet and self-effacing. Its movements are deft, imperceptible, tactful—underscoring a moment or a detail or an expression by tracking gently forward, for example. But mostly it stays still, changing position only to see and hear a bit better or to slightly revise our view of things. As it does, to quietly dramatic effect, in an early scene between Kralik and Pirovitch.

They are in the stockroom, preparing to begin their day's work. Kralik wants to know if his friend would like to "hear something nice." Pirovitch would, of course, and so Kralik produces a letter and reads.

KRALIK: "My heart was trembling as I walked into the post office, and there you were, lying in box 237. I took you out of your envelope and read you—read you right there—oh, my dear friend. . . ."
PIROVITCH: What is all this?

It started, says Kralik, when he decided that he wanted to buy an encyclopedia. He was looking through the ads when he came across a "modern girl" who wished to "correspond on cultural subjects anonymously with intelligent, sympathetic young man." And they have now exchanged four letters. "Four letters," repeats Pirovitch wonderingly, with his long neck and walrus mustache and shrewd eyes, gleaming with humorous consciousness. Kralik assures him that she is "no ordinary girl, either," and offers the following to prove it: " 'Are you tall? Are you short?' " Pirovitch looks off, listening, while Stewart, towering over him (as he does over everyone), reads. " 'Are your eyes blue? Are they brown? Don't tell me.' " "Mm-*hmm*," says Pirovitch, emphatically. " 'What does it matter so long as our minds meet?' " And Kralik pauses for a response. Pirovitch is still looking off, in his listening attitude. "That's beautiful," he says after a moment, seeming somewhat dazed. "Isn't it?" says Kralik. "Mm-*hmm*," says Pirovitch. "Now wait a minute," says Kralik, as he returns to the letter for more.

All this has been in a single take, a two-shot favoring Kralik and his transports, shooting past Pirovitch in the foreground. Now there is a cut in which Lubitsch reangles the shot to favor Pirovitch as well as moving it closer in, heightening the intimacy. So that now it is Pirovitch's reactions to the letter, as Kralik continues to read from it, which become the focus of the shot. With Kralik absorbed in his reading, Pirovitch permits himself a slight smile, looking down at the paper in the other man's hand. " 'We have enough trouble in our daily lives,' " reads Kralik. "Mm-hmm," says Provitch—and slowly raises his eyes to Kralik's enraptured face, beside and above him. " 'There are,' " he reads, " 'so many great and beautiful things to discuss in this world of ours' "—and Pirovitch looks at him tenderly. And then, as the letter reaches a kind of apotheosis of silliness—" 'it would be wasting these precious moments if we told each other the vulgar details of how we earn our daily bread' "—Pirovitch looks tactfully, sadly away. And the scene ends (with a summons from Mr. Matuschek).

What's special in the experience of this comedy is how the jokes, reflecting on the characters' absurdity, keep shifting into something else: into that same mixture of feelings as Pirovitch shows here, the same amusement and predominating tenderness, the same final fatherly sadness. We are always being surprised by affection in this movie—surprised at the tenderness of feeling lurking in a joke that we've taken to be merely clever in a way, those elaborate permutations of witty contrivance that Lubitsch and Raphaelson are so adept at involving us in. These scenes and situations achieve benignity in the same way that the characters do—gradually and at length, after going through and past the resentments and vanities that make them laughable. The same process, roughly, by which Matuschek is restored to his family at the store—once he has gotten free of the fake family he and his wife make at "home" (we never see this character, since she doesn't belong to the store—all she does is take money from it), once he has finally renounced his romantic obsession with her. "*This* is my home," he tells his little band of employees on Christmas Eve. Vadas, the false son, has been rejected—fired and turned out—and Kralik, the real son, has been reinstated, as manager. The point is clear: Matuschek becomes a real father only after he gives up the role of doting and jealous husband. And it's this renunciation, as well as the betrayal and pain which occasion it, that now makes possible the very powerful sweetness of feeling that suffuses the whole Christmas Eve sequence—over which Matuschek, just out of the hospital after his suicide attempt, restored to his patriarchy and reunited with his "son," handing out bonuses and stammering his thanks and beaming his affection, presides. And Morgan's famous vocalized pause—his trademark—becomes not, as it usually is, an expression of indecision or alarm or uneasiness but a hesitation before kindness—when, for example, he invites Rudi (Charles Smith), the delivery boy (Pepi has been promoted to clerk), the Matuschek family's newest and most hapless member, to have Christmas dinner with him.

But the pettiness and the generosity in this film are importantly connected. Just as calculation in Lubitsch often seems to authenticate ardor (see *Trouble in Paradise:* "Make that check out to cash," says Gaston to Mariette). It's the crass con-man side of our natures that he specially loves, and he is never more delighted than to find it in our most exalted moments and states. As when Kralik, in the midst of excited love for Klara, still contrives and maneuvers to get the Christmas present he wants (a leather wallet); or when Klara, in the same transported state, resolves to check out that bow-legs rumor about him. The penultimate shot of the film—the one just before the ecstatic fadeout kiss—is of Kralik pulling up his trouser legs so that she can see for herself. It's the sort of event that makes the kiss that follows seem, paradoxically, all the more intoxicated. And the sort of conjunction that accounts for the whole scene's queer and surprising emotional force: people both becoming wonderful and remaining incorrigibly themselves at the same time—which is in a Lubitsch film nearly always the most wonderful thing of all. Particularly in *this* Lubitsch film—the summit of the Lubitsch-Raphaelson collaboration (it was also their last important film together)—with its extraordinary final sequence. The one where Kralik finally discloses to Klara the identity of her "Dear Friend."

It's after the Christmas Eve festivity. Mr. Matuschek has left with Rudi, and the others have gone too. Kralik, the manager, is staying behind to lock up. "Oh," he says in the doorway of the stock room—as if he hadn't known that

Klara was still there. She is wrapping the wallet she has chosen for her suitor. "I decided to follow your advice after all," she concedes (she had wanted to get him a cigarette box, the "Orchi Chornya" one, but Kralik had urged the wallet). She doesn't quite understand it, but Mr. Kralik has been mysteriously nice to her lately. He has something to show her now: the Christmas present that he's chosen for his girlfriend. It's a locket, and he gets Klara to try it on to see how it looks. She goes to the mirror between the lockers, holding the locket up against her throat, with Kralik looming over her. She looks in the mirror; he looks down at her. "Oh, *my*," she says, "my . . ." as he looks at her, gravely.

But she didn't know, as she tells him now—turning almost reluctantly from the mirror and handing him back the locket—that he had a girlfriend. He replies that that's probably difficult for her to imagine. "Now, Mr. Kralik," she says, "don't let's start all over again. It's Christmas and I'd like to be friends with you." But she doesn't look at him when she says this—and it has her huffy, Miss-ish sound, in startling proximity to the dreamy young woman we've just seen at the mirror. And besides, he's wrong. She's ready to confess now—slowly and nervously (what harm can there be, since she is "very happily engaged, at least it looks that way"?)—that she had quite a crush on him when she first came to work at Matuschek's. He finds this hard to believe; he looks stunned, in fact. "You certainly didn't *show* it," he says. "Well, you see," she says airily—she crosses to her locker and he follows her—"I was a different girl then. I was really rather naïve." She hands him her coat and he holds it as she slips into it. "All my knowledge came from books." And she had just read about a Comédie-Française actress who roused men's interest by treating them "like a dog." "Yes," he says, "well, you treated me like a dog." She concedes this, but she still doesn't look at him; she never does through this whole scene.

"Oh, well," he says, "that's all forgotten now." But there is something in his tone that makes her glance at him, in her half-averted way. She turns quickly back to her locker. He is still looming over her. "So you're going to see your girlfriend," she says chattily, as she takes her hat out and puts it on. Then, turning to him as she adjusts the hat: "By the way, is it serious?" "Yes," he says gravely, "very"—hovering over her with a kind of avid benignity. She responds brightly, still not looking at him: "Maybe we'll both be engaged Monday morning." "I think we will," he says, with the same gravity, still looking at her, still looming above her. But she doesn't want him to misunderstand: in her case it only *might* happen. "Well, as a matter of fact," says Kralik, as she turns back to her locker again, "I can tell you it *will* happen." And he walks out of the shot and leaves her staring after him.

She follows him into the store as he goes about turning out the lights. What does he mean? Her fiancé has been to see him, he tells her. She is astonished. But she can't let Kralik know that she's never even met or seen the man (they have a rendezvous that night, and she is on her way to it now) or that she doesn't even know his name. It's Popkin, according to Kralik. ("*Pop*kin?")

KLARA: I think he's a very attractive man, don't you?
KRALIK: Oh, yes—yes, for his type, I'd say . . . *yes.*
KLARA: You would—uh—really classify him as a—a definite *type?*
KRALIK: Oh, absolutely. And—ah—don't you try and change him now. Don't put him on a diet.

And so it goes, with Kralik turning out lights and Klara slipping around behind him—and "Popkin" progressively revealed as bald, morose ("Didn't he impress you as being rather witty?" "Well—he struck me as rather depressed"), out of work, ready to live on her salary (especially considering the raise and the Christmas bonus), and a plagiarizer of the verses she thought he'd composed just for her ("That's Victor Hugo—he stole that"). Klara is devastated. She sits down on a customer's bench. Kralik eases himself down beside her, tactfully. They sit in the shot together. "And I built up such an illusion about him," she says tearfully, while Kralik looks sideways at her. "I thought he was so perfect. . . ."

But her putting this in the past tense, her suspicious readiness to give up this dream even before she's met the man who occasioned it, clearly has something to do with the way she sits in this shot with Kralik. They are very close, and she doesn't move. Kralik looks at her in his uneasy, sidelong way as he offers her his sympathy, his regrets at having to be the one who has dashed her hopes. "Oh, that's all right," she says weakly, still without moving. "I guess I really ought to thank you." But she is still not looking at him. He is uncertain, but he seizes the moment anyway. "Klara," he says softly, looking sideways at her, "if I'd only known in the beginning how you felt about me, things would have been different. I . . . we wouldn't have been fighting all the time." Her head is lowered as he begins this explanation, and it slowly lifts as he goes on. She has a faraway expression in her eyes, and she tilts her head to one side: she seems both listening and not listening. "If we did quarrel," he continues, slow and gingerly, looking at her fixedly, "it wouldn't have been over suitcases or handbags"—she gives a little sigh, still looking into the distance—"but over something like . . ."—he hesitates, then says the next words with great deliberation, watching their effect as he goes—"whether your aunt or grandmother should live with us or not. . . ." But there is no effect—no visible one, anyway. She is still looking off. After a moment she turns toward him, seeming at last to be about to meet his eyes; but then she doesn't again. "Well," she says, "it's sweet of you to try to cheer me up." And she rises. "I guess we better say good night. . . ."

It's the familiar juxtaposition—the one in the know and the one who isn't—but Lubitsch has raised it to a new power of feeling and delight. It's not just the way Stewart hovers over her, a figure of complex suspense and affection (where Matuschek had to get beyond love to achieve this sort of benignity, Kralik finds it *in* love). It's the way Sullavan "hovers" over her own consciousness here. Mooning, sighing, hesitating, looking off, looking down, looking away—it's an extraordinary, very Lubitschean mimicry of a state of complex consciousness. Klara may sense the happy news that is coming—as on some level she clearly does—but she registers its approach with hesitation, trepidation, contained excitement, maintaining to the end (when Kralik actually reveals himself) her same strange, funny, finally and triumphantly playful relation to it. They both seem extraordinary in this scene—both marvelous and familiar at the same time, this boy and girl with their common dread of being "insignificant" and ordinary (if this were a more American sort of comedy—like *Bachelor Mother*—they would hate their jobs, but as it is they are merely trying to rise above them), each with their own kind of slyness, their own kind of delight, and the passionate unspoken connection between them as the scene goes on. It's no wonder that this comedy—for all the depressiveness it sounds and evokes, the melancholia and touchiness and vanity—seems finally so elated. Lubitsch transposes it all onto new levels of sunniness and freedom and transforming tenderness.

"Oh, dearest sweetheart Klara!" cries Kralik, done at last with hovering. She starts to leave, and he takes her by her arms and looks at her: "Please," he says, "take your key and open post-office box 237, and take me out of my envelope"— she stares at him in amazement—"and kiss me." He takes a red carnation from his pocket, the sign they'd agreed upon in their letters, and puts it in his buttonhole. "Dear Friend . . ." he says. And she understands at last. Though she's not too carried away to think about those bow legs—before the final kiss.

Ninotchka was a big box-office success—Garbo's biggest ever, in fact. *The Shop Around the Corner* was a modest one. And different as the two comedies are, they both have a complexity and amplitude, a freedom and fullness of feeling, that seem to mark a new stage in Lubitsch's art. The Lubitsch of the forties. . . .

*Preston Sturges
with the stars
of* The Palm
Beach Story:
*Joel McCrea,
Mary Astor,
Claudette
Colbert, and
Rudy Vallee.*

PART 3

The Sturges Era, 1940-1948

*William
Powell, Asta,
and Myrna Loy
in* Another
Thin Man.

Decline of | 19
the Romantic Comedy

*There was such a steady flow of bright comedy that it appeared to be a Holly-
wood staple, and it didn't occur to me that those films wouldn't go on being
made. . . . The comic spirit of the thirties had been happily self-critical about
America, the happiness born of the knowledge that in no other country were
movies so free to be self-critical. It was the comedy of a country that didn't
yet hate itself.* —PAULINE KAEL, "Raising Kane"

THE MOVIES of the studio era had always been torn between broad conflicting impulses: between impiety and reverence, cynicism and sentiment, the
city and the small town, busting loose and staying put. And at least until the
forties, the struggle between these opposing tendencies might have seemed a
fairly equal one. But the more powerful and prosperous the studios became (and
the forties were their peak), the more the impious, irreverent, anarchic side
seemed to lose out, even to be systematically suppressed—in what Agee (in the
mid-forties) called "the slick, growing genteelism of U.S. cinema." It was in the
forties that the American Catholic Church consolidated its control over the movies' content and style, until at times the industry seemed almost like a branch
of the Legion of Decency. And with the onset of the war and the consequent
closing of European and international markets, the run of Hollywood films became more provincial, more smugly and narrowly "American," more commodified than ever before.

The times were hard on the more sophisticated stars. The preeminent example was Garbo, whose audience had always been more international than
domestic (most of her movies made their profits in Europe). If she was to survive,
she would have to be "humanized," connected to something less troubling and
forbidding than her previous lines—eroticism or romantic martyrdom or (as in
her last film) Bolshevism—appropriated to the particular meaninglessness of
American life and American aspirations. And so the heroine she plays in *Two-*

Faced Woman (1941) is an athlete, a ski instructor, a health nut. Though passionate about it all—being Garbo. "I get my stimoo-lation from the outdoors," she says to the hero—balefully. She is described as an "idealist," with her fanatic devotion to sports and clean living, and her insistence on sleeping with the window wide open in even the coldest weather.

But when her New York publisher husband (Melvyn Douglas)—who is no idealist and who likes the windows closed—stays too long in the city away from her, she undertakes an impersonation to win him back, another "going wild" act. She pretends to be her own twin sister and opposite number, a city woman of infinite sophistication. She changes from ski togs to an evening gown with a plunging neckline. She wears her hair in a frizzy, upswept "off the face" style ("the Garbo bob," as the ads christened it), decorated with little barrettes and embellished by a big curl in the center of her broad brow. She is meant to be kittenish, and she seems horsier than ever (it was Graham Greene, in his review of *Queen Christina*, who first noticed the equine resemblance). And this time she is meant to be kidding about all of it: doing a takeoff of the Camille character she so often played ("I see my future . . . a few more burning flamelike years, and then the end"). She even leads a spectacular dance number—haltingly at first (supposedly she has never danced before), but then turning it into a triumph, a wild galvanizing rumba step called the "Chica-Choca," complete with chorus and mariachis and enraptured onlooking extras.

It's not that Garbo hadn't played dumb formulaic trash before; with blazing exceptions like *Camille* and *Ninotchka*, that's nearly all she did play. But behind all that trash, in however debased a form, there was always the idea that somehow life was a serious affair. Behind *Two-Faced Woman* there is only a void—the "sophistication" of the past and the sit-coms of the future. She is infinitely less preposterous doing a cooch dance "to the goddess Shiva" in *Mata Hari* (1931) than she is in this nightclub sequence doing a rumba. It's not the high spirits that defeat her here but the emptiness. She *could* play gaiety after all, as she had shown in *Ninotchka*. What she *can't* play is "a new dance sensation," or an image reversal, or won't-they-be-surprised-when-they-see-me-do-*this?* And she is almost equally ill suited to the bitchy Clare Boothe–style banter she's required to exchange with the Other Woman (Constance Bennett)—as well as to the arch, rigorously sexless love scenes she plays with the bewildered husband, teasing and tantalizing him. As Lubitsch had observed, if she can't feel it, she can't do it. A judgment that is borne out by almost every frame of *Two-Faced Woman*. "They're killing me with this picture," she reportedly said on the set. And in fact they were, as it turned out: *Two-Faced Woman* was a resounding box-office failure and the last film Garbo ever made.

But if the attempt to demystify Garbo had failed, a similar attempt made upon Katharine Hepburn just the year before—at the same studio and with the same

director (MGM and George Cukor)—had succeeded splendidly. Philip Barry's play *The Philadelphia Story* had been written expressly for Hepburn—tailored to her in every detail, even written with her help (she and Barry spent two months together working on the script), and it became an enormous Broadway hit. It had the same sort of success on film in 1940, and it rescued Hepburn's movie career. Which had been more or less washed up. After six years at RKO and fourteen starring films (she never played a supporting part), most of them flops, both audiences and critics were finding her increasingly mannered and monotonous, both too much and not enough ("the least versatile of star actresses," as one reviewer put it), and by 1938 she was known as box-office poison. She made her comeback in the theater with the help of Barry's play, and then made her movie comeback with the same vehicle. *The Philadelphia Story* was the biggest audience success Hepburn had ever had.

And she gets it, partly, by apologizing. It's one of the most peculiar star vehicles ever constructed—and one of the shrewdest. Instead of trying to coax and cajole us out of our resistance to its leading actress—as *Two-Faced Woman* did, assuring us that she's just a nice girl at heart—*The Philadelphia Story* makes

Katharine Hepburn trying her best to make Ruth Hussey and James Stewart "feel at home" in The Philadelphia Story.

that resistance more or less its entire subject, if a disguised one. Though not *very* disguised. Everyone recognized that the character of Tracy Lord, aristocratic and beautiful and arrogant, was "about" Hepburn herself. Even about her career problems. Tracy, too, is having problems with her audiences: misunderstandings and misfired performances, walkouts (her ex-husband) and bad notices (her mother and little sister, her father and that same ex-husband)—all of which begins to reverse when she gets a rave from one of her most determined critics. "There's a magnificence in you, Tracy," says Connor the reporter (James Stewart) in one of the play's most heartfelt speeches (Donald Ogden Stewart adapted the play for the screen). "A magnificence that comes out of your eyes, in your voice, in the way you stand there, in the way you walk. You're lit from within, Tracy! You've got fires banked down in you, hearth-fires and holocausts! . . . Oh, you're the golden girl, Tracy, full of life and warmth and delight. . . ." A notice to die for.

But Hepburn warrants it in this film. She has never looked more beautiful (the MGM glamour style—Adrian's gowns and Joseph Ruttenberg's photography). And she *is* magnificent, especially when she is being funny. As when she puts on the two intruding reporters from *Spy* magazine (Stewart and Ruth Hussey), offering them her "calla lilies" persona, speaking in loud insistent French, sweeping into the room in a cloud of taffeta, with a large hat and a basket: "I'm Tracy Lord." "I'm—I'm Mike to my friends," stammers the unnerved Stewart. "Of whom you have many, I'm sure," she replies, as if she really hoped to reassure him. And she wants to know everything about them now, even their home towns. "Duluth, is that west of here?" she inquires. And then: "South Bend . . . it sounds like dancing, doesn't it?" She asks them embarrassingly intimate questions, waiting just long enough to see their discomfiture but not long enough to hear the answers—and so on, until the two wiseacre reporters are nearly gibbering with confusion and dismay. It's Hepburn's scene and it's lovely: played with an almost breathtaking assurance and precision, touching every nuance of outrageousness, and passing grandly on. At moments like this, calling for a kind of delicate, detached zaniness, she really does seem "lit from within."

But the film, for most of its length, asks us to consider what's *wrong* with her. She's priggish and arrogant, intolerant and impatient and unforgiving and so on—everyone tells us about it. They even tell her: it's the main activity of the other characters. And the most authoritative of them are her father and her ex-husband, Dexter (Cary Grant). According to the latter, her "magnificence"—all her beauty and brains, her wit and vitality—is just her problem. Because it compounds her arrogance and intolerance, her impatience with "human imperfection" (she divorced him because of his drinking), her "religion" of self-discipline and strength. It makes her a lousy lay, too—at least that's what he *seems* to be talking about when he calls her a moon goddess, "chaste and virginal," and when he tells her she is one of those "married maidens" who are "a special class of the American female."

One way or another she lets men down, that's clear. Even her father, Seth Lord (John Halliday). His problem is that he keeps getting involved in messy affairs with chorus girls. That's why her mother—at Tracy's instigation, as we are not surprised to learn—has divorced him. But then he turns up again for his daughter's wedding—a graver and wiser man, it seems, with a new understanding of things, and especially of the problem that broke up his marriage. He has given it a lot of thought, he tells Tracy solemnly. And he has come to the reluctant conclusion that his philandering was really her fault. No kidding. If only *she'd* been a devoted young girl to him, he might not have gone off after all those *other* girls—if he'd had "a girl of his own" at home when he got there, "full of foolish, unquestioning, uncritical affection" for him, instead of the handful he did have, with her tendency to impose her own high standards on others, her lack of what he calls "an understanding heart."

And that's the way it goes: almost everything in the film turns out to be *her* problem. Not his, or theirs, or even ours. It's the trouble with being a goddess, with being too magnificent. You lose the human touch. This was not only a consoling thought for the rest of us but an inspired solution (courtesy of Philip Barry) to the problem of Hepburn's career. Consequently, she spent most of the rest of it submitting to just such strictures—atoning before us all for the aristocracy that she could never quite disguise or entirely throw off. That's one reason audiences liked to see her with Spencer Tracy. They knew *he'd* make her sorry. And their first co-starring film, George Stevens' *Woman of the Year* (1942), set the pattern: the high-flying independent woman brought finally and comically to ground by the solid, complacent, implacable male.

The reverse of the old screwball pattern. And it more or less pertained throughout the decade. It was no longer the witty heroine who had the edge but the feet-on-the-ground hero. Melvyn Douglas in *Third Finger Left Hand* (1940) is, like many of his predecessors, a kind of free spirit—a painter who knocks around and does what he likes and doesn't worry about getting ahead. What he dreams of, though, is not adventure—the way Gable's Peter Warne dreams of the South Seas—but early retirement, right back in his home town of Wapakoneta, Ohio. The pictures in his wallet are not of some tootsie but of Mom and Dad. And the girl he is looking for is one he can take home to *them*. Career woman Myrna Loy hardly qualifies; she is too flip and independent, too much a city type. And she is too scornful of his certitudes. Doesn't he ever change his mind about anything? she inquires wonderingly. "Nope," he replies. "Well, almost never—nope." This self-assurance is one of the things about him she has to learn to like. But of course she does by the end. She and a lot of others—in the years ahead.

Garbo does the "Chica-Choca" in Two-Faced Woman.

MOVIE ATTENDANCE in the United States during and just after the war was higher than it had ever been (or would be again). Average weekly attendance in 1945, for example, was 90 million, as opposed to 75 million in 1935. At the same time, the movies themselves became fewer in number (350 U.S.-produced films in 1945; 525 in 1935) and greatly more standardized. Everyone who went to them registered the sameness, the iron predictability, of the experience. You never (or rarely) saw anything you hadn't seen before at the movies. That was partly their point. To soothe and reassure us. But they could also feel numbing. They were in fact getting more like their heroes (see Melvyn Douglas above)—smug, incurious, self-righteous. America's most celebrated "escape" was getting more and more to feel like a trap.

To take one instance: ever since their silent days, movies had become progressively less fanciful, more and more literal. The motion picture, it was said, was "growing up." And the industry's newly gained, solidly achieved respectability was a goal at least as dear to the hearts of the moguls as big profits were. So that the pictures themselves (with licensed exceptions like the Hope-Crosby *Road* films) were now expected to *behave* like grown-ups—to act nice and talk sense, not silliness. Above all, not to make things up (or at least not to get caught at it). And this literalism became almost fanatical. Even fantasies, if their budgets were big enough, would have to be "explained" to us at the end. A dream was the favored method. Just what Dorothy's Oz turns out to be. And the people of Oz, from the Wizard to the Woodman, are really all people from the farm where she lives. Of course—what else? To some audiences, such explanations must have been reassuring. But to many—and to children especially, perhaps—the message was a depressingly clear one. There is no escape from the commonplace. Not even at the movies.

And so the Garbo sort of star, far from commonplace, might also have to be "explained"—smoothed out, as it were, and rendered user-friendly. Certainly the new stars were that: personable and unproblematic. The dominating female image was the girl-next-door type. And "starlets" were suddenly everywhere, tirelessly promoted by their studios: Joan Leslie at Warner's; Jeanne Crain and June Haver at Fox; Joan Caulfield and Gail Russell at Paramount; Gloria De Haven and June Allyson and Kathryn Grayson at MGM. Even the major women stars, the ones whose names really counted for something at the box office— Betty Grable and Lana Turner and Gene Tierney—were much blander types than their thirties counterparts. And even the sultry ones—Rita Hayworth and Ava Gardner—were less exotic and more accessible. One of the ironies of forties moviegoing was the frequent contrast, more insistent than ever, between the determinedly prosaic doings on the screen and the fantastic surroundings that people watched them in—paying their admissions to enter some freehanded version of Versailles or a Moorish palace or even Paradise itself, going to Rothafel's Roxy or Loew's Paradise, to the Oriental or the Egyptian or the Carthay Circle, to see the Hardy family, or someone like Van Johnson, or *Going My Way* . . .

At the same time, movies *looked* more magical than ever—largely because of the new celluloid lacquers. Black-and-white photography in the forties had a glow and depth and tactility that were nearly unprecedented. Technicolor, used only for special suitable projects, was in its greatest period. And all this visual glamour suited the movies' new assurance, their confidence in their public, narrowed by the war to a mostly domestic one. Never had moviemakers been surer of that public, or clearer about their own relation to it. (All this certainty would collapse in the fifties, of course.) There was none of that experimentation and casting around that had helped to make the early thirties such an interesting and varied movie time. The forties filmmaker knew how to nail an audience from the start; with the right Max Steiner score, for example, you could do it with the opening credits. Big-budget dramas in particular gained a kind of operatic sweep and amplitude. Warner Brothers films, once noted for their quick nervy fast-paced style, were now almost always sprawling and overlong, but done with such panache and forward impulsion and urgency that audiences were carried irresistibly along. It was a studio style—*Casablanca* (1943) was its apogee. And so it hardly seemed to matter who the director was—Sam Wood's *King's Row* (1942) or Vincent Sherman's *Old Acquaintance* (1943) or Jean Negulesco's *The Conspirators* (1944) or Delmer Daves's *Dark Passage* (1947). Standard sorts of movies, but made by teams of people who knew what they were doing and did it with passion and mastery. Or so it seemed. And when a director as gifted as Raoul Walsh deployed this studio style—in *The Man I Love* (1946), for example, with a script which is like a loosely connected anthology of favorite Warners scenes—it could become almost inexplicably stirring and expressive.

Because the most extraordinary thing of all about this time in Hollywood—with its standardization and "genteelism" and studio dictatorships—was that so many wonderful films still got made. As many as ever. Even if the general level of filmmaking was less interesting. Sturges' major films all belong to this decade. So do some of Lubitsch's richest and most surprising. It was in the forties that Howard Hawks really came into his own; so did John Ford. The newcomers to Hollywood included Alfred Hitchcock and Orson Welles and Robert Siodmak at the start of the decade, Max Ophuls and Douglas Sirk and Nicholas Ray toward its end. And an exciting new trend took hold (Welles and Hitchcock both contributed to its beginning)—an explosion of somber, Germanic-looking thrillers, "film noir," as it was later called. Like the screwball comedy inspiration, this, too, seemed infectious for a time, prompting the best work of the best people. It was a dissident style, subverting the piety and self-congratulation of the war and postwar years with expressions of menace and paranoia and fatalism, visions of entrapment and hopeless corruption. Not surprisingly, it was never a mode that was very popular with audiences; but it was irresistible, apparently, to filmmakers, who turned out these doom-ridden melodramas in great numbers into the fifties and beyond. "From now on, every picture I make will be done in flashback," said Jerry Wald (to screenwriter Catherine Turney) after seeing *Double Indemnity* (1944). And his next picture was *Mildred Pierce* (1945).

*The Other
Man, so to
speak—in the
"small, perfect
kitchen":
Spencer Tracy,
David Wayne,
and Katharine
Hepburn in
Adam's Rib.*

Bᴜᴛ ɪᴛ was not a good time for the romantic comedy. Even if the screwball inspiration hadn't been wearing down (the gloom of film noir had more staying power), the spreading atmosphere of religiosity-cum-patriotism would probably have been enough to do it in. Hollywood—at least as submissive to the State propaganda system as it was to the Catholic Church—was off to war well before the country was. And suddenly, ordinary movies began to take some very odd turns. Like *They Met in Bombay* (1941), with Clark Gable and Rosalind Russell: its first half is a traditional sort of romance-with-badinage about competitive jewel thieves; its second half, with Gable joining the British army to fight the Japanese, a kind of recruiting poster. As more and more films were turning out to be, with the heroine inciting the hero not to romance but to enlistment. As Judy Garland does to draft dodger Gene Kelly in *For Me and My Gal* (1942)—about the First World War—and making it seem quite worthwhile after all. But that's the way that war was seeming in all the movies now—no hint of the horror and waste that it had been in earlier films like Lubitsch's *The Man I Killed* (1932). There are people who oppose the war in these films (just as there were pacifists and isolationists and anti-interventionists in the movie audience); but they generally turn out to be afraid and unmanly, or self-centered—like Kelly's slacker—or not to believe in God—like James Cagney in *The Fighting 69th*. But a saintly priest (Pat O'Brien) sets him straight finally. And God Himself—riffling the pages of a Bible with a mysterious wind—seems to do the same for Gary Cooper in Howard Hawks's *Sergeant York* (1941), the "true story" of World War I hero Alvin York, a onetime conscientious objector (due to his quaint backwoods religion) who becomes "the greatest civilian soldier of the war," picking off Germans in the trenches like birds at a turkey shoot.

And the smarminess grew like a smell, getting into everything. In Billy Wilder's *The Major and the Minor* (1942), a relatively "sophisticated" sort of comedy and a big popular success, Rita Johnson as the Other Woman is snobbish, nasty, and materialistic. But the main way she shows her bad character is by plotting to keep Ray Milland safe from the war's action in his job behind the lines. (Heroine Ginger Rogers outwits her, though, and he gets sent to the fighting zone.) This was one of those "issues"—whether to prefer a safer war post to a more dangerous and active one—that forties movies (made by people whose "posts" were, and remained for the most part, very safe indeed) often pretended to explore, before reaching their utterly foregone conclusions about them. Like the question of whether young couples in wartime should enter into hasty marriages, a favorite movie dilemma. In which characters opposed to their doing so were always creeps or fools or else fated, like the draft dodgers, for a climactic conversion.

For at the same time as movies were commending the risks of marriage and the battlefield, they were getting harder than ever before on most other kinds of risk. The screwball heroine's kind, for example—which was bound in this climate of right-think to seem trivial and out of place even if it didn't already seem out of date. But though her day may have passed, the stars who embodied her were still around, and still important stars. One of the solutions to this situation was the career-woman comedy—which both featured the heroine's independent spirit and portrayed it as a violation of nature. Claudette Colbert, for example, who had played one of these "boss lady" heroines in the thirties (*She Married Her Boss*, 1935), played three of them in the forties (*No Time for Love*, 1943; *Practically Yours*, 1945; *Without Reservations*, 1946). Even Carole Lombard was scheduled to do one at Columbia, *They All Kissed the Bride* (1942)—replaced after her death by Joan Crawford. And Rosalind Russell, once she got started, seemed to play almost nothing else—from the secretary in *Hired Wife* (1940) to the college dean in *Woman of Distinction* (1950), with six such comedies (a judge, a literary agent, a psychiatrist, etc.) in between.

Another persisting plot was the platonic-marriage comedy—a movie situation that was already so epidemic by 1940 that Lubitsch even blamed part of his own

creative impasse on it. Every script he got, he complained to the New York
Times,

> deals with a marriage of convenience which turns into a love match after
> propinquity has done its work. He says that the fact that Universal recently
> used the situation in *Hired Wife*, that Columbia treated it thoroughly in *The
> Doctor Takes a Wife*, and that Metro is exhausting it in *Come Live With Me*,
> seems to discourage neither writers nor their agents.

By the time Donald Ogden Stewart did *his* version of it for Tracy and Hepburn—
Without Love in 1945 (from a Philip Barry play, also written for Hepburn)—this
story with its complications was as familiar as anything else in the movies. And
it was nearly always combined with the career-woman one, as it had been back
in 1935 in La Cava's *She Married Her Boss*, and as it was in two of Lubitsch's
examples (*Hired Wife* and *The Doctor Takes a Wife*) from 1940.

But there was a difference. In earlier versions (like La Cava's) of the in-name-
only marriage joke, it's the hero's complacent egoism just as much as the heroine's presumption in stepping outside her womanly role, that postpones the lovemaking. Later on, however, that postponement is mostly linked to her—to her
career obsession and to her crazy dumb-ass ideas. It's always—as in *This Thing
Called Love* (1941), where Rosalind Russell insists on a three-month delay of
her wedding night with Melvyn Douglas—or in *Appointment for Love* (1941),
where Margaret Sullavan insists on separate apartments for herself and Charles
Boyer and no wedding night at all—either a function or a result of her determined absurdity, of which the hero is always the victim. Romantic comedy
shifted from a fantasy of freedom to a joke about entrapment: women by their
nonsense, and men by their women; she trying to escape her nature, and he
trying to fulfill it, and both without success. *You Can't Run Away from It* (1956)
was the new title Columbia gave to *It Happened One Night* in its remake—and
no wonder.

Because in fact it was the heroines, and the inevitably aging stars who played
them, who were really trapped—in movies that seemed to embody an animus
against them, against the style and wit that made them special. The alternative
to the girl-next-door type (once likely to be the Other Woman, now more likely
to be the heroine) was not the screwball comedienne but the "black widow" siren
of the film noir. The independent heroine of the forties tended to be a killer—
and worse. As if the movies had lost some crucial element of belief in romantic
love. At least the kind of belief needed for romantic comedy.

Still, the comedies got made. They weren't so popular anymore, but they were
popular enough. They were part of what people expected from the movies. And
so the *It Happened One Night* model, for one example, continued to reappear.
Except that the whole feeling was different: it had become less a comedy about

falling in love than about trapping a man. In *A Lady Takes a Chance* (1943) Jean Arthur gets on a cross-country bus in New York and ends up at a rodeo out west, where a bronc tosses cowboy John Wayne into her lap. And at the movie's end, this glamorous hero bursts into the New York bus station where she is being met by her three ludicrous and quarreling "boy friends," and literally sweeps her off her feet and into his arms. But in between times—and after his first flirtatious come-on—he is the one who needs to be chased and followed, the one who is reluctant to be "hog-tied," as he puts it. And the Arthur heroine must contrive a series of misjudged and humiliating little strategies to lure and cajole him, culminating in a ghastly, tearoomy kind of supper (showing him she can cook, etc.) that she prepares for them in the motel, causing him to gag and flee when he tries to eat it. And her general style—in this scene as elsewhere—is aggrieved, as far as could be from the dashing and gallant Arthur heroines of the thirties. She is less a romantic heroine than an anticipation of the "little woman" she will turn into: kinda cute, maybe, but a pain—beseeching and whining and querulous. (And a prelude to Arthur's retirement—this was the last such comedy she would ever make.)

The Wayne hero is pursued by Claudette Colbert in Mervyn LeRoy's *Without Reservations* (1946). On a train instead of a bus this time. And Colbert has even more strikes against her than Arthur had: not only does she know nothing about life, she writes books about it too. She reads highbrow political journals and wants to talk about things like politics and justice and world government and the direction of the postwar world. Her book is a big best-seller (she's on her way to Hollywood, where it's being filmed) but an idealistic one, starry-eyed and do-goodish. So it's not surprising that she's without a man. She can't even understand why Wayne, an Air Force pilot, should be so indifferent to her. Until she talks to a girl known as "the Beetle" (Ann Triola), who manages to turn every male head on the train. *She* knows men; and she tells Colbert, who only knows books, what they go for in a woman: chattering and emptyheadedness, egostroking and expensive tastes, deferring to *him* in everything but the amount of money he spends on you, and so on. What's specially interesting about this character is how stridently unattractive she's made out to be, how firmly *un*sexy. She wears awful clothes, talks in a screech, walks in a kind of waddle with her butt stuck way out, and glows with malicious high spirits, so that you really wince for the men she gets hold of in the club car. Although *they* smile. We're meant to think they like it. Just as we're meant to know she's right about what "they" want. And Colbert is meant to know it too: she listens to the Beetle's advice in the powder room with wide solemn eyes. She's being taught a lesson, of course. That's why her instructor is made so comically grotesque. But the revulsion behind this characterization feels strong even for this ugly and misogynist comedy.

The romantic comedy not only lost its conviction; it also lost its class. More and more films like *Without Reservations* (in spite of its big budget, its prestige director, and "guest appearances" by people like Cary Grant and Jack Benny) were aimed at a fairly rube-ish and unsophisticated sort of audience—the small-town trade. As, unmistakably, were Colbert's next two comedies, *The Egg and I* (1947) and *Family Honeymoon* (1948). Under the circumstances, then, it's no wonder that the Tracy-and-Hepburn comedies—and most especially *Adam's Rib* (1949), at the end of the decade—seemed to fans and reviewers like a return to the old magic. But in fact it was more a gentrification of it, as it seems now. *Adam's Rib* was less a fantasy of wit and love and freedom than of urban gentility and success. Adam (Tracy) and Amanda (Hepburn) are the romantic couple turned into the cute couple. They are married lawyers, hard-nosed and competitive yet very much in love. And the one-sided battle of the sexes with its inevitable male triumph that audiences in the forties were getting used to, is replaced here by a mutual respect and civilized balancing: the battle is at least a draw.

Adam and Amanda may be respectful opponents in court—on opposite sides of the same court case in the film's main plot—but at home, in what the Ruth Gordon–Garson Kanin screenplay describes as their "small perfect kitchen" ("copper pots and pans, a huge herb stand . . . A kitchen you can live in"), they cook gourmet dinners together. And in the bedroom they give each other Swedish massages (with a lotion made of "cold cream, alcohol, and almond oil"). And at all times and wherever they are, they call each other by a large and various repertoire of playful names: "Hello, thing." Or: "You were pretty cute in there today, my little." He is "Pinky" and she is "Pinkie"—the difference in spelling is insisted upon, archly. Even requests for ordinary information are inflected whimsically. "What's this some of?" asks Adam, holding up the cocktail shaker. "Some of daiquiris," replies Amanda. And so on. They are meant, it is apparent, to be irresistible. But the void that yawns behind all this banter and Bloomingdale's life-style is sufficiently apparent in exchanges like the following. Adam is worried about being pitted against his wife in the courtroom the next day. But she is keen on the case—a young woman has been indicted for shooting at her erring husband—because it has turned into a women's rights issue, both in the press and in her own view of it. They are in their kitchen:

ADAM (*as they prepare the lamb curry*): Pinkie?
AMANDA: What, Pinky?
ADAM: Do me a favor?
AMANDA: Not too much salt?
ADAM (*gravely*): No. . . . Give up the case.
AMANDA (*equally gravely*): I can't.
ADAM: Why not?
AMANDA (*in a small voice, with hint of a trembling lip*): It's my cause. . . .

They have their alarms and adventures, of course—especially in the court-room. And they even have their "causes"—the same way they have kitchens and summer places, with an air of wistful attachment. But finally there is noth-ing, they make us feel, that can't somehow be reduced to the manageable di-mensions of that "small perfect kitchen" and the life of discreet, tasteful affluence that the movie both evokes and enacts. This coziness was precisely the sort of feeling that screwball comedy at its best had seemed to challenge. It's no wonder that Adam and Amanda have to work a bit at sparkling. But there are always, it seems, plenty of cute ideas to go on—like deciding to distinguish between "Pinky" and "Pinkie"—or imitating characters in a silent melodrama when they make a home movie, twirling imaginary mustaches and burning the mortgage on the new country place they've just bought.

In this world of measured playfulness and enlightened privilege, it's the Other Man—Kip, the fey songwriter down the hall (David Wayne)—who is the lively one and a threat to the stuffed shirts. And in fact he is less an Other Man (his pursuit of Amanda never seems quite serious) than an extra man, bringing a whiff of audacity (and sexual ambiguity) to the dinner party. Kip doesn't care what he says. "You always have judges here," he comments to Amanda, as he surveys the elderly eminences in the parlor. "Why is that? To get in good with them?" He even makes fun of the home movie. Adam detests him. "All right, Kip," says Amanda, amused in spite of herself, "that's enough." But she keeps an eye on him—the rascal. . . .

George Stevens | 20

GEORGE STEVENS not only directed Hepburn (twice, in *Alice Adams* and *Woman of the Year*) but Dunne, Arthur, Rogers, and Lombard as well. The only great screwball women he didn't work with were Colbert and Loy. Stevens—who began his career as a cameraman for Hal Roach, working on many of the Laurel and Hardy shorts (including the McCarey ones)—was mainly known as a director of comedy. And yet when he came to work with Lombard and then with Dunne in the early forties, the result in each case was a film of almost unrelieved solemnity. *Penny Serenade* (1941), starring Dunne and Cary Grant just after their big success in the farcical *My Favorite Wife* (1940), is a tearjerker about a struggling married couple who adopt a child who falls ill and dies. *Vigil in the Night* (1940), with Lombard, Brian Aherne, and Anne Shirley, is a stately melodrama (from an A. J. Cronin novel) about nurses in a London hospital struggling under gothic archways against poverty and disease. And it begins the same way *Penny Serenade* ends: with the death of a child.

And with a terrific rainstorm—a virtuoso tracking shot (accompanied by the plaintive Alfred Newman score) that moves from storm-tossed seas in the distance, over a bluff, across a lawn, to a cliff-side hospital—traveling along the bleak stone walls until it reaches a lighted window. The first close shot of Lombard, in nurse's cap, sitting by a sleeping child's bedside, is a stunning one. Not lush or rapturous, but sharp and intent—the kind of "glamour" that makes you sit forward in your seat, makes you feel the full force of the actor's attention. Lombard's whole performance is like that: not sentimental (in spite of a script which makes the heroine into a saintly masochist) but heroic, and businesslike. There are lives to be saved in this picture—and no time for nonsense. (Anne Shirley as Lombard's sister is the frivolous one, responsible by her negligence for the child's death.) It's not a very interesting role or film, but you feel that Lombard comes to it with relief. It has a moralistic severity, accommodating her quality of fierce, steady intelligence as almost no other film of hers has done.

And it's a genuine transformation: it's Anne Shirley here, in their many scenes together, who looks like the "pretty" one next to her plain, careworn older sister.

Irene Dunne seems similarly transformed in another, later Stevens film, *I Remember Mama* (1948), where she plays an immigrant Norwegian woman in turn-of-the-century San Francisco. As with Lombard, it's clear from the film's beginning that Dunne has found a special identity with the role. The result is not so much a miraculous piece of acting as a mysterious seeming-not-to-act. It's an utterly plain and undecorated performance: everything, including the Scandinavian accent, done from the inside out. What's most distinctive about it is apparent in an early scene between Mama (Dunne) and her two awful sisters, "the aunts" Jenny and Sigrid (Hope Landin and Edith Evanson). A third sister, Trina (Ellen Corby), a pathetic and trembling spinster type, has become engaged to the local undertaker, a Mr. Thorkelson (Edgar Bergen). It is up to Mama to make the announcement of this event to the formidable sisters—while Trina cowers in the adjoining room, afraid she will be laughed at, not only for her

Irene Dunne in I Remember Mama.

belated engagement but for her taste in fiancés ("Mr. Thorkelson—from the *funeral* home?" says Mama herself when she first learns, having to struggle with her own mixed feelings). And the sisters, just as Trina feared, are full of scorn and malicious amusement at the news. Until they are checked by Mama—who reminds them that she knows some wedding-day stories about *them*—which she will certainly repeat if they insist on humiliating Trina. When the aunts begin to protest, Dunne shuts them up by relating the stories (a wedding-night panic in one case, a recalcitrant bridegroom in the other), which are both grotesque and comic.

It's a conventional sort of reversal, giving a conventional sort of pleasure. We are meant to take satisfaction in the stories on the two unpleasant aunts, and we do. What is striking, though, is that Dunne does *not*—though she recites them determinedly, and with full appreciation for what makes them so embarrassing. But it remains clear in this scene what Mama is doing and not doing. So that when a moment later she turns and says to her amused and gratified husband (Philip Dorn—he doesn't like the aunts either), "I do not tell these stories for spite, only so they do not laugh at Trina," the speech only makes explicit what Dunne has not only shown us in the scene but also made us feel the importance of: the fact that this woman is exactly the sort of person who does *not* enjoy petty triumphs over others. Though she is smart enough to know how such triumphs happen, even how they might be managed, she is too smart—too serious and intelligent, finally—to take satisfaction in them. And the lovingness and generosity that the movie (from a Broadway hit by John Van Druten and a best-selling novel by Kathryn Forbes) celebrates so predictably in this idealized mother become in Dunne's performance not clichés but functions of her fundamental seriousness. And her plainness. A woman who never (as her daughter Katrin points out) talks about herself or her feelings: one of what Orwell calls "the great mass of human beings" who "live chiefly"—unself-consciously and matter-of-factly—"for others."

And it shouldn't be surprising that the two great screwball comediennes, Dunne and Lombard, different as they otherwise are, should still come near the climax of their careers to an identification with women like these—figures of gravity, stolidity, and wholly unplayful temperaments. Roles which are like categorical denials (at least as they are played) of anything actressy in their own temperaments, or in their futures. It's a measure of Dunne's distinction as a comedienne, for example, that no one would ever have thought of her for *Auntie Mame* or its equivalents later on—that such female caricatures, widely felt to be suitable to aging actresses, would always be beyond her range. Just as (for different reasons in each case) they would be beyond Arthur's and Loy's and (presumably, had she lived) Lombard's. One of the strongest things the screwball heroine's style conveys is her own mixed feelings about it, her skepticism about self-expression even while she pursues it—feelings that surface in Hazel Flagg's panic and Lucy Warriner's mockery, in Loy's sardonic reserve and Arthur's double take and so on. Her "madness" is finally an expression of her common sense, which is inescapable. As Theodora's uncle says: "A Lynn may go wild but never silly."

Mama's world, it would seem, is far from such issues—but not entirely. There is a moment at the end of the film when we see this extraordinary "ordinary" woman tempted by self-consciousness, struggling against it, then looking out the window and succumbing to it, at least momentarily. And Dunne makes the moment very powerful. The family is gathered in the kitchen, seated around the table; Mama is standing apart from them. Katrin, the budding writer (Barbara Bel Geddes), has had her first story accepted by a magazine, and now she is reading it to them all. But Mama is upset, because she had told Katrin, who had asked her what she should write about, to "write about Papa." And now it's clear that the story (like the movie we're watching) is mostly about her. Mama fusses as Katrin reads, but she shushes an interruption by one of the children and turns away to the window—where, face averted, she gives in: she is helplessly—movingly—eager to hear this. Dunne makes us see how deep and important to her the satisfaction of it is—unlooked for, and given to her by her daughter.

LIKE DUNNE, George Stevens was a comic with a talent for seriousness. He knew how to encourage and exploit just the sort of thoughtful, inward performance Dunne gives in this film—this living into a role. A Stevens set had the kind of concentration that promoted such work. He was dogged, determined, painfully slow. And often what came out on the screen seemed that way, too—that was his failing. But often too, as in Dunne's *Mama* performance, the obsessiveness paid off. As it had done thirteen years earlier, in Katharine Hepburn's *Alice Adams* (1935). This was Stevens' first important RKO feature, and it is probably Hepburn's best work of the thirties. It's a stately film, with a fussing, dithering heroine at its center: it regards her gravely. Which turns out to be the best way to register the kind of shamed consciousness that Hepburn gives to the character, the unappeasable intelligence behind all the airs and chatter and silliness. As when she tells the hero (Fred MacMurray)—she's sitting on the front porch swing and hoists her legs up beside herself in a seizure of coquetry—that she has been thinking of all the different kinds of girl she might pretend to be in order to impress him: "Yet here I am," she says archly, and in extreme close-up, "just being myself—after all." And we not only see the pain at the center of her eyes but a kind of panicked self-dislike as well. Fred MacMurray later claimed that it took some eighty takes before Stevens was satisfied with this scene.

Carole Lombard with Brian Aherne in Vigil in the Night.

Most actors—like Dunne and Joel McCrea—liked to work with him, though. Lombard once claimed that he knew more about lighting than anyone else in Hollywood, though she was less sure about his directing: "You know what that s.o.b. is thinking about when he's in one of his trances?" she once said (according to Larry Swindell). "Not a fucking thing." Orson Welles recalled visiting the set of *Vigil in the Night* to see a master at work and finding Stevens asleep in his director's chair: "I never did get to see him direct." Stevens liked to claim (apparently without any warrant) that he had "Indian blood." He was "a great bear" of a man (Shelley Winters), imposing and genial but withdrawn. There was no piano music on his sets: only long brooding silences while cast and crew waited for the word. As time went on, the waits got longer and the silences more reverential. There was no "fooling around" on the set of *A Place in the Sun* (1951), according to Shelley Winters: "everyone was quiet and concentrating," feeling that they were involved "in the creation of something timeless and extraordinary."

It was on *Gunga Din* (1939) that Stevens first slowed down—and he was replacing Howard Hawks, who was fired for being too slow. By the time Stevens

George Stevens directing Joel McCrea and Jean Arthur in the lunch-counter scene of The More the Merrier.

was done, *Gunga Din* had become the most expensive RKO film ever. But at least it was a box-office winner. *Vigil in the Night,* Stevens' next RKO project and done at an equivalently painstaking rate, was not; and the studio let him go. Harry Cohn then signed him for Columbia—getting him on the rebound, the same way he'd gotten McCarey from Paramount a few years before. Stevens, it seems, was the kind of director who hardly ever visualized a scene ahead of time. He liked to shoot from many different angles, then choose the shot or combination of shots that he wanted in the cutting room. Like McCarey and Hawks, he valued spontaneity in front of the camera, and he drew directly on his actors for inspiration, searching for that nuance or detail that might be lost in a set performance. But unlike McCarey, he tended to find what he was looking for only after it was filmed. "I rehearse on film," he said in 1974; and the number of takes on a Stevens scene was likely to be the stuff of legend. But Harry Cohn more or less gave him his head, just as he'd given McCarey his. The result was a trio of hits: the Dunne-Grant tearjerker *Penny Serenade* (1941) and two wonderful Jean Arthur comedies (Stevens called her "one of the greatest comediennes the screen has ever seen"), *The Talk of the Town* (1942) and *The More the Merrier* (1943). This Columbia period comprises what is probably the best work of Stevens' career.

Everyone said he was changed by the war: he had been in the Army Signal Corps and had photographed the death camps during the liberation. He had a hard time adjusting to postwar Hollywood—a harder time than "any of us," according to his friend Frank Capra (who had a hard enough time himself). *I Remember Mama*, though notably overblown in its direction and style, was Stevens' last "light" film for a while. He then embarked on what would later be known as his "American trilogy"—three films united only by their grandiloquence and common attempt to represent some salient aspect of American culture and history: *A Place in the Sun*, based on Theodore Dreiser's *An American Tragedy*; then the super-Western *Shane* (1953); followed by *Giant* (1956), about modern Texas—the longest and biggest of them all. They were all box-office successes; and Stevens himself, probably more than anyone else in fifties Hollywood, fulfilled the industry's idea of a major and important filmmaker. He won an Academy Award as best director for *Giant*. And his next picture, *The Diary of Anne Frank*, though widely conceded to be overproduced and miscast (especially the title role), still sustained his prestige, garnering several Academy Award nominations, including best picture and best direction. Stevens then spent the next six years—his longest silence yet—preparing and filming *The Greatest Story Ever Told* (1965), a grotesquely misjudged retelling of the New Testament with guest-star cameos by people like John Wayne, Pat Boone, and Shelley Winters and on one of the biggest budgets and most extended shooting schedules in Hollywood history. It was a critical and financial disaster, and the effective end of Stevens' career.

In a way it's a classic Hollywood story: a successful and talented director of modest comedies (see *Sullivan's Travels*), done in at the end by his own pretensions and success, until everything he touches turns "epic" and leaden. But the truth is that the "epic" Stevens was lurking even in those early comedies. Even in such a slam-bang, happily raucous affair as *Gunga Din*, there is a turgid overripe flavor. And even in his first RKO feature assignment, *Bachelor Bait* (1934), a B-picture comedy with Stuart Erwin, Stevens maintains a strangely inappropriate tone: the pace is so slow that the film feels lugubrious and depressive in spite of its lighthearted intentions. And watching Stevens mimic gaiety, in a meant-to-be-buoyant comedy like *Vivacious Lady* (1938), can be painful: where high spirits are called for, he offers a kind of persistence. His favorite comic devices are usually those of overextension and stasis—shticks like the slow burn or the double (or triple or quadruple) take, group routines like the infectious crying jag, which are meant to get funnier the longer they go on, and so on. In fact, there is nearly the same deliberateness in his comedies as there is in his serious work. The touch is always heavy. He shows us nuances—but only one at a time, as it were, stopping everything else on the screen so we can see it.

And in the comedies the absence of elation can make the camera's scrutiny seem almost morbid at times. As in the hair-pulling match in *Vivacious Lady* between Ginger Rogers and the Other Woman (Frances Mercer), with the two women frozen like statues in a contorted and painful-looking wrestling hold so that the two men coming upon the scene (Charles Coburn and James Stewart) can react and then react again. And again. Jokes in this film are so drawn out that they begin to seem prurient even when they're not. Though often enough they are—since the central joke is the one about the wedding night endlessly and excruciatingly postponed by various accidents and mistimings. And Stevens' style makes the fun even creepier than usual. Even when the ideas in a Stevens film are better than that, his camera seems drawn to the squirmy moment, whether it's Astaire and Rogers looking coy after kissing behind a door (*Swing Time*) or Irene Dunne trying to bathe her new baby with everyone in the house watching her do it (*Penny Serenade*).

But probably his most serious liability as a comic filmmaker is his apparent lack of any anarchic or subversive or even dissident impulse. He has the temperament of a solid citizen, and he tends to temper and meliorate whatever is harsh or abrasive or unsettling in the familiar people and plots. He makes a Ginger Rogers comedy, for example (*Vivacious Lady* again), in which she *never* wisecracks. Invariably his films take a moderate, balanced, fundamentally "constructive" view. Over and over again the people you expect to be awful turn out to be not so bad really, even sort of okay, like the millionaire uncle (Herbert Heyes) in *A Place in the Sun*, or the big-mouth Texans in *Giant*. Although reviewers were ludicrously mistaken to take McCarey's *Make Way for Tomorrow*— that tormented and despairing film—as a call for moderate social adjustments (Social Security, or a more enlightened kind of social worker), Stevens really did make films you could describe that way. That's one reason *Giant* seems so oddly pointless, given its length and scale, its apocalyptic look and sound. In the end there seems to be nothing much wrong with this new oil-rich barbarianism that won't be cured by a growing tolerance of interracial marriages. And that nightmarish new hotel (Jett Rink's "folly") might be okay too, it seems, if only the beauty salon didn't refuse to do Mexican women's hair. It's this sort of "reasonableness" that makes Stevens almost the definitive middlebrow filmmaker. Even when he embarks on a mad and ludicrous enterprise like *The Greatest Story Ever Told*, the result, though elephantine, turns out to be impersonal, perfectly without religious feeling of any kind, and in its way rather modest: a life of Jesus drawn not only from Scripture but from a *Reader's Digest* rewrite of them (by Fulton Oursler), and "in creative association with Carl Sandburg."

For in fact Stevens seems really not qualified for "epic" filmmaking or for trilogies about American life. One of the most striking patterns in his work is his tendency to isolate the central characters. He has no special gift, it seems, for creating milieux or social worlds, for evoking backgrounds or locales. There is less sense of a convincing small town in *Alice Adams* or of a convincing newspaper office in *Woman of the Year* than in many less distinguished movies: small towns and newspapers were, after all, Hollywood staples.

Nonetheless, Stevens quite often turns this limitation to good account. The most stirring thing in *A Place in the Sun* is the remarkable early love scene between Elizabeth Taylor and Montgomery Clift ("You'll be my pickup"). And a hero who seems meant—at least part of the time—to be a victim of society (as in the Dreiser novel) becomes more than anything else a doomed and tragic lover. In *Penny Serenade*, Irene Dunne and Cary Grant move from New York to Tokyo to an unnamed small town back in America. But it hardly seems to matter where they go: *they* create all the world the film is about. Other people and places impinge on this world, even threaten to destroy it, but they never suggest even a remotely equivalent reality. It's a resolutely mundane story, about the kinds of problems—job changes and money and having a family—that almost everyone faces. But the strange, luminous isolation of the stars at the center of it—their intense, rather melancholy conjunction with each other—gives the whole thing a surprising power, a sickly irresistible romanticism.

For Stevens' romanticism is less a liberating impulse than a nesting one. His two best comedies are both about people being crowded into living quarters against their wills and expectations and then learning to like it. In *The Talk of the Town*, Jean Arthur rents her house to Ronald Colman. But then, instead of moving out as agreed, she stays on—because Cary Grant is in the attic, hiding from the police and the town, and he has to be hidden from Colman as well. Just as Joel McCrea, invited into a Washington apartment by the sub-let tenant Charles Coburn in *The More the Merrier*, must then be hidden from Jean Arthur, the apartment's owner. But these triplings, awkward as they are at first, are full of excitement and ultimate goodwill. Not triangles, but three-way love matches.

The Talk of the Town is a conscious attempt at a kind of Capra comedy—a mixture of romance and social significance. And Sidney Buchman's screenplay (co-written by Irwin Shaw), like his *Mr. Smith Goes to Washington*, offers a fairly bleak view of the workings of American democracy. The New England small town is even more sinister than the one he gave Theodora to live in—a place where even the baseball games look ominous, in long shot and under lowering skies, and where the one champion of justice (Cary Grant) has been framed on an arson charge by the local mill owner. "He's the only honest man I've come across in this town in twenty years," says village sage Edgar Buchanan, "so

*Cary Grant,
Ronald
Colman, and
Jean Arthur in
The Talk of the
Town (above);
Jean Arthur
(with cold-
cream mask),
Charles
Coburn, and
Joel McCrea in
The More the
Merrier
(right).*

naturally they wanta hang 'im." But Grant has broken out of jail; that's why he has to hide out with Arthur—and with Colman, as it happens. And even though the latter is a jurist of national prominence, on the eve of his appointment to the Supreme Court itself, he and Grant and Arthur finally make common cause against the mean-spirited town: three comrades.

Of course, we only *hear* about the activities that got the Grant character in trouble—handing out leaflets, haranguing the workers on street corners, denouncing the town bosses. And although we never see him doing such things, still it's a nearly breathtaking piece of miscasting: Cary Grant as a left-wing agitator. To another sort of movie it might even have been damaging. But to a Stevens film, where the outside world remains dim and insubstantial, as distant and dreamlike as that baseball game, it hardly matters. Grant may be unbelievable as a radical firebrand, but as the brusque charmer of Arthur's hearthside, full of insinuation and verbal challenge directed at Colman's primness and conservatism, he is perfect. And Stevens banks everything in this film, strikingly deficient in even the usual degrees of "reality," on the casual charms and skills of its three stars. Which are very real indeed.

So are the props in a Stevens comedy, especially the ones that take on a life of their own: the big propeller blade Joel McCrea wanders around with in *The More the Merrier*, looking over the apartment; or Charles Coburn's missing pants, flying out the window on the recoil of their suspenders while he looks for them in the room; or the waffle iron that regurgitates its batter and makes urping sounds while Hepburn is preparing Tracy's breakfast in *Woman of the Year*. Stevens is a master of timing—and cutting—for comic effect. As when Arthur in *The Talk of the Town* has to catch and conceal Grant's shoe (it's just fallen from the attic window above her) while chatting in her doorway with Colman, or when she rushes in from the kitchen in time to slide a fried egg onto a newspaper Colman is about to read (he doesn't yet know that Grant is a fugitive). Neither of these gags is intrinsically very funny: what makes them take off on the screen is not only Arthur's virtuosity but Stevens'—who knows just how and when to juxtapose reactions and movements, when to speed up or slow down or cut away, to evoke just the right demented effect. This basic slapstick skill—an instinct for comic *rhythms* in a gag—is something in which he surpasses both Capra and McCarey.

Like McCarey and other veterans of the silent two-reel comedy, Stevens liked to improvise on the set. The famous front-stoop scene in *The More the Merrier*—with the McCrea character copping feels from the Arthur character while she tries to talk about her fiancé—originated (according to McCrea) from the two actors horsing around between takes, Arthur expressing her usual disabling fears of performance and McCrea trying to kid her out of them by making mock passes at her. *The Talk of the Town* has the same spontaneous feeling. There's a wonderful moment with Arthur, thinking she's alone, making faces at herself in a full-length mirror, pulling a handful of hair down under her nose to make a mustache, and then, inexplicably, making sounds at herself like Hepburn: "Lovely, lovely—*rah*lly lovely." The moment is wonderful just because it's so *dumb:* just the sort of thing people do do when they're absolutely alone. Or think they are: here, of course, Colman (who probably *doesn't* do such things) is watching her from the doorway.

T*he More the Merrier* is Stevens' funniest and most inspired comedy. And it gives Arthur her best role since *Easy Living* six years before. It's built on almost nothing but the often uncomfortable proximity of its three leading characters. For some reason (it's never quite explained, beyond the fact that we share the wish), one of them, Mr. Dingle, the older, fatherly one (Coburn), becomes instantly determined that the other two, Joe and Connie (McCrea and Arthur), should be married, and sets out to bring them together. The problem with Connie—apart from her rather rigid character—is that she already has a fiancé. He is, of course, a stiff—"the youngest man," as she patiently explains (he is 42), "ever to occupy the position of assistant regional coordinator" of the OPL. His name is Mr. Pendergast (Richard Gaines). And having to explain about him to her two nosy tenants almost inevitably makes her exasperated. "Don't you ever brush your *hair?*" she says at one such moment to Joe (McCrea). "I suppose," he says, swiping futilely at it with his big hand, "Mr. Pendergast combs his hair every hour on the hour," and he exchanges a look with Mr. Dingle (Coburn). Connie draws herself up: "Mr. Pendergast," she says coldly, "has no hair"—and she closes the door behind her, while the two men in the kitchen laugh and whoop in triumph. And on the other side of the door, she smiles. She can't help herself—nor can she quite help betraying Mr. Pendergast to them, even in this early, bristling encounter.

And after a while she is simply lost, though she fights it to the end. Arthur gives a hilarious movie-long impersonation of this struggle against the flesh. The way she frowns when Joe tells her she looks lovely tonight ("Oh," she says, like someone getting the expected bad news), or the way she keeps walking backward into his chest. The way she refuses him when he asks her out—"You forget I'm engaged," she says weakly, "and . . . uh . . . I don't think *he'd* like it." And so on. It all culminates in that scene on the front stoop. They are walking home together (Mr. Dingle has detained Mr. Pendergast back at the nightclub), in a haze of longing for each other. He isn't fighting it; but she is, and trying to keep the conversation going. She is asking him about his old girlfriends back home. He answers her indifferently; he keeps fooling with this little cape she wears above her off-the-shoulders evening gown. She keeps talking and walking—and finding his hand on her arm, on her shoulder, on her throat. She lifts the cape and finds the hand inside it. She removes it. She doesn't protest exactly. But she does keep talking, loudly and hollowly, like someone who suspects a wire tap. They arrive at the house and sit on the stoop, almost falling over as they land. Her cape is off again, leaving her shoulders and her back bare. She is still talking. His head disappears behind her back, and her chin shoots suddenly upward. She is trying to tell him about Mr. Pendergast's "dinner conference with Leon M. —" His head behind her shoulder makes a nuzzling motion, she breaks off and leans forward intently, as if struck by a sudden thought—then continues:

McCrea and Arthur are in separate rooms but dancing to the same samba, in The More the Merrier.

"—Henderson, and Donald—" She raises her head and closes her eyes, rapturously: "—M. Nelson," she says, finishing her sentence at last. He draws back and looks at her now, dreamily. She looks at him. Then repeats, for the record: "Leon Henderson and Donald M. Nelson." But her voice is thick. "Must be an important man," he says, as he puts his hand back on her shoulder. "*Yes,*" she says, so relieved he's been listening to her. "And so considerate, you know." And so it goes.

Stevens shows the same tendency to milk his gags here as elsewhere. But in this picture, for the most part, the jokes *are* funnier the longer they go on—like this front-stoop scene. Or the scene where McCrea and Arthur mutter together over the new traveling case he's just bought her, something to take on her "honeymoon" (each time they think they've exhausted its features, a new compartment falls open to be exclaimed on). It's partly that the improvisations seem so natural and unforced, extended by their own logic rather than by the director's will, and because the performers (particularly Arthur) are so good at them. But it's mostly, I would think, because the central joke of the film—Connie's divided consciousness, the desire that drives her into a kind of helpless hypocrisy—seems so endlessly rich. "Yes," she says, as Joe nuzzles her on the stoop, "I consider myself a very lucky little lady"—she is trying to interest him in Mr. Pendergast's engagement ring, holding up her ring finger to show it off—but his head, as usual in this scene, is somewhere down her back.

The More the Merrier is one of the greatest comedies of this romantic comedy time. But it belongs to the end of that time in more ways than its date. Connie Milligan is less a thirties kind of heroine than a forties kind of stereotype: a woman who *needs* to be married (as Mr. Dingle's approach to her suggests), and desperately. She is closer to the "little lady" she calls herself than to the big glamorous one of Arthur's earlier films. She is in fact a version of the girl-next-door. Or at least she tries to be. And it's in that effort that she and the wonderful movie she appears in reflect some of the hidden conflicts of their time—the *tensions* of being mealymouthed—in a remarkably candid and funny and liberating way.

Howard Hawks | 21

I was going to prove to somebody one night that The Front Page *had the finest modern dialogue that had been written, and I asked a girl to read Hildy's part and I read the editor and I stopped and I said, "Hell, it's better between a girl and a man than between two men," and I called Ben Hecht and I said, "What would you think of changing it so that Hildy is a girl?" And he said, "I think it's a great idea," and he came out and we did it.*
—HOWARD HAWKS, to Peter Bogdanovich, 1962

HOWARD HAWKS'S career offers a kind of antithesis to Stevens' gentility. Take the Hawks heroine, for example. There are no tough women in Stevens' movies—not even in the thirties, when such heroines seemed nearly unavoidable. While in Hawks's films there is almost nothing but—particularly in the forties, when such heroines went against the grain. Hawks remade *The Front Page* in 1940—as *His Girl Friday*, with Cary Grant and Rosalind Russell—solely, he claimed, because he got the notion to change its tough newspaperman hero, Hildy Johnson (the Lee Tracy–Pat O'Brien role), into a heroine. An idea that Lubitsch later called "a stroke of genius."

Rosalind Russell wasn't, reportedly, Hawks's first choice for the role. (According to a New York *Times* story, it was offered previously to Dunne and Arthur and Rogers.) But having cast her (at Harry Cohn's insistence, Russell later said), he proceeded to shape the role around her, as he almost always did with his actors. She walks into the office of the *Morning Post* at the film's opening—it's clear she hasn't been around in a while, and she causes a stir as she strides through the newsroom, in her loosely tied coat and black flop-brimmed cylinder-shaped hat, exchanging greetings, basking in the attention, looking down at all the fuss through half-closed eyes, half smiling—guarded but genial and very much at home. She is both regal and ungainly, with a clear element of parody in the down-looking style. That parody is partly self-protective—part of her geni-

*Howard Hawks
with Cary
Grant and
Rosalind
Russell on the*
His Girl
Friday *set.*

ality, too. And we see the office she strides through in traveling shots from her point of view. It isn't like one of Jean Arthur's offices, in *Easy Living* or *The Whole Town's Talking:* those familiar dismal places full of putzes and pensioners and assorted dim bulbs. This is a Howard Hawks place: a newspaper office, full of women just like Russell, just as assured and independent and self-possessed as she is. "Hiya, Hildy," says one of them, hand on hip, leaning over another woman at a desk, giving Hildy a big, friendly smile as she passes. Another—a grimmer type but no less authoritative—falls into lockstep beside her. "Hiya,

Beatrice," says Hildy. "How's advice to the lovelorn?" "Fine," the other replies.
"My cat just had kittens again." They walk without looking at each other, in
perfect sympathy. "'S her own fault," says Hildy dropping into her deepest basso
register, going on her arm-swinging way down the aisle—to the door of the
editor-in-chief. And we understand the cynicism: she is going to see Cary Grant.
Walter Burns in this version is not only Hildy's ex-boss but her ex-husband. And
Peggy Grant, Hildy's "nice girl" fiancée in the original, has been turned into
nice-boy fiancé Bruce Baldwin—Ralph Bellamy again as the Other Man—an
insurance salesman from Albany who almost glows with his own uncomplicated
goodwill. He makes Hildy glow too, in their very first scene, just before her
stride through the newsroom. She leaves Bruce in the outer office, telling him to
wait for her just ten minutes. "Even ten minutes," he replies, "is a long time to
be away from you." She's not used to this sort of thing, and she asks him
to repeat it before she goes. To confront Walter Burns.

Her gracelessness—that touch of awkwardness, the suggestion of being *too*
tall—never affects her self-assurance, even seems to enhance it. When she gets
excited she flaps her hands from her wrists—or she looks for her watch on the
wrong wrist and to hell with it. She dodges through street traffic with her skirt
hoisted up and her knees together like someone wading through a stream. When
she wants to stop a man running down the street, she tackles him and sends
them both sprawling. It's not grace she aspires to but composure. And when she
achieves it—as she often does in these games—she seems transported by it,
turning well-being into a peak experience. She lights a cigarette and lords it
over the smoke: head tilted back, looking down along her face as she towers
above the smoke, her I-don't-know-how-I-got-here-but-I-love-it look. But she is
also at such altitudes dangerously exposed; and when she is rocked by something it's like a seismic shock, the head unmoored, tilted even farther back, the
eyes jolted open, the half-smile gone. Never mind: towering is really her specialty—and casting sardonic glances, with half-closed eyes, on the world below.
Her *other* specialty is the low crouching run, maniacal and banjo-eyed, slapping
the brim of her hat back like a comic-strip character, usually cradling something
in her arms, like a typewriter or a suitcase, as she scuttles between desks.
Russell is like Groucho *and* Margaret Dumont, zany and dowager, alternating
in the same person. Composed and then discomposed: towering and collapsing
and then towering again.

Hawks uses this startling changeability to shape the tone and structure of
Hildy's first long virtuoso scene with Walter, with its slam-bang pace, its dizzying shifts of sound and direction, its crackle and energy and constant surprising
life. Hildy (after that walk through the newsroom) has come to tell Walter not
only that she is leaving the paper for good but that she is marrying another man;
but she has a hard time getting the news out, since Walter is behaving with such

infuriating obtuseness, as usual. Russell told in an interview how Hawks egged the actors on in this scene—encouraging them to ad-lib, invent bits of business, step on each other's lines, and generally "let go." And then when she asked him how she was doing, he replied: "You just keep pushin' him around the way you've been doin'."

But of course it's Walter who's been pushing Hildy around—just how much so, it's one of the functions of this scene to reveal ("I intended to be with you on our honeymoon, Hildy—honest I did")—though she seems in this contest to be more than equal to him. How long has it been? he inquires, by way of openers, and his self-satisfied smirk here leaves no doubt what he means by "it":

> HILDY (*a pleasant blank*): How long is what?
> WALTER: You know what. How long is it (*a slight hesitation*) . . . since we've seen each other?
> HILDY (*tapping her cigarette, ruminating into the air*): Well, let's see—uh . . . I spent six weeks in Reno, then Bermuda. . . . Oh, about four months, I guess. Seems like yesterday to me.
> WALTER (*grinning, pointing at himself*): Been seeing me in your dreams, Hildy?
> HILDY: No, no. Mama doesn't dream about you anymore, Walter. You wouldn't know the old girl now.
> WALTER: Oh, yes I would. I'd know you (*with great emphasis*) anytime, anyplace, anywhere.

But as he says these last words (obviously meant to trigger a romantic memory) she says them along with him, in a loud nasty jeering voice even louder than his, as they circle the desk, he bearing down, she eluding. Russell's sound is a funny surprise: a yah-yah schoolyard noise, and she makes a schoolyard face to go with it. That done with, she resumes her hauteur and points out that he is repeating himself: "That's the speech you made the night you proposed." He notices that she remembers it. "'Course I remember it," she says. "If I didn't remember it, I wouldn't have divorced you."

They are both consummate stylists—and conscious self-parodists. And their way of quarreling, as in this case, is to *perform* to each other, their best and most challenging audience. A way of quarreling without losing your class. It's this element of performance—the *ritual* of personal exchange and expression— that interests Hawks in a particular way. Hawks and his players make us feel not so much that we're seeing a particular quarrel or a particular turning point, as we do with Connie and Joe in *The More the Merrier*, for example, or Jerry and Lucy in *The Awful Truth*, but rather that we're seeing *the* quarrel, the one these people must always have: the one they create themselves by. And it's this element of triumphant self-creation, taking place before our eyes—even taking place *because* of our eyes, a collusion of characters and actors and filmmaker and audience—that gives this scene (and this movie) its special unflagging zest and delight. Screwball characters like Lucy and Theodora may impress us by impersonating their opposite numbers: Hildy and Walter are the kind of characters—Hawks's kind of characters—who impersonate themselves. And are knockouts.

As when Hildy decides for some reason, at the height of their altercation, to make herself up. And why not? Walter is carrying on behind her—she is in the foreground of the shot—muttering about Sweeney the reporter and what will he do; it sounds as though something unfortunate has happened to Sweeney. "Dead?" inquires Hildy, applying the lipstick—so much for the appeal to her feelings, in case he was thinking of trying *that*. No, Sweeney's wife is having a baby, but that puts the paper in a terrible spot. She looks at him—and powders her nose. He is working hard now to sell this to her. "This'll break me," he says (and she goes on powdering), "un*less* . . . !" he cries (a sudden thought). She

Walter Burns (Grant) invites Hildy and Bruce (Rosalind Russell and Ralph Bellamy) to lunch in His Girl Friday.

snaps the compact closed. Unless *she* could cover the story! They do another dance around the room, and she does a nasal reprise of "anytime, anyplace, anywhere" as they go. "Don't do it for me, do it for the paper," he pleads. "Scram, Svengali," she says—opening her purse and popping the compact inside. Makeup job done.

Hildy's control is always impressive, since she is the human one of the pair. And since Walter is so *in*human, her performance, unlike his, is always on the edge—and frequently over it—of exasperation and anger. As when she throws her purse at him (an improvisation, as was Grant's line when she misses: "You're losing your eye"). Or the hand dance they get into in the middle of a wrangle, a quick shuffle and flash of clutches at each other's wrists. Until Hildy ("Whatta you playing, *osteopath?*") finally puts an end to it and pushes him away. "I'll tell you what I'll do," he says in his most reasonable manner. "You can come back to work on the paper, and if we find we can't get along in a friendly fashion, we'll get married again." Even she is impressed by this one, in spite of herself, remarking that he is "wonderful—in a loathsome sort of a way." He claims now that she would never have accepted his first proposal if she'd been "a gentleman." That's when she throws the purse.

But of course she *is* a gentleman—the only real one in the film (as she shows when she sides with Molly Malloy later on and confronts the "gentlemen of the press" in the newsroom). And an even more convincing one than the original Hildy. But being a screwball heroine as well, she aspires to a more conventional femininity. You can't quit, says Walter: "you're a newspaper man." "That's why I'm getting out," says Hildy. "I want to go someplace where I can be a woman." But for *that* sort of thing you have to get out of Chicago. And her problem in this version is that she has to get Ralph Bellamy out with her.

Not an easy thing to do—since he keeps getting arrested: once for "mashing," another time for stealing Diamond Louie's watch, and so on. "I'm innocent," he cries—a fact his being behind bars would confirm even if nothing else did. The only people in jail in this film are the ones who are too dumb or too nice to be running loose. Poor Bruce still can't figure it out, as he and Hildy (who has just bailed him out) drive away from the jailhouse in a cab. "I can't imagine who'd do a thing like that to me," he says. "I can't think of any enemies I have." "I'm sure you haven't any, Bruce," says Hildy tenderly, watching him as he searches his pockets. Once again he is astonished: "I've lost my wallet!" "Don't bother, Bruce," says Hildy wearily, "you'll find lots of things missing."

But Hildy can't escape Walter Burns any more than Bruce can—any more than Grant could escape Hepburn in Hawks's *Bringing Up Baby*, to be a respectable dinosaur specialist. This time Grant is the pursuer, the Susan Vance figure, crazy and ruthless and amoral, and the heroine is his victim. But the parallels to the divorced-lovers comedy of *The Awful Truth*—not to mention the borrowings—are even more striking, especially in the first half-hour or so. "So you two are gonna get married, huh?" says Grant to Russell and Bellamy, just as he'd said it to Bellamy and Dunne. They are seated around a table in a café, and just as in the nightclub scene in *The Awful Truth*, the hero is trying to embarrass the heroine over the Other Man. The jokes this time are not about Oklahoma but about Albany—"a mighty good insurance town," as Bruce explains it. ("Most people take it out pretty early in life." "I could see why they would," replies Walter.) But once Walter has maneuvered Hildy into covering the Earl Williams hanging, one last job before she leaves with Bruce, the action moves to the locale of the single-set play—the press room of the criminal courts—and mostly stays there, following the plot and sequence of events of *The Front Page* to the end, even using most of its dialogue. And yet the film remains, remarkably, a divorced-lovers comedy. It would be hard to overstate, I think, the boldness and brilliance of what Hawks has done here: not only an astonishingly funny comedy but a fulfillment of a whole tradition of comedy—the ur-text of the tough comedy appropriated fully and seamlessly to the spirit and style of screwball romance. *His Girl Friday* is not only a triumph but a revelation.

It seemed less special at the time (1940 was a good year for movies). And a lot of the reaction to it was of the oh-not-*The-Front-Page*-again kind: like Frank Nugent's *New York Times* review, where he professes to being more than a "little tired" of "the frenzied newspaper comedy." But "they've replated" it again, he says, in "a special woman's edition . . . slapped *His Girl Friday* on the masthead and are running it off at the Music Hall"—where you can hardly hear the lines ("all cute if you can") for all the noise the audience makes, infected by the movie's "hysteria." This was the most "frenzied" newspaper comedy of all, faster and noisier than any of them yet: "It takes you by the neck in the first reel and it shakes you madly, bellowing hoarsely the while, for the remaining six or seven." No one would accuse this comedy of gentility.

It wasn't just the noise and the frenetic style that seemed excessive. The tone of the original play, with its rampant cynicism and its vision of a universal corruption, was not the sort of thing the movies felt comfortable with by now. And so the Hawks film is preceded by this interesting disclaimer, on title cards after the opening credits:

> It all happened in the "Dark Ages" of the newspaper game—when to a reporter getting that story justified anything short of murder.
> Incidentally you will see in this picture no resemblance to the men and women of the press of today.
> Ready?
> Well once upon a time . . .

And that "once upon a time" (unlike the "mythical kingdom" introduction to the earlier film, which was a joke about a joke) seems meant to reassure us. This is the new, more respectable Hollywood, condescending to its own past—pretending that we have to be reminded that we ever saw things in that bleak way. For by 1940 most movies as well as most other features of the culture were conspiring to make us forget that we ever did. And so the play is in many ways bowdlerized—much more so than in the 1931 movie. Chicago isn't even named this time, though New York "under La Guardia" is—cited by Walter Burns as the kind of outstanding mayoralty the city of the movie can have, too, once it gets rid of its crooks. And the screenplay (credited to Charles Lederer, who also cowrote the 1931 version) jettisons any of the play's troubling or controversial political references. The condemned man, Earl Williams, is no longer a political radical and an anarchist, as he is in the play and the earlier film—a man who knows exactly how to distinguish between anarchism and Bolshevism, and who proclaims that it's "better to die for a cause than the way most people die." Here he's just a nut with a gun. And although the mayor and the sheriff are still ludicrous red-baiters ("Reform the Reds with a Rope" is the sheriff's campaign slogan), the movie is clearly a little nervous about this joke. "The sheriff has just put two hundred more relatives on the payroll," says a reporter into his phone, "to protect the city from the Red Army, which is leaving Moscow in a couple of minutes." This is a line from the play. But the movie—lest we feel sanguine about the Red Army—adds another: "Trouble is," says another reporter nearby, "when the *real* red menace shows up, the sheriff'll still be crying wolf." A statement worthy of the mayor himself.

Yet except for these omissions and an occasional mealymouthed new line, in most ways it's still the same Chicago, even if it does go unnamed. A place where even a casual remark can open up dazzling, unthought-of new vistas of corruption and control. As when the mayor (Clarence Kolb), trying to bribe a minor functionary named Pettibone (Billy Gilbert) with an important new job in the city, finds the man concerned about whether his kids will miss out in school if the family has to move: won't they lose a grade? "No they won't, they'll skip a grade," says the mayor peremptorily, as he hustles Pettibone out the door. "And I guarantee you that they'll graduate with highest honors." A place where delicacy, such as it is, takes the form of not "hanging a man in his sleep," at five a.m. instead of seven, just to make the city edition. "There's such a thing as being humane, you know," says the sheriff (Gene Lockhart), when the request is made of him by the jokers in the press room. He says this with a whine in his voice—the same aggrieved way he tells them not to call him "Pinky" ("'Cuz I got a name, see—and it's Peter B. Hartwell"). But the whine turns to a bleat when he talks to his friend and mentor the mayor, who doesn't suffer fools gladly, even though he's stuck with one. He and Pinky are on the same ticket, and the ticket is in trouble. "It frightens me," says the mayor, looking at his running mate with harrowed eyes, "to think what I'd like to do to you." "Do you realize," he demands, "there are two hundred thousand votes at stake, and if Williams don't hang we're gonna lose them!" As Hildy later remarks: "You'd hang your own mother to be re-elected." But the mayor is not about to let *this* pass: "That's a horrible thing to say about anyone, Miss Johnson," he assures her gravely. He knows a tasteless suggestion when he hears one—just as the sheriff knows an inhumane one. Chicago is never more wonderfully itself than when it is pretending to a moral sensibility.

But if it's still the same Terrible Place, it's no longer a place that you have to leave to find love, as the original Hildy was trying to do. *This* Hildy stays behind with Walter Burns in the end—and sends the nice person away. Back to Albany—"where he belongs." But before that, and through most of the movie, Hildy—being a bona fide screwball heroine—is determined to have just what she really knows better than: "a halfway normal life," as she calls it—a man who lets a lady go first and helps her with her coat and tells her that even ten minutes is too long to be away from her, someone who is "kind" and "sweet" and "considerate" and who "wants a home and children." "He sounds like a guy *I* ought to marry," says Walter. Who is neither kind nor considerate, never mind "sweet."

What he is instead is an incarnation—more extreme than usual—of those subversive energies and impulses that the movies, to the dismay of watchdogs and moralists, so often seemed to be recommending to us. He doesn't believe in anything, it's clear. You can't even divorce him and count on his noticing it. "Why, divorce doesn't mean anything nowadays, Hildy," he tells her, "just a few words mumbled over you by a judge." If the mayor conjures up visions of power in his conversation, Walter enacts them in front of our eyes: not only having Bruce arrested, over and over again, but kidnapping his old mother as well; stashing Earl Williams in a rolltop desk ("Get back in there, you mock turtle!") and planning to have it hoisted out with pulleys or even moved by the sheriff himself; hiring the obsequious Benziger (Ernest Truex) away from a rival newspaper (he writes verse) and then giving orders to have him kicked down the stairs. Walter is an inveterate double-crosser. But then, as he points out, so are most of the people he does it to. "Well, Walter," says Hildy, as she enters his office just in time to hear him on the phone setting up the governor for a con, "I see you're still at it." But, as he points out to her, this is the first time he's ever double-crossed a governor. And with that one line alone, he defines both his appeal for her (and for us) and his moral stature. Double-crossing important people is part of what this hero is all about—and what Hildy is mistakenly (and temporarily) turning her back upon. She wants to live in Bruce's world now, in Albany—where governors are *respected*.

But Hildy is a Chicago person herself. Her expressions of conventional feeling, for example, can sound almost as grotesquely unconvincing as the mayor's do. "Don't worry, Mother, this is only temporary!" she cries, as silver-haired

Mother (Alma Kruger) disappears out the door with her eyes rolling, tied and gagged and slung across the shoulder of Diamond Louie (Abner Biberman). And later, when Bruce, out of jail for the moment, wants to know where his mother has gone to, Hildy replies, "Out someplace" (what else can she say?), busy at her typewriter now on the Earl Williams story. But Bruce persists: *where* has she gone? "She couldn't say," says Hildy (a tactful allusion to the gag); she is getting irritated with these questions. But when it later develops that Mother might be killed, Hildy is very upset. "Dead, dead—oh, this is the *end!*" she cries, clutching her head and reeling out of the frame. "What am I gonna say to Bruce?" she wants to know, "—what can I *tell* him?" But Walter is at her side now. "Look, honey," he says tenderly, "if he really loves you, you won't have to tell him anything."

It turns out that Mother is not killed. She returns, more or less alive, after all, to where all paths converge in this movie—the Criminal Courts Building. Where she is reunited with her anxious son. But there is a lot going on when she gets there. Earl Williams' concealment in that desk in the press room has just been discovered by all the cops and reporters—all guns and eyes are trained on it now, waiting for the fugitive to emerge and surrender. Just then Bruce arrives in the hallway outside and Mother rushes out to greet him. "Mother!" he cries, as they fall into each other's arms in the doorway—and just as they do so, an anonymous cop standing by the door pushes it closed on them. Cancelling them. A lovely offhand gesture, perfectly expressive of the movie's (and Hawks's) attitude toward such moments (somebody shut that door, please).

For, in spite of minor bowdlerizations, Hawks has made a version of *The Front Page* that is even tougher in spirit, bolder and more daring than the original. For one thing, there is almost none of the play's occasional nervousness about the inhumanity of the reporters. Nor any suggestion, as there was in the 1931 movie, that we are watching something about the Decline of the West. Nor is there any reneging—as there is in both the play and the earlier movie—on the wise-ass fun; any attempt to strike a more "responsible" tone. Not in a Hawks movie. He handles the Molly Malloy (Helen Mack) scenes, the most "serious" and bathetic in the play, briskly and unsentimentally. Her jump out the window, for example, is done with maximum despatch, not milked for pathos the way it is in the Milestone version. And the earlier scene of Hildy—more responsive to a hooker than to a mother—going to Molly's side when the reporters are baiting her, seems to have its main point in this demonstration of Hildy's brand of womanliness.

Most important of all, perhaps, by changing Hildy into a heroine Hawks has changed Walter Burns into a hero. The editor is still essentially what he was in the original: a comic scoundrel, a triumphant amoralist, close to a character role. He is a center of life, an unfailingly energizing presence, but a monster too—someone to be wondered at. Now, it seems, he is someone to fall in love with as well. And he is still a monster.

But he is also Cary Grant, with his extraordinary power and charm. Hawks has turned the editor's role into a kind of extension and expression of Grant's own extrahuman quality, that seeming detachment from ordinary life and feelings, that standing-apart quality that marks Grant more than almost any other major star. Walter Burns may not be as intelligent or incisive as some Grant heroes are—he is a vulgarian, and sometimes (though less often than in the play) the joke is on him ("Leave the rooster story alone, that's human interest!"). But he is still the romantic hero, tough newspaperman version. And where earlier screwball comedies tend to tone down this hero's more disreputable side, to suit him for the romance—to sweeten and soften him, like *It Happened One Night*, or to make him reform in some way, like *Libeled Lady*—Hawks and Grant do just the opposite. Take, for example, Grant's ineffable way of responding to the news of an employee's illness, a reporter he was particularly depending on. "Where *is* Duffy?" he shouts into the phone. "Dia*betes!*" he shouts even louder, making it sound not only loathsome but obscene. "I should know *better*," he says, hanging up, flinging his arms wide and dancing with impatience, "than to hire anybody with a *disease!*" And this apparent inhumanity isn't (as it is in the more conventional *Only Angels Have Wings*) a cover for a deeper, more genuine humanity underneath. This Grant hero is just as outrageous as he seems, and remains so to the end. It's true he loves Hildy (it's almost surprising how convincing that is) and that he fights the crooked mayor and sheriff; but in every other respect he is unregenerate. Not only is he going through the door first in the last shot of the film, but Hildy is carrying the suitcase—in her arms. And he is taking her for a honeymoon not to Niagara Falls, as she had so wistfully hoped, but to Albany, to cover a strike there. "I wonder if Bruce can put us up," he says, as they go out the door—his last audible remark, and a staggering one.

That unregenerate quality is at the heart of this movie, and it's triumphant here as it's not quite in the play. The Hawks version is even clearer and less apologetic about its own subversive instincts—and the joy that goes with them. Grant's outrageousness is so wonderfully elated. That's one reason we don't squirm—just the opposite, in fact—to see Hildy scuttling out the door after him at the end, or feel that she's abasing herself. She's following the Wizard, so who cares if she has to carry the bags? Where cynicism and romanticism may seem to go together in other comedies, for Hawks they are almost the same thing: the cynicism *is* the romanticism. Above all, it's the deliverance from cant: the absolute refusal, in the fantasy of this comedy, ever to talk shit again. It's easy to be crooked or ruthless in the Chicago of this movie—but it's hard to be dishonest, at least in a convincing way. You can fool others, but not yourself. For that you have to go to Albany. Or to another movie.

That's why Hildy and Walter's single overtly romantic scene—it comes at the end, of course, just before they go out the door with the suitcase—has such curious force. "I thought you didn't love me," says Hildy through her tears. "What were you thinking with?" responds Walter, with real tenderness and concern now. She thought he was going to let her go ("What did you think I was," he says, "a chump?")—that he was even going to let Bruce go. She didn't know that he's had Bruce locked up yet again (for passing counterfeit money). And the revelation that he has—Bruce having just phoned from his jail cell—now affects her powerfully. Because a minute ago she really thought he was kissing her off, letting her escape to her "happiness" in Albany. "I was jealous," he had said, pretending to be giving her up for her own good. "That's why I made fun of Bruce and Albany . . . because he can offer you the kind of life I can't give you." She had thought for a frightening moment or two that he actually *meant* all this. But now it turns out to be another con, and Bruce has to be bailed out again. Hildy's emotion now, surprisingly infectious as it is, is as much relief as admitted love. And ours is something like it, when this wonderful comedy confirms its own exhilaration. It *remains* unregenerate. This Wizard is the real article, not a fake behind smokepots. And we don't have to go back to Kansas, after all.

As far as Howard Hawks is concerned, we never do. While those around him were making movies and movie stars more and more like some prosaic illusion of "real life," Hawks was making them more movielike. And doing this—paradoxically—in a serious way. Just as in *His Girl Friday* he takes the Grant hero's inhumanism seriously, refusing to rationalize or domesticate or regenerate it. More than any other major filmmaker of his time, Hawks is involved—within the terms of classical Hollywood filmmaking and its commitment to "reality"—in just those aspects of the conventional movie experience that seem most magical. In a way, his whole career is an exploration of that magic—*as* magic, and not something to be explained away. Hawks illustrates the Godardian reflection that you touch depths mainly by fixing on surfaces ("How can you render the inside? Precisely by staying prudently outside"). And Godard, writing in a 1952 *Cahiers du Cinema*, calls Hawks "the greatest American artist" of all.

From the art of *Only Angels Have Wings* to that of *His Girl Friday, The Big Sleep* and indeed *To Have and Have Not*, what does one see? An increasingly precise taste for analysis, a love for this artificial grandeur connected to movements of the eyes, to a way of walking, in short a greater awareness than anyone else of what the cinema can glory in . . . through a rigorous knowledge of its limits, fixing its basic laws.

And it's because of this "greater awareness . . . of what the cinema can glory in" that Hawks had the remarkable, uniquely protean kind of career that he did. He worked in every major genre, reconstituting them all in his own spirit and style, making a notable or even definitive movie (or movies) in each one of them: from the western (*Red River*) to the screwball comedy (*Bringing Up Baby*) and the film noir (*The Big Sleep*) to the musical (*Gentlemen Prefer Blondes*) and the sci-fi thriller (*The Thing*) later on. He made the best of all the gangster movies, *Scarface* in 1932, and the best newspaper comedy, *His Girl Friday*. Hawks could move around like that—with the same apparent mastery—because he was centrally interested in something about the movies themselves, something that could be as intrinsic to the effect of a musical as to that of a western or an urban comedy: "this artificial grandeur connected to movements of the eyes, to a way of walking. . . ."

When Tony Camonte (Paul Muni in *Scarface*) in a barber chair unwinds the towel from his face and first shows himself to the camera, the effect is like unwrapping something from a tomb. But the face is creepily alive, with its thick lips and black button eyes and heavy dark-shadowed eyelids, stupid and crafty, simian and sensual—and oddly, disturbingly glamorous. "I'm gettin' a massage too," he says when the cop (C. Henry Gordon), a functionary with a natty mustache, tells him to come along for some "questioning." Tony rises and crosses in front of the cop. He picks up a hand mirror to study his haircut: "Hey, how's it look in back, huh?" "Very good," says the barber offscreen. "Ummm," says Tony, and smooths the top of his hair with his hand. This isn't showing off for the cop, offering a provocation to him the way Cagney might do: Muni seems really, and almost spookily, absorbed in his haircut. This is what makes him so compelling: he has this eerie energy of concentration. Whether he's spraying a wall of billiard cues with his machine gun, or arranging a flower in George Raft's buttonhole to confirm a rival's "rubout," or attending a play about Sadie Thompson ("She's what you call . . . disillusioned"), or watching the boss's girl pluck her eyebrows ("It takes a long time with the pinchers, huh?"), or propositioning her in the stairway later on. He has a new place, he tells her. "Come up some time?" he says, earnest and pleading. "Yeah, and I'll bring my grandmother," she replies. But her wan sarcasm is no match for the force of his longing. "No kiddin,' come up," he says, urgently. She can try to get by this hunger, but she can't turn it aside. It's this ability to give himself to the moment—*any* moment ("Hey, lookit," he cries gleefully, "they been here too!" when he returns to his "office" to find the walls spattered with bullet holes)—that makes him remarkable and scary. It's like some native gift, this capacity for excitement, marking him off from all the dimmer people around him.

The opposite of Cagney in *Public Enemy*, Muni's Tony Camonte seems almost explosively sexual—an id on the loose—swinging his arms from his shoulders as he walks, with the taut, straight back that seems never to relax, as unrelenting as the eyes. While his sidekick Guino (George Raft), an impassive and menacing presence, seems hardly to move at all (except for the incessant, suggestive coin-tossing), Tony careens and lunges around when the rage or the fever is on him like some mad, terrifying ape. But he strikes a chord in Karen Morley's Poppy, his boss's mistress, with her tough weariness and her sad, unsettling laugh, this exhausted, sensual woman whom nothing surprises. Though *he* does, a little. That's why she laughs, in that sudden, eloquent way, and why she strolls into his new place one day, with her lounging, hip-sprung walk ("Kinda gaudy, isn't it?" she says) while he prowls around her ("Aint it, though? Glad you like it," he says).

But Tony's sister Cesca (Ann Dvorak) is even more disturbing. While he pursues Poppy, she (unknown to her brother) pursues Guino. "You're only a kid," Guino says, when she turns up at the nightclub wearing a sexy gown. Dvorak has a witchlike beauty, with her broad brow and pointed chin, her frizzed black hair and wide brilliant eyes. It's these eyes, with their candor and life, that make her seem girlish. She walks forward into the close-up—a shot from over Raft's shoulder—shining and brimming and smiling to herself as she moves close to him. It's a stunning moment and there is a pause: as her smile passes. "I'm eighteen," she says rather wanderingly, as if that number had just occurred to her—and offscreen a saxophone blares, the opening bars of "Some of These Days." She wants him to dance with her—and in medium shot, her eyes fixed on his (his back, as impassive as his face, is still to the camera), she does a lumbering, snake-hipped dance step—like some speakeasy temple dance. Dvorak is *very* disturbing: unlike her subhuman brother—unlike almost everyone else in the film—she seems fully and attractively human. But she also seems dangerously, even thrillingly exposed in everything she does, with that same lunging, thrusting forward impulse that Tony shows. Even when she does something conventional and coquettish, like showing her face from her window to Guino on the street below, she seems undefended and reckless. The same little smile, but this time the wide eyes are heavy lidded, half-closed, as if she were offering herself even here, in some insolent heedless way. Like Tony, she is expressive, fierce-eyed, giving herself to the moment. In early scenes her lids are darkened just the way his are. This gives their eyes an unsettling expanse of white—makes them seem wild and startled and rolling. While Guino's and Poppy's eyes are narrowed and watchful.

If *His Girl Friday* is about the fun of anarchy, *Scarface* is about the thrill of it—and the scariness, too: the eye whites and the uncontrol, the shadows (Lee Garmes's photography) and the omnipresent X's (marking the victim's spot) and the horrified whispering shouts they talk in when Tony drags Cesca in her evening gown back to the house, to a darkened room in front of a window where

they are outlined by light, locked in an appalled impasse, eyes starting out, lace-curtain shadows on their faces, exchanging their hoarse shocked threats— even *they* seem involved in the thrill. Hawks was proud of this incest motif, discreet (necessarily) and yet plainly there (he got the idea from the Borgias, he said). But his major use of it, as with all forms of inner life in this film, is to turn it into a spectacle. Scarface himself is a spectacle, unnerving and riveting at the same time. So, finally, is Cesca—stepping out of the shadows with a gun aimed at Tony, her long throat swathed in a black scarf, her eyes ringed with mascara, her face pallid and set: she has become an image more than a person, powerful but theatrical.

Hawks especially likes to stylize his women: to give them that remote, mysterious, imponderable quality that we associate with the more exotic kinds of movie star. There is an extraordinary sequence in *Fazil* (1928)—a wildly pulpish romance (Hawks always dismissed the film in his later interviews) with Charles Farrell as perhaps the silent cinema's most improbable sheik—where the camera, in company with the heroine (Greta Nissen), tours the hero's harem. He is an Arab prince who, after quarreling with his Parisian bride (Nissen), has been forced to console himself in "the traditional way of his people." He gets himself a harem, that is. And soon the bride arrives from Europe, not knowing anything about this family tradition and hoping to make everything up with her husband. Instead, she gets shown to the women's quarters. She is supposed to be shocked by what she finds there—reeling from it, in fact—but the sequence itself, as she tours the wives' abode, is charged with wonder and erotic excitement. The women are so provocative, so odd and various—walking and lounging, smoking and dressing themselves, being manicured and pedicured, even (most surprisingly) reading. They wear coronets that look like insect antennae; huge, curly blond wigs; long trains that fan out behind them. They glower at the intruder as she passes, or watch her with alarm, widening their eyes, shrinking down into their pillows—or else they appear not to see her at all. And on the wife goes, down passageways and past cubicles; there seems no end to the women. One of them, a sinister Madame Butterfly type, gabbles something in an unknown tongue. Another, like some dazed grounded bird, spreads her skirt and turns slowly around in front of the visitor. And so on: you get no more than a glimpse of anyone, but each seems special, eccentric and inviting in some way, and absolutely opaque. And the excitement builds as they keep coming on. It's a vision (derived from the showgirl spectacles of the musical review), even a delirium, of sexual largesse and variety. But invested with that formal, distant, even ceremonial quality that seems always important to Hawks—especially in his vision of terrific women.

Because he doesn't just want us to stare—he wants us to catch our breath, too. And to be a bit baffled by what we see. Both dazzled and bemused. The Hawks woman is nearly always a plain sort, with no airs or aspirations to elegance, but she is always offered in some mode of "artificial grandeur" that distances her from us. Like Hildy's fast-talking turn with Walter—or Cesca's appearance with scarf and gun. And when she is a show-biz type, as she more and more often is—a chorus girl or a saloon singer—she can create her own artifice, "doing her number" for us, singing or (if that seems unthinkable, as with Jean Arthur) playing the piano. After Cesca's snake-hipped shuffle-and-tap, she never again dances. She moves too slowly, too hieratically for that. Like Frances Farmer in *Come and Get It* (1939), she is moving toward apotheosis. And in Farmer's Lotta Morgan in that film, she reaches it—probably the Hawks heroine's single most stunning incarnation.

There's an earlier try in *Barbary Coast* (1935)—like *Come and Get It*, also a Goldwyn film—and a misfire. Miriam Hopkins' Swan, like Lotta, is a saloon girl and a toughie. She stands at the beginning of the movie—like Dietrich at the beginning of *Morocco* (one of the films Hawks later claimed to have contributed to, through his friendship with the screenwriter Jules Furthman)—at the railing of a ship coming into port, and makes sibylline remarks to the man next to her about liking the fog (because it hides things). But when she lands on shore (the men on the dock instantly show her to the city's biggest and best saloon), it's apparent that the movie's in trouble. Partly because of the overwritten script—one of the most verbose, self-indulgent Hollywood jobs Hecht and MacArthur ever perpetrated, either singly or together. And partly because of Hopkins. Who keeps sighing and raising her eyes heavenward (she can't seem to control it) to indicate her own hard luck, even after she has become the "star" of the Belladonna Saloon. Instead of being tough and insolent, she seems irritable and martyred. Instead of sauntering and strolling among the crowds of male customers, she hunches her shoulders over and slips around them—in her long-suffering way. You can almost feel Hawks' chagrin at this performance: whenever she has to move across the room, he starts cutting away to get her there. "I don't remember the story too well," he told Peter Bogdanovich in 1962, "except it was about a girl who arrived in San Francisco Bay in a ship that came around the Horn. . . . As Ben Hecht said, 'Miriam Hopkins came to the Barbary Coast and wandered around like a confused Goldwyn Girl.'"

F RANCES FARMER, on the other hand, was something else altogether. "I don't think there's any doubt," Hawks later said—to Joseph McBride in 1977, two months before Hawks's death—"that Frances Farmer was the best actress I ever worked with." She plays a double role in *Come and Get It*, appearing in the second and longer section of the film as her own daughter, a nice-girl version of the saloon-singer mother—as if the character had grown finally and in fact into Edward Arnold's first, idealized impression of her when he comes upon her in the saloon.* Farmer is beautiful and touching as the daughter. But it's as the saloon singer—the pure Hawksian vision—that she makes her most astonishing impact, in the opening scenes of the film.

She emerges, almost without emphasis, from out of the crowd at Arnold's elbow. He is at one of the gaming tables, a lumberman who's just struck it rich, and now he is betting five hundred dollars on a shell game that seems sure to be fixed. Naturally he attracts a crowd. He looks at her as she appears at his side. "Hullo," she says in her deep, surprisingly boyish voice, assured but a little

---

*This sort of idealization seemed to be Arnold's line at the time. In *Diamond Jim* (screenplay by Preston Sturges, 1935), Jean Arthur plays a similar "double" heroine to Arnold's hero, but reverses the progression: the nice girl turns into the worldly one.

Osgood Perkins and Paul Muni lighting Karen Morley's cigarette in Scarface *(above); Edward Arnold plays the shell game and Frances Farmer kibitzes in* Come and Get It, *with Walter Brennan at left, Edwin Maxwell at right.*

tentative, too. He grins at her, and she smiles back—a side-of-the-mouth smile, hiked up at one corner—revolving some gum in the front of her mouth as she looks him over. She is very beautiful in this first big close-up (Gregg Toland is the photographer), with her crooked smile. She has the air of someone who's just gotten the joke—and liked it, too. She looks at him now as if he could know an even better joke—why not? In the meantime she revolves her gum and waits. "You gonna bring me luck?" he says. "If I do it'll be the first time," she answers, on an escaped, barely perceptible sigh, a don't-remind-me sound. "So you're not lucky, eh?" he says, still grinning. "Think I'd be here if I was?" she says, seeming amused at the idea. But she is still waiting for *his* joke. It turns out to be worth the wait. Once he's picked out the shell with the pea under it, he demands that the man running the game lift not that shell but the other two; if there is nothing under them (as of course turns out to be so), that has to mean he wins—unless, of course, the house is cheating. He wins. "Coming with me?" he asks Farmer, triumphantly, while the customers shout and whoop in excitement and the saloon boss (Edwin Maxwell) seethes on the sidelines. "Sure," she says, taking his arm and giving the boss a big happy grin as she passes.

Arnold pays her a compliment—his real luck, he says, was finding her—which she acknowledges with a laugh and a comradely salute of the hand. He asks her name. "Lotta," she replies, leaning against a pillar. "Lotta Morgan." And he offers to share some of his winnings with her; she accepts. But then they are interrupted by a call from the piano player: "Come on, Lotta—let's go to work!" "Stay right here, I'll be with you in a minute," she says to Arnold, clapping him on the shoulder, and walks off. The camera follows her as she crosses the room. When she is turned away, we see that she walks with a rather slumped swagger—the counterpart to her crooked smile.

This brief walking sequence—less than a minute long, from the moment she leaves Arnold to the moment she begins her song—is a single tracking-and-panning shot, entirely controlled, so it seems, by Farmer's movements. But she does a great number of different things in this brief shot: crosses the room, parks her gum behind the bar while she makes an under-the-breath offer to Sid, the boss ("Hullo, Sid. Want me to get your money back?"), laughs at his reply ("I'll give you a hundred if you do") as she crosses in front of him, salutes some customers who call out her name, greets the singing waiters who are just joining her ("Feel like workin', boys?"), picks up her parasol (a prop for the act), returns to the bar in time to hear the boss's new offer (two hundred dollars), which she accepts ("All right, give me something to put in his drink")—then leans out of the frame to begin her song in the next shot.

It's a prosaic sequence, with nothing in the shot or the movement of the camera (in fact quite complicated) that calls attention to itself in any way; and yet it's magical. And it makes us experience the actress—not the filmmaker or the film itself—as the source of the magic. She makes us feel the kind of awe we can feel in front of anyone who shows familiarity and control in a world or a place that's strange to us. But the movie actor not only may control the world on the screen; in a traveling shot like this one she controls our access to it, too—by her movements, by her own easy, multiform mastery of the complex, shifting, tricky milieu. And what Hawks emphasizes is the continuity of Farmer's movement, of her "walk" to "work." Although we certainly register her doing a lot of different things in the course of it, what we are watching throughout, it seems, is a single seamless movement, going through different and surprising phras-

Frances Farmer in Come and Get It.

ings, like a complex dance passage. Just a girl doing her job—but Hawks makes us feel the wonder of it. Which gets stronger as it goes along, almost sneaking up on us—and climaxing in a song. She now walks into the next shot, gives the downbeat to the pianist, leans insouciantly against the railing—she is at the top of a short stairway, in a low-angle medium shot, with appreciative men below and around her—and begins to sing.

At first she seems to sing the way she smiles: with the side of her mouth, in a husky contralto. And yet it's not exactly the sort of song we expect to hear from such a singer in such a place: no raffish love song or barroom anthem but a familiar traditional ballad, "Aura Lee," gentle and sad and yearning. And she delivers it with professional pathos:

> As the blackbird in the spring
> 'Neath the willow tree,
> Sat and piped,
> I heard him sing . . .
> Singing of the lea. . . .

Arnold looks impressed—almost beside himself, like someone who's been granted a vision. And this is only the opening verse. She knows what she's doing: she directs the last line, with its dying fall, at him. Now she comes to the refrain, hoisting her parasol and opening it behind her, so that she is framed by it when she gets to the good part, with its sudden surge of feeling, its poignant sudden change of pitch:

> Aura Lee! . . . Aura Lee! . . .
> Take my golden ring. . . .

It's not just her beauty that fills the screen here but a kind of intoxicated consciousness. She is in touch with so much when she sings—the waiters, the pianist, the rhythm and sound and sentiment, not to mention her infatuated audience—just as when she walks. And all on one soaring, continuous line of control. Except that here the line is a melodic one, full of feeling. But what's also clear is that she is somewhat detached from that feeling: it's fine with her, she is certainly enjoying herself, but it's really for *them*, and we can see that it even amuses her a little. There's the slightest edge of mockery when she gets to "Take my golden ring"—she comes down on each syllable almost jovially, heightening the barbershop-quartet sound. But at the word "ring" she lowers her eyes and cues the harmonizing waiters for a diminuendo, and a change of feeling in the refrain's final lines:

> Love and light . . . return with thee . . .
> And swallows with the spring.

The close-up now is extreme—and ravishing. "Love and light . . ." she sings, in a high, delicate voice, drawing the words out tenderly, then hesitates in the middle of the line, then completes it: ". . . return with thee"—lifting her eyebrows and turning her head in Arnold's direction. This is the other side of the light mockery—the mysterious side. This extraordinary and moving raptness— qualified by the consciousness. She is still looking the place over, casing the action, as always, but from a different height. As if using this song full of pain and sadness to float above the pain and sadness. Hovering—lifting her chin, arching her eyebrows, drawing out the sound—then coming back to earth again: "*And* swallows . . .": she lands, swaggering in place, her good-humored style. The same hesitation in the middle of the line again, but this time with a smile— as if to say: here it comes, boys, the payoff. And then here it is: ". . . *with* the spring!" Pretty good, huh?—and she's done. Folding her parasol and going off. To cheers and wild applause. It's only been a snatch of song (there is an encore coming up in a minute or so), but the on-screen cheering for once seems appropriate.

I N T H E original novel by Edna Ferber, the heroine was "a little lame girl who sang so badly that the woodsmen hooted at her," Hawks later recalled; and changing her to the "good lusty girl" that Farmer played was one of the things he got fired from the picture for. Sam Goldwyn had been in the hospital, and when he found out that Hawks had been rewriting the script (Goldwyn thought that directors should stick to directing, especially when they were filming Goldwyn-approved scripts), the two men argued so bitterly that Hawks had to leave the picture. William Wyler was brought in to finish it, and the completed film bears both his name and Hawks's—with Hawks getting top billing, reportedly at Wyler's insistence. "The best parts," Wyler said later, ". . . were done by Hawks," including all the Lotta Morgan scenes in the first part of the film. To Wyler it was always a Hawks film. (Hawks claimed that in the end all his rewrites were used.)

But Hawks had total control over *To Have and Have Not* (1944) at Warner Brothers. The kind of tough comedy-melodrama where, as Agee said in his 1945 review, the lovers "seem to do even their kissing out of the side of their mouths." And it was in this movie, a Humphrey Bogart vehicle, that Hawks produced the quintessential Hawks heroine. If Farmer is the most moving of these heroines, Lauren Bacall is the most stylized and outrageous, a lean, rangy, sexy big-cat of a woman. "Anybody got a match?" she says in her startling deep voice—she is off-screen, we just glimpsed her the moment before this in the hallway. And now we see her, in a long shot, with Bogart in the foreground of the shot looking at her as she leans against the doorway of his room, in her checked suit, touching the unlit cigarette to her mouth and eyeing him. He throws the matchbox and she catches it in a casual overhand reach, still leaning against the doorway. He stares at her—speculatively, hitching up his belt, looking her up and down. She eyes him—with absolute, devastating evenness—before looking down and striking the match. She lights the cigarette and looks up again, in close-up, taking the cigarette from her mouth. She tosses the dead match over her shoulder, leans forward to go, and tosses the matchbox toward him and toward the camera: "Thanks," she says, making it sound like some variant of "Up yours," and swings out of the frame.

It's a come-on, of course. That's how Bogart sizes it up in his reaction shots, with the help of some frantic back-and-forth eye dartings from Frenchy (Marcel Dalio), who is also on the scene—as if we needed the clue. But no ordinary come-on: it's too outré. And the insolence at the end ("Thanks")—unprovoked (though we know it isn't: Bogart almost requires it in a way, and this is no Ingrid Bergman type)—is almost as surprising as it is delightful. From her first moments on the screen, she gives the kind of pleasure that audacity generally gives—excitement, some suspense, and almost unreasoning satisfaction when the boldness works. "Thanks"—and up yours.

Walter Brennan, Lauren Bacall, and Humphrey Bogart in To Have and Have Not.

."Wha'd you do that for?" says Bogart, much later on, after she's sat on his lap and kissed him. "I've been wondering whether I'd like it," she says. "What's the decision?" "I don't know yet," she says, implacably—then kisses him again, more lingeringly. Then she rises, in her indolent way, her long tawny hair falling forward across her face as she does so. "It's even better when you help," she says, from behind her hair, and walks off.

She slouches and saunters and lounges. She sits looking off and down, framed in a corner of light. She speaks and moves slowly; she even *looks* slowly, head down and looking up and out from under her eyebrows: slow lateral track of eyes, slow pan of face, as she sizes up the room for a likely prospect. This stare (soon christened "the Look") is like all her movements: insistent, insinuating, oddly momentous. The way she passes through a crowd at the bar, taking some guy's elbow, moving it aside as if she were parting a curtain, easing herself across his back. She is on her way to sing her song, wearing a slinky black bare-midriff gown. And the song itself, "How Little We Know" (written for her and for the film by Hoagy Carmichael and Johnny Mercer), is an inspiration. Like the singer herself, it's full of odd disjunctions and small opacities, and all about love: will it last? can it? or should it even?

> Is this what I've waited for?
> Am I the one?
> Oh, I hope in my heart that it's so,
> In spite of how little we know.

But the formulaic romanticism is at odds with the growling suggestive delivery. And the oddity is compounded by the band's percussive, twittering bird-sound accompaniment, including synchronized breathing and gasping from the backup group behind the piano. The discordances are intentional: it's like a cubist version of a sexy number—less a sexy number than a ceremonial one.

She has this hieratic air even when she's being funny. The sultriness seems almost stately, as if the whole effect might fall apart if she moved too quickly. And indeed it might have, it seems. Bacall was very nervous and inexperienced. She says in her autobiography that "the Look," her most famously sexy effect, came about when she found that if she held her head down she could keep it from shaking. And Hawks makes this unease (as he does to a lesser extent with Farmer's) part of the effect. If Bacall's crossing a room—or even looking it over—seems like an event, it's partly the threat of her not making it. The performance exerts control precisely because it's so close to losing it. She has to swagger and bluff her way through this role (whereas someone like Miriam Hopkins merely cheats), bringing out just those qualities that Hawks values. The inexperience becomes part of the audacity, of the wonderful chutzpah of the whole thing. It's less the tough type that Hawks is interested in than women like

Farmer and Bacall who can *become* that type, in amusing and interesting ways.

More than anyone else he had worked with, Bacall was his creation—from the beginning. "She was about sixteen or seventeen," he later said—erroneously: she was nineteen—"and you had to give her everything she did." Which suited him just fine. "And she did it well," he added. His wife, Slim, first saw her on the cover of *Harper's Bazaar*. Hawks met her, signed her to a personal contract, and brought her to Hollywood, where she learned over long periods of coaching and training to embody the woman he had in his head—and who had been up there for some time, it seemed. "Jean Arthur was very difficult to work with," he claimed in a later interview. "She didn't understand until after the film [*Only Angels Have Wings*] was done what it was I wanted—which was Bacall." Bogart calls her "Slim" in the movie, without apparent cause: her name is Marie. *His* name is Harry Morgan, and she calls him "Steve." Why? Hawks was asked. Because these were the names he and his wife gave each other. And where did he get the Bacall character from? "I was merely doing somebody that I liked," he replied.

That somebody had to be Dietrich—at least in part. And Hawks admitted it was. He told a story of screening the movie for her: "That's me, isn't it?" she said to him (in one of the versions he told), and he conceded it was. But Bacall is an American-girl version of Dietrich—Dietrich plain, so to speak, without filters or gauze or shadows, without spangles or trappings or veils. Where von Sternberg emphasizes the delusional aspects of his heroine, Hawks does just the reverse. Bacall can look ravishing, but she never looks hallucinatory or surreal—always casual, natural, perfectly palpable. Through most of the film she wears the same sort of tailored checked suit with big lapels that Jean Arthur, her unsatisfactory predecessor, had worn. She also appears in a bathrobe. The only glamour outfit is the one she sings the song in. And even on this occasion she performs in a bright, evenly lit area. (Frenchy's Café is always well lighted, in contrast to the more cavernous, "native" sort of place she and Bogart drop into on their way back from the police station.)

She is, after all, *not* Dietrich. Any more than she is Mae West—whom she also often sounds like ("It's even better when you help"). Though she could hardly have existed, it seems clear, if *they* hadn't. "It was that quality of insolence" in Bacall, Hawks said, that bowled audiences over. "*That* hadn't been seen. It *had*"—in Dietrich, of course—"but people didn't remember it." "Nothing like Bacall," proclaimed a Warner Brothers memo (from publicity chief Charles Einfield), "has been seen on the screen since Garbo and Dietrich." And clearly Hawks has a special feeling for the exotic star, who was quite out of fashion in the mid-forties (it has to heighten any pleasure you take in Bacall to remind yourself what her competition was like). Bacall belongs to the spellbinders, outsized and outlandish, who take over the screen just by walking across it. The heroine who gives herself to many but never quite gives herself away, not to anyone. Bacall may be brightly lit and casually gowned, but she is still in this larger-than-life tradition, riddling and mysterious. In some ways she is even more oblique, more angular and abstractionist, than her predecessors. "'Will it say a farewell?'" she sings, referring to "love." "'Who can tell?' " she answers, making this line sound almost unspeakably raffish, with the force of a stripper's bump and grind. But the stripper's grind has a clear meaning. So, for the most part, do Dietrich's "double meanings." But the Bacall line is meaning-less—so, in fact, is the emphasis given to it by her and Hawks (it coincides with a nice close-up). Many of her spoken lines, too, seem equally empty of meaning or point. We laugh—her "'Who can tell?'" is as surefire as her "Thanks"—even without understanding, responding to her sound and style, to the image and idea of her, rather than to any perceived point. She is like those harem women in *Fazil*, showing themselves, talking in unknown tongues, turning around in front of us, insistently expressive—but expressing what?

For one thing, all that manner—this theatricalized version of the sexy girl—really stands for non-manner: the Hawksian paradox. For honesty, plainness, unaffected common sense. The opposite of formal virtues, expressed in a figure with her own striking formality. And the more formalized she becomes, the more Hawks insists on the point. Bacall isn't even as duplicitous, for example, as Farmer tries to be—who tries to put something in the hero's drink but then can't go through with it. Bacall steals the wallet of a character named Johnson (Walter Sande) because she needs the money and because she doesn't like him. "That's a good reason," the Bogart hero tells her, perfectly without irony. And of course she is right about not liking Johnson—an American businessman type, a kvetch and a bully and a deadbeat (he was trying to skip out without paying Bogart what he owed him). She is unfailingly right about important things. Early on, she passes what turns out to be the movie's crucial moral test: i.e., Eddie's bee question. Eddie (Walter Brennan) is an old rummy ("a good man on a boat once") and the hero's inseparable companion. To someone like Johnson this is incom-prehensible. "Why d'you look after him?" he wants to know; he's not a relative or anything. "He thinks he's looking after me," Bogart replies with a grin. Eddie interrupts a conference in Bogart's room: some Gaullist Resistance men are trying to enlist Harry's (Bogart's) aid, a life-and-death matter for them. "Was you ever bit by a dead bee?" the addled Eddie asks. The preoccupied Resistance leader dismisses him testily ("I have no memory of being bit by any kind of bee"). But Marie (Bacall), also on the scene, doesn't: "Were you?" she replies, in her deep friendly voice. The excited Eddie—before launching into his long unfunny story ("Does he always talk so much?" asks the impatient Resistance man; "*Always*," says Bogart, menacingly)—tells her that she's the only person besides Harry who ever responded that way. "And Frenchy," Harry carefully reminds him—Frenchy being the *other* character the hero gives his friendship to. "And Frenchy," Eddie concedes. It's clear (and it's easy to see why) not many people have passed this test. But Marie was bound to. She's not only nice; she's perfectly untouched (unlike the heroic Resistance leader) by any form of snobbery or self-importance.

The Hawks heroine is never destructive or deadly, like some of the Dietrich heroines or the black widows of film noir. Hawks is really not interested in or impressed by femmes fatales. Nor is he drawn to the conventional feminine types, like Mme de Bursac (Dolores Moran) in this film. She is the Ilsa Lund–Ingrid Bergman figure, though not, this time, the heroine. She was originally meant to be a rival to Bacall in a triangle over Bogart, but Hawks kept cutting the part down. Until now she's more or less just this nuisance—who faints and complains and makes problems. She can't stand Bogart at first and lets him know it. But then she comes round. "You don't make me angry when you say that. I don't think I'll ever be angry again with anything you say," she tells him glowingly, surprised at her own relenting. But she is too surprised—and too guileless and open about all her feelings. Her candor is really a form of coquetry, as Bacall makes clear when she does a wonderful eye-batting imitation of her. Not that Mme de Bursac is easy to figure out ("Another screwy dame!" exclaims Bogart). She's puzzling and unpredictable; but all that only makes her tiresome. In a Hawks film, it's the down-to-earth, no-nonsense woman—the "good lusty girl," in his phrase for Farmer—who is finally and wonderfully mysterious.

I said, "Howard, if you will permit me, I don't think it should go like that." He gave me his reptilian glare. The man had ice-cold blue eyes and the coldest of manners. He was like that with everyone: women, men, whatever. He was remote; he came from outer space. He wore beautiful clothes. He spoke slowly, in a deep voice. He looked at you with those frozen eyes. And you did what he said. And he usually damn well knew .

—NIVEN BUSCH, in a 1985 interview

HAWKS, unlike most of his Hollywood colleagues, came from money and "background"—a family of wealthy paper manufacturers in Indiana. He went to schools like Phillips Exeter and Cornell, working on his vacations as a prop man at the Famous Players Lasky studio and graduating with a degree in mechanical engineering. He joined the Army Air Corps in the First World War but never left Texas. After the war he was by turns a racing car driver, an aviator, and an airplane builder, before being drawn back to moviemaking. He used his own money to produce and direct some short comedies, and in 1922 he joined the story department at Paramount, where he wrote or contributed to some sixty

*The first un-
mistakable
"Hawks family
group," in*
Only Angels
Have Wings.
*Standing: Sig
Rumann, Allyn
Joslyn, Noah
Beery, Jr., and
Cary Grant,
cadging a
light for his
cigarette from
Jean Arthur.*

screenplays. It was at Fox that he began his career as a feature director in 1926. But once the sound era began, he managed his jobs so as to escape the dominance of a single studio. He worked on all the major lots except Paramount in the thirties and forties (he liked MGM the least—too regimented). And for the most part he made deals with them that insured his autonomy, or at least a high degree of it.

He was tall and slim and patrician-looking, and a fashion plate. John Bright called him "a fake Englishman." Ben Hecht described him as "a-purr with melodrama." He was "an inveterate gambler and man-about-town," his friend Jean Negulesco said, with "a busy and turbulent social life." John Ford called him "the gray fox of Brentwood." He was also intimidating. Rosalind Russell remembered his "eyes like two blue cubes of ice." Lauren Bacall, when she first knew him, was struck by his absolute self-assurance, as if he never had any doubts or hesitations. In fact he was—and was well known to his friends as—"a preposterous, imaginative, and inspired liar," in Negulesco's words. Film historian Joseph McBride said that Hawks in his late years showed "the highest self-opinion" in a director that he had ever encountered. And along with this went an incredible, relentless boastfulness, in that slow, steady, low-pitched drawl of a voice. A willingness to claim some credit (mostly as a writer or a contributor to the writing) for almost any movie achievement an interviewer was likely to mention, from *Gone With the Wind* to *The French Connection*. But then a lot of the stories turn out to be true after all (*The French Connection* one, for example), as McBride admits he found out. "He took me to lunch," writes Bacall in her autobiography, describing her first days in Hollywood, "and told me about his directing experiences with various actresses. It was always what he said to them, or to Howard Hughes, or to Jack Warner—he always came out on top, he always won." This was also the style of his interviews later on.

But when he was explaining something, like "a complicated card game, for instance," you were struck by "his patience and simplicity," said Negulesco, even his "humility." Frances Farmer was struck by how "sensitive" he was as a director (in *Will There Really Be a Morning?*): "he gave every scene a minute examination, both psychological and visual," she said, and made her feel "full of anticipation" for every take. In the end he tailored nearly everything to his actors—lines, camera movements, characterization, story, which might take a whole new direction (as *To Have and Have Not* did) if the performances suggested it. And in spite of his personal reserve and ice-cold eyes, the atmosphere on his set was relaxed and spontaneous. "Word has reached me," Jack Warner memoed him during the filming of *The Big Sleep*, "that you are having fun on the set. This must stop."

Like McCarey and La Cava, Hawks was an improviser by inclination. But unlike them—probably because of his early tenure as a screenwriter—he generally prepared a complete script beforehand, and with great care. Although he collaborated on these scripts, he never took a writing credit. If he had, he later said, he'd never have gotten all the best writers to work for him—people like Jules Furthman and William Faulkner (his two favorites) and Ben Hecht and Charles Lederer. But the "final" scripts were always rewritten, often extensively, on the set—day by day, through extended colloquies and rehearsals with the performers. Hawks, unlike Stevens, didn't use an inordinate amount of film; but he did use a lot of time on the set, running through scenes and reworking them in the morning before filming in the afternoon. "The reason he was slow," said Niven Busch, "was he didn't want to make any mistakes." And "he always knew, looking at a scene, if anything was wrong."

Though he made the remarkable *Scarface* much earlier ("my favorite film, even today," he said toward the end of his life), it's in the late thirties that Hawks really hits his stride. This period—beginning with Frances Farmer and going through three sensational Cary Grant films in a row (*Bringing Up Baby, Only Angels Have Wings, His Girl Friday*)—seems to have consolidated his special relation with his actors. There is a feeling of spontaneity in *Only Angels Have Wings*—the first unmistakable "Hawks family group"—that is never so clear in his earlier films, even the ones, like *The Dawn Patrol* (1930) and *The Road to Glory* (1936), that have nearly identical situations. The experiences with Farmer and Grant and Russell, in succession more or less, seem to have made a turning point for him, showing how far he could go both in bringing a talented actor out and in shaping the movie character around him. In any case, these are the pictures and performances that most clearly anticipate the great Hawks comedies of the forties and beyond.

The Hawks film offers the same sort of casual behavioralism that you find in McCarey and (sometimes) Capra. But not even McCarey ever made a film as relaxed and meandering in its overall style as *To Have and Have Not*. Hawks really went farther in the improvisatory style than almost anyone else, especially in the capturing of a certain conversational sound—almost a drone, uninsistent but resistless. Hawks people talk *at* as well as to each other; often they just talk, interrupting, talking at once, cutting in or breaking off or going unflappably on. This was one important way scenes got rewritten on the set—to accommodate these real-life sounds, the obliqueness and overlap and even confusion, to a degree that no writers working beforehand ever could. Hawks called it "three-cushion dialogue," and he offered it in many different modes and styles, different pitches and tempos and orchestra sizes: from the machine-gun snap of *His Girl Friday* to the drawling sotto voce of *To Have and Have Not*, from the one-on-one encounters of *The Big Sleep* to the team sounds of *Only Angels Have Wings* and *The Thing* and others. There is even a conversational death—in *Air Force* (1943), with the captain (John Ridgely), out of his head, imagining he is giving orders for a takeoff, surrounded at bedside by the men of his squadron, who chat him gently into the beyond. The scene is effective partly because Hawks has already made that sound of chat—of these interacting voices, a sustaining sound, even a life-giving one—so central to the movie.

And that is of course exactly the sort of thing he does that sets his work apart from the other improvisers. He evokes the real sound and look of things, in a way that emphasizes everything most casual and spontaneous—and then he ritualizes it. Whether it's Bogart pulling his ear, or Cary Grant or Lauren Bacall passing through a crowded barroom, or Frances Farmer revolving her gum in her mouth, or John Wayne striding through a cattle herd—such images have a gravity and momentousness, an independent sort of interest, that they don't get from other filmmakers. They are also closer to being devoid of meaning, at least in the usual way. McCarey's casualness is comic, Capra's is likely to be charming; in any case, the randomness turns out to have some point or function of a rather easily nameable kind. Not so with Hawks.

Take the operation scene in *To Have and Have Not*, in which Harry (Bogart), at Frenchy's pleading, performs a makeshift surgery on the wounded de Bursac (Walter Molnar). The scene is long, portentous, and thickly detailed. But it's hard to tell *why* it is any of these things, or even why it holds our interest as much as it does. It's supposed to be dangerous for all involved, this operation (de Bursac is a fugitive); but that is more something asserted than dramatized by the scene itself (someone might come in?). The operation itself, inevitably, is unshown, taking place well below the frame line. And as movie operations go, it's a minor one: removing a bullet from a man's shoulder. The man in question is still a rather dim and faceless figure at this point in the narrative (his principal scene with Bogart is the postoperative one). And most surprising of all, everything goes perfectly smoothly, without a hitch. Practically the only interruption in the placid course of things is a moment when Marie, who is assisting Harry in the operation, gets a chance to express her animus against Mme de Bursac, who faints at the first incision: Marie fans ether fumes in her direction.

And what's astonishing is how absorbing it all is. Because by this time in the film—well into it—we're accustomed to watching these scenes of almost pure "behaving," with occasional incidental pleasures like the ether-fume gag. Now, as the operation proceeds, the patient also faints. "He's out too," announces Bogart, and refers to the prone, unconscious woman on the floor beside them (no time to pick her up) as "Nursie." And the satisfaction of the scene is of course in just this sort of authority—the competence of the two stars as compared with the incompetence of the two "fainters." We like to be around this competence—as Hawks knows—even if we don't know exactly what's going on all the time, or can't really see it (the operation), or don't even particularly care. Hawks makes scenes out of "real" behavior, but it's the real behavior of *stars*. He knows that a triumphant personal style is something self-justifying—that it can make considerations like logic and motivation, narrative sense or dramatic point, seem almost unimportant. He not only knows it, he seems determined to prove it—what Godard calls his "taste for analysis."

From the forties on, this master of all the genres begins to experiment with the limits of those genres, to make recognizably and even eccentrically "Hawksian" films out of them. He likes to take the big moment and deflate it, take the surefire effect and make it chancy. It's as if he's trying to get at the essence of movie excitement—"fixing its basic laws" (Godard)—by stripping away everything inessential. Increasingly, for example, there's near-perversity in his relation to conventional narrative. And in his interviews this hostility to "story" comes up almost obsessively. There are only so many of them, he says. About twelve, in fact. You can't keep telling them over. Nobody really cared about the story of *To Have and Have Not*. Nobody really understood the story of *The Big Sleep*. And what does it matter, anyway? What matters is good *scenes*—as many of them as you can manage. If you have to do the others—for the sake of that "story" again—all you can do is try not to "annoy" the audience too much with them. "We had to have a plot," he said later about *To Have and Have Not*, "but it was just an excuse for some scenes." A case in point: "Out of the wounded man, we got a marvelous scene about one girl fainting and the other girl fanning ether fumes on her." And what made *The Big Sleep* so special, he claimed in 1962, was that "we decided we were going to make every scene we made have something in it that would be fun."

To Have and Have Not was an obvious imitation of *Casablanca*, the Bogart blockbuster of the year before, not only in story and situations (Bogart, after refusing at first, aids a Resistance hero and his wife) but in details as well: the exotic locale (Morocco into Martinique), the international saloon the hero lives in (Rick's into Frenchy's), the sympathetic piano player (Dooley Wilson into Hoagy Carmichael), the police raid at the beginning (Captain Renault into Captain Renard), and so on. Such spinoffs weren't uncommon at the time, certainly not at Warner Brothers. But the imitation in this case is also a devastating one. *To Have and Have Not* is like a common-sense version of *Casablanca*—and an implicit critique of its pretensions. Everything in the earlier film that was the least bit pious or inflated or grandiloquent (all-but-inevitable characteristics of the wartime thriller)—the patriotism, the tragic romanticism, the hero's moral conflict—is cut carefully, scrupulously down to size. The romantic made prosaic. Instead of Bogart's Rick, mysterious boss of a glamorous café and gambling casino, Hawks gives us Harry, owner of a shabby fishing boat that hires out to tourists. While "everyone goes to Rick's"—the place always crowded and humming with exotic and soigné types—Harry gets exactly one unappetizing customer, a porcine, complaining American. We see Rick establish his authority in the opening scenes—barring an arrogant German aristocrat from the gambling tables, refusing to drink with the women customers ("Madame, he never drinks with customers. Never. I have never seen him.") in spite of their importunings, and so on. And we see Harry *trying* to establish his—arguing with the American over an unpaid bill for the fishing trip, including a tackle that got lost at sea. And where Rick has a background (before his present cynical phase) of fighting for the "lost causes" of democracy and antifascism in Spain and Ethiopia, Harry, it seems, has just enough political savvy to explain to Marie (who has even less) who the Free French are—although she is clearly more interested in cadging a drink than in hearing about it. When people ask Rick to join the fight for freedom again, his reply is characteristically hyperbolic: "I stick my neck out for nobody," he declares. Harry, to the same appeal: "Boys, don't make me feel bad. I tell yuh true, I can't do it." Rick is torn by an agonizing conflict between love and duty, but there is no such problem for Harry. Nor could there be in a Hawks movie, which makes us feel—sensibly enough—that you could never get a terrific girl like that if you were a fink or a coward. And though Rick, by his own account, is "no good at being noble," he finally comes to see that the struggle against fascism must outweigh everything else and "that the problems of three little people don't amount to a hill o' beans in this crazy world." "Someday," he tells Ilsa helpfully, as he bids her goodbye, she'll "understand that." At the parallel moment in *To Have and Have Not*—as Harry prepares to ship off with the de Bursacs and Marie on a dangerous mission to Devil's Island—Frenchy asks him why he is "doing this." Harry laughs. "Well, I don't know," he says. "Maybe because I like you"—i.e., Frenchy—"and maybe because I don't like them"—i.e., the Vichy police and their henchmen. The "three little people" in a Hawks film, far from not mattering, are almost the only things that do. It's precisely because of Frenchy and Marie—who *both* got Eddie's bee questions right—that Harry is converted to the Free French cause. A conversion so uninflected as to be almost unnoticeable when it comes. No wonder. Harry is converted from neutrality but not from skepticism about big words and big causes. His final choice is merely another expression of that skepticism, of his remorselessly common-sense nature. It's not Vichy or fascism he's come to hate, but Captain Renard. "Pickin' on a poor old rummy that never— . . . Slappin' girls around!" That kind of thing really drives him crazy.

Hawks, like Harry, is radically common-sensible, committed to the plainest, most sensible, most *personal* view of things. He's the opposite of Frank Capra: he *doesn't* believe in belief. That's why Hawks feels so bound up with what we specially like about "movies": the unpretentiousness, the feeling of rough honesty, the conjunction of commonness and magic, the repetitions and deep, instinctive ritualism, the commitment to personalities—all functions in one way or another of their skeptical, reductive, anarchic inspiration. And Hawks represents this Hollywood genius in almost its purest form. And its most unregenerate. Unlike George Stevens or the moguls, he had no pillar-of-the-community impulse. That's why he often went too far for official Hollywood—in *Scarface*, for example, where the imagination of anarchy was almost *too* complete. Other comic filmmakers, like Capra and even McCarey, were more afraid of such experiences, just as they were afraid of disbelief itself. Hawks and his characters thrive on them. *His Girl Friday* is not only the most unapologetic of tough comedies—it's also the most exhilarated.

But Hawks also reflects the madness of this common sense. Just the problem with the "sensible" view of things: it's often the most deeply crazy. So it is with Hawks, particularly in his war films—which are also exhilarated. Hawks heroes don't kill or die in battle with any high-flown rationalizations or invocations of principle to spur them on: they do it all unquestioningly. And the fact that they do—that ordinary men will obey these orders to kill each other without ever raising a difficulty about them—moves him not to rage or incredulity but to admiration. As it did (and does) large parts of his "sensible" audience. "They're stout fellows, aren't they?" says Major Brand (Neil Hamilton) in *The Dawn Patrol*, choking with emotion. "They just say 'Righto!' and go out and do it." Just like the pilots of Baranca in *Only Angels Have Wings*. It's peacetime in this film, but it's also business: the establishment of an air transport line in the remote Andes. Whether that business might be finally worth all the lives he's expending to build it is something that boss Cary Grant is only briefly troubled by: he's running an airline, he says, "and I'm not running it any different from anyone *I* ever flew for." And although he deals briskly with doubts, still he suffers—more than you'd think, really. It was a familiar movie dilemma. The movies were always urging audiences to consider their poor oppressors (you think it's *easy* to be an executioner? day after day after day?).

Hawks named Lubitsch, McCarey, and Ford as his three favorite directors. Joseph McBride asked him which of Lubitsch's films he had "studied" or been most influenced by. Hawks replied:

> I studied them all. . . . We became very good friends. . . . He was quite a character. When he saw *Sergeant York*, he said, "Howard, how can any man in his right mind make two or three reels of a picture about a man shooting a gun?" I said, "I don't know, Ernst. How the hell can a man in his right mind make two or three reels of people coming in and out of doorways?"

It's amusing to imagine Lubitsch sitting through *Sergeant York* (1941)—a solemn and pious Gary Cooper film about a religious pacifist during the First World War who saw the light, joined the army, and ended up killing more people than anyone else: an immensely popular movie, said to be influential in preparing American audiences for the next war. There seems no way Lubitsch could have confronted such a character or experience without registering the lunacy and horror. We would know that, I think, even if he hadn't made *The Man I Killed* in 1932. But since he did, we can compare it to Hawks's *The Road to Glory* in 1936. In both films Lionel Barrymore plays a soldier's father. But where in the Lubitsch film he reviles himself for cheering his son on to the war that took his life, in the Hawks film he takes him by the hand (the son has been blinded) and leads him there himself, proudly. So that they can die together in the front lines, taking a few more of the enemy with them.*

"I don't give a goddamn for taking sides," Hawks replied when asked if his projected film about the Vietnam War (never made) would do so. "I've *never* made a statement," he said—only "entertainment." And almost certainly he

---

* What makes it even more obscene is that *The Road to Glory* was based on, and even used extensive footage from, a 1931 French film, Raymond Bernard's *Les Croix de Bois*, that was one of the most harrowing and uncompromising antiwar films ever made. It was never released in the U.S.

believed that. But then he was much more of an aesthete than Lubitsch ever was or could be. And he loved the masculine heroics of films like this—all that showy stoicism and *Boy's Life* posturing about danger and death. And the essential emptiness of it all (at least in his version of it)—the fact, as his films register it, that it's really all for nothing—only adds to the thrill. All those fliers in *The Dawn Patrol*, for example, saluting and drinking to their enemy, both before and during the kill, even embracing him if they can get close enough: a *real* triumph of form over reality, style over content. Hawks's militarism is mostly a function of his love of ritual, and especially of rituals between men. And it's partly a miscalculation—like his aversion to displays of feeling, which so often results in displays of nondisplay (as in the famous "Who's Joe?" sequence of *Only Angels Have Wings:* mourning by ostentatious forgetting).

And finally he felt the strain of it. His questioning, skeptical side recoiled. He was drawn to these heroics, and he always would be, but he was also uncomfortable with them—more and more so as time went on. He didn't really *like* all that killing and dying. He decided later on that he had nearly "messed up" (as he put it) *The Dawn Patrol* that way, "and I didn't want to monkey with that again." And so as movies in the wartime years grew more militarist, the Hawks film grew rather less so. One of the most interesting things about *To Have and Have Not* is the way Hawks on the set consistently modified the patriotism and bloody-mindedness of Faulkner's screenplay. (Faulkner also co-wrote *The Road to Glory*.) The way Hawks changed the script's ending, for example. Faulkner had written a concluding scene in which Harry, before leaving on his mission to Devil's Island, delivers a short, stern lecture to Frenchy, rebuking him for his squeamishness. ("It's time you fellows started on the offensive, Frenchy. No fooling.") Harry and the others depart, and Frenchy climbs the stairs "to do what he has to do"—i.e., gun down a room full of imprisoned Vichyites. (Harry has made this killing necessary by deliberately telling the Vichyites about the Devil's Island expedition.) While Cricket (Hoagy Carmichael) and the band play extra loudly to drown out the gunfire. But in the ending that Hawks filmed, Cricket plays not for a patriotic killing—that whole incident is omitted—but as an accompaniment to Marie's happiness, as she goes hip-switching up to Harry and out the swinging doors to their new life, with Eddie doing a jig behind them and bringing the bags. It's Hawks's idea of doing what you have to do: bringing your friends.

In *Red River* (1948), Hawks's first great western, nearly the whole movie—as well as the laws of its genre—has led us to expect a confrontation and shoot-out at the end between Dunson (John Wayne) and Matt (Montgomery Clift). Matt has responded to Dunson's tyranny on the cattle drive by finally taking over both the herds and the men and pushing on to Abilene. Dunson has been left behind, but for the last third of the movie he is in pursuit, with every man on the drive worried about his catching up with them, but above all with Matt, whom he has vowed to kill. And from the adroit way that Hawks builds to this climax—the showdown in Abilene—there can be no doubt that he relishes the prospect, or that he means us to. There is always an element of thrill to these ritual masculine standoffs in a Hawks film—something almost erotic.

But when Dunson does catch up with them—striding through the cows and down the main street—Matt refuses to draw his gun. So they have a fist fight instead. But the heroine, Tess Millay (Joanne Dru), breaks *that* up by waving a gun at them and telling them, in effect, to be sensible. More than that, she is

John Wayne and Robert Mitchum shooting up the local church in El Dorado.

mad—she says so repeatedly. And she is mad because she's had just the impression the movie has contrived to give to the rest of us—that one of them might get killed. But she was taken in, as she now sees: "Everyone can see you two love each other." She is also, and primarily, relieved—like the audience by now, and like Hawks himself. "I certainly would have hated to kill one of them," he later conceded. "It frustrates me to start killing people off for no reason at all," and especially at the end of a movie. But "no reason at all" would be every reason in the world in a conventional western. What else have we been waiting for? And yet in fact Tess Millay is right, as we are reminded that we know. *Sensible* people don't kill or maim each other for revenge or honor or empty matters of pride—especially if they are friends. Hawks may love these confrontations, and he may know (no one better) how to convey their excitement; but he is finally too sensible, *really* too sensible, to follow through. And the surge of good feeling that now invades the film turns out to have been waiting in it all along, transforming even what's gone before, making those earlier excitements seem almost dim by comparison. It's this final powerful realization that makes the movie feel so distinctively Hawksian in the end. A *sensible* western . . .

Howard Hawks approached [Robert Mitchum] about costarring with John Wayne in El Dorado. . . . *[Mitchum] inquired what the story was. "Story? There's no story," he later claimed Hawks replied. "You and Duke play two old cowboys." Intrigued, Mitchum accepted. "He was right. There was no story. It was all character development. Hawks would stand there and stand there just before a shot. The crew would say, 'Shhhhh! He's writing.' Once he stood there for so long I thought he was going to fall asleep on his feet. Finally he said, 'That's all for today.' He had a mystique about him."*
    —GEORGE EELS, *Robert Mitchum*

AND THERE were more to come: his last two comic masterpieces, *Rio Bravo* (1959) and *El Dorado* (1967), arguably his two finest films, certainly his most original and eccentric. Hawks's overall career was long, prolific, and uneven. There were stretches—the late thirties, the mid- to late forties—when he seemed hardly able to put a foot wrong, producing one extraordinary (and commercially successful) genre film after another. But there were a lot of misfires, too. And the more "Hawksian" his successful films became, the more insistent and even grotesque were the failures surrounding them: the two Bogart-Bacall films and *Red River* followed by *I Was a Male War Bride* (1949); *Rio Bravo* followed by *Hatari!* (1962), not to mention *Man's Favorite Sport?* (1963) and *Red Line 7000* (1965); *El Dorado* followed by *Rio Lobo* (1970), his fortieth and final feature film. Hawks thought at times that he was getting a better grasp of what he was doing ("Sometimes it takes you a little while to realize what you did unconsciously, and then you can begin to do it purposely"), but he never really gained the control he wanted from film to film. That failure has something to do with the ritualized, even totemic quality of the films. For all his skepticism, he also knew—and felt—that he was dealing with magic. If something worked, you repeated it—*many* times—like casting a spell.*

It was in the fifties that he first wondered if the magic hadn't entirely deserted him. His output in that troubled movie decade, when both the genres and the studios themselves seemed imperiled, covered the usual (for him) mix and range—a western (*The Big Sky,* 1952), a crazy comedy (*Monkey Business,* 1952), a musical (*Gentlemen Prefer Blondes,* 1953)—but without the same assurance, and culminating in a CinemaScope historical spectacle, a contemporary genre that had been created more by Hollywood panic than by audience demand: *Land of the Pharaohs* (1955), about the building of the pyramids (Faulkner co-wrote the screenplay), and a terrible flop. Hawks then decided it was time to lie low for a while and to take stock of what he was doing. It was three years—an unprecedented inactivity for him—before he made another movie. He used the time, he said, to think about "how we used to make pictures, and how we were making them now, and I reviewed a lot of pictures that I had liked. Today they want you to stick to a script. . . . So I determined to go back and try to get a little of the spirit we used to make pictures with. . . ." The result was *Rio Bravo,* and it was even a big box-office hit. And then eight years (and three problematic films) later, when the western he had planned on making ("I bought a story"—Harry Brown's novel *The Stars in Their Courses*—"that was a Greek tragedy where everybody got killed") just wasn't working out at all, he decided to go back and do another version of *Rio Bravo* instead, calling it *El Dorado.* Why not? He had "enough good notes" from that earlier movie, he said, to make a whole other one.

In both films, both in Technicolor, four lawmen are holed up in the town jail, defending their lives and their prisoner from his friends' attempts to set him loose. The four men are an experienced gunfighter (John Wayne in both films), a drunken ex-gunfighter who has to rehabilitate himself in the course of the siege (Dean Martin in the first film, Robert Mitchum in the second), a tetchy old man (Walter Brennan, then Arthur Hunnicutt), and a feisty kid from out of town

---

*But you'd have to look hard in other filmmakers to find an equivalent to Hawks' repetitions in their insistency and frequency. He called it stealing from himself. He repeats not only situations and characters but lines and jokes and details, over and over again. There are several versions of Bacall's "It's even better when you help" moment: Montgomery Clift has one in *Red River,* Angie Dickinson another in *Rio Bravo.* Even the hayloft scene from *The Outlaw* (1940)—which Hawks co-wrote with Jules Furthman, before Howard Hughes took over the direction—turns up thirty years later in *El Dorado,* and in detail. Not only does the girl in each film prowl around the barn with a rifle, and the boy disarm and sit on top of her, but both girls are named McDonald, and both boys tell her to stop struggling or she'll lose her clothes—and so on.

(Ricky Nelson, then James Caan). There is also a "supportive" woman (Angie Dickinson, Charlene Holt), but she isn't inside the jail.

It's a surefire situation. But then Hawks does with it just what he did to the dramatics of *Casablanca:* makes it prosaic, toning it down rather than hyping it up. *Rio Bravo* is the most minimalist of all his films in everything but its length (141 minutes)—a kind of chamber western, without landscapes or wide open spaces, taking place almost entirely in small rooms, in the jail or the hotel or on the main street between. Dude (Martin) has turned into the town drunk, but after being humiliated by the saloon crowd (someone tosses a dollar into the cuspidor for him) and getting into a fight with his best friend, Sheriff John T. Chance (John Wayne)—all of this in the film's first scene—he gives up drinking. And the hard part begins. "You don't look so good," says Wayne, almost with surprise. "I *feel* worse," growls Martin, saying it as if he were tearing the line from his bowels. He is Chance's deputy again, like old times. And he sits in the jail—he and Stumpy (Walter Brennan) are the sheriff's men, guarding the prisoner—and pounds on his leg: there doesn't seem to be any feeling left in it. Neither of his friends knows quite what to do for him at such moments. As Chance says, he'll just have to sweat it out. But then Dude redeems himself spectacularly when he and Chance follow a killer on the run into the enemy's saloon. Dude, in spite of the sheriff's misgivings about it, wants to handle the front door: "I *been* goin' in the back door," he explains. "They wouldn't let me in the front." They will now, says Chance, after they've nailed their man and lined up and disarmed all the rest—and both of them trying not to smile too much. But redemption is one thing; still not being able to roll a cigarette because your hands shake too much (Dude's condition in the next scene) is another. "Think I could get one out of a whole pack!" But he can't, and he tries repeatedly.

He can't shave himself, either, because of that hand. So Chance's girlfriend, Feathers (Angie Dickinson), shaves him in her hotel room. We get to watch that, too. Just as we watch the endless comings and goings from the hotel (Chance sleeps there) to the jailhouse and back again. And they have to be careful when they get up to the front of the jail to yell, or else Stumpy, sitting in back with the prisoner, will shoot. He even shoots the door out once, because Dude didn't yell—then they have to fix the door. They also have to be sure to have enough beer and coffee—and blankets and matches and tobacco. "Did you get Stumpy his coffee?" says Chance. "Can I make you some coffee," says Feathers at the hotel, "or fix you a nice hot bath?" And sometimes these matters become truly urgent—like the time when Dude comes back after a brawl in a horse barn. Of *course* he'll take a bath—didn't he *say* he would? "Why, Dude," says Stumpy, "I never had no idea you wouldn't—I was just wonderin' when."

They are in danger, of course; that's what draws them together and keeps the movie going. But the danger gets engulfed by these details as both the movie and the siege go on. And that danger is really more discussed than shown. No one ever storms the jail or even threatens to. The main problem, we're told, is that the bad guys, Burdett and his gang, have the town sealed up. Eventually the kid, Colorado (Ricky Nelson), joins the sheriff's side—and they sit around the jail and sing: "Better'n bein' on the street and gettin' shot at," as Stumpy, who plays the harmonica, points out. It's then that it occurs to them that they really are safe in the jailhouse, after all—if they can only hold out three or four more days until the marshal arrives. But then Dude goes out and gets kidnapped, and so they have to get up the next morning and get him back. This means a gunfight with the Burdetts, and the canny use of some dynamite to blow up their headquarters in the course of it. But the sheriff and his friends attend even this big event—the obligatory showdown at the end—imposing their style on it like picnickers spreading their blankets, bickering and chatting and bantering and joking as they fire and miss, then fire and don't miss, as they reload and change their positions and cover each other and fire again, as Stumpy throws dynamite sticks and Chance detonates them with his gun. ("Throw it *farther* this time!" "There you go again, never *can* satisfy you!") And they win of course. The next day, we're told, there "isn't a Burdett man left in town." Not that we'd notice the difference—we hardly saw them when they were there.

But this movie takes you by surprise as it meanders along. It's a daring, moving, and utterly original piece of filmmaking—composed of scenes whose primary effect is to give the feeling of an almost astonishing depth—in spite of what they seem to be about or not about otherwise. *Rio Bravo* fulfills the Hawksian experiment that *To Have and Have Not* seemed most strikingly to begin: seeing how far you can defuse the conventional effects and moments. *All* the scenes of *Rio Bravo* are scenes of pure behaving, and dependent on the authority of its stars—most of all on John Wayne, who defines the personal style of both *Rio Bravo* and *El Dorado.*

Hawks said that Wayne had "more force, more power than anyone else on the screen." (That was one reason, according to him, that *Hatari!* didn't work: because the other actors in that film couldn't stand up to him, as Martin and Mitchum and Dickinson *could.*) Wayne plays the main honcho in both *Rio Bravo* and *El Dorado.* "Do I get to play the drunk this time?" he asked Hawks about the latter film. No: he is still the leader and the group's mainstay—it's almost inconceivable that he should be anything else. But his authority isn't like Bogart's, whose serenity and competence, star magnitude in action, offer such a satisfying if easy contrast to the maladroits and fainters around him. But in these westerns, anybody might faint. And the people in them are neither serene nor always quite competent. Their star quality hasn't such a conventional, daydream source as in earlier Hawks films. And the hieratic note has all but disappeared.

Forceful Wayne may be, but he has almost no talent for one-upmanship, as Bogart does. When the Wayne hero gets the last word, it's usually because he's been maneuvered into it, because the other person (the fool) hasn't left him anything else to say. Like James Caan in *El Dorado* trying to explain why he wants to come with Wayne into the dangerous town ahead: "You saved my life two times," he says. "But I'm gonna be too busy to keep *doing* that!" says Wayne, exasperatedly. Later on, Caan (he is a very bad shot) is trying to turn a miss with his shotgun into a hit—of some kind. "He was limping when he left," he says hopefully of the "victim." "He was limping when he got here!" cries Wayne. He always seems surprised by such easy verbal triumphs (unlike Bogart, who seems almost unsurprisable), and perplexed. That perplexity, in fact, is engraved on his face: his eloquent "what the hell is going on *here?*" look. He turns it on everyone: looking up smilingly at newcomers to town, watching Caan mix his horrendous antidrunk medicine, listening to Angie Dickinson explain her feelings. He's this big, badly aging man with this unshakable boyish puzzlement: he'll never lose it and he's learned to live with it—gruffly. Far from having the Gary Cooper hero's sort of composure, Wayne is pettish and fretful and irritable. And he worries a lot about his friend Dude—in a way that Wayne in *Rio Bravo* makes almost painfully palpable. Not so much in words or even actions as in all those looks he directs at him—when Dude is pounding on his leg or trying to roll a cigarette or losing his temper with Stumpy, Wayne is noticeably in the background, looking. In the foreground, though, he's likely to be stern. "We been pampering you too much," he says after Dude has thrown another tantrum over Stumpy's garrulousness. And when Dude hits him (the second time) and then says he's sorry: "*Sorry* don't get it done, Dude," says Wayne, solemnly. But friendship does, it seems: he never does hit him back, in spite of the provocation and challenge.

Our sense of all the relations in this film accumulates through just such details. Slowly, imperceptibly, undramatically, we get to be inside all these motions and inflections of friendship. Not the friendships of the Dawn Patrols or the flyers of Baranca ("ravished with each other's *soigné*," as Manny Farber puts it) but friendship without postures or gestures or attitudes—the friendship of jokes and irritations and impossible behavior. Wayne's concern for Martin becomes powerfully moving. And the heroine's falling in love with Wayne seems another expression of this concern, which the film develops like a passion. "John T. for trouble," she says, knowing what she's in for. But then everyone we care about in this film is trouble for everyone else. That's finally the way it understands friendship. A nuisance that makes people glamorous.

El Dorado is a tougher, harder-edged film. It's also more eventful and various (although the jailhouse siege is the center of the movie again, it takes up only about half its length), with funnier lines, a more elaborate plot, and more colorful situations. Instead of the bad guys being dim and nearly faceless as they are in *Rio Bravo*, they are fully and interestingly characterized—especially in the person of Christopher George's hired gun, a figure who is both sinister and sympathetic. And although the central four—or five, including the helpful girl—reappear, the point about them seems different. The tone is lighter, the pace is brisker, and everything seems more professionally distanced than before.

And more familiar, too, in a way. The town this time is like a Wild West version of Chicago ("There's somebody out there with a *gun!*" "Everybody in *town's* got a gun!"). It's a tough-comedy tone. Mississippi (James Caan) can't shoot, so Cole (Wayne) gets him a sawed-off shotgun guaranteed to hit anything. "The fella who had it before," explains Swede, the gunsmith (Olaf Wieghorst), "couldn't see too good. He jus' shoot where he hear somebody talk." The heroes shoot up a church. They have a good excuse for doing so (a killer loose inside), but the destruction is shown in lascivious detail. And J.P. (Mitchum) shoots up a piano (a killer behind it). Later on, when we hear piano music offscreen, it turns out to be the same one. They are stalking the outside of the saloon, a prelude to the final shoot-out. "Joe never was much good on that piano, was he?" says J.P. "No, and shootin' them strings out didn't help much neither," says Bull (Arthur Hunnicutt). It's not just the bad sounds in this picture: there are more bad tastes (Mississippi's antidrunk concoction) and bad smells (the bath routine is now *very* extended) than in the earlier film, and *many* more jokes about physical pain. "This may hurt," says the oily young doctor (Anthony Rogers). "It did," says Wayne—and you believe him.

Pain is inescapable in this film. Where Dean Martin's alcoholism had seemed as much a moral condition as a physical one (his "I *feel* worse" evoking every kind of discomfort, including self-loathing), Mitchum's just *hurts*, so much so that it's almost hard to watch when he has one of his cramps, crumpling and doubling up nearly to the ground. But where Mitchum—characteristically—folds inward, Wayne arches up and backwards and falls off his horse, hitting the ground with sickening impact. *His* problem is an old bullet wound that has lodged against his spine. And when the spasm hits him, he is paralyzed on one side, like a stroke victim. Though he eventually comes round—often too late. There are no overt references to getting old anywhere in the film, but there hardly needs to be. (There are none in Beckett's *Happy Days*, either.) *El Dorado* is unflinching in its way—relentlessly, even triumphantly tough-minded. It may be, in fact, the funniest movie ever made about the "joke" of old age and dying.

So that finally it's a much darker movie than *Rio Bravo*—even literally so. Once the jailhouse siege begins, it all seems to take place at night, under or near yellow lamplight. The "open spaces" in this film are black and encircling and right next to you—appropriate to James Caan's frequent allusions (by way of the Poe poem he keeps reciting) to "the valley of the shadow." And the emphasis of most of the action and humor is on mortality and impairment. Mississippi is young, but he can't shoot. He has a big gun, but it goes off indiscriminately (Hawks's joke about youth). Bull is old, and he uses a bow and arrow. J.P. has the shakes and the cramps, and Cole has his stroke problem. In addition to all this, they both get shot in the leg at different times, making them cripples as well. None of this makes them nicer, either. They are much more violent than their counterparts in *Rio Bravo*, and much less controlled, given to sudden murderous outbursts of rage at their enemies. And when they have control, they may use it to cheat, as Cole does when he gets the drop on Nelse McLeod (George) only by tricking him. "You didn't give me any chance at all, did you?" says McLeod as he lies dying. "You're too good to give a chance to," says Cole. They are becoming more and more—as they advance into "the valley of the shadow"—like that former shotgun owner who "couldn't see too good," who "jus' shoot where he hear somebody talk." And as we see them in the final shot of the film, they are walking down main street—the town brought to order at last—on their crutches.

What keeps these two wrecks—and the movie as well—going, along with their variously enfeebled friends, is a common comic style, a kind of disaster humor, a constant, affectionate sick-joking, different in substance and feeling from the banter of *Rio Bravo*. *El Dorado* is a grimmer film—grisly, queasily comic, almost viscerally painful at times, full of dark good humor. An unsettling combination of despair and high spirits, but with the same powerful evocation of friendship as before, the same ill-assorted but deeply yoked group at its center. What Hawks particularly liked about the movie, he later asserted, was that it began "tragically"—with the death of a boy (the only thing he retained, he said, from the original novel)—and then turned into clowning and joking. But in a way everything that's most serious in the work of Howard Hawks finally turns into joking. He is a transcendent—in every sense of the word—comic artist. And the whole force of his work gathers in this final great film. To Hawks, joking is no light matter. It's one of the most important things people can do for each other.

Charles Boyer finds himself in the wrong bedroom—or is he? Before he can decide, Helen Walker screams—in Lubitsch's Cluny Brown.

Lubitsch in the Forties

In years to come, the fact that Hollywood could convert part of a world crisis into such a cops and robbers charade will certainly be regarded as a remarkable phenomenon. —*Life* magazine's review of *To Be or Not To Be*

To say it is callous and macabre is understating the case. . . . — BOSLEY CROWTHER, in the New York *Times* review of the same film

It is true that I have tried to break away from the traditional moving picture formula. I was tired of the two established, recognized recipes: drama with comedy relief and comedy with dramatic relief. I had made up my mind to make a picture with no attempt to relieve anybody from anything at any time. — ERNST LUBITSCH, in the New York *Times*, March 29, 1942

IN 1939 Lubitsch made his second attempt to form an independent production company, this time with mini-mogul Sol Lesser. They signed an agreement with United Artists to deliver two pictures a year. The first of these was *That Uncertain Feeling* (1941), a Park Avenue marriage comedy with a screenplay by Donald Ogden Stewart, starring Merle Oberon, Melvyn Douglas, and Burgess Meredith. It was not only Lubitsch's first independent production but his first film with a contemporary American setting. (It was his last as well.) It should have been a breakthrough, but it was a disappointment. Especially after the two brilliant and adventurous films that he had just done at MGM, *Ninotchka* and *The Shop Around the Corner*. In some ways *That Uncertain Feeling* seems almost the least of Lubitsch's American films. It's deft and proficient and often quite funny (there's a wonderful running joke about the husband poking the wife in the stomach and saying "Keeks!" under the mistaken impression that she likes it). But the whole thing has a kind of sit-com tepidity: Lubitsch has done all this before—all too often, it seems. (It's a remake in some respects of his silent *Kiss*

Me Again in 1925, and both films are drawn from the Sardou play *Divorçons.*)
And the attempted satire of psychiatry and modern art ("modernistic sacred
cows," as Lubitsch called them) showed the same complacent ignorance of these
subjects that almost every Hollywood movie of the time did.

Even Lubitsch seems to have felt he was marking time with this project. His
interviews during the shooting sound defensive even before the fact. He complains of the "sterility of the story market" in Hollywood. So why shouldn't he
do a remake? On the other hand, it's not really a remake, since the current script
uses "only two or three situations" from the silent film—and so on. The fact is,
he didn't enjoy being an "independent." Sol Lesser said in 1976 (in a letter to
Lubitsch scholars Barry Sabath and Robert Carringer) that Lubitsch had missed
the big studios too much—"contact with the stars and other professionals he
associated with at MGM." In any case, Lesser and he agreed to dissolve their
partnership. And Lubitsch promptly signed a three-year contract with 20th Century–Fox. Back to the studio. But in the meantime *That Uncertain Feeling*
opened (April 1941) to indifferent notices and business. And Lubitsch still had
an unfulfilled commitment with United Artists—that second picture agreed to
in their contract.

It was, to begin with, a very personal project: the only one of his major films
that was "original" from its inception and not drawn from an existing source.
The story was credited to Melchior Lengyel ("Writing for Lubitsch," he later
said, "is just kibitzing"), as was the original story of *Ninotchka*. But *Ninotchka*
had been a studio idea, underway even before Lubitsch came on the scene. *To
Be or Not To Be* was Lubitsch's, from beginning to bitter end. It was his first
movie about the war—his first act of artistic "engagement," as it were. That's
how he meant it, at any rate, even when others were appalled by it. A comedy
about a troupe of Polish actors outwitting the Nazi command in occupied Warsaw, it drew not only on his hatred of Nazism but also on his memories of the
theater when he was a young actor in the Max Reinhardt company. To many—
including Samson Raphaelson—it seemed an unpalatable mixture. Lubitsch
had, of course (as always), wanted Raphaelson to work on the screenplay with
him. Raphaelson was otherwise committed at the time, but he was also repelled
by the project. "I didn't have it in me," he later said, "to make gags about the
Nazis in 1941." One of the first signs of the reaction to come.

And so Edwin Justus Mayer—another distinguished New York playwright
(*Children of Darkness*), who had co-written *Desire* six years before—became
Lubitsch's collaborator on the script. The leading role—of "that great, great
Polish actor Joseph Tura"—was conceived from the start as a Jack Benny role.
Benny, of course, was delighted: no director of Lubitsch's stature had ever of-
fered him a picture before (though he'd had a big hit in Warner Brothers' *Char-
ley's Aunt* the year before, his movie career was fitful, and he was mainly a radio
star), let alone written the leading part specifically for him. Miriam Hopkins,

The stage of the Theatre Polski in To Be or Not To Be. *Maria Tura (Carole Lombard) is wearing her "concentration camp gown." Joseph Tura (Jack Benny) is in his Nazi costume.*

who had been signed to co-star, as Maria Tura, the other half of "the Polish Lunts," was less happy about her role—smaller than Benny's, less important and less comic—and finally withdrew. When Carole Lombard, who had recently gone "independent" herself, heard about this event, she asked her old friend Lubitsch for the part. Lubitsch thought it would be wrong for her at first, too much a "straight woman" to the leading man. But Lombard, who had read the script and loved it, insisted. And anyway, Benny let her have top billing—once she pointed out to him, as the story goes, that "you already have all the lines." With Lombard's name added to the cast, Lubitsch had no more trouble raising the necessary money. And though there were other problems (Walter Wanger withdrew as producer and was replaced by Alexander Korda as co-producer with Lubitsch), shooting got underway in November 1941 at the Samuel Goldwyn studios. "It was the happiest experience of her career," asserts Lombard biographer Larry Swindell, "the one time, she said, when everything began right, stayed right, and ended right."

But by the time filming was completed (December 23, 1941) America was in the war. And three weeks later, Lombard herself was dead—shockingly: killed in a plane crash on a bond-selling tour. The grief over her loss was a national,

even an international, event. And under the circumstances, *To Be or Not To Be* when it finally opened (March 6, 1942) seemed like an offense: a tasteless, gaggy farce about ham actors tangling with cartoon Nazis and winning a comic-strip triumph over them at the end—at just the time when the real Nazis seemed to be winning the war in Europe too. Audiences wanted to remember Lombard, but not as the star of *this* movie—a heroine, if that's the word, who is not even notably sympathetic, a woman who (it's implied) cheats on her husband with not just one (it's implied) but several young wartime flyers. But then it's all a joke—

or is it? Like the joke of her first appearance: wanting to know if the director will let her wear this sexy silk gown she's got on for her big concentration-camp scene. And so it went. "A weird mixture," wrote the reviewer in the New York *Sun* (Eileen Creelman), "of melodrama, anti-Nazi propaganda, and low comedy. Mr. Lubitsch lays on his effects with a heavy hand, permitting his actors to indulge in the broadest of burlesques." And according to the same reviewer (and others), he'd done something even odder yet:

> Apparently bursting with indignation, he has interjected into his comedy plot scenes of the destruction of Warsaw, with ruined homes and frightened children. This is not funny, and Mr. Lubitsch treats it with due seriousness. He seems, however, to have forgotten that the introduction of such grim material destroys like a bomb any hope of comedy atmosphere. . . .

In any case, "bomb" was the appropriate word. United Artists, in tax court, wrote off the film as a "salvage operation," claiming among other things that its lighthearted treatment of Nazism made it unmarketable.

Some people liked it, of course—quite a lot. Even some reviewers, if nervously. Lubitsch would claim that it always played well with *audiences*—once they were in the theater, anyway. That was the problem. And to the end of his days he was touchy about the whole issue, particularly about the charges of callousness and insensitivity. But in some part of himself he should have been pleased—or so you hope, at least. After all, in spite of the outcry, he *had* gotten away with it.

Publicity over-rates everything. Picasso's over-rated. I'm over-rated. Even Jack Benny's over-rated.
> —GEORGE BALANCHINE, quoted by Bernard Taper,
> in *Balanchine, A Biography*

He was the greatest director in the motion picture industry. He was also very easy to work with, as he always played a scene first and just by watching him you knew exactly what to do.
> —JACK BENNY, in a 1968 letter to Herman Weinberg

All his life, Lubitsch told me, he'd wanted to be a policeman.
> —MARY LOOS, in conversation

PARTLY IT'S a comedy about the theater. But it's utterly unlike any *other* such comedy. The actors—the Theatre Polski, with their star couple, Joseph and Maria Tura—aren't even very actorish. At least not in the usual ways. They don't shout or carry on or throw tantrums; they don't orate or domineer or have hysterics when things go wrong—the way they do in *Twentieth Century,* for example. Nor do they posture or attitudinize the way they do in *The Guardsman.* (The one actor in the company who does behave this way—the Lionel Atwill character—is a dimwit and a joke to the others.) The Turas, compared with the *Guardsman* couple and all their many spin-offs, seem like fairly plain folks. Like Jack Benny and Carole Lombard, to be exact. It's just that they *happen* (part of the time, anyway) to be dressed as Hamlet and Ophelia. And except for Benny's three aborted attempts at his "To be or not to be" soliloquy, we never see them performing onstage. Mostly they seem to be backstage, in rehearsal or between acts, walking around in that familiar Lubitschean dream state. When we first see Benny in his Hamlet costume, he is at the wall phone backstage ordering a salami and cheese from the local deli. As he hangs up and walks away, his wife—as Ophelia—walks slowly, dreamily past him. "Audience is a little cold tonight," he says. "Not to me," she says—and goes raptly on.

She sits in front of her dressing-room mirror (i.e., facing the camera and us) in that same state—and talks about meeting that handsome young flyer in the second row who's been sending her flowers. While Anna, her maid (Maud Eburne), sits behind her and sews, giving her what she wants by way of answers without once looking up or varying her sardonic tone. "I love my husband dearly," says Maria to the mirror, "but he gets so unreasonable, so upset about little things." "Like the little thing in the second row," observes Anna, who—it's clear—has been through all this before. This not only gives her some license but some impatience, too, so that she finally cuts short—still without looking up—Maria's "debate" with herself: "Darling, don't waste any more time in excuses—if you want to see him, see him, while he's still young." Maria decides to see him: she sends him back a note telling him to come to her dressing room when Hamlet begins his "To be or not to be" speech. "How's it sound, Anna?" she asks. "Safe," says Anna, as she sews. And the young flyer, Lieutenant Stanislaw Sobinski (Robert Stack), turns out to be a dazzler. But not too bright: he tells about seeing her picture in the paper—she was behind a plow on a farm. "By the way, where was that?" he asks. "In the *Chronicle*," she replies. When he insists that he means the farm, she changes the subject. He's handsome, but he's also something of an intrusion, requiring her to pay more attention than she likes. She looks at him dreamily later on—he is now a frequent visitor, it seems, and she is brushing her hair in front of the mirror while he sits next to her—regarding him with real tenderness as he talks but also attending to her hair. When he suddenly asks her what they are going to "do with" her husband. She is shocked (now she *is* paying attention). They are going to "tell him," of course, persists the young man. But I love my husband, she tells him. He doesn't believe her.

But her manner with her husband is entirely different. Lubitsch offers a marvelous image of the two of them together at the beginning of the film. It's the first time we see them together, and it conditions the way we see them for the rest of the movie. Dobosh, the Theatre Polski's producer (Charles Halton), has just been chewing Maria out for her inappropriate costume. Tura in his costume, a Gestapo uniform (they are rehearsing their anti-Nazi play), saunters onto the scene, a cigarette between his fingers, and stands beside her. "What do you mean, talking to my wife like that?" he says to Dobosh, with a deceptively mild air. And as he does so, Lombard leans into him, her hand on his shoulder, her chin on her hand—and together they regard the offender in almost Olympian conjunction, she idly, he sternly. "I'm sorry," says the extinguished Dobosh, "I lost my temper"—and retires from the scene. They are a formidable couple— especially as a couple. They have a way of doing this sort of thing throughout the movie: turning and looking together when someone else speaks or challenges or threatens in some way, even though they may be quarreling—as they are at the very next moment here, and do, in their quiet way, through most of the action. But when Maria reminds Stanislaw that she is a married woman, the fact has a force and a reality that it has in almost no other Lubitsch movie.

They are both hams, of course. And in a way they pool their solipsism— looking out of a self-enclosure for two. And although their milieu is a specifically theatrical one—with quarrels about billing and worries about mood and performance and audiences—the emphasis on the characters' self-absorption is the most familiar sort of Lubitsch territory, seeming only the slightest bit heightened by the backstage setting. But there is another "setting," too: the backdrop of Nazism. And the effect of this on the familiar Lubitsch gag is more substantive. The difference between being a solipsist in Marshovia, say, or a make-believe Paris, and being one in a world of pogroms and concentration camps and the Gestapo.

So that there are times when the self-absorption of these actors seems almost a kind of sick joke. Lombard's first entrance into the movie is one breathtaking example. She wanders onto the stage during the rehearsal of the Gestapo play in her stunning white silk evening gown ("Miss Lombard's costumes by Irene"), the kind she used to pose in so much in the early thirties, clinging and backless, with a fur-trimmed hem and train. Dobosh, the director, is aghast. He's just been telling the rest of the actors that this is "a serious play, a realistic drama . . . a document of Nazi Germany." "Well, why not?" says Maria about her costume. She thinks it would be "a tremendous contrast" to the background of the concentration camp: "Think of me being flogged in the darkness—I scream and suddenly the lights go on and the audience discovers me on the floor in this gorgeous gown." "It'd get a terrific laugh," observes Greenberg (Felix Bressart) in passing. But Dobosh doesn't *want* laughs. "That a great star," he cries, "an artist, could be so inartistic! You must be out of your mind!" (This is where he gets reprimanded by Tura.)

But the point is not exactly what it first seems. Because Maria does get to wear that gown, after all—not for a play about the Gestapo (the censors prevent them from putting it on) but for the real thing—and it turns out to be entirely appropriate. She wears it to Nazi headquarters (she even goes home to change) for her rendezvous with Professor Siletsky (Stanley Ridges), the spy from London. Just as the absurd Tura ("that great, great Polish actor") not only plays a hero but gets to be one, the savior of the Polish Underground—and remains absurd. Just as Greenberg, a spear-carrier and supporting actor in the troupe, dreams of playing Shylock—and finally does. In front of an "audience" of Nazi storm troopers, who don't know that they are hearing an actor's speech or that they are providing an escort for escaping saboteurs. It seems impossible in this movie to escape the theater—even if you are dying. When Siletsky, the spy, is finally trapped and then shot down as he attempts to escape, it's on the stage of the Theatre Polski. The troupe has been pursuing him through the empty auditorium. Suddenly he is onstage in front of the curtain, pinned by the spotlight. He disappears through the curtain—and a shot rings out. The curtain rises. He is center stage—with his assassin, Sobinski, in the background. Siletsky clutches his back and falls, raising his hand and gasping out one last "Heil Hitler." His pursuers in the auditorium—professionals all—look on with awe: what a death scene!

In some ways *To Be or Not To Be*, which seemed such a formal offense at the time (and still seems so to many people today), such a hodgepodge of conflicting voices and modes—farce, thriller, propaganda film—is the most "formalist" Lubitsch film of all. It begins, in the best modernist tradition, with a deliberate confusion of appearance and reality, showing a man in a Hitler costume (Tom Dugan) standing in the midst of a Warsaw street crowd. Is this really Hitler? asks the stentorian narrator on the soundtrack. It's clear to us, of course, that it's an actor playing Hitler; but it's not at all clear whether we're to take him as that or as the real Hitler. And so on. (It turns out he is a character named Bronski playing Hitler.) On into the next scene, which we are told is Gestapo headquarters in Berlin—but turns out to be a rehearsal of the Theatre Polski's anti-Nazi play. Such confusions and manipulations of reality are much more than incidental effects; they are imbedded in the structure of the film, which is marked by doublings and triplings of events at every level. We see three samples not only of Benny's Hamlet but of Bressart's Shylock. Tura becomes "Colonel Ehrhardt," the Gestapo chief, in order to trap Siletsky. *Then* he gets to become Siletsky—in order to meet Colonel Ehrhardt. And meets "himself" again—when Ehrhardt confronts him with the murdered Siletsky's corpse.

So it is that we see Tura's impersonation of the Gestapo chief before we see Ehrhardt himself. The point is to keep Professor Siletsky, who has just come from London with a list of the Polish Underground, from getting to Ehrhardt with it. So Tura plays Ehrhardt—and the Theatre Polski "plays" Gestapo headquarters—where Siletsky, set up by Maria and then escorted by fake storm troopers, arrives bearing the fateful list. "You know, you're quite famous in London," he tells the "Colonel" (Tura in his Gestapo costume) as they sit down together in his office. "They call you 'Concentration Camp' Ehrhardt." That's right, rejoins the Colonel: "we do the concentrating and the Poles do the camping"—and they both laugh.

But then it turns out that there is a duplicate list back at Siletsky's hotel room. Tura excuses himself to confer with his colleagues in the other room—which is really the theater's balcony. They tell him to stall. He goes back to Siletsky, but he's having trouble sustaining the scene now. Siletsky is helpful: is there anything you'd like to ask me, he inquires. "Lots, lots," says the affable Colonel. "There are many, many things I want to ask you." And there is another pause. "So they call me 'Concentration Camp' Ehrhardt?" he says at length, chuckling and slapping his hands together. Is there something Siletsky wanted to ask *him*, by any chance? But there isn't. And Siletsky is already suspicious. "So they call me 'Concentration Camp' Ehrhardt?" says the Colonel, chuckling again. "Well, well . . . Excuse me a minute." And he goes out the door again. Another hurried—and unavailing—conference with the others. And he comes back: "So they really call me 'Concentration Camp' Ehrhardt?" he says as he enters. But the game is up. Siletsky pulls a gun—then makes that run through the theater that leads to his death.

The comic strategy in this scene mirrors the whole film. You probably don't laugh at "'Concentration Camp' Ehrhardt" at first; in fact, there are strong considerations to *prevent* you from laughing. And Benny's first response—which *is* funny ("the Poles do the camping") in a way—reminds you of them. But you do laugh at last, almost certainly. Benny is of course something like the all-time world master of such scenes—of this false, fussy, utterly unfelt heartiness, struggling unsuccessfully with panic. And he gives the disastrously recurring line just the right hollow, stomach-sinking cadence—"So they *call* me . . ."—making the genial chuckle that follows it, that *must* follow it, all the harder to produce—and funnier each time. But you notice, at the same time you're responding to this mastery, that the monstrous soubriquet the scene began with is being reduced to something like a token of social embarrassment. Though of course it never quite loses its monstrousness. You laugh, but you're uneasy—which makes you laugh more. It's Lubitsch's favorite kind of joke—the kind that implicates the one who laughs as well as the one who tells it.

And that unease has a marvelous, surprising, explosive resolution later on, when at last we meet the real "Concentration Camp" Ehrhardt—in the person of familiar Sig Rumann, with his furious look, his pop eyes and bulbous nose and walrus mustache, a Captain Katzenjammer type. Shouting over the phone when Tura, now disguised as Siletsky, enters the office: "Arrest him too! Whenever in doubt arrest him! How many times do I have to tell you, *arrest* him!"—then turning warmly and expansively to greet "the professor." Whose "old friend the Führer" will soon be in town, too, as it emerges when they chat. By the way, says Tura-Siletsky amiably, "you're quite famous in London. They call you 'Concentration Camp' Ehrhardt." "Oh, they *do*, do they!" Ehrhardt shouts, all but erupting with delight. They both laugh. Then it comes: "So they *call* me 'Concentration Camp' Ehrhardt?" says the Colonel—and laughs even more loudly. "I thought you'd react just that way," says Benny, in his mildest, most poisonous manner.

The point about "tastelessness" is that it's finally irresistible—drawing people like a magnet. You can't *help* but make jokes about things you shouldn't joke about. Not even Nazis can help it. It's no wonder that the Gestapo in this film is on the track of jokes—and that they execute people for telling "outrageous, supposed-to-be-funny stories about the Führer." But the trouble is, you can never tell where such investigations may lead. Hitler jokes seem to be particularly irresistible, even to Hitlerites. And even if they are as lame as the riddle we hear at the very beginning of the film: If they named a brandy after Napoleon and a herring after Bismarck, what's Hitler going to be? The answer—a piece of cheese. It first turns up in the anti-Nazi play about the Gestapo that the Theatre Polski is rehearsing. But then Ehrhardt, in his genial and expansive mood, tells it to "Siletsky." The unhappy Gestapo chief is always making these slips, and in front of the very man he presumes to be Hitler's close personal friend. It comes to him what he has done almost as soon as he starts to laugh—"Don't you think it's funny?" he says, bug-eyed with sudden terror, to the unsmiling "Siletsky."

In the play-within-the-movie, Tura playing a Gestapo commandant is trying to get a boy in a Hitler Youth uniform to answer questions about his father, who is suspected of not really *liking* the Führer. But then *anyone* might be suspected of this, as everyone in this movie knows. And in certain circles it makes conversation about the Führer very difficult. "I know you'll be delighted to see him again," says Ehrhardt to "Siletsky." "Who wouldn't?" comes the suspicious reply, causing another flutter of terror in the Colonel. A great deal is made of Hitler's being a vegetarian. And so, it develops, is Colonel Ehrhardt's orderly, Captain Schultz (Henry Victor)—who also declines when invited to drink or smoke. "*Just* like our Führer," says Tura-Siletsky admiringly. But this Schultz is a trial to his boss at times—reminding him aloud, when it turns out that they've inadvertently shot a key witness ("Why don't we look *over* people before we shoot them!" says Ehrhardt), that it was Ehrhardt himself who signed the execution order. "Oh, well, I sign so many every day," he blusters; then to "Siletsky": "You see I can't rely on my own people anymore." "Siletsky" has his own sly comment to make, once Schultz has withdrawn: "I didn't like the way

Captain Schultz shifted the responsibility back to you," he says. "Neither did I," says Ehrhardt, wiping his brow with a handkerchief. "You know, there's *always* something wrong with a man who doesn't drink, who doesn't smoke, who doesn't eat meat—" And he's done it again, as he realizes as soon as he's said it. "You mean our Führer?" says "Siletsky," coldly. But there's no way, it seems, Colonel Ehrhardt *can't* mean just that, even when he tries.

And the movie itself is in the grip of a similar compulsion, an idea with an almost embarrassed inevitability, once you've thought of it, that is—namely, Jack Benny as Hamlet. Once you've *had* that idea, you could hardly expect to escape it. And although Lubitsch handles it with his customary restraint, he's clearly aware what he's got in it: the literary-cultural equivalent of a *very* dirty joke, reductive and subversive and philistine. And it's almost enough, it seems at first, to see Benny backstage in his Hamlet costume, with his puffed sleeves and marcelled hair. But it seems daring to actually show him acting the role, even minimally. (He never gets beyond the first words of the soliloquy, of course—since this is always a signal for someone to get up and leave for his wife's dressing room.)

"Oh heavy burthen," intones the Claudius (Lionel Atwill) in his furs and crown. "I hear him coming," says the Polonius with the same elocutionary deadness. "Let's withdraw, m'Lord." And they go off into the wings, leaving the stage free for Hamlet's entrance. A pause. He comes in from the back of the stage, and walks slowly and portentously, holding an open book in front of him as if reading, to the footlights. A *long* silence—reproaching the audience even before he speaks to it. It's an extraordinary vision: an *aggrieved* Hamlet. He closes the book—with limp wrists—and looks up, pettish and wounded, in almost a trance of irritable self-love. By the time he begins the speech—whereupon the scene dissolves to his wife's dressing room—he's already "said" everything. (He performs the same scene, with lovely and subtle variations, twice more in the film.) And in some way he *is* a convincing Hamlet. Or at least we're reminded that there is nothing in the idea of Hamlet—or at any rate in the tortured romantic consciousness he's come to stand for to us—that's altogether inconsistent with Jack Benny's pursed-lips suffering, his snits and fits of pique.

"I thought you'd react just that way," says Tura-Siletsky to Ehrhardt; but in fact *we* hadn't thought so—not quite. That's one way the "Concentration Camp" Ehrhardt joke works—surprising us and persuading us at the same time. In the structure of this film, theater always precedes reality. We always see the fake, "ham" version first, then the real thing—which is always grosser and more fantastic than the prediction. Reality is more theatrical than the theater. At least in occupied Warsaw. It's the special vision of this comedy to see Nazism as a form of theater. Just as bullies—even the most laid-back ones (the "Make my day" style)—are always more theatrical than other people, always a bit too much.

And always in some way dependent on a receptive audience, as Maria reminds us in a wonderfully funny exchange with Professor Siletsky (the real one). "This lady is permitted to leave," says the professor to the armed guard by his door at Nazi headquarters, where he and Mrs. Tura plan to rendezvous that evening. "This is a very difficult place to get in," he says as he bids her *au revoir*, "but much more difficult to get out." "Oh, I'm terribly frightened and terribly thrilled," says Lombard, and exits.

There is a dispute early in the film, among the Theatre Polski company, about whether Bronski, who is playing Hitler, looks sufficiently like him. In fact he's a marvelously comic version of Hitler: his good-natured face gives him a rather startled, confused look when he's in full Hitler costume, with mustache and cap and belted coat. Most of the other actors think he's fine in the part. But to producer Dobosh he just isn't convincing. "To me he's just a man with a little mustache," he says. But what else is Hitler? says someone else. And the question hangs over the movie from then on. Indeed, what else *is* he?—if Hamlet is a ham. Because *To Be or Not To Be* invokes a tradition of lowbrow comedy that's impressed by nothing or no one—certainly not cultural monuments or tragedies about unhappy princes. Its coarseness and crudity ("If Napoleon is a brandy . . .") are not slapdash and inadvertent but aggressive and purposeful, aimed at all forms and degrees of power worship. Pauline Kael has regretted that "Lubitsch abandoned his famous light touch" in what she calls this "melodramatic burlesque" of a comedy. But the film's "heavy" touch sets it squarely at the center of a triumphant Hollywood style: the vaudeville-comic movies of W. C. Fields, Bob Hope, and Benny himself, with their revue-sketch scenes and their inconsistent, anything-for-a-gag relations to verisimilitude. This is a movie in which "Hitler" enters and says "Heil myself"; in which the villain shoots himself behind a door and then shouts for his stooge ("Schultz!") to blame it on. It is also something else, of course— and something more. "Call it a tragical farce or a farcical tragedy," said Lubitsch in the New York *Times*. "I do not care." But it gets a lot of its energy and conviction from this crazy vaudeville tradition— the sort of movies that gave you the feeling that *any*thing in the world would yield to the right gag or wisecrack. And *To Be or Not To Be* belonged to a time, says Pauline Kael, "when a lot of people thought that if you showed how ridiculous the Nazis were they would—magically—lose their power." It seems likely Lubitsch felt something like this, which accounts, in Kael's view, for the movie's feeling of "enthusiasm." But it's also true that he knew and felt more complicated things about power, both the Nazis' and other people's, than this formulation suggests.

The operations of personal power, of dominance and submission ("All his life . . . he'd wanted to be a policeman"), almost displace sex as a Lubitsch theme at this time. It's no accident that Ehrhardt and Schultz carry strong if distorted echoes of Matuschek and Kralik, or that Lubitsch seems to make inadvertent reference to the world of *The Shop Around the Corner* when he defends *To Be or Not To Be* in his New York *Times* article:

> Do I really picture the Nazis so harmless that it might be a dangerous misleading of the American people by making them underestimate the enemy? I admit that I have not resorted to methods usually employed in pictures, novels and plays to signify Nazi terror. No actual torture chamber is photographed, no flogging is shown, no close-up of excited Nazis using their whip and rolling their eyes in lust. My Nazis are different; they passed that stage long ago. Brutality, flogging and torturing have become their daily routine. They talk about it with the same ease as a salesman referring to the sale of a handbag. . . .

The single most monstrous character in this film about monstrousness is not a handbag salesman but a harried bureaucrat: a thoroughly prosaic figure as well as a comic one. "Concentration Camp" Ehrhardt, in Sig Rumann's transcendent performance, is a harassed man doing his job under trying circumstances, full of suspicion and mistrust not only of his underlings and associates but of his superiors, too, all the way up to that nutty Führer. It's a nightmare version of office politics: in other offices it's your job, in this one it's your neck. No wonder he is always shouting "Schultz!," wiping his brow and falling apart and telling impolitic jokes. He is an ordinary man under extraordinary pressure. And he bears out in his comic way the argument Professor Siletsky (the real one) makes to Mrs. Tura when he is trying to recruit her to the Nazi side: the run of Nazis, he says, are just like human beings everywhere. Only Hitler—and the insufferable Schultz—it would seem, are "different." "We're just like other people," says the amorous Siletsky—not puritans or fanatics at all. "We love to sing, we love to dance, we admire beautiful women. . . ."

EVEN ALLOWING for the tragedy of Lombard's death, it's not entirely clear why people should have been so repelled by this comedy when it first opened. Hitler jokes and gags about boobish Nazis were already a staple of the popular culture, in comic books, radio shows, movies with Bob Hope and Red Skelton and Kay Kyser and even Donald Duck. The most notable Hitler joke of all, of course, was Chaplin's *The Great Dictator*, the fourth-highest-grossing movie of 1940, outdistancing even *The Philadelphia Story* and *Rebecca* in ticket sales. So why, then, was Lubitsch's joke taken so badly in 1941, so widely regarded as going too far? Given the precedents, you would think that would be hard to do.

To Be or Not To Be, it should be noted, offers different varieties of "tasteless-

Now Tura (Benny) is playing Professor Siletsky— whom they have just killed. Maria (Lombard) has been waiting for him here at Gestapo headquarters. Captain Schultz (Henry Victor) looks on approvingly.

ness" in its humor. Some of the jokes seem close to the edge even today—like the exchange between Maria and Lieutenant Sobinski during their first meeting in her dressing room. Tell me about *you*, she says. He gangles and looks at the floor. "Well, there isn't much to tell," he says. "I just fly a bomber."

MARIA: Oh, how perfectly thrilling!
SOBINSKI: I don't know about it's being thrilling—but it's quite a bomber. You might not believe it, but I can drop three tons of dynamite in two minutes.
MARIA (*in close-up*): Really?
SOBINSKI: Does that interest you?
MARIA: It certainly does. . . .

He makes a date with her to take her up in his plane. And as he leaves, he pauses in the doorway to apologize for his awkwardness: "This is the first time I ever met an actress," he explains. "Lieutenant," replies Lombard, looking at him dreamily, "this is the first time I've ever met a man who could drop three tons of dynamite in two minutes.—Bye!" It's the same general style ("Oh, how perfectly thrilling") that she uses later with Siletsky. This time, of course, with Sobinski, she's not exactly faking—the hungry close-up assures us of that. But the ironic distance on male potency, particularly the enlarged forms of it that war encourages, is still there. It's an essential component in Lombard's performance.

But a risqué exchange based on bombing raids wouldn't have struck anyone at the time as particularly "callous" or "macabre" (Bosley Crowther's words for the film in general). And a lot of audiences who might have been shocked or titillated by the sexual meaning probably wouldn't (remarkable as that seems now) have gotten it—at least not collectively and out loud. No, the sort of thing people objected to in this comedy was quite different, and crystallized around a single line. Which *everyone* objected to, or so it seemed.

Tura-Siletsky leaves Colonel Ehrhardt's offices after gaining assurances of his safe conduct out of Warsaw to London. But he wants, he tells Ehrhardt, to take Mrs. Tura, whom he has recruited as an agent, along with him. Ehrhardt is doubtful about this: "Frankly, I don't believe in women agents," he says, but promises to think it over and let the professor know. By the way, says the latter, "her husband is that great, great Polish actor, Joseph Tura—you've probably heard of him." Nobody has up to now (that's been a running gag); but Ehrhardt, it seems, is going to be an exception. "Oh, yes . . ." he says, remembering. "As a matter of fact I saw him on the stage when I was in Warsaw right before the war." "Really?" says Benny, nearly as surprised as we are. "What he did to Shakespeare," says Ehrhardt, as he ushers him out the door, "we are doing now to Poland."

Lubitsch's close friend Walter Reisch has recalled how the first Beverly Hills preview audience, which had been "cracking up with laughter" up to then, responded to Rumann's line in stunned silence. There was a parallel silence afterwards among Lubitsch's "inner circle" (Charles Brackett and Billy Wilder, Henry Blanke, S. N. Behrman, producer Alexander Korda) as they sat in the restaurant with no one quite saying it, until Lubitsch's wife did: why not eliminate the offending line? And there was a chorus of agreement, even insistence, that he should do so. What Reisch particularly remembered—some twenty-five years later—was how angry this suggestion made Lubitsch, angrier than he'd ever seen him, making "his face waxen and the long cigar tremble in his mouth." People were avoiding their table, Reisch said. Until Samuel Hoffenstein, the screenwriter (*Desire* and *Cluny Brown*) and noted New York wit, stopped by "and bent down to the Master, expressing his grief that the fate of Poland, the destruction of a country, the annihilation of millions, should have been grabbed up for the sake of a laugh. Lubitsch had no answer to that, no further argument, no smile. . . ." But "the Master" kept the line in. And "later on, when practically every review in the American press, with the exception of *Time* magazine, took exception to this very line," he was still unrepentant, and defending it as if an attack on this joke (to Reisch and the others, it was an expendable gag, so why *not* cut it out?) were an attack on his film. As indeed it was. Lubitsch knew what he had wrought better than his friends did.

There were, for example, no objections to this line: "We do the concentrating and the Poles do the camping." Though surely here "the fate of Poland" had been treated with an equivalent flipness—"grabbed up for the sake of a laugh." And yet no one seemed to notice, and the audience laughed on cue—precisely because it's a Jack Benny line (it could have been a Hope or a Cantor line as well). Even though the gag enters a villainous point of view, it can be taken as a rejection of that view, a joke *against* it, in a familiar American wisecrack style. But Ehrhardt's crack about Tura is actually made by a Nazi, not by someone pretending to be a Nazi. It's no wonder audiences were put off. This was the sort of joke we told about our victories over them. To suggest that *they* might tell the same sort of joke, on the same sort of occasion, about us—*was* shocking, and not what people were used to. This was just the sort of distinction, however— between Them and Us—that Lubitsch was incapable of making.

And his failure to make it was precisely what made *To Be or Not To Be* seem "tasteless" where other Nazi farces weren't. For all his antifascist intentions, it *felt* as if Lubitsch were somehow muddling and subverting those boundaries between the enemy and us that were becoming clearer and more emphatic as the war grew more desperate. And Lubitsch, many suspected, was simply too "sophisticated" to serve these distinctions anyway—the "cynical playboy" of Graham Greene's description. But *To Be or Not To Be* is surely one of the least cynical comedies ever made. The Nazis in this film *are* like ordinary people. They are also monsters. Evil is clearly named; but it is also brought closer to familiar feelings and situations than people expected it to be in such a film. This, finally, is what gives it its special quality of hilarity—and its force. And its combination of clarity and power makes it almost the peak of Lubitsch's work—attaining just that adversary force that had eluded him earlier, in the comedies of the late thirties.

In any case, the perception that we are more like Them than we want or like to remember leads, in this particular fantasy, not to a shrug or a sigh but to saving the Polish Underground, as Tura and his colleagues finally do. The Nazis here are not defeated by our ridiculing them—but by our knowing them: being able to imitate and predict and finally understand them ("I thought you'd react just that way"). This knowledge *is* power—even if it goes with self-enclosure. In the world of Lubitsch comedy we know too much about ourselves to be taken in by them—or by "a man with a little mustache" who may be taken in by himself. It's an odd and surprising development of the so-called Lubitsch "cynicism," of his emphasis on our frailties of solipsism and self-concern. *To Be or*

Not To Be is not only a climactic masterpiece. This comedy about power is also a refusal of powerlessness.

L UBITSCH REPORTED to the Twentieth Century–Fox lot to begin his new contract in February 1942. But he spent his first months there in indecision, beginning new projects and then giving them up, or rejecting them (in the case of a proposed Ginger Rogers comedy) as too "frivolous" for wartime. But in May he and his favorite collaborator, Samson Raphaelson, were together again, writing the screenplay of *Heaven Can Wait* (1943). That completed, Lubitsch eagerly took up an assignment for Lieutenant Colonel Frank Capra's film unit: a training film called *Know Your Enemy: Germany*. He prepared the script in the summer and shot the film in the fall, only to have the result summarily rejected by the army: they thought it was "ponderous" and unsuitable for its military audience (it was later redone by others). And so Lubitsch returned to Fox, to begin his first feature there and his first film in color. He started shooting *Heaven Can Wait* on February 1, 1943, and finished it over two months later.

For him that was a bit longer than usual. But *Heaven Can Wait* was an elaborate production. It was also—by Lubitsch standards, anyway—a troubled one. Gene Tierney, its star, would be the first Lubitsch leading woman since Mary Pickford in *Rosita* to speak coldly of him. In her autobiography, *Self-Portrait*, she describes him as a "tyrant" and "the most demanding of directors," reducing her almost to tears by his incessant "shouting." The film was based on the usual Hungarian play (*Szuletesnap* by Laszlo Bus-Feketè) but was about a New York family at the turn of the century. The hero, Henry Van Cleve (Don Ameche), is an incurable woman chaser, from his boyhood to his old age. The movie covers both stages, as well as the young manhood and middle age in between. And although Raphaelson has recalled—in his remarkable and moving memoir, *Freundschaft*, written in 1981—how happily he and Lubitsch worked together on this script, he also remembered on another occasion how the conception of this womanizing hero marked, to his sense, a division between himself and Lubitsch.

Lubitsch really *loved* this hero, Raphaelson said, this amiable European-style rake, with an affection and enthusiasm for him that Raphaelson, with his very different background, could never quite share. And when the playwright watched the film again in 1977, on a special occasion at the Museum of Modern Art, he confessed afterward in his public remarks that he had gotten "a little tired of the variations on lechery." He cited the "occasional difference" that he and Lubitsch had in "our outlook on human behavior" and remembered that he hadn't at first wanted to do this picture—especially once Lubitsch had given him "a notion of what he expected." He described Lubitsch as almost literally "smacking his lips" over the prospect of "this thirteen-year-old American boy being seduced by a voluptuous eighteen-year-old double-buttocked kitchen wench" (replaced in the final film by a much tamer sort of joke, with the French maid telling the thirteen-year-old that he doesn't *have* to marry the little girl he's just kissed). And the older Henry Van Cleve seemed to Raphaelson finally "a pretty monotonous old Casanova," with too little beyond his "bungling infidelity" that might claim anybody's interest.

But to Lubitsch this character had a very personal interest. If *To Be or Not To Be* was for Lubitsch a kind of reflection on his art, *Heaven Can Wait* seems a reflection on his life—or at least on the kind of life he might have had *without* the art. And where the earlier film dealt with some version of the present, this one looks back over a life and forward into a fanciful hereafter, imagining how such a life might finally be judged. But since it is committed from the beginning to finding in its hero's favor, it amounts to a kind of comic brief for the charming roué and gallant lover of women. Probably only a Lubitsch would undertake such a project (even in the advance publicity it sounded "daring") in the midst of wartime sanctimoniousness, and perhaps only a Lubitsch could get away with it. Even *he* would have to be careful.

But *Heaven Can Wait,* for all its daring, had the look and many of the attributes of a standard Twentieth Century–Fox line: genteel Americana, a studio style marked by child actors and family narratives and "gay nineties" nostalgia, with cluttered and overstuffed sets in garish candy-box Technicolor. *Heaven Can Wait* had all of it, along with two of the wet-wick stars the studio also fielded. Gene Tierney—who would be memorable a year later in *Laura,* and even more so in John Stahl's *Leave Her to Heaven* the year after that—gives a cloying performance here; Don Ameche gives a proficient and charmless one. It is probably the most unhappily cast and performed of all the major Lubitsch films, except for the customary brace of wonderful supporting players: including Charles Coburn as Grandfather Van Cleve, and Eugene Pallette and Marjorie Main as Mr. and Mrs. Strabel.

The Strabels are among the sublimest creations in the Lubitsch-Raphaelson canon. A gruff, portly couple locked into a marriage of pure and energizing hatred, seething grossly at each other in their Kansas mansion, where their elegant black manservant (Clarence Muse) performs the role of conciliator and anxious message-bearer, mediating an argument at the breakfast table over the Sunday funnies, turning threats into requests and challenges into endearments, while all the while he tries to get them to eat their wheatcakes. The precarious harmony he maintains is shattered, however, when Mrs. Strabel gives too detailed a description of the way one of the characters in the funny papers gets squeezed by a snake. "It *wound* itself *around* the barrel, and then—*cr-r-runch,*" she says, aiming a salacious and glittering look at her husband and squeezing

*Allyn Joslyn
introduces the
Strabels—
Eugene
Pallette, Gene
Tierney, and
Marjorie
Main—in
Heaven Can
Wait.*

an imaginary object between her hands. "I can't live in this house any longer!" he cries, almost in tears: she knows it's no fun unless he reads it himself.

When the movie opens, Henry Van Cleve, who has died at the age of seventy, is presenting himself for admission to Hell. "I have no illusions. I know the life I lived. I know where I belong. I'd like to get it over as quickly as possible." But "His Excellency" (Laird Cregar), a suave type in a cutaway, has his doubts and asks to hear more about Henry's life. The movie then returns to the 1870s and unfolds in flashbacks: a scene from each decade, more or less, of Henry's life. "Perhaps the best way to tell you the story of my life," he says, "is to tell you about the women in my life." And so he proceeds, in the early reels, from mother and nurse (infancy) to girl playmate (childhood) to French maid (adolescence). At twenty-six, he abducts Martha Strabel (Tierney), the fiancée of his dull cousin Albert (Allyn Joslyn). They marry, and ten years later, when she leaves him over his philandering, he abducts her again—out of her parents' Kansas mansion. At fifty, he visits a Follies girl (Helene Reynolds) in her private apartment, but it turns out that he is only trying to extricate his young son (chip off the old block) from her control. The following year (1923) Henry and Martha celebrate their twenty-fifth wedding anniversary, dancing alone together in the hallway of their Park Avenue home. Martha will soon die, Henry's voice on the soundtrack tells us—and so she does, between scenes. And so at sixty, Henry is asking his son, Jack (Michael Ames), who now runs both the house and the family business, to give him a "reading companion," a young cutie he's just met at another old boy's house. At seventy, he has to be put to bed on doctor's orders for celebrating too much on his birthday—or so we are told, as the son and his wife prepare to go out for the evening, leaving the old man at home with the nurse.

And he resents it very much when this nurse (Maureen Rodin-Ryan), a spinsterish type, wakes him up from a wonderful dream he's been having. He was "on a big luxury liner, floating on an ocean of whiskey and soda . . .":

> . . . And on top, in a lifeboat, sat the most beautiful blonde, wearing a Merry Widow costume. . . . "Henry," she said, "how about a little dance?" And suddenly the man from the boat took an accordion and played "The Merry Widow Waltz"—and the girl held her arms out to me and started to dance. . . . I put my arms around the beautiful girl and was about to dance away with her when, of all people, *you* cut in—*you*, yes, *you!*

But the nurse is occupied with taking his temperature. She removes the thermometer from his mouth and turns down the light. He has fallen asleep again. Someone knocks softly at the bedroom door and she goes to it. It's the butler. "The night nurse is here," he says to her. She goes to the bed, takes her bag from the night table beside it, crosses to the door again, and goes out into the hall, which is very brightly lit. She turns and walks to the right with the camera tracking laterally beside her. She stops when she comes to a mirror and sets her bag on the table beneath. This is the first good look at her we've gotten: she is severe but not unkind-looking—prim, thin-lipped, middle-aged. She looks at herself and pats her straight dark hair into place, takes up her bag again, and walks out of the shot. The camera does *not* follow: empty shot, empty mirror. It's a Lubitsch delay—and because of the mirror, perhaps, more than usually dramatic.

Then, off-screen, we hear women's voices. An exchange of greetings: "Good evening." "Hello." "First door to the right." Another pause—and then suddenly the night nurse (Doris Merrick) appears in the mirror and pats *her* hair—which is long and blond and gleaming. She's a Hollywood cutie, forties style, lacquered and lustrous and red-lipped. She takes her bag and goes left, the camera following, to the bedroom door. She goes in and closes it behind her. We look at the door. The shift from mirror to door is upsetting somehow. Still we look at the door. Then the faint sound of an accordion . . . growing louder . . . playing "The Merry Widow Waltz" as the camera pulls slowly back to the music . . .

tilts down to the lower hall . . . and sinks into a dissolve, where we find Henry again in the afterworld talking to "His Excellency":

> . . . I was awakened by a caressing touch on my forehead. I opened my eyes and there she was, sitting on the edge of my bed . . . Nellie Brown, registered nurse. . . . Your Excellency, one look at her and it didn't matter whether she was registered or not! And then Nellie took out a thermometer, and she said, "Open your mouth." Who wouldn't for Nellie? . . . Then she put the thermometer in, and my temperature went up to a hundred and ten. Who could ask for a more beautiful death?

As usual with Lubitsch, what he *doesn't* show us becomes most eloquent. Every time we shift from one sequence to another in this movie, someone we've gotten used to seeing around in the family is simply missing, and without comment. It's this absence of comment that gives the death theme a kind of gathering power, that makes it seem insistent, almost obsessive. And we know, even when she first appears in the mirror, what Nellie Brown is really bringing to Henry. As usual again, Lubitsch makes us collusive—surprising us by *not* surprising us, implicating us in *his* knowledge. And the association of sex with death, implicit in so much of his film work, is now overt. What was an overtone in *The Merry Widow* has become—with this latest use of "The Merry Widow Waltz"— an explicit meaning. Earlier on, Henry is upset because he suspects Martha of seeing another man. What else is he to think? She goes out in the afternoons without telling him where; she talks at length on the phone and won't tell him who it is. "My lover," she says jokingly. But it's no joke: "There were only a few months left for Martha. . . ." She *is* seeing another man: the doctor who is seeing her through her unnamed terminal illness.

There is, clearly enough, something grisly at the heart of this movie—and Lubitsch tries to make it winsome. The greater explicitness about death seems to inspire a kind of panicked archness. There is none of the real tough-mindedness of *To Be or Not To Be*—of *The Merry Widow* even. And the movie never confronts the pain at its center the way *The Shop Around the Corner* does. So that even the moments of Lubitschean mastery—like the Nellie Brown sequence—leave a disagreeable afterfeeling. The mood of sugary nostalgia that belongs to the genre and the studio style is never entirely defeated, nor is it really challenged in the end. Raphaelson told Herman Weinberg an interesting story in 1967 (reported by Weinberg in *The Lubitsch Touch*): he said that he and Lubitsch had written a sequence for the last part of the film where Henry the old man "gets into a mess" with his grandchild's nursemaid. "A scene of grisly humor, inspired completely by Lubitsch," Raphaelson recalled, "it came out of *his* knowledge, out of his European savvy." They were both delighted with it, in any case, until Zanuck made them take it out of the script. They had to substitute the "reading companion" joke, one of the movie's feeblest episodes. But surely Zanuck must have been right in a way. If the deleted sequence was even partly as "harsh" and as "mean" as Raphaelson gleefully remembered it to be, it would have been strikingly out of place in the movie that Lubitsch made.

Partly, of course, the problem was the Production Code. For once, it seems that Lubitsch—who prided himself both on never having vulgar run-ins with the censors and on outsmarting them more consistently than almost anyone else—had outsmarted himself. He set out to make a case for a kind of life that everything in the climate of American piety around him seemed to be discounting. But *Heaven Can Wait* is the story of a philanderer in which no philandering ever occurs, at least so far as we can tell. If it had, the hero would have been required to be punished in some way (the Production Code)—which was *not* the kind of movie or moral that Lubitsch had in mind. Since he means to forgive, even to eulogize, this amiably lecherous hero, he has to seem at least to deny the lechery. And so a pattern is set up. From the French maid to the Follies girl, Henry always turns out to be innocent, in *spite* of initial appearances. The only one he seems to make any real headway with is his wife. And he seems indeed a very contented sort of husband. And yet the implication of adultery—of even a habit of adultery—is clear, if carefully handled. Martha discovers a bill for a diamond bracelet and leaves him. And we discover in the scene that follows that there have been many such quarrels before this. But when? And over what exactly? We know even less about Henry's infidelities than he contrives to let his wife know. But since this is a problem the film is importantly about, the effect is of a peculiar smarminess: as if there really *were* things you never discussed, no matter how insistent or obtrusive they became. Lubitsch and Raphaelson undoubtedly felt that their techniques of eloquent reticence would carry the day. But never before had these techniques been required to carry so much—so much necessary meaning and information left out. The film gives less a feeling of double entendre than of massive denial.

"That's the story of my life," says Henry to His Excellency, "and now I'd be grateful if you'd push that button and have it over with." But His Excellency refuses. "Sorry, Mr. Van Cleve, but we don't cater to your class of people." He suggests that Henry try "the other place," above. Where he'll probably find that Martha and all the other ladies he's made "pretty happy" will be ready to plead for his admittance. "Down?" asks the operator as Henry steps into his elevator. "No," says His Excellency, "*up*"—as the last door closes and the film ends.

But the happiness Henry gives to the ladies (his "bedroom benevolences," as Raphaelson sarcastically called it) is not something the film has been allowed to show us. So that it ends up seeming less like a brief on his behalf than a kind of whimper: he's lovable and harmless and kind of cute. And *both* his mothers (the real one and the wife one) loved him. This condescension seems finally and fatally the movie's point. It's certainly at the essence, as it turns out, of Martha's devotion. She tries to leave him, to resist him; but then he reminds her of this little boy—and never more so than when he's lying and trying to cover up. And as they get older, she finds to her delight that he gets even cuter, more harmless and lovable than ever. As she explains to him when he's fifty:

> Nearly fifteen years ago, when you and Grandfather brought me back from Kansas, I still didn't feel that you really belonged to me—and only to me. . . . Whenever I wasn't with you, I was always uncertain and nervous about my little Casanova. And one day I noticed that you began to have a little—well, just a little tummy. *Then I knew I was safe.* From that moment on, you were really mine. . . .

This is offered as sympathetic (though comically discomfiting to Henry and his surviving illusions)—an instance of Martha's uncomplicated warmth and niceness. (And Tierney makes it even worse, if that's possible: even her beauty in this movie seems syrupy.) It's a moment—and indeed a movie—that even Louis B. Mayer might have envied. Lubitsch set out to confront the times, it seemed, and ended up by illustrating them. *Heaven Can Wait* is his most sentimental comedy. And the reviewers and the critics who had been so appalled by *To Be or Not To Be* rallied to him once more. Lubitsch, they said, was back in form again.

Walking with his nurse in a nearby park one day, he was talking politics at machine gun speed, throwing gestures in all directions. They passed a large flower, which, blown by the breeze, seemed to nod at them.

Lubitsch went ahead with his conversation. Twenty minutes later they were back at the same spot.

Again the flower nodded.

"Thank you very much," Lubitsch bowed. "I saw you the first time too."
—J. M. KENDRICK, in the Baltimore *Sun* (March 26, 1944)

"Who wouldn't for Nellie? . . ."
—HENRY VAN CLEVE, in *Heaven Can Wait*

THE NEXT few years were difficult ones. He was divorced from his wife, Vivian Gaye, but he had his little daughter, Nicola, to dote upon. And he drew closer to his European friends, says Samson Raphaelson in *Freundschaft*, to German-speaking cronies like Reisch and Billy Wilder. "And he had probably for the first time in his life," Raphaelson writes, "a real camaraderie with a lovely woman. She was Mary Loos (niece of Anita)—young, beautiful, splendidly tall, a blueblood of California-pioneer ancestry—whose platonic devotion Lubitsch received, to the surprise of everyone, with gratitude and affection."

The next film he planned was to be a comedy-fantasy with Irene Dunne and Charles Boyer, which then got deferred in favor of something more timely: a comedy about the WACs. He had already begun the screenplay, with Henry and Phoebe Ephron (he had even conferred with Colonel Oveta Culp Hobby), when in September 1943—just one month after the successful premiere of *Heaven Can Wait*—he had his first heart attack. After a party at Sonja Henie's, where he had danced ("incessantly," according to a news report) and played the piano. He was unconscious for three days and confined to bed for two months after that. When he began to recover—at the beginning of 1944—he signed a new contract with Twentieth which took account of his diminished strength: he would produce three films, with the option of directing the third if his health permitted.

The first Lubitsch production under this new arrangement was a remake of his 1924 silent *Forbidden Paradise*, with Tallulah Bankhead in the Pola Negri role as Catherine the Great: *A Royal Scandal* (1945). Lubitsch prepared the script with Edwin Justus Mayer (of *To Be or Not To Be*) and directed the rehearsals but was "not yet strong enough," reported the New York *Times*, "to expose himself to a full day on the set." Otto Preminger was assigned to direct—and later confided to interviewers his lack of sympathy for the whole project. It showed on the screen. It's Lubitsch shtick, mechanically performed, and coarsened even more by Bankhead's camp bawdiness. It was an inexpensive film but a flop: the studio dumped it on the market, almost surreptitiously, relegating it to second bills.

But the next Lubitsch production was unlike anything he'd ever done: *Dragonwyck* (1946), based on a best-selling gothic romance. Joseph Mankiewicz was assigned to both write and direct—a dream come true, said Mankiewicz, since he idolized Lubitsch more than any other living filmmaker. But the dream turned sour. Mankiewicz found the Master "stubborn and touchy," overconcerned about his health, and argumentative about the direction—"mostly about where I put the camera." Finally, according to one account, Mankiewicz barred Lubitsch from the set. What is incontestable is that Lubitsch withdrew his name from the production and refused to speak to Mankiewicz for some time afterwards. And the Lubitsch influence on the final film—a combination of *Jane Eyre* and *Gaslight*, with Gene Tierney as an innocent bride and Vincent Price as her sinister husband—is perfectly undetectable. The whole thing seems to have been, in every sense, an error, though the film itself enjoyed a modest box-office success.

But Lubitsch's health was improving, and by November 1945 he was ready to direct again—the film version of Margery Sharp's international best-seller *Cluny Brown* (1946), with a screenplay by Samuel Hoffenstein and Elizabeth Reinhardt. The British novelist had sold the rights to Fox on the eccentric condition that Jennifer Jones be cast, however improbably, in the title role; and so she was. But more important to Lubitsch was the opportunity to cast Charles Boyer (they had long hoped to work together) opposite her, as the anti-Nazi refugee Adam Belinski. The film—begun in December 1945 and completed in February of the following year—is major Lubitsch, and a fitting final work, as it turned out to be. It attracted upon its release (June 1946) neither the obloquy visited upon *To Be or Not To Be* nor the praise lavished on *Heaven Can Wait:* in fact, it didn't arouse much notice of any kind. Business was modest and reviewers treated it perfunctorily. Except in England, where it was something of a scandal, excoriated in the press for its inaccuracy about English life, for making everything (cars, riding clothes, dining halls) too expensive-looking, and for lighting it all too brightly. The *Sunday Express* was astonished to find the English "upper classes" portrayed as "amiable half-wits" and the "lower orders" as "smugly servile morons." It was as if they'd never seen a Lubitsch film before.

In April 1946 Lubitsch was given a special Academy Award: "He advanced

Mrs. Wilson (Una O'Connor) blows her candle out—or so it seems, Mr. Wilson, the chemist (Richard Haydn), holds the cake for her. This is just before Cluny (Jennifer Jones, at right) gets up to fix the plumbing. Cluny Brown.

the technique of screen comedy as no one else has ever done," said Mervyn LeRoy in his presentation. But it was over a year later before Lubitsch could go back to work—when he called on Samson Raphaelson to write with him again. This project, *That Lady in Ermine* (1948), was no advance but a return to the naughty operetta style of the old days. It was, ironically, the same property he had originally intended for Dunne and Boyer (its source was a German operetta), transformed now into a Technicolor vehicle for Betty Grable, Fox's most important star. For Raphaelson, it was all a kind of going through the motions, a favor to an ill and depleted friend. Lubitsch had had two mild heart attacks in the year just past—which he kept a secret from the world and most of all from Zanuck. "To impress Zanuck," Raphaelson recalled, "we worked on the lot." Lubitsch began filming in October. But after five weeks he died of a heart attack—at the age of fifty-five, on November 11, 1947. Otto Preminger completed the film.

He also rushed to Lubitsch's home the night of his death. So did Marlene Dietrich. Mary Loos thinks Lubitsch would have enjoyed the irony of this—that two of the people he liked least in Hollywood should be the first ones to gather at his deathbed. There was also—apart from the doctor (who was Mary Loos' father) and Otto Werner, Lubitsch's valet of twenty-two years—a woman who had been a longtime friend of his. She was also a close friend of Mary Loos. But her name and the fact of her presence were, for the conventional reasons, suppressed. In any case, it seems that Lubitsch—with uncanny appropriateness, almost as if fulfilling the foreboding of his films—died in the act of lovemaking. "And after all," Mary Loos said to me in 1984, "what more beautiful way to go?"—in an unconscious echoing of Henry Van Cleve's line to His Excellency.

I N HIS six years at Twentieth, then, he completed only two films. And *Cluny Brown* in particular was made under such poor auspices of health and personal fortune that it seems all the more remarkable that it should have turned out to be marvelous. It is reasonably faithful to its best-selling source (much more than Lubitsch ever was to those Hungarian plays, anyway), following Margery Sharp's plot and general patterns of character and event. Lubitsch broadens and simplifies some of the characters (Sir Henry and Lady Carmel, for example, are much dottier and funnier than they ever are in the book), deepens and complicates others (Adam Belinski, the hero). But the movie is altogether richer and stranger than the pleasant, amusing, intelligently romantic novel. And everything in it that's richest and strangest is certifiable Lubitsch.

In both the book and the movie, Cluny (Jennifer Jones) is a plumber's assistant, working for and living with her Uncle Arn (Billy Bevan) in London—until her fancy notions, and her facility for getting into embarrassing scrapes, prompt her uncle to send her into service as a maid. She ends up at Friars Carmel, where Belinski is a house guest. In the novel Cluny's enthusiasm for plumbing is merely one of her eccentricities, a mildly comic circumstance that is more or less forgotten after the first chapters, when she leaves London to become a parlormaid. But in the movie, plumbing is an obsession for her—and a source of upset for others, especially after she leaves London. She is being courted by a country chemist in the village where she spends her day off, a priggish, pompous little man named Wilson (Richard Haydn), who plans to announce their engagement at his aged mother's birthday dinner. But then the pipes in the bathroom start to growl and belch, and Cluny rushes off from the party to take care of them ("I may not cook the best tripe and onions in England, but whoever gets me won't have to worry about his plumbing!"), thumping and pounding them into submission off-screen while the appalled guests sit silent and stiff-backed around the birthday table. The plumbing gets fixed—we hear the rush of relieving water, announcing Cluny's success—but there is no engagement announcement. As Cluny later points out, and as Mr. Wilson's reaction confirms, "men just don't marry plumbers." "When I was young," Sir Henry says, "we never even discussed plumbing."* Times have changed, of course—but not that much.

The chemist's elderly mother, Mrs. Wilson (Una O'Connor), enters when she first appears from behind an ominously footlit bedroom door ("Mother's been resting"), and then, with her son taking her arm, clears her throat violently all the way down the stairs and into her chair in the parlor. The occasion is her first meeting with Cluny, an event that Mr. Wilson later describes as a success. "Mother's taken a great liking to you," he tells Cluny—who is puzzled, since, as she points out, Mrs. Wilson never uttered a word in her presence. "That's the point," says Mr. Wilson, pleased that Cluny has registered it. "Mother doesn't waste words on flattery. If she speaks, it's to correct faults." But in fact, so far as we can tell, Mother simply doesn't speak—not ever. She doesn't even look up. She only clears her throat—though she manages to make the sound a various and expressive one. She is the ultimate solipsist: totally absorbed in this most minimal movement of the self. And if outside events ever do reach her, she gives only slight, occult signs of it—though occasionally she is taken off guard, as when, after clearing her throat with particular violence in front of her birthday cake, she sees the candle go out. She looks startled. But to the other people around the table, who applaud and cheer, she has blown it out. Neither we nor she is quite so sure. She is nonetheless—like almost everyone else in this film—alert to the real meaning of plumbing. And it's Cluny's zest in going at

---

* There are the usual double-meaning jokes for the rowdier sections of Lubitsch's audience: e.g., two servants overhear Cluny telling Belinski about the pleasure she gets from "unloosening the joint" and then just "banging" away.

Cluny tells Adam Belinski (Charles Boyer) that she dreamt about him last night. He listens with guarded hope.

those pipes that sends the old woman back up the stairs again to "rest," clearing her throat all the way, like an alarm that has gone off and can't be silenced.

But to Cluny herself this is all just as it should be—the cramped parlor behind the shop, the censorious guests, the grotesque, domineering old lady. To Cluny, who's never had or known one, it's a home. And those are the sounds of a mother. She even rather likes the after-dinner snoring ("You see, I'm an orphan, I never heard my mother snore"). And she is nearly transported—in radiant close-up—by Mr. Wilson's rendition of "Flow Gently, Sweet Afton" on his hideously wheezing harmonium. And later, when Belinski, in love with her himself, tries to indicate in the most tactful way that she is making a serious error, even suggesting that Mr. Wilson is really quite stuffy and dull, it turns out that stuffy-and-dull ("with everything cozy and peaceful and so homey") is just what Cluny is after, like so many comic heroines before her. "Oh, I'm so glad you like him!" she says.

Her impenetrability on this score seems to throw him, at least for the moment. But for the most part, the impenetrability of others is Belinski's element. He's a man who has learned to be at home with out-to-lunch types—and he is surrounded by them. At times they almost make him buoyant, in his melancholy way. Why not? Like his trying to convince the two eager young men he meets at a London cocktail party that his life is *not* in immediate danger from Nazi agents. But it's no use: they are not only fervent antifascists but even more fervent melodramatists. They insist on taking "the Professor," as they call him, "somewhere safe," instantly. But where? "I should say," says Belinski, giving in at last, "the Ritz is a good safe place." And so off they go. "It takes a lot of nerve," says young Andrew Carmel (Peter Lawford) to his friend John (Michael Dyne) as they all go out the door, "for a man in his position to show himself at the Ritz."

But the Ritz is just the sort of place Belinski usually has the nerve for, just as he calmly accepts Andrew's invitation to come for an indefinite stay on the family estate. He has noplace else to go. Never mind that Sir Henry and Lady Carmel (Reginald Owen and Margaret Bannerman), the master and mistress of Friars Carmel, have never seen anything quite like him—and that their faces, as they regard him across the dinner table, show it. He quotes Shakespeare to them, a special tribute to generous English hosts: "'This royal throne of kings, this sceptred isle. / This other Eden, demi-paradise. / This land of such dear souls. This dear, dear land. / This blessed plot, this earth, this realm, this England. . . .'"* They stare at him. "To Shakespeare," he says in conclusion, raising his glass in toast. "How well you speak English, professor," says the always gracious Lady Carmel. "Rolls right out of him," adds Sir Henry, and comments that he himself never speaks anything else, even the one time he went rather unwillingly abroad. "English is my husband's hobby," says Lady Carmel, and remarks later, as she is showing the professor to his room, that she has never seen her husband "so stimulated" before. "Well, he's a very stimulating man himself," says Belinski, without apparent irony. And Lady Carmel prattles on in her soothing way: she will arrange for the butler to "valet" him while he's with them. But Belinski is embarrassed: he only has one suit. It doesn't matter, she explains graciously; it's mainly not to hurt the butler's feelings that she will ask him to do it, if Belinski will oblige. They reach his door and say their goodnights. "By the way," she says, "there's a nightingale under your window." "Oh," says Belinski, "you shouldn't have gone to so much trouble"—leaving her looking as bemused as she did at the dinner table.

But there is one person at Friars Carmel whom he never bemuses—the one person of an almost equivalent sophistication. Belinski and the Honorable Betty Cream (Helen Walker)—the astonishingly beautiful young woman whom Andrew is in love with and always proposing to—share a wary instinctive understanding. It's apparent whenever they're alone together—as when Belinski goes to her room to ask the day off for Cluny; they hardly know each other, and they

---

*The lines—from John of Gaunt's deathbed encomium of England (*Richard II*, I, 2)—are quoted out of order here, a frequent custom in such tributes as the one Belinski is making.

have the bantering, challenging style of people who "know" each other only too well. "I like you," says Belinski, "and you *do* sit a horse well, hang it!"—echoing Andrew's exclamation earlier on. "Shall we get back to Cluny Brown?" says Betty Cream, in her wariest and lowest voice.

Belinski belongs to a class of movie hero that became briefly popular in the forties, with the impact both of the war and of film noir. A hero marked by exhaustion, depletion, and bitter knowledge—a onetime man of action and accomplishment gripped and baffled by inaction and despair. It was the figure preeminently embodied in Bogart's Rick. But in Boyer's version there were suggestions of an almost Garbo-like range and depth: a capacity for implying the world's sorrow as well as his own. Boyer was to play this figure—the refugee hero with a tragic and partly mysterious past—three times during the decade: in *Confidential Agent* (1945) with Lauren Bacall; in *Arch of Triumph* (1948) with Ingrid Bergman (both films were notable flops at the box office); and in *Cluny Brown*. But in the Lubitsch film, this melodramatic hero is placed in a context of comic irony—troubled not by Gestapo agents and obligations to revenge but by penury, sexual and romantic frustration, and the necessity of maneuvering in the insane world of the British upper classes.

Belinski is a Czech refugee, a writer, "a professor at Prague," and "one of Hitler's worst enemies," debarred from his country (it's 1938) by the Nazi occupation and making a temporary residence in England. Where he finds himself broke and homeless. He may indeed be a hero, as Andrew believes (the point, though vague, doesn't seem to be at issue), but the man we see is only trying to get by—not freedom-fighting but sponging, looking for ways (not too humiliating) to get free meals and pound notes and lodging. He is infinitely and genially adaptable, the sort who might have operated as adroitly and imperturbably in the front offices and back lots of wartime Hollywood as he does in the town and country houses of wartime England. Belinski is the most Lubitschean of all Lubitsch heroes—in his reserve and detachment, his amused melancholy, his quizzical tenderness toward the women in the film, his rather bemused lust. Skeptical, pragmatic, humorous and rather sad—an exile among madmen, a stranger in a *very* strange land.

Where, among other problems, it gets lonely. Though about this, as about everything else, he is discreet and uninsistent. Even when he finds himself—for the second time—in the Honorable Betty Cream's room. This time it's late at night, and she is in bed, reading. And just as he had come to talk about Cluny before, now—he claims—he's come to talk about Andrew. "What does one do with a woman like you?" he says. "One feels like a fool and gets out." she says. "In a hurry, professor." But he has to talk about Andrew—and about why she is so unkind to him. And he insists that her "blue eyes" and "rounded shoulders" (staring fixedly at her breasts as he says this) mean, well, "very little to me."

Then why, she asks, is his hair so carefully combed, and why does he smell "like a perfume salesman"? He sniffs the air: "It *is* me, isn't it?" "I'm afraid it is," she replies. "Betty," he announces complacently, "I'm beginning to doubt my motives." She has no doubts, however—and since he won't go, she screams, just as she has been threatening to do, and wakes the whole household. And the considerable tact of Lady Carmel has to be employed to avert a general sort of unpleasantness.

But this is a slip—it comes near the end of the movie—and signals the extremity of Belinski's frustration by then. Cluny, after all, is committed to Mr. Wilson. Not that she has ever been encouraging to Belinski—even when they first discover each other at Friars Carmel and he is kind to her. She kisses him, out of sudden grateful emotion; but as soon as she's done it, she wants to take it back. "I don't know what came over me," she says. "It isn't as if you were my type. Believe me you aren't." He looks at her kindly: his mouth forming an "oh" of chagrin before collapsing into the accustomed smile. "I'm sure I'm not," he says. "I understand perfectly. You were just happy to find a friend here. And so am I. And we must go on being friends. And as we're not our types, that should be easy." "You know," says Cluny, her eyes glowing, "we're like two people on a desert island, waiting for a ship to rescue us." He agrees—"but you know how it is on a desert island. You wait—and wait—and then you don't wait anymore. . . . Today we're not our types. But as time passes, we might not look so bad to each other. . . ." But he doesn't press the point.

He is used to such disappointments, as we can see. He is almost airy about them. But he's not at all above seizing petty advantages where he can. Or even trying to where he can't. As when Cluny confides to him, solemnly, her belief that Mr. Wilson is getting serious. "What would *you* think," she asks, "if a gentleman invited you to tea, and to meet his mother, too?" "I wouldn't go," says Belinski, half ashamed of his words but half hopeful about them, too, fingering his tie and looking sheepishly at her. "But I've already accepted," she says, "and I'm certain I did the right thing." "I'm sure you did," he says—accepting the inevitable, as he has learned to do. But he has also learned that there are little vengeances he can take, satisfactions to be gotten in even the most hopeless situations—like ringing Mr. Wilson's shop door every time he passes it, just to discommode the owner. It's not much, but it's something—under the circumstances.

There's a strange autumnal buoyancy to this film. It casts a spell like the wonderful old house it takes place in might be supposed to do. In the midst of the mockery, there are moments of strange, unexpected, half-mysterious dignity. Like the unspoken rapport between Belinski and Betty Cream—or the unfailing, graceful authority of the vague, lamebrained Lady Carmel. Even the Lubitsch comic servants, Syrette, the butler (Ernest Cossart), and his consort, Mrs.

Maile (the incomparable Sara Allgood), have such a moment when they stand in the shadows of the kitchen and listen to Belinski's melancholy goodbye to them: they are like people in the throes of awesome thought—particularly Mrs. Maile, as she repeats Belinski's cryptic final message to Cluny ("Squirrels to the nuts") as if it were a magic formula, to be spoken with utmost care and reverence. And Belinski *is* a kind of magician, in his odd, reductive, carefully balanced way. "Where are we going, Mr. Belinski?" says Cluny as she gets on to the train with him at the end, at his command. "General Delivery," he replies, alluding to his homelessness.

> CLUNY: Are you expecting a letter?
>
> BELINSKI (*as the train starts to move*): Always. That's what's so wonderful about General Delivery. Letters pour into it. Millions of them. Greetings from all over the world. . . .

It's outrageous in a way that this infinitely knowing man, with those infinitely pained eyes, should talk in this style: "Greetings from all over the world." It's what Cluny likes, of course. "You do make one see things," she says. And in fact he does. Boyer's absolute poise in this whimsy—his detached, clear-eyed assessment of what he is saying and doing at such a moment—is breathtaking. How could the postal service sound sadder?

Earlier on, Cluny tells him that she had a dream the night before—but he mustn't tell Mr. Wilson. "Does he forbid you to dream?" exclaims Belinski. But she dreamt about *him*—Belinski. "Cluny, you did?" he says, hope rising in spite of himself. He was riding an Arabian stallion, and he swept her up off the sands onto the saddle ("My, did we sit a horse well"). But just as he was taking her into his tent, she kicked herself—according to their pact—and woke up. He looks dispirited but not surprised. "Mr. Belinski," says Cluny, noticing his face, "do you wish I'd gone to your tent?" Boyer at this moment is extraordinary. "No, Cluny," he says on a sigh—and he smiles: "You did the right thing." What's extraordinary here is the note of exhilaration—unexpected and powerfully convincing. "I have no tent," he goes on. "Not in the desert or anywhere. But you better run along now. Good luck." And he sends her off to Mr. Wilson. Boyer's Belinski is an eloquent culmination of the Lubitsch vision—especially in this moment when he relinquishes (as he supposes) not only Cluny but the fantasy of her. It's Boyer's peculiarly glamorous relation to defeat and disappointment that ties him to Lubitsch and that makes this final triumphant collaboration. Tempted by enervation and somehow—magically, almost—getting beyond it. What we feel in that sigh is the exhilaration of despair. And it's powerfully moving.

Sturges: "Genius at Work" | 23

Make no mistake—this new American cinema is strictly the opposite of what we have seen in the past. Sturges is the anti-Capra. . . .
— ANDRÉ BAZIN, in a 1949 review

PRESTON STURGES was unique. He came on the directing scene at roughly the same time Orson Welles did, that other movie "genius" of the early forties; but in some ways Sturges' career was even more astonishing. In his brief tenure as a Paramount contract director he wrote and directed one marvelous movie after another—eight extraordinary films in four years, and each one an "original"—a burst of achievement without precedent or parallel in Hollywood memory.

Sturges' first year at Paramount (as a screenwriter)—1937—was Lubitsch's last. He idolized Lubitsch. And Lubitsch's career in American films—as a major director, not a performer, who more or less limited himself to comedies—was the kind that Sturges himself had embarked on. He had meant to begin *The Great McGinty* (1940), his first film as a director, with an on-screen dedication to Lubitsch; but Paramount wouldn't permit it (Lubitsch had been gone from the studio for over two years). But Lubitsch's name is dropped so pointedly and often in *Sullivan's Travels* two years later—when Sturges had almost total control of his own work—that the studio may have wished they'd consented to that earlier dedication. And as eagerly as Sturges associated himself with Lubitsch, he seemed impelled to *dissociate* himself from Capra—in a very precise way. Indeed he becomes, as André Bazin says of him, "the anti-Capra."

Sullivan's Travels is a movie about moviemaking. And it begins with a movie-within-the-movie, though we don't know that at first: the opening is a deliberately disorienting one, with two men fighting fiercely on the top of a speeding freight car until they topple off and fall into the waters of a river below, disappearing into its depths—at which point the music goes up, there is a close-up of the rushing black waters, and THE END comes rippling into view. We are in a projection room; and as the lights go up, Joel McCrea, looking a little insane, is standing and turning to confront the two queasy faces behind him. "You see!" he says, pointing at the screen. "You see the symbolism of it? Capitalism and labor destroy each other! It teaches a lesson, a moral lesson. It has social significance. It—" But a small, dyspeptic-looking man (Porter Hall)—he is named Hadrian and he is a studio executive—interrupts him: "Who wants to see that kind of stuff?" he growls. "It gives me the creeps." The other man, Le Brand (Robert Warwick), tall and imposing-looking, is also a studio boss. And Sullivan (McCrea), one of their most valued directors of box-office comedies, has just been showing them the kind of picture he *wants* to make: "a commentary on modern conditions" and "the problems that confront the average man," "a picture with dignity, a true canvas of the suffering of humanity."

> SULLIVAN: . . . I wanted to make you something outstanding, something you could be proud of, something that would realize the potentialities of film as the sociological and artistic medium that it is. With a little sex in it. Something like—
> HADRIAN: Something like Capra, I know.
> SULLIVAN (*bristling*): What's the matter with Capra?

In a way, Sullivan spends the rest of the movie learning the answer to that question—finding out why he's mistaken to want to make a movie like the one he's just shown them.

And though that movie hardly *looks* like Capra, we realize in some way that it *feels* like him—once Sullivan begins to talk, anyway. That it has the essence of "Capracorn," in fact: the reduction of its human figures to a kind of embodied significance—whether "capital and labor," as in the movie-within-the-movie, or the common man, as in *Meet John Doe* (Capra's most recent film at the time). In a Sturges film, on the other hand, there *are* no common men. Not even among the supporting players. Take Hadrian in this scene, for example: the movie-mogul type (much more than Le Brand, who is classier), rat-faced and disgruntled. He has the movie's second line of dialogue—when he interrupts the first (Sullivan's speech of enthusiasm, above)—and it, too, is perfectly according to type, surly and philistine, the sort of thing a mogul-in-a-movie *would* say. With one important difference: that it's a wonderful remark—"It gives me the creeps"—of stunning, magisterial accuracy about exactly the sort of feeling such experiences of "symbolism" can produce in us. It has an Orwellian force ("the creeps" is beyond praise), making us discover what we already knew, unforgettably. A mogul-type remark—that utterly transcends its category. As Sturges people, even the walk-ons and bit players, characteristically do.

*Preston Sturg
at a preview
of* Christmas
in July.

Like the avuncular guard at Penn Station (Edward J. McNamara) who calls Joel McCrea "laddie" and hustles him out the door for attempting to "molest" Claudette Colbert—while advising him as they go: "You let the dames alone in Pennsylvania Station and Pennsylvania Station will let you alone and vice versa." Or the Pullman porter (Charles Moore) in the same movie—*The Palm Beach Story* (1942)—handing people off the train while he answers McCrea's questions about the escaped Colbert. "Was she alone?" McCrea wants to know. (She is with Rudy Vallee.)

> PORTER: Well, you might practically say she's alone. The gentleman who got off with her give me ten cents from New York to Jacksonville. (*To a woman getting off*) Watch your step, please. (*To McCrea again*)—She's alone but she don' know it.

Or the forbidding Miss Swerf (Nora Cecil), the censorious office manager in *Easy Living* (1937), rebutting Jean Arthur's denial that that's a mink coat she has on: "Well, *I* ought to know mink. My mother had a little tippet." Or the wife (Jan Buckingham) in *Sullivan's Travels*, slapping some flowers down on her husband's grave and looking at the headstone ("John L. Sullivan, 1909–1942") with narrowed eyes: "You don't suppose this is a gag, do you?" she says to her boyfriend as she rises. Or the saleswoman fitting Linda Darnell's gown in *Unfaithfully Yours* (1948), a chic, svelte woman with gypsy eyes and black hair. "What a lollipop!" she says to another saleswoman when Darnell turns from the fitting to answer a phone call from her husband—who has just had a fire in his dressing room. "He set fire to it himself!" says Darnell at the phone, in disbelief. And the saleswoman responds with a dreadful certainty, involuntary and barely audible: "Insurance!" she murmurs, folding her hands at her waist and lifting her eyes heavenwards. And there are even people we only hear about who still end up seeming unforgettable—like Woodrow's departed grandfather in *Hail the Conquering Hero* (1944). Why *can't* Woodrow (Eddie Bracken) wear his marine uniform at home, his mother (Georgia Caine) wants to know. So does her friend Martha (Elizabeth Patterson). And they call the other marines standing around to witness. Woodrow protests that it's against regulations to wear it. His mother can't believe that.

MRS. TRUESMITH: Your grandfather wore his Civil War uniform the rest of his life.

AUNT MARTHA (*explanatory, to the others*): Kept having new ones made.

MRS. TRUESMITH (*also to the others*): He said he had to remind people that brother fought brother. . . .

You always think you know these people (they are nearly always familiar), but then it turns out that you don't quite (they are nearly always surprising). There is usually something slightly askew, slightly *beside* our expectations—often quite a bit so. We expect Betty Hutton to be showing off for the soldiers in the record store where she works in *The Miracle of Morgan's Creek* (1944)—we've already heard how "popular with the boys" she is, to her father's shame. But should she be imitating a tuba sound when we first see her, mouthing the words of something called "The Bell in the Bay"—

Boom, boom, tolled the bell in the bay,
As the wind sang a dirge overhe-e-e-e-ad—
And the roll of the waves
Marked their watery graves,
While the bell chimed the toll of the dead.

—to a basso profundo recording of the song? (Still, it's no wonder they're crazy about her.) And why should tough Brian Donlevy in *The Great McGinty* (1940) take such flamboyant exception to William Demarest's ordering orange juice from the bartender in the back room? "Orange juice!" Donlevy whoops—he hardly even knows this man, or anyone else in the room, but he is suddenly, unaccountably provoked. "How's my back hair, Flossie?" he says in an effeminate voice, smoothing the back of his head. While the other people at the bar just look at him, baffled. "What'd he say?" says the Boss (Akim Tamiroff) to the little mayor (Arthur Hoyt). The mayor shrugs—staring in alarm. "Give me a double pecan twist with two cherries in it," says Donlevy in the same mincing voice. The mayor looks even more alarmed ("What'd he say?" persists the Boss). Donlevy returns to his real, "manly" voice: "Gimme a boilermaker," he says. "A what?" says the bartender—his first question so far.

There are always a hero and heroine, of course. But they play out their destiny in these films against milling backgrounds of people. Never before, it seems, have romantic comedies been so densely populated, or these background figures so heightened and galvanized. The privileged spaces at the center occupied by romantic couples like Dunne and Grant are unknown to the Sturges couple, who always have someone, or several someones, pressing from behind—who are surrounded not by spectators but by eager participants, full of their own vivid, jostling, eccentric life. And even when they come in groups—like the ineffable Ale and Quail Club in *The Palm Beach Story*—these figures retain their conten-

Sturges and Colbert on the Penn Station set with The Palm Beach Story's Ale and Quail Club: (standing) Dewey Robinson, Robert Greig, Robert Warwick, Arthur Stuart Hall, Torben Meyer, Jack Norton, Vic Potel, Jimmy Conlin; (seated) Chester Conklin, Sturges, Colbert, Roscoe Ates, William Demarest.

tious uniqueness. Compare the press-room crowd in *His Girl Friday*, all familiar character players: Tom Jenks, Porter Hall (again), Cliff Edwards, Regis Toomey, Roscoe Karns. But Hawks doesn't use them for their individuality—more for their ability to speak in a common voice, to express a common style, even to look alike (after a while, anyway). And their bitter, funny, wisecracking lines are—as we hear them—interchangeable. Of course, this is one of the things Chicago can do to people—to the run of people, at any rate: wearing them down, absorbing them into the collective character.

But not Sturges people—who are just as vivid and intrusive and appallingly distinctive in Chicago (his version of it is in *The Great McGinty*) as anywhere else. One reason they're intrusive is a simple one: they turn up in all Sturges' films. Other filmmakers might have been attached to the same supporting players, using them again and again—but never before to forty of them(!), as Sturges was, using nearly all of them in every film. They came to be known as the Sturges Stock Company. And from movie to movie he seemed not only to be casting them to type (their value to other filmmakers, and to the studio system itself, was the vividness with which they could evoke a type) but exploring their range and variety. So that they were rarely cast the same way twice in his films. Arthur Hoyt, the milquetoast type, goes through a variety of occupations, from mayor to lawyer to preacher. Al Bridge, the house-detective type, goes from department-store clerk to brutal prison guard to kindly small-town lawyer to house detective. Esther Howard, the sexy mama type, goes from streetwalker to fortune teller to small-town widow to mayor's wife. Jimmy Conlin, the comic stooge type—who looks and behaves like a manic cricket—goes from tout to convict to mayor to judge. And Harry Hayden, the embodiment of dull solidity, with his round face, thick little glasses, and thin, droning voice, moves between representatives of unimpeachable integrity (Doc Bissell in *Hail the Conquering Hero*) on the one hand, and serenest corruption on the other (the nameless pollwatcher in *The Great McGinty*).

For the character actor, as it's been said, physiognomy—or its equivalent—is destiny. But in a Sturges film you're not so sure. He casts Jack Norton, the movies' resident souse, sober—and Franklin Pangborn, the movies' resident pansy, straight. And it's Frank Moran, the definitive plug-ugly, a hulking, gravel-voiced ex-fighter, who identifies a paraphrase from the Bible in *Sullivan's Travels*, and who shudders with distaste at a sight of the hero's new clothes in *The Great McGinty*. "Quite a suit," he remarks to the gunsel next to him in the front seat of the car, as McGinty gets into the back. And the gunsel (Harry Rosenthal) gestures dismissively, as if to say, "What can you expect?" Sturges loves it that private detective Edgar Kennedy ("a vulgar footpad," as Sir Alfred, with his imperfect command of the jargon, calls him) should turn out in *Unfaithfully Yours* to be a connoisseur of classical music performances and an inveterate concert-goer. Or that almost everyone in the orchestra that makes such glorious sounds in the rehearsal sequence should look—under the camera's extended scrutiny—either like an insurance agent or a manicurist. The point is that people are always unexpected in some way. That's what gives the Sturges comedy so much of its excitement. As if the liberated feelings we associate with the hero and heroine in screwball comedy had somehow spread through the whole cast.

Sidney Fox and Paul Lukas in John Stahl's film of Sturges' Strictly Dishonorable.

A T THE time—1940—Sturges seemed to belong to a new "generation" of filmmakers, like Welles (born 1915) and Wilder and Huston (both born in 1906). But in fact Sturges (born 1898) was a year older than Capra, two years older than Hawks, and only six years younger than Lubitsch. But Hawks and Capra and Lubitsch, all veterans of the silent film, had begun their movie careers as very young men. Sturges was middle-aged before he got round to movies: he didn't arrive in Hollywood until he was in his mid-thirties, in 1933. And then he spent seven years as a screenwriter before being allowed to direct his first film, at the age of forty-two.

Before that, he was a playwright, an inventor, an airman during the First World War (though, like Hawks, he never got overseas), and the survivor of one of the most outrageous childhoods anyone had ever told an interviewer about— being trundled across Europe and America by his restless, much-married mother, the incredible Mary Desti (née Dempsey), who was the best woman friend and nearly constant companion of Isadora Duncan. The anecdotes all this supplied were numerous—and Sturges the adult told them with relish (and without apparent bitterness): about being made to wear a toga to school in Chicago; about being oppressed in different ways by his mother's various lovers and husbands (among them a discipline-prone Turk named Vely Bey, and Aleister Crowley, the world-famous satanist); about being "dragged . . . into every goddamn museum in the world" for his education; about being awakened in the middle of the night when he was eight to be told that Solomon Sturges, the "father" he loved so dearly, was not in fact his father—and then being spirited back to Paris, and Isadora again, by his mother. (His real father was a dim, banjo-playing traveling salesman named Biden, who had decamped for good long ago. Solomon Sturges, a stockbroker, one of the richest men in the Midwest and his mother's fourth husband, had adopted Preston when he was three.) What's striking in Sturges' accounts of all this life with Mother, in his interviews and occasional autobiographical writings, is the good humor—as if it were the plot of one of his movies. But he may have had his revenge, all the same: "They did everything they could," he later said, "to make me an artist. But I didn't want to be an artist. I wanted to be a good businessman—like my father."

But even his father didn't want him to be a stockbroker. He said it was too much like being a betting commissioner. For a while, young Sturges ran his mother's business, a cosmetics firm called the Maison Desti. And in 1919, as he later recalled (in 1949), "I invented a lipstick compounded of dyes so violent that even the most lascivious kisses failed to remove it—for several days." But even the first "kissproof" lipstick failed to save the business. And now married to an heiress with the improbable name of Estelle de Wolfe Mudge, Sturges began to indulge his passion for the invention of machines (an automobile engine, a flying machine, a photo-engraving process, etc., etc.) on a full-time scale. Until his wife left him—after four years of marriage. His despair and subsequent illness, he later claimed, prompted the reassessment that turned him to writing. *Not* "artistic" writing, of course—but the commercial stuff. First he tried songs (no luck there), then Broadway plays. His second play, *Strictly Dishonorable*, produced by Brock Pemberton, opened on September 18, 1929— and became one of the biggest hits in Broadway history.

It's about an Italian opera star who tries to put the make on an innocent Southern girl. It takes place in a speakeasy, which the girl visits with her dull fiancé from New Jersey. The fiancé departs, and the girl is finally about to yield to the opera star, when he is stricken with qualms of conscience and backs off. The girl feels rejected and has resigned herself to returning to the fiancé and to New Jersey—just as the singer returns and proposes to her for the final curtain. "No, I am not joking," wrote George Jean Nathan in his rave notice. "That by God is actually the plot!" But he added: "The playwright has done wonders with it." And Nathan wasn't alone in noticing the disproportion. Since even by the then-prevailing standards of the commercial comedy, *Strictly Dishonorable* was strikingly formulaic. Its characters were like an inventory of stock types: not only the European lothario hero and the blushing Southern-belle heroine and the stuffed-shirt Other Man but also a bibulous Irish cop, an effusive Italian restaurant owner, and a kindly elderly judge. As Gilbert Seldes pointed out in *his* rave notice, these figures were "assembled" not from life but "from literature and the stage," and yet by some miracle, "by a real humor, both in speech and in motives," the playwright had brought them fully to life. He had also, it was generally agreed, avoided "bad taste"—by devices no one could quite explain. Since the play was such a transparent and calculated sort of tease, with so much on-the-brink stuff about the girl's deflowering, much play with things like pajama tops and teddy bears (as well as teddies, in which the heroine appears in the second act), and so on. But it was just this "thin ice" aspect of the play that made for its "essential satisfaction," observed Thornton Delehanty in the *Post*, two years after its opening—adding that only people who hadn't "been around much in the last year or two" would need to be told this.

And it's just in these ways—stereotypes embraced and somehow transcended, "offensiveness" risked and redeemed—that Sturges' first great success prefigures his great movies later on. Though it doesn't otherwise much resemble them, or come close to their brilliance and adventurousness. Sturges himself felt that the play had been taken away from him by the extensive rewrites that Pemberton had insisted upon. He even thought that it had been ruined—until it turned into this enormous, career-making success. And his next two plays were disasters. *Recapture*, a romantic tragicomedy, opened January 29, 1930, and closed after twenty-four performances. The critics cited its oddly conflicting tones and intentions—John Mason Brown called it "that play about an elevator" (the heroine dies in one in the third act). At this time, Sturges married again—another heiress, Eleanor Post Hutton—after a much-headlined romance (her prominent family was against it). Then he embarked on his next theatrical venture, which seemed to everyone around him (except, apparently, his wife, who bankrolled it as a wedding present) a peculiarly wrongheaded one. He acquired an expensive musical production, *Silver Swan*, an operetta that had flopped out of town, and undertook to write a whole new play—new story, new dialogue and lyrics—to suit the existing music and sets, even the cast and the costumes. This scheme, which seemed so loony to others, seemed irresistibly sensible to him. Even practical: think of the savings. The inventor-artist. Later on, in Hollywood, he would offer to "re-dialogue" (his word) somebody else's film for them. And this was the kind of writer he at least partly meant to be, it seems: the consummate pro, to be called in on any case. *The Well of Romance*, as the "re-dialogued" operetta was called, opened on November 7, 1930, and closed after eight performances. It was, said John Mason Brown, "old-fashioned enough to seem like a revival."

Nineteen thirty was also the year that Sturges wrote his first screenplays, both filmed at Paramount's Astoria studios outside New York: *The Big Pond* (1930), with Maurice Chevalier and Claudette Colbert, and *Fast and Loose* (1930), Miriam Hopkins' debut film, with an important supporting role for his friend Carole Lombard. Although Sturges in each case shares screen credit with several writers, both these scripts seem to be largely his. Especially *The Big Pond*, with its European hero who finds American success by inventing a whiskey-flavored chewing gum. There was another Broadway play in 1932—*Child of Manhattan*, about a Brooklyn taxi dancer, notable for its cinematic structure of many scenes (Lubitsch attended a rehearsal and praised the experiment to the press)—but also a failure (eighty-seven performances). And Sturges' second marriage collapsed at the same time.

He was ready for Hollywood. Though apprehensive about it, too. He signed a screenwriting contract with Universal—the studio that had produced the 1931 movie of *Strictly Dishonorable*, directed by John Stahl. It was a "Universal Super Attraction," playing two-a-day road-show engagements—like a play. Too much so, perhaps. Reviewers were disappointed, complaining of the picture's stiltedness, comparing it unfavorably with the "vitality" and "verve" of the stage production. And even today, the movie seems cautious and sedate—almost more concerned to replicate a success than to have one. But since it's so faithful to the play, it does convey its force and interest. Stahl and his actors (Paul Lukas, Sidney Fox, Lewis Stone) have caught the real generosity of feeling behind the winking-and-leering mode. Sturges thought so, too, and liked the film enormously. He wrote Carl Laemmle to tell him so, and a correspondence ensued that led to his taking the screenwriter's job.

BUT THE Universal stint didn't work out well. He wrote a script for the movie version of H. G. Wells's *The Invisible Man*—entirely original and "an excellent hair-raiser" by his own account. But director James Whale rejected it, and Sturges was dropped from the salary rolls. It was then—just when his Hollywood career seemed to have been aborted—that he pulled off a coup that shook the movie industry. He sold a completed and original shooting script to Jesse Lasky at Fox. Sturges wasn't even asked to rewrite: Lasky, in interviews, called it "the most perfect script I'd ever seen." Sturges had even negotiated some control of the production—and the signing of this precedent-shattering contract was much photographed: Sturges and Lasky and director William K. Howard—and Sturges looking *very* pleased. But others, like B. P. Schulberg, were alarmed at so much power ceded to a writer.

"I wonder if you ever saw *The Power and the Glory*," Sturges wrote of this film in 1948, in a letter to British film critic Peter Ericsson of *Sequence* magazine,

> . . . called in England *Power and Glory* and in France *Thomas Garner*, which was the first film I did in Hollywood? It is the film which started Spencer Tracy off on the right foot in Hollywood and made me a host of enemies. I was not allowed to direct it of course, but I did write it alone and directed the dialogue and received a percentage of the gross. . . . Writers at that time worked in teams, like piano movers, and my solo effort was considered a distinct menace to the profession. My credit, as it is called, was inserted modestly between that of the gentleman who did the music and the lady who did the frocks. . . .

The Power and the Glory (1933) was released to much fanfare—and much publicity for Sturges the screenwriter (contrary to his later recollections, suggesting he was ignored more or less). It's the story of a railroad tycoon (Spencer Tracy), which begins with his funeral and then recounts in flashback his life and eventual suicide. A lot was made at the time of Sturges' invention of what the Fox publicity department termed "narratage" (coined from "narrative" and "montage")—a technique involving voice-over narration and a novelistic freedom of structure. "The first *narrative* screenplay ever made," boasted Jesse Lasky in the souvenir program, and "I believe Mr. Sturges is the first author to avail himself of the full resonance of the new medium" (i.e., talkies). The most daring aspect of the screenplay and final film was its fractured chronology: jumping back and forth in time as it ranged over the hero's life. In its subject, style, and framing device (after-the-funeral reflections), *The Power and the Glory* prefigured both Sturges' *The Great Moment* and Welles's *Citizen Kane*. And Sturges, it seems, meant it as a kind of breakthrough film, not unlike *Kane*. "Great filmwrights will come," Sturges wrote to Burns Mantle, the New York critic and theater anthologist, in a "confidential" letter almost as grandiloquent on the subject of his film as Lasky's program blurb—and "small potatoes like myself" will show the way:

> . . . I wrote it as a play is written, complete and final. I sold it that way. We shot it that way. I was on the set during the entire filming of the picture, rehearsing the actors in the reading of the lines just as we do in the theater. . . . It will be as obvious tò you then as it is to me, that the writers and the writers alone can bring motion pictures to the high level they are destined to occupy. . . .

All this Importance was ratified by the reviews in many cases—but in many cases not. The dissenters found the picture thin, glum, and pretentious. *Time* complained that for all its fanciness the film was still about "the simplest characters" and "the simplest possible problem." *The New Yorker* (John McCarten) was very unimpressed by the experiment in discontinuous chronology, calling it a "hodgepodge," asserting that it "by no means serves to freshen that old bromide about the ruthless financier who destroys everything before him in his march to glory and disillusionment." If the reviews were divided, the box-office reaction wasn't: audiences found it depressing and confusing.

Spencer Tracy in The Power and the Glory.

It's a curious exhibit in the Sturges canon, even for an early work. Lifeless, characterless, mostly humorless—and grindingly predictable in almost everything but its "narratage"—it seems to be his one stab at a kind of art film. And however he may have disavowed that sort of thing in his subsequent work, he seems always to have had a not-so-sneaking fondness for this try at it—as if it proved something about his credentials. If *Variety* over a decade later referred to it as a "flop," he wrote them a letter claiming it wasn't (it was). And he tells Peter Ericsson in 1948 this story about it: "To this day visitors from Europe flatter me by saying: 'Do you know, Mr. Sturges, some of your films remind me a little of that great European masterpiece *Thomas Garner?*' I thank them."

It's true that *The Power and the Glory* broke several Hollywood rules: its fracturing of the narrative line can seem risky even now. But the film's "daring" (unlike the very real daring of the Sturges comedies to come) is fatally genteel— just as that fantasy (as I take it) of its being confused with a "European masterpiece" suggests. The combination of "experimental" technique with solemn and empty cliché evokes the whole tradition of Theatre Guild seriousness; and the movie suggests by inversion just how much Sturges had to gain from Hollywood crassness, how much he (and all of us) might have lost if he'd learned to suit himself to the requirements of Broadway "class," to the ideals and ambitions of a New York theater artist.

But the career gamble he had taken with this script hadn't paid off, at least not by Hollywood standards. And now Hollywood, as was its custom, proceeded to humble him. For the next year or so he went from studio to studio, job to job, mogul to mogul—from Irving Thalberg to Harry Cohn to B. P. Schulberg (his enemy) to Sam Goldwyn (who called him "Sturgeon"). He worked on several pictures, credited and uncredited; his name appeared on three of them, though not much of his work survived in any but one: the Goldwyn film, *We Live Again*, an "adaptation" of Tolstoy's *Resurrection* directed by Rouben Mamoulian, is mostly Sturges' work (an early, gently comic scene of challenge and banter between Fredric March and Anna Sten even sounds like his later comedies), and he was given credit in Hollywood for having "licked a tough property." He returned to Universal—where things began to look up again.

A ND HE gained more control of his next two films there than he had had since *The Power and the Glory*—getting sole screenplay credit on both, and once again working on the set with the director and actors. The films even include in their casts an embryo version (i.e., Eric Blore, Al Bridge, Torben Meyer, and Frank Moran) of the soon-to-be Stock Company. And the Sturges quality—his sound and feeling—began to emerge on the screen more distinctively than it ever had before. Both *The Good Fairy* (1935), with Margaret Sullavan, Herbert Marshall, and Frank Morgan, directed by William Wyler, and *Diamond Jim* (1935), with Edward Arnold, Jean Arthur, and Binnie Barnes, directed by Edward Sutherland, are full-blown Sturges works, despite their sources (Molnár in the one case, a conventional biography in the other). He wrote on the set on both productions: on the first, because there were so many problems with the temperamental Sullavan; on the second, because the movie went into production with only seventeen pages of the Sturges script completed. Originally Sturges had been hired only to do a patch-up job on some other people's screenplay. But once he got into the material, he was so carried away by the story of Diamond Jim Brady that he insisted upon doing the whole script over again. And Sutherland, the director, supported him, against much studio opposition. The biggest fights came at the end of the shooting schedule: the arguments over what Sturges had invented for an ending—when the ill, gourmandizing hero, having lost both love and hope, repairs to the dining room to eat himself to death. The front office was appalled, but Sturges and Sutherland persisted and won this issue, just as they had the others.

Sturges' Hollywood stock was now very high. And he was enjoying it. His "charismatic charm" was "almost legendary," and his "festive and brilliant" talk "kept a hundred colorful friends flocking around him": that is how Frederick Kohner recalls the Sturges of this period. And in 1936 Paramount—the most important studio in his career, just as it was in Lubitsch's—signed him to a screenwriting contract, on the basis of a script he had done for Burns and Allen (it was made in 1937, with other actors, as *Hotel Haywire*). And he worked cheerfully, more or less, on such assignments as *Never Say Die* (1939), a very funny Bob Hope–Martha Raye film (originally written for Jack Benny), and *If I Were King* (1938), with his good friend Ronald Colman, the warhorse play about François Villon revamped. But what Sturges wanted to do—what he had been devising fruitless plans and strategies to do from his first days in Hollywood— was confirmed in this intention more than ever by the common fate of his two most important Paramount screenplays, *Easy Living* (1937) and *Remember the Night* (1940): i.e., they were both directed by

Herbert Marshall, Frank Morgan, Margaret Sullavan, and Reginald Owen in The Good Fairy.

Mitchell Leisen, the former art director now become one of the studio's top film-makers. And *well* directed, too, as most people would—and did—say. But not Sturges—who objected to Leisen's pacing, his cuts in the scripts (done, Sturges thought, only to assert control), his arrogance and pretension, his fussiness over costumes and sets (he cared more about the background, Sturges claimed, than the scene in front of it), and so on. (Leisen's contribution to the writer-director movement, in fact, seems to have been inadvertent but considerable: Billy Wilder also detested him.)

Sturges was a genuine studio asset at this time, and his unhappiness had to be addressed; on the other hand, it was generally agreed that writers had to be kept in their place. (At Warner's, for example, they were barred from the set of any movie they had written for.) Sturges made production chief William Le Baron an offer: he would *give* the studio an original screenplay (the nominal purchase price was ten dollars) if they would let him make the picture for them. Le Baron agreed—shattering Hollywood precedent even more decisively than Jesse Lasky had in his deal with Sturges six years before. Art directors might aspire to the director's chair, but not writers, who were hard enough to control as it was. Preston Sturges, then, was the first of the studio writer-directors (others, like Wilder, soon followed)—and he began shooting his own script of *The Great McGinty* on December 11, 1939. And in spite of needing help at times (i.e., how to look through the camera) and falling sick in the middle of the schedule (losing four days), he proved to be surprisingly efficient, finishing in mid-January, three days early and a thousand dollars under budget.

And the movie itself (released in August 1940) was a sensation. "The answer to any exhibitor's prayer," said the *Hollywood Reporter*, in spite of its being a B film and without major stars. So pleased had the studio been with the rushes, in fact, that they'd let Sturges begin a second picture (another original script) even before *McGinty* was released. So that one sensation was followed by another, only three months afterwards: *Christmas in July* (1940). But even this was just a warmup, as it turned out, for *The Lady Eve* (1941), an A film with major stars (Henry Fonda and Barbara Stanwyck) and one of the biggest hits in Paramount history. This "genius" made money, it seemed—unlike that other one at RKO (1941 was also the year of *Citizen Kane*)—and he played the Hollywood game, not reluctantly but eagerly. Or so it appeared at the time.

He even opened a restaurant on Sunset Boulevard, The Players—another longtime dream realized. He conceived it as a special convenience to movie people—a kitchen that was both first-class and late night, so that people working late on the set would have someplace besides home to go to. One of the striking things about Sturges' movie career at this time is how much fun he had with it—and how many people he invited to it, whatever way he could, either at the restaurant or on his sets, which were always open and convivial. He once said that he did his real directing at the typewriter. Like Lubitsch and Hitch-cock, he mapped it all out beforehand. But writing could be an agony to him, something to be put off as long as possible—done in a panic, under the wire, in the middle of the night. Filming was something else, at least in the good days—a kind of party, with lots of guests, noisy and friendly and bustling. There was the inevitable piano: either he played it himself ("to keep actors going," says the *Life* photo caption—cryptically) or Stock Company player Harry Rosenthal did. Sturges often wore outlandish costumes, like a red fez (so people could find him in the crowd, he said), and was accompanied by one of his Dobermans. He liked everybody to watch the rushes with him, whether they were involved in them or not. Just as he wanted his wife, Louise (his third marriage), to be on the set with him, whether others thought she was in the way or not. When he found out that Cecil B. De Mille had a special table for his staff at the studio commissary, Sturges finagled one right next to him—for his Stock Company. He was "crazy," said W. R. Burnett in a 1981 interview—"one of the best" but "nutty," too: "He had a big desk and a horn on it that honked. Honk, honk. He thought it was goddamned funny."

He laughed a lot at his own jokes. So did the actors. Barbara Stanwyck, said a reporter (the Pittsburgh *Press*) on the set of *The Lady Eve*, became "hysterical" during the filming of her love scene with Henry Fonda—the one on the chaise longue with Fonda on the floor beside her ("Snakes are my life . . ."). And it took four hours to stage the scene because the two stars kept breaking up at it. And yet once they settled down, the whole thing was done in a single four-minute take, then repeated once for insurance, and wrapped—a total of fifteen minutes altogether, said the impressed reporter. Sturges rarely did more than two or three takes of a scene, and he neglected close-ups and covering shots (making a problem for his editors at times). "For an artistic genius type of direc-tor," said Joel McCrea, "he wasted less time and less film than anyone, except maybe Hitchcock." Particularly if a sequence was long and intricate, Sturges liked to do it all at once and without cutting—in a single uninterrupted take. The long walks through town in the two Eddie Bracken films were done that way—in one or two takes. And the opening sequence of *Sullivan's Travels*—Sullivan's argument in and out of the screening room with Hadrian and Le Brand—a scene scheduled for two days of shooting, was accomplished on the first try in a single take and on the production's first morning—a feat that be-came the talk of the lot.

But *Sullivan's Travels* (1942)—a film about a filmmaker—was too unorthodox a picture to be really popular. Though it had (at Sturges' insistence) new star Veronica Lake in it, who was *very* popular. Sturges, who by now could do pretty much as he wanted at the studio, decided to hedge his bets with his next pro-duction: *The Palm Beach Story* (1942), with Claudette Colbert and Joel McCrea, is classical screwball, marital-mixup variety—or so it was meant to be. It was a stranger film than Sturges probably knew—colder and odder than audiences of the time were ready for. In any case, the returns were disappointing, and this time—the first time—even the reviews were mixed. Nevertheless, Sturges proceeded with his riskiest project yet: a costume film about the American dentist who discovered anesthesia. And this film—*The Great Moment* (1944), as it was finally called—effectively ended his career at Paramount.

Buddy De Sylva was now the production chief, replacing Sturges' friend Le Baron (who had once replaced Lubitsch), who had departed for Fox. De Sylva hated the whole idea of this dentist picture—certain that the title alone, *Triumph over Pain*, after the best-selling book (by René Fulop-Miller) it was based on, would sink it—but Sturges' contract rendered him powerless to stop it. Sturges renamed it *Great Without Glory* and began filming on April 9, 1942, with Joel McCrea and Betty Field in the leads. If the studio couldn't avert the disaster, they could at least keep it quiet, and they discouraged the sort of on-the-set press coverage that a Sturges production normally got—and that Sturges himself loved. But with his usual efficiency, he brought the film in on budget and a day ahead of schedule. And it was then that his troubles really started.

De Sylva detested the completed picture even more than he had expected to. And the first preview in Glendale was not heartening. Sturges, however, felt he had made just the film he meant to: when De Sylva demanded changes, Sturges fought back and refused. De Sylva shelved the picture, postponing its release indefinitely. And Sturges—determined not to get hung up in a studio battle he would be almost certain to lose—went on to the next project. He wanted to do a film with Betty Hutton, and so he wrote *The Miracle of Morgan's Creek* (1944) for her, a wild wartime farce about a girl who gets impregnated by a soldier she can't even remember meeting.

You'd think they might almost have preferred the dentist. The sexual promiscuity of wartime was one of the movies' most resolutely unmentioned subjects. And a *comedy* about it? How could he get such a project past the Production Code? But he was determined—and so the negotiations began. And they were endless, with censors worrying him about everything in the script from a mention of "screeching tires" (the waste of rubber) to an "unnecessary indictment of the motor court industry" (the seedy motel where Trudy and Norval get married) to Emmy's "lack of reverence and respect" for her father, Officer Kockenlocker (apparently that name got by them). Even the War Department got into the act, with an urgent wire requesting the "picture to make clear that husband is father and no other soldiers involved." But the amazing thing in all this is not that Sturges finally won so many of these minor battles—that the picture appeared with wasted rubber and dingy motel and filial disrespect intact—but that he won the major one. And totally, it would seem—to the astonishment of audiences everywhere when the film finally opened (a year after its completion). "The Hays Office," proclaimed the delighted James Agee, "has been raped in its sleep."

But the filming itself had been a hassle from the start. Because of all the negotiations over the script, Sturges had to begin shooting (in November 1942) without a finished screenplay, filming in the daytime and writing at night. And there were more problems on the set than he was used to, as well as more complaints and interventions from the front office. At times the legendary Sturges efficiency asserted itself (as when he filmed Diana Lynn and Betty Hutton's long walk through downtown Morgan's Creek in only two takes, fifteen minutes of shooting, and after only an hour of preparation)—other times not. And those were the times when De Sylva—who had already decided that Sturges was probably more trouble to the studio than he was worth to them (*The Lady Eve* had been his only really big moneymaker)—would strike. As in the following memo, upbraiding Sturges, in the time's most patriotic style, for "sabotaging" the war effort:

> . . . I really mean sabotage, as the same materials that are used to make film go into the making of munitions. No other director on the lot needs fifty takes to get a scene. Either you do not properly explain to the actors what they are called on to do or you engage inadequate actors. Or perhaps the actors are so upset after takes #15 or #20 that you are no longer capable of getting what you desire. . . .

And so on. But what Sturges now desired more and more was to be free of Paramount—where, as he pointed out in one of his many letters of protest to the front office, he was never given credit for achievement or even ordinary competence ("How many years and how many pictures does it take to win the confidence of Paramount?"), where he was treated either like a wayward child or a suspicious person: "checked, cross-checked, tabulated, reported upon, and as closely watched as a paroled convict." On the other hand, he said—quite truly—"I love Paramount and do not want to leave." But De Sylva was making it impossible to stay.

With two pictures completed and unreleased, Sturges began a third in July 1943, his eighth (and final) Paramount production: *Hail the Conquering Hero* (1944), which he shot on the same back-lot "town" he'd done *Miracle* on, and with the same star, Eddie Bracken. It was a comedy with another touchy subject—about a war hero who's a fake. But at least it wasn't about sex—and so at first, anyway, there were fewer problems. Until De Sylva began his campaign against the leading lady, Ella Raines, who had done only three minor films before that and who wasn't even a Paramount player (she was a Howard Hawks protégée, under personal contract to him and to Charles Boyer). In any case, Raines stayed on, the film was finished in September, shelved for the moment like the two before it, and Sturges—after an unsuccessful attempt to negotiate a contract that would give him more autonomy (and less De Sylva)—left the studio for good in December 1943.

BUT HE still wasn't done with them. De Sylva, who had recut and rearranged the footage of *The Great Moment*, was now threatening to do the same thing with *Hail the Conquering Hero* after some disappointing previews. And Sturges, of course, was more helpless than ever. Until the opening of *The Miracle of Morgan's Creek* (January 1944)—in the Sturges version—seemed to turn the situation around. *Miracle* was a smash, an even bigger hit than *The Lady Eve*. And when, shortly after this triumph for Sturges, De Sylva previewed *his* version of *Hero* in New York, the response was disastrous. It seemed that Sturges did know better, after all, and he was now permitted to return to the studio to restore *Hero* to its original form. He did more than that: he improved it—tightening it, doing retakes, writing and filming a new ending. And when *Hero* opened, just seven months after *Miracle* had, to nearly the same acclaim and excitement, Sturges really did seem like a miracle man—his reputation higher and his success more dizzying than they had ever been.

But he still couldn't rescue *The Great Moment*—and he was still trying. There is still time, he urged Y. Frank Freeman, the studio head, in an urgent "hand-delivered" letter, "to save *The Great Moment* from the mediocre and shameful career it is going to have in its present form." But on this issue, it seemed, the studio wouldn't be budged. And in November 1944, just three months after the triumphant premiere of *Hero*, Paramount released—very quietly—the De Sylva version of *The Great Moment*. The critics, Sturges' friends up to now, hardly knew what to make of this one, especially after the epiphany of his last two films. And audiences just stayed away—those who didn't reportedly wished they had. "Come now, Sturges—surely you were kidding?" wrote a serviceman fan in a typical response. "All I want is a reassuring word."

After all this, then, Howard Hughes looked good. Hughes was just the sort of figure—the rich, eccentric inventor—that Sturges would be attracted to anyway. Sturges was "hot," and he had a lot of offers from other studios, but what Hughes promised him was freedom—and the sort of financing that meant he could set himself up like Chaplin, with his own studio, and as his own studio boss. And so Hughes and Sturges established California Pictures (whose motto was "Non Redolemus Pisce"—i.e., "We Do Not Smell From Herring," in Sturges' translation), and in September 1945 Sturges began shooting *The Sin of Harold Diddlebock* on the Samuel Goldwyn lot, with Harold Lloyd, one of Sturges' idols, making his long-deferred return to the screen. Sturges had also rounded up as much of the old Stock Company as he could collect (it would be his first film without William Demarest, whom De Sylva refused to lend), and cast his then-current girlfriend, the attractive Frances Ramsden (his third marriage had all but broken up), in the ingenue role.

This set was a *real* party—and filming often wasn't allowed to interfere with it. So it appeared, anyway, as the production schedule stretched on and on—fifty-two days over the original schedule of sixty-four, and more than six hundred thousand dollars over its million-dollar budget. It's my money, said Sturges (who was listed by the IRS in 1947 as the third-highest earner in America)—just as it was his time. But "freedom" really had its problems for him. And they showed in the film, too, which was without the tightness or discipline of his Paramount work—with its inexpressive star and all its signs of imaginative depletion. When it was finally finished in January 1946, Hughes reacted like another De Sylva. He was disappointed with it, and after a few scattered engagements in early 1947 he pulled it out of release and proceeded to re-edit it. Three years later it was released nationally in the Hughes version, retitled *Mad Wednesday,* nineteen minutes shorter than the Sturges version and with a talking horse super-added for a joke at the end. It was of course a flop.

Now the *studios* looked good. And the offer that Sturges accepted, after his

Diddlebock (Harold Lloyd) finds a use for his hungry circus lion: to scare mean bankers like Jack Norton (on the desk). The Sin of Harold Diddlebock.

breakup with Hughes, was Darryl Zanuck's at Twentieth Century–Fox. Zanuck was as appreciative of Sturges' gifts as De Sylva had been carping and mingy— and he was more generous than anyone else, giving Sturges the biggest budget of his career for his first Fox assignment. It turned out to be his last great film: *Unfaithfully Yours* (1948), with Rex Harrison and Linda Darnell, an unsettling comedy about the indomitability of romantic love, done in a dazzling film noir style. Rex Harrison has recalled how happy the filming was, and how elated the "extraordinary and ingenious" Sturges seemed throughout—so amused by his own actors that he had to stuff a handkerchief in his mouth so as not to spoil the take by laughing.

But the laughter stopped when the film opened in theatres. Audiences, it was reported, were sitting through the jokes (as when the hero seems to slash his wife with a razor to the strains of Rossini) in dumbfounded silence. Receipts at New York's Roxy Theater were so calamitous that the studio decided on a whole new selling approach: if people couldn't take it as a comedy, maybe they could be persuaded to take it as a thriller—it certainly looked enough like one. "The hands around her neck," said the new ad campaign, "will hold a *RAZOR* to-night!" But nothing helped. For the public, it was the first Sturges movie in four years (Hughes was still sitting on *Diddlebock*); and like the one before it (*The Great Moment*), it seemed inexplicable.

The next one seemed even worse. *The Beautiful Blonde from Bashful Bend* (1949) was the movie that Sturges had promised Zanuck he would do for Betty Grable, the studio's most valuable star. But Sturges' heart was never in this project—and after a while neither was Zanuck's, as the rushes began to look more and more ominous. There were no reports of fun on this set. Grable was discontented and peevish—just as she had been with Lubitsch (she accused Zanuck of saddling her with has-beens) on the set of *That Lady in Ermine* the year before. So both Sturges and Lubitsch, by some strange and troubling fluke, made their last, disastrous Hollywood movies with this same star—the top female star of the forties, presiding like a kind of Nellie Brown (Nurse Cutie at the bedside) over the demise of their careers. But it was *her* career that worried Zanuck now. "He crucified her in it!" he later said to Mel Gussow. "We previewed it in Pomona and I walked around the block ten times. My God, I didn't know what to do." But as it turned out, he did: he let Sturges go—in spite of the director's pleas to be allowed to stay and to make the kind of modest, low-budget pictures he knew about.

Sturges never made such pictures again. The last decade of his life was an active one. He made a final and happier marriage—to Sandy Nagle. They had two sons. He still—for a while—had The Players. He moved from Hollywood to New York to Paris in pursuit of projects, in film or theater or even television, that for one reason and another never seemed to come off. Except for a botched

European film with Jack Buchanan, *Les Carnets du Major Thompson* (1956). He died on August 6, 1959, at the age of sixty-one, of a heart attack, at the Algonquin Hotel in New York. His friend Katharine Hepburn put it differently: "He died of neglect," she said.

Not only was Sturges the first writer-director to emerge from the studio ranks (John Huston and Billy Wilder soon followed, but they were writers, as Sturges was not, in a more conventional studio mold—adapters and collaborators), in some sense he was the only one: a top-rank filmmaker who filmed nothing but his own original scripts and who wrote them alone. Even his "adaptations," like *The Lady Eve* or *The Great Moment*, were originals, so much did he transform or leave behind their sources. He was not a displaced writer who made movies— a literary artist with no particular talent or bent for films, or a theatrical one who might just as well have directed his talents to the stage so far as we can tell: a Joseph Mankiewicz or a Nunnally Johnson. Just the opposite: Sturges was a writer of genius who fulfilled that genius in making movies and only in making movies. He came closer for his short time to an ideal of personal filmmaking— "writing with the camera"—than almost anyone else in Hollywood.

And yet his achievement is also, in some important way, an *im*personal one. Unique as he was, he was before everything a *movie* artist. We're certainly aware of the distinctiveness of a Sturges movie as we watch it: it couldn't have been made by anyone else. But we're also aware—and it's part of the very deepest pleasure his movies give us—of how he fulfills the movies themselves. As James Agee put it: "'Hollywood' was made for Sturges, and he in turn is its apotheosis." For Agee, though, this was a sign of his limitation, the reason he could never be (in Agee's view) a really first-rate artist. For us, though, it's likelier to seem different: the apotheosis of Hollywood—at least the Hollywood of the past— doesn't sound so bad. And Sturges was in fact just such a culmination: it even defines his special glory. Rather than being caught and hobbled by the formulas and stereotypes of movie custom, he was inspired by them. Like almost everyone else in Hollywood, he made movies from other movies. But he did it with a degree of consciousness and sophistication of purpose—as well as a depth and an originality—that hardly anyone else matched.

Jimmy MacDonald gets his name on the door— temporarily: George Renavent, Ellen Drew, and Dick Powell in Christmas in July.

Sturges: American Success | 24

Iɴ *Diamond Jim* (1935) Edward Arnold and his crony Eric Blore are having a drink at the bar when a horse walks through the swinging doors and joins them, so to speak, taking his place at the rail beside them. The horse is pulling an open carriage containing a well-dressed, rather vague-looking man, who orders two crèmes de menthe. Neither Arnold (as Diamond Jim Brady) nor Blore (as his sidekick, Sampson Fox) seems particularly startled. And since no one, not even the bartender, comments on the horse, we know that the man with him must be very rich and important. He is: his name is Horsley (Hugh O'Connell), and he turns out to be a valuable business connection for Brady, who soon becomes rich and important himself.

In *Diamond Jim* and then in *Easy Living* (1937), Arnold was Sturges' favorite plutocrat. And he has in these films an almost magical quality. We are not really taken aback, then, by the horse at the bar, or by the blackbirds that fly out of the pie at one of Brady's banquets, or by the fur coat that J. B. Ball (Arnold) flings out of the sky onto Jean Arthur's head, changing her life forever after. He is like some rich, wonderful father, and the glamour he has for Sturges comes no doubt from the latter's feelings about his own father, who was such a reassuring counterforce to his mother's scattiness and frightening caprice.

I adored this big man I had been re-united with, this ex–football player, this ex–bicycle champion of Illinois (on the high bicycle, of course), this man who brought me home another present every night of my life when I was little, and whose unfailing tenderness toward me extended back into the diffused twilight before my memory began. It was heaven to sit on his lap and the perfume of my father—a mixture of maleness and the best Havana cigars—was the breath of Araby to me. . . .

Whether he is irascible, as in *Easy Living*, or broken-hearted, as in *Diamond Jim*, this figure has great sweetness of nature. And it's the specifically masculine

*He gapes at
her in Dia-
mond Jim
(above) and
fumes at her in
Easy Living
(right):
Edward
Arnold and
Jean Arthur
in their
two Sturges
films.*

character of this sweetness ("a mixture of maleness and the best Havana cigars")
that interests and compels Sturges throughout his career.

And in some Sturges movies this character is explicitly magical. In *The Good
Fairy* (1935) and *The Palm Beach Story* (1942), he is a fairy godfather. "I thrive
on obstacles!" cries the determined-to-be-benevolent Konrad (Frank Morgan).
"All my plans are foolproof!" "The enchanted woods!" exclaims the childlike
heroine (Margaret Sullavan). More like "the enchanted bankroll," he rejoins.
And the Wienie King (Robert Dudley) takes just one look at Claudette Colbert
and whips his bankroll out ("I'm cheesy with money!"): how much does she
need? He does the same for Joel McCrea a bit later on. What he gives to the
hero and heroine—as these fantasies make clear—is the grown-up world itself,
the world of power and affairs, which he stands at the entrance to. His money
and goodwill not only make that world possible for them, but his example makes
it enviable. Of course, *they* will never be as grown-up as he is. How could they?
He is so large and solid and authoritative—especially in his Edward Arnold
versions. Where his size is like a metaphor for his nature. Just as Diamond Jim's

overeating (much referred to but sparingly shown) seems almost more like a spiritual activity than a physical one—his suicide by gourmet dining a final gesture of largesse and expansiveness.

He is a lonely figure—either in love, like Brady, with a woman he can't finally have or married, like J. B. Ball, to a woman without sympathy. But the contrast he makes to this wife (Mary Nash—who is also Arnold's wife, and the same *sort* of wife, in *Come and Get It*) is an instructive one. She is always calculating advantages (the narrow way she looks at him) and assessing personalities. She seems almost reflexively invidious. She wouldn't blame him, she announces, if he found another woman (he hasn't, in spite of what she thinks). "After all," she says, "I'm not the debutante you married." But he is preoccupied at that moment with a collapsing financial empire, and not able to deal with the reproaches she's aiming at him—"out of simple decency" he asks her to stop. "Well, I wouldn't talk about *decency* if I were you," she replies before stopping. Where he is self-forgetful, absorbed in his work, she is self-absorbed: when we first see her she is painting her toenails and guarding her furs. His authority comes from just such self-forgetfulness—which finds a counterpart in the heroine, Jean Arthur's Mary Smith (in their argument over compound interest), if not in the woman he's married to.

The city he presides over in *Easy Living* is not Chicago—gray and dingy and cramping—but that other screwball place, New York—light and sparkling and airy, a place of crowds and avenues and sunshine and skyscrapers. Like the building Louis Louis (Luis Alberni) stands in front of and contemplates: his own hotel, two gleaming towers soaring into the sky above him—and empty. "How can such a phenon-nee-num be a flop?" he says, in hopeless admiration. But then anything, or anyone, can be a flop in New York—and then just as suddenly be a hit. It's that dizzying roller-coaster changeability that makes the place so bracing. Sturges parallels the stock market, J. B. Ball's domain, to an Automat riot: a lot of gray-hatted people going crazy when all the little doors open at once. It's the familiar movie New York, but it's also a heightened, manic version of it—as a kind of delirious free-for-all. Where a wife leans from a penthouse window to drop a goldfish bowl onto her husband's head—and where a cook

Ellen Drew and Dick Powell in Christmas in July.

rushes outside to throw his apron into his boss's face ("You dirty capitalist!")—and the boss throws it right back. It's not a classless place—it's very far from it, in fact. It has a seemingly infinite number of arrangements for keeping people out and for keeping them apart—from tones of voice to privileges of office to solid walls. But nothing entirely works: the energy is too high and the madness too strong. There is finally no line that can't be crossed—no party that can't be crashed—no putdown that can't be put down again, crushingly. "Ah-uh-*ah!*" exclaims the salesperson (Franklin Pangborn) when he sees a customer (Arnold) removing the lady's hat from its model. He retrieves it: "We *prefer* to handle these ourselves," he says, with killing hauteur. "Uh-uh-ah yourself," growls Arnold, snatching the hat back and slapping Pangborn's hands. But Mr. Ball can't see you now, says the receptionist to Jean Arthur—whereupon Arthur takes her two sheepdogs and charges (on a signal) through the swinging wooden gates and into the center of Ball's office, landing sprawling on the floor. One reason it's so hard to keep people in their places is that hardly anyone seems to be in the right place to begin with. Louis Louis looks ill at ease in his own hotel, just as Mrs. Ball does in her boudoir, or Mary Smith (Arthur) in her penthouse. One of the deepest, most energizing convictions of the Sturges vision is that all these arrangements are arbitrary ones—capricious, predictable only in their nuttiness, and subject to instant revision. America is the land of scary fun—and New York is its capital.

B<small>UT</small> *Christmas in July* (1940) offers another view of New York. The hero and heroine, Jimmy MacDonald (Dick Powell), and his girlfriend, Betty (Ellen Drew), belong to an East Side tenement neighborhood, with its mandatory ethnic mix. And Sturges doesn't leave out a single stock figure, from Italian organ grinder to Irish cop to Jewish mama. Apart from this, however, the place has all the signs and virtues of a movie small town: warmth and loyalty, tradition and community ("I know this boy," says Mrs. Schwartz, "since his papa and mama wasn't even married yet"), as well as a suspicion of outsiders. This latter comes into play when Jimmy is pursued to his doorstep by two powerful, important men, Dr. Maxford (Raymond Walburn) of Maxford House Coffee and Mr. Schindel (Alexander Carr) of Schindel's Department Store, both of them calling him a swindler and demanding his arrest. But the cop on the beat (Frank Moran) wants to arrest *them.*

Jimmy and his girl have just been at Schindel's spending the check he won in the Maxford House Coffee contest on presents for the whole block—which is now out on the street en masse enjoying them. A scene of Sturges-like prodigality. That's when Maxford and Schindel come along. It seems that Jimmy hasn't won the Maxford House Coffee contest after all (it was just some wiseacres in his office, who sent him a phony telegram). And Dr. Maxford, who has discovered the fraud, is now demanding his check back. "You know perfectly well you didn't win!" exclaims the indignant Maxford. But of course Jimmy didn't know—and the discovery is a sickening one. He registers the blow—numbly—in close-up. And then walks out of the shot. Leaving his girl Betty to occupy the center of it—watching him go. And as she walks off in turn, to go after him, she leaves his mother (Georgia Caine), following them both with stricken eyes. The actors are placed in the shot, surrounded by the street crowds, so that each one's departure seems to *disclose* the other (we don't see the mother at all until Betty moves away), as if the camera were peeling away the layers of Jimmy's distress, reflected on the faces of the people who love him. The contrast with Lubitsch is an instructive one. Where a Lubitsch crowd isolates the central figure, a Sturges crowd supports and upholds him.

And yet this is a movie about leaving "the crowd" behind. It begins on a tenement rooftop—with the usual nighttime vista of Manhattan lights in the background and "Penthouse in Manhattan" playing on the soundtrack (we hear it throughout the movie)—where the hero is dreaming about making it big, winning the twenty-five-thousand-dollar coffee slogan contest. The heroine isn't grandiose: she just wants to get married. But when he explains to her what marriage might be like on their present salaries—

BETTY: Well, I earn eighteen, and you earn twenty-two, and that's forty, and—

JIMMY: Sure, sure, and you got your ma and I got mine. You get a kid and you'll have to stop work and we're right back at the twenty-two again—except that there's you and the kid and the two old ladies and me.

—he seems (with the kind of quiet power Sturges gets into such speeches) like the realistic one. Happiness, he says bluntly—which means not being worn out by life the way his parents were—"costs money." Jimmy is dispirited in this style through a major part of the film. Dick Powell, who up to that time had made a specialty (it put him twice in the top ten box-office stars, seventh in 1935, sixth in 1936) out of an infectious, almost lunatic ebullience when selling a song (the more witless the lyric, the wilder the eye roll), most notably in Busby Berkeley production numbers, could also be glum—though he wasn't often allowed to be at Warner Brothers. He goes through Sturges' film, however, alternating glee and discouragement—and even the glee seems touched by a certain depressiveness. If *Easy Living* is about the fun of being on a roll in capitalist America (there's never any question about the good luck in that movie), *Christmas in July* is a lot about not being on one, and how bad that can feel.

And how good it feels to "crash through," as Jimmy calls it. There are a lot of scenes of festivity in this film: Jimmy standing on his desk to announce that he's won the big prize, calling his mother while his excited fellow clerks look on and listen, shopping at Schindel's with Betty until even Mr. Schindel himself is excited, and returning to the old neighborhood and the outbreak of joyfulness on the streets as he gives away the presents. Like *Diamond Jim* and *Easy Living*, *Christmas in July* celebrates prodigality. But the celebration of success in this comedy, as in all Sturges' work, is an ambiguous one.

Earlier on Jimmy tries to tell Dr. Maxford why winning the contest (as he supposes) means so much to him. It's not just the money. "But to be poor and unknown one minute, and to be sitting on top of the world the next minute, that's a feeling nobody can ever take away from me." What means the most to him is that he won the contest because he "thought of a better slogan than anyone else." It's given him a new sort of confidence: "You see, I used to *think* maybe I had good ideas . . . but now I *know* it!" But Jimmy isn't the only one who needs a contest to know what he thinks. "I didn't hang on to my father's money by backing my own judgment, you know," his boss, Mr. Baxter (Ernest Truex), tells him. "I think your ideas are good because they sound good to me. But I *know* your ideas are good because you won this contest over millions of aspirants." But he hasn't won the contest—and when Mr. Baxter finds this out, he's no longer sure that Jimmy belongs in that new office that his "success" had won for him. Oh, yes, he does belong here, says Betty, pleading for him and the new office: "He belongs in here because he *thinks* he belongs in here . . . because he thinks he has ideas." But Jimmy, as he confides to her in the next scene, no longer does think that. "You know you've got what it takes," she reminds him. But he doesn't know—and he never did until he "got that telegram—and now I don't know anymore." But then who does know? Does anyone? Can you have what it takes without knowing you do? Or not? "Having it," like "making it," is a trick with mirrors, it seems—happening only because of the people who certify that it's happening—who may know less about it even than you do. But still it happens . . . When even your girlfriend isn't so sure about you ("because he thinks he has ideas"). He deserves at least a chance, she tells Mr. Baxter. That's all he wants, and "that's all any of them want," a chance to succeed "while they're still young and burning."* Besides, she says, concluding her plea for him, "his name's already on the door." Whereupon Mr. Baxter relents: "Well, if anything decided me, that would be it." So Jimmy gets his chance—"for a very short time, you understand." It all goes to show what Sam the porter (Snowflake) had said when Betty and Jimmy had first entered the building that night and encountered a cat in the office. "Is it good luck or bad luck," inquires Betty, "when

---

* Harold Lloyd in *The Sin of Harold Diddlebock* is a depressed, middle-aged version of Jimmy, burned out instead of burning: someone who had his chance and muffed it—as his boss (Raymond Walburn) explains to him.

a black cat crosses your path?" Replies Sam: "That all depends on what happens afterwards."

What if you end up like Mr. Waterbury, though—the office manager? According to Betty, you won't mind so much, even if that happens, provided you've been given that "chance to succeed" she's asking for Jimmy. Mr. Waterbury, on the other hand, doesn't mind at all—so he says. And in the person of Harry Hayden, he is one of the movie's most inspired creations: a robot of a man, putting his voice and face on automatic pilot as he gives Jimmy a chewing-out by rote for his neglected work. He stretches his neck, glazes his eye, folds his hands on his desk—and drones away. Just before this, we've seen him passing down the rows of desks, looking furtively pleased with himself as he lines up the papers on each worker's desktop. But it turns out, as it so often does with such figures in Sturges, that he is a very serious man in his way, who feels strongly about both his workers (they are children in a family, he later says) and his own responsibilities toward them (he stands up fearlessly for Jimmy to the boss later on, in that same droning style). He is also, it seems, a little deranged—though in a helpful way. When Jimmy tells him that the reason for his neglect of work is his anxiety about the Maxford House Coffee contest, Waterbury wants to know how much the prize is. Jimmy tells him; and Waterbury recalls, stretching his neck and shooting his cuffs and giving a distant chuckle (the sound of a madman?), that he once longed for just that amount of money himself:

> . . . I used to think about twenty-five thousand dollars too, and what I'd do with it—that I'd be a failure if I didn't get ahold of it. And then one day I realized I was never going to have that twenty-five thousand dollars, Mr. MacDonald. And then another day a little bit later—considerably later— I realized something else, something I am imparting to you now, Mr. MacDonald. . . . I'm not a failure. I'm a success. You see, ambition is all right if it works. But no system could be right where only one half of one percent were successes and all the rest were failures. That wouldn't be right. I'm not a failure. I'm a success. And so are you—if you earn your own living and pay your bills and look the world in the eye. I hope you win your twenty-five thousand dollars, Mr. MacDonald. But if you shouldn't happen to, don't worry about it. . . .

Mr. Waterbury has come to terms with failure by deciding that it doesn't exist. ("I just don't believe in failures," Frank Capra once said in an interview, in 1973.) And he has the simple decent man's faith in the decency of the established order. But, like his decision to call himself a success, it's a willed faith, maintained against terrible odds, as the rest of the movie, and the deadness in his voice and eye, show us. A nice man—who gives you the creeps.

But then Baxter's Coffee, where Waterbury and Jimmy work, is a disheartening place, with its time clocks and rows of desks and cubicle-style offices and clerks in dust jackets filing to their places at the bell in ranks like prisoners (with *mécanique* music on the soundtrack). It could hardly offer a greater contrast to that *other* coffee place, Dr. Maxford's—where there's an enormous electric sign (on all night and visible from Jimmy's rooftop) and a contest and a network radio show. Where no one wears dust jackets. Where there's not a nervous, purse-lipped boss, unsure of his own judgment, but an irascible, bug-eyed one—who is sure of disaster and endlessly voluble about it. Where the only clerks we see—far from filing to their desks—are lounging around the "contest room," as it's called, and bitching at each other. Especially at Bildocker from the shipping department (William Demarest)—who has deadlocked the twelve-man contest jury of company employees just at the moment when the "Maxford House Coffee Hour" has gone on the air to announce the winner. "Muffing" the biggest moment "in the annals of commerce"—not to mention giving "heart failure to the Western Hemisphere." These are the words—characteristically overheated—of Dr. Maxford himself. Who rushes to the contest room to tell Bildocker that he has been getting into his hair for the past twenty years—"and I meant to mention it before." Now he is giving him and the rest of them just four seconds to end their deadlock and arrive at a verdict—and "the next nitwit who talks to me about a contest had better *duck* before I swing on him!"

But ultimatums are wasted on Bildocker. He is too busy fending off the impatience and rage of the other jurors—"a bunch of fatheaded mealymouthed lamebrains," as he calls them. Nevertheless, they have chosen such a *nice* slogan—"just what the doctor ordered," says their foreman (Robert Warwick)—why can't Bildocker *see* that? And the foreman reads it to him again, in his dulcet and magisterial voice: "'Maxford—Magnificent and Mellow.'" And once again, with extreme patience, he tells Bildocker why they have chosen it: "It's brief, it's smooth, and it's pungent." Says Bildocker: "It's putrid." "But *why* is it putrid, Bildocker?" says the foreman, in his infinite sadness. "Because it stinks," says Bildocker—which is what he's been saying all along.

And so it goes in the contest room—with Dr. Maxford in *his* room, circling the desk and fulminating to his companion, the radio announcer Don Hartman (Franklin Pangborn). Who is also full of grievance ("I thought I'd die of embarrassment," he says, recalling his on-the-air hang-up) but who is having a hard time getting a word in—while his employer inveighs against "a gang of horse whistles who wouldn't know a slogan from a-a-a-a poke in the eye with a pointed stick!" "What *good* are these contests anyway?" he demands. "They disrupt your entire organization, they make you millions of enemies and all they prove is that you're making too much money in the first place since you can afford to toss a large chunk of it to some saphead who probably never had a cup of your coffee in his life and lives on goat's milk!" And so on. People are locked into terrible enmities in this place, where the uproar is constant. And they are very happy—or so it seems, anyway.

It's another world from Jimmy's office. It's another world even from his block—which is noisy and lively and friendly but hardly so exciting or funny or individualized (Sturges, at this early point, seems more interested in marshaling that street crowd than in characterizing it vividly). And it hardly seems to be quite the world for Jimmy—with his gee-whizzes and his eagerness to please and his undifferentiated sort of niceness (in the shooting script he is referred to throughout as "The Boy," and Betty is "The Girl"). But as it turns out, he has the key to it—in his slogan.

Just as Jimmy has built his hopes on this slogan, Sturges has—with almost equal quixoticism—centered his movie on it: a whatsit play on words, a kind of lunatic haiku, so labored as to be puzzling, so dumb-smart that it's arresting. It captures the attention, anyway, but it leaves everyone who hears it (as gradually and eventually everyone does) feeling uneasy and perplexed. Including Betty— in that opening rooftop scene—who has heard it "a thousand times" and *still* doesn't understand it. *"Maybe,"* Jimmy suggests darkly, "you don't *try* to understand it." "Maybe I don't," she concedes wearily. She has just tried telling him that she *did* understand ("Well—do you get the point?" "Yes." "What do you mean, *'Yes'*?")—but she didn't get away with it. He made her explain it, and then got angry when she couldn't: "It's clear as crystal" and "A kid of two . . ." and so on. "Can't you just see it over there?" he says, pointing toward the Maxford House Coffee sign in the distance, with a coffee drinker outlined in moving lights. "The guy swallows his coffee and it says: 'If You Don't Sleep at Night, It Isn't the Coffee, It's the Bunk.' You've got to admit that's some slogan."

But on their portable radio the "Maxford House Coffee Hour" has just signed off with no contest winner announced. Did you really expect to win? she asks him. He points out that he hasn't lost yet. "How many [contests] *have* you lost?" she asks, with more than a hint of acerbity. He doesn't know, but he does know that every time he's lost one he's doubled his chances on the next: "It's what you call the law of averages." Like the time he lost the "How Many Peanuts in the Window?" contest. "They put boxes under the peanuts," says Betty, still bitter at the memory. "They have a right to do that," he says defensively—anxious not to jeopardize a single loss—before going on to recall some others. The list is a long one, and makes his chances in *this* contest, he believes, "a cinch." And besides, there's that terrific slogan. . . .

JIMMY: I tell you it's a new scientific theory. It's the basis of my slogan. People think coffee keeps them awake, those kinds of people are nervous wrecks and can't sleep anyway, so why blame it on the coffee? . . . (*very patiently, repeating*) So I say . . ."If You Don't Sleep at Night, It Isn't the Coffee, It's the Bunk." Do you *get* it?

BETTY: I guess so.

JIMMY: You guess so? What does it mean?

BETTY: It's the bunk.

JIMMY: Yes, but do you get the play on words?

BETTY: Oh, but you don't *need* a play on words, Jimmy! Anytime somebody tells you coffee makes you sleep, you don't need a play on words to know it's the bunk!

JIMMY (*maniacal now, in close-up*): Don't you understand, it's *funny!* People are going to *laugh* at it when they hear it! It means if you don't sleep at night it isn't the coffee that keeps you awake, it's the bed.

BETTY: With me it's the coffee.

She comes round when he "wins," of course—like everyone else. Though she still can't get it right when she tries to repeat it ("It isn't the bunk, it's the coffee"). Nor can Mr. Baxter: "Isn't that marvelous? 'If You Don't Sleep at Night, It Isn't the—It's the . . .'" But coffee keeps you awake, he points out. Still, no one argues with success.

Except, perhaps, Dr. Maxford—who finds his worst forebodings about Bildocker and his "gang of horse whistles" more than confirmed when the winner of the contest turns up unannounced, without any fanfare or even a call from the contest room to prepare him for the visit. Jimmy shows him the telegram (the phony one that his friends sent). Dr. Maxford takes it and holds it away from himself like something smelly and mouldering.

MAXFORD (*reading*): Yes, yes, yes . . . *oh*, yes . . . (*aloud, mutteringly*) "great pleasure . . . informing you . . . twenty-five thousand dollars . . . kindly call and pick up your check." (*looking up; scathingly*) Bildocker has a great sense of the dramatic. You aren't by any chance a coffee drinker, are you, Mr. MacDonald?

JIMMY: Yes, sir, I am.

MAXFORD: Well, that's surprising. You don't by any chance drink my coffee, do you?

JIMMY: Well, no sir, you see I—

MAXFORD: Ah, yes, that sounds more natural.

JIMMY: But I could easily change.

MAXFORD (*drily*): That won't be necessary, Mr. MacDonald. I wouldn't want anybody to think that I had any base commercial motives in all this. I just give my money away because I can't sleep at night. I have a guilty conscience—

JIMMY: That's my slogan! The one I won with . . . Oh, well, I guess you know all about that. . . .

MAXFORD (*stares at him—before speaking*): "A Guilty Conscience," eh? I can see that my money is well spent. That's a great slogan.

JIMMY: No! "If You Can't Sleep at Night, It's Not the Coffee, It's the Bunk."
MAXFORD (*staring again*): . . . I beg your pardon.
JIMMY: It's a pun.
MAXFORD: . . . It certainly is. (*as the situation sinks in*) It's great.
JIMMY: Thank you.
MAXFORD: I can hardly wait to give you my money.

But he does give it to him. And then, when the mistake is discovered, he has to try and retrieve it—in that brawl on Jimmy's block. It's when he's changing his clothes after the fight (he got smacked with a fish among other things: "Were you to a fish fry, Dr. Maxford?" says his valet) that Bildocker bursts into the office to announce the glad news: "It took a little doing, but I won those clucks over in the end." And he reads the winning slogan: "If You Don't Sleep at Night. . . ." "Is that a slogan!" he wants to know. "It's what you call a pun. And believe me, it's some pun." They've just sent the author a telegram, he says, and the guy's name is—But he is interrupted by Dr. Maxford throwing a lamp at him.

And just at this moment—the movie's concluding scene—Sturges "throws"

McGinty (Brian Donlevy) becomes governor; Allyn Joslyn and Muriel Angelus look on. William Demarest, at right, is not visible in this scene in the film itself—for good reason (see text).

his camera (a zoom shot leading into a dissolve) back across the Manhattan rooftops to the offices of Baxter's Coffee. Just as Jimmy and Betty are leaving the building (after their scene with Mr. Baxter), stepping into the elevator and going down—unaware how Bildocker has now changed their fates. And as the frame is vacated by the elevator (and "Penthouse in Manhattan" comes up on the soundtrack), it is filled by the face of the cat—the one who'd crossed their path earlier. It's an oddly moving final shot, displacing the fadeout clinch, or even a fadeout *smile* (Jimmy and Betty are still very dejected), reminding us that the real happiness of this movie is in the sense it gives us of an observing presence, both sardonic and generous, both personal and impersonal. That final rapturous camera movement, the zoom across rooftops, brings us to a cat looking at us— implacably. It's not really the American Lottery, with its caprice and craziness, that takes over Jimmy's fate, as it more or less takes over Mary Smith's in *Easy Living*. It's something more like a providence—or a fairy godfather: that aspiration toward impersonal generosity, toward an ultimate magical fatherliness. And it's a spirit we can locate not in any one person or couple but in places like Maxford House, conundrums like Jimmy's slogan, impulses like Bildocker's intransigence: that community of indomitable singularities and offbeat inspirations and odd, passionate energies that this movie—Sturges' second—only begins to explore.

B UT *The Great McGinty* (1940), the film before it, is an even more impressive performance. Like Welles, Sturges seems to make his debut as a director with his powers and talents fully and astonishingly formed. There was a lot he didn't know when he made this first film, especially about the camera. He got too much opposition, he felt, from cameraman William C. Mellor, whom he never used again.* And he tried to bluff his way through too many situations where he was really at sea, his assistant director and friend George Templeton later said. But the sheer filmic intelligence of *McGinty* is apparent from its very beginning. There is an odd framing device around the main story, which is told in flashbacks. And the way *into* that story turns out to be almost labyrinthine— like the movie itself, full of unexpected turnings.

The opening title—

This is the story of two men who met in a banana republic. One of them was honest all of his life except one crazy minute. The other was dishonest all of his life except one crazy minute. They both had to get out of the country.

---

*He alternated thereafter between Victor Milner, Lubitsch's favorite Paramount cameraman, and John F. Seitz, one of the greatest cinematographers working anywhere.

—is superimposed over the swinging doors to a very lowdown-looking dive, while cucaracha music plays wheezingly on the soundtrack. The camera tracks through the swinging doors and into the dive. It's one of those movie places— like the newspaper office or the ocean liner—that movie audiences automatically felt at home in: the tropical saloon, with the smoke, the ceiling fans, the slatted windows and doors, the cucaracha-style band and the tinny-sounding upright piano, the sexy girls and the sleazy men, an atmosphere of raffish, boozy, horny happiness. A girl (Steffi Duna) is dancing to the music in the center of the room. But she can't, it appears, get this disorderly crowd's attention, no matter how much she flings her shoulders about. She looks puzzled and distressed— until she thinks of lifting her skirts up and showing them her legs (shades of Colbert's Ellie Andrews). Close-up of legs. Close-up of her: she looks knowing and amused. Now we see what she sees—a tracking shot from her point of view: the people at their tables (mostly sailors) gawking, the waiters above them bumping into each other.

But clearly none of it matters to her once she sees Thompson (Louis Jean Heydt), a sozzled-looking man in a dirty white suit, moving through the tables. She leaves the dance floor and catches him by the arm, beseechingly: "Tommy? You buy me a drink, Tommy?" "Okay," he says. She helps him to a table and sits across from him. It's clear that for her it's almost enough just to be near him—without having any real idea who he is. She is in love. It's equally clear that for him she hardly exists—as she pulls the handkerchief from his breast pocket and arranges it for him. "I had a wife and a couple of kids," he tells her, apropos of nothing, and she listens raptly. "And the house was almost paid for. It was what they call half-timbered." A close shot of the girl listening as he goes on: "With a tapestry brick underneath." "My father," she says brightly, "he live in a big house, too, with many butlers and maids." (How could she match "tapestry brick"?—though she tries.) People used to say, he tells her, that he'd go "a long way in this world." "I came a long way all right," he says bitterly, over a close-up of the girl—then back to the shot of them both: "One crazy minute," he says—reminding us of the opening title. "Do you want the tabasco in it?" calls out McGinty (Brian Donlevy) from behind the bar, where he is making the drinks that the girl has just ordered. The girl puts her hand on Thompson's arm and repeats the question tenderly. He does, of course, want the tabasco in it, however irritably he may reply when asked. He is the kind who *always* wants the tabasco—or whatever else is coming to him on the menu. And who reflects moralistically on the money he's just scattered (quite a lot of it: that "one crazy minute," presumably) while trying to pay for the drinks. "That's right," he says, as the girl stoops to gather the bills up. "Don't lose any of it, wonderful stuff." But she's not just gathering it, she's stealing it, too—tucking the extra notes into her glove but still looking at him adoringly as she does so. He rises unsteadily;

she gets up with him. Is he going home? "No, I'm going in *there*," he says—and sets off. She is behind him and holding him up now. They make their slow progress through the tables, while the tinny piano plays bluesily ("*She* used to play that," he says mournfully). In a lovely, long tracking shot they pass along the bar to the music—with McGinty behind it, at his post in the background, busy making a garnish and looking at them. The girl signals to him frantically, supporting Thompson with one hand and doing a pantomime of upchucking with the other. McGinty responds in a distant voice: "What's that got to do with me?" But he throws the garnish down and follows them, walking behind the bar. He comes out just as they reach the end of it, and in front of the men's room door, he takes him from her: "I've got him," he says, and guides him inside.

The two men enter the john, the door closing on the girl's concerned face in the background of the shot. "Go ahead, heave ho," says McGinty, as Thompson walks out of the frame. And while McGinty is spraying himself with some perfume from a vendor on the wall, Thompson—in the mirror—is ending it all, raising a gun to his head. McGinty sees him and jumps him, wresting the gun away as it goes off, and pinning him against the wall. The girl bursts in: "What'd you do to him!" she demands. "Somebody lit a firecracker," says McGinty, pushing her out again. And Thompson, pinned and wriggling on the wall, cries for his gun back. "Let me have it, Dan," he pleads. "What do you care? Go on, let me do it. I'm not like the rest of the trash around here. I don't fit, see? I'm not a crook." But McGinty is unmoved, and he pushes him toward the door: "Come on," he says. "Don't you under*stand?*" cries Thompson. "I was the cashier of the First National Bank! I was going places!" "Come on, come on—outside," says McGinty. He pushes him out and then gives him a shove into the bar, where the girl is waiting for them. "Guy wants to burn his brains 'cause he was cashier of a bank, no foolin'," says McGinty. "And I suppose you was the president of the bank!" says the girl as McGinty steps back behind the bar again. "Who, me?" he says reflectively—as he pours Thompson a drink. "Nossir . . . *I* was the governor of a state, baby." "What you were?" says the girl. "Oh yeah," says McGinty. And the scene dissolves into the past: "Oh yeah. . . ."

And so the real story begins—*not* "the story of two men" but the story of one (the second man, Thompson, is around for a point that doesn't become really clear until later on). It starts with an overhead long shot of a park and a statue, a trolley passing, and a sign on a banner: "Donated by Mayor Wilfred H. Tillinghast. Don't Forget Your Friend." We are back in Chicago. ("The locale," wrote Sturges in an early draft of his screenplay, "is the mythical city of Chicago in the imaginary state of Illinois.") Bums are standing in line at a soup kitchen, the hobo McGinty among them. Go around to the toolshed, the man serving the soup (Vic Potel) tells them—there's a couple of bucks in it for you. And don't forget who gave you the soup, says the cop who ushers them along (Emory Parnell), "on this cold election night." In the toolshed McGinty meets the man known only as the Politician (William Demarest). "Some soup, ain't it?" he says. He is paying the tramps two bucks a throw for a vote under an assumed name. "What do you get for repeatin'?" McGinty asks. The Politician is indignant: "Who said anything about repeatin'? What do you think this is—Hicks Corners?" You vote and the watcher gives you a ticket—two dollars for each ticket. McGinty comes back with a hard-to-believe thirty-seven tickets, having cast thirty-seven ballots for the mayor—a record even for Chicago—voting under such names as Rufus J. Whiticomb ("Whi-tee-comb," says poll watcher Harry Hayden over his shoulder, as McGinty painstakingly signs the name), Emmanuel Goldberg, and Heinrich L. Schutzendorf. And so his political career begins, when his achievement catches the attention of the Boss himself (Akim Tamiroff)—as he arrives at party headquarters for the victory celebration, with the little mayor (Arthur Hoyt) dithering at his side. Thirty-seven times! "See the kind of service I'm giving you, Wilfred?" says the Boss to the mayor. Then, turning to the Politician: "Bring the lug here. I want to look at him." And he strides off. "We certainly do," quavers the mayor, before following him off the screen.

But the Boss, who is used to imposing on the people around him, finds McGinty ("A tough guy, huh?") maddeningly impervious. "I guess you don't know where you are," says the Boss, who has brought this lug into his private office. "That's right," says McGinty, "and I don't care neither." The Boss persists in trying to impress him: "The gentleman to your right," he says, "happens to be the mayor of the city, the honorable W. H. Tillinghast." This does catch McGinty's attention: "That gink?" he says disbelievingly. Finally the Boss—"just to help you remember"—hauls off and slaps him: McGinty slaps him right back. And in spite of his fury, the Boss decides he can use this gorilla—someone who doesn't need a rod to be a tough guy. He gives him a job "collecting."

Thus begins their long and exasperating association. The Boss, a tough guy himself, is determined to show that he can take McGinty any time he wants to. And though he never does, he's always trying. So that any chance remark or look askance ("All right, you asked for it!") is likely to end in a brawl. With these two short, beefy men—one round, the other wide, and both the huff-and-puff types—falling upon each other and rolling around on the floor. Or in the backseat of the Boss's soundproof limo. In the front seat, the chauffeur (Frank Moran) is telling the bodyguard (Harry Rosenthal) about how he told his girlfriend off the night before. "You let 'em get an angle on you, you're a goner." "You said it!" "You tellin' me?" And they chat away in this amiable style while above their heads, behind the soundproof glass, there is a silent, frantic flurry of flailing arms and upended legs. The movie even ends with just such a brawl—revealing the Boss in the final scene to be the owner of that banana republic dive McGinty is bartending in. He catches McGinty stealing from the cash register. "So I caught you again, you cheesy cheapskate!" "Listen, you fat little fourflusher!" "Fat!" And they start pummeling each other again, with the same frantic, ineffectual zest as before. "Here we go again," says the Politician, who is a waiter in the same place—signaling the final fadeout.

One problem with McGinty—apart from his ingrained dishonesty, of course—is that he doesn't listen. He never pays attention when you're talking to him. The Boss is explaining his philosophy in the backseat of that limo—how "this is a land of great opportunity," where "everybody lives by chiseling everybody else"—and McGinty is looking around the limo trying to figure out why it's so quiet inside. "It's armored," says the Boss irritably. "Armored for what?" "So people shouldn't interrupt me!" yells the Boss. "I got it," says McGinty, moments later, snapping his fingers. "Bullet-proof!" Later on, he is absorbed by the heroine's search for her key as they stand outside her door—he peers into her purse as her hand moves through it, suggesting that next time she put the key "on a little chain and hook it on the bag." Just as he is equally distracted, once they get inside, by the way she keeps rubbing the felt on his top hat, which she is holding in her hand, the wrong way. "Rub it the other way, will you?" All the time she is trying to tell him about the two children she has in the other room, whose existence he doesn't even suspect as yet. But it's always difficult to get his attention when you want it. He is too quirky and wayward. He looks and listens, but not where he's supposed to look and listen—like a hypnotist's subject who keeps looking away. That's one reason he's not impressed by mayors— or Bosses. Or unduly *de*pressed by being a bartender. He is too distractible to be imposed on.

"I guess you don't know where you are": and he really doesn't know. He never does. That's his strength in a way. He *can't* be impressed—it simply can't be done to him—no matter how much it's tried: "The gentleman to your right happens to be the mayor of the city. . . ." McGinty is like a natural cynic. He seems to know instinctively what other people may learn only after bitter experience— that worldly trappings and honors are undependable and meaningless. He has no interest in them, in any case—not in titles of any kind. He has a lot of drive, as we see—a kind of dumb, brute ambition once he gets started. But it's for money and classy suits, not for respectability or prestige. *Those* are things he never sees the point of. He is *very* low-class—hopelessly so, in fact.

But this obtuseness gives him a paradoxical sort of sanity—even a kind of moral stature, as it turns out. "If it weren't for graft," observes Demarest the Politician, "you'd get a very low type of people in politics." Exactly. People like Thompson, even—who believes in all those institutions and who *still* cheats on them—and then can't even enjoy the money he's stolen. That he is the relevant contrast to McGinty is something Sturges makes us feel by the way he keeps bringing the movie back to the tropical saloon. After the limo scene, for example, with that silent brawl in the backseat. "Boy, we had some brannigans," recalls McGinty with relish behind his bar. "I thought you said you were governor of a state," says Thompson ("a little drunkenly and very sourly," says Sturges' screenplay). "Yeah," says the girl, "you was just a cheap crook." McGinty doesn't deny it. "You got to crawl before you can creep, don't you?" he replies—before going on to tell about being alderman. Compare this sobering observation to Thompson's outcry in the men's room: "I was going places!" And it's the respectable view, not the crooked one, that seems most profoundly delusional.

McGinty at home: the "Willie Rabbit" scene. Brian Donlevy and Muriel Angelus in The Great McGinty.

BUT JUST as the movie has established its credentials as a tough comedy, it takes another unforeseen turning—into a different, but equally familiar, movie mode. The shift starts to take place when the Boss decides that McGinty the alderman should run for mayor—on the Reform ticket ("Whatta *you* got to do with the Reform party?" "I *am* the Reform party, who do you think? . . . In this town I'm *all* the parties"). But a mayor has to be married. McGinty refuses. The Boss is dismayed—calling marriage (after a slight hesitation) "the most beautiful setup between the sexes." "All right, why don't *you* try it?" says McGinty. "Because I ain't running for mayor," says the Boss. But McGinty is, after all. And so his loyal secretary, Catherine (Muriel Angelus), suggests an arrangement: since neither he nor she really *wants* to get married, they might as well marry each other. She could run his house for him, be photographed with him, make speeches for him at women's clubs—be his "lawful wedded wife in everything except when we were alone," as she puts it. It's a deal—and it's the old platonic-marriage plot.

A Lubitschean moment: "*Well?*" barks the Boss, stepping from the church in a cutaway and confronting Louie, the bodyguard, lounging on the steps outside—and Louie, snapping to, throws rice in his face. McGinty and Catherine follow in their bridal outfits. But then, once they are all three in the back of the limo, Catherine announces that she won't be able to come to the reception: it's six o'clock and she's expected at home. McGinty is disappointed, but the Boss—who ordered the food—is positively indignant: "What kind of a wedding is this!" She's sorry, but she can't help it. "All right," says the Boss, "send her home in a taxi—there's plenty o' dames." "Listen," says McGinty, "she'll go home in any kind of rig she wants to and you keep your big trap shut!" There is almost another "brannigan"—except for Catherine's intervention. So McGinty takes her home and meets the two children as well, a little boy and girl ("I did tell you I was married before, didn't I?"). She also has a black maid. And a dachshund.

So they all move into a mansion, suitable for the mayor and his family. And what's even more surprising, perhaps, than the intrusion of this new marriage-of-convenience plot is the way Sturges uses it: without any of the usual jokes and situations. Mostly he uses it to establish McGinty's aloneness, which is more than situational: a kind of deep, permanent bachelorhood, only slightly tempered by his new situation in life. He takes a distant but genuine interest in the kids, buying them toys, electric trains and playground slides. And they in turn remember him in their prayers at night. But he lives in a different part of the sprawling house, and everyone in the other part calls him *Mr.* McGinty. Just as his wife does. He is a patriarch without a hearth—just a big house. Treated with respect and even some affection—and tactfully left alone. He comes home alone even on his own election night, stewed to the gills, and knocking over the new furnishings in the dark. When Catherine tucks him into bed, she removes his shoes, his watch, and then the wad of bills from his trousers. *This* wakes him up: "Oh, no you don't!" he says, grabbing her by the hand. "That's been tried before, sister!" Old habits die hard.

There is even an Other Man in this part of the film—named (as he often is) George and played (as he often was) by Allyn Joslyn, an actor with a mouth inclined to purse and eyes both close-set and startled looking (Albert in *Heaven*

Can Wait). But like the others in this film, George both is and isn't the stereotype he evokes. He proposes to the heroine a lot, it's true—and she is never really interested. But he is never mocked, and though he looks like a stuffed-shirt type, he doesn't really behave like one. When we—and McGinty—first see him, he is playing with the kids, who really do like him. It's a point that isn't lost on McGinty, when he comes home from his mayor's work (a lovely scene where he extorts some graft from a sweating Thurston Hall as the owner of a city bus company) and sees this tableau of domestic happiness in his own house, with George at its center. McGinty appeals to Catherine: "Who's this lug who gives me the 'Good evening' every night when I get here?" Catherine is obliged to explain that since McGinty is never home, she likes to go out with *some*one—even if it is George. This explanation leads to a remonstrance, an apology, a kiss—"I musta been blind," says McGinty, and Catherine calls him "Daniel," and there is a fadeout. Once again we have been waiting for "propinquity to do its work," and once again it has—just as we knew it would.

What we couldn't know so clearly is that Catherine is something like a time bomb ticking away in this film. Muriel Angelus makes her very attractive—warm and humorous and generous spirited. And she and McGinty have at least one early moment of real romantic élan when together on an impulse they join a parade passing by: it happens to be his parade, and they swing along together under the McGinty for Mayor signs. She's a conventional heroine in many ways—but also anomalous. What is such a ladylike type (that *is* her type) doing among these crooks? Since she knows what they are—that's clear from her first scene, when we see her in McGinty's outer office, as his secretary and receptionist. Demarest as the Politician is reading aloud to her from the newspaper reports denouncing Mayor Tillinghast (it's McGinty's alderman days). But it doesn't really matter about the graft, she volunteers—"especially since you can't rob the people anyway." "Sure," says Demarest, then does a double take: "How was that?" "What you rob, you spend," says Catherine cheerfully, "and what you spend goes back to the people—so where's the robbery? I read that in one of my father's books." "That book," says Demarest reverently, "should be in every home." Catherine is a sort of New Right type—as this early version of supply-side economics suggests—with a theoretic base for her amoralism and for her deferral to the purposes of the "fathers" around her, even the ones that are thugs. But she is very nice, too, and it's no surprise to us later on when her toleration of injustice turns out to be *merely* theoretic.

In any case, the propinquity plot is over—and the movie clearly isn't. What next? The answer comes quickly this time. In the following scene, McGinty has come into his hearthside at last—sitting in a dressing gown on a couch by the fire, a kid on each side of him under his arms as he reads them a story, the dog on the floor—while Catherine knits and looks on. Instant domesticity: the kids and the big book and the father's enfolding arms. No sooner has he kissed her, it seems (in the scene just before), than it all materializes—like a fairy story.

MC GINTY (*reading*): ". . . You had to get up pretty early to be smarter than Willie Rabbit, because he was as full of brains as a dog is full of fleas. Just as he got to the edge of the field by the old split rail fence, a shadow fell across his path. And who do you suppose it was? I'll give you three guesses and then three more and then three other ones. But you can try all night without guessing who it really was because it was none other than—"

CATHERINE (*very gently*): Darling . . .

MC GINTY (*looking up*): Hunh?

(*In pantomime Catherine indicates that the children are asleep.*)

MC GINTY (*looking down at them*): Oh . . . (*He looks back at the book.*)— Just a minute. (*reading*) "—none other than our friend Muggledy-Wump the Tor-toys. . . ." (*looking up again*) . . . That's who I thought it was.

Catherine had earlier reproached George for not being sufficiently polite to "Mr. McGinty." "Why should I be polite?" replies George. "I don't like him." And George's presence reminds us that from one point of view there's not so very much to like about this hero. He's a thug and a crook, and he's no charmer: he's Brian Donlevy, not Jimmy Cagney. But that unguarded reaction to the "Willie Rabbit" tale (". . . That's who I thought it was") reminds us of what we like about him. It has to do with that distractability of his—shading into an impersonal kind of wonder at times. He is a tough guy, but in some ways he is exceedingly open. And he is about to show how dangerous that condition can be.

Catherine has something on her mind: the little boy got into a fight at school today, because someone called his "father" a grafter. "I thought you didn't care about that stuff," says McGinty mildly, speaking softly because of the children. "What's that slogan of yours? You can't rob the people because what you rob you spend and something or other. . . ." "I wasn't married to you then, Dan," she says—unanswerably. As their dialogue goes on—she sits on the floor next to his chair while the children sleep peacefully in his arms—it develops that it's not so much what he does that concerns her ("shaking people down a little" is how she puts it) as what he doesn't do: with "all the power and opportunities you have to do things for people." "What are you trying to do—reform me?" he says. "Oh, I'm just being dull," she says, but she's been hearing so much lately "about sweat shops and child labor and the firetraps poor people live in." McGinty takes alarm at this: "I couldn't do anything about those things if I wanted to, honey," he says. "Those are the people he works with—they're the people that put me in. You've got to understand how those things work." But when she presses him anyway, he responds in exasperation:

Don't you know those people just want to be let alone? They *want* to be dirty. They don't like people fooling around with them. Give them a bathtub, they keep coal in it!—You've got to understand, honey, no man is strong enough to buck the party . . . no matter how much he wants to make his wife happy.

The emotional line of this speech is intelligible exactly because the arguments are so familiar. The arguments for inaction: moving from blaming the victims to "you can't buck the system" (or the party)—the appeal to "realism" ("no man is strong enough . . ."). But then that diminuendo climax comes—"no matter how much he wants to make his wife happy": said so uninflectedly, so matter-of-factly by Donlevy that we hardly register what he's said, let alone its importance, until it's over—and it hangs in the air afterwards.

Suddenly, everything in this odd, wayward movie comes together—the conjunction of tough comedy, marriage games, and domestic romance makes sudden and total sense at last. We've come to what the movie is about, and has been moving toward all along—and with what simplicity and power Donlevy conveys it here: the temptation of goodness—to cite Brecht again. And though it's a complicated moment, it is also among other things a romantic one—evoking what can be the most romantic yearning of all: to be splendid in some way, to be beneficent and grand and good—the longing that love can give us to be somehow better than we are. "You'll be strong enough someday," she tells him—sealing his doom.

It seems the right moment to go back to the tropical dive—to that "reality" again. McGinty tells Thompson and the girl that he knew that what he was about to do now was "wrong," but he went ahead anyway: "I like the way it made me look in her eyes and the kids." In the next flashback he is running for governor. And the next parade we see him in is not so lighthearted and informal as the one before it—that McGinty for Mayor bash that he and Catherine had joined on an impulse. Now the two of them are riding in an open limousine, making slow, stately progress through throngs of onlookers—going to his inauguration at the state capitol. "You're strong enough for anything now," she tells him, as they both smile and wave at the crowds.

MC GINTY (*not hearing*): What?
CATHERINE (*as she waves*): I said you're strong enough—
MC GINTY (*hearing*): Oh.
CATHERINE: —to do good for people. To justify the faith of your constituency.

They both look very diminished in their open car in the middle of the crowds—and McGinty's voice, as it reaches us now over the cheering and noise from the throngs lining the streets, sounds aggrieved and small. "You're the governor's lady—isn't that enough for you?" he says, trying feebly to impose on her, just as the Boss had once tried to impose upon him ("The gentleman to your right . . ."), with pride of office. "Why can't we let well enough alone?" he asks, waving and nodding to right and left. No answer. And he gives it his last shot: "Everybody don't get to be governor," he says, almost plaintively. She really ought to remember that. But it's too late.

As the next scene suggests, something unappeasable has been set in motion. McGinty is taking his oath of office, his right hand in the air, his left on the Bible, surrounded by men in high silk hats—as the camera tracks imperceptibly, slowly, remorselessly in on him. While he swears an oath that he will "do equal right to the poor and to the rich." The only faces besides his that are turned toward the camera in this tableau are the two immediately behind him: Catherine and George. The conscience faces. The rest are just tophats—nobodies.

"Well, here we are," says the Boss, sitting in the governor's chair behind the governor's desk as McGinty, coming from the inauguration, enters his new office—grimly. "You don't look as happy as you should," says the Boss. "Don't you feel good?" He is going to feel better when he hears about all the things they are now going to "build." . . .

> BOSS: And you'll kiss me for this one—a new dam!
>
> MCGINTY: Yeah?
>
> BOSS: I can see from your expression you don't know what a dam is. You think a dam is something you pour a lot of water in. A dam is something you put a lot of *concrete* in—and it doesn't matter how much you put in, there's always room for a lot more. And any time you're afraid it's finished, you find a crack in it—and you put some more concrete! It's wonderful.
>
> MCGINTY: What's the matter with the old dam?
>
> BOSS (*with widened eyes*): —It's got a crack in it.

It's as if the movie itself were trying to get back to its own earlier mode: the tough comedy again, with all its insouciance and paradoxical innocence. This statehouse reunion with the Boss is a lovely scene, as stylish and funny as anything before it (Tamiroff's comic timing, for one thing, is something close to a wonder). But for McGinty, and for the movie, it's too late—the innocence is gone. When McGinty tells the Boss what he really intends now—"no dam, no bridges, no buildings that the people don't need from now on"—the Boss's response is predictable. "The people? Are you sick or something?" But when he hears the rest of McGinty's new program—a child labor bill, action against sweatshops and tenements—he's even more outraged. "You're spouting like a woman," he says; then understanding dawns: "Your wife! That cheesecake you married!" At this, they have another "brannigan," rolling around on the floor. But this time the

Boss has a gun—and he ends up being arrested for an attempt on the life of the governor.

But even with the Boss—for the time being at least—put away, McGinty is fearful. They have too much on him. "I feel leery about the whole setup," he tells Catherine, once they are back by their fireplace. "Sweatshops and tenements are very hot stuff to handle." He sits down, undone—he leans forward on his elbows, his voice shaking: "Child labor is just plain *dynamite!*" "Doesn't it mean anything to you," says Catherine, really trying to be encouraging, "to stop little children from being exploited in dark airless factories when they ought to be out playing in the sunshine?" But McGinty isn't buying this. He wants to know if *she* has ever worked in a factory. But "exploited in dark airless factories" is not, of course, the language of someone who has: "You know I didn't," she says coldly. And McGinty replies, in excitement:

> Well, *I* did—see? When I was seven years old. Instead of playing on the streets learning a lot of dirty words, I earned four dollars a week for mother. And it *wasn't* dark and airless—it was very neat and clean. We folded the boxes (*he gestures folding*) . . . and then we twisted the oil paper on the toffee (*his voice breaking*) . . . what we didn't eat. (*defiantly*) And I want you to know that we *liked* it. . . .

This unexpected defense of child labor—extraordinary and touching as it is—is the cry of a man at bay. That he can't get past the toffee twisting without losing his control is, of course, a powerful, unlooked-for demonstration of his wife's point. She is inescapable—and she even brought George to the inauguration. It's not surprising that McGinty is unstrung.

But he is himself again the next moment—after the cops have come for him ("I'm afraid I got some bad news for you, Governor McGinty"). He is calm, reassuring, taking charge—telling Catherine not to be upset and trying not to wake the children when he visits their room. Catherine has been tucking the little girl in when McGinty comes in to tell her that he has "to go away tonight for a little while." But the girl wakes up and wants to know where "Daddy" is going. "By golly," says McGinty in a whisper, looking at her with calf eyes of love, "I went and talked too loud," as if he can hardly get over the wonder of it—that even her waking at his voice was another proof of the marvel. Oh, well—he tiptoes out. "She's going to break a lot of hearts when she grows up," he says—happily—as he leaves the room. On his way to the state pen. He didn't even get to serve one full day as governor.

But he *did* turn into this wonderful father—just about. The kind of father who protects *other* children, too. At least he almost did. In the "real world" of this movie, however—the wised-up world of the tough comedy—*those* kinds of fathers don't make it. What's irresistible about McGinty is that he wanted to make it—that he understood, even against his own better judgment, what there was about being governor that might in fact be important. Though there was a lot he never did understand. And never would, it seems. "Everybody don't get to be governor," he says: he *still* doesn't know where he is—and still doesn't care really, in some fundamental way. "So long, honey," he says in his final goodbye to Catherine over the phone, after he has made his jail break with the Boss. "I'm sorry it didn't work out, but . . . you can't make a silk purse out of a pig's ear." No indeed. He is irredeemable. But he makes a fine bartender.

*Barbara
Stanwyck,
Henry Fonda,
and Charles
Coburn in*
The Lady Eve.

*She impressed me all the time as someone—what can I say?—someone who
had a great experience, someone who had been touched deeply by life in some
way. . . . That insignificant little picture she did with me [All I Desire, 1953]
and she played it all out of herself. . . . And there is such an amazing tragic
stillness about her at the same time. She never steps out of it, and she never
puts it on—but it is always there. . . .*
—DOUGLAS SIRK, *in a 1976 interview*

STURGES' TWO Barbara Stanwyck heroines are both—like McGinty—seduced by innocence. And Stanwyck is remarkable . . . standing in the
middle of Fred MacMurray's Indiana Christmas in *Remember the Night* (1940),
leaning on the piano while he plays and sings "Swanee River" for his admiring
family. It's such a warm, comforting, storybook sort of Christmas scene. And
she is a lady up against it, on her way to jail because she heisted a diamond
bracelet from a department store. In the meantime, she is grateful to be here—
and she is falling in love with the man at the piano who brought her. She looks
at him with a fond little smile as he sings. She looks around at the others, the
mother and the aunt and the hired man—the same fond little smile—all around
the room. She notices the framed picture by her elbow; she picks it up and looks
at it: it's a picture of him as a boy. She looks up at him now, singing away at the
piano—and her smile is gone.

In *The Lady Eve* (1941), she has just dealt Henry Fonda a hand of cards in
the three-handed poker game they are playing with her card-sharp father. But
she is at least as good at cards as her father is, and she is seeing to it that the
rube-ish Fonda—whom she has fallen in love with—is not bilked of any more
money. Quite obviously she's given him a winning hand this time: he starts with
pleasure, his eyes bug, and he starts to smile, then quickly affects a kind of
scowl—what he thinks of as a poker face. Stanwyck sees it all (she is sitting

next to him), and she looks away smiling, a sort of I-can't-stand-it roll of the eyes, a sardonic, helpless tenderness. Later on, when they are getting married (he is no longer so lovable, and she is setting him up for a little revenge), she exchanges a look with him at the altar. It's a killing look in many ways—a predator regarding the prey (who looks *very* fatuous and proper)—and also very funny. It's her cryptic, self-possessed look, with that sense of a smile behind—far, far behind—the eyes that miss absolutely nothing.

Sturges first thought he was writing *Remember the Night*—among his original screenplays, the closest thing to a tearjerker—for Carole Lombard. But then the studio assigned it to Stanwyck instead. And, unhappy as Sturges professed to be with Mitchell Leisen's direction of the film (as well as the numerous cuts he made in Sturges' script), he thought Stanwyck was terrific. "I'm going to write a great comedy for you," he told her at the time, as Stanwyck told Sturges' biographer James Curtis: "I told him I never get great comedies, and he said, 'Well, you're going to get one.'" It turned out to be from a 1938 screenplay he had originally prepared for producer Albert Lewin, now reconceived and completely rewritten and called *The Lady Eve*. And it was a great comedy indeed.

She was right, though: she never got them. Maybe because she seemed too downright—her effects too plain and undecorated—for comedies. Though she did them (just like everyone else at the time), her "great" roles weren't comedies: they were films like *Annie Oakley* (1935) and *Stella Dallas* (1937) and the Capra heroines of *Ladies of Leisure* (1930) and *The Miracle Woman* (1931) and *The Bitter Tea of General Yen* (1933). And then there were the roles she *made* "great," in such lively Warner Brothers melodramas as *Baby Face* (1933) and *Gambling Lady* (1935). But the Stanwyck comedies of those days were pale or worse, ways to keep working mostly—things like *Breakfast for Two* (1937) and *The Bride Walks Out* (1936). She did the runaway heiress, but her version is not so much a fool for love as a dupe of the communists, and she is set right by a patriotic soldier (Robert Young) in the low-budget, independently made *Red Salute* (1935)—a movie that went in "for the most embarrassing chauvinism of the decade," according to the New York *Times*'s Andre Sennwald.

But no matter how poor the movies, Stanwyck went on being impressive somehow. *She* never seemed foolish or strained, and she became over the years a powerful accumulating presence for audiences, one of those stars whose existence seemed almost to define the movie experience at its most satisfying and sustaining. She was both sensible and sad—a conjunction that was noticed early on in her career. "There is something," said the New York *Herald Tribune* review of *Shopworn* ("That unfortunate, but descriptive, title") in 1932, "about the simple, straightforward sincerity of Miss Barbara Stanwyck which makes everything she does upon either stage or screen seem credible and rather poignant." All her gaiety in *The Lady Eve*, for example—her flights of comic invention, her self-delighting feats of impersonation and deception—seems superimposed on something immovable and deeply reserved, what Douglas Sirk calls her "amazing tragic stillness." Her voice, for example, as distinctive in its way as Arthur's or Sullavan's, is both flat and eloquent, oddly and always both nasal and husky.* Though what that huskiness suggests is not whiskey or disillusion or sexual provocation—but tears. Tears which have been firmly and sensibly surmounted but somehow, somewhere, fully wept—the voice of someone who is "cried out."

She is a paradigmatic woman star of the thirties: tough and independent and *very* smart. But she also suggests the ambivalence of these qualities, in ways and moments that can be startling. It's no wonder that Sturges was drawn to her. See what she does with a characteristic bit of Sturges dialogue in *The Lady Eve*, when she first threatens to beat her card-shark father at his own game. "You'll find out I can play a little cards myself!" she says. "You think so?" he says. "I *know* so!" she says. "I'm not your daughter for free, you know!" Stanwyck makes this sort of "crack"—with its surprising echo of a really felt self-judgment—seem almost indecently forceful. And troubling. The Sturges gift for a kind of offhand profundity has its ideal exponent in her, with her directness, and the feeling she gives of so many levels of comment *behind* the directness: the smile behind the eyes. The Stanwyck temperament and style are at the heart of that tension between experience and innocence which so much preoccupies Sturges, even more than it did most other filmmakers. She has the same value and interest for Capra, of course, in *Meet John Doe* (1941). In this film as well as in Sturges' *Remember the Night*, an overly "experienced" heroine is finally regenerated by the innocence and unworldliness she encounters through the hero. But as always in Sturges' work, it's the *differences* from Capra that turn out to be most determining.

Lee Leander (Stanwyck) is on trial for stealing a bracelet in the opening scenes of *Remember the Night*. She has a wonderfully preposterous defense attorney (Willard Robertson), who (we are told) used to be on the stage, and who pleads on her behalf "a temporary loss of will and consciousness, now known as schizophrenia, but formerly known as hypnotism" (an effect of the diamonds' brilliance). Jack Sargent (Fred MacMurray), the assistant DA who is prosecuting the case, seizes this opportunity to ask for a postponement until after Christmas—so that a hypnotist may be consulted, he says. His real motive, though, is the difficulty in getting a jury to convict a woman during the holidays; it will be much easier afterwards. But when the woman in question complains loudly about having to spend Christmas day in jail, he is visited by some remorse and sends a bondsman to bail her out. But the bondsman, thinking "the worst,"

---

*In Robert Altman's *The Long Goodbye* (1973), the parking-lot attendant (Ken Samson) who does movie-star imitations for incoming cars captures it perfectly.

brings her directly to the attorney's apartment. Where it soon comes out that she has no place to stay (her unpaid hotel bill) and no money. "Well, come on," he says. "I'll buy you that Christmas dinner I cheated you out of"—the one they serve in jail—"and maybe we can figure out something." He takes her to a nightclub. They sit in a booth overlooking the dance floor and contemplate the problem (she tells him not to worry: "I can always chisel a hotel for a week or so," a suggestion he describes as "cheesy." "Well, I'm not going to sleep in the subway," she says) as well as each other. And the disapproval—as well as the attraction—is mutual. She supposes that "somebody" has to do "the dirty work" he does; it's "just too bad it had to be somebody as nice as you." While he is trying to think of extenuations for *her* career. For the fact is—and it's apparent on his face—he really can't figure her out at all.

> JACK: How long have you been swiping things?
> LEE: Always.
> JACK: Did you ever get caught before?
> LEE: Uh-huh.
> JACK: Did you take things you didn't need?
> LEE: Sure.
> JACK (*undeterred*): In the presence of beautiful things, did you have the sudden irresistible urge to take them in your hand and hurry away with them?

She is really touched by this last one, though slightly disbelieving—"You mean was I hypnotized?" she says, smiling radiantly at him. They are sitting very close together. No, he means maybe she's a kleptomaniac. That one's easy: "Oh, no, no," she says. "They tried that, though. You see, to be a kleptomaniac, you can't sell any of the stuff afterwards. Or you lose your amateur standing." He doesn't understand it, as he now says. Obviously, she is nice in some way; and yet here she is, apparently without a conscience. She won't even plead diminished responsibility. "First you think it's heredity," he says, reflecting on crooks in general, "and then you get some guy with seven generations of clergymen behind him." He just doesn't get it. But then she says something he *really* doesn't get: "I don't think you ever could understand it because your mind is different. Right or wrong is the same for everybody, you see, but the rights and the wrongs aren't the same. Like in China they eat dogs. . . ."

It's extraordinary: Stanwyck is evoking an inner life and an ethical dimension that we hardly expect in such a familiar figure as this glamorous lady thief. In Lubitsch, for example, stealing is just another form of unconventionality—like adultery, or an undue interest in plumbing. His crooks no more have an ethical life than his businessmen do. But now we are being reminded by this heroine, in this conventional movie comedy, that there are people (she is one) for whom stealing a bracelet from a rich department store *isn't* wrong, people who don't

believe or take quite seriously the values and arrangements by which such an action is judged as wrong. In this respect, Lee is an articulate, self-aware version of McGinty. But she doesn't really expect Jack to understand—and he doesn't. He calls her "theory" a "lot of piffle." But she tries again to explain, in this wonderful exchange:

LEE: Oh, well, uh . . . try it like this. Supposing you were starving to death and you didn't have any food and you didn't have any place to get anything. And there were some loaves of bread out in front of a market. Now remember, you're starving to death. And the man's back was turned. Would you swipe one?

JACK (*proudly*): You bet I would.

LEE: That's because you're honest. You see, I'd have a six-course dinner at the fancy restaurant across the street and then say I'd forgotten my purse. Get the difference?

He doesn't really. "Yeah," he says. "Your way's smarter." So was her question about the loaf of bread: a kind of trap, and he walked right into it. But what she says now complicates the matter again: "That's it," she says softly—and bitterly—in close-up. "We're smarter . . ."

She is touched by his unworldliness—when he suddenly realizes how his being seen with her might "look" (they have just run into the judge from the trial). "Gee, you're sweet," she says, in genuine wonderment. And: "You never think of anything wrong, do you?" Now he asks the orchestra to play "My Old Indiana Home." They dance—and discover that they are both from Indiana ("No wonder I like you," she says), with the difference that he makes it home to his mother's farm every Christmas, and she hasn't been "home" in years, ever since she ran away. He offers to take her with him—he's setting off by car tonight—and to drop her off in her hometown. For Christmas.

The trip is a success, but the drop-off isn't: Lee's mother (Georgia Caine) is censorious and unwelcoming ("What'd you come here for? What do you want?"). So he takes her on to *his* mother for a "real" Christmas. And not a single cliché is neglected or overlooked, it seems, in the scenes that follow back at that old Indiana home (the song was a clue). But in all the formulas that Sturges invokes and that Leisen skillfully and lovingly fills out—the fireplace and the Christmas tree and the cookies in the oven, the kindly mother and the acerbic spinster aunt, the shawls and hooked rugs and hurricane lamps, the rocking chairs and four-posters, the apple bobbing (cut from the final film) and piano singing and church bazaar and barn dance—we are moving not just through evocations of the past but through the furniture of the American mind. To Sturges' audiences—and even to audiences today—these images were the tokens of a vanished or imagined innocence. And Lee Leander is no more immune to their power than the audience is—or than Sturges himself.

And it's that power that *Remember the Night* conveys—in a somewhat troubled fashion. No sooner has Stanwyck announced a level of consciousness that threatens almost to explode the film ("That's because you're honest . . .") than the girl in front of the band is crooning "Back home in Indiana . . ." and Stanwyck on the dance floor is melting in the arms of Fred MacMurray, this hero who can't or won't understand that someone like her might not simply be "crooked" but might have her own ideas of right and wrong. But it's partly this obtuseness of his that she is drawn to: "You never think of anything wrong, do you?" Reflecting a simpler view of things. Like Aunt Emma's (Elizabeth Patterson's) belief, reiterated while she shows Lee how to make popovers, that "the shortcut to a man's heart is through his gizzard." Or John's mother's (Beulah Bondi's) reaction when he tells her that unfortunately Lee is a crook: "That girl's as honest as all outdoors—why you can tell just by looking at her face." Nice people. Just as simple and generous as their notions of life are. But glamorous lady thieves should stay out of Indiana; they should probably even stay away from men who were raised there. Or so it seems. "That's right . . . we're smarter." She's already beginning to feel ashamed.

Not that she doesn't go on having fun in her own style: telling the justice of the peace (another crook) who has hauled them up on phony trespassing charges that her name is Mary Smith and that she is from Roaring Falls, Ohio ("Don't give your right name," Jack, the pro, cautions her; "I never do," she replies—a *real* pro); and giving a high sign of approval to Jack when he tells the JP that his name is Henry Wadsworth Longfellow and his occupation is steam fitter. But he disapproves when she sets fire to the place so that they can escape; she might have burnt it down. "It's better than going to jail, isn't it?" she answers testily, and adds: "I *told* you my mind worked differently." And although she can't do much with Jack's angelic mother beyond responding tearfully to her kindness, she finds a kindred spirit in Aunt Emma, the spinster, who has her own streak of lawlessness. A pretty girl like Lee will be a great help to them at the church bazaar, says Mother: "Why, the men are so tight we almost have to pick—their pock—" She stammers and halts in an agony of sudden consciousness (Jack has told her about Lee). A painful silence. "Well," says Stanwyck, with her most radiant and confiding smile, "I'll do my *best*." "My specialty," says Aunt Emma with nervous pride (in a medium close-up to herself) "is shortchanging 'em."

But Stanwyck's "we're smarter" has reminded us that the prospects for a lady thief—at least in the real life this movie so oddly and fitfully impinges on—are not lighthearted ones. Christmas alone (or in jail) for a start. And we feel all Lee's relief in escaping that fate—at being taken into a family without question or judgment or reservation, welcomed not only into a home with a history and a ritual and an ongoing life, but into that America we've all heard about. Lee is threatened by her own recklessness—and redeemed by goodness and community. "'The Lord is my shepherd,'" reads the minister in the pulpit on Christmas Eve (this scene was also cut from the final film). "'He maketh me to lie down in green pastures . . .'"—and Lee begins to cry. "'Surely goodness and mercy shall follow me all the days of my life . . .'"

In some way she remains always and fatally *outside* this rural idyll, no matter how urgently and admiringly she may respond to it. And as an outsider she becomes a more ardent proponent of its values in the end than even the hero himself is—and collusive with his mother to save him from *his* recklessness (he wants to throw the case to save her from a prison term). His mother, like Armand's father when he visits Marguerite, asks Lee to give him up, not to ruin his career by letting him fall in love with her. Lee agrees. And she does her best to live up to the promise. She sees what he's doing in the courtroom—using tactics that will make the jury sympathetic to her—and she stops him by pleading guilty and going to the slammer. When he visits her in the last scene, he asks her—in loving exasperation, in anguish because of what's in store for her now—if she knows what she's *done*: does she *really* know what she's done? But she does. And if he still wants her when her prison term is over, she may come to him then. "I love you so," she says—and they embrace for the final fadeout.

Because part of what she's been admiring in this idyll is the dumbness of it all ("the shortcut to a man's heart," etc.). And now she is part of that dumbness: sacrificing herself for the hero's "career." She is inside the idyll at last. But now he isn't. "I know what you were trying to do," he says bitterly. "Save little Willie's career from the bad, bad woman." And he's exactly right, of course. But the fact is that she *is* "smarter," just as she said she was; and while a Capra film might suppose that she could undo that, and even that she should, a Sturges film knows better—as the complicated feeling in this last scene shows. But finally it's a feeling of impasse, of something unresolved. The movie itself makes us feel that there's more to be said for Stanwyck's lady thief, even for her way of life, than *this* film, with its formulaic regeneration at the end, ever really manages. Indeed there is. And *The Lady Eve* ("I'm going to write you a great comedy . . .") says it all.

ALMOST FROM the beginning there is a peculiar tone of exultancy: from Stanwyck's first appearance, leaning over the rail of the ship with her father, Colonel Harrington (Charles Coburn), watching the new arrival, the very rich young Charles Pike (Henry Fonda), come aboard from a steam-powered launch he has just sailed out of the Amazon jungle on. Jean Harrington can't wait to get at him—she is almost jumping with it, in fact, while she banters with her father, almost chattering with excitement: "Gee, I hope he's rich," she says, pressing against the railing and straining to see below. "I hope he thinks he's a wizard at cards." But the effect is a curiously distanced one: Sturges shows us the heroine's high spirits well before he's begun to induce our own.

JEAN (*excited*): And I hope he's got a big fat wife so I don't have to dance in the moonlight with him. I don't know why it is but a sucker always steps on your feet.
COLONEL: A mug is a mug in everything.
JEAN: I don't see why I have to do all the dirty work. There must be plenty of rich old dames waiting for you to push 'em around.
COLONEL: You find 'em, I'll push 'em.

Their colleague, Gerald, the colonel's "valet" (Melville Cooper), joins them now with the news that Pike is very rich indeed—the heir to the Pike's Ale fortune. "I wonder if I could clunk him on the head with this?" says Jean—and she drops the apple she's been eating ("Don't do that!" cries her father, too late) on Pike's head, "clunking" him on his pith helmet just as he is starting up the Jacob's ladder from the launch.

She is on the same odd high—and even more so—in the next scene in the ship's dining room. She is sitting at a table with her father, looking into the

*The Lady Eve
at the races:
Charles
Coburn,
Melville
Cooper, Eric
Blore, and
Barbara
Stanwyck.*

mirror on her compact and conjuring it like a crystal ball: watching Charles, the center of attention for everyone in the room when all he wants to do is read his book (*Are Snakes Necessary?*—he is an ophiologist). The women circle him; they pass his table and drop handkerchiefs, or approach him with a story about someone he looks like, or catch his eye and raise a beaker of Pike's Ale at him. And we see all of this in Jean's mirror—a series of silent images, with Jean supplying the thoughts and words, and directions for action, too, of all the people caught there, as if she were the author of the whole event. Her father is waiting for her to make her move—not knowing, apparently, that she is making it. "What did you say?" he asks. But she is not talking to him; she is talking to the mirror—to her own sense of life and power, to her own energy of creation. "Look over to your left, bookworm," she conjures Pike. "There's a girl pining for you. A little further . . . just a little further . . ." And he does. "I wonder if my tie's on straight," she says, thinking his thoughts for him. "I certainly upset them, don't I? Now who else is after me?"—as Pike looks uneasily around. "Oh, you just can't stand it anymore, you're leaving?"—he closes his book and rises. "These women don't give you a minute's peace, do they?" Once again Stanwyck is giving the impression of someone in a state of high excitement, controlling and exalted. And yet we are still so much outside this elation of hers (it's amusing but slightly off-putting, too) that the effect is unbalancing. Creating a tension ("Well, go ahead, go sulk in your cabin," she says as he leaves his table—"Go soak your head and see if I care.") that isn't ended until Pike passes her table and hits the floor (she stretches out her leg and trips him) on his face. And she rises—in full deadpan imperiousness, no trace of unholy glee: that familiar sad-contemplative presence we recognize as "Stanwyck" looking down at him now. "Why don't you look where you're going?" she says in her dry voice—and we're "home," balance righted, back in the familiar screwball world—and off. "Why don't *I* look—?" he says, aghast. "Look what you did to my shoe," she says. "You knocked the heel off." Now he is penitent—and confused. Did he do that? "You did, and you can just take me right down to my cabin for another pair of slippers." She introduces herself and her father, clasps him by the arm, and steers him limpingly to the exit—while the crowd in the dining room stares. "Funny our meeting like this, isn't it?" she says—the glee breaking out once again.

"Because you were so polite," she tells him when they reach her stateroom, "you can pick them out and put them on if you like." But there are so many shoes in the closet she has pointed him at, and he is already reeling from her perfume: where he's been, as he explains—"up the Amazon for a year"—they don't use it. He looks at the shoes. She looks at him, leaning insinuatingly against an open wardrobe: "See anything you like?" she says. He kneels at her feet to put the shoes on; she crosses her legs and extends her foot. He's an ophiologist, he tells her, and he's been looking for snakes. One of the things he has against ale—apart from its taste (it makes him sick just to think about it) and in spite of the family fortune ("Pike's Pale, the Ale That Won for Yale")— is the nickname he got as a child: Hopsie. "Hello, Hopsie," she says brightly. "Make it Charlie, will you?" he says. But she thinks that "Hopsie" is "kinda cute." ("And when you get older I could call you Popsie. Hopsie Popsie!") He holds on to her ankle and looks faint. She looks down at him gravely: "We'd better get back now," she says. But he tries to explain: "You see, where I've been, I mean up the Amazon, you kind of forget how—I mean, when you haven't seen a girl in a long time . . ." They stand, together. "I mean, there's something about that perfume that . . ." "Don't you like my perfume?" she says. They are *very* close together. "Like it?" he says. "I'm *cockeyed* on it!"—and he leans, half staggering, as if he's going to kiss her, but it's hard to tell. "Why, *Hopsie*," she says, pushing him backwards and off balance with the flat of her hand and walking off in front of him, "you ought to be kept in a *cage*. . . ." That glee again. She leaves Fonda alone in the shot, swaying woozily and looking after her.

And then when it turns out that he does card tricks, too ("Have you seen this one?" he asks. "You palm it . . . that means you grip it in the palm of the hand—like this . . ."), the delight of Colonel Harrington and his daughter is almost too much for them to contain. "Bless my soul," says the colonel, once "palming" has been explained to him. "Do that again, will you?" And then, when he does: "Amazing . . ." As indeed it is—more than they could have hoped for, almost. They let him win the first evening's play ("sweetening the kitty," as the colonel calls it), and Pike is both shocked and embarrassed by the large amount he has won. He hadn't even thought they were playing for money. "Oh, Father's in the oil business, dear," says Jean. "It just keeps bubbling up out of the ground." She herself has lost a hundred dollars. Charles is appalled. But she insists on paying it to him anyway.

JEAN: Don't you worry—I'll get it back.
CHARLES: Well, if that's a promise . . . (*He gathers the money up reluctantly.*)
JEAN: You can depend upon it.
CHARLES: . . . I'll certainly feel better.
JEAN (*brightly*): You certainly will.

And she laughs out loud, as if the thought had just struck her.

That's just it. He's come to them like a happy thought. And he *keeps* coming—as in the exchange above: not only with "if that's a promise" but "I'll certainly feel better," too. Or in this exchange, after the colonel has left Jean and Charles alone ("to talk about whatever young people talk about"). "A nice fellow, your father," says Charles. And a good card player, remarks Jean. "You think so?" says Charles, rather surprised. "I don't want to be rude, but I thought he seemed a little uneven." "He's more uneven some times than others," says Jean, laughing, with that same air of being struck by the thought. "That's what makes him uneven, of course," explains Charles—before going on to pay *her* card playing a little compliment.

He is incredible. A nice fellow—almost unbelievably nice, in fact—but asking for it with every breath. How could anyone resist? Certainly not a company of pros like Jean and her father and Gerald. That unholy, let-me-at-'em glee ("Gee, I hope he's rich" and "You find 'em, I'll push 'em") that Stanwyck and Sturges showed us at the very beginning no longer looks so unholy to us. We are inside it by now, a party to it even, to every joke at Hopsie's expense, every knowing remark, every nuance and frisson and anticipation of the con. We've been here before, of course—many times: in all those Cagney and Gable con-artist comedies, in Cary Grant's Walter Burns, and so on—but probably never so richly and fully as now, with the kind of heightened, elated awareness that Stanwyck makes so vivid.

One of the boldest things Sturges does in this film—one way *The Lady Eve* goes farther and deeper than the comedies before it—is to make explicit in the

Stanwyck figure what has been only implicit in earlier versions of the screwball heroine: an element of destructiveness in her authority and style. What seems an underlying complexity in movies like *Libeled Lady* and *Shall We Dance* and *The Awful Truth* is here an overt meaning—and a central one. The special tone of *The Lady Eve* is a kind of energetic cruelty, a malicious exuberance, reflected chiefly in Stanwyck's treatment of Fonda: a kind of relentless and systematic humiliation, extending over the whole film with all its changes of direction and transformations of character. Their romance begins when she trips him. It climaxes when he steps off the honeymoon train in his pajamas and slides into the mud. In between times, she has him tripping himself. And their final reconciliation is signaled by her tripping him still again. But all this is only secondary to the moral and psychological punishment she visits on him: the famous wedding night on the train, with the virginal new husband forced to hear his upperclass Englishwoman bride recollect, in the best *Private Lives* style, a romantic past that seems to have been both rollicking and insatiable. And even when she is first seducing him, she does it with casual, happy, open contempt. What's puzzling—and even disturbing at times—is how little Fonda seems to deserve all this, at least at first. After all, when Dunne embarrasses Melvyn Douglas in *Theodora Goes Wild*, it's because he's asked for it: he isn't unoffending like Fonda. And the embarrassment the heroine occasions in *Theodora*—as in *The Awful Truth, Bringing Up Baby*, et al.—is public, a way of detaching the romantic couple from the public world. Fonda's humiliation in *The Lady Eve* is an almost intimate thing, requiring no audience but Stanwyck and us, it seems. And there's something solemn about her manner of inflicting it, even at its funniest. "I need him," she says, her face in close-up, framed by a large, round hat, filling the screen darkly and beautifully, "like the axe needs the turkey." This is certainly an odd moment (coming at the movie's midpoint) for a romantic comedy, ambiguous and troubling—but, like the movie itself, not really unpleasant, in *spite* of what it seems to be saying. For almost the oddest thing of all about this exuberant, coldly brilliant comedy about the humiliation of a man by a woman is that its final effect is not only exhilarating but positively goodnatured.

THE FONDA hero, it turns out, has three almost different characters—corresponding to the three-act structure of the movie—and each of them a stereotype. The first is the absentminded professor, the male virgin with arcane intellectual interests ("I'm an ophiologist"). He is boyish, innocent, almost unbelievably naive—literally just out of the woods (that Amazon jungle). He is also possessed of a nearly unshakable equanimity as he is cheated, mocked, tripped, dragged down three flights of stairs by the heroine (she's in flight from his snake), and, in the midst of swelling passion for her, bumped onto the floor. That's where he is when their first love scene takes place. She has disposed herself on the chaise longue in her stateroom, recovering from her snake fright; he is below and beside her on the floor, where he has fallen—both in a medium close-up ("Comfortable?" "Yes, very")—his head back, his eyes starting out: "Hold me tight," she says, her cheek nuzzling his. "I wouldn't have frightened you for anything in the world," he somehow manages to say. "I mean, if there's anyone in the world I wouldn't want to . . ."—she is playing with his ear now, and his eyes close "—it's you," he concludes. "You're very sweet, don't let me go," she says, with her cheek nestled against his, her finger in his ear. He looks downward and sees that her dress has fallen away from her knees, baring them. He replaces it, with a limp extended hand and tactfully lowered eyes. She opens her eyes and stares as this tactful procedure takes place. "Thank you," she says . . . then sighs, closes her eyes again, and nestles against his face. "How *was* everything up the Amazon?" she says, fondling his hair. "All right, thank you." A slight pause. "What are you thinking about?" she says. "Nothing," he replies in a strangled voice.

> JEAN: Are you always going to be interested in snakes? (*She strokes his cheek.*)
> CHARLES: Snakes are my life (*his voice breaking*) . . . in a way. . . .
> JEAN (*round-eyed and thoughtful*): What a life . . .

Charles illustrates Sturges' way with stereotypes: his tendency both to emphasize their familiarity and essential artifice and at the same time to open up their richness and paradoxical "reality." A line like "Snakes are my life . . . in a way," for example, works in both these ways. A Sturges character never tries to disguise his formulaic nature: he proclaims and fulfills it, makes it vivid and wonderful, as Charles does in this couch scene with Jean. He is the bumpkin in excelsis.

The second Fonda surfaces when he finds out that Jean is a professional card sharp and con woman, at the end of their shipboard idyll. This version of Charles is smug and self-righteous. And as Stanwyck transforms herself into the Lady Eve Sidwich to get back at him, he seems to become even more so. Closer to the Other Man than to the romantic hero: he is a stuffed shirt, a snob and a phony even. He is still a bumbler (that element remains constant)—falling over the couch, knocking a servant's tray over, sliding into a mudhole. But that haplessness no longer reflects innocence and inexperience so much as it does simple (and deserved) cloddishness. *This* bumbler is a prude and a pompous fake.

But the third Fonda, who appears triumphantly at the very end, seems for his brief moment on the screen to be just what a romantic lead should be. This time he drags *her* down the three flights of ship's stairs, manfully ignoring her father's

The chaise longue scene from The Lady Eve.

protests, and disappears with her into a stateroom. "A mug is a mug in every-thing," her father has said—but now "mug" has a different meaning: "Don't you know I couldn't look at another man if I wanted to?" she says as the door closes on them. "Don't you know I've waited all my life for you, you big mug?" Though he still doesn't understand who she is, it seems: "It'd never have happened," he says (starting to explain to Jean about his marriage to "Eve"), "except she looks so exactly like you."

It's not that these three Fondas are inconsistent with one another, even ac-cording to the conventions. There is ample precedent for uniting in the same character the male innocent and the stuffed shirt—Ralph Bellamy in both *The Awful Truth* and *His Girl Friday*, among other examples. Ample "precedent" in life, too: the probability that innocence sustained past a certain age will congeal into self-righteousness and emotional fakery. So that it even seems "realistic" that the second Fonda, with all his ungenerosity and reactionary spirit, should be living at home with his parents when we first get to know him (his father contemptuous, his mother protective and concerned), in a fundamentally child-ish sort of relation to them. But Sturges doesn't so much unite these character-istics in the same figure as *layer* them in, so that we experience them successively. We don't really expect Hopsie to turn into the second Fonda—in fact, we're given almost no clue from the first Fonda that he will do so. Though of course when he does, we see the point.

More than that, we *feel* it—with all the power of emotional conviction that this comedy carries. And it's less because of Fonda than of Stanwyck: because our collusion with her in this film makes Hopsie's transformation seem not only deeply right but necessary. Because the deep delight of this film lies so much in our enjoyment of Stanwyck's power, her triumphant self-assertion—so wonderfully credible every moment she's on the screen—as a woman, a seducer, or a card player. A high point in that delight is the three-handed poker game in which she outwits even her father ("Know any more games, Harry?"). We have no idea how she does it, of course—how she even seems to know what cards he's pulled from his pocket. It's like watching a magic act—except that we never really *see* the trick itself, except as it registers on the faces of the players and in occasional close-ups of the cards. Still, we believe in it all, eagerly—not only because of Stanwyck but because we want to.

But this happy collusion has a significant catch. Sturges is testing the moral limits of the delight he's giving to us by insisting, as he does always, on something outrageous, even vindictive, in Jean's treatment of Hopsie.* Stanwyck's heroine carries us into a troubling and ambiguous area of feeling, and our consciousness of that is part of the whole rich effect. Part, even, of our laughing so much. In a way we are in the same relation to the heroine's personal authority, her triumphant assertion of intelligent power, as she is: enjoying it, but somewhere uneasy about it, too. And this uneasiness suggests a larger point, already familiar to movie audiences from all those other tough-girl heroines who seem weary of their own toughness: that it's nice to know your way around, all right—but surely nicer in a way *not* to ("You never think of anything wrong, do you?"). So that it makes perfect sense that Stanwyck should fall in love with Fonda—just as it did before when she fell in love with Fred MacMurray ("That's right . . . we're smarter")—not only in spite of his obtuseness but because of it. As Jean puts it when she is trying to explain it to her disapproving father: "I think I'm in love with the poor fish, snakes and all. Oh, I don't know, he's kind of touched something in my heart." And she has, of course, like McGinty with Catherine, fallen in love with Hopsie's idea of *her*, too: "And I'd give a lot to be—well, I mean I'm *going* to be exactly the way he thinks I am, the way he'd like me to be. . . ."

But then her fondness for Hopsie has been something Stanwyck has managed to convey even through all the torment she inflicts on him. "You have a definite nose," he tells her, referring to her card-playing skills. "I'm glad you like it,"

---

* Jonathan Demme's *Something Wild* (1986) is in many ways a less sophisticated, less coherent version of the same screwball plot—even including the changed perception of the hero in the middle of the film.

she says—they are sitting nose to nose in the dining room. "Do you like any of the rest of me?" And assures him when he gets flustered that she was "just flirting" with him. And this flirting seems at least as powerful an impulse for her as the mocking one. "Oh, now you're kidding me," he says, during the chaise longue scene. "Not badly," she replies, almost tenderly—and meaning it, before going on to kid him some more. And it's precisely the ambiguity of her responses here—somehow her tenderness is never in doubt—that makes the scene not only funny but in some way fascinating. "You have the darnedest way," he tells her the morning after, "of bumping a fellow down and bouncing him up again." "And then bumping him down again," she replies in her sad-laughing way. As Hopsie himself puts it the night of their first encounter: "You're certainly a funny girl to meet for anybody who's just been up the Amazon for a year." The morning after the chaise longue encounter, she wakes up screaming, dreaming of snakes. And reminiscing once she's awake about the hapless victim: "The poor sap . . . that *card* trick!" "Tragic," replies her father as he sits down by her with a deck of cards and starts dealing hands on the bed. "I don't believe it," says Jean, reacting to the deal he's just shown her ("Like heck you're dealing fifths!" "You wanta bet?" He shows her) with open wonderment. "You don't really need it," says her father with becoming modesty as he gathers up the cards. "It's just virtuosity." "Harry," says Jean, after a thoughtful moment. "Yes, darling?" "Tell me my fortune," she says, almost shyly—smiling (the Sturges screenplay says) "like a little girl."

That, of course, is just the sort of thing that Hopsie means to her—recovering that little girl again in some way. He unwittingly makes that point himself in their love scene on the bow of the ship, against a moonlit sky—in the sort of night air, as Jean remarks, that "makes you feel all clean inside." "Don't move!" says Charles suddenly. And then he explains, in this unaccustomed rush of words:

. . . I've just understood something. You see, every time I've looked at you here on the boat, it wasn't only here I saw you. You seem to go way back. I know that isn't clear but I—I saw you here and at the same time further away and then still further away and then very small—like converging perspective lines. . . . No, that isn't it. It's like—like people following each other in a forest glade. Only way back there you're a little girl in short dresses and your hair falling to your shoulders and a little boy is standing with you holding your hand. In the middle distance I'm still with you and not holding your hand anymore because it isn't manly, but wanting to. And then still further we look terrible. You with your legs like a colt and mine like a calf. . . . What I'm trying to say is—only I'm not a poet, I'm an ophiologist—I've always loved you. I mean I've never loved anyone but

you. I know that sounds as dull as a drugstore novel—and what I see inside
I'll never be able to cast into words . . . but that's what I mean. . . .

And she loves it.

But the sort of magic that Jean and her father can work ("It's just virtuosity"
and "Tell me my fortune") is not something to be lightly renounced, even for this
promise of recovered innocence ("I'm *going* to be exactly the way he thinks I
am"). "You'll go straight too, won't you, Harry?" says Jean, upon first broaching
her marriage plans to her father. "Straight to where?" he replies. He can come
and live with them when they're married, and Gerald, too, she says—and "think
how peaceful you can be." "Playing cribbage with Gerald," he says. "I can just
see myself roaming around your estate with a weedsticker and fifty cents a week.
And a pair of new slippers for Christmas. The trouble with people who reform
is they always want to rain on everybody else's parade too. . . . You tend to your
knitting. *I'll* play the cards!"

But then, of course, we don't want to see either his parade or hers rained
on—though the movie seems dangerously close to one or the other such outcome. And it's rescued, just in time, by Fonda's first transformation. For it's
been clear all along that Hopsie's innocence, which makes Jean fall in love with
him, threatens to undo *her* just as much as it does her father: to make her feel
"cheap," as she later says, and humiliated, and to deprive her of her energy and
style. More or less just what happens to the tough-girl heroine in *Remember the
Night*, and in *Meet John Doe* and *Mr. Deeds Goes to Town* and countless other
movies. But Hopsie's transformation into a jerk, into the second Fonda of the
stuffed shirt, saves this heroine, for herself and for us. *This* time she meets
exposure and rebuke when they come not by penitence and reformation but by
becoming more wonderfully herself than ever: beating her father at his own game
and then, best of all—in the second part of the movie—transforming herself
into the Lady Eve Sidwich: beating the respectable ones at *their* game. But
finally it's the second Fonda who makes all this seem right—not only her mid-
movie imposture but her earlier punishment of him. And as the movie goes on,
we feel and understand more and more clearly what this punishment, so seemingly undeserved, has really been about.

"THESE RIGHTEOUS people," the colonel reminds her, "are apt to be slightly
narrow-minded." Jean replies to this with a kind of serene confidence: "A
man who couldn't forgive wouldn't be much of a man." But then Hopsie, as it
turns out, *can't* forgive. Jean had told him that he didn't know "much about
girls." "The best ones aren't as good as you probably think they are, and the bad
ones aren't as bad," she says. "Not nearly as bad," she adds. But Hopsie has

found out about her—that she and her father are well-known con artists and card sharps—and he is shattered. After the first shock passes, though, his mouth sets in a grim, tense line, and he looks straight ahead while Jean looks at him with disappointed love. He even tells her that he was playing her for a sucker—that he knew about her all along. She doesn't believe this story, but she is still hurt by it. "I hate that mug! I hate him!" she cries, sobbing in her room while her father tries to comfort her. The next time we see her, she is composed again, standing at the ship's railing with the others, looking cold and imperious—and ready to take her revenge. "When I think we let that sucker get off scot free, it makes my blood boil. . . ."

Her chance comes when they run into their old friend Pearlie (Eric Blore)—"Sir Alfred at the moment"—at the races. Where he tells them about his adventures in "the contract bridge belt" ("*Won*derful game!"), living in a town that's full of millionaires.

> COLONEL: How do you meet them?
> SIR ALFRED: The chumps? . . . Oh, my dear fellow, when one's name is
>   Sir Alfred McGlennan-Keith, R.F.D., one doesn't have to *meet* them—
>   one fights them off with sticks. . . .

When Jean discovers that Pearlie knows the Pikes ("Do I know them! I positively swill in their ale. Good old Horace—oh-ho, what a card player!"), she asks him—over her father's strenuous objections—if she can visit him and be introduced as his niece. "My dear girl, there's only one thing—you'd have to be English, you know." "I've been English before," says Jean. "I shall be as English as necess'ry"—clipping the words in the English style. Then, very much in her own style: "I want to see that guy. I've got some unfinished business with him. I need him like the axe needs the turkey. . . . Better go make your bets."

And so the Lady Eve appears, at a reception given for her by the Pikes themselves. And she wows them all—with her beauty and her quaint upper-class English ways, her English slang, and all her funny stories about her mixups in America, as well as rumors of her being almost mysteriously well-connected ("She must be very—very—?" "Oh, *very!*"). Above all, she is so natural and unassuming—no airs at all, just herself at all times ("Oh, please, just call me Eve"). Even Charles is beguiled by her, once he gets over his initial shock ("Well, I mean to say, haven't we *met?*")—and dazzled. It shows in the falls he takes during the party ("Anybody's apt to trip," says Eve, coming to his defense. "Not over a sofa," snarls his father—Eugene Pallette) as well as in the new, ingenious form his mental muddle takes. He soon convinces himself—in spite of his valet Muggsy's (William Demarest's) vigorous dissent ("That's the same dame. She looks the same, she walks the same, and she's tossing you just like she done the last time!" "She doesn't talk the same.")—that Jean and Eve "look too much alike to be the same." Anyway, why should she do such a thing?

The Lady Eve
gets flowers
from a sucker:
the marriage
proposal
will be next,
she tells
Eric Blore.

MUGGSY: I don't know. Maybe she wants you to fall for her again.

CHARLES: Do I look that dumb?

MUGGSY: You wouldn't be the first one. I knew a guy married the same
dame three times and then turned around and married her aunt.

But she hasn't even *tried* to disguise herself, says Charles, "with her hair dyed
yellow and eyebrows different" or something. No, she can't be the same. "If she
didn't look so *exactly* like the other girl I might be suspicious." And so he goes
back to the party—and to more falls.

His most telling scene, however, is the next one—"about two weeks from
now"—when he and Eve go horseback riding. This is the occasion he takes to
propose to her. They have stopped and dismounted to admire the sunset: "There
against the glory of Mother Nature," says Eve—who is foretelling the scene to
Pearlie (reminding us of her conjuring over the compact mirror) at the same time
as it fades into view on the screen—"a horse will steal up behind me and nuzzle
my head. And so will Charles . . . the heel!" In his screenplay, Sturges gives

this scene a preliminary title: "Eve and Her Horse's Head—Against the Sunset."

"Stop that!" says Eve. She thought it was the horse—or so she says—but it was Charles being amorous. They are in a medium two-shot, facing away from each other and into the sunset, Eve with a kind of fixed, sunset-watching smile, Charles looming above and just behind her, looking stricken and solemn. His consciousness of the occasion ("I suppose you know what I'm thinking about," he begins, looking into the sunset. "Possibly I have an idea," she replies) has made him sententious. "The union of two people for life," he reminds her, is not a light matter.

EVE: How wise you are.
CHARLES (*continuing*): Men—that is, lots of men—are more careful in choosing a tailor than they are in choosing a wife.
EVE (*playfully*): That's probably why they look so funny.
CHARLES (*looking down at her, thinking she must not have heard him*): No, dear—they're *more* careful in choosing a tailor than in choosing a wife.
EVE: Oh . . . (*turning to face him, eagerly*) But not you, Charles.
CHARLES: That's right. (*She turns back.*) I think that if there's one time in your life to be careful, to weigh every pro and con . . . that this is the time.

He has in this last speech attained a kind of exaltation, it seems—in a quiet way. The prudent man's high. He looks up and off as he speaks—and he has that father-of-us-all quality, that foursquareness and solidity that Fonda brought to the playing of so many American heroes. Particularly when he gets to: "to weigh every pro and con." That image of weighing seems to move him inexplicably, and he seems to be looking into the ages as he says it. He is a man who is stirred at the thought of his own caution—and about to do (as we know) this utterly mad thing. In fact, the mad thing is right there in the shot with him—and smiling. "Oh, *yes*," she says, "you can't be too careful."

And now Sturges adds another detail to this scene of apotheosis. Just as Charles is launching himself (in his stately fashion) into the marriage proposal ("Now you might think," he says, "that having known you such a short time . . ."), the horse behind them starts to move around restlessly. So that in the same tightly framed shot, above the faces of the two people, there is now this mad, rolling horse eye—as the animal hits Charles in the head with its nose, interrupting him. Eve takes up the thread: "I feel I've known you always," she says, encouragingly. "That's the way I feel about you," says Charles imperturbably, as the horse jostles him again—and whinnies. And then Charles, with the same controlling complacence that has marked his demeanor throughout the scene, begins a speech that Eve (and we) have heard before—but to a very different effect now. "I don't just see you here in front of the sunset," he says.

"But you see, we go way back. I see you here—at the same time further away, and still further away, and way, way back in a long place like a—" And the horse nuzzles him again. "Like a forest glade?" says Eve. He is surprised. "That's right, how did you guess?" he says. "Because that's where I see you always," says Eve, turning toward him eagerly (but not looking into his eyes). "We held hands way, way back." "Why, that's remarkable," he says. "That's like telepathy." "I can read many of your thoughts," she says, turning back to the sunset, with her smile.

And just at this juncture, as the joke reaches a kind of intensity of pleasure and irony, Sturges pulls us up with a rather surprising cut: to a reverse angle. We are now looking into the sunset, too: we are at the same medium distance from Charles and Eve but looking now at the backs of their heads, framed against "the glory of Mother Nature." Nevertheless, Charles is still talking—in his reverent, solemn way. "Oh, then I need hardly tell you," he says, "of the doubts I had before I brought myself to speak like this." Now we see the back of the horse's head, moving undiscourageably into the frame—and Charles pushes him away. "You see, Eve, you're so beautiful, you're so fine, you're so—" and pushes the horse's head away again. "I don't deserve you," he concludes. And for Eve's reply to this, Sturges cuts back to the head-on shot: "Oh, but you *do*, Charles," she says, turning to him ardently. "If anybody *ever* deserved me" (the horse's eye again), "you do. So richly!" They embrace—with Charles with one hand holding off the horse—who whinnies dementedly. End of scene.

It's an extraordinary sequence, in every detail. For one thing, there is a way—and different ways, too—in which the horse and the sunset place even Eve, in all her controlling splendor, in a larger context of feeling and experience, enriching both the joke and the film. But above every other wonderful thing here—capping the whole sequence—is Eve's final, dizzying line: "Oh, but you *do*, Charles. If anybody *ever* deserved me, you do. So richly!" The reserves of bitterness (in *all* directions) that this hints at, and then turns into a joke (successfully), without at all troubling the dominantly sunny, irresistibly good-natured tone of the film: it's the sort of feat that makes you both laugh in surprise and leaves you slightly gasping; you're still taking it in even after you've stopped laughing.

This is also one of those moments that remind us how powerful the feelings behind this comedy are—far, far behind it, like the smile behind Stanwyck's eyes. What we feel the force of at these comic high points is a kind of transmuted anger. Is *that* what the sunniness is about? It certainly accounts for the headiness. *The Lady Eve* is one of the most intoxicating comedies ever made. And it gets plainer as the movie goes on—and as Charles keeps coming on, in more and more awful ways (there is worse to come even than this proposal scene: i.e., the wedding night on the train)—what the anger behind it is about. Charles may be a butt and a victim, it's true. But the more he is—the more he gets dumped on, by Jean, by Eve, by the movie (by us)—the more provocation he seems to offer, revealing yet another dimension, unsuspected up to now but wholly convincing, of his complacency. He is a "developing" character in this respect, unfolding himself with a kind of terrible inevitability: his snobbery, his self-importance, his numbing male thickness. He not only gives a kind of permission to our cruelty, he even does it retroactively, so that the uneasiness that Sturges has inspired in us from the beginning is finally and hilariously resolved. The movie's instinct about this figure, enacted by the Stanwyck heroine from the opening scenes—that he was asking for it even when he seemed not to be—turns out to have been the right one. This is a Mr. Deeds we *can* punish—without feeling guilty about it. A Capra hero in his way—but one who demonstrates that the other side of "innocence" is a stubborn refusal of knowledge and experience. A patriarch in the making—an old fart before his time.

But what is she going to do with him now? wonder her father and Gerald. She has married him, and they are on their wedding trip. Cut to a night train moving toward the camera. Cut to the train interior. Charles, in robe and pajamas, knocks and enters the compartment. Eve, in her negligee, is sitting on a chair, looking at him. But when a piece of luggage falls on his head from the rack above, she goes to comfort him, sitting by him on the bed, petting and soothing him—until something starts her laughing, something that reminds her of "that other time." Oh, yes? "Haven't you noticed that I never eat cheese?" she says, still laughing. "Oh, it was *so* unromantic." The classy Englishwoman who emerges *now*, before his horrified eyes, is like a combination of Noel Coward's Amanda and Evelyn Waugh's Miss Runcible, though more insatiable than either. "That other time" was someone named Angus—whom she "eloped with" at the age of sixteen. "It was really nothing, darling . . . you know how romantic young girls are. It wasn't of the slightest importance, I assure you. I'm sorry I even mentioned it. . . ." But now, as she observes regretfully, she has "planted a seed" in his mind. Who was *Angus?* he wants to know.

EVE: Oh, I assure you, darling, he was no one of the slightest importance. Oh, what a way to make me spend the wedding night. He was just a groom on my father's estate. . . .

CHARLES (*bugging eyes, choked voice*): A groom? . . .

EVE: Well, not really the groom, of course. He used to put on the groom's uniform on his day off and then he'd be the groom that day. The rest of the time he was just a stable boy! (*She laughs at the memory.*)

CHARLES (*ditto*): A *stable boy?*

EVE: Yes, the boy who cleans up the stables. . . . Oh, you mean you don't think much of my choice? But he didn't look so bad, darling, in the groom's uniform, with the little tight pants, and the boots with the yellow tips. . . . (*laughs again*) Don't you think they're cute?

Anyway, they were caught and brought back—and that was that. Except that Angus, she adds wistfully, was "discharged." Charles "trusts" that they were brought back "before nightfall"? This inquiry sends her again into little peals of laughter: "Oh, my dear, it took them *weeks* to find us!"—because of all the funny names they made up at the different inns and hotels. And so on. Cut to the train exterior again, hurtling and whistling through the rainy night. Cut back to the compartment: Charles is pacing, silently and deliberatively—while Eve regards him from the bed, with her level deadpan gaze. He breaks the silence: he has decided, he tells her (to the strains of the "Pilgrims' Chorus" on the soundtrack), to appeal to such virtues as "the ability to understand" (that faculty, as he points out, "that distinguishes a man from a beast") and to the ideal of "sweet forgiveness." But she makes him repeat the last one: "Sweet what?" she says blankly. "Sweet *forgive*ness," he replies, through clenched teeth. And then explains his decision: "A girl of sixteen is practically an idiot anyway, so I can't very well blame you for something that's practically done by somebody else . . ." and so on. She is ecstatic. She puts her arms around him. "I knew you'd be that way," she says. "I knew it the first moment I saw you standing beside me—I knew you'd be both husband and father to me, I knew I could trust and confide in you. I suppose that's why I fell in love with you. . . ." And she wonders if now would be the time to tell him about Herman. And as he repeats the name in a shout, Sturges cuts again to the outside of the train, now going through a tunnel. The rest is handled in montage: each new name (there are several) provoking another shot of the speeding train, another cry of the train whistle. Until finally the train slows to a stop. And Charles, in overcoat, hat, and pajamas, carrying a suitcase, appears on the platform. As the train slows, he throws the suitcase off. And as it stops, he steps down—into the rain and mud and slipping, falling flat on his back. It's a lovely *slow* fall because of the mud—unlike all his other falls, which were swift and loud and violent. This one has something inexorable about it, and an almost sensuous relish—the loss of control (except for the hand holding onto his hat) is painfully gradual, with one impotent, upraised leg in the air, as he sinks slowly into the ooze. The wages of dumbness is mud. . . .

But then Sturges does something extraordinary again: he cuts back to Eve inside the train—now alone, and slowly, sadly drawing the shade on her window as the train pulls out. It has been, we are suddenly meant to recognize—even before we've stopped enjoying it—an empty victory. Even a self-defeating one. For one thing, it isn't Allyn Joslyn or Ralph Bellamy out there in the mud. It isn't even Melvyn Douglas. Charles is Henry Fonda, and in some way, even at his worst ("A *groom?*"), somehow likable. And this is precisely the complication that Eve and the movie are hung up on. It's not only that we expect and want the inevitable romantic ending. But even more that we don't want—any more than Eve does—the movie simply to expose this figure as a fraud. Eve's consciousness ("I'm not your daughter for free, you know!"), her sense of herself and her attitude toward her own powers, are all too ambivalent for that. And this comedy hasn't prepared us, we realize, for a blanket endorsement of worldliness and sophistication—or of cynicism. Just the opposite, in fact. Because Charles's emblematic innocence, shaky and ambiguous as in fact it is, has reminded Eve—and us—of the limitations of her own "experience" and worldliness. And so, having exposed him finally—having enacted this final satisfying understanding of him—she will take him back. She is hopelessly attracted, after all—like Sturges, like most of us—to this image of a kind of American niceness, this version of Mr. Deeds, however much she may deride him. And although Sturges himself may be angry at the tyranny this image exerts in our lives and imaginations, he is also and always, like Eve herself, drawn to it. As much as Capra is—and perhaps even more genuinely. But Sturges knows—as Capra does not—how complicated and even painful, how ludicrous and contradictory, our relation to this figure must be.

And so the third Fonda: he has been punished into maturity, it seems—into valuing and loving Jean again. He refuses to talk to Eve after that honeymoon experience. He won't even see her again, even to dissolve the marriage. But he is sailing on another ocean voyage, and Jean is in the dining room again with her father. Once again she trips him. He is overjoyed. "We must play cards this trip," he says to the colonel, "lots and lots of cards!"—as he spirits Jean off to a stateroom to be alone with her. He loves her, but he still doesn't "understand." "I don't want to understand," he says. "Whatever it is, keep it to yourself. All I know is I adore you." But he has no right to be in her cabin, he tells her—as the door closes on them and the movie ends:

JEAN: Why not?
CHARLES: Because I'm married. . . .
JEAN: But so am I, darling. So am I. . . .

Sturges: The McCrea Films | 26

THE GIRL: *There's nothing like a deep dish movie to drive you out in the open.*

SULLIVAN: *What are you talking about? Film's the greatest educational medium the world has ever known. You take a picture like* Hold Back Tomorrow—

THE GIRL: *You hold it. Did you ever meet Lubitsch?*

—*Sullivan's Travels*

STURGES WROTE *Sullivan's Travels* (1942) in the exhilaration of his new success. In comparison with the long gestations and multiple rewrites of his earlier films, he practically dashed this one off—a film *about* success—in two months. He began it in February 1941, just at the time *The Lady Eve* was opening across the country, to universal acclaim and huge returns. So he pretty much had the freedom now to do what he wanted. He took it. *Sullivan's Travels* is sui generis: there is nothing else quite like it, not even in Sturges' work. It's a movie about wanting to make a movie: people later on would see a parallel to Fellini's *8½* (1963), but the Sturges film ("Sturges' *8½*," as it's come to be called) is in some ways even more daring.

A comedy about a Hollywood director who is noted for his comedies but who wants now to do a serious film full of idealism and social relevance, suitable to troubled modern times. When it is pointed out to this rich and famous man that he doesn't know much at all about "trouble," he sets out to find it, disguising himself as a tramp and taking to the road in the travels of the title. Like Swift's Gulliver, he makes four "voyages." And just as in Swift, it's the fourth and final voyage that transforms him.*

---

* The film's title card is a book cover: "*Sullivan's Travels* by Preston Sturges," designed to look like all those children's book editions of Swift, with Sullivan and the Girl in place of Gulliver in the cover drawing, in their tramp costumes and towering over masses of tiny people below.

"I'll never get rich." "You're a little richer than you were." Pat West, Veronica Lake, and Joel McCrea in Sullivan's Travels.

This picaresque framework makes the movie feel as random and seemingly aimless as *The Lady Eve* seems finished and symmetrical—a notebook film, with a kind of freehand energy and boldness and an almost bewildering variety of scenes and tones and styles. But the prodigality and invention are controlled by a "meta-filmic" self-questioning structure. Sturges, characteristically, is both enjoying his powers and thinking twice about them. But *Sullivan's Travels*, brilliant as it is, doesn't quite have the depth or density of his other great comedies. There is *real* randomness here, in substance as well as in feeling. That is part of the point, of course. "How's the girl fit into this picture?" the policeman (J. Farrell MacDonald) asks Sullivan (Joel McCrea) after arresting both him and the Girl (Veronica Lake). "There's always a girl in the picture," retorts Sullivan. "Haven't you ever been to the movies?" And that's just why the Girl (she never gets a name) *is* there—because in the movies she always is. She may be necessary in that way, but in the logic of the material she seems dispensable. And her extraneousness may have something to do with the fact that she is rather halfheartedly executed, less interestingly written and played than most of

Sturges' other heroines. Other parts of the film, too, have this casual, not-quite-realized quality. The slapstick set pieces, for example, and a small-town sequence involving Sullivan in a brush with a man-hungry widow, though pleasant enough, don't seem really inspired. Sturges may have felt this problem himself—or so it seems from the number of reaction (and overreaction) shots he sticks in, like television laugh tracks, nudging us to a response in a way that he does in no other of his films.

But then you get the feeling that some of the material of the first three "voyages" is there mainly to fill out the structure and to set us up for the fourth "voyage," which is the film's real heart. When Sullivan, looking so vainly for "trouble" up to now, finds it at last—by losing his identity, and all the power and privilege that go with it. No longer just traveling in the world of the wretched and the powerless, he is now trapped in it. If the movie has been marking time, so to speak, so has he. No longer: "Sullivan" is reported to be dead—no one knows who *this* bum is, and no one cares. He has been arrested for slugging a railroad detective and is sentenced to six years in a rural southern prison camp.

Where at least they take them to the picture show on Sunday—to a ramshackle Negro church in the middle of the swamp, where the Preacher (Jess Lee Brooks) shows movies to the congregation on a clattering silent projector. It's the sort of place that isn't likely to mind convicts too much, even when they enter in chains. Before they do, the Preacher enjoins his flock smilingly, in his rich basso voice, not to "act high toned" nor to "draw away from them"—"I'm going to ask you once more, neither by word nor by action nor by look to make our guests feel unwelcome . . . for we are all equal in the sight of God." To which the congregation returns a chorus of heartfelt "Amen"s.

> PREACHER (*incantatory*): And He said, "Let him who is without sin cast the first stone!"
> CONGREGATION: Amen! Hallelujah!
> PREACHER: "And their chains shall be struck from them, and the lame shall leap, and the blind shall see, *and glory in the coming of the Lord!*"
> CONGREGATION: Amen!
> PREACHER (*normal voice, very genial*): Now let's give our guests a little welcome. . . .

And as the prisoners enter, filing down the middle aisle in their leg irons, shuffling and swaying in unison, the congregation, led by the Preacher, sings "Let My People Go."

The whole movie is a kind of "what next?" experience. And this Negro church is one of the things that seem almost to come out of nowhere. In more ways than one: it isn't, after all, the sort of place we're used to visiting in a Sturges film. But at the same time it has a familiar feel to it. These poor blacks show the same sort of helpless kindness that Sturges' most sympathetic characters nearly always betray at some point—whether it's McGinty reading a bedtime story or Jean looking at Hopsie's "poker face." This is a hyperbolic version of that kindliness, of course—fantasticated and dreamlike. This poor, rundown backwoods church almost seems enchanted—rising out of the bayou in the night mist, with its lighted windows and welcoming voices as the convicts approach, with their clanking chains and shuffling feet. And the kindliness is different from its counterparts in the other films, where it amounts to the condescension of the powerful to the weak, whether a man to children or a terrific woman to a dim-bulb man. Here, it's the meek comforting the rejected, the despised comforting the despised. And though it may come out of nowhere, it has extraordinary power when it comes. It comes partly, of course—and as usual—from other movies. A place full of beaming, chuckling, dulcet-voiced stereotypes of "Negro life," from the *Green Pastures* preacher to the angelic Hall Johnson–style voices of the congregation to the lovable lady dimming the lights for the picture show while she lights up the screen we're looking at with a hearty "How *do!*" to a neighbor she's spotted. There are no surprises here, to say the least—except, perhaps, the surprise of how strongly felt it all seems. That comes through in the extraordinary care with which Sturges registers all the details—in the Preacher's sermon and the congregation's response, in the contrast of all this life and concern to the convicts' despair, but above all in those biblical invocations, both spoken and sung.

But in fact we have been somewhat prepared for this sequence—even set up for it—by the even more powerful scene that precedes it. Sullivan has talked back to "the Mister," the brutal commandant of the prison camp (Al Bridge). For punishment, he's been put into the sweatbox—a tin structure, "not quite high enough to stand up in, not quite wide enough to sit down in" (Sturges' screenplay), without light or air and exposed to the heat of the sun. It's nightfall, and the fellow prisoner known as the Trusty (Jimmy Conlin, one of the most familiar and redoubtable members of Sturges' Stock Company) has come to take him out. He shines a lamp on the door and unlocks it, fumbling and pulling it open. McCrea is slumped inside, shirtless, like some great limp doll, knees buckled, head lolling on his shoulder. He tries to speak but can't. The little Trusty takes him in his arms—and McCrea falls on top of him. They are locked together for a moment, the frail, fussy little man all but collapsed under the big, inert one—holding and soothing him, talking consolingly to him as he eases him to the ground. "You gotta learn, that's all," he says to this "newcomer"—learn not ever to talk back to the Mister is what he means. "It ain't so easy at first, but after a while you don't mind." It's the almost cartoonlike Tom-and-Jerry contrast in their sizes, the *power* of the little man's concern as he supports and cradles the big strapping one, that makes the image so moving. It becomes even more so in a way when we realize that the little man, in the course of his meant-to-be-soothing chatter, is offering some observations about the Mister. "He ain't bad according to his lights," says the Trusty, pursuing his consoling line of talk. Adding: "He has to deal with some pretty tough hombres. Got us chicken last Thanksgiving, and some turkey once for Christmas. And there ain't another Mister takes his gang to the picture show. . . ." And so on. This isn't the first time that Sturges has reminded us that this monstrous figure—who comes on from the first like the most detestable sort of movie villain, shouting at Sullivan and slugging him brutally for speaking before he's spoken to—is probably a man like other men, some kind of ordinary fellow "doing his job." We have seen him in some homey exchanges with the bailiff (Dewey Robinson) earlier on—"Give my regards to the missus," and so on. But these reminders don't have the force of the Trusty's goodness behind them—and are therefore less disturbing. It's probably true that this cruel man "ain't bad according to his own lights," but it's upsetting to be reminded of that here. Because we're also reminded—by the whole situation—that such a recognition can't change anything. It doesn't even mitigate the horror; it only connects it to reality.

And this is really what *Sullivan's Travels* is all about: Sturges' attempt at connecting what he does—his "comedy"—to the un-comic realities beyond it. Just as he feels impelled to connect his good fortune to the incalculable bad fortune of all those others. It's characteristic that the Sturges comedy that is most directly about his own success should also be the one "comedy" that most directly—and worryingly—confronts such realities as failure and poverty and injustice. And the act of confronting such things while still maintaining the comic movie mode becomes the center of the film—a kind of moral testing of that mode, and of Sturges' own investment in it. He mocks Sullivan's seriousness. The McCrea hero here is a kind of butt from the opening scenes, foolish in his naiveté about both life and art ("It has social significance!"). But at the same time we take him seriously—and not only because Joel McCrea is playing the part. But most importantly, because Sullivan's ambition for "social significance," ludicrous and misguided as it is, reflects an ambition *within* the film itself. It's not only Sullivan who is trying to make a connection with "trouble": so is this movie.

Not an easy thing to do. Sturges knows this—uncomfortably—even if Sullivan, who wants to be like Capra, doesn't. For filmmakers like Capra, in the idyllic-sentimental vein, acts of individual beneficence—like Deeds giving his inheritance to the deserving farmers, or Ellie giving away her last money to the hungry boy on the bus—are central and defining. So they are in Sturges. But they are also complicated in his films in ways that challenge our complacency about such things. Sullivan and the Girl get off the freight they've hopped and go into a roadside diner, but it turns out they have no money to pay for the coffee and doughnuts they've ordered. When the counterman (Pat West) sees how long-ingly the Girl is looking at the doughnuts, he breaks down and hands them over anyway. Irritably: "I'll never get rich," he says, slapping the plates down in front of them. But for Sullivan this is a big moment, just the sort of experience he's looking for: "You're a little richer than you were," he says. And when he gets back to his staff in the "land yacht"—a deluxe trailer parked watchfully nearby—he has one of them run over with a present of a hundred dollars for this goodhearted man: "Never mind from who," says the messenger (Byron Foul-ger). When we last see the counterman, he is standing at the door of his diner and scratching his head, staring at the handful of bills. "A great human-interest story," exults Sullivan's Press Agent (William Demarest), 'as the land yacht speeds off. And the episode is over—except for this comment, thrown out in passing by the pretty, wry-voiced Secretary (Margaret Hayes): "It'll probably ruin him," she says to the Press Agent. "He'll give turkey dinners to every slug that comes in and never hit the jackpot again."

Because this movie mistrusts "human interest." Just as it mistrusts intentions like Sullivan's. "I'm doing it for the poor," he tells his disapproving butler, Bur-rows (Robert Greig), an imposing and authoritative man. "I doubt if they will appreciate it, sir," he replies. "They rather resent the invasion of their privacy—I believe quite properly, sir." As for making a movie about the horror of being poor: "If you'll permit me to say so, sir, the subject is not an interesting one. The poor know all about poverty and only the morbid rich would find the topic glamorous." Burrows himself, it seems, has known what it is to be poor—as well as thought about it (he is, we are told, "always reading books"). And in trying to dissuade his employer from what he regards as a dangerous and futile venture, he makes the following speech:

> You see, sir, rich people and theorists, who are usually rich people, think of poverty in the negative as the lack of riches, as disease might be called the lack of health. But it isn't, sir. Poverty is not the lack of anything, but a positive plague, virulent in its soul, contagious as cholera, with filth, criminality, vice, and despair as only a few of its symptoms. It is to be stayed away from, even for purposes of study. It is to be shunned. . . .

"To be shunned" but *not* shunned—that places the film's exact uneasy and guilty relation to the subject. Because Sullivan goes on his journey (this scene is just before his first setting off). And though he may be unconscious of the risks and the traps, the movie isn't. Poverty, whatever the delusion of the rich may be, does *not* build character—and its evils are contagious. This argues either for staying away from it—which is Burrows' point—or, even more perhaps, for trying to "do" something—which is Sullivan's. And the movie's. But Burrows reminds us of another trap: if the poor shouldn't be sentimentalized, neither

The flophouse in Sullivan's Travels. *Joel McCrea and Veronica Lake are in the center of the first "row."*

should they be patronized—that "privacy" he speaks of and counsels Sullivan against invading. He makes the same point when he first sees his employer dressed like a hobo ("Isn't that overdoing it a bit, sir?" says the valet [Eric Blore]. "Why break their hearts?")—trying on costumes for the road, as it were. "Fancy dress, I take it?" says Burrows, with great coldness. "What's the matter with it?" Sullivan demands. "I have never been sympathetic," explains Burrows, "toward the caricaturing of the poor and needy, sir."

But neither is Sturges. But then what are we watching in this movie if not just such a caricature? How, in fact, can that caricature be avoided—if you're safe and privileged and comfortable? As Sullivan is? As Sturges, and presumably his audience—at least to the degree that we're not desperately poor—are too? And it's Sturges' consciousness of this problem that controls the film finally. At times, *Sullivan's Travels* almost looks like a precursor of the self-reflexive European film of the sixties—one of those films that insists on admitting that it's a film. "There's always a girl in the picture." And when things look darkest for the hero: "This plot needs a twist," Sullivan cries—which it speedily gets. And these meta-filmic touches underscore the deliberate unreality of even the film's most apparently serious moments—the Negro church and the chain gang scenes, for example. Almost like Bresson or Godard in their different ways, Sturges seems to understand that often the best and clearest way to look at something in a movie—especially something whose pain strikes you mute—is to look away from it. The way Godard's *Masculin-Feminin* (1966), for example, "shows" us a Vietnam war protester immolating himself—by the sparest of allusions to the actual event: a man passing in front of the camera, asking for a match and mentioning Christ. The counterpart to that is Sturges' way of showing us the "virulent plague" of poverty—by shunning it and not shunning it, by admitting that he *can't* show us, under the circumstances of a movie comedy and its limits, of our comfort and his. And by reminding us that this is only a movie.

These reminders here come not from any modernist consciousness, some variant of the Brechtian alienation effect, but from the most lowbrow Hollywood precedents. That style of anarchic movie comedy deriving from burlesque and vaudeville which had a very particular currency at Paramount, from the early sound films of W. C. Fields and the Marx Brothers to the Hope-Crosby *Road* films of the forties. These were movies where people joked from the screen about the movie they were in, shattering the "illusion" that "serious" movies work so hard at. *Sullivan's Travels* evokes these comedies that kid themselves, just as it evokes the days of silent slapstick and melodrama. Whatever it does, in any case, it never gets very far away from the movies. Just as Sullivan himself can never get out of Hollywood.

Or so it seems at first. The studio reluctantly lets him go on his mad expedition, but it considers him really too valuable ("We better insure him for a million"—"He's worth more") to be let out of their sight. And so as Sullivan, on his way at last, walks hobo-style with a bundle over his shoulder down a country road, he is followed by a huge land yacht, tracking him remorselessly, containing a full publicity staff, a secretary, a chauffeur, a personal physician, a radio operator, and others. But then when a makeshift, souped-up auto pulls up, driven by a maniacal little boy in a crash helmet (he is "studying to be a Whippet Tanker"), Sullivan sees his chance to escape. And Sturges gets *his* chance to stage a slapstick chase—with a motorcycle cop in pursuit and a hay wagon in the way and a cook falling around in the galley and everyone else falling on top of each other as vehicles go bouncing and careening over the countryside, filmed by a speeded-up camera. Sullivan has shown his entourage that he can shake them if he wants, and so now he proposes a compromise—that they go their way and he'll go his and he'll meet them in two weeks in Las Vegas.

In the next sequence he is chopping wood in a small-town backyard, while the widow who has hired him (Esther Howard, at her most coquettish and eye-batting) yoo-hoos at him from an upstairs window. Inside the house she dusts and flutters ("He seems very strong. Did you notice his torso? . . . Oh, I do hope he likes it here. It's so hard to keep a man") and trades gibes with her acerbic sister (Almira Sessions). That night, they take him to the movies for a triple feature (*Beyond These Tears,** *Valley of the Shadow, The Buzzard of Berlin*) plus a game of "Swingo"—where Sullivan sits uncomfortably and looks around at the audience, which is both noisy (popcorn munching, hiccuping, crying babies) and totally absorbed. Except for the widow, perhaps, who tries to hold his hand. Back home, she locks him in his room: "Do you think he'll stay?" asks the sister. "I do, do hope so," says the widow, turning the key in the lock. But he escapes by climbing down the drainpipe and then hitching a ride on a truck. Getting off the next morning, he asks where he is. "Hollywood," says the driver ("You'll get a chance to see the moving-picture stars"), as he guns his motor and speeds away. Disgusted, Sullivan goes into a nearby diner. This is where he meets the Girl, who takes pity on him (his hobo outfit), even though she is nearly broke herself. She tried to break into the movies, and now she is on her way home— or would be if she had the money to get there. That Sullivan is really not a hard-luck case at all doesn't really get through to her until he takes her home and shows her around his swimming pool: she pushes him in.

But on the second "voyage," she goes along. As his "frail" or "beazle" (i.e., his girl). A black limousine pulls almost stealthily into the freight yards and comes to rest among the crowds of tramps (the real ones) who are assembled there to board the train: it's one of the film's grandest, most sardonic and haunt-ing images. Sullivan and the Girl get out of the limousine, dressed as tramps. And as the train starts to move, tramps from everywhere, in magisterial hordes, converge on it and jump on. Sullivan and the Girl join them. And that night, in their open boxcar, they cross the desert. The next morning they decide to get off, in sight of a lunch stand. "What town is this?" says Sullivan to the count-erman (the one who gives them the free doughnuts and coffee). "Las Vegas, Nevada," he replies. And there, sure enough, is the land yacht, waiting outside for them—benign and fateful. Oh well. They eat and clean up. And Sullivan, afflicted with a temperature now, is ordered immediately to bed by the doctor (Torben Meyer). It's while he's there—protestingly—with the land yacht headed back to California, that he reflects on his strange fortunes: "how everything keeps shoving me back to Hollywood or Beverly Hills—or this monstrosity we're riding in—almost like—like gravity. . . ."

It isn't just that he can't get out of Hollywood: he can't get out of the movies, either, it seems. Either the small-town comedy of his first voyage, or the riding-

---

*This was Sturges' original title for *Remember the Night*.

the-rails melodrama* of his second. Now the third commences—and it turns out to be a silent, mixing comedy and pathos, looking like Griffith at times, Chaplin at others, and soundless except for the emotional music that wells up to accompany it. *The Hobo Jungle*, it could be called: Sullivan and the Girl stand in a soup line, sleep in a flophouse, get showered and deloused, attend a Bowery-style mission service, and so on. A movie with everything: it has laughs (when they scratch for fleas or walk around with sandwich boards) and romance (when they look at the moon on the water) and grim realism (when they start to go through garbage cans). It's at this last point that Sullivan looks strickenly at the Girl and decides they've had enough of *this* movie—grabbing her by the hand and running Chaplin-style down the alley with her and off. Back to Hollywood . . .

Where there is general excitement and relief all round. With the ecstatic Press Agent declaring that "the greatest expedition of modern times, almost the greatest sacrifice ever made by human man," is now completed. Sullivan is back where he belongs. He is also (there's always love in a movie) in love, in his grumpy, low-key way; but he can't get married because he already is, and his estranged wife ("the Panther Woman") refuses to give him a divorce, for her own mercenary reasons. It seems that he can't get away from anything—that he always ends up right where he began. But by now it's clear to us, if not to him, that he'll never find "trouble" as long as he has the option—as people in real trouble don't—to leave it at any time, to exit running. But in the fourth "voyage" he loses that option. And so he enters there a different kind of movie as well, much grimmer than the ones he's been in up to now: a social exposé film ("torn from the headlines!") like Warner Brothers' *I Am a Fugitive from a Chain Gang* (1932—which Sturges borrowed and screened when he was preparing to shoot this film).

And Sullivan enters this movie by disappearing, temporarily, from the one we're watching. For a moment at least, it's as if a new consciousness—certainly a new destiny—has taken over the movie: the most unexpected thing yet, and by far the most startling shift of tone. It happens when Sullivan goes back among the tramps for what he thinks is the last time. This is how the Press Agent describes the idea, reporting over the phone to Le Brand:

> He's all washed up except tonight he's just going through for a quick tour—and do you know what for? . . . It'll tear your heart out. He calls it the payoff. . . . He's taking a thousand dollars in five-dollar bills and he's going to hand them out to these bums—in gratitude for what they did for him. . . . Now is that a story? Does that give you a lump in your throat or does that give you a lump in your throat?

---

* Like William Wellman's *Beggars of Life* (1928); Veronica Lake's "look" and costume in the tramp sequences seem modeled on Louise Brooks' in the earlier film.

But as Sullivan is walking his "tour" that night, handing out bills to each person he passes along the squalid streets, an old tramp (George Renavent) robs him—rising up out of the shadows where he's been crouching and hitting Sullivan from behind, knocking him unconscious. He drags the body to an empty freight car and stows it away there. Then he goes dancing across the railroad tracks with his incredible loot—more than he's ever seen probably—clutched in his hands. But he stumbles and drops some of it on the tracks—and then scrambles after it. But there is a train coming: the whistle sounds and the camera moves down the tracks. The old tramp, in a panic now, is still grabbing at the money—until he looks up, caught in the oncoming light, and blinded. He is—we can see now—on a maze of intersecting tracks. Which one is it coming on? He dances back and forth in the light—"like a rabbit between the moving headlights of a car" (Sturges' screenplay)—to the right, to the left, then back to the right again. He gives up and starts to run away—running toward the camera now with the train light behind him, bearing down on him. Until it runs over him. A shoe and a flurry of bills are blown into the frame as the train whooshes by.

It's the most upsetting moment in the film up to now. And even more so because we hardly know this character—it's puzzling and disorienting. In fact, we don't know him at all. He is furtive and anonymous, and we hardly even get a good look at him in the shadows and the long shots; nor does he ever say anything. Neither does Sturges offer to "know" him. What he does do—in one of the movie's most brilliant strokes—is to make sure that for a moment at least we identify with him powerfully—in an irresistible, visceral way. When we see the train coming (we see it even before the tramp does)—and he and we have to choose the track it's *not* coming on, without being able to see properly, and with almost no time to do it in, and almost no chance of getting it right anyway—and then it's here. . . . When we first see this old tramp—dimly—he seems sinister, forbidding, "alien." And then when he attacks and robs Sullivan, he is "criminal." But none of that matters by the end of the sequence. When he has to "choose" the right track (a *real* contest), he is us.

And what happens to us here in a small way is precisely what is going to happen to Sullivan now: he is going to lose the identity that separates him from the poor and wretched. At first, when he wakes up the next morning, he can't even remember it himself—who is he? And by the time he does, he can't get anyone else to believe it. "Look," he explains to the Trusty as they both face the rock pile, "they don't send picture directors to a place like this for a little disagreement with a yard bull." And they certainly don't: that is one thing this movie makes clear. But Sullivan is no longer a picture director (the cops found Sullivan's ID on the old tramp's mangled remains); he is a vagrant. And it isn't until he reaches this point of degradation—until the first becomes last, as Scripture says—that he learns anything at all. His moment of illumination comes in that backwoods church—where they all, convicts and congregants together, watch a Mickey Mouse cartoon featuring Pluto. And not only does Sullivan ("the Caliph of Comedy," as the studio calls him, but notably humorless otherwise) laugh out loud and quite spontaneously (it sounds like a bark), but he learns at last the value of laughter. It's what he has left—with his importance and everything else gone now. It's what they all have, laughing in the church. And it joins them—and us—together.

So when he gets back to Hollywood *this* time (he gets the idea in the camp of confessing to his own murder, so that his picture will appear in the papers and he can be rescued, as he is), he no longer wants to make *O Brother, Where Art Thou?* He is too happy, he says now. And what's more, he hasn't suffered enough. Le Brand and the others can hardly believe their ears—hasn't suffered enough?! "I want to make a comedy," says Sullivan in the film's final scene. But what about all the publicity! "Nobody's had more publicity since the Johnstown Flood!" says Casalsis (Franklin Pangborn). It's going to be "the greatest tragedy ever made," says Le Brand. "The world will weep! Humanity will sob!" he orates over the rescued Sullivan, who is sitting in a chair with the Girl beside and just above him, her arm around his shoulders. "Your personal courage and your sacrifice," exults Le Brand, "the lengths to which you went to sample the bitter dregs of vicissitude, will make *O Brother, Where Art Thou?* positively—" But Sullivan is looking at the Girl (his wife has remarried and set him free)—and he is thinking about making people laugh. "Did you know that's all some people have?" he says. "It isn't much, but it's better than nothing—in this cockeyed caravan. . . ." And his final, eloquent word is "Boy!"—as his face and the Girl's merge into a montage of superimposed faces of all varieties: men and women and children, the convicts in the chain gang and the blacks in the church, soldiers and hospital patients and old people—they are all in audiences and they are all laughing. What had begun as "echo of distant laughter" (Sturges' screenplay) mounts to a sound that is "wild and deafening," as these images jostle the screen and THE END—the real one—appears over them all.

It's an extraordinary ending. It's powerful in its way, but it also leaves you feeling a little uneasy. Sturges is not only flirting with mawkishness here but with something like complacency. After all, any hack might be able to show us people in a hospital or a prison or a nursing home enjoying his shows. That, in fact, is the customary way of defending the most numbing kinds of commercial entertainment. And it isn't much to say for any film that it might, for example, help people to forget their operations. But on the other hand, perhaps it *is*—as *Sullivan's Travels* reminds us. And the materiality of this justification would appeal, of course, to an inventor-artist. Sturges doesn't mind risking philistinism. Quite the contrary.

But like much of the movie, this final scene seems almost too explicit. The points Sturges often seems to be making in this film—often working too close to the surface of his own attitudes and feelings—seem greatly more simplified than the film is. He was addressing himself, he said in the New York *Times*, to those "friends" of his who had gotten, in his opinion, too "deep-dish" for their own good, "wasting their excellent talents in comstockery [sic], demagogy and plain dull preachment." His friend Frank Capra's latest film was *Meet John Doe* (1941)—without a laugh in sight, so to speak—called a comedy only because Capra was supposed to *make* comedies, and because it used comic stereotypes for serious effects. But the business of making people laugh, wrote Sturges in the *Times*, is an important and dignified one. And so his hero Sullivan in the end regains "the dignity of his profession" and returns "to Hollywood to make laughter." Sturges, on the other hand, dissociates himself from Sullivan ("I am not Sullivan. He is a younger man than I, and a better one") and from Sullivan's final stand on comedy. Now is the time, Sturges concludes, for all kinds of art, and all kinds of movies, not just comic ones—"and now is always with us."

But we can't dissociate Sturges from his creation quite so neatly. Nor from the blatancy of the film's "conclusion." That blatancy is central to what Sturges is all about. He was not—and he would insist on the point—an artistic filmmaker. But then of course he was. And what makes *Sullivan's Travels* so interesting, so oddly and finally effective, are its convolutions and contradictions: a preachment against preaching. The final claim that Sturges makes for his "laughter" is on the one hand minimal and modest to a fault; on the other hand, breathtaking: that final vision of the earth's dispossessed, with their desperate but sustaining ("wild and deafening") laughter—while the two stars listen to it, with the same far-off look in their eyes, the same "Boy!" of reminiscence in both their faces. This final image is the most "romantic" moment in the film—with the hero and heroine struck by the same thought of beneficence, the same vision of community through the audience. Sturges is as serious about not being serious as it's probably possible to be.

A<small>ND AS</small> if to prove the point (one part of it, anyway), his next film, *The Palm Beach Story* (1942), is the most unserious one yet—the most deranged and off-the-wall and liberated from the constraints of ordinary sense: Sturges' version of Oz. There is even a character named Toto (Sig Arno) in it, not a little dog but a "house guest"—a natty little gigolo who follows Mary Astor around, running errands for her, providing her some amusement ("We might put Toto in the army!"), twitching his little mustache and speaking in a foreign tongue that sounds like an articulated sneeze but that no one can identify. "I think it's Baluchistan," says Astor, after one of Toto's alarming verbal flights, "but it's impossible to tell." "Allo!" he says in conclusion, proudly—while they all stare. He

*Gerry (Clau-
dette Colbert)
meets the
Wienie King
(Robert
Dudley)—and
leaves her hus-
band, Tom
(Joel McCrea),
"while we're
still young
enough to
make other
connections."*
The Palm
Beach Story.

appears in various costumes: evening dress and yachting whites, polo togs and tennis togs and perky little berets—ready for any kind of fun or party, it seems. But he is mostly not invited, once Astor sees Joel McCrea. "Nitz," he says, when she asks him to go back to the yacht and get her handkerchief for her. "*Yitz*," she replies firmly. "Nitz," he says again. "It'll be nitz to *you*, Toto," she says threateningly. And he goes, even though his arms are already full of packages.

It's the kind of movie where someone speaking an invented nonsense language and carrying a lot of packages seems perfectly in place. It's also a classic sort of screwball comedy (Toto clearly derives from such earlier gigolo figures as Mischa Auer's Carlo in *My Man Godfrey*), with all the generic marks of the tradition. Tom and Gerry Jeffers (McCrea and Claudette Colbert) are Sturges' version of the screwball couple. Living in a penthouse apartment—bright and white and gleaming, with an elegant curving stairway to the bedrooms up-stairs—and dining in the nightclub below. The central action begins, as in *The Awful Truth* et al., when they split up, enabling them to become involved with inadmissible Other People (Rudy Vallee and Mary Astor) before reuniting at the end. The split-up this time, however, is entirely the heroine's idea. Gerry Goes Wild—and Tom goes after her.

But in Sturges' version of screwball, no one seems to notice when you do go wild—except possibly your husband. No one gapes at you at the country club or makes a circle around you on the dance floor. After all, how do you astonish— or outrage—a world where a Toto or a Princess Centamillia (Mary Astor) is perfectly at home, or where an organization like the Ale and Quail Club flourishes? Here is another place where Sturges is more like his model, Lubitsch, than he is like Hawks and McCarey in their romantic visions. Like Lubitsch, he is less likely to see the romantic couple as autonomous, standing against and apart from the world around them in some way—more likely to see them as an expression and extension of that world.

And in *The Palm Beach Story* at least, the world is a remarkably unresistant place. It's true there are money problems. The couple can't pay the rent on their posh apartment—in fact, they can't pay any of their bills. Tom is an inventor, and he is currently trying to sell a device enabling planes to land in the middle of a city: by an enormous steel mesh stretched over the top of it. He needs ninety-nine thousand dollars. Gerry decides that she is just holding him back. After all, she can't *do* anything—she can't sew, she can't cook ("You certainly can't," he echoes gloomily, with a distant, stricken face); and whenever she *really* tries to help him—as with that president of the smelting company ("He liked you *very* much, he said," she reminds Tom)—he gets jealous and tries to punch the man in the nose. She decides the time has come for them to split up, for the good of his career—"while we're still young enough to make other connections." And she leaves the next morning without even any money. It's her idea that an attractive, smart woman doesn't *need* money to get by—not with men around.

"Look," she says to the cab driver (Frank Faylen)—with Tom at her elbow, still trying to keep her from leaving—"I'm in awful trouble. I haven't got a dime." Would he take her to Penn Station for nothing? We are surprised at the flatness of this appeal—but even more so by the cab driver's response, after only the slightest of hesitations: "Oh, sure," he says. "Hop in, babe." And so she does. (Compare her earlier cab-driver encounter in *Midnight*.) It's at Penn Station that she connects with the Ale and Quail Club, composed of armed millionaires with their own private railway cars, on their way to Savannah: "You can be our mascot!" cries Asweld (Jimmy Conlin). And when she escapes from them—in terror—she meets John D. Hackensacker III (Rudy Vallee), one of the richest men in America, on the same train. He takes her by yacht to his Palm Beach palace. Tom turns up there, too—and is introduced as her brother, "Captain McGloo." Hackensacker's highly susceptible sister, the Princess Centamillia, falls for the "brother" while Hackensacker pursues the "sister." He even offers to build her brother's airport for him. And so it goes—until Gerry can no longer fight her yen for Tom and ends up making love to him again, while Hackensacker serenades her under the window. "Oh, darling, darling, darling!" she says as Tom kisses her and Hackensacker sings. "I hope you realize this is costing us a million dollars."

But in fact nothing costs anything in this movie—not even money. Hackensacker is too determined a benefactor. He is certainly thrown for a loss when it turns out that the brother is really the husband—he's sure he'll never get over it. But at least, he says, he'll have the airport to occupy himself with. "You mean you still want to go through with the airport?" says Tom, hardly daring to believe it. "If an idea has merit," says Hackensacker, "it has merit." So the hero and heroine (not exactly a moralist's film) get to eat their cake and have it, too. But what about the cake *suppliers?* Nothing for them, as usual, but the spectacle of the romantic couple's great happiness at the end? Not in *this* comedy—where even the Other Man and Other Woman are to be provided for. "I don't suppose you have a sister?" says the disconsolate Hackensacker, attempting a joke. "Only a twin sister," says Gerry.

HACKENSACKER: A twin sister!
GERRY: Oh, didn't you know about that? That's how we were married in the beginning—both being twins. . . .

TOM: Of course that's another plot entirely. . . .

HACKENSACKER AND THE PRINCESS (*at once*): Both *twins!* Are *you* a twin?

TOM AND GERRY (*at once*): Yes. . . .

HACKENSACKER AND THE PRINCESS (*at once*): Well, what's she/he *doing?*

TOM AND GERRY (*at once*): Well . . . *noth*ing. . . .

And in the next—and concluding—scene (wedding march swells), they are all six getting married: a triple ceremony. With the newly unearthed "twins" looking especially bemused.

But we have seen the twins before, as we can now reconstruct: under the credits at the very beginning of the movie, a confusing and soundless succession of melodramatic vignettes. A maid is talking excitedly on the phone when a shadow falls over her: she screams and faints. Freeze frame: "Claudette Colbert and Joel McCrea in—" And then, for the rest of the credits, shots of the maid in various stages of distress are intercut with shots of the minister waiting at the altar; of McCrea, still dressing, dashing there in a cab; of Colbert undressed, bound and gagged in a closet and kicking her legs through the door while the other(?) Colbert leaves in a wedding gown—causing the maid to faint again (the third time) as Colbert steps over her, trailing the wedding train over her prostrate form. It all ends with bride and groom at the altar and exchanging a smile—along with a final shot of the unconscious maid.

This episode is never explained; it's never even alluded to again until the end of the movie, when we are back at the same altar, with six instead of two. But it sets the appropriate delirious tone. These are sights—coming in wonderful and hectic profusion here—that announce "screwball comedy" to us. Sturges knows that we really don't require such images to be explained (as they nearly always are in other comedies, often with a distinct feeling of letdown): sights like the maid fainting, and the legs breaking through the door, and the bride in her wedding gown hailing a taxi with her bouquet, and the groom still dressing on his way down the aisle to the altar—images of conventional life spinning out of control but not quite, of conventions like the wedding day mocked, transcended, and somehow made wonderful again. Sturges knows, too, that what we value in the experience of these comedies is the special feelings of release and liberation that they give at their best. He even breaks some of the usual rules—like the one requiring explanations—to remind us of that. *The Palm Beach Story* announces from its bewildering opening montage that it will concede nothing at all to literalism. This is going to be an adventure—with no wet-blanket types worrying about whether the audience for it all is sufficiently resigned to its lot or adjusted to "reality." In this movie, whenever reality becomes a problem—on the way to Penn Station, for one example—it's simply revoked. And it's the movie's relation to reality—not Colbert's chutzpah, not the cab driver's wise-cracks—that makes the real and best joke at such moments. When Don Ameche searches for Colbert in *Midnight*, we know that he'll put a stop to the fun when he finds her, reclaiming her for true love and real life. When Tom finds Gerry among the Hackensackers, however, nothing changes but the addition of another character to the mixup. When the Colbert heroine of *It Happened One Night* tells the bus driver to please wait for her, the joke, of course, is on her. In this movie it's on us—if we expect him not to. Here, everything gives way to her—and to the adventure.

Sturges has turned screwball into an idyll in this film. As a result, however, events are more than ever without suspense—or even a certain kind of sub-stance. There seems less at stake in Gerry and Tom's initial breakup than there was even between Lucy and Jerry in *The Awful Truth*. Sturges' version of this essential scene is almost affectless, reminding us how conventional it all is. "You mean the bust-up?" says McCrea in a distant voice, as if he were foresee-ing a turn in the weather. That's just what she does mean, of course. But as she describes it, it sounds more like a continuation of marriage by other means—"while we're both still young enough to make other connections." The joke is in how coldblooded it is: it is, after all, about money, not about two people who can't get on together (in fact, they can't even quarrel convincingly). The cold-bloodedness reminds us of the classy comedy in a way—except that the point here is not sophistication but practicality. And the amorality, like the language it's couched in, belongs not to some aristocratic freedom from restraint and con-vention but to the American success ethic. "Nobody who's been married to *me* for five years," says Gerry later on, "is going to be a flop. You're going to get your airport if I have to build it myself. *After* I'm married." "After you're married . . ." says Tom (they are on the dance floor together), in the same distant tone with which he contemplated her first departure. "It's a funny thing to hear your wife say."

The Palm Beach Story has the usual conflicts for such a comedy—Gerry's deception of Hackensacker about Tom, Tom's jealousy of Hackensacker, and so on—but none of them seems serious. After all, the only real threat to the ro-mantic couple that this Other Man and Other Woman seem to pose is that they might bestow their largesse too soon, and end the movie (which nevertheless gets dangerously limp toward its end, with desperate little bits of business like a mock marriage proposal and a lovebird statue used as a signal that "it" has happened—scenes so feeble and uninflected that they hardly seem to be hap-pening at all). In fact, the whole thing is a vision of largesse—a comic adventure in which the funny thing that happens is how everything keeps going *right*.

But there is an unsettling sort of candor behind this make-believe. The shamelessness of it reminds us how much and how simply we want the triumph of this heroine. So that the movie becomes a kind of unimpeded gratification.

From the beginning she is surrounded by enchantments. And so are we: it's an uncommonly handsome film, with the kind of sights and backgrounds the movies taught us to love: Penn Station (one of Paramount's largest standing sets) and the train itself, the penthouse and the yacht and the dance floor surrounded by palm trees and the art deco mansion with its vaulting white rooms and staircases. And then there are all those helpful funny people: the cab driver and the Irish cop (two of them, in fact) and the ticket taker at the train gate and the Ale and Quail Club—who enter one by one, like a parade, passing through the gate in their sportsmen's regalia, taking note of Gerry ("No ticket?"), and finally taking her along. It's a pattern of generosity that reaches its apex in Hackensacker himself—whom she meets when she tries (in flight from the club, who have formed a posse to go through the train after her) to climb into the upper berth above him.

But in a Sturges success story, there must always be victims. Just as, when Tom and Gerry finally reach the altar together in that opening sequence and look at each other lovingly, we are then accorded a vision (a very funny one) of the maid laid out on the floor back home—a casualty of their bliss even before it's begun. We can't be too surprised, then, when Hackensacker turns out to be, rather spectacularly, the patsy type. He sticks his head out through the curtains of his Pullman berth just as Gerry, wearing oversized striped pajamas, is hoisting herself up into the empty berth above; and when he turns to look up at her, she steps on his face, mashing his pince-nez into his eyes. "Oh!" she cries when she realizes. "Oh, I'm terribly sorry"—climbing down again. "I hope I didn't hurt you." "That's quite all right," he says, with the equanimity that turns out to be characteristic of him, blinded but smiling. "Just pick off any little pieces you see, will you?" he says, proffering his face to her. And when he finds out what she is trying to do, he insists—after replacing his broken glasses from a supply of spares—on helping her to climb up, advising her where to place her feet in order to get the best lift-off and so on. "Would you mind giving my foot a little push?" she says, and he sticks his head out again, looking up and grasping her foot. And then there is that exquisite moment when her foot hesitates just inches above his face—his hands around the ankle—before descending once again to grind his glasses into his eyes.

And when she jokes at his expense, he responds with the same imperturbability. If there's anything he admires in a woman, it's "the homely virtues," he tells her as they seat themselves in the dining car for breakfast—"a woman who can sew and cook" and who can "whip something up out of nothing" (she lost her clothes to the club and has just made a dress for herself from a Pullman blanket). "Were you going to buy me breakfast, or would you like me to bake you something right here at the table?" she says. "I like a witty woman too," he replies, with his little smile, opening the menu.

Once she finds out who he is—not the tightwad eccentric she thought, but one of the world's richest men, and a spender, too (as he demonstrates when he takes her shopping to get some clothes)—her tone changes. But not the essentials of their relationship. He is—just as she remarks about one of the many openings for a wisecrack that he gives her—"too easy." He seals his own doom when he decides to serenade her under her bedroom window, singing "Good Night, Sweetheart" accompanied by a full-size orchestra. He puts her in a romantic mood—but the mood is for Tom. Who is in the room just across the palatial hallway. Which she eventually crosses (her hesitant progress is beautifully timed and modulated to the music)—to get help in unzipping her dress. Tom makes her sit on his knees in the light for this—and when she falls into his arms, the scene concludes not with the usual fadeout but in a medium shot of Hackensacker singing, below, the last bars of his song ("Good night, sweetheart—good night . . .").

The joke here is not only in the inevitability of Hackensacker's humiliation (at least that's how we perceive it; he never does understand the full extent of it himself) but in the sense we have that it even enhances the romantic occasion, just as that out-cold maid adds something to the wedding occasion—something we recognize as *belonging* to it, even. In this film there's a kind of impersonal necessity to these bodies at the feast, just as there is to that dainty feminine foot hovering remorselessly over Hackensacker's glasses. The joke on Hackensacker hardly seems to be a personal matter at all—in contrast to the joke on Hopsie, for example. It's just the way things are. This is an idyllic comedy about the cruelty of things.

And it really is idyllic. Hackensacker may be exploited and dumped on, but what he can't be, it seems, is discomfited. "Is that right?" asks Gerry, as she tries to follow his instructions about climbing into the upper berth. "You're standing on my hand but otherwise it's perfect," he replies, adding that she is "light as a feather." He is part of the movie's enchantment, and he is protected by it. But he also bestows it. He is genuinely gallant and generous. Just as the Ale and Quail Club are—in their roughhouse way. There is a pattern in this movie of benign avuncular figures. Gerry's mobility (and even Tom's) is sponsored by them at every step of the way. They come singly—and in droves. And they begin with the Wienie King.

It's the Wienie King who first starts her out—who starts the whole movie out, in fact, appearing right after the credits and that opening montage. He (Robert Dudley) and his wife (Esther Howard) are coming down the hall of a posh apartment house, escorted by the manager (Franklin Pangborn). The Wienie King (that's how he identifies himself later to Gerry: "Invented the Texas Wienie. Lay off of 'em! You'll live longer") is a little elderly man with close-set, glinting eyes behind thick spectacles. He wears a long, shapeless overcoat and a large, broad-brimmed black hat. He carries a cane, which he wields like a club—he looks feisty and mean. And he makes a marvelous contrast to his blowsy, big-eyed wife, as well as to the oleaginous Pangborn. He raps on the walls with his cane as they pass along the hall. His wife likes the quiet here, she says. *He* likes "a little life" ("We'll be dead soon enough"). And since he is deaf, there are frequent misunderstandings with the manager—especially about the opera singer who is vocalizing loudly in her rooms as they pass them. "What's that?" cries the Wienie King. "A canary? I *love* birds." The manager tries to explain that this noisy tenant is leaving the first thing in the morning ("She got in by mistake"), but it's no use. "I understand it's a bird," says the Wienie King. "What about it? I *like* birds." But he doesn't like Pangborn. "What's he say?" he demands of his wife. And then, before she can answer: "I don't like him to talk to me."

So he goes upstairs—they are in a duplex apartment, available because the current tenants have fallen behind in their rent—and meets Colbert. She is standing behind the shower curtain in the bathroom, trying to dodge the manager. "I don't suppose you go with the flat," says the little old man. "No—that'd be too much to hope for." Now *she* has a voice he likes ("like a bell")—as well as the outline of a bird stitched on her wrapper ("I love birds," he says, pointing at it with his cane). When he finds out that she lives here and can't pay the rent, he insists on giving it to her ("You thinkin' about money, forget it. I'm cheesy with money"), along with some money for a new hat and dress, too. "You're a fine girl," he tells her. And departs. When he appears again (he and his wife have moved into the opera singer's place), it's to find Tom in the apartment alone, coming to terms with Gerry's absence. And the Wienie King gives *him* the money to fly after her, once he finds out that's what he needs. "Then why didn't you say so instead of standing there like a big stinkweed?" he demands, taking out his roll again and unpeeling the bills.

But this character sounds another sort of note, too—and with comic insistence. No sooner has he first complimented Gerry on her voice and looks—she has just stepped out of her hiding place behind the shower curtain—than they have this exchange:

WIENIE KING: You have a lovely clear voice. . . . Why if I were married to you I'd hear everything you said almost. But *you* wouldn't enjoy it. Besides, I'm already married.
GERRY: So am I.
WIENIE KING: Me too. Anyway I'd be too old for you. . . .

And he proceeds to recite a poem (it's a poem that Sturges himself had once written and recited to his friend Bertie Woolfan)—full out and in a nasal drone, looking straight ahead, like someone in an old-fashioned declamation class:

Cold are the hands of time
That creep along relentlessly
Destroying slowly but without pity
That which yesterday was young. . . .

Colbert's look as she listens to all this is particularly wonderful: both knowing and uncomprehending at the same time—with a little smile and a "what the hell is *this* now?" expression in her eyes. Reminding us that there are some things that the Colbert candor does *not* comprehend or know quite how to respond to. "'Alone our memories resist this disintegration,'" he concludes, "'And grow more lovely with the passing years.'" And he adds: "That's hard to say with false teeth." Colbert laughs. "You're a funny old man," she says. "I didn't get it," he says, "but you looked very pretty when you said it."

And *not* so funny, too. Because the gaiety of this airy comedy is sponsored—as this black-hatted fairy godfather reminds us—by a certain grimness, a sense of painful disproportion, whether in the nature of things or the arrangements of men. "You'll get over it," says the Wienie King about Gerry's trouble. "You'll get over being young, too. Someday you'll wake up and find everything behind you. Gives you quite a turn." But this remarkable and funny film has its own "turn" to give—however delayed it may be in coming to us. Sturges calculates what he's *really* saying when he makes everything so free and painless. The tone is idyllic-sardonic. There is a slyness, even a wickedness, to the cheeriness: happy endings that remind us of the real endings—a pastoral with a kick to it.

I did the best I could—without trying too hard.
—JOEL MCCREA, 1978

I finally ran across the man I consider the greatest pure cinema actor I ever worked with—Joel McCrea. . . . I used to watch scenes on the set [of The First Texan, *1956], and I'd think, Jesus, there wasn't anything to him—and I'd see him in the rushes the next day and it'd knock you off your seat, because of the hemming in of the camera on the sidelines, focused on Mc-Crea. . . .* —BRYON HASKIN, in a 1984 interview with Joe Adamson

STURGES HAD a special relation with Joel McCrea. He was at the peak of his success when he made three pictures in a row with McCrea—more than he made with any other star. McCrea has remembered that Sturges told him even back in the early thirties that whenever he got the chance to direct he wanted them to work together. And when that finally happened, they seemed to have a special rapport. "He never used Fonda again, and he's a better actor than I am,"

Betty Field
and Joel
McCrea in The
Great Moment.

said McCrea in 1978. "But Fonda wasn't in love with Sturges and I was." And
though the first of the Sturges-McCrea films was fairly risky (none of them were
great hits), the third was even more so. René Fulop-Miller's *Triumph over Pain*,
a controversial best-seller about the Massachusetts dentist who discovered ether
anesthesia, had been a Paramount property for several years. It was originally
slated for Gary Cooper, with Henry Hathaway directing. But instead Sturges
made it, and with Joel McCrea. And *The Great Moment*, as it came to be called,
was a project close to his strongest feelings.

It was also a project spoiling for trouble—from its inception. If Sturges had
shown that he knew how to play the Hollywood game, now he seemed to be trying
to beat the odds. This was how he originally proposed to begin this new film,
with a shot of the hero's grave, while a narrator speaks the following:

> One of the most charming characteristics of Homo sapiens, the wise guy
> on your right, is the consistency with which he has stoned, crucified,
> burned at the stake, and otherwise rid himself of those who consecrated
> their lives to his further comfort and well-being, so that all his strength and

cunning might be preserved for the erection of ever larger monuments, memorial shafts, triumphal arches, pyramids and obelisks to the eternal glory of generals on horseback, tyrants, usurpers, dictators, politicians, and other heroes who led him, usually from the rear, to dismemberment and death. . . .

This sort of "kidding"—even if you supposed that it applied exclusively to the *other* side's generals—was hardly acceptable at the height of America's war effort. And it wasn't helped by the misanthropy of this conclusion, as the narrator goes on:

> . . . We bring you the story of the Boston dentist who gave you ether. Before whom in all time surgery was agony. Since whom Science has control of pain. It is almost needless to tell you that this man, whose contribution to human welfare is unparalleled in the history of the world, was himself ridiculed, burned in effigy, ruined, and eventually driven to despair and death by the beneficiaries of his revelation.

Of course, this prologue was never filmed; the studio nixed it as soon as they read it. But it's an accurate index to the movie that was, and even to the movie that survives after studio interference. A movie where Sturges adds, to his customary jokes about malfeasance and corruption, a new field of sardonic reference—jokes about war and the spending of blood. As when, for example, Dr. Morton (McCrea) tells President Franklin Pierce (Porter Hall): "I hate to have it look as if I was making the Government pay to relieve wounded soldiers from pain." To which the coarse and stupid President replies: "The Government pays for the guns, don't it?" And laughing sharply: *"Huh?"*—as Morton looks dumbfounded. "Well, good day, good day," says the chief executive, who also tells the hapless inventor: "Believe me, I'd rather be you than President any day."

Corruption and stupidity are conditions as epidemic here as they are in *The Great McGinty*. But here they're not so funny—more sort of maddening, less likely to provoke a joke than fits of anger and hopelessness. *The Great Moment* is a bristling, craggy, and intransigent movie, and it has a hero to match. Who is ideally embodied by McCrea. In this film Sturges exploits the actor's irritable, grumpy side—a kind of premature elderliness in his look and sound. Morton combines touchiness and remoteness. He is crotchety and preoccupied and intractable. If he can't remember what Dr. Jackson said about anesthesia, why doesn't he *ask* him? inquires Morton's wife (Betty Field). "Because I despise him so," replies Morton, full of grievance as always. No wonder: he didn't have the money to finish medical school and so now he's a dentist instead of a doctor. "And as I remember," says Dr. Jackson (Julius Tannen), his former professor at

Harvard Medical School, "you were a rather dull student." ("You didn't keep us in stitches, either," recalls Morton sullenly.) Morton has neither the equanimity of Tom Jeffers ("like Sitting Bull in a new blanket," as his wife describes it, "breathing through your nose while we both starve to death") nor the condescension of John Sullivan. But the McCrea hero in a Sturges film is always the same sort of figure: whether he wants to discover anesthesia or build an airport over the top of the city or "realize the potentialities of film as the sociological and artistic medium that it is," he is an inventor-artist. And a crackpot.

And the casting of McCrea safeguards the purity of this cracked state—keeps it from being contaminated by little egotisms. McCrea is self-contained but never complacent. He can be pretentious (as Sullivan is) without seeming self-important. The effect that Fonda as Hopsie gives when he is talking about the time "to weigh every pro and con" or invoking the power of "sweet forgiveness" is outside McCrea's range—and for good reason. McCrea is utterly—remarkably—without narcissism (maybe that's what he means when he says he never

She thinks he's drunk; it's only that he's bungled another experiment. The Great Moment.

"tried too hard"). And for Sturges, it's clear, the McCrea hero embodies a kind of ultimate masculine value, operating in a contemporary time but stemming from an earlier one ("the perfume of my father"), when being a man was equated with a kind of plainness, was all but defined by a refusal of certain kinds and degrees of self-consciousness (one reason male movie stars of Sturges' and McCrea's generation so often felt demeaned by what they did and were), by an absolute distance from such things as vanity and preening and pettiness. The almost palpable solidity of McCrea's presence grounds both the sophistication of *The Palm Beach Story* and the pretension of *Sullivan's Travels*. And he gives the idealism of *The Great Moment* an inescapable common-sense center, in *spite* of the craziness. Morton is originally impelled to discover anesthesia because he can't stand (that irritable tone) the sounds that his dental patients make. "But they yell so, Lizzie," he complains to his wife. "It's bloodcurdling. It gets on your nerves." "Why don't you try stuffing up your ears?" she replies, missing the point as usual. Missing *his* point, anyway. The McCrea hero is always a little out of step, in conversation with others or in his dealings with the world. It's not that he's dense or naive exactly, but rather that he's preoccupied—thinking about those screams, or that airport, or "trouble" itself. And it's his preoccupation, finally, that gives him his special quirky dignity—and finally his "greatness," too. When he becomes *this* hero—the ultimate fairy godfather, the one who freed us from pain.

Paramount Pictures Incorporated has the honor of bringing you, at long last, the true story of an American of supreme achievement: W. T. G. Morton of Boston, Massachusetts, in a motion picture called The Great Moment. . . .
—Studio press release, 1944

Only the Woman He Loved Believed in Him . . . and Sometimes Even She Had Her Doubts. . . . —Ad for *The Great Moment*

Many of the reviews have been bad and many more will be. However, as I believe Orson Welles said: "When the world agrees with me, I start to suspect that I was wrong. . . ." —PRESTON STURGES, in a 1944 letter

The Great Moment (1944) is a major Sturges film, but it presents problems that none of the others do. Because the film that Paramount finally released—and that still survives—is not the version that Sturges himself completed and edited. *That* film is now lost, surviving only in Sturges' screenplay. And Sturges was emphatic about the damage done. "My next picture is coming out in its present form over my dead body," he wrote just before the movie's disastrous opening. "The decision to cut this picture for comedy and leave out the bitter side was the beginning of my rupture with Paramount. . . . The dignity, the mood, the important parts of the picture are in the ashcan." And the story of Morton—"serious, thrilling, and a little sad"—is simply "not told."

The damage is severe, certainly. But probably (and understandably) Sturges overstates it a bit, too. In *his* version (I'm drawing from the final screenplay) the movie falls into two distinct parts. Both these parts are—like the basic structure of *The Power and The Glory*—flashbacks from a scene in the present in which an elderly man and woman reminisce about the dead hero. Eben Frost (William Demarest) visits Morton's widow, Lizzie, with a medal he's redeemed from a pawnshop for her. It's a citation from the French government: "To the benefactor of mankind, with the gratitude of humanity." This souvenir stimulates the first long flashback, in which Lizzie recounts (supposedly) the last twenty years of Morton's life, the years of decline and frustration and neglect. It ends with his death; and the movie returns to the present, to the kitchen where Eben and Lizzie are talking. When it moves into the past again (as it quickly does), it's to take up the first part of Morton's life, the years of struggle and final success. This second long flashback (roughly two-thirds of the film) begins with Morton as a very young man—courting Lizzie, setting up his dental practice, beginning his search for anesthesia. It takes him through his discovery of ether narcosis and into the fame and prosperity that—briefly—follow. It ends with his gesture of self-sacrifice, when he gives away the "secret" of his discovery so that a servant girl can be spared the pain of an operation without it—an event whose bitter results we already know about from the first flashback. This gesture is the "great moment" of the title, and it is the image upon which the film ends.

It's a movie with many of Sturges' most obsessive concerns: the dizzying ways success and failure keep turning into each other; all the ways in which virtue is *not* rewarded; the passion of the inventor and the excitements of discovery; and so forth. And the movie's structure gave him—the filmmaker in control—a chance to enact the arbitrariness he liked to contemplate: by reversing the order of events in Morton's life (like most lives, a decline toward the end) to please himself and his audience. A biographer, he later wrote about this film, has two obligations: not to lie and not to bore his audience.

> . . . Since he cannot change the order of events, he can only change the order of their presentation. Dr. Morton's life, as lived, was a very bad piece of dramatic construction. He had a few months of excitement ending in triumph, and twenty years of disillusionment, boredom, and increasing bitterness.

My job was not to show the meanness, lack of gratitude, suspicion, and general stupidity of Homo sapiens, which are well known, but rather to show a play about Dr. Morton's life. To have a play you must have a climax and it is better not to have the climax right at the beginning. . . .

And unorthodox though this procedure may have seemed to the studio (it's much less so than the scrambled chronology of *The Power and the Glory*), it's a model of clarity compared with the version *they* produced when they recut it. They retained Sturges' structure of first and second flashbacks, with Morton's end preceding his beginnings—and confused it. It's true that they made the film a bit shorter; but then it had never threatened to go over normal feature length. And the omitted scenes (Al Bridge as a softhearted moneylender in one; Dewey Robinson in another, as a quartermaster colonel chuckling over the latest model in revolving pistols: "Nasty little things . . . we don't believe in them. Of course, if the *other* side should start using them—") are neither long nor numerous. And yet in order to get them out—almost all of them are from the first long flashback—the studio version reduces the opening section of the film, the flashback describing Morton's last years, to an almost total incoherence. The scenes that survive are rearranged, taken puzzlingly out of their original contexts, or given whole new meanings (a scene of Morton in bed which is meant to show him getting well is now a prelude to his death). Not only is Sturges' perfectly clear narrative line confused, so is his characterization. In the original film, Morton breaks up a prosperous medical-goods store because he's just discovered that they've stolen his inhalator device from him. In the studio version, this scene is moved to a later point (after Morton has lost his court case), so that he no longer seems to have a clear reason for what he's doing to the store but seems instead to be in a kind of undiscriminating rage. With the result that he seems loonier than Sturges ever means him to be. And so on. It seems likely, to be sure, that even the Sturges version of *The Great Moment* would have been too strange for popular success. But the studio version ensured its failure.

It wasn't just the "mutilation," according to Sturges: they upset "the balance of the picture" by cutting "the unpleasant part of the story"—i.e., the first flashback—"to a minimum." But at least they left the rest of it alone, more or less. The second flashback—the bulk of Sturges' film, covering the earlier part of Morton's life and ending with his "great moment"—is close to intact. There are some minor cuts within scenes, and one brief scene (Morton and Lizzie talking on the stairway of their grand house) pointlessly transposed from the first flashback. But otherwise this part of the film follows the Sturges cut. So that audiences who are patient with the confusion and disconnection of the first twenty minutes can see in the rest at least (an hour or so) the film that Sturges intended and made.

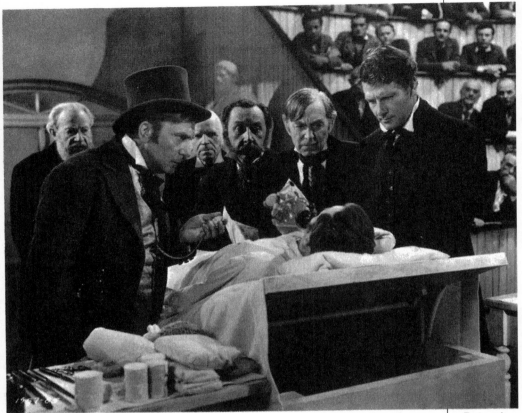

Testing ether anesthesia in the operating room: William Demarest, Franklin Pangborn (with mutton chops), Harry Carey, and Joel McCrea.

Of all the things in nature, great men alone reverse the laws of perspective and grow smaller as one approaches them . . .
— From the prologue to *The Great Moment*

IN SOME ways *The Great Moment* is like a revised version of *The Power and the Glory*. The great man is no longer so imposing as he was in the earlier film. Just the opposite: he's become more like one of the Stock Company. The young Morton seems to be a series of comic stereotypes: the young man of such prodigious appetite ("Tonight he had three plates of soup and twelve slices of bread, not that I counted them, four helpings of roast beef, six potatoes . . .") that he threatens to eat his landlady and future mother-in-law (Georgia Caine) "out of house and home"; the awkward suitor on the front porch, trying to kiss his intended while she has her little dog in her arms, and "venturing to say" that he might soon be "in a position to support . . . a family of reasonable size"; and finally and foremost, the dentist ("Oh," says the landlady when she learns, "—and he seemed like such a *nice* young man"), doing comic routines with reluctant patients. "While you're at the office," says the little idiot wife, "I'll be at home taking care of *my* end of things." She has just tried out his new dentist's chair: "Oh, it's deliciously comfortable, William—one would be reluctant to leave it." But the next occupant of that chair (Vic Potel) has to be held down in it by main force while Morton tries to get a drill (an enormous corkscrew instrument) into his mouth—which has, of course, to be pried open, enabling the patient to scream. This sound causes a mass exodus from the waiting room, which Morton is then obliged, drill in hand, to go out and intercept—enabling the patient in the chair to escape. And so on, like a comic strip. So is life at home, where the dizzy wife nags and prattles, saving her little dog from his attempts to catch and anesthetize it ("This is *my* dog, you know!"), declaring her intention to "go home to Mother" ("Is that a promise?" says Morton), and evincing her unfailing instinct for property of every kind (". . . and we'll take the furniture," she says to the dog, "because, after all, Daddy gave it to me anyway"). She is not much help to his experiments, either. "Drunk again!" she cries, when she finds him passed out from one on the floor of the parlor.

But then she has a point. Not that he drinks, exactly; but he *is* a bumbler. He falls around a lot, chasing patients at the office and the dog at home—where he ends up futilely trying to anesthetize the goldfish. He never seems too bright; he asks dumb questions ("He goes to school with me for years," exclaims the acerbic Dr. Jackson, "and now he doesn't know what ethyl chloride is! Morton, you are the living proof that ploughboys belong behind the horse!") and then forgets the answers, mixing up chloric ether and sulfuric ether. And then, when he finally gets it straight and is about to anesthetize his first subject, he sends his wife to the wrong pharmacy for the ether. "The trouble with you," says Jackson later, "is you can't remember anything." The consequence of this blunder is that the patient, Eben Frost (William Demarest), gets ether that is not "highly rectified": instead of putting him to sleep, it sends him crashing out the window and running down the main street, at the head of an imaginary cavalry charge.

The cartoon-strip flatness of this world is almost without precedent in Sturges' work. It's a more strictly male world, without any of the strong feminine components of his small towns or modern cities. The public world of affairs, of business and politics and professions, of clubs and saloons and storefronts and banks and newspapers, a world where women are either safely tucked away at home ("taking care of *my* end of things") or "lost" on the streets (Esther Howard's streetwalker). And even where you most expect to see them—in, for example, the hospital—they're not in evidence. Instead of a nurse in the operating room (what woman could stand it?), there is an unsmiling Frank Moran in what looks like a butcher's apron: he is the one who holds the patient down. The Stock

Company appears in this film in the same profusion as in the others. But the effect, instead of being transforming, is almost depressive: it's not so much that it's a shock to see them in nineteenth-century costumes as that they seem muted and held back. Jimmy Conlin's pharmacist, for example, might have been played by anyone. And the ones who do make a vivid impression are figures like Porter Hall's President or Julius Tannen's Dr. Jackson or Louis Jean Heydt's Horace Wells, who represent various kinds of venality and stupidity and hypocrisy—the mean-spirited ones, in a public world marked by greed and ambition and petty striving.

But it's also a world in thrall to pain—a point that Sturges' prologue underscores: "It does not seem to be generally understood that before ether there was nothing. The patient was strapped down . . . that is all. . . ." But this film *has* "understood" it—has imagined it fully, and even obsessively. Pain does flatten things out, after all. And in this world—the world before Morton—it is pervasive. And it can reduce experience to the kind of comic-strip flatness we see at the dentist's office. That's one of the risks Sturges runs in this movie: the discomfort of these jokes—the succession of routines about things like toothache pain and dentist's chairs—gets to you after a while. Like the joke that makes you laugh because you're embarrassed—here you laugh because you're squirming.

So that it's almost a relief when we get to the hospital, where everyone talks in a hush and the halls are long and vaulted and cathedrallike. Here, where the pain is most intense, it at least has some dignity. The chief surgeon is that ultimate gentle patriarch, Harry Carey, with his craggy face, spaniel eyes, and soft, suffering voice. Morton and his friend Eben (Demarest) enter the auditorium above the operating theater, where Dr. Warren (Carey) is performing an amputation. The rows of seats are empty and dark. The two men enter, come slowly down the steps, and sit—drawn toward the light and the terrible process below. They are watching what the movie averts its eyes from (of course). Morton looks intent and grave and leans slightly forward. Eben, next to him, leans slightly backward, as if not wanting to see; his eyes roll up in his head and he falls soundlessly to the floor in a faint—a kind of lapsing into the darkness behind. It's a haunting image: a fall with solemnity to it. It's as if a new contract with the subject itself were made at this moment, a new understanding entered upon—no more vaudeville. Won't it hurt his dental business if he gives Dr. Warren his ether to use and then it doesn't work? wonders his wife that night in their room. "You've helped so many people already—why endanger that?" "Did you ever see an amputation?" says Morton. And that's all he does say—the scene ends.

And that sort of response defines him, as far as Sturges is concerned. Morton embodies the materiality, the concreteness and factuality, of Sturges' own idealism. It's true that Morton is not very gifted. And he doesn't seem to be very knowledgeable, either. The "benefactor of mankind" is also, like most Sturges heroes, the beneficiary of his own luck (as when he sets the ether bottle near the heat of a candle, causing the fumes to escape by accident)—even of his own bumbling (that mix-up of sulfuric and chloric ether). Above all, he has his doggedness—McCrea's air of stubborn, mute resolve, his Sitting Bull side. It gives him a way of transcending his own limits—becoming absorbed, just as the movie itself does, not only in the goal of discovery but in its process (the properties of sulfuric acid appear on the screen at one point as if it were a blackboard, à la Godard). Morton may be mired in ordinary life, in all its indignities and irritations and limits, as much as or more than anyone—finally he is even swamped by it. But he has that impersonal determination. And ultimately he achieves a kind of impersonal grandeur. The film suggests that he could never live up to his own discovery ("great men alone reverse the laws of perspective . . ."). But then in a way he does—if only when he renounces it.

"Never again," Morton had promised Dr. Warren in the emotion of seeing that amputation, "will you have to go through what you've just gone through in there." For the next such operation, Morton promises, he will supply an anesthesia that works. But when Morton arrives at the hospital with his ether inhaler, the Medical Society is there, too—demanding to know what's in the stuff. "As you probably know, Dr. Morton, physicians may not use nor prescribe patent medicines the ingredients of which they ignore." But if he tells them, Morton protests, while his patent is still pending, he would be throwing away "the secret of my business, the one advantage I have over my rivals." Surely they can't ask him to do that. But they can and do. "You mean you're going to continue to let people be tortured when it isn't necessary?" cries Morton. But Dr. Warren intervenes: "We will share the blame, Dr. Morton, you and I." And he gives instructions to his staff: "I shall operate in the usual way."

So the dilemma is clearly posed. And we already know its outcome from the first flashback: that Morton will give in over the issue of this operation and will therefore lose not only his rights to Letheon (his name for his anesthesia) but ultimately almost everything else, including his good name. We know about this event already; now we wait to see it. But what follows is nearly the most astonishing thing in the whole movie: we've been prepared for the event of Morton's renunciation, but not for the way Sturges shows it to us.

Once Dr. Warren has issued his order to begin the surgery, the room empties out and Morton is left alone (even Eben for once seems to have disappeared). He walks out of the office and proceeds down the corridor, a long stone hall with high leaded arches. He is a very dejected figure, in medium long shot. But the tone of the film has changed oddly: for the first time Morton really does look like a storybook figure, distanced and framed in a conventional theatrical style. The next image is even more conventional: the girl for the operation—a servant

(Sheila Sheldon, who played the crippled girl in *Christmas in July*) whose leg is to be taken off—lying on a stretcher outside the operating theater, forming a tableau with the priest (J. Farrell MacDonald) who is comforting and praying over her, while Schubert's "Ave Maria" (a violin arrangement) begins to play on the soundtrack. ("Come now, Sturges, surely you were kidding?" wrote a fan— see above.) Morton sees them and stops. Now he enters the tableau; they are all framed in a medium shot—behind them are the doors to the operating theater. There are fan-light windows above the doors where we see what looks like a choir loft full of people—the audience in the balcony, as it were. Of course— historic operation, et cetera—these are the medical-student observers. But they seem, in the arrangement of this shot, to be spectators to the exchange between Morton and the servant girl. Which now begins. "Are you the girl?" he asks hesitantly. "The girl for the leg operation?" "Yes, sir," she replies. "I'm terribly, terribly sorry," he says, looking down on her. "It isn't as bad as it sounds, sir," she says. "Some gentleman has made a new discovery and it doesn't hurt any- more." "That's right," says Morton. "It doesn't hurt anymore. . . ." Whereupon he throws his head back and speaks in a loud, declamatory voice, not to her but into the air: *"Now or ever again!"* At which signal, trumpets sound, the operat- ing theater doors swing magically wide to reveal the surgical team, Dr. Warren at their head, waiting in their gowns like welcoming seraphs. And Morton steps into the background to surrender his discovery—all of them freezing (the girl still in the foreground) for a final tableau, Historical Moment Department, over which suddenly appears (it's all handled very briskly) THE END.

No wonder De Sylva was furious. . . . When had anyone pulled anything like this? It's as if Sturges were short-circuiting his own movie with this deliberate, self-proclaiming theatricality. Or at the least, sabotaging a response he had seemed to be asking for (if you were going with those violins), undercutting what should have been the point of maximum emotional impact. But Sturges isn't after that sort of impact—any more than he has been earlier in the film. What he's trying for here (the boldness is still impressive) is something much more com- plicated. He gives us nobility in the final scene—the real thing, too—but laced with bitterness and overarching irony, with reminders of the way of the world and of men ("the wise guy on your right . . ."), even while he shows us someone temporarily transcending these conditions. There is no incentive or payoff for uncommon virtue in the world of this film. Quite the opposite. The only way an ordinary sort of "great man" like Morton can achieve greatness is by wrenching himself into it—and into history, or at least history as he conceives it: in tab- leaus of greatness (*"Now or ever again!"*)—like the one that ends the film. In Sturges' view, heroism isn't subverted by its theatricality but sustained by it. There is—in the world of *The Great Moment*—almost nothing else to sus- tain it.

The point is clearer in Sturges' version of the film—precisely because the "bitterness" is clearer. Sturges makes a point in that version of showing how Morton's sacrifice is forgotten almost as soon as it happens. ("It says here that I did a very generous thing," he says, reading the newspaper the next morning, "giving my secret to the world.") We see the widow who praises him sincerely, with tears in her eyes and voice, for his unselfishness—juxtaposed (through the flashback) with the young wife who scolds him for it ("I mean, you weren't such a fool as to give away the most valuable secret in the world—just for the *asking!*"). And so on. Yet in spite of such gaps and imbalances, and even in this "mutilated version," *The Great Moment* remains a powerful and fascinating film. But even in the Sturges version, had it survived, it seems doubtful that the movie would altogether have "worked." The depression and misanthropy are almost too palpable—too heavy, even—for the sort of strong and liberating ironies that Sturges intends at the end.

Sturges made films about idealism at a time when that was a "hot" movie subject. But unlike more sentimental filmmakers who set out to forget what they know (or could know) when they are trying to be high-minded, Sturges sets out to remember. He wants to be high-minded *and* knowing. If screwball comedy unites the cynical mode with the romantic one, Sturges attempts something even more paradoxical: combining the unillusioned and the inspirational. As he attempts to do with the inspirational biography film in *The Great Moment*—where it doesn't entirely come off. But he attempts a similar sort of reconciliation in his next two films—in the genre of the folksy comedy. And he pulls it off in both of them—stunningly.

"Be vulgar by all means, but let me hear that brazen laugh!"
    —SIR ALFRED DE CARTER, in *Unfaithfully Yours*

The Miracle of Morgan's Creek *is so filled with violence, disorder, and misunderstanding that I have known people to emerge from it trembling.*
                                                    —DAVID THOMSON

*. . . Many letters have been received here, including bitterly denunciatory
ones from analphabets who believed the sextuplets were the result of the heroine having been promiscuous with six different men. Education, though com-
pulsory, seems to be spreading slowly. . . .*
                                    —PRESTON STURGES, in a 1945 letter

IF JOEL MCCREA is Sturges' movie alter ego, his favorite image of comic
masculine assurance, Eddie Bracken is his demon, his favorite image of
human extremity—a performer of a desperation so intense that it touches a
Higher Composure, and the perfect actor to express Sturges' extremest ambiv-
alences, his most contradictory feelings about American life and values. That
ambivalence in Sturges isn't nervous or uncertain or apologetic—it's passionate
and energizing. And it produced these two mad, sublime, passionate comedies:
The Miracle of Morgan's Creek and *Hail the Conquering Hero*—both of them
centered in Bracken's performance.

Norval Jones (Bracken), the hero of *The Miracle of Morgan's Creek* (1944), is
a 4F bank clerk. An orphan with no family, he rooms with the Johnsons (Al
Bridge and Georgia Caine), the town lawyer and his wife. Norval is ruled by two
passions, one more hopeless than the other: his desire to get into the wartime
army like everyone else (every time they examine him he gets excited and starts
to see "the spots," and they reject him for high blood pressure); and his love for

the boy-crazy Trudy Kockenlocker (Betty Hutton), the daughter of the town constable. Officer Kockenlocker (William Demarest), a widower presiding with mounting desperation over a family of two teenage girls, is the sort of American father who likes to sit on his front porch and clean his guns. In spite of his vigilance, Trudy goes to a soldiers' party, where the high point seems to have been (as she remembers it, anyway) something about everyone getting married. And it soon develops that she is pregnant—by a man she has no memory of, not even his name (she thinks it's Ratzkiwatzki), and who is in any case now gone off to war. She decides to use Norval to get out of her dilemma, marrying him as quickly as she can. But then she can't go through with the deception. And the loyal Norval becomes, instead of her dupe, her co-conspirator. When they run off to get married, they are apprehended and Norval is arrested. But on the day of the birth, Trudy redeems their disgrace by having sextuplets, all boys (the "miracle" of the title). She becomes an international heroine—and Norval, the presumed father, a hero. "Some have greatness thrust upon them," as the post script to the film tells us.

This strange and wonderful comedy—it looks like a rube comedy, with its rubber-faced cast and its hard-core slapstick (the sort of programmer Universal specialized in), and it turns out to be one of the most sophisticated films ever to come out of Hollywood—works in some very peculiar ways. Take, for example, Emmy (Diana Lynn), Trudy's younger sister—a fourteen-year-old, very soignée in bobby sox, with shrewd hard eyes and a hair ribbon, and the social manner of a mature and sardonic hostess. She regards her blustering, coarse father with a kind of far-off distaste—which *he* responds to by trying to kick her. "If you don't mind my mentioning it, Father," she says, "I think you have a mind like a swamp!" "*What!*" cries the enraged man; and as she turns away, he takes a flying kick at her backside—missing, flying off his feet, and falling backwards out of the shot with a thud. And later, after Emmy has just pulled him off the hapless Norval, she inquires—in her ineffable snooty manner—why her father can't "learn to be a little more refined." (He has just been strangling Norval against the lintel post on the front porch.) "*Refined!*" he screams, and tries to kick her again—again landing on his back. At other times, the violence is merely verbal: referring to her as "ladder legs" or "zipper puss"—as in: "Listen, zipper puss! Someday they're just gonna find your hair ribbon and an axe someplace—nothing else! The mystery of Morgan's Creek!" Such threats, of course, only confirm her disdain—which only heightens his rage—and so on.

But then it turns out that she likes to sit on his lap—at least when she's upset or nervous, the way she is the night she's waiting for Trudy and Norval to return from their furtive attempt to get married. It's like the way she keeps calling him "Papa," with almost childish determination, even when she's cracking wise at him. It's as if she meant to insist on something: and so she sits on his lap (they are on the front porch). "Git off my lap!" cries the startled Kockenlocker, trying to read his paper. "What's the matter with you?" "I've got a right to sit on your lap," she says, staying hostilely and firmly put. "I'm your daughter, aren't I?" "That's what they told me," he says. But she stays on his lap. Emmy really is a tough number—not the Diana Lynn kid sister type who appears in Billy Wilder's *The Major and the Minor* (1942) and other films of the time (a tough talker, who is really a perfectly nice little girl behind it all, standing by all the proprieties and conventional notions). She really is unillusioned and cynical—and she is the smartest person in the movie. "We'd better warn Norval," says Trudy. "We'd better marry him," says Emmy—succinct as always. She knows just how narrow-minded these people are—"a town that can produce schnooks like Papa." She is a city type, in fact. That doesn't make her out of place in a Sturges small town. Any more than it precludes her needing to sit on her father's lap— or needing him. Or loving him: *that* issue never comes up of course—exactly because it would never occur to us (or to Sturges) to doubt it, if we should think of it.

Sturges favors such paradoxes, as we've seen. In the same way, he centers the sentiment of this comedy around a dirty joke. And by the standards of the time at least, it was exactly that. Not only did the film touch on a taboo subject (wartime promiscuity). But Trudy's situation was precisely calculated to remind audiences of two shockingly incompatible archetypes: the traveling salesman joke, which was categorically cruel and scabrous; and the Nativity story. This flirtation with blasphemy—the several implied parallels to the first Christmas (the livestock in the living room when Trudy is near her time, for example)— struck some as the most shocking thing of all. These hints were sly enough to get past the censors but persistent enough to amplify the feeling of "bad taste" that the whole movie gave—very deliberately. Like his Paramount colleague Billy Wilder, Sturges courts "bad taste"—he delights in it even. But unlike Wilder, he also gets—in some mysterious way—quite beyond it. That's what he means to do, it seems—insisting on the scabrousness in order to redeem it.

Just as he "redeems" the vulgarity Betty Hutton had come to embody. That, presumably, was an important part of her attraction for him (he wrote the role of Trudy for her). The type she represented—in her four Paramount films before this one (three of them with Bracken opposite her)—was the frustrated, man-hungry hoyden. It was a type that enjoyed a particular currency during the war years, with several new young actresses specializing in it (Cass Daley, Virginia O'Brien, Nancy Walker, etc.), though Hutton was the only one to achieve stardom playing it. In publicity stills she was often shown getting a hammerlock on her bug-eyed boy friend (Bracken's usual role), the befuddled and terrified prey. She was usually a contrast to the sweet, bland heroine—and she was understood to be unattractive. Though this fact—like her sexuality—seemed more theoretical than real: like a metaphysical category. And though she was avid and wild and out of control, she was never allowed to be bawdy: she never even came close. What was striking, in fact, was how asexual she seemed—less like a person seeking a mate than an athlete having a workout. But she was nearly the best the movies could do in those straitlaced days by way of joking about sexual frustration. And so she was understood to be funny. Though it became less and less clear as she kept reappearing what the funniness was *about*. Except loudness. Which was Hutton's specialty, whether acting or singing.

Sturges reminds us what it's about. He makes the whole wild girl conception Hutton was identified with intelligible and funny in a way that it hadn't been before (or would be again, unfortunately). He does it in part by a shift in the character—making her not a wallflower but the life of the party, not the Girl Who Gets Left Behind but the one Who Never Stays Home—that makes everything else fall into place, everything that had seemed arbitrary or formulaic in previous roles suddenly seem wonderfully right: the asexuality, the charmless energy, the terrifying willfulness. "You know me," Trudy says to Emmy, "I never get tired." And the joke is as much about the Hutton persona as about Trudy herself. Sturges evokes that persona memorably when he first shows Trudy in her room—in her bouffant party dress, jitterbugging to the radio and going "Yip-yip!" as she wheels and jumps gracelessly around. And his collusion with the moment when she gets hit on the head at the dance (she springs into a lift and bangs her head into the reflector globe on the ceiling—loud sound effect: *crash!*) is very funny. He lets us know that he shares all our apprehensions about this inescapable forties type.

And he associates her with that nightmare out of American adolescence: the Popular Girl, ruthless in her pursuit of distraction, and merciless to her admirers, especially the abject ones like Norval. Trudy not only uses him as a decoy, getting him to take her out and then leaving him alone at the movies while she goes to that soldiers' dance her father's forbidden her to attend; she asks to borrow his car, too. "The boys mightn't have any," she explains. And, after all, the boys are going to war—in contrast to Norval. So she tends to couch her appeals to him in patriotic terms—and when he resists, to accompany them with tears. "Go ahead, cry all you like," says Norval. "I've seen you cry before." In fact, he's been through it *all* before. So has Trudy. What about saying we had a

*Frank Moran
(the sergeant),
Betty Hutton,
Eddie Bracken,
Diana Lynn,
and William
Demarest in*
The Miracle of
Morgan's
Creek.

flat tire, he says ("That's old, but it's reliable") when he's obliged to bring her home the next day at eight in the morning and is trying to think of a story for her father. "I don't think Papa goes for that one," says Trudy, "—he makes you show the patch." As she reminds him: "You shouldn't have kept me out so late. . . . Papa will be sorer than a boil."

But at other times she has a strange and affecting sobriety. As in her first scene in the film, when Norval approaches her in the record store where she works and finds her "singing" that basso rendition of "The Bell in the Bay" for a group of the boys. They leave—and Norval is left behind to ask futilely for another date. The striking thing is how Trudy seems to identify with him in this scene—to enter into his pain and disappointment. He is concerned with his own despair; she is concerned with him. She even knows ahead of time when he is going to mention "the spots" (he is talking about being turned down by the army again—his other obsession), not only saying the words with him but pointing to them, too.

Trudy, it's clear (Hutton's performance is extraordinary), doesn't really want to hurt Norval, nor is she even insensitive to what he's feeling. But she is driven—toward uniforms and parties. And Sturges shows us what that forbidden party, when she gets to it, does for her. Trudy fulfills that dream of happiness the movies so recurrently evoke: being at home in a happy crowd. Surrounded by soldiers, riding in a crowded convertible (Norval's) while everybody sings, gathering at the punch bowl, or "cutting a rug" on the dance floor—she looks in all this oddly composed and serene. This whole sequence of Trudy's party night—full of noise and bustle (including that hit on the head), quickly shifting scenes and oddly angled shots, as Trudy and her anonymous gang of soldiers and girls go from dance to dance, dance hall to nightclub, singing in Norval's car en route and in between times—has a remote, dreamlike quality. "Merrily, merrily, merrily, merrily / Life is but a dream," they chant tunelessly in the car, in a sound that has the same thin, detached, vaguely narcotized quality as the images in this sequence. This is fulfillment, but it's also fatality. And its name is Private Ratzkiwatzki, as it finally happens. This improbable name (in every sense) is all that Trudy will retain of the man she "marries" that night. And her encounter with him—which becomes the most fateful of her young life—is finally inaccessible, both to her and to us. The parallel to the Nativity here is more than just a daringly impious joke. Sturges is serious about the comparison—as he fully persuades us by the end of the film. Trudy and Norval are involved not just in a joke or an irony but in something strange and marvelous.

And there is a solemnity about them both at the beginning of the film. Norval's demeanor has the dignity of his own unhappiness: in the record store, for example; and later that night, when he sits on the Johnsons' front steps, while Georgia Caine's Mrs. Johnson rocks and knits on the porch behind him. Bracken has that toneless sound here that Sturges actors often have (Dick Powell in *Christmas in July*)—before the craziness hits. What's nice here is that Mrs. Johnson has it, too—an expression of her tact, of her feeling for Norval—never once looking up from her knitting through her delicate, sympathetic questioning:

MRS. JOHNSON: Aren't you going out, Norval?
NORVAL: No, ma'am.
MRS. JOHNSON: I thought you were going to the picture.
NORVAL: I thought I would . . . and then I figured I wouldn't. . . .
MRS. JOHNSON: Oh . . . (*then—after a pause*) Isn't there a dance or something tonight?
NORVAL: For the soldiers.
MRS. JOHNSON: Oh . . . (*then—after a pause*) I'm sorry, Norval. . . .
NORVAL: If they don't want me . . . they don't want me.

The quiet is shattered by Trudy's phone call, summoning Norval to "take her out," after all. And Norval is suddenly beside himself—the beginning of a hysteria (mostly his) which grows over the course of the film.

The "miracle" itself . . . the count grows . . . and the hospital whoops. Julius Tannen, Vic Potel, William Demarest, and Diana Lynn are the ones on the bench.

. . . You tell me that you saw The Miracle of Morgan's Creek *and that it is very funny. I am relieved to hear it, but did you notice and file away in your memory the pure gold perfume of Al Bridge as the small town lawyer? I doubt it. Did you notice Georgia Caine rocking on her front porch in the twilight? I doubt that also. In other words, my dear young lady, whereas I thank you for your letter and the stamped envelope, which I shall use, I suggest that much more has been placed on the screens of our picture houses than your young eyes have yet received. You have been getting a great deal for your $1.10, probably even $3.30 or $4.40's worth. . . .*

        —Sturges' reply (1946) to a young fan's letter of complaint

I am sorry that you did not see The Miracle of Morgan's Creek. *I don't think you would hate me for it, because it is not unkind, nor does it derive its comedy from the embarrassment of the poor young girl. The story has much love and tenderness. At least I think it does. . . .*

        —His reply to another fan (1949)

NORVAL IS one of Sturges' patsies, but he has none of Hopsie's smugness or Hackensacker's obliviousness. He may be taken advantage of, but he is never taken in. He registers every nuance of Trudy's chutzpah. He is irritable and exasperated—and helpless. But it's this helplessness that finally makes him an authentic romantic hero—wholly committed to his love for her, resourceful and brave and finally triumphant. All this in spite of his terror—which grows incrementally, until it becomes nearly his most characteristic condition. He is terrified of losing his job, of enraging Trudy's father, of going to jail. But justifiably, in each case. In each case the thing happens just as he dreaded—and even worse. Norval and Trudy are not just playing at outrage, as the screwball comedy lovers do, they are really incurring it. Trudy is really going to have a baby—and she isn't going to be able when it comes to hand it over to the *real* unwed mother waiting in the wings, as Theodora does at the end of *her* movie.

Take that town, for one thing. It's a Hollywood sort of small town (a standing set on Paramount's back lot, scheduled to be razed until Sturges offered to make these two movies on it), idealized and picturesque and anachronistic (a horse and buggy, a stereopticon, etc.). Nevertheless, Sturges makes sure we see the place, and that we are never really unaware of it. Trudy and Norval take three extended walks through it at various intervals. And Trudy and Emmy take another. (There are three more such walks through the same place in *Hail the Conquering Hero*.) Past the front yards and the picket fences and the front porches, past the drugstore and the movie house, the gas station and the pool hall and the lending library and so on. It's not an idealized place, like Mr. Deeds' home town; nor is it the sort of awful place Hazel Flagg comes from. It's really, for good or bad, not all that different from the city. Sturges makes a point of its connection to the city by his framing device, which has Governor McGinty and the Boss (Brian Donlevy and Akim Tamiroff making a reappearance) doing a *Front Page* routine over the telephones while they hear the story of the "miracle" that's taken place in their state—i.e., the story of the film, reported to them by the editor and Mr. Rafferty back in Morgan's Creek. (The Governor and the Boss issue instant orders for turning the whole thing to commercial advantage: "This is the biggest thing that's happened to this state since we stole it from the Indians!" cries the Governor. "Borrowed," corrects the Boss.) The Sturges small town is a place you don't exactly leave, and never entirely love. Like your family, it's not exactly a field of choice. It stands for community, but in much the same way that Officer Kockenlocker's house stands for a family home. It really is, of course. It's also hopeless—ghastly in its way—but still sort of terrific. "The mystery of Morgan's Creek!"

But the place can kill. Take Mr. Tuerck (Emory Parnell), for example—the president of the bank, and Norval's worldly, genial, beady-eyed employer. Who stops by Norval's cashier window one morning to inquire about his "engagement." Something he heard about from Mr. Shottish (the one who saw Norval coming home at eight in the morning after his fracas with Constable Kockenlocker on the front lawn). "My enga—" replies Norval as the terror strikes. "My enga—enga—" "Yes," says Tuerck. His friend Shottish "kinda had a wild idea that maybe you'd eloped or something." Norval denies it. And Tuerck—taking note in passing of Norval's apparent nervousness (he is nearly fainting)—observes that while it's none of *his* business what Norval does ("what time you get home in the morning, or how drunk you are when you do get home"), it is the *bank's* business. "Th-th-th-the bank," echoes Norval.

> TUERCK: That's right. A man in a bank is like a fellow crossing Niagara Falls on a tightrope. He cannot be too careful.
> NORVAL: Oh, yes, I—I get what you mean, Mr. Tuerck.
> TUERCK: Fathers taking pokes at you and all that sort of stuff. Very bad for a banker.
> NORVAL: Oh, you sa—you said it, Mr. Tuerck, y-y-y-y-you—you said it.

Norval is a creature—and a respecter—of convention. So is Trudy—unlike her sister, Emmy, who seems to be beyond pieties of any kind. When Kockenlocker orders Trudy to hit him on the head with the blackjack he's just given her (they are trying to make Norval's flight look like a jailbreak), all she can do is tap him, wincingly. "Harder!" he says. "How could that knock anybody out!" And she tries again, with her eyes closed. "Oh, here!" says Emmy, who has just finished tying her father up with a rope—taking the blackjack and knocking him cold. But there are freedoms that Trudy can neither permit herself nor even imagine, in spite of Emmy's example. And Emmy takes a very dim view of Norval: he was *made* to be a patsy, she tells Trudy, "like the ox was made to eat, and the grape was made to drink."

But Norval has his own kind of acuity. For example, it's Mr. Tuerck who disguises the real stakes in the scene above—Norval who exposes them, embarrassingly. "Th-th-th-the bank" is right. But what's most impressive finally is that Norval's fully justified terror of the bank—even his respect for it—doesn't prevent him from robbing it later on (he breaks in to get his own money out). And that's only one of the crimes he commits in the course of the film. He may be a ludicrously conventional type, cautious and timid and law-abiding, working in the bank and aspiring to the army; but when he is pushed to the limit, as he is by his love for Trudy and all its complications, he becomes that most miraculous of human figures: someone sensible—even radically so. As when Trudy explains to him why she can't marry him: "I couldn't let you run the risk of going to jail for twenty years for bigamy." He is willing, but she isn't. Anyway, there is always "the creek" . . . "It may be the only way," she says dramatically. "What are you talking about, Trudy!" he exclaims (they are walking past the front yards again). "That's the *last* way—when everything else has failed. Before I tried that, I'd try b-b-bigamy, f-f-forgery, b-b-b-burglary—anything!" But she doesn't give up the idea so easily. "Maybe we could jump in together," she says, as they walk and he subsides into depression beside her. "There's not much water this time of year, Trudy," he says. Then she remembers the swimming hole. But he points out to her that he is "a very good swimmer—and being a very good swimmer, they say that whenever they get in a situation like that, they—they just naturally sw-sw-sw-swim right *out*." She is a very good swimmer, too—she hadn't thought of that. Of course, they could tie rocks around their necks. But he nixes this firmly. They come to Trudy's front gate. She turns to him—a sudden happy idea. "What's the matter with *gas?*" she says. "What's the matter with *bigamy?*" he rejoins, at the end of his patience with this conversation. It's Norval's finest moment—so far at least. But it is instantly undercut by the voice of Officer Kockenlocker, calling from the front porch: "*Hey!*" he shouts, and Norval nearly collapses on the spot, cringing imbecilically behind Trudy as they approach her father. Who announces that he wants to have "a little talk . . . with your gentleman friend there." This is the scene in which Kockenlocker ("When is the happy event?") cleans his gun and it goes off accidentally, causing Norval to get up and walk through the screen.

Norval (Eddie Bracken) has asked to see "the baby"; Emmy (Diana Lynn) is about to tell him.

Bᴜᴛ ᴛʜᴇ fact is that Norval's terror gives him a kind of eloquence, a candor and felicity that go beyond even what Emmy can muster. He is the most expressive figure in the movie—especially when his language is impaired. What could improve on "my enga—enga—"? Or on "they just naturally sw-sw-sw-swim right *out*"? When Trudy first tells Norval about her middle-of-the-night marriage and then about her impending "happy event," his reactions (they are taking one of their walks through town) are divided between panicked, disbelieving questions and visions of "the spots": "How could you do it—the spots!—to me, Trudy?"—as the terrible story unfolds. "You're going to make me cry," says Trudy. "Well, go ahead, cry—cry all you like—see if I care! The spots! Who did you marry?" She tells him she doesn't know. But then *how* does she know she's married "if there's no name on the r-r-r-record? How can you pos-pos-possibly be su—Trudy, you don't mean—?" He stops—and they stop. They look gravely at each other. "That's right," says Trudy. "The spots!" he cries—and staggers to a nearby bench. Where he manages enough composure after a moment to ask what her father is going to say, who he's going to—But as soon as he asks it, he sees the spots. "I can almost see them myself," says Trudy.

And soon, of course, she does. His terror takes her over, just as it takes over the movie—culminating in her attempt (mostly unsuccessful) to say "Kockenlocker" to the justice of the peace (Porter Hall) when they are contracting their guilty and bigamous marriage. They are both stammering and staggering by this time, united in terror—virtuoso performers of their own gibbering dismay. It's a nightmare refraction of the screwball lovers' competition, with their feats of wit and daring. Norval and Trudy have achieved panic. So that the movie's "wit" rises almost onto another level, displacing ordinary words and ordinary sense—becoming a matter of expressive sounds. Take Norval's unforgettable invocation—when the justice of the peace marrying them asks him where he is stationed (Norval is impersonating a soldier, pretending to be Private Ratzkiwatzki)—of the place he calls "C-C-C-Camp—uh—Camp Sm-Smum."

JUSTICE: Camp what?
NORVAL: S-S-S-S-Smum.
JUSTICE: Where is it located?
NORVAL: It's located in—in—S-S-S-Smum—Smum County.

"Suppose I just put 'U.S. Army'?" says the justice. "Oh, f-f-fine," says Norval.

But behind all the escalating hysteria—in Norval, in the movie itself—there is a kind of insane hopefulness: "What's the matter with *bigamy?*" For that matter, what's the matter with "Camp Smum"? The terror in this film is curiously liberating—and the hopefulness grows even independently of Norval (he leaves the film for a short while near its end, to escape the charges against him and to search for Private Ratzkiwatzki), reaching its climax with the birth of Trudy's babies. This event is beautifully performed and modulated, and curiously moving: it has that mingled excitement and awe that Sturges always brings to scenes where people's destinies are being settled by forces beyond themselves. With Kockenlocker and Emmy, Mr. Rafferty (Julius Tannen) and the newspaper editor (Victor Potel), waiting on a bench in the hospital's long hallway, while nurses go running in and out, for linen and baby baskets, going back and forth until they start to dance and whoop, as the "miracle" gathers to its final count: "Six! All boys!" And the news spreads over the world. (Including the almost obligatory Hitler and Mussolini gags.)

But it hasn't reached Norval, we learn. He is stashed away in jail again, where they put him after Mr. Tuerck apprehended him outside the bank—the fugitive returned. Norval is unprepared for Officer Kockenlocker's appearance, in the full magnificence of his new chief-of-police uniform, with an excited crowd surging behind him. He unlocks Norval's cell, but Norval is nervous about leaving.

"I wouldn't want to get you in wrong again," he says. "Get me in wrong!" cries Kockenlocker. "I'm the *Chief!*" And he laughs insanely.

KOCKENLOCKER: Haven't you heard about—about—?
NORVAL: About what? (*Kockenlocker's mouth moves, but no words come out.*) You mean she's had it?
KOCKENLOCKER: Has she had it!—You'd better come and see your wife.
NORVAL: My wife? B-B-But I'm not m-m-m-marr—
KOCKENLOCKER: Oh, yes you are, my boy!

And the people outside push into the cell—led by the Johnsons and Mr. Rafferty, the editor and the tailor, Mr. Schwartz (Harry Rosenthal). They are carrying a clothes box, and as Norval falls back in astonishment and alarm, someone pushes it toward him, someone opens it and someone else claps a braided officer's cap on his head. It all seems to happen at once, and then to explode into the next scene, bursting into view on a quick dissolve (it's a galvanizing effect) to the rousing opening roll of the "Post March" blasting off the soundtrack—and there is Norval, in full colonel's regalia, in the popping of flashbulbs, on the shoulders of a crowd, seeming both buried and surging forward, both held back and borne aloft. He is resplendent, looking terrified, and smiling witlessly—drawn along by Kockenlocker through the throng of reporters and townsfolk and hospital people. He is being taken to see his "wife."

"You're a papa now," Trudy tells him from her bed. He concedes that he feels like one, anyway. "You *are* one," she says—the point is important to her. "The papa gives love and protection," she says. But he still doesn't know (neither in fact does she, it seems) the full extent of his new fatherhood. Appropriately, it's Emmy—the wised-up one, who has been standing at the foot of Trudy's bed for this scene, overlooking it all with her lovely shrewd tenderness—who gets to lead Norval to the nursery, beckoning with her finger and a *very* knowing look, taking him by the hand . . . while she points out the babies behind the glass, and *keeps* pointing them out. Until Norval is gibbering again: running back to Trudy and sprawling across her bed. "*The spots!*" he cries—and the spots themselves appear on the screen (now *we're* seeing them)—as the movie ends with this written postscript . . .

> But Norval recovered and became increasingly happy—for as Shakespeare said, "Some are *born* great, some *achieve* greatness, and some have greatness *thrust upon them.*"

The special exhilaration of this comedy—more than exhilaration, the contagious happiness of this ending, that peak of excitement and gratification to which it's all been building—is without parallel in Sturges' work, or elsewhere, so far as I know. Is there anything else like it? Not just that it rises to a kind of manic high of elation and triumph and hilarity—but even that Trudy's calm assertion at the height of the lunacy, "The papa gives love and protection," seems to connect with it all. The sense that the awesomeness of the papa's love, of the undertaking to be a papa, fits the film's general, insistent and inescapable atmosphere of terrified hope. Because ordinary life is terrifying in this comedy—and awesome. And Norval takes its measure—for all of us. And the laughter it occasions here is not only the kind that leaves you feeling limp at the end, but that seems to give you for a while a new power of feeling and seeing. Where we can accommodate even the connection that Trudy makes—the serenity beyond the hysteria: "You're a papa now."

The next one is called Hail the Conquering Hero. *It also has Eddie Bracken and although it is not quite as funny, it has some sentimental passages which I think make up for that. Let me know what you think of it. . . .*
                                   —Sturges' letter to a theater owner (1944)

I saw Hail the Conquering Hero *the other night and at once came home and ordered the firing of twenty-one guns. You are an original. You have done that amazing thing—created a new style out of the best of the past in film, plus a thousand units of Sturges vitamins, and a dash of pure courage.*
                                   —DUDLEY NICHOLS, in a 1944 letter to Sturges

EDDIE BRACKEN —who had been a professional performer from his childhood, in vaudeville, legitimate theater, and movie shorts (some "Our Gang" comedies)—was a comic juvenile under Paramount contract since 1940 and specializing in anguished twerps. So far (by 1943) his career at the studio—partnering Betty Hutton and supporting stars like Bob Hope—had been unexceptional. But after *The Miracle of Morgan's Creek* (and well before it was released) Sturges was so excited about Bracken that he proceeded to write another film for him: *Hail the Conquering Hero* (1944), to be filmed on the same backlot town as *Miracle* had been.

Another twerp hero. But then not exactly: there are important differences. Far from being on the margins of his small town's life, as Norval (the orphan) was, Woodrow—the hero of *Hero*—is a favorite son, very much at its center. That, in fact, is just Woodrow's problem. He is trapped by the town's adulation. And where Norval seemed panicked, Woodrow seems exasperated. Where Norval gibbered, Woodrow seethes. He is acclaimed as a hero, and he is a fraud—though a reluctant one. "I'm a haunted man for the rest of my life," he says midway through the film. But in fact he even looks like one at the beginning, sitting at the bar of a San Francisco waterfront café. He is already involved in imposture, as we learn—pretending to the folks at home that he's in the marines when he's really working in a shipyard. The marines have discharged him after a month because of his chronic hay fever.

Hero was the last of Sturges' Paramount films, and it's among his densest, richest, most oddly beautiful works. It's some people's favorite of all. Sturges later said it was his favorite—mainly because of its impeccable construction. The tempo is headlong and the plot snowballs deeper and faster into lunacy and chaos with each scene. There are none of even the mild longueurs that occur at times in *Miracle* (the long jailhouse sequence between Norval and Kockenlocker, for example). And in this film the shots are more congested than ever—as if Sturges were seeing just how many discordant, expressive faces he could crowd into the same frame and still maintain its coherence. But underpinning all the clutching and clinging and furor is something quite the opposite—something quiet, fierce and remorseless: a peculiar sort of intensity—that may be hard to name but is nearly everywhere to be *seen* in this movie. And it moves around—scarily. It's in the way that Bracken's initial distress yields more and more to a kind of burning-eyed, zealot-faced look and manner—as his fraud becomes more outrageous, his imposture more desperate. Until he seems almost to *glow* with his own torment and anger. (There was plenty of anguish in *Miracle* but it stopped short of luminescence.) It's also visible in the grave, sweet faces of the townspeople—led usually by Jimmy Conlin—as they gather in delegations to confront Woodrow with their concerns. It's in the six marines—and their square-jawed determination to coerce Woodrow into his "heroism" and even into the job of the town's mayor. Most of all it's in the disturbing presence of Bugsy (Freddie Steele), the one of the marines who "got a little shot up, that's all," with his frightening power of concentration and his obsession with mothers. He is, in fact, a madman. We are told that early on. But it doesn't make him any the less disturbing—nor does it prepare us for the way he takes over the movie, the way the madness seems to spread.

It seems extraordinary to audiences now that Sturges could have gotten away with this wartime satire—joking about patriotism and American values and public bellicosity at the height of the war effort. But what seems satiric now, or at least ironic, didn't necessarily seem so to audiences then. *Hail the Conquering Hero* is like the joke that's *so* raunchy that it gets by—people either really don't get it or won't admit it if they do. In any case, like *Miracle*, it's a movie full of the excitement of its own risk. But it's a more delicately balanced, more inward-turning sort of comedy. And both the excitement and the delicacy are reflected in its opening sequence, with its witty juxtapositions and inventions, its slightly skewed version of reality, its triumphantly controlled cross-currents and tensions.

A chorus girl is tap-dancing in front of a band in a sailor costume—a child's dancing-school outfit, satin and with a bare midriff. She twirls and taps and then suddenly leaps into an entrechat—as the camera pulls back through the café to follow a waiter with a tray, and then tracks along the crowded bar (the place is full of servicemen) to discover Woodrow at the end of it, alone and dejected. The music has changed now—from perky to dreamy—as Woodrow has a disconsolate exchange with the bartender ("Why don't you grab yourself off a skirt," says the latter, "and have yourself a time?"): a woman's voice is heard off, singing a sentimental old ballad (written by Sturges). She is a classy chanteuse (Julie Gibson), we see as the film cuts back to the dance floor, with an upswept blond hairdo, in strapless gown and elbow-length gloves and carrying a handkerchief. "'Home to the arms of Mother,'" she sings, as a quartet of singing waiters comes up behind her and joins her in close harmony. "'Safe from the world's alarms'"—as they all move forward through the tables. "Why don't they sing something gay?" says Woodrow at the bar. "Why don't you acquire a gay viewpoint?" retorts the owlish-looking bartender. "It's all mental, every bit of it," he goes on sneeringly. "Smile and the world smiles with you, frown and you frown alone." A familiar streetwise tone: both cynical and defiantly credulous at the same time. "Yes, well I'd just as soon be alone if it's just the same to you," says Woodrow. "Gratitude," says the bartender, turning away to listen to the song.

Woodrow thinks they've come to arrest him; they've come to ask him to be mayor. The delegation includes Harry Hayden (extreme left), Jimmy Conlin, and Franklin Pangborn; Freddie Steele is between Ella Raines and Bracken, and William Demarest and Georgia Caine are to Bracken's right. Hail the Conquering Hero

The chanteuse is familiar, too, in her radiant self-composure. She is a witty parody of a familiar movie type—a figure like Frances Farmer's Lotta in *Come and Get It*. So detached and so sure of her effects—the glowing eye and uplifted face, the confiding spread of arms, the jaunty little hitch of poignance she gives to the first extended syllable of "Mother." "'Safe from the world's alarms,'" she sings—looking nearly as "safe" and as pleased about it as anyone could possibly be—as she and her huddled quartet go implacably among their audience. Sturges calls attention to the way her effects are contrived (a shot of the man operating the filters on her spotlight, a view from behind of the waiters' posteriors as they jostle into place to frame her pleasingly)—and to the distance she is at from her lumpish audience's emotions (truck-driver types crying into their beers), the serenity and unconsciousness, sailing in front of her waiters, with which she wreaks her havoc:

> . . . As you stood in the gloaming
> To welcome me home . . .
> Home to the arms of *Mo*-ther . . .
> Never again to roam!

And just as the strains of this song are dying out, we see the six roaming marines outside on the street—Sergeant Heffelfinger (William Demarest) and his buddies, quarreling about the money the corporal (Jimmy Dundee) has lost in a crap game. Now they have five days of leave left and no money—except the fifteen cents that Bugsy (Freddie Steele) announces ("He laughs a little queerly," says Sturges' screenplay) he is about to spend inside. And they all follow him into the café. Where—after a bracing exchange with the manager (Sergeant Heffelfinger tries to sell him "General Yamatoho's tooth," an old Elk's tooth: "Big man, wasn't he?" says the manager—before offering to sell *them* the flag they buried the general in: he has it in his pocket, along with several other such items he's gotten stung on), they meet Woodrow—who stands them all to drinks. "I can't think of any other way I'd rather spend my money," he says, "than for marines . . . from Guadalcanal." He tells them how he'd been in the marines himself—for a month—and about his medical discharge. Even though he "was kinda born to be a marine"—his father was a marine sergeant who died at Belleau Wood the day Woodrow was born. And Woodrow can "tell you every battle the marines were in from 1775 down to now." He does so. And the camera tracks in on Bracken's transfigured, oddly beautiful face (the profile doesn't look out of place on a Roman coin, the way Sturges shows him in a joke under the opening credits). The historic names ("Tripoli in 1805, Nukuhive in 1812, the Battle of Hatchee-Lustee River, 1837, Vera Cruz in '46 . . ." and on and on) have a rapt, incantatory tone as he says them—and something more upsetting, too, when he gets to the recent names (the sound of "Taps" replacing the martial music on the

soundtrack): ". . . and now—Wake Island . . . Guam . . . Bataan . . . Correg-
idor . . . Guadalcanal. . . ." His voice winding down: "They bled and died"—
he says in extreme close-up, and there is the discreet sound of a cash register
ringing. The camera tracks backward again: "They gave me a big send-off when
I left home," he says, almost without pausing—and he tells his own story.

It's a story of shame—it has the plangency of that cash-register sound—
because Woodrow has been living a lie for over a year now, pretending to his
home town not only that is he still in the marines but even that he is overseas.
The marines are sympathetic, but Bugsy is horrified. "You mean you ain't been
home?" he says. He can't get over it: "That's a terrible thing to do to your mother.
You ought to be ashamed of yourself." "I am," says Woodrow quietly, but Bugsy
still can't get over it. And while the rest of them talk—the sergeant, it turns out,
had served under Woodrow's father, "Hinky Dinky" Truesmith, in the First
War—Bugsy keeps bringing up that mother—before going off to make a phone
call. "He never had any mother," explains the sergeant about this peculiar figure, "—he's from a Home." "He's a little bit screwy, too," says the corporal.
"He's all right," says the sarge, "he got a little bit shot up, that's all—nothing
serious."

But they should have watched him anyway: he calls Woodrow's mother and
tells her that her son is coming home—that he's just back from Guadalcanal,
wounded in action and discharged ("Then she won't have to worry no more," he
explains). Or so Woodrow discovers when he takes the phone and talks to her,
trying to straighten it all out. Of course he *wishes* he could come home—But
now Sergeant Heffelfinger has a brainstorm himself. "Mrs. Truesmith," he says,
taking the phone from Woodrow, "I fixed it up with the colonel and your boy's
comin' home tomorrow!" In fact they are all coming—that's the idea. The only
reluctant one is Woodrow—especially when they put him back in uniform and
start pinning their own medals on him, practically having to drag him onto
the train.

A genial general (Robert Warwick) passes by on the platform. "How are yuh,
boys?" he says as he salutes and strolls slowly by, accompanied by his aristocratic wife and beautiful blond daughter—and nearly giving Woodrow a heart
attack. Even more: evoking in one unforgettable image nearly everything that's
most threatening to a type like Woodrow, and most alien to him—the fat, oblivious well-being, smiling and condescending, of the ones who've got theirs. It
only takes this group a moment to pass, but it's a rich and wonderful event.

Woodrow's idea is that he'll just slip off the train and then change out of his
uniform as soon as he gets home. But the marines' idea, once they see and hear
those bands at the station of Woodrow's home town, is that he should have more
medals ("I told you he ought to have the Battle Blaze—with all those people
. . ."). No problem, since they have plenty. The whole town of Oakridge, the

mayor and everybody else, has turned out to meet them. And now Woodrow has to be more or less dragged *off* the train. Not that anyone seems to notice—with all the excitement and the reunions and the bands playing, all four of them, each of them a different piece. "O Death, where is thy sting!" cries Mr. Pash, the chairman of the entertainment (Franklin Pangborn), who has tried so hopelessly to coordinate it all. But then it's been out of control from the beginning. Woodrow does manage to get home and take off his uniform—though not without having to hear about his grandfather who "wore his Civil War uniform the rest of his life" (see above). But then they all go to church and it turns out that the Reverend Dr. Upperman (Arthur Hoyt) has a surprise to announce: the grateful citizens of Oakridge have gotten up a subscription to pay off the mortgage on Woodrow's mother's home. And they "have asked me," he says, "to perform the following ceremony." He holds up the "document in question," the mortgage— "You will notice I have nothing up my sleeve," he says (a little laugh here)— and then touches the rolled paper to the flame of a candle. A single organ note sounds. And as the paper burns and the organ tootles (Dr. Upperman does a sort of nervous little magician's pass with his hands), the horrified Woodrow sinks lower and lower into the pew between his mother (Georgia Caine) and the sergeant—who looks edified.

And Woodrow's girlfriend, Libby (Ella Raines), still hasn't broken the news to him yet about her engagement to Forrest Noble (Bill Edwards), the mayor's son. (Woodrow had written her a letter from "overseas" calling off *their* engagement.) At first she doesn't want to spoil his homecoming; after that, she never seems to get a chance to. As she explains to her fiancé, Forrest: "Every time I started to, a band started playing or they burned the mortgage on his house or— or . . ." Or they're nominating him for mayor. Judge Dennis (Jimmy Conlin) leads a group of citizens into the Truesmith living room to ask Woodrow to run against the corrupt and fraudulent incumbent, Mayor Everett Noble (Raymond Walburn). They need an honest man who'll tell them the truth, he says, someone to jar the town out of its selfishness and business-as-usual spirit. They've got an honest man who tells them the truth—Doc Bissell, the veterinarian (Harry Hayden)—except that "nobody votes for him but his brother and his wife," says Mr. Schultz (Torben Meyer). "And I'm not even sure about her," adds Doc Bissell. "I have everything but popularity." "In other words, Woodrow," says the judge, "we want you to take Doc Bissell's place." Woodrow hardly even begins to take in what they're talking about ("But I'm not a . . . a veterinary. I hardly know one end of a horse from another . . .") before he finds himself on the front porch (the marines carry him out) facing a cheering crowd. And all his modesty and disclaimers ("The medals you saw on me you could practically say were . . . pinned on by *mistake*") only make them cheer for him more. "He has a natural flair for politics," observes the judge. Woodrow firmly declines to run, but that is regarded as more evidence of his "flair," it seems—especially once the sergeant and the others start campaigning for him, recounting his battle exploits to the crowd. "I'm gonna tell you how he saved my life," says the sergeant, to wild hurraying. ". . . Now a voice says, 'Keep cool, pal'—and beside me I see . . . *Woodrow!*" As the judge and the doc and the Reverend Dr. Upperman all agree, only "a miracle" could stop him from being mayor now. "Don't drink that, dear," says his mother, "it's cooking wine." "Well, *I'm* cooked," says Woodrow.

He is certainly surrounded. Almost the last time we see him alone on the screen is at the beginning, when he's sitting at the end of that bar. From the moment he gets on the train he is nudged and pressed from all sides. Sturges takes something like the Lubitschean two-shot, with all its discordances and cross-currents, and turns it into a five- or six- or even more–shot, discordance in *all* directions—and Woodrow at its center most of the time. People collect into groups in this movie—like the judge's delegation, and like all those bands at the station. They move in groups, speak from the center or sidelines of them—to other groups. The marines, for example, who almost always appear as a crowd—either in medium or close shots—even in the middle of *other* crowds. And even the close-ups of people's faces show us four or five at once, with more in the background. As when Woodrow finds himself on his porch in front of that cheering crowd that wants him for mayor. Just behind him to one side (the left) is Sergeant Heffelfinger; Libby and his mother are to the right, his mother slightly in front. The four of them are crowded together by the crush of people, and they are strikingly lit (from above, by a high key light) in a way that makes their faces seem luminous and extraordinarily handsome. Woodrow's extreme anxiety is framed throughout the sequence—impinged on, even—by these other quite different reactions to the event, these different understandings of even what the event is. His mother is looking at him proudly. Libby is looking fondly at her. While Woodrow looks at the sergeant. And the sergeant looks away. One of the points of these groupings is the way they refract in all directions. A Sturges frame, even a comparatively static one like this, is always involved and kinetic and alive.

No one in a Sturges crowd fails to register his special and unique relation to it, and to the others. No detail of even a glance fails to establish the character's waywardness, his intractability and dissent. The way Mayor Noble looks at his wife (Esther Howard), who's usually just said something he's irritated by. The way she looks at the person looking at them (never at him) when he answers. "He talks that way in public," she says, putting a good face on it. The way Libby looks at Forrest when his father (she is the mayor's secretary) is being particularly fatuous—the way Forrest looks at the floor. The mayor in particular feels the power of such glances: it is a function, ironically, of his general obliviousness that *these* messages (not meant to do so) do reach him, if only in a confused way. Especially when he is pacing and orating in his office—as he generally is when we see him. So carried away, for example, by a turn of phrase about the stupidity of his constituents ("but the poor misguided voters, without a brain to bless themselves with, without a cerebellum to the carload . . .") that he tells Forrest to make a note of it: "I'll use it." "I wouldn't," says the Boss (Al Bridge), his drawling, laid-back sidekick, enigmatic but ever present, whose main function seems to be to restrain the mayor from just such impulses ("Save your voice, Evvy").

"What are you gaping at?" asks the mayor, nervously, when his son looks momentarily up from the transcription of his father's oratory. Libby is out for the moment. When she returns, the mayor gets going again. Winding to a climax, his subject is his own reluctant submission to the people's call: "*Mine* not to reason why, mine but to—" "Do or die," volunteers Forrest, out of his boredom. "When I want your assistance I'll ask for it!" the mayor says. He resumes: "Mine but to—" And stops: Libby is looking at him. "Well, what're you looking at?" he says. "Nothing," she says. "Well, cut it out." She looks down at her pad again and repeats: "'Mine not to reason why, mine but to—'" "Harken and obey," says the mayor, looking blissfully into the air. He is launched again: "Heaven knows I did not *seek* this distinction, but since you force it upon me, what alternative have I but to—" . . . and once again beyond their reach.

If Oakridge seems more richly characterized than Morgan's Creek, it's partly because these interactions, even between minor figures or people on the edges of a shot, seem so consistently witty and exact and full of nuance. The feeling of a community is very real in this movie. It's powerfully present in those crowded frames—with everyone registering themselves in dissident ways. The Sturges frame contains the dissidence as naturally as the Sturges town does. It also—like the Sturges town, or the Sturges family (e.g., the Kockenlockers)—promotes it. The six marines, with their own kind of community, offer a similar sort of paradox. They give Woodrow a very bad time, causing, in fact, most of his troubles; but they also protect him, standing loyally and unfailingly between him and whoever they imagine may threaten him (they tend to mistake those delegations of townspeople for lynching groups) at the same time as they expose him to risk and compel him to an imposture. It's no wonder the movie is so rife with double feelings—with hardly a person or a major circumstance that doesn't inspire them.

The marines are interesting. In a way they are behaving quite conventionally—good-hearted strong-men types with their little weakling buddy. But in another way they are mysterious, to put it mildly. They go so *far:* all but making Woodrow run for office finally, virtually holding him prisoner in his own house (they guard his room at night)—"forcing their victim through the show," as James Agee puts it. And Agee, in his highly influential review of the film, objected strongly to all of this, accusing Sturges of (characteristically, in Agee's view) faking and dodging, using his "power to entertain," in this "bewilderingly skillful picture," to distract his audience from a basic implausibility.*

For the marines, of course, the whole thing starts as a way of helping Woodrow out—and having a way to spend the last five days of their leave. The medals they insist on his wearing are a matter of marine honor, as they say (all those bands). And it's not just Woodrow, it's his mother they're thinking about, too. Nor is it just Bugsy who is moved by her or even by the *idea* of her. They all want to make a mother happy somehow. And then she takes them all in to see the shrine in the living room to her dead husband, Hinky Dinky. He was a young man just their age when he died, as the photo sitting above the medals tells us. Now, she says tearfully, she has not just two heroes (Woodrow and his father) but eight. And when Woodrow protests against the sergeant's campaign oratory, with its excited accounts of Woodrow's exploits in battle, the sergeant retorts: "We're doin' this for your ma, kid." And, in fact, it's all beyond her wildest dreams: the mortgage, then the mayoral campaign . . . "Isn't it wonderful, darling?" she says to Woodrow in the midst of all the excitement. "I'm so proud of you." And that, of course, was just the idea.

And what a ma she is. "Does your ma put up preserves?" asks Bugsy on the train. And of course the answer is yes. Just as it's true that she's a wonderful cook. Woodrow's mother does everything a down-home sort of mother is supposed to do—and be. She is another version of the Beulah Bondi mother in *Remember the Night*—idealized and widowed and the epitome of small-town life and warmth. She even has the same actress sidekick: Elizabeth Patterson, who was Aunt Emma there, is Aunt Martha here. And in fact the six marines are in roughly the same relation to the small-town idyll as Barbara Stanwyck was: outsiders sponsored by an insider, wistful about this enchanted world but also fatally alien to it.

For it's clear that they are all in some way homeless. Urban rather than country types, slickers among the squares, rootless and without connections. The most we ever hear about from them is an occasional girlfriend—like the one the corporal is reminded of by Woodrow's chronic hay fever ("Every time you'd get close to her, she'd sneeze right in your kisser." "She wasn't so dumb." "It was the excitement"). What this partly means is that they are heroes without an audience. "I been a hero, you could call it that, for twenty-five years," Sergeant

---

* And Agee broadens his indictment to cover Sturges' work in general. "In thoroughly good pieces of work," he writes in the *Hero* review, "there is an aesthetic and moral discipline which, however richly it indulges in certain kinds of illusion, strictly forbids itself others. It never fakes or dodges a motive, a character, an emotion, or an idea." But Sturges does. And it's this sort of sleight-of-hand in Agee's judgment that makes Sturges, for all his gifts, "a never-quite-artist" of "not-quite-genius," and films like *Hero* "wonderfully, uncontrollably, almost proudly corrupt."

Woodrow confesses to the town: "The coward is at last cured of his fear. . . ." Hail the Conquering Hero.

Heffelfinger tells Woodrow, "and does anybody ask me what I *done?* If they did I could hardly tell 'em, I've told it so different so many times." He compares himself to General Zabriski, the neglected unknown figure out of history whose statue stands in the town square: "All everybody knows is he's a *hero,* and the birds sit on it. And except I ain't got no birds on me, I'm in the same boat." Until Oakridge, that is—and Woodrow's mayoral campaign. Which gives them a chance to tell all their stories—to cheers. *True* stories, too, "except they change the names a little so's not to give out military information."

What impels Sergeant Heffelfinger and his buddies—as it impels the whole movie, supplying its special demoniac energy—is the excitement of a dream come true. A dream of pleasing the folks—a dream you may have, and have even *more* deeply (as Bugsy most of all reminds us), even without the folks: real folks only complicate it (as Woodrow reminds us). And not just pleasing them but *showing* them: turning out to be more splendid than even they could have ever expected or guessed, even at their fondest—coming back to town to be mayor of it. Oakridge is a town of "folks," in fact—much more so than Morgan's Creek was. The character of this town is entirely set by these older parental types—Mr. Schultz and Judge Dennis and Mr. Pash and Doc Bissell, men with clear connections to all those decencies and stabilities and traditions that, even when they are not quite fully achieved (Doc Bissell), and even when they are grossly parodied (Mayor Noble), remain powerful and attractive to us all. The *ideal* of small-town life.

But just as the heroes need Oakridge, so Oakridge needs them—and just because of its own failures and limitations. As Judge Dennis says when he first asks Woodrow to be their mayor, they need someone who will get them beyond themselves, someone who will move them to transcend their own narrow lives and interests. And so they welcome the heroes, who stand for bravery above and beyond the call of ordinary life. And no one in this town is immune to "heroes," as it turns out: not even Mayor Noble and the Boss (who both subscribe, in spite of themselves, to the mortgage fund); not even Forrest, who even in his jealousy of Woodrow is still concerned whether Libby will break the news of their engagement to him gently enough ("Be sure and put on something pretty," he tells her gloomily). And at the center of all this yearning and idealism is, of course, a fake. And behind *him* is a madman. . . . "Does your ma put up preserves?"

WOODROW CALLS it a "mother complex." The corporal, who presumably knows Bugsy better, simply describes him as "screwy." The sergeant, as we saw, puts it more tactfully: "He got a little shot up, that's all." He is, in any case—in his quiet, lowering, steadily watching way—a monomaniac. No matter what else is going on in a scene, Bugsy is thinking about those preserves, or about what a wonderful cook she is, or about the look in her eyes when she's happy: "That's what we're working for, see?" he tells Woodrow, warning him against making any more "cracks" about his mother (that's what "mother complex" sounded like to *him*, anyway). And he even seems to have—just as we fear about "maniacs"—powers beyond the normal. "I don't care much about sleeping at night," he says to Woodrow, as he sits guard, as he does every night, outside Woodrow's bedroom door. Finally, driven to his limit by Bugsy's watchfulness (he has just taken the cooking wine away from him: "Your ma said not to"), Woodrow puts the issue squarely: "Are you nuts or something?" he says. They look at each other. "Maybe," says Bugsy. (But he keeps the wine.)

In fact, Woodrow seems almost the only one who does put things squarely—and hopelessly. "Don't you understand this is all based on *lies?*" But the sergeant sees it differently: "They want heroes? We got six of 'em. . . . All right, we throw in a seventh for good luck. . . . Who's counting?" Woodrow is not only burdened with everyone's dream, both the marines' and the town's, with that wonderful mother, with that awful shrine in the living room, with the Congressional Medal of Honor awarded posthumously to his father ("I grew up with it. They hung it on *me* . . .")—but with a knowledge of a reality that no one else in the movie has any comprehension of. Finally it's what gives him his terrible glow—the agony of consciousness. And what makes even those passing representatives of *un*consciousness in this film—like the chanteuse and the general at the beginning—seem so full and so funny. Even an innocent and sensible person like Libby is made to seem dim and dithering when she shares the screen with Woodrow's gemlike flame. Witness the wonderful walk they take after she has told him (at last) about her engagement to Forrest—"That's marvelous!" says Woodrow. "At least I don't have to worry about *you*." This was not the reaction she expected from him exactly, and she is hurt by it. But she is still in love with him and can't quite give him up, it seems—even now. He runs after her and they walk together. He thinks his own terrible thoughts while she reminisces about the idyllic past—the days before he was "famous," as she puts it. "I'm going to be famous all right," says Woodrow, with horrible emphasis. He doesn't have anything to say at all when she starts to speculate about the girl he threw her over for, as she believes (his letter)—first hoping she's nice, then hoping she's "*awful!*": he just looks despairingly into the distance and slaps his arms against his side. They pass a tree where they once carved their initials. Their names will be there always, she says. "Naturally," he says. Then adds, through his teeth: "Unless something happens to the *tree*. . . ." She doesn't understand these remarks—any more than she believes him when he tells her he's a phony. "You—a phony?" she says, tenderly. It's really beyond her imagining. Why should she imagine it—when the marines come along just in time to take him off to bed, reminding her before they go of his "jungle fever" disability?

And that night at least, he *is* a hero—in this terrible dream he has—leading a charge against thousands of the enemy. But he only ends up on the floor beside his bed. Bugsy comes in and picks him up, puts him back in the bed, and then tucks him in, in his forbidding, avuncular way. "I must have had a nightmare, I guess," says Woodrow. "You're lucky," says Bugsy. "Hunh?" says Woodrow. Bugsy stands and looks down at him, his hands on his hips: "You're lucky you don't have them all the time—like some guys." And he goes out again, closing the door behind himself.

But what was that again? It's one of those problematic exchanges that now begin to dominate the movie, or so it seems. Bugsy is talking to Woodrow as if he really were a combat veteran. Bugsy is screwy, of course. But such is Freddie Steele's power by this time in the film—the authority of his gaze and presence—that we're no longer at all sure that "screwiness" is the point. This scene with Woodrow is too suggestive, too disturbing, even: it *feels* as if some revelation has been made—but what? One of the screwiest things about Bugsy all along has been the way he (quite unlike the sergeant and the others) seems to reproach Woodrow for not *wanting* to lie. As if in not wanting to fake it, Woodrow were refusing not only a promise to his mother but a community with the wounded and battle-marked—all those guys who have the nightmares. It's all crazy, of course. But now Woodrow himself has had one of those nightmares. And Bugsy, we find, is not surprised.

Nor, in a way, are we—and that's more surprising. Under the movie's reasonable, sensible surface—our identity with Woodrow's knowledge and point of view—things are shifting about upsettingly, getting displaced and confused somehow, and ambiguous. It's still clear, at least—just as it is to Woodrow—that the logical thing is for him to get out of town. (It's even clearer to *us*, since we know that the mayor and the Boss will soon have the scoop on his discharge.) If he can. And why not?—once he gets his terrific idea (it comes to him the same night as he has his nightmare), a story that will both liberate him from his captors and placate his mother and the town. But it's already too late, as it turns out. Too many things have shifted around.

Next morning at breakfast, Woodrow gets the marine named Juke (Len Hendry) to phone him from the drugstore. Then Woodrow gets on the phone in front of everybody—the five marines, his mother and Libby, Judge Dennis and Doc Bissell (who've just come to get him for the parade and the big rally at the town hall)—and pretends that it's the marine base in San Diego, calling him back for limited service—*today*. "You were our only hope," says the judge mournfully. "When duty calls, duty *calls*," says Woodrow, in the direction of the sergeant and with a nasty emphasis. "It will be so lonely without you," says his mother tearfully—and Bugsy has to be restrained. But he can't be restrained when Juke comes in from the drugstore. He rushes Juke in the hallway, "like a bat out of hell" (the screenplay), and they tangle at the bottom of the stairs until the sergeant and the others pull them apart. When Woodrow bursts through the group, Juke is sitting on the stairs, eye closed and mouth bleeding, and the sergeant and the corporal are holding Bugsy by the arms. Woodrow confronts him in a fury (from Sturges' published screenplay):

WOODROW (*through clenched teeth*): You meant that for me, didn't you?
BUGSY: What about it?
WOODROW: You think I'm afraid, hunh?
BUGSY (*sneeringly*): Well, I'm glad I wasn't never in a foxhole with you.
WOODROW: Let him go.
BUGSY: You yellow-bellied . . .
WOODROW (*nearly crying with rage*): Let him go, I tell you!
(*Bugsy laughs in his face and Woodrow hits him a terrible punch in the mouth. The corporal and the sergeant exchange a glance, then drop Bugsy's arms. Bugsy looks at Woodrow for a moment, spits some blood out of his mouth, then speaks:*)
BUGSY: Go find a woman to fight with . . . that's all you know how to hurt. (*He leans over and helps Juke to his feet.*) Come on, kid.

And together they go up the stairs, Bugsy helping Juke—leaving Woodrow behind to face the others, his mother and Libby and the other marines, who move in on him accusingly as the scene fades out.

There is such a tangle of ugly and painful feelings in this scene that it seems almost out of control. It is certainly risky, given the overall tone of the movie. Woodrow's humiliation here—brandishing his fists in an impotent rage, massaging the knuckles of the hand he hit Bugsy with while the others stare at him— is almost unwatchable. Even more so because his feelings are so sympathetic— and infectious even. He has been pushed so far, by Bugsy most of all. Not just the guarding and the reproaching but something more. It's Bugsy who enforces all those confusions which are beginning to seem both more and more crazy and more and more threatening. Who implies that walking out on a scam would somehow be a failure of nerve and courage. Who confuses a "mother complex" with love of your mother, putting up preserves with a home, and an impersonation of something (like a hero, or a mayor, or even, perhaps, a loving son) with the real thing. More than all that even, it's Bugsy who makes you feel that the confusions—crazy as they are—are hopeless. It's that burning gaze partly, the intentness and passion behind it—the whole force of his demented, square-jawed, *Boy's Life* manliness. It's no wonder Woodrow wants to punch him— "nearly crying with rage"—to kill him even. Nor that almost as soon as the blow is landed, he is consumed with self-loathing.

For though Bugsy's view of things may be deranged, we recognize that that's partly a function of the powerful longings—for home and mother, for community and familyhood, for an ideal America—he stirs up. He is the hero some part of us wants—a *mad* hero even. And his confusions are not unique to him, as the movie points out. They are present in diluted and more reasonable forms not only in the other marines but in the town of Oakridge—which, like America itself, stands for ideals that in its actions and its public life it tends to parody. As Woodrow puts it in his last speech to the town: "Doc Bissell here . . . has tried so long to serve you—only you didn't know a good man when you saw one—so you always elected a phony instead. Until a still *bigger* phony came along. Then you naturally wanted him. . . ." Bugsy is not the only one who confuses substance with the signs and imitations of it. He is only that confusion's most attractive exponent: purer, more passionate, more compelling than the others.

And Woodrow is right, of course. Woodrow is *sane*. But he can't, as it seems, turn away from Bugsy—not without cost. It's the painful *unresolved* feeling of that scene on the stairway—with Bugsy returning to the community of his friends, and Woodrow, alone and distraught, massaging his bruised hand while the others look on accusingly—that primes us for the next exchange between Woodrow and Bugsy, which has a curious and enigmatic power. It's an exchange of looks: Woodrow is riding in an open car, with his mother and Libby on either side of him, on the way to the rally at the town hall (where he plans to announce his sudden "reinduction" into the marines, and to give his endorsement to Doc

Bissell). Bugsy is in the crowd on the street, standing by a lamppost. Woodrow turns and looks at him as the car goes slowly by. It's a mysterious, many-sided sort of moment. Simple in one way: Bugsy (his eyes are shadowed by his cap but we still "see" them) looks grim and accusing, even disgusted. Woodrow looks ashamed. But it's also as if Woodrow, in returning that gaze so long and so steadily, is accepting at last the claim that Bugsy is making on him.

And so he does an extraordinary thing when he gets to the rally—standing on the platform, with his mother and Libby sitting just behind, Mr. Pash and Judge Dennis and Doc Bissell, and the five marines (Bugsy, the sixth, is sitting pointedly among the audience) standing in a military line behind the chairs. Woodrow tells the truth about his discharge and his deception. He counters "heroism" with heroism. He exonerates the marines and takes the blame on himself: because he didn't want his mother to know, he tells them. "Well, it wasn't to save *her*, it was to save *me*. . . . I stole your admiration, I stole the ribbons I wore, I stole this nomination. . . ." And at this, Bugsy rises from his place in the front row and walks noisily up the wooden steps onto the platform—taking his place with the others behind Woodrow. "The coward is at last cured of his fear," says Woodrow. And he concludes: "There's no use telling you I'm sorry, because I wish I was dead. . . ." No one gloats at this self-exposure (except, of course, the mayor and the Boss). Everyone is silent and embarrassed—like Mr. Pash on the platform, who looks eloquently at the floor as Woodrow's story unfolds.

But his mother stands by him—as she makes clear when he goes home to pack. She only wishes he didn't have to leave town. But, as he says, no one here would be likely to give him a job now. And Libby joins him, too—since she's never stopped being in love with him (she also has the satisfaction of walking out on Mayor Noble at the end). "You can't say it's because you're a hero I'm running after you, can you?" And they go to the train station together—the marines, as always, in protective attendance. Except that Sergeant Heffelfinger seems to have stayed behind at the rally. And now it looks like the whole town is coming after them—a mob striding purposefully down the street toward the station, with Judge Dennis and Doc Bissell and Sergeant Heffelfinger at its head. And it turns out, in the comedy's final twist, that the town really *does* want an honest mayor. After an explanation by the sergeant, and a speech by Doc Bissell. "I made a very good speech on your behalf," he tells Woodrow, "better than I ever made for myself." "The guy had us all blubbering," adds the sergeant. Woodrow is nominated again—"I think it's a vindication campaign," says the Boss, and the mayor faints. And in the final delirious scene, the marines pull out on the train—with Woodrow and the town waving after them.

It's partly as an American artist that Sturges seems so special. Not only because he drew so much of his inspiration from explicitly American sorts of character and subject, not to mention American movies—but because he cut through the knot of smugnesses and self-deceptions and half-truths that the idyllic Americanists had made of the American subject matter—and because he deals so directly with our love affair with innocence. Where Lubitsch ran afoul of it (in the reception of *To Be or Not To Be,* for example), Sturges confronts it. He used the fantasies of the common imagination (certainly his small towns were that) not just because they were tested and surefire but because they were interesting and true in some way. Or so *he* found them. And through them he finds a special and excruciatingly funny way to talk about American life—a way to express its strange and often panicking energies, even its peculiar decencies—without ever telling us comforting lies about it. And in this respect at least, *Hail the Conquering Hero* is nearly the summit of his work. His last great comedy about community (the next one is about solitude) is also about a hero, the one Woodrow finally becomes—strange and transfigured and irresistible—who makes Americans see and understand, at both his expense and theirs. And in the comedy's final blissful irony (like Trudy's sextuplets), they vote for him anyway.

Sturges: A Black Comedy

*Unfaithfully Yours is a good picture which suffered from too much master-
minding and not enough previews. The performances, I thought, were very
good, and my favorite parts are the three prospects which I tried to do as if
written and directed by Sir Alfred. . . .* —STURGES, *in a* 1949 letter

*[I especially liked] the stiff marionettish quality of Lady Daphne in all the
fantasy sequences . . . what the figures in one's own heroic dreams always
are: lay figures responding in the exact way which will give us our cue to be
magnificent. Mr. Sturges, that was genius!*
     —MRS. MURIEL K. PALER, *a fan, in a* 1949 letter

*I cannot thank you enough for your perfectly charming and heartwarming
letter which came today. It so happens that what I like best about* Unfaithfully
Yours *was the marionette-like behavior of the other characters in Sir Alfred's
prospects. Of all the critics throughout the world, you, and you alone, noticed
the direction of those scenes. It pleases me very much. . . .*
     —Sturges' reply

U*nfaithfully Yours* (1948), the last of Sturges' great films, is the only one
without either a parade or a train. The hero of this film arrives in it in
a plane—a fragile-looking two-propeller model, making its way through a
fog, while the people waiting below worry about whether it will make it at
all. It's also the only Sturges film to take place in the milieu of high culture
(the hero is a conductor), to have a hero whose eloquence and volubility
are dazzling, who is accurately polysyllabic, and whose brilliance with
words seems nearly equivalent to Sturges' own. He is, in fact, a version of
Sturges—to the people who knew him, anyway*—the closest thing to a self-

---

*Sandy Sturges says that to this day the movie evokes him for her just as he was. Frances Ramsden says (in
the Curtis biography) that it's "autobiographical": "It is Preston's relationship to me. . . ."

portrait the filmmaker ever did. Sir Alfred de Carter (Rex Harrison) is also a hero *without* a community—and he is also without America, in some essential sense. Although he lives in it (apparently), he is a foreigner—an Englishman and a baronet. And an artist and an intellectual.

He is one of the world's foremost conductors (the character makes allusions both obvious and subtle to Sir Thomas Beecham), and he is characteristically surrounded by people. He has a manager (Lionel Stander), a valet (Robert Greig), a secretary (Kurt Krueger), and a beautiful young American wife (Linda Darnell), all in more or less constant attendance on him. And beyond them there are still others, always: people waiting for him everywhere—to step out of a plane, to arrive at a concert, to appear at a restaurant. Wherever he goes, he is looked after, and applauded. But on the screen—unlike any Sturges hero before him—he is characteristically alone: on a podium or in a phone booth, looking at himself in the bathroom mirror, or walking down a long, empty hotel corridor with the sound of the maid's vacuum cleaner whirring in the background, abstracted, obsessed, isolated. And even when

Rex Harrison dressed for a murder in Unfaithfully Yours. *(He has to keep adjusting the hat.)*

he shares the screen with others, they generally keep their distance—he is never crowded or jostled or leaned on. It hardly seems like a Sturges world at all. It is more, in fact, like Lubitsch.

According to a story that Sturges' cinematographer, the legendary John F. Seitz, told to James Ursini in 1971, Sturges had offered one of the early screenplay versions of this project (called "The Symphony Story") to Lubitsch back in the thirties. And Lubitsch had refused it, advising Sturges that it was "caviar" for an audience that preferred "corned beef and cabbage." But *Unfaithfully Yours* is probably Sturges' most Lubitschean film: a comedy about isolation. Although that isolation hasn't the same melancholy, sardonic inflection it has in most of Lubitsch. At least not at *first* it hasn't. For Sir Alfred, it seems almost energizing, in fact. His day-to-day life seems to be an almost continuous experience of mastery—of colleagues and friends and even strangers, of words and of music. And the enjoyment of that mastery is part of the daydream fun the movie offers. Entering a restaurant with Sir Alfred, or watching him deploy his staff and dispose of interviewers. Conducting his orchestra, or even making love to his adoring wife—it all seems to belong to the same serene pattern of control (his) and willing deference (theirs). Dealing with an obtrusive hotel detective (Al Bridge)—"You're what's known as the house dick, aren't you?"—or an obnoxious brother-in-law (Rudy Vallee)—"Today you've sunk below even yourself!"—even his anger is controlling. No one offers any real resistance to it: he tells them off and they cave in. Even the fire in his dressing room cooperates. He set it himself? Never mind. There are plenty of people to put it out. He trains the fire hose on the "house dick," gets "sloshing wet" himself, calls the fire captain (Frank Moran) "colonel" and "general" ("Be with you in a second, general") while talking to his wife on the phone to tell her he'll be late for their luncheon appointment and instructing her to buy some more dresses to make up for it.

But just as *Unfaithfully Yours* gratifies (as movies so often do) our fantasies of personal power, it then proceeds to demonstrate to us with a wicked sort of delight how truly limitless those fantasies are—in the movie's brilliant middle section. Sir Alfred—who discovers (as he thinks) that Daphne, his devoted but much younger wife, has been unfaithful to him with Tony, his handsome secretary—fantasizes his response to this situation while he is conducting. There are three pieces of music on the program that night, and Sir Alfred fantasizes three separate responses, corresponding to the music in question. To Rossini's *Semiramide* Overture, he murders Daphne and frames Tony, who goes to the chair. To Wagner's *Tannhäuser* Overture, he forgives her and magnanimously sends her away to her "happiness" with a large check. To Tchaikovsky's *Francesca da Rimini*, he confronts the adulterous pair and challenges the craven

Two faces of Daphne (Linda Darnell), both upsetting. (The first is a fantasy, but what is the second?)

Tony to a game of Russian roulette in Daphne's presence. These are Sir Alfred's "three prospects," as Sturges calls them, "as if written and directed by Sir Alfred."

Each one begins—after a virtuoso tracking shot that seems to take us from the orchestra up to Sir Alfred's eye and into his head—with the same sort of image: a medium long shot down the semidarkened entrance hall to Sir Alfred's apartment, as the door at the back opens and Daphne enters, returning from the concert, walking solemnly, looking regal in her black low-cut gown and the sumptuous white fur around her shoulders. She is followed by Sir Alfred. (In the third fantasy, Tony is with them.) She walks ahead—he gives her the camera, so to speak, and the forefront of our attention.

In the first fantasy, that is done so we can register every nuance of her duplicity. "Would you like to go dancing?" he asks her. "Oh, wouldn't that be *wonderful!*" she exclaims toward the camera, as he patrols implacably behind her. But *he* can't go—until later. Can't she think of anyone she might like to go with in the meantime? "Think hard," he says. "I *am* thinking hard," she says, "but I——" and he crosses behind her, the shifting of her

eyes registering his change of position (she is still facing us)—"I can't think
of anybody," she finishes. "How about Tony?" "Tony?" she repeats—who is
Tony? "Oh, you mean *Tony?*" she says. "Well"—savoring her little joke
here—"why should I want to go out with Tony?" But Sir Alfred persists—
and she reluctantly consents: "If you really want me to." "I really want you
to," he says. She'll go and call him then. "Do you know his room number?"
She hesitates. She speaks very slowly when she replies, as he watches her
from behind—patrolling, while her eyes shift to follow him as before. "I
could get it from the operator," she says, then adds in a very small voice:
". . . I guess." "Oh, yes," he says, "of course." And she smiles to herself.

Except that he sees that smile, of course—since this is *his* fantasy. And
she is betraying herself with every detail of it. Even to the eagerness with
which she skips off now to phone Tony: the same girlish breathlessness she'd
greeted the first suggestion of dancing with. Sir Alfred has urged her to
change her dress, too—to "something younger" (for the younger Tony),
"something a little less conservative. It's not as if you were going out with
. . . *me*." "Oh," she says, again rising to the bait, "you mean that purple

one with the plumes at the hips?" This dress, as it turns out, is one of Sir Alfred's obsessions—or, rather, the phrase (his phrase really, not hers) that describes it is. "Then go and put on the purple one, with the plumes at the hips," he says, sounding the plosives and sibilants, the luscious little popping and hissing sounds, like someone pronouncing an epitaph, combining relish with a dying fall.

And so it goes through the second and third fantasies. They have different emotional modes (revenge to forgiveness to manly challenge), but they all belong to the same dream world—a world where the people you're talking to will *never* say "That's ridiculous" or "Come off it" or (as Daphne says to Sir Alfred later) "And I thought my sister was the one who married the jerk!" Nor, for that matter, will they ever say "What did you say?" Even in his real life, people seem to listen to Sir Alfred quite closely. But we discover through his fantasies that as far as he is concerned they could be listening even *more* closely: they don't actually *hang* on his words, the way they do in these fantasies. The way Daphne does when she enters the room in the second fantasy (to *Tannhäuser*)—waiting, hardly daring to breathe, with just the slightest glance over her shoulder (she is again facing the camera) as he removes her wrap and speaks: "Poor baby," he says softly. "Why?" she says, looking fearful. "Because you know that I know," he says. "You can feel it." It's because he understands so completely what she is feeling ("as if we could control our love," he says, "lead it by the hand and order it to do our bidding") that he can forgive her. "I don't know what you're talking about," she says—but it's no use. When he describes for her her first vision of Tony ("see how gently the tendrils of his lustrous hair curl behind his ears . . ."), she bursts into uncontrollable weeping. And when he comes to "the spark that leaps from his skin to yours when accidentally your hands meet," she cries out: "Oh, no! No!"—it is too much. But he reminds her as she weeps that *he* is the one who should feel ashamed, that the older one should bear the blame: "The union between a man of the world, a seasoned traveler, and a child of Port Hole, Michigan, I suppose was doomed from the start. . . ." He has the name of her home town wrong ("Port *Hall*," she says, sobbing into her handkerchief; "I'll *never* remember it," he says with a little smile), but he has everything else right. She shouldn't be surprised at that, or alarmed. "I couldn't understand music as well as I do," he says, as he writes her a check for one hundred thousand dollars, "if I didn't understand the human heart a little." Needless to say, she is no longer occupying the forefront of the shot—nor has she been for some time.

Nor does she get it at all in the next fantasy (to *Francesca da Rimini*)—the one where Sir Alfred confronts both her and Tony. He is neither murderous nor sentimental in this one, but manful and forthright—in contrast to Tony, who tends to snivel. Sir Alfred shows his executive style, accusing the guilty pair openly; they gasp out loud when he says the word "mistress." "Didn't you know that I knew?" he says, almost amused, as Tony hides behind Daphne. And once again—as in the murder plot of the first fantasy ("Oh, look!" says Sir Alfred, "a razor!"; and everybody in the room looks, heads turning as one, toward the telltale object)—every gesture and word has its intended effect. And more. "You're wondering what I'm going to do, aren't you?" he says now to Daphne and Tony—and indeed they are, nearly expiring to know. And when he takes a gun out of the desk, they cry out and clutch one another, as they do when he puts it to his temple to demonstrate "this enthralling little game called Russian roulette." They even react pleasingly when he tells them what he *might* have done. "I thought of killing you, my dear. I cut your throat with my razor, your head nearly came off!" "Oh!" exclaims Daphne, putting her hand to her throat. "But it was *your* fingerprints they found on the razor, Tony—and you they burned, screaming your innocence!" And at this Tony and Daphne clutch one another and cry out together: "*Alfred!*"

And so it goes. Not just exposing Sir Alfred, but reminding the rest of us, too, the dumber it gets, of our own most wretched and awful longings. One of the most extraordinary things of all here is the way Sturges uses Darnell, one of the forties' most attractive new women stars. But she *is* a forties star: no Stanwyck or Lombard, she has less edge of temperament or personality than the thirties stars generally had. She is intelligent and looks gorgeous (breathtakingly photographed here, by Victor Milner), but she also seems a bit blank at times, even bland. Like Daphne herself, Linda Darnell seems made to order, so to speak— *not* to give trouble or to make problems. But when Darnell plays the Darnell/ Daphne that Sir Alfred sees in his fantasies, so wittily as she does here, she is suddenly and devastatingly *inside* the mind that "ordered" her, inside all the fatuousness about herself, in a way that makes the joke on that fatuousness very rich and specially delightful. It's a special kind of victory—a more obviously knowing and wised-up sort of actress couldn't have had it. (And it was confirmed by Darnell's wonderful comic performance in her very next picture, Joseph Man- kiewicz's *A Letter to Three Wives*, 1949.) It's a sly and subtle variant of the screw- ball heroine's triumph—her ability to transform herself and to escape her own limits. She escapes *us* in a way, too, just as Daphne "escapes" Sir Alfred. Be- cause the final joke of all this fantasy—its single most disturbing effect—is to suggest that perhaps our grossest delusions of control and power, our maddest dreams of glory, are about knowing the human heart "a little."

H E WOULDN'T have doubted her at all if it hadn't been for August (Rudy Vallee), his dismal millionaire brother-in-law, who had responded to Sir Alfred's parting injunction before he left on his tour to "keep an eye on my wife" by hiring a private detective to do it. Sir Alfred is both flabbergasted and incensed. "Good heavens, I merely had her tailed," protests August. "You merely had her *what!*" cries Sir Alfred, grabbing him by the lapels and lifting him up off the floor. "I give you my solemn word, August, if I don't regain control of myself in a few minutes—" He pulls down on the lapels and rips them off.

AUGUST (*stammering*): Please k-k-keep cool, Alfred.

SIR ALFRED: Keep cool, Alfred, my sainted aunt! I am outraged!

AUGUST: Please, Alfred.

SIR ALFRED (*pacing and shouting*): Low as my opinion has always been of you, August, little as I ever expected of chivalry or even common dignity, today you've sunk below even yourself! This is the sewer, the nadir of good manners!

AUGUST: I really think you're exaggerating a little, Alfred. (*Sir Alfred flips August's torn lapels with his hand, noting the damage.*) I've always used detectives to some extent, and so has my whole family. . . .

SIR ALFRED: Then your whole family is contaminated! (*pacing*) No man who employs detectives should ever be disappointed. I hope every time you've engaged these vermin you've discovered that you've had antlers out to here (*holding his arms out*), that you were the laughingstock of the city, that you came crawling out of the agency, (*walking toward the camera*) your face aflame, (*turning back to August*) your briefcase stuffed with un-deniable evidence of your multiple betrayals, dishonor dripping from your ears like garlands of seaweed—

AUGUST: I forgive your insults on the grounds that you are excited, Alfred.

SIR ALFRED (*driving his finger into August's chest*): I forbid you to forgive me anything on any grounds whatsoever (*holding up his fist*) and I may still punch you in the nose at any instant! Now get out of here and never speak to me again unless it is in some public place where your silence might cause comment or embarrassment to our wives!

This invective is a lot of fun. No matter what tumult his feelings may be in, Sir Alfred can express them in such a *satisfying* way—in a way that transforms both the situation and even (it would seem) the feelings themselves. As here with August: a potential humiliation turns into a triumph and a rout—a wipeout, in fact. Sir Alfred's language is more than a grace: it's a way of life. It brings him control, and freedom—above all, freedom from intrusion. His eloquence (along with his eminence: the two things go together in this film) reduces the others either to victims—gasping and stammering like August or the "house dick" later on—or to onlookers—like the ambiguous Tony, or even like Daphne herself, enjoying themselves but lying low all the same. And that's where the problem is finally. If the great Brando heroes—Terry Molloy and Stanley Ko-walski—are tragically inarticulate, then Rex Harrison's Sir Alfred is tragi-cally—or comically—the reverse.

For Sir Alfred, there are no competing voices. And there is a vivid reminder of what's missing in one untypical sequence: the one time that Sir Alfred ventures out of his penthouse–concert hall world, when he goes to visit the office of Sweeney, the detective. Sweeney (Edgar Kennedy) isn't there when he arrives, but the tailor from next door (Julius Tannen) is, eating his lunch from a metal pail and watching the office. Or at least trying to eat it—after Sir Alfred walks in and launches into a tirade against detectives and their profession: "a criminal invasion of the rights of decent people, an assault upon the very privacy which is the cornerstone of self-respect, an infamous pursuit . . ." and so on, ending with such appropriate climactic phrases as "the cesspools of humanity" and "the seepage of civilization." The little man closes his lunch pail and rises.

TAILOR (*with a Yiddish accent*): Look, mister, I am the tailor from next door. I'm just here to eat lunch—I mean I was trying to eat my lunch and answer the telephone, a favor, that's all. (*He crosses to the door.*) With much of what you got to say—and believe me, whatever you are doing you are wasting your time, you should be in Congress—confidentially I agree. But what good is that going to do you? About a blue serge suit my opinion is worth something. But from ethics? . . . (*He shrugs.*)

It's a brief exchange, but under the circumstances a striking one. This tailor is the *first* person in the movie to reduce Sir Alfred—even if only for a moment—to a listener, to silence and even to a hint of uncertainty. And the second one is coming up the stairs now. "Here he is now," says the tailor with relief, as he sees Sweeney mounting the noisy metal stairs to the office, "—climbing. Tell him."

But Sir Alfred hardly gets a chance to do that: Sweeney is so thrilled at meeting the great man himself, so determined to tell him how he's followed his career all these years now, never missing one of his concerts, in the New York area, that is—washing his hands and drying them, setting out glasses on the counter and pouring two drinks, raising a toast to "the world's greatest living conductor." "Which is hardly," says Sir Alfred, for the second time (and even more seriously) at a loss on this visit, attempting at last to reclaim the initiative, "what I came to see you about, Mr. —" "The way you handle Handel, Sir Alfred . . ." And so the praise flows. But Sir Alfred finally gets a word in—a withering one: "I'm bitterly sorry," he says, "to hear that you're a music lover." Sweeney's face falls: "I *live* for music," he says. "Without music, I wouldn't—" But Sir Alfred interrupts, taking off again: "Because I'd always hoped that music had a certain moral and antiseptic power, quite apart from its obvious engorgement of the senses, which elevates and purifies its disciples. . . ." And so on. But as he declaims, a look of understanding comes over Sweeney's face. "You're just hurt, I can see that," he says, under Sir Alfred's continuing fulminations. A nice moment: for the first time in the film someone has really *heard* Sir Alfred—not just his words, so to speak, but his music. "The flattery of a footpad is an insult in itself," he says, and much more to the same effect ("You mean a flatfoot, don't you, Sir Alfred? You don't mean a footpad." "I mean a *footpad!*")—but still, he remembers before he departs to leave the two extra tickets he has for tonight's concert with this unexpected music lover ("Sir Alfred!" exclaims Sweeney, touched), even after the revelation about Daphne (that she was observed going into Tony's room in her negligee) has been made. And there is a memorable image near the end of the sequence, when Sir Alfred pauses in the hallway— before taking the tickets back—troubled and frowning, with the tailor behind the glass of his shop in the background, finishing his interrupted lunch.

The tailor and the detective represent just the kind of life, fractious and un- expected and eloquent, that is missing from Sir Alfred's sphere. They are, of course, Stock Company figures. But in this picture the Stock Company is only nominally represented. The members who do appear (apart from Tannen of course)—Robert Greig is Sir Alfred's valet, Al Bridge is the hotel detective, Frank Moran is the fire chief, and there is even a brief glimpse (you have to be alert to catch it) of Georgia Caine in the concert audience—don't in this film have the force and life and quirkiness that mark them in the others. But Ken- nedy and Tannen do, and they remind us of the vision of community the Stock Company stands for to Sturges. The sort of thing Sir Alfred knows nothing about.

But then there is something like it here—in that orchestra. Which Sturges shows us with such lingering and loving attention when Sir Alfred in an early sequence (just after the blowup with August) rehearses the Rossini overture for the concert. And Sturges gives us this music without distraction or interruption (except for one cutaway shot to show Al Bridge arriving backstage)—a very daring thing to do at the time. Even more daring: the music here is really the *point* of the scene. We are meant to be as involved in the excitement and wonder of these sounds as Sir Alfred himself is in this sequence. But it also shows us another kind of wonder: the look of the orchestra itself. Beginning with a lateral tracking shot, a back view of the back of the orchestra (the percussion section), moving past the timpanists, rising and passing over the string section, hovering over two harpists (who are *not* playing at the moment; one of them is knitting, the other doing her nails), then passing down through the violins as we hear Sir Alfred's voice over the music ("And now, gentlemen, merely to follow the wishes clearly expressed by the composer: *pizzicato con molto vibrato*—like a dentist chipping out an old filling"; and the orchestra laughs), then tilting upward to show Sir Alfred on the podium: the wonder *is* (confirmed by the camera's inven- tory) that such exultancy as we hear should come from the people we see, so prosaic-looking, so settled and middle-aged and nondescript, and with such impassive faces. Like a convention of insurance agents. There are repeated shots of the kettledrummer, for example, a small, bald, portly man with collapsed jowls, in shirtsleeves and opaque glasses—a very Harry Hayden–ish type. And he of all the players has to make the most violent exertions, on those drums, and does it as unflappably and impassively as Hayden himself might do it ("I'm not a failure, I'm a success . . ."). And as if to confirm the point, Torben Meyer himself—addressed here as "Dr. Schultz"—is nearby. He is the one playing the cymbals, which are much used in this rousing music. "My favorite instrument in the entire orchestra," Sir Alfred tells him, "but I can't hear you." Dr. Schultz sounds his cymbals again (quite loudly enough, you would think) and then speaks above the music:

DR. SCHULTZ: I was afraid of being a little loud, Sir Alfred. You know—
   vulgar. As a small boy, I was learned always never to be vulgar.
SIR ALFRED (*as he conducts*): Be vulgar by all means, but let me hear that
   brazen laugh!

And he puts a cigarette into the corner of his mouth and turns to the woodwinds. Harrison looks very raffish in this sequence, in his turtleneck shirt and with his

Finale: Sir Alfred on the podium.

glinting eyes, more like a pirate than a conductor. But in the meantime, as the music rises to a particularly galvanizing climax, we see Dr. Schultz go hurriedly offstage, down behind the orchestra, then return—the music pumping brilliantly away—with a pair of perfectly enormous cymbals, Cleopatra's barge-size, borne high and triumphantly over his head as he rushes back to his place. Now the cymbals *do* sound—nearly knocking Sir Alfred (to his delighted surprise) off his podium. He is transported. And as he makes Zeus-like stabs in the air to set this sound off again—and *again*—a demonic, exultant laughter is heard on the soundtrack—and grows and grows as the monstrous cymbals clash again—and then is replaced by Sir Alfred's humming, and his dum-de-duming, as the music comes to its extraordinary climax and ends.

"Out of what dogs have I seen him coax it out of," says Hugo, his manager, at another point, describing Sir Alfred's orchestra. But for Sturges that's just the point: the kettledrummer who looks like an office manager, the private eye who lives for music, the cymbalist who is deferential to a fault, hoping above all never to be vulgar but able to play the biggest, vulgarest pair of cymbals that anyone ever saw. It all comes together in the surprise of people and the surprise of art—in the surprising sudden ways we can transcend not only propriety and decorum but our own limits, in the release and fulfillment of that "brazen laugh."

"If it was me, I'd never have 'em tailed. I'd never try to find out nothing!"
—SWEENEY, in *Unfaithfully Yours*

BUT TRY to transcend that detective's report. And Sir Alfred really does try. It's an insult and beneath notice. As he has more than adequately explained to August—who is now at last venturing to leave, torn lapels and all. "I suppose I'll see you at the concert this evening," he says. "I suppose so," barks Sir Alfred. "I'm usually there on the nights that I conduct." And of course, August doesn't suppose now that Sir Alfred would be interested in the detective's report—which he produces nervously from his inside coat pocket. "Oh, yes I would!" Sir Alfred says, grabbing the report and shredding it in August's face. He throws the pieces in a wastebasket, takes it to the door August has just left by, and drop-kicks the whole thing into the hall. He shuts the door and kicks that, too. *Would* he be interested . . . ! But perhaps if he'd been a little less emphatic about it—if the wastebasket hadn't gone flying out into the hallway and been seen (as we later learn) by a maid who was alarmed enough to report it to the hotel security—then the house detective wouldn't have turned up later that day at the rehearsal, in Sir Alfred's dressing room, with the report in hand ("I glued it together myself"), requiring Sir Alfred to destroy it once again, this time by setting a match to it, waving the flaming paper in the intimidated detective's face ("Cut it out, boss—take it easy, will you!"), and inadvertently setting fire to his own dressing room.

The fire, however, is quite enlivening—just the sort of overstatement Sir Alfred likes. Still, it doesn't entirely solve the problem. Suppose there are *other* copies in the private eye's possession? He approaches his detested brother-in-law again—in a restaurant, where August is dining with his wife, Barbara (Barbara Lawrence)—and demands the detective's card: "Will those people who shall be nameless be apt to have additional copies of that which I did you know what with this morning because I *will* not have them around!" He takes the card from August ("Thank you very much"), glances at it, tears it up ("Thank you"), and stalks off, leaving August and Barbara gaping. "He's getting nuttier than you are," she says. But he's also getting closer—each time he tears something up or kicks it into the hall or sets it on fire—to a knowledge he wants to deny. (He is at Sweeney's office in the next scene.)

It's important to note that *Unfaithfully Yours* isn't the usual sort of comedy (*Hay Fever, The Guardsman*, et al.) about outrageous artistic types—the sort of characters whose feelings and gestures are always larger than life but who are marvelous in their way just because of that. Sir Alfred, even at his most extreme and self-centered and overbearing, is never posturing or camping or swanking. He is dealing with painful issues of truth and falsehood, of knowing and not knowing, as best he knows how—blunderingly, and with real anxiety. He's outrageous, but he's serious, in a wholly recognizable way—never someone we watch from an amused distance. Nor is he someone who plays to an audience— as the Noel Coward hero tends to do—either the one onstage or the one beyond. He does indeed play *before* an audience. But how that audience responds, or whether it does at all, is a secondary matter to him at best. He knows, for example, that his *Tannhäuser* Overture was sodden and exaggerated, even though the audience went wild over it. ("What visions of eternity," asks Hugo about the Rossini piece that preceded, "did you have in your head?" "You'd be enormously surprised if you knew," Sir Alfred replies.) It's the music he serves, not the audience.

The same relation operates in his private life, too. His wit and expressiveness, his bountifully flowing eloquence in all situations, seem independent of the people they are performed before—the unreadable Tony or the thick-witted brother-in-law ("Now, my dear August, what happy updraft wafts you hither?" "Thank you") or even sometimes his wife. Who is too upset, after his unexplained absence, to respond to the rush of angry words with which he describes the movies he's spent the afternoon seeing:

SIR ALFRED: I saw a very long picture about a dog, the moral of which was that a dog is a man's best friend, a companion feature which questioned the necessity of marriage for eight reels and then concluded it was essential in the ninth—

DAPHNE: Alfred—!

SIR ALFRED: Also something about time marching on and a newsreel of the Royal Family christening something, extremely out of focus, a lot of people being saved from a sinking freighter, and a cat which had its kittens in a harmonium and frightened a Harlem congregation nearly out of its *wits!*

DAPHNE (*putting her hand on his forehead*): You feel quite hot. . . .

SIR ALFRED: I feel anything but *quite hot!*

This sort of outpouring is another sort of music in a way, and he makes it out of the same sort of compulsion—the same sort of expressive need, independent of the listener. So that Sir Alfred's relation to his audience is more indirect and more complex than that of other Sturges heroes who also find themselves on public view. The sense of an audience that impels Woodrow to heroism, for example, or Dr. Morton into history, is a relatively clear one. The analogous sense in Sir Alfred is more like an uneasy, unformed, tormenting awareness. *His* audiences are a reminder of his relation to himself. And of his aloneness.

And in no other Sturges movie are the physical props quite so prominent (like the indestructible detective's report)—so full of a cantankerous kind of life of their own, it almost seems. Like the sandwich which gives off a loud exhaling sound when touched, or the zipper on August's wallet, or the telephone that keeps saying "Number, please" ("Some jerk on the line") when Sir Alfred keeps kicking it over. Like Sir Alfred's straight-edged razor (a very ominous presence), or Daphne's purple-plumed dress, or the mantel clock that plays a few bars of "Jingle Bells" before cutting itself off with a sound like a Bronx cheer. Or the enormous oblong box Sir Alfred's flowers come in ("It could be a skeleton," says Hugo), or the negligee on the bed that stirs him to putting his murder fantasy into action, or the curtain he gets his foot caught in climbing back through the window with the recording machine, or the two-headed art-moderne statuette that keeps turning up in the cabinets when he is looking for the machine. And so on. It's almost as if the importance usually reserved to all those jostling supporting people in a Sturges comedy had been displaced here onto the objects. It's the inanimate physical world that really impinges on Sir Alfred's expressive freedom, that baffles and beleaguers him in a way that the people around him would hardly dare to do. In his fantasies, he has an ordinary unthinking mastery of such objects. This is revealed as a delusion—and an extreme one—in the extraordinary and very extended slapstick sequence where he tries to put his murder fantasy into action (razor, recording machine, and all) and nearly dismantles the apartment. At this climactic point in the movie, Sturges almost eliminates "character" altogether, focusing our attention and our hilarity on the smallest details of the objects giving Sir Alfred so much trouble: the phone, the curtain, the chair with the seat out, the three-legged table—above all, the Simplicitas Home Recording Machine, with all its refinements of frustration (with its baffling instructions, its simplified diagram, the device that carefully picks up the record and ejects it to the side): "Remember, it is so simple that *it operates itself.*"

It seems, after all, that Sir Alfred *would* kill her—if only he could *find* anything ("Where are the bullets to my revolver?") or if he could make anything work. At least he sets out to kill her. (It was the matter-of-factness of all this that made the movie unsettling to audiences at the time.) Even after the recording machine has undone him, he is still experimenting with the razor, testing its sharpness in the bathroom on a hair from his own head—except that he keeps dropping the hair on the floor. It's less something in himself that keeps him from acting out his fantasy than something intractable in the things and circumstances around him. He may be a great man and a great musician, but he is finally just not dignified enough to be a murderer. He is conscious of the problem: between pratfalls with the recording machine, for example, he keeps adjusting his hat in the mirror.

And *she* is part of the same problem—offering the same kind of intractability, the same kind of dumb, maddening intransigence. "By the way, I will not be able to take you dancing tonight," he announces (carrying out the fantasy). "Why? Who are you taking?" she says over her shoulder. Not that *she* wants to go. Not even with . . . Tony? "Have you ever *seen* Tony dance?" she says. "He gets up on his toes like a rooster and he pushes you over sideways, and then he shoves your head back till you think it's going to drop off—why, compared to him, you look like Arthur Murray." Anyway, she feels about as much like going dancing as cutting her throat. "How did you happen to use *that* simile?" he says. She hesitates a moment: "What's a simile?" she says. And when he tries to forgive her, she doesn't even know what he's forgiving her for. "Have you ever heard of Russian roulette?" he inquires, removing the pistol from the desk drawer. "Why, certainly," she replies. "I used to play it all the time with my father."

> SIR ALFRED: I doubt that you played Russian roulette all the time with your father!
> DAPHNE: I most certainly did. You play it with two packs of cards and—
> SIR ALFRED: That is Russian bank. Russian roulette is a very different sort of amusement—which I could only wish your father had played continuously before he had you!

At other times—as at the end of the film, when they are reconciled—he sees her as "a wonderful, wonderful, wonderful child." She tells him she had never been in a man's room before ("except yours, of course") until that night she went into Tony's: she was looking for her sister, Barbara (whom she suspected of getting something on with Tony), and was trapped there when she saw Sweeney, the detective ("A large, lumpy man, with a face like an orangoutang?" "That's right—like a gorilla"), watching outside the door. So *that's* the explanation. Sir Alfred is exultant. She is delighted, of course, but she doesn't really understand yet what he's been so upset about. He asks her to put on her "lowest-cut, most vulgarly ostentatious dress" and go out with him: "to the vulgarest, most ostentatious, loudest, and hardest-to-get-into establishment this city affords!"

He'd reacted somewhat like this in the earlier part of the film, just after he's come home from his tour and August has planted the first seeds of suspicion in his mind. He approaches Daphne in their bedroom:

SIR ALFRED: . . . You really do love me, don't you?

DAPHNE (*looking up at him*): —What?

SIR ALFRED: You really do love me, don't you?

DAPHNE: I don't know what I'd be doing here if I didn't.

SIR ALFRED: No, I don't either. . . . By the way, you didn't do anything you shouldn't do while I was away, did you? I mean like falling in love with anyone else or anything like that?

DAPHNE (*leaning forward and looking into his eyes*): How could I fall in love with anyone else . . . when you took my heart with you?

SIR ALFRED: No man ever had a better answer than that.

And he asks her to meet him, before their luncheon date, at a store he names: "because you haven't a thing to wear!" She protests that she has "closetsful." "I'd like to buy you a little something," he says. "Would you do that for me?"

And of course it *is* for him—the nightclubs and the dresses and so on—much more than it is for her. "Will you do me a very great favor?" he says at the end of the film, as a prelude to inviting her to "accompany" him to that hard-to-get-into club. It's meant to be a specially gallant way of asking her, but it seems even more importantly to be an exactly accurate one. And we are reminded that whenever he makes his most ardent love to her in this film—their reunion at the airport at the beginning or their reconciliation at home at the end—it is in front of interested and appreciative onlookers. Barbara tells August to put on his glasses and "learn something" at the airport. At the end she just says "Shhhh!" Even in the boudoir Daphne and Sir Alfred are interrupted by Tony—he knocked but they didn't hear. Sir Alfred's "audience" never deserts him, it seems—not only confirming his relation to himself but to Daphne as well.

"No man ever had a better answer than that"—nor a better explanation for thirty-eight minutes (Sweeney's count) in another man's room in her negligee. That's just the trouble. There *is* something childlike about her of course. Or is it exactly *child*like . . . the way she keeps turning to the sheltering men around her? "Take me home, Tony" comes as easily to her lips as an ordinary greeting, it seems. Or take her first words in the movie—at the airport. The airlines officer is explaining to them all about the fog and the delay, but she turns to the man at her side: "Is it a very bad fog?" she says. "Make him tell me the truth, Hugo." And even in moments of intimacy with her husband, there is something almost formal about her spontaneity ("You sweet love!"), something a bit learned, perhaps, and even unreal.

Or *is* there? Because she is really beyond reproach or cavil. How can he fault a woman who, as she later tells him (he asks), takes his picture to bed with her? But on the *other* hand—what does he make of her? And as the movie makes clear: there is no answer. She is mysterious without ever offering to be. So extraordinary in her common American way that she could be anyone or anything. "I have no secrets from you," she says—and keeps her secret to the end.

It's no wonder, then, that he looks for witnesses. "There's nothing the matter with me," he says at the end of the movie, a moment both funny and moving—while the strains of the *Tannhäuser* Overture sound under his words—"that a few magnums of champagne won't cure." And he goes on, in his most elated vein, pacing and gesturing:

> SIR ALFRED: . . . I happen to want to celebrate. I want to be seen in your exquisite company. I want the whole world to know that I am the most fortunate of men in the possession of the most magnificent of wives. I want to *swim* in champagne—and paint the whole town not only red but red, white, and blue! (*going toward her*) I want everybody to see how much I adore you (*taking her by the shoulders and looking at her*)—always have adored you, revere you, and trust you. Also how much I hope you have of warmth for me. . . .
>
> DAPHNE: But my darling, I worship you.
>
> SIR ALFRED: Then put on your most outrageous dress!
>
> DAPHNE: Shall I wear the purple, with the plumes at the hips?

He is a little taken aback by this at first—but then: "By all means. And let it be a purple lesson to me." And the "audience" now enters: Hugo and Barbara and August and Tony open the door and come quietly down the hallway, getting in place in the doorway to watch the final clinch. Daphne still doesn't understand what was wrong. Sir Alfred begs her—humbly—never to make him tell her. Of course she won't, if that's what he wants—compliant as always. And they embrace. "I know what it's like to be a great man," she says in his arms. "That is, I don't really—but having so many responsibilities, so much tenseness, watching out for and protecting so many people . . ." But she doesn't know *him*, of course, any more than he knows her. There is no rhetoric by this time about understanding the human heart. Just the opposite.

He really is alone. In a way there is no one in this movie but him—and the people he refracts from his own consciousness. It's a severer kind of entrapment than anything Norval or Woodrow could know. But like most Sturges heroes, Sir Alfred is making the best of it all by the end—coming to terms with his own limits: the "great man" who learns to make something out of his own littleness. And unlike Hopsie, for example, who never does seem to understand about Eve, Sir Alfred takes the full, bitter measure of his own ignorance. And he speaks— before the fadeout, and before the last, staggeringly beautiful close-up of Darnell in his arms—the movie's final, remarkable line, summing up the whole mixture of love and anxiety and defiant final exultance that this powerful sardonic-romantic comedy conveys. "A thousand poets dreamed a thousand years," he says, "and *you* were born . . . my love." Still on the podium. And making music out of what he *doesn't* know.

Conclusion

I like to yodel and dance and fuck a lot. . . .
                                    —SAM SHEPARD, in an interview

BUT THEN we have always preferred to believe that we were innocent. Just as Capra and so many others have told us.

The stars and movies this book has been about have rarely been among the most popular with American audiences. In a fairly recent listing of "All-Time Hit Comedies" in David Pirie's *Anatomy of the Movies* (1981), among the 68 titles, there is not a single screwball comedy. And in the mid-thirties, when screwball was at the peak of its popularity, the top box-office star was Shirley Temple. Before that, it was Will Rogers.

The most popular star of the war and postwar years—the mid- to late forties—was Bing Crosby. And he is an interesting transitional figure. By the time he had become a major star, his main characteristic was a kind of relaxing blandness, omitting all trace of the exciting young singer he had once been—both wide-eyed and savvy, with a kind of animal moan behind the crooning sound. He became instead (no hint of a moan now) the most affectlessly genial of stars—only, it seemed, in the *Road* pictures rousing himself to something sharper, as a waspish con man opposite Hope and Lamour. In his musical numbers he had perfected the ability to make any song he sang—whatever its tempo, mood, or style—sound exactly like the last song he'd sung. Where a singer like Astaire served the composer, Crosby obliterated him, reducing everything to the same unmistakable but eerily impersonal Muzak sound. And his recordings were as popular as his films. He was the consummate commodified artist.

And everywhere he was recognized as a distinctively American type—that was one reason he was such a favorite. But he was neither a big-city nor a small-town sort; by the time of his heyday, those categories had come to seem outdated. What he really was was a suburban type: at home in the outdoors, but generally

on some kind of lawn—with golf clubs and Hawaiian shirt. Anyway, he was inescapable, and his prominence banalized our lives in the same comforting way that advertising did: suggesting that there was very little at stake in them— beyond a choice of lawns. It's no wonder, then, that the apocalyptic tone of film noir—a movie genre even less generally popular than screwball comedy was— found appreciative and receptive audiences, and to some of them even seemed oddly cheering. It was not about ordinariness, at least, not about comforting everydayness. It was about failure and doom, but it testified to immanence.

Probably all mass culture involves a certain amount of denial, and in the postwar era we had more to deny than ever. We had not only just dropped the Bomb but we had made, in Mary McCarthy's phrase, "a kind of hole in human history." We never quite took in what we had done. We had been the good guys in the war, and now we were the good guys in the Cold War. For most of us in those days, the worry about the Bomb was that those others had it. We knew, at least, that *we* could never be the first to use it—forgetting that we already had. And twice.

Today, of course, we have gotten far beyond that contradiction. We even refuse to say that we *won't* use it first. We are still the good guys, of course—more ever, perhaps. Almost as if the conviction of our innocence—which we have lived with so long—has carried us at last beyond the need for evidence of it, become so powerful that we no longer need to square it with reality, with our announced policies and actions.

America has come a long way since 1945. We have both made the ultimate Faustian bargain, with the planet itself as the stakes—and refused to notice what we have done. Although not quite. Because it's a bargain that calls for constant renewal and growing commitment—as our government constantly reminds us—with each day that passes. And though the Bomb may not be quite at the center of our consciousness, it is now at the center of our national life. As E. L. Doctorow writes: "It was first our weaponry and then our diplomacy, and now it's our economy." Our destiny. Or so it seems. No wonder we are forgetful— and drawn to banality and emptiness. Genial and waving to the world and not quite at home upstairs sometimes. Although we are too sophisticated in other ways—too wised up, too far beyond the naïvetés of the past—to have Mr. Deeds in our movies. But we must have him—we have always had to have him. And so we have installed him in the White House. Or at least a facsimile of him.

I take it that Frank Capra is a much nicer and much smarter man than Ronald Reagan is.* But they are both involved—along with the rest of us—in the triumph of wishes over evidence. So that the most popular President of modern times is admired not in spite of his befuddlement and willfully reduced consciousness, his tranquil imperviousness to knowledge and experience, but precisely because of these qualities. He represents the ultimate American freedom: the ability to believe whatever you want to believe. And although it necessarily gets harder, in our ongoing bargain with the devil, to see ourselves the way we

---

* Reagan is also reputed to be a nice man, of course. And clearly he aspires to that description as Richard Nixon, for example, never did; for many people (not to mention most American voters) he seems to merit it. The question is complicated, perhaps; but Reagan seems to be to "niceness" what Bing Crosby's Father O'Malley is to piety. Compare, for example, Capra's reaction to revelations of the Holocaust: by all accounts he was genuinely shaken, not only in a personal way but in his view of human nature. Reagan's reaction, as we know, was Bitburg—and a repeatedly told lie about being on the scene when the camps were liberated by the American armies.

*Bing Crosby in
Leo McCarey's
Going My Way.*

want to—as the good guys of the world—in some ways we manage that feat even better, more determinedly, than ever. But only in some ways. Neither *Rambo* nor Dan Rather could be the product of a truly convinced innocence. Nor is the Reagan administration. We simply *know* too much by now—about Vietnam, about Central America, even about the terror in our own streets—to really buy into the old certainties and simplicities and optimisms.

But we want them anyway—more than ever. More, even, than Americans in the thirties did. But as our belief wanes, our *will* to belief—something much scarier—grows stronger. That's why there seems so clearly to be a "camp" element to the "new" patriotism, the new "Pride in America." We don't quite believe it really, and we don't really care if we do—so long as we can have the *feeling* of belief. And it's here at least—in the assertion of will over reality, "image" over substance—that we are most deeply at one with our mad and evil leaders.

None of this would seem to have much to do with the movies—or with a movie book. Except that the movies have so much to do with us and with our lives in America. And a present as frightening as this one is (in 1986 as I write this) is bound to make the past seem more culpable. Even—maybe even especially—

our movie past. It's instructive in a way to look at that past and realize how many clear connections with the madness of our present it has. And although that hasn't exactly been the subject of this book, it's been on my mind as I wrote it—and it's affected in essential ways what I've written. But then I think it should do. To all of us, the past must seem less benign, less "innocent" than it would have even ten years ago.

But there's something else, too. Maybe an even more important point—or at least there's a chance that it is. If in some respects the old movies look worse to us, in others they look better. All those elements of sanity and resistance—in the screwball comedy, in the work of the great directors, in the stars themselves—seem even more miraculous. And even, perhaps, encouraging. In a way, that's been the real subject of this book. Or so I hope, anyway.

KATHIE *(at the roulette table)*: *Is there a way to win?*
JEFF: *There's a way to lose more slowly.*
     —JANE GREER AND ROBERT MITCHUM, in *Out of the Past*

THE DECLINE in movie attendance in the fifties (the average weekly attendance, which had been around 90 million in the mid- to late forties, dropped to almost half that by 1953, and has been declining more or less steadily ever since) profoundly affected the movies themselves. If one thing had marked a studio product of the forties, that was its confidence in itself, so to speak—its assurance that it was being watched and responded to in the intended ways. Even the emptiest and dumbest of these films carries even today an uncanny sort of conviction—even if it's only a conviction about what makes a successful movie. In the fifties, however, no one quite knew what did anymore. And it showed in the product.

So that although fifties movies were more outspoken than ever in their endorsements of ordinariness and conventionality and "normalcy," they were also more likely than ever to show signs of nervous breakdown. You never quite knew now when you went to the movies, in spite of the prevailing predictability, what in fact you might come across—when the dullest, most well-behaved film might suddenly lose its balance or go "funny" or start sending off mixed signals. And many of those signals, as more and more of them kept coming across, began to seem intentional.

The genre film felt outdated after the war, anyway. And though it wasn't abandoned, it was made more "real" in various ways. Movies began to escape the studios and to shoot in real places and locations. The set-bound film—along with that other bastion of unreality, the minor comic player—was eventually phased out. Hollywood had exchanged wartime duties for peacetime ones: less "escapism" and more "maturity," of style and subject matter. The movies took on such topics as psychoanalysis, juvenile delinquency, postwar readjustment and Cold War jitters, even racism. But the odd thing was that however "explosive" the subject, it always took place in these films against a backdrop of social harmony. America was pictured as a place where the political problems had been solved. All we had to do now was solve the "personal" ones, as it seemed. Movies not only offered us a vision of social consensus; they told us it had been achieved.

But *other* movies, it was clear, had joined the modern world of absurdity and anguish: Richard Burton carrying a dead man to "safety" in Nicholas Ray's *Bitter Victory* (1957)—or Susan Kohner on a conveyor belt of showgirls, drinking from an empty champagne glass, pouring from an empty bottle, in Douglas Sirk's *Imitation of Life* (1959)—or Jerry Lewis as a monster of vanity named Buddy Love in *The Nutty Professor* (1963), kissing his own hand. Because the *real* movie life of the time seemed not to be in consensus but in excess, in images of dismay and insanity. The noir film of the forties was followed by the wide-screen melodrama of the fifties, "the cinema of hysteria," with its visions of living-room apocalypse. And even the western—a genre that regenerated itself in the fifties, attaining a greater glory and prominence than it ever had before—became less a stage for action than for its hero's aloneness and angst.

The competing genres of urbane and folksy comedy, however, did really seem dead. Though there were attempts to reanimate them. Capra's *It's a Wonderful Life* (1946) was a relative failure at the box office because it was based on oppositions and arguments that most audiences by that time had either forgotten or no longer cared about. And yet, paradoxically, it was the old-fashioned genre films like Capra's in this period—rather than the "mature" and "controversial" ones, the so-called "new Hollywood"—that turned out to be most daring. Hitchcock's *Vertigo* (1958), for example, and Ford's *The Searchers* (1956), and Hawks's *Rio Bravo* (1959). These were just the kind of movie—"personal," obsessed and quirky, slow and repetitive and open to charges of self-indulgence—that the old studio system had functioned to prevent. And yet it was in this period, when the studio controls were beginning to lapse, that directors like Hawks and Hitchcock did what was arguably their finest work of all. They revealed things in their "genres" that no one had ever suspected before. And more.

It was not, however, a great time for comedy—of the intentional kind. Certainly not for romantic comedy. Hawks's attempts to regenerate the screwball style—*Monkey Business* in 1952 and *Man's Favorite Sport?* in 1964, even *I Was a Male War Bride* in 1949—are all horrendously unfunny examples. The genius of the time was for melodrama and grotesquerie. And the sort of comic impulse that it did nourish was the sort that realized itself, however fitfully, in the films

Jane Greer
and Robert
Mitchum at
the casino in
Out of the
Past.

of Jerry Lewis and Frank Tashlin—or, later on, "Monty Python" and John
Waters. Lewis's *The Nutty Professor* is, I think, the boldest and funniest American comedy since Sturges—and yet it could hardly be more different. In some
way, it's an almost illiterate film: the language functions in an expressive comic
way ("I hope you find what you're looking for," says the psychiatrist to the demented hero) *because* it's limp and banal. The origin of this movie is in the comic
strip, which it parallels in looks and style as well as content. The whole thing
seeming less a product of controlling comic skill than of demonish inspiration—
springing out of deep and alarming fissures in the comic's temperament—
dramatized in the Jekyll-Hyde parody of the plot. Almost as aggressive toward
its audience as it is toward its material, it's a comedy *about* aggression—and
about the deep and furtive love of the bully that infects American life and culture. It's also—significantly—a movie with two endings (quite literally): the
first, conventionally sentimental and "warmhearted"; the second, cynical and
wise-ass and absolutely reversing all the meanings of the first, as if in a kind of
afterthought. A joke on us (especially if we really bought the first ending), and
yet audiences missed it: it was done so brusquely, and a lot of people were
already up the aisle.

But then it was no longer, as it had been at the movies, that the *whole* audience had to get the point—so long as some of it did. In the studio days, any attempt to divide the audience in this way—like *The Great Moment*, for example—was likely to be suppressed or at least impeded, as Sturges' film was. And yet it was partly through Sturges that the situation had changed. It was with Sturges, according to André Bazin (writing in 1951), that "the humor of the American comedy" was transformed into irony: Sturges had "protracted" the genre of the romantic comedy, but his irony also brought it to an end. So that what we are really laughing at in his comedies, says Bazin, is "the death of laughter."

Billy Wilder is a case in point, I suppose. He was thought of, by himself and others, as carrying on the traditions of Lubitsch and Sturges—even doing it at their same studio, Paramount. And yet he is nearly always less effective as a comic artist than he is as an ironist, even a rather heavy one: in movies like *Ace in the Hole* (1951—where even the title, later changed to *The Big Carnival*, is a nasty joke, referring to a man who is buried alive) and *Kiss Me Stupid* (1964), in films noirs like *Double Indemnity* (1944) and *Sunset Boulevard* (1950). And certainly irony is the dominant note of film noir in general. For example, it's almost *like* a joke when Jane Greer, the murderous heroine of Jacques Tourneur's *Out of the Past* (1947), comments on the run of bad luck that's just prompted her to kill Kirk Douglas: "I think we deserve a break," she says to the benumbed hero (Robert Mitchum). This is the noir version of a joke: beyond belief, really—and no surprise at all. A stimulus to chagrin rather than amusement. "The death of laughter . . ."

When you're watching a comedy at least, the sound of the audience around you can be almost as important as the sounds on the film. That's why the same film or routine that seemed feeble on the TV late show, for example, may seem sharp and hilarious later on in a movie theater. And not even the most brilliant of the old movie comedies ever seems *quite* as brilliant if you watch it alone or even at home with family or friends. But that's the way it should be: the people who made those comedies (at the time, of course, they had no choice) intended them for a *public* experience. And as they knew, seeing a smart comedy with a smart, responsive audience—where everybody's perception seems to sharpen and heighten everybody else's, where the intelligence as well as the hysteria becomes infectious—is an experience like nothing else.

But where a successful joke connects you to an audience, an irony may do just the opposite. Mostly, an audience "gets" a joke or else it falls flat, as we say. But an irony—of the film noir kind—may only confirm itself, may begin to seem richer than it did even at first, if half the audience misses it. The ending of *Out of the Past*, for example, which seems at first to be a simple, rather sentimental affirmation of the good girl's middle-class world and values (Virginia

Huston, Jane Greer's blond and "innocent" rival for the hero—and now the only principal in the movie who is left alive), also turns out to be a reminder of how deeply she relies on denial, on a principled ignorance of all the things the movie has been about. (In an earlier scene, she discusses Greer with Mitchum: "She can't be all bad—no one is," says Huston. Replies Mitchum: "She comes the closest.") Max Ophuls' great film noir *The Reckless Moment* (1949) offers a more or less straight-faced account of an upper-middle-class housewife (Joan Bennett) in a jam, haplessly involved because of her daughter in the concealment of a corpse. The movie shows the heroine as selfless and courageous and resourceful throughout—just as the love-struck hero (James Mason) sees her, even though he is blackmailing her. But it also shows her—it becomes clearer and clearer as the movie goes on—in some crucial and fascinating way, as perfectly unconscious, leading and promoting a deranged life both in herself and in those who depend on her. The irony is movie-length, developed with the most marvelous tact and complexity as well as accuracy about contemporary American life. And yet it wasn't a meaning that audiences of the time necessarily got, or needed to get in order to make sense of the movie, which seemed to most a perfectly conventional (if not very exciting) thriller.

But then there was no framework in movie precedent for what Ophuls was trying to do—no convention for talking about the *wrongness* of the suburban American family or the collective delusions that had produced it. But more and more filmmakers like Ophuls—dissenters from the consensus—were learning to use the conventions that existed. Just as Sturges, in Bazin's view, had used the tradition of American humor to criticize the "assumptions" behind it. The fifties were a time of disarray in the movie business and inattention in the movie audience. It was the beginning, as we now know, of the end of the old system. But for many Hollywood filmmakers it was a time of rich opportunity, unlike anything that had come along before: a time when movies were still in touch with a mass audience but no longer had to identify with it so completely and simply as before.

But for audiences it was like messages in a bottle—or feeling sometimes that you might have stumbled on a code. Could this movie really be saying this? ("Come now, Sturges—surely you were kidding?") On the movie surface, "maturity" and "normalcy," the successful adjustment to American life, were unquestioned values. And the opposition between the neurotic and the healthy dominated the mainstream movie the way it had once been dominated by arguments between city and town. But in this new opposition, there could hardly be argument—only consensus. Healthy was better than sick—who could deny it? And yet was there ever a time in popular entertainment when so many repugnant versions of the healthy—in a seemingly endless profusion and variety—had been paraded before our startled eyes? Or, for that matter, so many alluring versions of the sick? Was this intentional? Sometimes it was, no doubt—mostly it probably wasn't, or at least not exactly. But the revulsion was everywhere, it seemed, and thick enough to taste.

This was one of the things that made the period so rich and stimulating—at least for moviemakers who could tap into the emotional line. As Nicholas Ray could—with the middle-class household of *Bigger Than Life* (1956), keeping up appearances while the mad killer Dad rages inside; or the dilemma of Gloria Grahame in *In a Lonely Place* (1950), whether to choose a normal life or Humphrey Bogart. "He doesn't act like a normal person. Why can't he be like *other* people?" For one thing, he's violent and paranoid—and for another, he might even be a murderer. But "normal" in this film seems to mean Frank Lovejoy—and Jeff Donnell, his perky, humorless, troublemaking little wife. *She* doesn't like Bogart at all (we're not surprised). He seems *very* sick to her. But Lovejoy defends him: he's a genius, he tells her. "I still like the way *you* are—attractive and average," replies the loyal wife, rather testily.

But it's very hard indeed to like the "attractive and average" Rock Hudson

The persistence of shadows in Douglas Sirk's Imitation of Life *with Lana Turner.*

and Lauren Bacall (come a long way since her Hawks days) in Douglas Sirk's *Written on the Wind* (1957). This pair are impugned throughout the movie for their cold, self-satisfied "normalcy"—but by such subtle strategies of design and detail that most audiences hardly notice at all. After all, Hudson and Bacall are the "sympathetic" ones; that's what the very familiar plot tells us, anyway. All the more so since the pair that we *do* like—Robert Stack and Dorothy Malone—are so flamboyantly sick. But they are also the ones who show up the prim lifelessness of the nominal hero and heroine. Sirk was a specialist at this kind of invidious and killing parallel—between people in extremity who suggest depths within and those who seem depthless—and "normal." And he sees this shallowness as a choice: that makes him eloquent about contemporary life in a way that almost no one else is. His masterpiece is *Imitation of Life*. There the parallel is between the Lana Turner heroine, with her fussy driven emptiness, and her black "maid," in the extraordinary person of Juanita Moore.

Filmmakers like Sirk and Ray may have been testing and subverting these conventional forms. But, like Sturges, they were still essentially reliant on them, even defining themselves by them. And however trickily and ambiguously, however subtly or ironically they were doing it, their movies were still addressing themselves to a homogeneous mass audience. But by the late sixties, that audience—along with the particular sort of movie that was made for it—had pretty much disappeared, seeming as much a thing of the past as the studio system or the censorship codes.

We are creating an esthetic community, a religion more of women than of men. The essence of the metropolis is that in it women find a worthier place than they do in the masculine provinces.
          —GEORGE KONRAD, "Homage to New York"

IT ISN'T now that there aren't wonderful filmmakers still more or less working—Altman, Kubrick, Scorsese, Leone. But even if there were many, many more, the aggregate today still wouldn't add up to "the movies." That experience belongs to the studio days, and to the classical Hollywood cinema, as it's now called. Though we can still have the experience to some degree—especially in the movie revival houses of our big cities—"the movies" themselves are gone.

"The movies" had a special relation to American culture—even to American democracy. It wasn't just that they drew more people than any other leisure pursuit in America did, but that they drew all *kinds* of people, all classes and types, ages and backgrounds, from the most to the least "educated." Everyone went to the movies, and mostly they went to the same movies. Only the most marginal sorts of film were aimed at special audiences (sex films, low-budget westerns, documentaries, etc.)—in contrast to today, when almost every movie is targeted at a "market" (teens or "art" or redneck, etc.). The studio film—*each* studio film—was for everybody. The "woman's film" had to be endurable to men, the male action film to women, and so on. Of course the movies—it went without saying—were for grown-ups. So that the occasional children's film (*The Wizard of Oz* or the Disney cartoon features) had to appeal to parents too. And it followed as well that "adult" films should never be "harmful" to children. There was one audience then, and it was all of us.

Probably enough has been said by now about the obvious baleful effects of all this—the eight-year-old mentality of the movie audience, the reduction of everything to the lowest common denominators of perception and taste, and so on. But the fact still remains that intelligent and serious and grown-up films got made in this system—many more than are made today, in fact. By *that* standard, the old repressive system seems to have worked beautifully, even if it's still a little mysterious to us how that could have happened.

And as a result of this system, the movies themselves had a special feeling—even a special bias. They were a public event—and they celebrated public life. First of all, we went out to see them. And if we lived in a city, the chances are that we saw them in almost unspeakably splendid surroundings. We were certainly never meant to be alone with them, but together in front of them with strangers, as it were. And when the movies themselves praised—as they so often did—the freedom and impersonality of the city, that was something the audience experience seemed to verify. Especially if the movie itself was wonderful.

Not that it usually was—mostly it wasn't. Nobody you ever heard of claimed that the movies were "good." On the contrary, everyone knew they were "silly," unreal, always the same, and so on. But everyone still went. Because it was never just a matter of going to this or that good or bad movie. You didn't pick a movie the way you chose a book or a record, for instance. When you went to a movie you were doing something else—entering a public continuum, a community of common experiences and shared consciousness. You might complain about the experience; you usually did, in fact. But you were still part of that community—connected through your dissidence, even. Movies could be seductive, but they could also be a place to hone your resistances at. There were always, of course, people who didn't go at all—often people who were too highbrow for them, or people who had no interest in *any* kind of imaginative product, high or low (men stayed away more than women). But not going was like refusing a connection to the public world—like refusing to live in America, in a way. And many people did refuse—quite consciously.

But for those who went—for everyone who went—the question before going or deciding to go was always (and sensibly) the same: "Who's in it?" We all understood the point of this—whether we put it into words or not: the movies were about their stars. That's why they could be wonderful even when they weren't good.

And yet the great stars—the Garbos and Bogarts—like the most virtuous people, have rarely been the most popular ones, as I suggested at the beginning of this chapter. Not, anyway, in their own time. And women stars have always inspired more ambivalence of response, even from women audiences, than men. In David Pirie's list of the top ten "all time" stars, for example, the only woman is Doris Day (number 8). Men stars are more popular probably because in some way they reassure us about the patriarchal values that the movies, like the rest of society, always finally endorse. And by that standard the women—the best of them, anyway—have always been a bit subversive: more challenging than reassuring. They were wonderful, of course (everyone could see that), but they made us a little nervous. And there was even something unpleasant about them to the sort of audience that preferred Bing Crosby, or even Doris Day.

Whatever it was, there was something special about the thirties star, as almost everyone now agrees. "And what stars they were!" as David Shipman writes. "They captivated audiences then, and they have captured the imagination since"—and in the decades since then, he adds, there have been only a few stars ("perhaps less than a dozen") even comparable to them. It seems clear now at least that that was a special time. That there was a moment in our history when we *understood* something about human nature—and we understood it collectively—both about how to look at it and how to show it, how to feel the special excitement of it. It was the mystery at the heart of all our experience—and the movie star, alone among our daily experiences, it seemed, permitted us to *look* at it directly. If the stars of the time seem unique now—almost, at times, like members of a vanished species—it's not so much, I think, that they *are*, that someone like a Lombard or an Arthur *couldn't* recur, so to speak—but that if she did, we wouldn't know how to *see* her. The movies taught us how to look—that is, that there were certain *ways* of looking that made all the difference.

Those glamour stills, for example. The point was never to reveal their subjects, as the movies did, but to do just the opposite: to associate them instead with an ideal, to move them toward abstraction. And *that* seemed appropriate. There was something impersonal in the personality of the thirties star: something in the inevitable narcissism that essentially contradicted it. That's why a down-to-earth sort of star like Lombard, famous for being without "airs," could pose for endless studies which were entirely composed of such "airs," and yet no one felt this to be anomalous in any way. The stars touched sublimity—that was almost a requirement of the job—but they took its measure, too. And that was finally what made them so thrilling. Diverse as they were, they all had this extraordinary *shrewdness* in some form, of perception and affect, a certain irony and standing-apart quality. (Compare the woundedness and winsomeness that soon began to take its place—and continues to do so, even in grotesque ways: any current image of Sylvester Stallone with his shirt off, for example.) What they had, what they showed on the screen, what we learned to see, was a kind of impersonal relation to themselves. And that seemed very wonderful—especially in action.

And in our attention to them, we had the same relation. The stars, like the movies themselves, were both real and unreal. They balanced the two polarities. They didn't make us—most of us, anyway—want to go to Hollywood. They didn't seriously propose that we could *be* them—or even that we could exercise our way into looking like them (a lot of the men at least were out of shape anyhow). We didn't really know about their private lives (not the "truth" anyway), and we didn't really want to (at least not most of the time): that was personal, and a distraction from what we really cared about. And though they did connect with our personal lives, they did so obliquely—just as they connected with themselves, it seemed.

And most extraordinarily of all in a way, just like the best of their movies, they were *about* common life—or at least its possibilities. They stood for equality—but an equality without illusions. It wasn't their job (unlike the left-wing rhetoric of the time, with its sentimental populism) to flatter us and to tell us we were wonderful. But they made us *feel* wonderful, and they gave us hope. Because what they were, so to speak, in front of our eyes—in their different forms of toughness, commonness, openness, in their glamour, in their final mystery and inviolability—testified to the possibilities of American community, to the freedom of the city. It was no accident that so many of their movies had them escaping from small towns. They belonged to the city—and especially the women did. There were thirties stars who were small-town boys—Cooper, Fonda, Stewart—but (apart from a holdover from silent days like Janet Gaynor) there were almost no small-town girls. It was the women especially—"love's anarchists," in George Konrad's phrase for the city spirit, and "sworn to impertinence"—who challenged the complacency of American life, who suggested that we might grow up and live together with the kind of candor and risk and honesty that seemed specially, even dangerously American. And each time we saw them again, and found them as interesting as ever, they confirmed that promise.

But probably the most astonishing thing is that all this *keeps* happening—that they somehow go on confirming it even now—when we see their movies.

Appendix:
Interview with Irene Dunne

(September 1978)

THERE SHE is in her Holmby Hills mansion—a sensible woman. I told her she reminded me of Garbo. (And if you're sensible, what do you say to *that?*) She looked blank for a moment, then said that was "interesting"—"because, you know, I met Garbo once." Yes? "Yes." On a picnic with Gayelord Hauser and Brian Aherne. Dunne remembers a general good time, that Garbo relaxed, that "she has almost a corny little sense of humor," and that she laughed a lot— but that she seemed indeed "terrified" of strangers. This led Dunne to reflect on the shyness of many actors and how they love to lose themselves in "character parts." Like her own Queen Victoria in *The Mudlark* (1950). "Nobody liked it, but I loved playing it." She recalled her first morning's appearance on the film's set—in her Victoria costume and some pounds of makeup—and how the British crew was struck dumb by the transformation. "Yes, character parts are fun," she said of the experience. "There you *really* hide. . . ."

She lives at a considerable distance from her famous past—"a lifetime ago," as she puts it. She looks ageless, and her present life is, I gather, both full and busy. But my questions were about the past—and she thought I was "a fiend for detail." She doesn't like interviews; she gives no sign of encouraging "fans" or of waxing nostalgic. But when she learned I was writing a book—presumed to be serious—about the romantic comedies of the thirties and forties, she agreed to talk to me. She likes the idea that people in universities are "teaching" *The Awful Truth* ("I would think that is one film that *could* be dissected"), and she asked questions on how I went about it. She wondered about the plethora of film books ("Do they *do* very well?"). At one time she thought she might do her own book; Harcourt, Brace had approached her. She had even begun it. But one day her husband said to her: "Do you think people really care about your grandmother?"—and that ended it. She asked about the new (at that time) Joan Crawford revelations (*Mommie Dearest*) and what I thought about it all—"though I never really knew Joan," she said. She occasionally sees what she calls "celebrities" on the Merv Griffin show and movies like *Rocky* on the Z channel. She rarely goes to the movies. "I certainly don't want to stand in line to see a new film—and that's what we get out here because we live near the university, and the college students just line up for miles." Does she go to the Academy Awards? No. "Though I was a presenter a couple of years ago—of the humanitarian thing." I said I had heard from sources in New York that she had been asked to play the older Roberta in a projected Broadway revival of the Jerome Kern musical—was that true? Yes, she seemed to remember she had heard about such an idea. "But why would I want to do that?" she said. . . . No answer.

She is glad, as she puts it, that her work has "stood up through the years"— or at least that so much of it has. Out of all her films, she is ready to inform me, she likes sixteen (the total is forty-one). But her list could be anyone's—a roll call of her best-known movies. So of course it excludes some of her most interesting work—like *Sweet Adeline* (1935), where she sings "Why Was I Born?" and moves like a sorceress through masses of chorus dancers, and the feminist heroine of *Ann Vickers* (1933), like Mamoulian's *High, Wide and Handsome* (1937) and La Cava's *Unfinished Business* (1941), and so on. Of La Cava, about whom so many in Hollywood speak so warmly, she has mostly painful memories. He was in bad shape in 1942 when they did *Lady in a Jam* together—drinking a lot and with a psychiatrist in attendance while they filmed. (This same doctor told Dunne she was the "most normal person he'd ever seen.") About Mamoulian she remembers how they would sit and wait for the right cloud formation ("Can you believe it?")—"I didn't think I was good in it," she says of the film. But she never seems to have minded waiting for George Stevens, whose slowness was legend, nor for Leo McCarey, whose delays and chaotic working methods on *The Awful Truth* reportedly so unnerved Cary Grant that he tried to get out of doing the picture. "It's true, we were putty in their hands," she says of directors in general. "I was one of the first free-lance artists—and what I had was the okay of my director, never the picture or the script. I made sure the director was someone I wanted to work with, and then I left it to him."

We had two meetings at her house. It's difficult to imagine a more recessive "star" or a manner less actressy. She is also powerfully—quietly—charming. She is perfectly matter-of-fact. She never tries to be funny, or consciously charming, or even to be "Irene Dunne." She sits back, talks quietly, listens carefully. She is thoughtful and careful almost to a fault. Anything in her own words that sounds to her like pretension or exaggeration gives instant alarm. She looks small and vulnerable. She is sometimes rather nervous, always friendly, and altogether rather anonymous. Except that nearly always—as there is on the screen—there is something unmistakable, something funny and secretive, at the center of her eyes.

But toward the end of a very agreeable hour and a half—on a rainy afternoon,

Irene Dunne in Love Affair.

in the library of her home—it's clear that something has gone wrong. This is the first meeting—a preliminary one, as far as I was concerned—and now she is making gentle difficulties about the next one. She does consent to it finally, but only after letting me know by her hesitations that she was unhappy about something. I have an interval of several days to figure out what it is. That first "interview" must have seemed more disorganized than she expected or could feel comfortable with: I had no written questions, no tape recorder, no clear sequence to the questions I did ask, and I finished with a request for more. "I really only have an hour," she told me over the phone when we set up the appointment for the second meeting: it was said with concern (concern for *me*, I thought) and was the kindest possible warning. And it worked. I like to think I would have been better prepared for that second meeting in any case—but perhaps not so *well* prepared. . . . It's clear she knows how to have her effect.

We sat on the patio—a beautiful sunny day. The tape recorder on the table between us was something we could both "play to." And she seemed very much more relaxed than on my first visit. When we were some minutes into the tape, she noticed that I had a lot of written questions, on the thick yellow tablet in front of me. She looked knowing. "Uh-hmmm . . . That will teach you," she said, both pleased and amused. And I laughed—so did she. A mutual recognition: she knew exactly what she'd done, and knew that I knew too, and so on. In fact it was a moment that had exactly the kind of complication that I'd come to explore and pay tribute to—in the person of this extraordinary and beautiful woman I was now sitting across from.

I turn the tape recorder on, and we both look at it.

ID: . . . Don't you have to take it out of its package?

JH: No. That's for carrying it.

ID: That shows how much I know about it. —Is it on now?

JH: It's on now.

ID: Oh . . . (*laughs*) Well, we won't talk about *him* then . . . Although I did know Ernst Lubitsch.

JH: You did?

ID: Well, I didn't know him well—but he lived up here right next to Merv LeRoy. I always remember the cigar. . . . And he did some brilliant things, I thought—just lovely.

JH: Have you seen *The Awful Truth* lately?

ID: No, I haven't.

JH: Is that one of the prints you own? You said you had prints of some of your films.

ID: I know I did. I have to stop and think . . . whether I own that. I never run them. I wonder . . . if they deteriorate. They would deteriorate whether I ran them or not, I suppose. . . . No, I haven't seen *The Awful Truth*, but I'll always enjoy it.

JH: When you say that you improvised on that film . . .

ID: Well, Leo wrote an awful lot of it. While we sat on the set and waited.

JH: Did you or Grant ever supply dialogue?

ID: Oh no, never. I don't think we ever supplied any dialogue. But McCarey was very good about sitting down and wanting to talk things out. . . . The scene, if you remember, where she plays the part of the nightclub dancer who is supposed to be Cary's sister . . . that was really all written right on the set. . . . Do you know what the bumps are? You do? —Well, I could never do those bumps the way they were supposed to be done. I think she must have done them in the original scene and now I was trying to imitate her. And this was so typical of McCarey—we came to that part, and I tried . . . and I said, "I never could do that"—and he just left it in the film that way. . . . No, the only writing I did, as I have told you, was my own—when I went back to my dressing room.

JH: To write thoughts about the character?

ID: Yes. I'd write and write and write—isn't that strange? If anybody had read it ever, they would have wondered about my sanity, because I would just ramble on, just to have thoughts of my own. . . . I suppose other people do that, but I've never discussed it with anybody.

JH: Did McCarey ever talk about the character with you? About her motivation?

ID: Not really. He'd give you the scene and see what happened. And of course he was a great man for routines. Like that part when she had this long chiffon handkerchief, and this grande dame who was sitting next to her thought she was sitting on the handkerchief—and then *she* was sitting on the handkerchief—and this went on and on like a regular comic routine. But that was Leo's early training—that was his background.

JH: Did you have many takes on that film?

ID: No. This was a director who loved spontaneity above everything. No, I don't remember many takes at all. The only one, as I mentioned to you earlier, was Mr. John Stahl—he was the one who wanted take after take after take.

JH: McCarey would do it in one take?

ID: Sometimes. Yes, sometimes. But then we'd sit and wait. It was a lot of fun, but my goodness, we used up an awful lot of time.

JH: Was *Love Affair* the same sort of experience? Did you do any improvising?

ID: I'm sure we did lots of it. Yes, lots of it.

JH: The serious scenes as well? It wasn't just comedy McCarey took this approach to?

ID: As I say, he kept handing us pieces of paper all the time with new dialogue. So there wasn't much sense in ever learning anything—you only had to unlearn it. It was a different way of working—I'm sure it could never happen today.

JH: How did you prepare?

ID: Well, as I say, with this particular director I couldn't prepare much beforehand. I had to stop off all the time and prepare as I was shooting. Which kept you on your toes, all right. . . . But ordinarily, if you had a full script you could prepare thoroughly. And you had to. Well . . . most thinking actresses—as they say, if an actress is falling down the steps, she's analyzing it—how she feels when she's falling down the steps. I don't know . . . that's going a little far, perhaps. . . .

JH: *Love Affair* falls into two parts, it seems—the first half is sophisticated comedy, the second is sentimental. Do you have any idea how or why that happened?

ID: I do remember one thing. You know yourself if you've ever been on a trip, a cruise for instance, and then you land back home, there's a terrible letdown. That's what happened to us in the filming. Everything on board ship was amusing and fun—they fall in love and this, that, and the other. Then when they arrived home it was a terrific letdown. I remember that Leo called in two or three writers immediately. He said, "You know we are sinking right here in the middle of this film."

JH: Did he have a script for the second part of the film then?

ID: I imagine so, but it wasn't working. However, I know I never saw a finished script of *Love Affair* before I did the movie.

JH: McCarey was a sentimental man?

ID: Oh, yes. He was an Irish sentimentalist. As you saw in the—what did he do? . . . *Going My Way.* (*She makes a face. I laugh.*) . . . He was a delightful man to work with.

JH: You were good friends.

ID: Yes, we were good friends, but we really didn't see much of him. He lived at the beach, he and his wife, and he had one daughter. They weren't social at all.

JH: He had a drinking problem, didn't he?

ID: Yes, but never on the film.

JH: Was he much on the set when you did *My Favorite Wife?*

ID: No, he was hurt then, he'd had this accident. He was never meant to direct that, you know. He was to produce it and Gar Kanin was to direct it, just as they both did. . . . You didn't particularly like that film?

JH: No. But you like it?

ID: I thought it was . . . kind of amusing. I love the bit players in it. The little fellow who comes to sell insurance was marvelous, I thought. . . . It was fun.

JH: But you didn't want to do *Theodora Goes Wild?*

ID: That film . . . was the biggest surprise of my life. I still don't see how it was so successful. They showed it about a year and a half ago—something to do with the Screen Actors Guild, and would I make an appearance later? I went in and here were all these young people—and they were really quite respectful of the whole thing. You remember, she moves into this fellow's apartment, and the minute she moves in, he moves out—because that was the Hays Code. I thought, these kids are just going to laugh this off the screen. They didn't . . . funnily enough.

JH: When I show it to students, they love it.

ID: They do? It seemed to me very . . . well, *un*sophisticated.

JH: Why were you so very reluctant to do it? You stayed in Europe three months to avoid coming back and doing it?

ID: I stayed there two. Well, I'd never done a comedy before. I'd done serious parts like *Back Street*—and here was this little flipperty small-town dummy, and I just didn't want to play her at all. But I got back here and there she was waiting for me. . . . You know, none of us wanted to do that picture. The director—Boleslawski—was being penalized for something. I was threatened with suspension if I didn't do it, so *my* nose was out of joint. We all got together like a bunch of rejects. But then the front office liked everything so much that it became a happy film. We had no problems. I enjoyed working with Melvyn Douglas, and everything rolled along beautifully.

JH: What was Boleslawski like to work with?

ID: Very kind. He too was not in good health. Neither was Victor Fleming when I worked with him. I'm surprised they both made films as good as they were.

JH: How did that affect *Theodora*—Boleslawski's poor health?

ID: Well, evidently it didn't affect it much. But he never struck me as a man with any flair for comedy. . . . Douglas was very good—and I guess the story . . . was kind of cute. I know lots of friends of mine like it better than almost anything I ever made. Because they say, now that's the real *you*. . . . Well, I don't know what that means. (*pause; then in a small voice*) She's supposed to have gone wild, but she didn't go very wild really. . . .

JH: No. By the way, is it true you were offered *His Girl Friday* and turned it down?

ID: No. My pal did that. Rosalind Russell. (*pause*) I suppose the film I thought was most difficult was *A Guy Named Joe*. It was winter, it was dark and raining and the whole set was gloomy. Then Van Johnson had this terrible motorcycle accident, so we discontinued shooting. And when we started up again, I had to jump back and forth between that and *The White Cliffs of Dover*. Spencer Tracy didn't like to rehearse, and he was sort of calling the shots on that picture. I don't particularly like to rehearse a lot, but I don't like not rehearsing at all.

JH: You had trouble with Tracy?

ID: We had trouble understanding each other. We really did. He was my hero. Then when we started working he got the idea that I thought he wasn't a hero anymore. Which was not true. But he had this big mental thing, and there was even talk of taking me off the film. That's one thing I'll always say about L. B. Mayer. . . . I knew they were going to be looking at some film—and I made up my mind I was going to be . . . my *best* . . . my best, my best, my *very* best. . . . So they came out of the projection room and Mayer said, "If we're going to replace anybody, let's replace Tracy." Which they never would have done, of course. But I'll always remember that. And we ironed everything out, Tracy and I.

JH: You did?

ID: Oh, sure. We became very good friends.

JH: What was the nature of—?

ID: Just what I said. He felt I didn't regard him—that my hero had feet of clay. . . . And that really wasn't true.

JH: Did you watch other movies in those days? Did you learn from watching them ever?

ID: No. I just took my characters as they came and tried to be that character. I had a one-track mind when I was working. I excluded everything else. I had no social life. I just lived that particular part. It wasn't a job. I just *was* that character. I used to drive my husband and my family crazy because I'd talk about "her" all the time—she did this and she did that. They'd say, "Are you talking about your*self* now?"

JH: Were you ever troubled by a character you had to be? Did you ever play a character you didn't like?

ID: Well, I didn't like the one in *Life with Father*. I thought she was really unbelievably rattle-brained. . . . But the critics liked it. They loved the picture. They loved the New York stage show, as you know.

JH: Were there any actresses you watched in those days, any you particularly admired?

ID: I always admired Lynn Fontanne, on the stage. I liked Katharine Hepburn, on the screen—though of course I would never try to emulate her. I loved Garbo, because she was so romantic. . . . I admired Bette Davis; she was such a vital actress. But as far as studying . . .

JH: Did you watch Lombard, Jean Arthur, and the other comediennes?

ID: I didn't admire them.

JH: You didn't?

ID: No. Not really.

JH: Why not?

ID: I don't know. . . . I never admired a comedienne. I never wanted to do comedy, and yet it was very easy for me. Very natural. It was no effort for me to do comedy at all. Maybe that's why I wasn't so appreciative of it. I liked the heavier things. I liked doing the woman in *Magnificent Obsession*. And as I told you, I liked playing Mama in *I Remember Mama*.

JH: Do you think you learned from Lynn Fontanne, from watching her?

ID: Well, I admired her so much. I loved her delivery. I liked the way she and Alfred Lunt played together—all that dovetailing and overlapping of lines. They must have rehearsed and rehearsed at home together—because that's the way we talk in real life. And I liked the way she carried herself—even up to the very end. I saw one of her last plays—I've forgotten the name, but she was quite elderly. So she wore these high collars, and everyone thought, well, of course. . . . Then in the last act she came out in a décolleté down to *here* . . . looking just divine, you know—and all those old hens in the audience were going: look, look, look . . . Sen*sa*tional . . .

JH: You and Grant have something like the Lunts' rapport together.

ID: I think so. Yes, I think so. *(laughs)* Cary was quite a mumbler.

JH: Was he?

ID: He'd go mmm-mmm-mmm—he'd throw in little yeses and nos and mumbles all the way through. . . . He was a lot of fun to work with. He was a lot of fun *between* scenes as well—and I was probably his best audience. I used to die laughing at him, and of course the more I laughed the more he went on. He does a cockney thing that is too funny for words. I'd always get him started on something like that. . . .

JH: In *Mama* there seems to be such total identification between you and the character that it doesn't seem to be acting at all. When that happens, do you know it's happening?

ID: No—because you're so out of sequence all the time. Actually, it's remarkable—you don't know whether you're giving a performance or not half the time. [In] that particular film all the exteriors were shot in San Francisco. So you go up and you shoot the beginning and you shoot the end, then a little something in the middle—and you just hope you've gotten a handle on the whole thing. But I don't think anybody's ever quite sure.

JH: You played a lot of tearjerkers early on. Did you ever feel oppressed by the sentimentality of those scripts? Especially since you got so close to the characters.

ID: You know, in a film like *Back Street*, that was so curious. I cannot tell you the mail I got on that film—from women who said it was their story. . . . No, I don't think so. I've heard and I've read about people who play a part where they are mentally deranged . . . or some of these rape scenes or something like that. I should imagine *that* would keep you awake the night before. (*I laugh.*) You know? . . . But I never had anything quite that drastic. The closest I came, I suppose, was the blind woman in *Magnificent Obsession*.

JH: One of the problems with the *Back Street* kind of heroine, I should think, is that she is constantly sacrificing herself. How do you avoid giving her a conscious nobility, a self-congratulating quality?

ID: I understand that in one of the remakes she was a very successful decorator. But that's all wrong. This woman was a pathetic character. She loved this man so much that she could never have her independence. And you can say, well that's just so soapy, so unrealistic—but it *was* that woman. She used to sit in her little apartment and do—in those days—painted china. You know, I still have some painted china my mother did. . . . No—she just had to be . . . a very, very *alone* woman. That was the whole idea. And he was a very selfish man.

JH: She was never self-pitying, in your idea of her?

ID: I don't think so. I hope *I* wasn't.

JH: No, no.
ID: She accepted it. . . .

When the first side of the tape ran out, I played a bit of it back to make sure we'd recorded something. "I always sound like I'm in bed" was Dunne's comment upon hearing herself. I turned the tape over and we went on.

ID: . . . We've been listening to this tape and I've found that I'm much too relaxed. So I'm going to sit up straight. . . . You know, when I did *The Mud-lark* I had to speak, of course, in this very *clipped* English accent. I was born in the South. I don't have a southern accent, but I do drawl at times . . . and I find when I'm sitting back like that, in a *very* lazy mood . . . and we're sitting out here on the patio . . . and it's a beautiful day . . . and I *drawl* . . . So that clipped accent was very difficult for me. Especially the word "cour-age"—the English have a very distinct way of saying that, and I still can't say it. . . . *Courage.*

JH: Lucille Ball gave an interview at an AFI seminar here and said that you were the actress at RKO she most liked to watch—that each take you did would be different and wonderful.

ID: Did she? Well, that's very sweet, coming from, I think, the top comedienne of all time.

JH: Really?

ID: Yes. Because, well, comedy is timing mostly—and Lucille has always had perfect timing.

JH: You think so?

ID: Oh, I do think so. She's been a great clown.

JH: *Your* timing is pretty good.

ID: Well . . . Cary Grant always said that I had the best timing of anybody he ever worked with. But that's unconscious, I think—comedy timing. Nobody can give you that—you just have it or not.

JH: According to Lucille Ball, you used to vary what you did when you did a lot of takes.

ID: Oh, really?

JH: Do you think that was true?

ID: Well, I suppose . . . the director was looking for me to improve . . . each time. Maybe that was it. Anyway, I don't think you can ever be completely identical, especially if you're working with a lot of props and other people.

JH: Do you remember if Tay Garnett did a lot of takes on *Joy of Living?*

ID: I don't remember anything about that picture. . . . I remember that Douglas Fairbanks—funny the things you *do* remember—that Douglas had been in England and was quite an Anglophile. There was a scene where he wanted to say "fu-*tile*"—and Tay Garnett said, this is an American picture, and you are going to say "*fewtle*" if we have to stay here all day. And we nearly did.

JH: Douglas Fairbanks said in an interview that you were terrific to work with.

ID: He did? Well, we had a lot of fun on that picture. I don't remember the story very well because I haven't seen it. I've seen the different ones we've talked about, like *Love Affair* and *The Awful Truth* and *White Cliffs of Dover*. I have seen them through the years, but I haven't seen *Joy of Living* and I've forgotten it.

JH: It's a fine performance.

ID: She was an actress, I believe?

JH: Yes. . . . Which directors gave you a lot of interpretation of the characters?

ID: Those were the directors I didn't like. I wanted to do my own thing. If they didn't like it, then we would do something about it, but as it turned out most times they seemed to like what I was doing and most times they would leave it at that. George Stevens was specially good that way—at letting you try your own wings.

JH: Which directors discussed motivation with you a lot?

ID: Well—I think Michael Curtiz, for instance—in *Life with Father*, because I didn't like the role very much, and he had to placate me and make it more palatable. But not many of them would sit down. . . . Rouben Mamoulian kind of liked to tell you how it was to be done—until we got together and he sort of let me have my head. No, most of the directors—the really fine directors—want to see what you will give them first. The worst kind is the frustrated actor director—the kind who gets up and shows you all the moves, who wants to show you how it should be done before you even have a chance—instead of letting you try it first and then working it out together. That kind of director I couldn't work with at all. (*pause*) Only one argument I remember having with George Stevens—and as I look back at it, he was a man of very, *very* few words. It was on *Mama*. He said, "I want you to come in the door and walk here, about ten steps, and then I want you to cross the room." I said, why? He said, "*Do* as I say—ten steps, then cross." Well, I didn't like that; I have to know *why* I'm doing something. As it turned out, it was just for the cutting. But he wanted to be stubborn, to make me do it without telling me why. So we had a kind of upset.

JH: Stevens was slow. What took the time?

ID: He was a perfectionist. A perfectionist . . . he took a lot of preparation with his crew. He didn't do a lot of takes.

JH: John Stahl was slow, too?

ID: Stahl . . . was rough on his actors—I mean, on his extras and bit players. He and Charles Vidor. They treated the stars beautifully, but they were awfully hard on the bit players. That was upsetting. . . . Stahl would throw things around on the set. . . . At the time I didn't think that was funny. (*pause*) Even I was cured of a temper one time. I got so angry I threw a hairbrush, and it hit a standing mirror and this wardrobe girl was right there. It could have blinded her; it could have done awful things to this girl. As it happened, it didn't. But from then I said, never again. No more losing temper, never, never, never again . . . will I lose my temper on a set again. . . .

JH: That was on a Stahl film?

ID: It was on a Stahl film. (*She laughs.*) It was on *Back Street.* (*laughs again*) In those days I used to knit. Everybody else smoked, and they would take a cigarette, and I didn't smoke so I'd grab my knitting. I'd sit there very placidly. Finally John Stahl said, "You have got to put that *knitting* away! You are driving me *crazy!*" (*laughs*) I looked too complacent to suit him. He wanted me bothered. . . . You know, I hadn't been in the business very long then, and Stahl never allowed us to see rushes. I remember he had this secretary named Bernice, a lovely woman—and he never moved without Bernice. She would go to the rushes and then they would *huddle* . . . you know? You never knew what they were talking about. That used to upset me.

JH: Who was the leading man you felt the greatest professional excitement with?

ID: Well, I think the *two* would be of course Boyer and Grant—I would think. I would have felt . . . they were so attractive in them*selves*—I mean, *I* liked them. Even if I were not in a movie with them, I'd enjoy seeing them.—Yes, definitely those two.

JH: But you didn't enjoy making *When Tomorrow Comes*, the Stahl film with Boyer?

ID: No, I didn't. It's quite a nice way I have, isn't it, of blocking out things I don't like to remember? . . . I only remember one scene in that film . . . we were caught in a storm—in a church choir?

JH: Yes. It's a strange scene.

ID: And he was a pianist—or I was?

JH: He was. (*I laugh.*)

ID: Yes, I remember him sitting at the piano. . . . And was I a waitress?

JH: Yes, you were a waitress.

ID: I remember those early scenes, yes.

JH: You were very good in them, too. (*She looks at me dryly. I laugh.*)

ID (*softly*): I can't imagine that I was good in that.

JH: Really? Why not?

ID: Well . . . I don't know. I didn't like it.

JH: And even working with Boyer didn't help?

ID: Not in that.

JH: Did he dislike it, too?

ID: I don't think he liked it very much. . . . But he did say before he died, he told someone that his favorite film was *Love Affair.* . . . And he did a lot of films. (*She laughs.*) The last time I saw *Love Affair* I said to him, "You know, Charles, you really were *good.*" "Ah," he said, "so you finally looked at *me.*"

JH: You know . . . you have this extraordinary ability on screen—like no one else—to suggest craziness, breaking loose. . . .

ID: You think so?

JH: I do.

ID: I never thought so. I didn't think I ever broke loose. I always felt I could have had more abandon.

JH: An example is that wonderful moment in *Show Boat* when Hattie McDaniel sings "Can't Help Lovin' Dat Man" and you break into that wild shuffling and trucking step.

ID: Well . . . that routine was always in *Show Boat* . . . the way she emulates the blacks. . . . That's another one you liked that I didn't particularly like—*Show Boat.* I loved the show, but I didn't think it adapted to the screen well.

JH: One thing that's clear about people who become stars, especially in the days when you were a star, was that they had a certain sort of suitability for the camera—something quite different from stage presence. Don't you agree?

ID (*smiling*): That reminds me of a joke that they tell about . . . Marlene Dietrich, I think. She was doing a film with Charles Boyer—or maybe it was Ronald Colman. Anyway, the story goes . . . that she said to him, "Do you have a good side?" And he said, "Well, *I* don't know . . . but"—he said—"they *tell* me . . . my right side is better than my left." (*I am laughing.*) You know the story?

JH: No, no.

ID: And so he said, "What about you?" And she said, "Neither one of my sides are good. . . . I have to look *straight* into the camera. . . . " (*I laugh. Dunne starts to laugh, too.*) . . . So . . . uh . . . what were we talking about before I got so funny? (*We both laugh.*)

JH: I like that story.

ID: Isn't it great? I don't know if it's a true story or not, but they tell it. . . . Of course in those days photography was more stylized. Today everything is realism.

JH: Did you ever have camera fright? It must have taken some getting used to when you first came from the stage—acting *to* the camera . . . or like Dietrich, looking straight into it.

ID: Well, I wasn't as free before the camera as some people, I think. (*pause*) I was . . . maybe at one time I had some mannerisms. I don't know. At least one critic said he was so happy to see that I had gotten rid of my mannerisms. I still don't know what he meant by it. I used to see the rushes and then come home in tears. And how unnecessary all of that was. Because many times it was cut out of the film—or it all went together in the end so you never noticed whether there was a shadow on your nose that made you look like you had two noses—it was all lost in the shuffle. . . . I was lucky with cameramen. Very lucky.

JH: When you say you weren't as free in front of the camera as some others, what do . . . ?

ID: Well . . . for instance . . . this is so silly . . . I used to think one side of my face was for serious scenes—and the other side of my face was for laughing scenes. Plain foolishness. But they were considerate . . . and would humor me along those lines, you know. . . . Or working with a man like Spencer Tracy—he couldn't care *less* how he photographed or where he photographed.

JH: One thing that people notice in your performances—even in films like *Sweet Adeline*, where nothing much seems to be at stake, or even to make much sense—what's striking is your intensity. It's one of the things that holds people when they watch your films.

ID: I think I am a serious person to begin with . . . and I took my work seriously. I don't think I take my*self* so seriously . . . but . . . —And I am a religious person also. And everything I did had a purpose—you know? . . . It wasn't just a superficial acting job for the moment. . . . It was tremendously important to me. . . . (*She stops.*)

JH: Can you expand—?

ID: Elaborate on that? . . . I don't know—how do we elaborate on that? (*Both laugh. Pause.*) Well . . . let's see. (*pause again*) I would dedicate certain scenes, for instance . . . (*pause again*) It *is* difficult to get into. It's—well, because I don't think I've ever told anyone. But . . . (*long pause; then, regretfully*) No, I guess I can't. . . .

JH: Of course. Certainly.

ID (*laughing*): Maybe I'll come *to* it . . . perhaps later. . . .

And we went on.

Index

Grateful acknowledgment is made to the following institutions, individuals, and enterprises for permission to reproduce illustrations on the pages indicated.

Academy of Motion Picture Arts and Sciences: 5, 8, 11, 23, 48, 70, 86, 111

Author's Collection: frontispiece, 109, 114, 168, 171, 195, 197, 252, 320. 402, 480, 511, 529, 536, 596, 597, 618, 624 (top, middle, and bottom), 628, 648, 657, 666, 671

Museum of Modern Art Film Stills Archive: 2, 32, 36, 41, 46, 55, 84, 96, 104, 120, 143, 145, 202, 205, 217, 225, 226, 227, 235, 267, 277, 288, 296, 298, 314, 317, 325, 328, 342, 352, 353, 355, 360, 361, 364, 368, 381, 390 (top and bottom), 393, 404, 410, 413, 428, 429, 447, 450, 451, 452, 455, 460, 476, 495, 501, 504, 520, 521, 523, 532, 534, 550, 558, 563, 572, 584, 619, 622, 633, 640, 650, 681

Phototeque (Carlos Clarens and Howard Mandelbaum): vi, 16, 28, 29, 39, 51, 60, 74, 82, 140, 147, 151, 154, 158, 164, 175, 178, 210, 211, 222, 238, 250, 258, 266, 283, 284, 293, 302, 337, 345, 372, 377, 407, 420, 423, 424, 434, 437, 468, 513, 515, 535, 544, 605, 607, 611, 651, 668

A NOTE ON THE TYPE

This book was set in a digitized version of Bodoni Book, a type face
named after Giambattista Bodoni (1740–1813), a celebrated printer and
type designer of Rome and Parma. Bodoni Book is not a copy of any one
of Bodoni's fonts, but a composite, modern version of the Bodoni manner.
Bodoni's innovations in type style included a greater degree of contrast
in the thick and thin elements of the letters and a sharper and more
angular finish of details.

Composed by Graphic Composition, Inc.,
Athens, Georgia

Designed by Peter A. Andersen